LEARN TO READ
THE GREEK NEW TESTAMENT

Also by Ward Powers

A Brief Outline of the Books of the Bible
The Christian and His Church
The Christian and His Salvation
Divorce
Principles and Practice of Religious Accounting and Taxation
To Take It Upon Himself

Contributor to

Faith Active in Love (edited by J. Diesendorf)

Dedicated to Rev. Howard Green, the Principal of the Sydney Missionary and Bible College, and Rev. Robert Emery, my colleague on the Faculty, who encouraged me to develop my ideas on a linguistic approach to Greek into a Course at the College, and thence into this book.

LEARN TO READ
THE GREEK NEW TESTAMENT

AN APPROACH TO NEW TESTAMENT GREEK
BASED ON LINGUISTIC PRINCIPLES

COMPRISING
A BEGINNER'S COURSE
AN INTERMEDIATE COURSE
A REFERENCE MANUAL OF FORMS AND PARADIGMS
FULLY INDEXED AND CROSS-REFERENCED

Ward Powers

B.A., B.D., B.COMM., TH.L., DIP.R.E., M.A., PH.D.

ANZEA PUBLISHERS
Sydney, NSW, Australia

THE PATERNOSTER PRESS
Exeter, Devon, U.K.

WM. B. EERDMANS PUBLISHING CO.
Grand Rapids, Michigan, U.S.A.

First Published: February, 1979.
Second Edition, Revised and Enlarged, in Two Volumes: March, 1980.
Third Edition, Revised, in One Volume: August, 1982.
Fourth Edition: July, 1983.

Published jointly by:

ANZEA PUBLISHERS,
3-5 Richmond Road, HOMEBUSH WEST NSW 2140 AUSTRALIA
ISBN: 0 85892 203 7

THE PATERNOSTER PRESS LTD.,
Paternoster House, 3 Mount Radford Crescent, EXETER, DEVON, U.K.
ISBN: 0 85364 291 5

WILLIAM B. EERDMANS PUBLISHING COMPANY,
255 Jefferson Avenue S.E., GRAND RAPIDS, MICHIGAN 49503 U.S.A.
ISBN: 0-8028-3578-3

Library Cataloguing in Publication Data
Powers, Beaumont Ward
  Learn to Read the Greek New Testament
  Includes index
  1. Greek language — Grammar. 2. Linguistics.
  I. Title
  487´.4'421

Typeset in 11 on 12 point Times Roman and Greek by Shirley King/University of New England, Armidale NSW AUSTRALIA. Printed in Australia by Knudsen Printing Pty. Ltd., Waterloo NSW AUSTRALIA.

AN EXPLANATION

ABOUT THE AUTHOR:

WARD POWERS has his B.A. in Greek from the University of Sydney, his M.A. in Linguistic Science from the University of Reading, U.K., and his Ph.D. from the University of London for New Testament research. He is in charge of the Department of New Testament Language and Literature at the Sydney Missionary and Bible College, Croydon, Sydney, N.S.W., Australia.

ABOUT THE BOOK

THIS BOOK is intended for use by those without any prior knowledge of Greek who would like to learn to read the Greek New Testament for themselves (and it will also be found useful by those who have already commenced the study of New Testament Greek by traditional methods). It is suitable for private study by individuals and groups, and for classroom instruction.

This book is based upon the researches of Dr Powers into the best method by which an adequately-motivated person without any knowledge of Greek can be enabled to commence the reading of the Greek New Testament for himself.

ABOUT THE METHOD

THE POWERS METHOD of learning to read the Greek New Testament applies the principles of linguistic science to the analysis of New Testament Greek, and to its teaching and learning. The Powers method is based on these six principles:

1. FRAMEWORK LEARNING

The student is introduced in the shortest possible time to the whole framework of N.T. Greek that he needs in order to be able to begin reading in the Greek New Testament: he is not required to master one section of the work before being introduced to the next. This framework of Greek is then progressively reinforced, "fleshed out" and built upon by means of the student continuing to encounter the same features of Greek in the exercises that he works through in subsequent lessons, and then in his work in the Greek New Testament itself.

2. NATURAL LANGUAGE ACQUISITION

So far as possible the procedures followed are those of "natural language acquisition", i.e. those by which the student learnt his own mother tongue. This means minimal emphasis upon rote learning, and maximum emphasis upon exposure to the Greek of the New Testament — the student learns Greek words by encountering them in selections taken from the Greek N.T., and grasps his grammar by seeing how it functions in the actual words of Christ and the writings of the apostles.

3. IMMEDIATE INTRODUCTION TO THE TARGET MATERIAL

From the commencement of the Course the student begins working with actual extracts from the Greek N.T. N.T. extracts are used exclusively for all examples and exercises — there are no artificial sentences of pseudo-N.T. Greek made up by the author. Thus from the beginning of his work the student is introduced to, and helped to become increasingly familiar with, his "target material" which is the aim of all his study: the Greek N.T. itself.

5

4. LOW THRESHOLD OF UTILITY

The "threshold of utility" is the point where a student enters the stage of his learning in a subject when he can begin to utilize what he has been learning. A Greek Course with a heavy and lengthy emphasis upon acquiring grammatical expertise as a prerequisite to starting to read the Greek N.T. has a very high threshold of utility which may take a student a year or more to reach. The Course in this book is deliberately prepared so as to have the lowest possible threshold of utility — the student is able after completing Lesson Two or Lesson Three to see how his developing knowledge of Greek is already beginning to give him an insight into the nuances and emphases of parts of the Greek N.T. With every lesson that he completes, this utilization of his knowledge of Greek grows and expands.

5. MORPHOLOGICAL ANALYSIS AND PATTERN RECOGNITION

Some rote learning of basic paradigms is inevitable; but those that are required to be learned in this Course are kept to an absolute minimum: less than a dozen or so. Thus a student's progress in Greek is not hog-tied to his memorizing ability. Instead, the student is instructed in the use of the tools of linguistic science, and he is taught how to recognize recurring patterns in words, and how to interpret these by pattern recognition and morphological analysis. This is adaptable to the different levels of linguistic ability of different students, and allows each one to find and operate at his own level of competence: the able student is not held back, and the weak student is enabled to achieve the maximum of which he is capable. Differing levels of competence are recognized and provided for, so that even the poorer student can gain enough from his work to be able to make use of his level of knowledge.

6. PROGRESSIVE PRESENTATION FOLLOWED BY SYSTEMATIC REVISION

In the Beginner's Course the material is introduced in a progressive presentation, i.e. in an order which will enable the student as quickly as possible to work on N.T. sentences of increasing complexity and using a wide range of different grammatical forms. Then in the Intermediate Course there is the systematic presentation of the whole of N.T. Greek grammar once again, but this time in a comprehensive way, everything on the one section of grammar being dealt with in the one place. This thus provides a systematic revision of the whole field of N.T. Greek grammar.

ABOUT THE SCOPE OF THIS BOOK

THIS BOOK CONTAINS:

The Beginner's Course (with additional helps in Appendix A for students working on their own, or requiring the lessons to be broken into smaller steps)

The Intermediate Course, Parts 1 and 2 (with Reference Section giving a systematic presentation in Appendices C and D of all the paradigms of Conjugation and Declension, and Explanations in Appendix E of how the Greek language functions)

Teacher's Manual (Appendix B) on how to teach New Testament Greek according to modern linguistic principles

Also: Details of irregular words in the New Testament; statistics on word numbers in each paradigm category, and word frequencies in the New Testament; Greek word lists and indices to references in this book to each Greek word.

CONTENTS

LESSON EIGHT: USING NOUNS, PREPOSITIONS, AND THE ARTICLE 102

LESSON NINE: ADVERBS; COMPARISON; VERB CONJUGATION 124

THE WAY AHEAD

STAGE II: INTERMEDIATE GREEK COURSE

THE APPENDICES

A: A STUDENT'S GUIDE TO THE USE OF THIS BOOK

B: BASIC PRINCIPLES FOR TEACHERS USING THIS BOOK

WHY BOTHER WITH NEW TESTAMENT GREEK?

Why should the ordinary Christian — or even the Christian leader — take the time and effort to learn New Testament Greek? Are there not a dozen widely accepted English translations for us to use, and commentaries galore on every part of Scripture that we can consult?

But if we stop to think about it, the very number of translations that have been made into English points to the answer to these questions. If we compare these translations we can speedily see the problem. There are so many translations for the reason that there is no such thing as THE "right" translation of a passage. One language cannot be given an exact and final translation in another language because every word has an area of meaning, and the area of meaning for a word in one language will only partially and approximately represent the area of meaning for a word in another language.[1]

If we know only the English translations of the Bible, we will be in the hands of the translators (and commentators) and cannot go behind them, and our understanding of a passage will be largely restricted to the area of meaning of the English words. This is completely adequate of course for learning and understanding God's truth. We must never undervalue a carefully-made translation into English (or whatever other language) as the vehicle for the message of God to man. But God's New Testament revelation to man came in and through the Greek language. It is our task and responsibility to receive that revelation, to understand it, and to communicate it to others; and if we have no knowledge of Greek — and so have to depend upon translators — then we are halted one step short of being able to explore the fulness of God's revelation and plumb the depths of its treasures and mine them for ourselves.

This is not in any sense to decry the tremendous richness to be found in the Scriptures in translation. But we are that one step short of grappling with the original form of God's revelation for ourselves. And if we have no Greek at all, we will not even be able to read a commentary which refers to the Greek text, but whatever we derive of the message of God must be mediated to us through others.

Initially, we all MUST learn from others. And we never reach the place where we are beyond the need to learn from others. But when we ourselves become teachers of the truths of God to others, there is much to be said for being able to wrestle directly with the New Testament in Greek.

Therefore, whatever knowledge of Greek you can obtain will be of real value to you. By the time you have completed three Lessons of this Course you will be able to

---

[1] For this and other footnotes, see Appendix F.

make use of a Greek Lexicon and of commentaries and other books which use Greek words written in Greek characters. After the completion of six Lessons you will have translated dozens of sentences from the Greek New Testament into English, together with five passages several verses long where you will have learned to work from your own copy of the G.N.T. When you have completed the first nine Lessons you will have been introduced to all the basic grammar and syntax of the G.N.T., and to all the common vocabulary, and you will be equipped to begin the study of the G.N.T. itself. This is where (and how) your knowledge of Greek will be consolidated and expanded, and the gaps in that knowledge filled through practice and experience.

Students working on their own can progress through these Lessons at their own pace. You will find additional help in Appendix A, "A Student's Guide to the Use of This Book" — be sure to use this. The book has been specifically prepared for use in classroom situations, and alternative ways of using it with a class are discussed in "Basic Principles For Teachers Using This Book" (Appendix B).

The basic nine-lesson Beginner's Course will provide the framework for all your future work in Greek. There will still remain many things that you can learn about Greek after you finish Lesson Nine (and the Appendices at the back will provide you with the material for an Intermediate Course of a further eighteen lessons, and for general reference) — but all your later learning will be slotted into the framework provided by the basic Course, and you will have already reached a stage where what you know of Greek can be put to immediate use in your own study, in the preparation of talks and sermons, and so on.

So then: we are engaged in a worthwhile and important task. Let us commence work.

INTRODUCTION

HOW THIS COURSE OF STUDY WORKS

0.1 As the purpose of this Course is to equip the ordinary Christian with the ability to read and understand the Greek New Testament, the primary emphasis is upon learning to read Greek. There is no formal instruction in how to translate from English into Greek (on the assumption that it is not really the aim of students to learn how to do this — but guidelines for this task are given in #B7.45). Grammar is introduced and taught in this Course on an explanation basis — elements of grammar are explained which will enable the student to understand the sentences from the Greek New Testament that he is being given to work with. That is, you learn your grammar at the point where you will use it.

0.2 There is much less emphasis in the Course upon learning vocabulary than is usual in a beginning Greek Course. There are two reasons for this: First of all, it is because there is no actual word-for-word correspondence between Greek and English, but most words have a meaning which is context-determined to a considerable extent. For a new student of Greek to learn a single word of English as representing a particular word of Greek can therefore be misleading. Rather, the meaning of each Greek word is given for its particular context in a passage, and then these words are used and re-used in slightly varying contexts, in order to lay a foundation for the understanding of the "area of meaning" of each word.

0.3 The second reason is a firm conviction that, as a student has only a given amount of time available for spending on Greek study, he is much better employed in spending it, not in learning vocabulary lists, but in actually reading and grappling with a slab of Greek text, with an open word-list/vocabulary alongside. He will of course find that many word-meanings will "stick", and these will be reinforced and expanded as he reads more and more widely in Greek.

0.4 This does not mean that learning vocabulary is unimportant but, rather, that words are better learnt in context than in isolation. Aim therefore to master the meanings of words as you see them used — by the time you complete the nine Lessons of the Beginner's Course you will have been introduced to the three hundred words which occur more than fifty times each in the Greek New Testament. These are listed in Appendix G of this book. It is very useful to go through this list at least once every week or so, and tick off in pencil those that have been learnt: this enables you to see for yourself how you are progressing. These three hundred words are referred to as "common New Testament words", and in the vocabulary that is listed for each of the Lessons of this book these common New Testament words are marked with an asterisk, *, to indicate that it is particularly worthwhile remembering them because of their frequency.

0.5   In the early Lessons, the Greek reading material is printed in the Course itself; in later stages we will also commence to work from sections of the Greek New Testament. The books which will be required for this Course are:

ESSENTIAL

The Greek New Testament (United Bible Societies, Third Edition)
Greek-English Dictionary of the N.T. (Ed. B.M.Newman, United Bible Soc.)
(It is preferable to use the edition of these two combined in one volume.)
An Analysis of the Greek N.T. (Zerwick & Grosvenor, Bib. Inst. Press)
Or A Linguistic Key To The Greek N.T. (F. Rienecker, Zondervan)

OPTIONAL

Reader's Greek-English Lexicon of the N.T. (S.Kubo, Andrew's Univ. Press/Zondervan)
Greek-English Lexicon of the N.T. (Arndt & Gingrich, Univ. of Chicago Press)

0.6   Remember that the aim of the Course is not really to train you in translating the Greek New Testament into English, but to enable you to understand the meaning of the New Testament in Greek. Therefore, do not concentrate on translating it as an end in itself, but use your translation work as a means of reaching your real goal, which is to understand what the text says in Greek, and what it means by what it says. This is your first step towards putting it into practice yourself, and teaching its meaning and message accurately to others.

0.7   Important Note: Under no circumstances ever write an English translation above any of the Greek sentences in this book — this would restrict your later understanding to what you had learnt at the time that you wrote out that translation.

NOTE: # indicates a cross-reference to a paragraph in this book: # followed by a *number* refers to the Lesson with that number in the Beginner's Course; # followed by a *letter* refers to that Appendix in the Reference section.

LESSON ONE

GREEK LETTERS AND WORDS

1.1 SOME BACKGROUND INFORMATION ABOUT GREEK

1.11 The country now called Greece consisted in the centuries before Christ of a large number of separate city states. They shared a common culture and a common language, though with some differences from one area to another. There were four main dialects — Attic and Ionic (these two were related), Aeolic and Doric. In the period before Christ's birth Attic, the dialect of Athens, had become the main literary form of the language, and this is what is known now as "Classical Greek". It then became the official language of most of the Middle East through the conquests of Alexander the Great, and was used as the language of trade, learning, and administration throughout the whole Macedonian Empire.

1.12 In the process, however, the literary form of Attic became broken down into a somewhat simpler and less rigid pattern of grammar, and absorbed forms from other dialects and also from other languages (including Latin). This colloquial form of Greek is known as Hellenistic Greek, or *koine* ("common") Greek[2]. In the First Century A.D. it was spoken and understood throughout Palestine and around the entire Mediterranean basin as well as much further afield in the Roman Empire and beyond. As Rome now ruled the civilized world, Latin was the official language of government; but Greek continued as the common language of everyday concourse and communication. It is illustrative of the position at the time that the inscription on the Cross (see John 19:20) was written in Aramaic (the local language), Latin (the official language of government), and Greek (the common language that just about everyone could read).

1.13 It is highly probable that Jesus gave much of his teaching in Greek, and we may well have in the Gospels a great deal of material that is not in fact a translation from Aramaic into Greek but a record of his actual words in Greek[3]. Thus koine Greek naturally became the language in which the New Testament was written, as it was the ideal vehicle for enabling God's message to reach the greatest readership. Even the Epistle to the Hebrews was written in Greek, not Aramaic, and the Epistle to the Romans in Greek, not Latin.

1.2 THE ALPHABET

1.21 In ancient times, there were up to twenty-eight letters in the Greek alphabet[4], three of which (stigma, koppa and sampi) survive only as numbers and one of which (digamma) has dropped out of use altogether. They left behind just a few peculiarities in the words where they used to occur. As a result of a law passed in Attica in 403 BC[5], there came to be 24 letters in the language of Athens, and thus of Classical and New Testament times.

15

1.22 The common form of writing in the First Century is called UNCIAL, and this was replaced in the Ninth/Tenth Centuries by an alternative style called *cursive* or "running" writing[6]. The cursive style is used now for all printing and writing, while the uncial letters function (with slight variations) as capital letters. Capital letters are used in Greek for **(a)** proper nouns, **(b)** to mark the beginning of a paragraph, and **(c)** at the beginning of direct speech. Apart from these circumstances, a sentence does not begin with a capital. Capitals are thus relatively infrequent in Greek.

1.23 There were dialectic differences in the pronunciation of Greek (cf. in English today), and a considerable degree of uncertainty exists about the pronunciation system, especially in regard to the vowels[7]. In cursive script, accent marks were placed above one of the vowels of each word, as a guide to pronunciation, but the key to the meaning of this system is lost.

1.24 In the use of New Testament Greek today, no attempt is made to pronounce words in the way that a First Century Greek speaker would have done. Instead, a standardized pronunciation system is adopted which is frankly intended as an aid to memorization[8]. Even in this regard, however, there are variations of pronunciation to be found in use today. The pronunciation scheme adopted in this book is a common one used today which represents something of a compromise between how in koine Greek the sounds were actually pronounced (which in any case was not uniform throughout the area or the Hellenistic period), how they are spelt, and how they are best pronounced by students of New Testament Greek today in line with the goal of having a phonemic system, i.e. one letter, one pronunciation. This pronunciation scheme is superior on these grounds to the other alternatives, particularly in that it has the practical virtue that (with a minor exception) no sound has more than one spelling, so that if you can remember the pronunciation that is given you will have minimal trouble in remembering the spelling.

1.25 It will be noticed that Greek words carry a stroke or mark over one of their vowels. This mark is called an *accent*, and a word's accent will be one of three types: an *acute* (´), a *grave* (`), or a *circumflex* (really a combination of acute and grave, ^, but in some type faces it is written as ⌢ or ˜). The Greek words are given with accents in this book because they are printed with accents in the text of the New Testament for which the student is being trained. In a small number of instances accents serve to distinguish between word pairs which are identical apart from accent — attention will be drawn to these when they are encountered. In many words, accents can guide as to which syllable in the word to stress in pronouncing it. Apart from this, accents serve no real purpose for the beginning student of Greek, and can be ignored. The general principles of accentuation are set out in #E6, which is reached at the end of the Intermediate Course.

1.26 When a word begins with a vowel, that vowel has a mark over it which is called a *breathing*. This breathing is either a *rough breathing* (ʽ), which indicates that the word is pronounced with an initial "h" sound, or a *smooth breathing* (ʼ), which indicates that it has no initial "h" sound. If an acute or a grave accent fall on the same vowel as a breathing, the breathing comes first, followed by the accent: thus, ῞, ῍, ῝, ῎. Further details are given in #1.36-1.38.

1.27

NAME		LETTER	EQUIV.	PRONUN-CIATION	GREEK EXAMPLES	MEANINGS
ἄλφα[10]	alpha	α A	a	as in along, father	*ἄνθρωπος	man, human being
βῆτα	beta	β B	b	boiling	*βάλλω	I throw
γάμμα	gamma	γ Γ	g/ng†	got/boiling	*γράφω	I write
δέλτα	delta	δ Δ	d	feuding	*δύναμις	power, ability
ἐ ψιλόν	epsilon	ε Ε	e	penguin	*ἔργον	work
ζῆτα	zeta	ζ Ζ	dz	adze	*ζωή	life
ἦτα	eta	η Η	ē	there	*ἡμέρα	day
θῆτα	theta	θ Θ	th	throw	*θεός	God
ἰῶτα	iota	ι Ι	i	in, kiosk	*ἴδιος	one's own
κάππα	kappa	κ Κ	k	kiosk	*καρδία	heart
λάμβδα	lambda	λ Λ	l	lute	*λαός	people
μῦ	mu	μ Μ	m	chemist	*μόνος	only, alone
νῦ	nu	ν Ν	n	in	*νόμος	law
ξῖ	xi	ξ Ξ	x	six	ξύλον	wood, tree
ὀ μικρόν	omicron	ο Ο	o	kiosk	*ὅλος	whole, complete
πῖ	pi	π Π	p	put	*προφήτης	prophet
ῥῶ	rho	ρ Ρ	r	throw	*ῥῆμα	word, object
σίγμα‡	sigma	σ, ς Σ	s	soup	*σάββατον	sabbath
ταῦ	tau	τ Τ	t	put	*τόπος	place
ὐ ψιλόν	upsilon	υ Υ	u	put (lute)	ὑποκριτής	hypocrite
φῖ	phi	φ Φ	ph	photograph	*φωνή	voice, sound
χῖ	khi	χ Χ	kh/ch§	loch, Bach	*χρόνος	time
ψῖ	psi	ψ Ψ	ps	glimpse	*ψυχή	soul, life
ὠ μέγα	omega	ω Ω	ō	throw	*ὥρα	hour, time

* Re words with an asterisk, see #0.4
† See #1.46.
‡ Sigma is written ς at the end of a word and σ in all other positions.
§ For the correct pronunciation of this letter, see #1.45.

1.28 The Greek sounds represented by the letters are called *phonemes*; that is to say, phonemes are to speech what letters are to writing. (Phonemes are described in detail in #E1 and E2.)

1.3 VOWELS

1.31 *Vowels* are sounds (phonemes) that you make by the shape that you give to your mouth while you are breathing out air from your lungs.

1.32 There are seven vowels in the Greek alphabet, two of which are short, two of which are long, and three of which may be either short or long:

Short Vowels	Long Vowels
α (along)	α (father)
ε (penguin)	
	η (there)
ι (in)	ι (kiosk)
ο (kiosk)	
	ω (throw)
υ (put)	υ (lute)

The words in brackets indicate pronunciation when short and long for those three vowels which can be either. Short *e*, ε, followed by ρ and a consonant can be pronounced *er* as in English: e.g., ἔργον, pronounced *ergon*. Similarly, short *o*, ο, followed by ρ and a consonant can be pronounced *or*, as for ὀργή, pronounced *orgair*.

1.33 Two vowels, ι and υ , can combine with each of the short vowels and with each other into a vowel-pair which has a distinct pronunciation, and which is called a *diphthong* (pronounced *diff-thong*). There are thus these seven diphthongs:

DIPHTHONG	PRONUNCIATION	GREEK EXAMPLES	MEANINGS
αι	aisle	*αἰών	age, world
ει	eight	*εἰρήνη	peace
οι	boiling	*οἶκος	house, household
υι	penguin/suite	*υἱός	son
αυ	†Mau Mau, Strauss, Faust, kauri	*αὐτός	he; self; same
ευ	feuding	εὐχαριστέω	I give thanks
ου	soup	*οὐρανός	heaven

†See comment in #1.52

1.34 IOTA SUBSCRIPT: The long vowels (α, η, and ω) can also combine with ι, and the iota is then written subscript, i.e. below the main vowel, as ᾳ, ῃ or ῳ. A vowel is pronounced the same with iota subscript as without it. **N.B.:** As with the breathing, iota subscript is part of the spelling of a word and must never be omitted in writing a word in which it occurs.

1.35 OTHER VOWELS TOGETHER: In all other cases where vowels occur together they do not form a vowel combination but are each pronounced separately; e.g., κύριε, sir; Βηθλέεμ, Bethlehem. (Notice that it is not possible to use a rough breathing in the middle of a word to give an "h" sound, so the "h" is just omitted.)

1.36 BREATHINGS: Every initial vowel and diphthong must carry either a rough or a smooth breathing. This is part of the spelling of the word, and is not to be omitted. When an acute or grave accent also falls on the same letter, the breathing is written first followed by the accent. A breathing can also occur together with a circumflex, in which case the circumflex is placed over the top of the breathing: ῏ or ῟.

1.37 The breathing is placed:
  (a) over the top of an initial vowel if it is a small letter (e.g. ἡμέρα, ἔργον, ὅλος).
  (b) in front of an initial vowel if it is a capital (Ἐγω, Ἄλφα).
  (c) over the second letter of a diphthong, whether or not the first letter is a capital (e.g., υἱός, εἶ, Οὗτος).

(d) over the first letter of two vowels which are not a diphthong, or in front if the first is a capital (e.g. ἑορτή, Ἐάν).

1.38 The letter upsilon (υ) always carries a rough breathing when it is initial; all other initial vowels may have either a smooth or a rough breathing. The letter rho (ρ) is a semi-vowel and when it is the initial letter it carries a breathing, which is alway rough (e.g. ῥῆμα); if a double rho occurs in a word it may be found with a smooth breathing written over the first rho and a rough breathing over the second one. For example, ἐρρέθησαν (Gal. 3:16) may sometimes be found printed as ἐῤῥέθησαν. The breathing on rho need not be pronounced.

1.4 CONSONANTS

1.41 *Consonants* are sounds (phonemes) that you make by interfering with the smooth flow of air from your lungs when you breathe out. Consonants can be classified according to *how* you interfere with the flow of escaping air (this is called the *manner of articulation* of the consonant), and *where* you interfere with the flow of escaping air (called the *place of articulation*).

1.42 There are three possible places of articulation: at the lips (producing sounds that are called *labials*) or at the teeth, using the tongue (producing *dentals*), or at the palate, again using the tongue (producing *palatals*, sometimes called *velars,* or *gutterals*).

1.43 The manner of articulation can be either to stop the flow of air altogether for a moment (producing a *stop* consonant, sometimes called a *mute*) or to restrict the flow of air without stopping it, causing friction while the sound continues (and thus producing the *continuants*, sometimes called *fricatives*).

1.44 The stop consonants can be made either with or without the use of your vocal chords, so that they will be either *voiced* or *unvoiced*.

1.45 The continuants can be released either through the mouth or the nose. If released through the mouth, the continuant can be made as a hissing noise (called a *sibilant*, the "s" sound) or by putting your mouth in one of the three "place" positions and making an "h" sound (which will give you the three *aspirates*) or as a combination by adding the "s" sound to the stop consonant in each of the three "place" positions (which will give you the three "double" consonants — but note that two of these are unvoiced and one is voiced). There are also two "liquid" sounds which can be made in the mouth, the *oral liquids* ("l" and "r"). If the continuant is released through the nose, this produces the three *nasal liquids*, one for each of the three "place" positions, labial (giving "m"), palatal (giving "ng") and dental (giving "n"). The three aspirates were originally stop consonants and, consequently, in interaction with following phonemes (sounds) they usually behave like (and therefore are grouped with and treated as) stops. The correct pronunciation to use for χ is as a palatal aspirate, which is achieved by forming the mouth for κ and then pronouncing "h" through it, giving the sound of ch in Scottish "loch" or German "Bach", or similar Hebrew phonemes. This pronunciation is desirable in order to distinguish χ from κ, but as this sound does not occur in English some students find it hard to pronounce, and settle for the "ch" sound as in "chemist", i.e. the same as for κ, as in "kiosk".

1.46 The letter gamma, γ, is pronounced as a palatal nasal liquid (i.e., as the English "ng") when it is in front of a palatal (as in ἄγγελος, angel/messenger), and when it is to be pronounced in this way it can be called *enga* (ἔγγα)[11]. Iota, ι, is pronounced as "y" when it comes in front of a vowel (as in its own name, ἰῶτα, and as in Ἰησους, Jesus); and upsilon, υ, is pronounced as "w" when it comes in front of a vowel (υἱός, son). Zeta, ζ, is listed in the following table in two places; as a sibilant (it is the voiced equivalent of σ) and again as a dental in the "double letter" line, as it functions in the language at times as a sibilant and at times as a dental. In early times zeta had two pronunciations, as *zd*, and as *dz*, reflecting the two sources from which it developed, and of these alternatives the pronunciation adopted and recommended here is *dz*, paralleling the labial double letter ψ and the palatal ξ[7]. Rho, ρ, is both an oral liquid and a semi-vowel — at times it functions as a consonant, and at times as a vowel.

1.47 All the Greek consonants can be set out in a table which shows all their features of manner and place of articulation and so on:

MANNER OF ARTICULATION		PLACE OF ARTICULATION		
		Labials	Palatals	Dentals
STOPS:	**Unvoiced**	π	κ	τ
	Voiced	β	γ (gamma)	δ
	Aspirated	φ	χ	θ
	Double	ψ	ξ	ζ
CONTINUANTS:	**Nasal Liquids**	μ	γ (enga)	ν
	Oral Liquids			ρ, λ
	Semi-vowels	υ	ι	ρ
	Sibilants			σ, ζ

1.48 It is not necessary to learn this table of consonant types at this stage, but just to note the overall pattern. We will refer back to it from time to time when it can help clarify some change in consonants in words.

1.5   PRONUNCIATION GUIDE

1.51 The various English words used above (#1.27 and #1.33) as a guide to pronunciation of the Greek letters and diphthongs can be assembled into a sentence to assist in remembering them: "Strauss, Bach's father, got a glimpse along the kiosk aisle, and photographed six feuding Mau Maus there, putting a lute and a kauri adze in the boiling soup, and throwing in eight penguins from the loch."

1.52 It paints rather a gory and somewhat nonsensical picture of Mau Maus addicted to penguin soup, but it does have the virtue that all the vowels, diphthongs and consonants in it (except for "the") are pronounced as they are for New Testament Greek, and all the vowels, diphthongs and consonants of New Testament Greek are included in it. Remembering these English key words can assist in pronunciation in the initial stages. (There is actually no English word which contains the right pronunciation of "au" corresponding to the Greek, so three names and a type of tree are given, as most people will know one or more of these.)

1.53 It is essential to become completely fluent as quickly as possible in reading the Greek letters, and pronouncing words correctly. For help in this, use the detailed guidance and graded exercises given in #A1.

1.54 The following passage from Luke 14:27-28 should be read and reread out aloud until correct pronunciation is automatic, and complete fluency is attained — it contains all the 24 letters of the Greek alphabet:

ὅστις οὐ βαστάζει τὸν σταυρὸν ἑαυτοῦ καὶ ἔρχεται ὀπίσω μου οὐ δύναται εἶναί μου μαθητής. τίς γὰρ ἐξ ὑμῶν θέλων πύργον οἰκοδομῆσαι οὐχὶ πρῶτον καθίσας ψηφίζει τὴν δαπάνην, εἰ ἔχει εἰς ἀπαρτισμόν;

1.55 The syllables of a Greek word are pronounced so as to begin with a consonant. Thus φωνή is not pronounced φων-η but φω-νη, and εἶδεν is not εἰδ-εν but εἰ-δεν. Break up other words similarly. So these words in #1.54 are pronounced as ἐ-γε-νε-το, ἀ-γα-πη-τος, εὐ-δο-κη-σα. When there are two consonants between vowels, start the syllable with the second one, thus: ἐκ-βαλ-λει. Similarly divide up the pronunciation of a double letter — thus ἐξω is pronounced ἐκ-σω.

1.6   THE WRITING OF GREEK

1.61   The written form of Greek at which you should aim is a style similar to that of the Greek printed characters, but without any of its ornateness. Aim at simplicity, clarity, and ease of recognition — avoid frills and flourishes. Practice writing the cursive (lower-case) characters as they are given here:

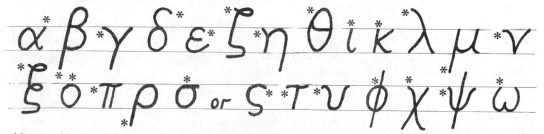

*Start writing each letter at the point indicated by the asterisk.

1.62 Note that β, δ, ζ, θ, λ and ξ, and these only, are double-height letters; that the two strokes of χ cross on the line; that the tails of ζ, ξ and ς go below the line, as do the stems or legs of β, γ, η, μ, ρ, φ, χ and ψ. All capital letters are of uniform height, and rest on the line.

1.63 TRANSCRIBING INTO ENGLISH: English words derived from Greek are usually spelt with the corresponding English equivalent letters. But note that Greek chi (χ) comes into English as "ch" (as in "Christ") and not as "x", which is ξ. However, upsilon (υ) usually comes into English as the vowel "y" (as in "hypocrite"), and the diphthong ου as "u" (as in "uranus" and "Jesus"). The diphthong ευ is sometimes still "eu" in English ("Eucharist") and sometimes "ev" ("evangelist"). The Greek γγ (i.e.

enga plus gamma — see #1.46) becomes "ng" in English ("angel"); κ comes across
into English as "k" when it is taken directly from the Greek, and as "c" when it has
come via Latin. Be careful to distinguish the Greek capitals P, X, H and Y from their
English look-alikes.

1.64 WORD ENDINGS: All Greek words end either in a vowel or else in ν, ρ or ς
(including ψ and ξ). The only exceptions are the words ἐκ (out of) and οὐκ, οὐχ (not),
which are always pronounced with the word which follows; and foreign proper names
(e.g., Βηθλέεμ). Whenever the inflectional changes that take place in a word bring any
other consonant to the end of that word, then that consonant is dropped.

1.65 MOVEABLE NU AND SIGMA: Numbers of words which end in -ε or -ι may
be found with an added -ν, especially before a following word beginning with a vowel, or
at the end of a clause or sentence. (Thus: ἐστι or ἐστιν, "is"). Similarly, ἐκ, out of, and
three other less common words have a moveable ς before a following vowel: ἐκ thus
becomes ἐξ. (Note that κ and ς coming together become amalgamated in ξ.)

1.7   PUNCTUATION

1.71 There are six punctuation marks in Greek:
  - **(a)**   , (The same as the English comma.)
  - **(b)**   . (The same as the English full stop, or, period.)
  - **(c)**   · (The high point — similar to the English semicolon and colon.)
  - **(d)**   ; (The Greek question mark — do not confuse with our semicolon.)
  - **(e)**   ' (The Greek apostrophe, similar to the smooth breathing in appearance,
             which is used — as in English, cf. "can't", "he's" — to indicate an
             elision, that is, where a letter has dropped out. Its use will be explained
             in due course.)
  - **(f)**   ¨ (The diaeresis, which is used — as in English, cf. "naïve" — where two
             vowels which normally combine to form a diphthong are to be
             pronounced separately, e.g. Ἡσαΐας, ἰχθύϊ, προϋπῆρχεν — Acts 8:9.)

1.72 This punctuation was NOT used in the earliest, uncial, manuscripts of the Greek
New Testament, where in fact the practice of the time was to run all the words together
without a space between them. Punctuation was later incorporated in cursive writing
and is used today in all printed editions of the Greek N.T.[12] Note that as there was no
punctuation in the original manuscripts, this has been added by later editors. Therefore
at a number of points it is a matter of interpretation as to whether a particular sentence is
a question or a statement. For example, are Romans 8:33b and 8:34b statements or
questions? — the Greek itself does not indicate which it is.

1.73 It will be seen that Greek has no quotation marks. The beginning of direct speech
is usually indicated by the use of an initial capital (see #1.22) and/or by the use of the
word ὅτι (="). The end of direct speech is often indicated by the words which follow it
being ὁ δὲ . . . ., and he . . . . (i.e., the other person in the conversation; and similarly for
the feminine and the plural). But in many places there remain uncertainties as to
whether something is a quotation or direct speech, or not, and as to where direct speech
ends.

1.8 GREEK WORDS

1.81 Greek words consist of two kinds, the "changing" and the "unchanging". The "changing" are nouns, pronouns, adjectives, verbs, participles, and the article, which have different *forms* to indicate number, case, tense, aspect, etc. The "unchanging" words remain unaltered in use, and comprise conjunctions, prepositions, adverbs, particles, negatives, and the infinitive.

1.82 The changes which take place in a word are called *inflection*. An inflected word consists of a *stem* (which is the *lexical part* of the word, i.e. the part that carries the lexical or dictionary meaning of the word), and an *ending* or *suffix* (which is the *grammatical part* of the word, i.e. the part which changes to indicate the function of the word in each particular sentence where it is used).

1.83 Greek words, especially inflected words, consist of a number of parts or segments each of which conveys a particular "piece" or unit of information. Each such segment of a word is called a *morph*[13], and a morph is described according to the information that it gives. Thus the "lexical part" of an inflected word can be described as the *lexical morph*, or *lexal*[14]. A suffix will usually be composed of several morphs, each of which conveys different information about a word's grammatical meaning. Sometimes a word may have a *prefix* or an *infix* as well (#2.74).

1.84 Thus, for example the word θεός (see #1.27) consists of the lexal θε-, which carries its lexical meaning of "God", and -ος, its ending, which indicates its grammatical information, i.e. that this form is nominative singular. With a different ending the word will have a different grammatical meaning — thus the form θεοῦ means "of God" (i.e., genitive singular).

1.85 Much of the work of the next eight Lessons will consist of learning the different types of inflection that can occur in Greek, and which words take one kind of inflection or the other, and the difference that is made to the meaning of a word by inflecting it, and how the words are assembled into sentences to express the author's meaning. The various morphs will all be identified and their functions explained. The assignments which follow lay the foundation on which this work will be built.

ASSIGNMENTS ON LESSON ONE

1. Read Lesson One through twice, aiming at understanding rather than thorough learning. Read carefully through Appendix #A0. and A1.
2. **LEARN** the Greek alphabet: the names of the letters, their order, their appearance, and their pronunciation. **LEARN** the diphthongs (#1.33). Master the pronunciation of Luke 14:27-28 (#1.54).
3. Note the Greek words in the column "Greek examples" (#1.27 and #1.33) — **PRACTISE** reading them out aloud, then **WRITE THEM OUT** to hand in (remember that you must put the correct smooth or rough breathing on initial vowels).
4. (Optional) Make out a list of English words that you can think of which are derived from the words in the "Greek examples" columns (#1.27, #1.33).
5. Do a quick preliminary reading of Lesson Two.

LESSON TWO

THE ARTICLE; SECOND DECLENSION;
THE PRESENT ACTIVE FLEXION

2.1 THE GREEK SENTENCE

2.11 A *sentence* is, in its simplest form, a statement about something; i.e. a topic, and a comment about that topic. The topic, the "something" about which the statement is being made, is called the *subject* of the sentence. Usually, the subject will be a *noun.*

2.12 A noun is commonly explained as the name of a person, place, or thing (such as "Jesus", "Bethlehem", "Jordan", etc.), or the term used to refer to a person, place, or thing (such as "man", "town", "river", etc.).

2.13 Each noun in Greek is of a particular *gender*. As in English, there are three genders in Greek: masculine, feminine, and neuter — but many things that are neuter in English will be found to be masculine or feminine gender in Greek, and vice versa. That is to say, gender is a grammatical category, and does not always correspond with the category of sex.

2.14 A noun can be either *singular* or *plural* ("man"/"men"; "town"/"towns") —this feature is called its *number*. Greek indicates whether a noun is singular or plural by the kind of ending or suffix which it adds to the word's stem.

2.15 In addition to gender and number, a noun has a third grammatical feature, *case*, to be discussed below.

2.16 There are words which can be used in the place of a noun as the subject of a sentence. Such a word used in the place of a noun is called a *pronoun*. Pronouns are of various kinds, to be introduced in due course. Some examples are: he, she, it, you, my, this, who.

2.17 In a sentence, the statement about the subject will be made by means of a *verb*. The verb will agree with its subject in number, so that if the subject is plural, the form of the verb will also be plural. Thus, the subject *selects* or determines the *number* of the verb.

2.18 A complete sentence can consist of just two words, a subject and a verb: "Jesus wept" (John 11:35). Usually, however, a sentence will contain more words which add further information about either the subject or the verb. These may be additional nouns or pronouns, or other words which further describe or identify them (words of this kind are called *adjectives* — examples are "my", "beloved", "good", and "your" in the following sentences) or words which show the relationship of a noun to the rest of the sentence (called *prepositions* — examples are "in" and "before" in the following sentences) or words which give more details about the action of the verb (and therefore called *adverbs*, i.e. adding something to the verb) or connecting words (*conjunctions*), or other words such as *negatives* or *exclamations* etc.

2.19 Examples of sentences which include these various kinds of words are:
"You are my beloved son."
"Did you not sow good seed in your field?"
"Behold, I send my messenger before your face."

2.2 INFLECTED FORMS FOR NOUN, PRONOUN, AND ADJECTIVE

2.21 A noun or pronoun can have different types of relationships to its sentence. Its relationship in a particular sentence will be shown by a preposition or by its *case*, or by the two together. The case of a noun (that is, its relationship to the rest of the sentence) is indicated by the particular ending which is added to the noun's stem: in general, each case uses a different ending.

2.22 There are four cases in Greek. Thus there are eight possible forms that a noun can have, four for the singular and four for the plural. (Sometimes two forms may in fact have the same ending.) There is also an additional, vocative, form for some words. Pronouns and adjectives, similarly, have a set of different forms to indicate number and case, and can have additional sets of forms to differentiate gender as well.

2.23 "Case" exists in English as in Greek, but in English only the pronoun retains special forms to indicate what its case is. Nouns do have an ending to indicate one kind of relationship (the use of "-'s" to show possession), but apart from this they indicate relationship by means of position in a sentence or by the use of prepositions such as "of", "to", and "for".

2.24 The cases in Greek, and their English equivalents, are as set out in the following table.

GREEK CASE	ENGLISH CASE	PRONOUNS				NOUN
Nominative	Subject	I	we	you	he/she/it/they	Before verb
Accusative	Direct Object	me	us	you	him/her/it/them	After verb
Genitive	Possessive	my	our	your	his/her/its/their	-'s/of ....
Dative	Indirect Object	{to me / for me	to us / for us	to you / for you	to him etc. / for him etc.	to ...... or / for ....

2.25 Pronouns have an additional feature called *person*. Those pronouns that refer to or include the *addressor* (the person speaking) are said to be *first person* (e.g. I, me, us, our, etc.); those relating to the *addressee* (the person/persons being spoken to or written to) are *second person* (you, your); and those referring to a person or thing spoken or written about (he, her, its, them, etc.) are *third person*. Nouns will usually be third person.

2.26 The different cases can be seen in these sentences (John 2:16; 16:7):

You	must not make	my	Father's	house	a house	of merchandise.
subject	*verb*	*possess.*	*possess.*	*dir.object*	*dir.object*	*possessive*
nominative	*verb*	*genitive*	*genitive*	*accusative*	*accusative*	*genitive*

But	I	speak	the truth	to you.
	subject	*verb*	*direct object*	*indirect object*
	nominative	*verb*	*accusative*	*dative*

Sometimes the word "to" is not needed in English for the indirect object — the second sentence could also be written in English as, "But I tell you the truth." "You" is still the indirect object, and the Greek would be identical for both forms of the English sentence.

2.27 In addition to the four cases mentioned, there is also a fifth case, the vocative, the form of address. The word "sir" is in the vocative case in the sentence, "Sir, we would like to see Jesus." In Greek the form of the vocative is the same as for the nominative (a small number of important exceptions will be treated separately, as we come to them).

2.28 As mentioned earlier (#1.8), Greek words show inflection by changes which are made to their endings. For nouns, pronouns, and adjectives these inflected endings indicate their number and case (and, sometimes, their gender also). The set of inflections for a word is called its *flexion*[15]. Where the same pattern of flexion (i.e., the same set of endings) is used by numbers of words, that pattern is called a *paradigm*, which means, etymologically, "showing the pattern" (of something). These two terms can be used for the inflections both of nouns (and pronouns and adjectives) and verbs.

2.29 Related paradigms for nouns are known as a *declension*, and to set out the pattern of inflected forms for a particular noun is called *declining* it. There are three declensions in Greek, each of which contains a number of paradigms. The nouns in the lists of "Greek Examples" (#1.27 and #1.33), and their Declension and Paradigm group, are:

FIRST DECLENSION

D1.2 Fem. Consonant Stem		D1.1 Fem. ριε Stem		D1.5 Masc. Consonant Stem	
ζωή	life	ἡμέρα	day	προφήτης	prophet
φωνή	voice/sound	καρδία	heart	ὑποκριτής	hypocrite
ψυχή	soul/life	ὥρα	hour/time		
εἰρήνη	peace				

SECOND DECLENSION

D2.1 Masculine		τόπος	place	D2.2 Neuter	
ἄνθρωπος	man	χρόνος	time	ἔργον	work
θεός	God (god)	οἶκος	house/household	ξύλον	wood/tree
λαός	people	υἱός	son	σάββατον	sabbath
νόμος	law	οὐρανός	heaven		

THIRD DECLENSION

D3.2 Fem. Vowel Stem   D3.14 Masc/Fem -ων Stem D3.9 Neut. Consonant Stem
δύναμις   power   αἰών   age/world   ῥῆμα   word/object

Note that all the words in each Paradigm or flexion group have the same ending. If you are at all uncertain about what a "noun" is, look carefully at these examples and see (from their English meanings) what kind of words they are.

2.3   THE ARTICLE

2.31 When Greek wants to indicate that a noun is *definite* it places a special word, ὁ, in front of it. This word is called the *definite article* or, more simply, just *the article.*The closest English equivalent is the word "the". Thus ὁ ἄνθρωπος means "the man", a definite man, the particular man, where the addressor or the addressee (or both) know which man is being referred to. In contrast ἄνθρωπος means simply "a man" or "man" — Greek has no *indefinite article* (English "a" or "an"), though where the Greek wishes to stress the indefiniteness of something it may use τις, "a certain", as in ἄνθρωπος τις, "a certain man" (Luke 10:30).

2.32 The article is an inflected word, changing its ending so that it always agrees with the noun to which it refers in number, gender and case. It therefore has a separate form for both singular and plural for each of the four cases, for each of the three genders —this means that it has twenty-four forms in all. (Some of these forms are spelt the same as one another, but most of them are distinctive.)

2.33 The feminine article is a paradigm for the First Declension.

2.34 There is a close similarity between the masculine and neuter flexions of the article and the masculine and neuter paradigms of the Second Declension. These are given here for ὁ κύριος the lord and τὸ ἔργον the work.

2.4   PARADIGMS OF THE ARTICLE & SECOND DECLENSION NOUNS[16]

2.40		MASC.	FEM.	NEUT.	D2.1 MASC.	D2.2 NEUTER
S	Nominative	ὁ	ἡ	τό	ὁ κύριος	τὸ ἔργον
	Vocative				κύριε	
	Accusative	τόν	τήν	τό	τὸν κύριον	τὸ ἔργον
	Genitive	τοῦ	τῆς	τοῦ	τοῦ κυρίου	τοῦ ἔργου
	Dative	τῷ	τῇ	τῷ	τῷ κυρίῳ	τῷ ἔργῳ
P	Nominative	οἱ	αἱ	τά	οἱ κύριοι	τὰ ἔργα
	Accusative	τούς	τάς	τά	τοὺς κυρίους	τὰ ἔργα
	Genitive	των	τῶν	τῶν	τῶν κυρίων	τῶν ἔργων
	Dative	τοῖς	ταῖς	τοῖς	τοῖς κυρίοις	τοῖς ἔργοις

Features to note in these paradigms:

2.41 The neuter nominative and accusative forms are the same as each other. This characteristic will be found to apply to all Greek neuter nouns.

2.42 The nominative and accusative neuter plurals end in -α, and all the genitive plurals end in -$\omega\nu$. These characteristics will be found to apply to all paradigms of all declensions.

2.43 The neuter paradigm differs from the masculine only in the nominative and accusative — in the genitive and dative they are identical.

2.44 The characteristic of the dative case is the letter ι (though in the First and Second Declensions in the singular it is written subscript; but this is still a part of the spelling of the word and must not be omitted).

2.45 The stem of the article is τ, which in the masculine and feminine nominative has become a rough breathing instead, over the ending.

2.46 The Second Declension masculine singular has a separate, special form for the vocative. This is one of the exceptions to the generalization that the vocative has the same form as the nominative (see #2.27).

2.5 INFLECTION OF ADJECTIVES AND PRONOUNS

2.51 An adjective, like the article, agrees with the noun to which it refers in number, gender, and case. The adjectives that have been listed so far ($\H\iota\delta\iota\iota\iota\iota$, $\mu\acute{o}\nu\iota\iota\iota$ and $\H\iota\lambda\iota\iota\iota\iota$ —see #1.27) each therefore also have twenty-four forms. These correspond with the eight forms each of the Second Declension masculine, the First Declension feminine, and the Second Declension neuter. Thus the possessive adjective "my" has the three nominative singular forms $\grave{\epsilon}\mu\acute{o}\varsigma$ (masculine), $\grave{\epsilon}\mu\acute{\eta}$ (feminine) and $\grave{\epsilon}\mu\acute{o}\nu$ (neuter).

2.52 Similarly, pronouns like $\alpha\grave{\upsilon}\tau\acute{o}\varsigma$ (#1.33) also have twenty-four forms. Thus $\mu\iota\upsilon$ is the genitive singular of the pronoun "I", and therefore means "my". The genitive of a pronoun is placed after the word to which it refers: $\grave{o}$ $\upsilon\acute{\iota}\acute{o}\varsigma$ $\mu\iota\upsilon$, my son; $\iota\grave{\iota}$ $\H\iota\alpha\gamma\gamma\epsilon\lambda\iota\iota\iota$ $\alpha\grave{\upsilon}\tau\H\iota\omega\nu$, their angels.

2.53 VOCABULARY LISTING: Adjectives and pronouns, like nouns, are listed in lexicons and vocabularies in their nominative singular form. Adjectives will normally be shown in the masculine, with the feminine and neuter endings, thus: $\grave{\epsilon}\mu\acute{o}\varsigma$, -$\acute{\eta}$, -$\acute{o}\nu$, my. The form of the genitive singular may be given with a pronoun, thus: $\iota\grave{\iota}\tau\iota\iota\varsigma$, $\tau\iota\acute{\iota}\tau\iota\iota\upsilon$, this. The genitive singular is always given with a noun (as this allows the identification of its declension), and this is followed by the indication of its gender, either by m, f or n respectively or by giving the article that it takes, thus: $\theta\epsilon\acute{o}\varsigma$, -$\iota\upsilon$, $\grave{o}$, or $\grave{\eta}\mu\acute{\epsilon}\rho\alpha$, -$\alpha\varsigma$, $\grave{\eta}$.

2.6 PREPOSITIONS

2.61 Many sentences contain nouns which are not the subject or object of the verb or related by the idea of "of" (genitive case) or "to" or "for" (dative case). For these nouns, their relationship to the rest of the sentence is usually shown through a preposition. A preposition is always located in front of the noun (or of the noun's article, if it has one) — hence the name, "pre-position", i.e. in the position in front of its noun.

2.62 When a noun is used after a preposition in this way, it can never be nominative or vocative, but it can be either accusative, genitive or dative. These three cases which are used with prepositions are called the *oblique* cases as they are capable of being related *obliquely* (indirectly, i.e. through the preposition) to the rest of the sentence; this is in contrast to the nominative case, which is called the *direct* case.

2.63 Each Greek preposition uses or *selects* or *governs* either one particular case, or two cases, or all three oblique cases. The preposition has a different meaning with each of its different cases, if it has more than one.

2.64 Most prepositions have a central or *core* meaning (which is the usual one), and a number of *extended meanings*, which are all part of its total *area of meaning* (see #0.2).

2.65 Each lesson, new prepositions will be introduced. They must always be learnt with the case (or cases) that they take. The following three prepositions, and the case that each takes, should be learnt this lesson:

- **(a)** ἐν Used 2,713 times in the N.T. Takes the dative. Core meaning: in. Extended meanings: within, among, by means of, with.
- **(b)** ἐκ/ἐξ (see #1.65) Used 915 times in the N.T. Takes the genitive. Core meaning: out of (indicating source or origin, or previous position). Extended meanings: from amongst/away from.
- **(c)** πρό Used 47 times in the N.T. Takes the genitive. Core meaning: before; used both of time (= prior to) and place (= in front of).

2.66 Thus a word that is declined (noun, pronoun, adjective, or participle) which is found in an oblique case (#2.62) will be in that case for one of two reasons: either **(a)** it has the *inherent meaning* of that case (#2.24; #2.26); in which circumstance you must give it that meaning in translating it; or **(b)** it is *following a preposition* which has selected the case it is in (#2.63): in which circumstance the meaning will be the meaning which the preposition has when used with that particular case. Thus: σοι is the dative singular of "you" and therefore has the meaning "to you" or "for you" (#2.24). However, the preposition ἐν, "in", selects the dative case: so ἐν σοι means "in you" and DOES NOT mean "in to you" or "in for you" — in this circumstance the dative case is not being used to mean "to" or "for" but the dative case is selected by the preposition ἐν for the word which ἐν governs. This is what is meant by saying (#2.65) that ἐν "takes the dative".

2.67 Always read a preposition in conjunction with what it governs in a sentence, and translate the preposition and what it governs as a single unit of meaning in that sentence.

2.7 THE VERB

2.71 The verb is the word in a sentence which makes a statement about the subject or transfers an idea or an action from the subject to an object (some other person or thing). In English it can consist of more than one word; in Greek it usually is a single word.

2.72 In its usual type of *mode* or *mood*[17] — the *indicative* — it can make an affirmation ("Jesus *wept*") or ask a question ("*Are* you the Christ?"). It has other modes also: It can make a request or give a command (*imperative* mode: "Lord, *save* us"; "*Take* and *eat* this"); it can make a statement about possibilities (*subjunctive* mode: "If any man *would be* my disciple . . . ."). The *infinitive* is also usually treated as a mode ("I will make you *to become* fishers of men . . ."). These four — *indicative*, *imperative*, *subjunctive* and *infinitive* — are the ones normally used (we meet the rare *optative* in #9).

2.73 Like a pronoun (see #2.25), a verb indicates *person* (first, second or third) and we have noted earlier (#2.17) that it agrees with the *number* (singular or plural) of its subject. When a verb has a multiple subject (such as "Jesus and his disciples") the number of the verb regularly agrees with the part of the subject which comes first or is nearest to the verb.

2.74 Like other inflected words, a verb consists of a word stem (the lexal — see #1.83) and *affixes*, i.e. morphs added to the stem to indicate the grammatical information about a word in a particular use. An affix added at the beginning of a word is a *prefix*, within a word is an *infix*, and at the end of a word is a *suffix*. Most grammatical morphs are suffixes. By means of these morphs, a verb indicates its five features: person, number, tense (including time and/or aspect), mode, and voice. To *parse* a verb form is to state each of these features about it, in the order given here, followed by the lexical form and meaning of the word.

2.75 The inflected forms of a verb that indicate person and number are grouped together into a *flexion* and (as for a noun) a pattern flexion is called a *paradigm*. Related paradigms for verbs are known as a *conjugation*, and setting out the pattern of inflected forms for a particular verb is called *conjugating* it.

2.76 Historical grammarians such as A.T. Robertson (on page 149) have concluded that the endings of a Greek verb which indicate the person and number of its subject had their origin long ago in the attachment of an unemphatic personal pronoun as a suffix to the stem of the verb (and such a suffix can thus be referred to as a *pronoun suffix*). For example: stem φα- or φη- means "say", and the pronoun suffix -μι means "I", so φημι means "I say". Similarly the stem of the verb "be" is ἐσ- and λυ- means "loose", while the pronoun suffix -μεν means "we". Thus ἐσμεν means "we are" and λυομεν means "we loose".

2.77 Notice that a joining vowel (called the *neutral morph*), -ο-, has been placed between λυ- and -μεν. This verb, and each of the other verbs that follow this paradigm, insert the neutral morph, either -ο- or -ε-, in this way. The neutral morph has a "neutral" influence in a word, i.e., it does not affect its meaning.

2.78 Sometimes in adding the pronoun suffix a change occurs in the stem or the ending, or both. Thus the original conjectural pronoun suffix -ντι became first -νσι, "they", and when this was added to λυο- the -ν- was pushed out of the word and in "compensation" the -ο- lengthened to -ου-, producing λυουσι, "they loose". Other changes have occurred over the years through some of the consonants dropping out of the endings, and the vowels thus juxtaposed have then combined into a diphthong.

2.79 All these various changes have resulted in the development over the years of two basic paradigm patterns (i.e., conjugations) for Greek verbs in the present tense. The older of these has retained the original -μι pronoun ending of its form for the first person singular present indicative active form (which is the *lexical form*), and is therefore often referred to as the -MI Conjugation. In the evolution of the later, Omega Conjugation, the -μι has been lost and in the first person singular its -ο- vowel, the neutral morph, has lengthened into omega, this lengthening indicating the pronoun "I".

2.8 PARADIGMS OF THE PRESENT INDICATIVE ACTIVE

2.81 In these paradigms for the Present Indicative Active it is possible to see how the original pronoun suffixes which Robertson has traced have been modified over the years prior to the period of Classical Greek. The first paradigm is that of εἰμί, "be", the most frequently-occurring verb of the -μι Conjugation (it is used about 2,500 times in the Greek N.T.). The second is that of λύω, "loose", which is the pattern verb for many hundreds of other N.T. verbs.

		Pronoun Suffix	Stem: ἐσ-		Stem: λυ-ο/ε-	
SING.	1	-μι	εἰμί	I am	λύω	I loose/am loosing
	2	-σι	εἶ	you are	λύεις	you loose/are loosing
	3	-τι	ἐστί(ν)	he/she/it is	λύει	he/she/it looses/is loosing
PLURAL	1	-μεν	ἐσμέν	we are	λύομεν	we loose/are loosing
	2	-τε	ἐστέ	you are	λύετε	you loose/are loosing
	3	-ντι	εἰσί(ν)	they are	λύουσι(ν)	they loose/are loosing

NOTE the further comments on these forms to be found in #A2.

2.82 Notice the forms which have *moveable nu* (shown in brackets — see #1.65). Learn this as part of the form.

2.83 Because an unemphatic personal pronoun is already part of each verb, that verb already has an *internal subject*. If a separate word in the nominative case is given in the clause (i.e., an *external subject* for the verb), then the internal subject is **NOT TRANSLATED.** Thus: ὁ Πιλᾶτος λέγει, Pilate says (and **NOT**: Pilate he says).

2.84 When there is no external subject in the sentence, the internal subject needs to be translated. (Note that as the pronoun suffix does not indicate gender, the 3rd person singular can be translated "he", "she", or "it", as the context requires.) Thus: καὶ λέγει τοῖς Ἰουδαίοις, and he says to the Jews.

2.85 We can see, then, that there is no separate word actually needed with a Greek verb for "I", "you", etc. When therefore such a pronoun *is* provided as an external subject, it is a way of indicating emphasis. Compare the shade of difference between saying, Εἶ ὁ Χριστός, and, Σὺ εἶ ὁ Χριστός. Always indicate this emphasis when translating by underlining an emphatic pronoun.

2.86 One accent needs to be carefully noted: the use of the circumflex on the form εἶ over the smooth breathing. This accent distinguishes this form, the second person singular present indicative of εἰμί, from εἰ, which has a smooth breathing and *no* accent, and which means "if".

2.87 The paradigms given for εἰμί and λύω are the paradigms for the Indicative Mode, i.e. where a verb is stating something as a fact. The Indicative also includes the Interrogative i.e. when a verb is asking a question — the fact that a question is being asked is shown by the use of a question mark (;) at the end of a sentence. NOTE: The first step in understanding the meaning of a Greek sentence is to check whether or not it is a question.

2.9 WORD ORDER

2.91 Greek sentence order can differ considerably from that of English. Word order is used in English to indicate the relationship of the words of the sentence (consider the difference in meaning, indicated solely by word order, between "The man ate a large fish" and "A large fish ate the man"). As Greek indicates case by its word endings, the position of a word in a clause or sentence is frequently used to indicate emphasis.

2.92 The beginning of a sentence is an emphatic position, and the most important word in a sentence may be placed first to give it emphasis. Often a word in this position is considered definite enough not to be given the article in Greek. A word can also be emphasized by being held back to the end of a clause or sentence.

2.93 It is normal for the subject to be placed *after* the verb to which it refers — it will be recognized as being the subject as it is nominative case, and will usually have the article. Exception: a pronoun subject usually comes in front of the verb.

2.94 The word (or words) coming after the verb "to be" to complete the thought is called the *complement* (i.e. the "completement"). Its customary position in Greek is prior to the verb. Thus κύριός ἐστιν ὁ υἱός means "the son is lord". Note that the complement normally has no article.

2.95 There are a number of words which can never be placed first in a Greek clause or sentence. The most common of these are the conjunctions δέ (and, but), γάρ (for) and οὖν (then, therefore). The translation of δέ and γάρ will be put first when rendering them into English.

2.96 The negative οὐ/οὐκ/οὐχ (not) comes in front of the verb to which it refers. Thus ἐγὼ οὐκ εἰμί, "**I** am not".

2.97 A genitive can come between the article and its noun, or (more usually) after the noun to which it refers. Thus ὁ υἱός μου, "my son". Similarly an adjective can come between the article and its noun (ἐν τῷ σῷ ἀγρῷ, "in your field") or after the noun: but in that case the noun's article must be repeated in front of the adjective (ὁ υἱός μου ὁ ἀγαπητός, "my beloved son" — more literally, "my son, the beloved one"). An adjectival prepositional phrase can be used in the same way, with the article. Thus τὸ πρόσωπον τοῦ πατρός μου τοῦ ἐν οὐρανοῖς, "the face of my father the (one) in (the) heavens", i.e. "the face of my father in (the) heavens".

2.98 Some words (mostly names) are indeclinable, and will be recognized as genitive (or one of the other cases) only by their position, and the sense of the sentence. Thus ὁ θεὸς Ἰακώβ, "the God of Jacob".

2.99 Thus for a basic sentence the normal Greek word order (from which there are however numerous exceptions, especially to indicate emphasis) is: conjunction, complement/object, verb, subject. A genitive will regularly follow the noun to which it refers. Other words and phrases will be fitted into this basic pattern. Be sure that you translate not only **Greek words** into **English words**, but also **Greek order** into **English order.**

YOUR ASSIGNMENTS are set out on the following page.

NOTE: for the assignments for this Lesson and for your subsequent Lessons, you should spend *five minutes daily* in learning the set paradigms. Read a paradigm aloud once or twice, then look away from the book and repeat it aloud again. Follow this procedure a second time if necessary. Then go on to the next paradigm. Go through only one or two paradigms each day in this way, then review all of them together at the end of each week.

In your study time, check through the Grammar Questions in #A1.95 and A2.8 (and for subsequent Lessons, at the end of each section of Appendix A for each Lesson) to see that you have understood the grammar that you need to know. But spend most of your available study time working on the set sentences from the Greek New Testament — these are the examples of the grammar set out in the Lesson. Note carefully the Principles of Translation (#A2.5) and Translation Techniques (#A2.6), and be guided by these in your work.

ASSIGNMENTS ON LESSON TWO

(Suggestions concerning the work of these assignments will be found in #A2.)

1. Read Lesson Two through twice, aiming for an understanding of the points raised rather than committing the details to memory. The material that *does* need to be **learned by heart** is: the paradigms of the Article (#2.4) and of the Present Indicative Active of εἰμί and λύω (#2.81). **Learn** these *down* the columns. Write them out from memory. Check them against the book and make sure that you have them word perfect.

2. Write out the English meanings for each of the forms of the paradigms of ὁ κύριος and τὸ ἔργον, with those paradigms (#2.4).

3. Read carefully through the Appendix Notes on this Lesson (#A2).

4. Work through the Selections from the Greek New Testament which follow. Aim to achieve an understanding of what the meaning is for each Selection, using the vocabulary below, and also that of the "Greek Examples" in #1.27 and #1.33. Write out a literal translation of these Selections on a separate sheet of paper (DO NOT under ANY circumstances write a translation above the Greek Selections).

5. (OPTIONAL COMPREHENSION QUESTIONS)
   a. What is the significance of the capital letters in Selections 1, 3, 4, 5, 7, 9, 10, 11, 12, 13, 14, 15, 16, 17, 18, 19, 20, 22, 23, 24 and 26?
   b. What is the significance of the capital letters in Selections 6 and 28?
   c. What is the subject of Selection 16?
   d. Is ἐγώ really necessary in Selections 1, 6, 7, 9, 12, or 15? Comment on its use, compared with Selections 18 and 27.
   e. What is the verb in Selection 17? Why is there no article with ἀρχή?
   f. Account for the word order of Selections 21 and 25.
   g. Why is ὁ repeated in Selection 8?
   h. What is the significance of ἐκ in Selection 28?
   i. Some Selections are very similar. Are there any exegetical points that can be noted by comparing these with each other?
   j. Are there any other points which you have noted which emerge from a reading of the Greek of these Selections from the Greek New Testament?

6. Do a quick preliminary reading of Lesson Three.

EXPRESSIONS (Not explained as yet)

διὰ παντός	always
ἐγένετο	there came
ἐκλελεγμένος	(the) chosen one
ἔσπειρας	you (sg.) sowed
ζώντων	living ones (gen. pl.)
λέγουσα	saying (participle)
σπείρων	the one who sows
τοῦ πατρός μου	of my father
χειρῶν	hands (gen. pl.)

WORDS

*ἀγαπητός, ή, όν	beloved
*ἄγγελος, ου, ὁ	messenger, angel
ἀγρός, οῦ, ὁ	field
*ἀκούω	I hear
*ἀλλά	but
ἀμνός, οῦ, ὁ	lamb
*ἀποστέλλω	I send
*ἄρτος, ου, ὁ	bread, a loaf
*ἀρχή, ῆς, ἡ	beginning (noun)

*βασιλεία, ας, ἡ	kingdom, rule		*ὅτι	that, because
*βασιλεύς, έως, ὁ	king		*οὐ/οὐκ/οὐχ	not, no
*βλέπω	I see		*οὖν	then, therefore
*γάρ	for		*οὗτος, τούτου	this
*δέ	but, and		*οὐχί; (introd.	not
*ἐγώ	I		question expecting	
*εἰμί	I am		"yes")	
*ἐκ/ἐξ (see #2.65)	out of		πόθεν;	from where? where?
*ἐμός, ή, όν	my (adjective)		*πονηρός ά όν	evil, bad, the evil one
*ἐν (see #2.65)	in		πρό (scc #2.65)	before
*εὐαγγελίον, ου, τό	gospel		*πρόσωπον, ου, τό	face
*ἔχω	I have		*σάββατον, ου, τό	sabbath
ζιζάνιον, ου, τό	darnel, a weed		σός, σή, σόν	your (sing.)
*ἰδού, ἴδε	behold! look! see!		σπέρμα, ατος, τό	seed (sperm)
*καί	and, also, even		*σύ	you (sg.)
*καλός, ή, όν	good		σου	your (sg.)
*κόσμος, ου, ὁ	world		*τίς;	who?
*κύριος, ου, ὁ	lord, sir		τί;	what? why?
*λέγω	I say, speak, tell		*ὑμῶν	your
*μου	my (pronoun)		ὑμῖν	to you (pl.)
*νεκρός, ά, όν	dead (dead person)		*φῶς, φωτός, τό	light
νεφέλη, ης, ἡ	cloud		*Χριστός, οῦ, ὁ	Christ, Messiah

NAMES: These will be self-evident. If in doubt, check in the Vocabulary in #G3.

*Re words with an asterisk, see #0.4.

SELECTIONS FROM THE GREEK NEW TESTAMENT

(NOTE: These are selections from the verses listed; in most cases only a part of the verse is being set for you to read at this stage.)

1. Ἐγώ εἰμι ὁ Χριστός. (ΚΑΤΑ ΜΑΘΘΑΙΟΝ 24:5.)

2. οὗτός ἐστιν ὁ υἱὸς τοῦ θεοῦ. (ΚΑΤΑ ΙΩΑΝΝΗΝ 1:34.)

3. ὁ Πέτρος λέγει, Σὺ εἶ ὁ Χριστός. (ΚΑΤΑ ΜΑΡΚΟΝ 8:29.)

4. Οὗτός ἐστιν Ἰησοῦς ὁ βασιλεῦς τῶν Ἰουδαίων. (ΚΑΤΑ ΜΑΘΘΑΙΟΝ 27:37.)

5. Σὺ εἶ ὁ υἱὸς τοῦ θεοῦ. (ΚΑΤΑ ΜΑΡΚΟΝ 3:11.)

6. Σὺ τίς εἶ; Ἐγὼ οὐκ εἰμὶ ὁ Χριστός. (ΚΑΤΑ ΙΩΑΝΝΗΝ 1:19.)

7. Ἐγώ εἰμι ὁ ἄρτος τῆς ζωῆς. (ΚΑΤΑ ΙΩΑΝΝΗΝ 6:48.)

8. οὗτός ἐστιν ὁ ἄρτος ὁ ἐκ τοῦ οὐρανοῦ. (ΚΑΤΑ ΙΩΑΝΝΗΝ 6:50.)

9. Ἐγώ εἰμι τὸ φῶς τοῦ κοσμοῦ. (ΚΑΤΑ ΙΩΑΝΝΗΝ 8:12.)

10. ὁ Πιλᾶτος λέγει τῷ Ἰησοῦ, Πόθεν εἶ σύ; (ΚΑΤΑ ΙΩΑΝΝΗΝ 19:8-9.)

11. καὶ λέγει τοῖς Ἰουδαίοις, Ἴδε ὁ βασιλεὺς ὑμῶν. (ΚΑΤΑ ΙΩΑΝΝΗΝ 19:14.)

12. Ἐγώ εἰμι τὸ Ἄλφα καὶ τὸ Ὦ, λέγει κύριος ὁ θεός. (ΑΠΟΚΑΛΥΨΙΣ ΙΩΑΝΝΟΥ 1:8.)

13. Ἰδοὺ φωνὴ ἐκ τῶν οὐρανῶν λέγουσα, Οὗτός ἐστιν ὁ υἱός μου ὁ ἀγαπητός. (ΚΑΤΑ ΜΑΘΘΑΙΟΝ 3:17.)

14. ὁ Ἰωάννης βλέπει τὸν Ἰησοῦν καὶ λέγει, Ἴδε ὁ ἀμνὸς τοῦ θεοῦ. (ΚΑΤΑ ΙΩΑΝΝΗΝ 1:29.)

15. Ἐγώ εἰμι ὁ θεὸς Ἀβραὰμ καὶ ὁ θεὸς Ἰσαὰκ καὶ ὁ θεὸς Ἰακώβ· οὐκ ἔστιν ὁ θεὸς νεκρῶν ἀλλὰ ζώντων. (ΚΑΤΑ ΜΑΘΘΑΙΟΝ 22:32.)

16. Ἀκούεις τί οὗτοι λέγουσιν; (ΚΑΤΑ ΜΑΘΘΑΙΟΝ 21:16.)

17. Ἀρχὴ τοῦ εὐαγγελίου Ἰησοῦ Χριστοῦ υἱοῦ θεοῦ. (ΚΑΤΑ ΜΑΡΚΟΝ 1:1.)

18. Ἰδοὺ ἀποστέλλω τὸν ἄγγελόν μου πρὸ προσώπου σου. (ΚΑΤΑ ΜΑΡΚΟΝ 1:2.)

19. ἰδοὺ φωνὴ ἐκ τῆς νεφέλης λέγουσα,
Οὗτός ἐστιν ὁ υἱός μου ὁ ἀγαπητός. (ΚΑΤΑ ΜΑΘΘΑΙΟΝ 17:5.)

20. Ἄρτους οὐκ ἔχομεν. (ΚΑΤΑ ΜΑΡΚΟΝ 8:16.)

21. ἔργα τῶν χειρῶν σού εἰσιν οἱ οὐρανοί. (ΠΡΟΣ ΕΒΡΑΙΟΥΣ 1:10.)

22. καὶ φωνὴ ἐγένετο ἐκ τῶν οὐρανῶν, Σὺ εἶ ὁ υἱός μου ὁ ἀγαπητός. (ΚΑΤΑ ΜΑΡΚΟΝ 1:11.)

23. Κύριε, οὐχὶ καλὸν σπέρμα ἔσπειρας ἐν τῷ σῷ ἀγρῷ; πόθεν οὖν ἔχει ζιζάνια; (ΚΑΤΑ ΜΑΘΘΑΙΟΝ 13:27.)

24. Ὁ σπείρων τὸ καλὸν σπέρμα ἐστὶν ὁ υἱὸς τοῦ ἀνθρώπου· ὁ δὲ ἀγρός ἐστιν ὁ κόσμος· τὸ δὲ καλὸν σπέρμα, οὗτοί εἰσιν οἱ υἱοὶ τῆς βασιλείας· τὰ δὲ ζιζάνιά εἰσιν οἱ υἱοὶ τοῦ πονηροῦ. (ΚΑΤΑ ΜΑΘΘΑΙΟΝ 13:37-8.)

25. κύριός ἐστιν ὁ υἱὸς τοῦ ἀνθρώπου καὶ τοῦ σαββάτου. (ΚΑΤΑ ΜΑΡΚΟΝ 2:28.)

26. καὶ φωνὴ ἐγένετο ἐκ τῆς νεφέλης λέγουσα, Οὗτός ἐστιν ὁ υἱός μου ὁ ἐκλελεγμένος. (ΚΑΤΑ ΛΟΥΚΑΝ 9:35.)

27. λέγω ὑμῖν ὅτι οἱ ἄγγελοι αὐτῶν ἐν οὐρανοῖς διὰ παντὸς βλέπουσι τὸ πρόσωπον τοῦ πατρός μου τοῦ ἐν οὐρανοῖς. (ΚΑΤΑ ΜΑΘΘΑΙΟΝ 18:10.)

28. Σὺ εἶ ὁ βασιλεὺς τῶν Ἰουδαίων; Ἡ βασιλεία ἡ ἐμὴ οὐκ ἔστιν ἐκ τοῦ κόσμου τούτου. (ΚΑΤΑ ΙΩΑΝΝΗΝ 18:33, 36.)

LESSON THREE

FIRST DECLENSION AND SECOND AORIST ACTIVE

3.1 COMPLETE PARADIGMS FOR THE FIRST DECLENSION

3.11 In Lesson Two, the feminine form of the article introduced the First Declension. The pattern of the article is in fact only one of four basic paradigms for this declension — the endings differ slightly according to the nature of the last letter of the stem to which they are being added, and according to whether the word is masculine or feminine gender (there are no neuter words of the First Declension). There is also a mixed or hybrid feminine paradigm, which changes from one to another of two of the basic patterns. These five First Declension paradigms are set out here:

		FEMININE NOUNS			**MASCULINE NOUNS**	
		D1.2 c stem	D1.1 ριε stem	D1.3 σ stem	D1.5 c stem	D1.4 ριε stem
		"voice"	"heart"	"glory"	"disciple"	"young man"
SING.	N	φωνή	καρδία	δόξα	μαθητής	νεανίας
	V	—	—	—	μαθητά	νεανία
	A	φωνήν	καρδίαν	δόξαν	μαθητήν	νεανίαν
	G	φωνῆς	καρδίας	δόξης	μαθητοῦ	νεανίου
	D	φωνῇ	καρδίᾳ	δόξῃ	μαθητῇ	νεανίᾳ
PL.	N	φωναί	καρδίαι	δόξαι	μαθηταί	νεανίαι
	A	φωνάς	καρδίας	δόξας	μαθητάς	νεανίας
	G	φωνῶν	καρδίῶν	δοξῶν	μαθητῶν	νεανιῶν
	D	φωναῖς	καρδίαις	δόξαις	μαθηταῖς	νεανίαις

3.12 It is not necessary for you to learn these paradigms off by heart; they are provided here for reference, and so that you can see how their flexions compare with that for the feminine article.

3.13 If the stem of a word ends in a phoneme (#1.28) other than -ρ, -ι, -ε, or a sibilant, then the word has -η throughout all its singular endings (like φωνή or the feminine article ἡ, #2.4). This is Paradigm D1.2 (i.e. Declension 1, Paradigm 2), referred to as the feminine "Consonant Stem" Paradigm, because almost all the words which follow this paradigm have consonant stems — it is followed by 191 New Testament words, 185 with consonant stems, four ending in -οη, one in -ωη, and one in ευη (these are listed in #D1.64).

3.14 If the stem of a word ends in one of the three phonemes -ρ, -ι, or -ε, then the word has -α throughout all its singular endings (like καρδία). This is Paradigm D1.1, referred to as the "ριε" Paradigm because the stem of all but one of the words which follow this paradigm — there are 310 of them in the New Testament — ends in a ρ, ι or ε. (The one exception is στοά, porch, which is also an exception to the expectation — see #3.13 — that an -o stem would end in -οη[38].)

3.15 If the stem of a word ends in a sibilant (ζ, σ, or a double letter containing σ), then that word follows the mixed pattern of $\delta\acute{o}\xi\alpha$, Paradigm D1.3, referred to as the "σ stem Paradigm". In addition, the Sigma Stem Paradigm is also followed by four New Testament words ending in -ρ, eight in -ν, and one each in -λ and -θ. As there are eight N.T. nouns with sibilant stems, there are thus a total of 22 N.T. nouns which follow Paradigm D1.3. These nouns, and the number of times each occurs in the New Testament, are set out in #D1.65. Paradigm D1.3 is also followed by pronouns and participles which have a sibilant stem in their feminine flexions.

3.16 Most words of the First Declension are feminine, belonging to one or other of the above three paradigms. There are also, in the New Testament, 112 masculine nouns of the First Declension, 111 of which have their stem ending in a consonant (usually -τ), and which all follow Paradigm D1.5, $\mu\alpha\theta\eta\tau\acute{\eta}s$. Note that this paradigm is similar to that of $\phi\omega\nu\acute{\eta}$ (D1.2), differing in two respects only — in the nominative singular the masculine words (Paradigm D1.5) are distinguished by having an additional -s as their final letter, and in the genitive singular they conform to the pattern of the Second Declension (see #2.4) and have -ov as their ending — which also has the effect of keeping the forms of the nominative and genitive singular different. Note that this paradigm has a vocative (#2.22, 2.27).

3.17 There is only one masculine noun of the First Declension with a "$\rho\iota\epsilon$" stem: $\nu\epsilon\alpha\nu\acute{\iota}\alpha s$. However, quite a few names occur (e.g. 'Ανδρέας) which follow Paradigm D1.4. This paradigm is identical with that of $\mu\alpha\theta\eta\tau\acute{\eta}s$ (Paradigm D1.5), but with -α instead of -η (i.e. it follows $\kappa\alpha\rho\delta\acute{\iota}\alpha$, but has the same two distinguishing features of the masculine: the added -s in the nominative singular, and -ov in the genitive singular).

3.18 In all cases the First Declension nouns, both masculine and feminine, adhere to the endings of the feminine article in the plural. As the article always agrees in gender with its noun, "the disciple" will be $\acute{o}$ $\mu\alpha\theta\eta\tau\acute{\eta}s$, and "the disciples" will be oi $\mu\alpha\theta\eta\tau\alpha\acute{\iota}$.

3.2   FEMININE NOUNS OF THE SECOND DECLENSION

3.21 The most common noun group in the Greek N.T. is the Second Declension (see #2.4), consisting of nouns which have their nominative singular ending in -os and are masculine (372 N.T. words) or ending in -ov and are neuter (196 N.T. words).

3.22 There are however a number of exceptions: Second Declension nouns ending in -os, and declined regularly, but feminine in gender. Twenty-eight such feminine Second Declension nouns occur in the Greek N.T. (listed, #D2.44), but most of them are used only a small number of times each. There are only five which are each used ten times or more in the G.N.T., and the two most commonly used words of these five are given in this Lesson's Vocabulary.

3.23 Twenty-two of the masculine words can also be feminine gender: e.g. $\theta\epsilon\acute{o}s$, $o\~v$, $\acute{\eta}$, a goddess; $\pi\alpha\rho\theta\acute{\epsilon}\nu os$, ov, $\acute{\eta}$, a (female) virgin — this word as a masculine form refers to a male who is a virgin. (Listed, #D2.45.)

3.3 PRONOUNS

3.31 The word that is used for the third person personal pronoun, αὐτός, he/she/it/they, also means (depending upon the context and the construction): "self, of oneself, even, very, the same". For the time being, in the Selections from the Greek New Testament in which it appears in this Course, it will always be the third person personal pronoun. Notice in the paradigm that follows that αὐτος has endings identical with those of the article (plus the standard Second Declension "-ς" ending in the masculine nominative singular which is lacking in the article).

3.32 The demonstrative pronoun and adjective οὗτος is very similar throughout to αὐτός, but has the additional feature that the *stem* itself changes in the feminine and neuter from "οὐ-" to "αὐ-" when the ending contains "α" or "η" (and not otherwise). You should note also that, like the article, it begins with a "τ" in all cases except the nominatives of the masculine and feminine singular and plural, where the "τ" is dropped and replaced by a rough breathing. This means that the only difference between the feminine nominative singular and plural forms for αὐτός and οὗτος consists of the breathing (and the accent): the letters of the words are the same. Care needs to be taken, therefore, to identify these forms correctly.

3.33 You will need to learn the paradigms for the 1st and 2nd person pronouns. You already know the pattern of endings for the other paradigms from the article — they are provided here for reference, and so that you can see how their patterns compare with that for the article.

		PERSONAL PRONOUNS				DEMONSTRATIVE		
SING.	1st	2nd	3rd m.	3rd f.	3rd n.	(Pronoun/Adjective)		
N	ἐγώ	σύ	αὐτός	αὐτή	αὐτό	οὗτος	αὕτη	τοῦτο
A	ἐμέ/με	σέ	αὐτόν	αὐτήν	αὐτό	τοῦτον	ταύτην	τοῦτο
G	ἐμοῦ/μου	σοῦ	αὐτοῦ	αὐτῆς	αὐτοῦ	τούτου	ταύτης	τούτου
D	ἐμοί/μοι	σοί	αὐτῷ	αὐτῇ	αὐτῷ	τούτῳ	ταύτῃ	τούτῳ
PLURAL								
N	ἡμεῖς	ὑμεῖς	αὐτοί	αὐταί	αὐτά	οὗτοι	αὗται	ταῦτα
A	ἡμᾶς	ὑμᾶς	αὐτούς	αὐτάς	αὐτά	τούτους	ταύτας	ταῦτα
G	ἡμῶν	ὑμῶν	αὐτῶν	αὐτῶν	αὐτῶν	τούτων	τούτων	τούτων
D	ἡμῖν	ὑμῖν	αὐτοῖς	αὐταῖς	αὐτοῖς	τούτοις	ταύταις	τούτοις

(The English meanings for these forms are given in #A3.21.)

3.34 Notice the alternative forms which are found for the 1st person singular accusative, genitive and dative pronouns. In the style of some writers, the longer form is more emphatic than the shorter form; at other times the alternatives appear to be used without any distinction of meaning.

3.35 οὗτος either refers to something of a grammatically masculine gender, or means "this man"; similarly with αὕτη, "this woman", and τοῦτο, "this thing". Thus ταῦτα means "these things". When used as a demonstrative adjective, οὗτος agrees with its noun in number, gender, and case, has the meaning of "this", and stands in what is called the "predicative" position, in front of the article, or after the noun without the usual repetition of the article.

3.36 ἐκεῖνος, the demonstrative pronoun/adjective meaning "that", is declined with the same endings as οὗτος, but without any change in the stem of the word, and it also takes the predicative position with a noun.

3.4   CLUES FROM THE AGREEMENT OF ARTICLE AND ADJECTIVES

3.41 Because the article and adjectives always agree with their noun in number, gender, and case, they often provide valuable clues to the identification of the number, gender, and case of nouns in a sentence when these might otherwise not be known to you.

3.42 Thus when you first see the word μισθόν, it is not possible for you to know whether it is the accusative of a masculine word μισθός or the nominative or accusative singular of a neuter word μισθόν. The query is resolved when one sees it with its article: τὸν μισθόν. Is βασιλείας the nominative singular of a First Declension masculine noun, or the genitive singular of a First Declension feminine? The article τῆς resolves the question. Again, there are many word forms ending in "-α": ὄνομα, πνεῦμα, πρόβατα, θύρα, and so on. These forms can be clarified and deciphered when we take note of their articles and/or adjectives: τὸ ἐμὸν ὄνομα, τὸ πνεῦμα, τὰ πρόβατα, ἡ θύρα.

3.5   THE PRESENT IMPERATIVE, SECOND PERSON PLURAL

3.51 In Lesson Two we noted the paradigm of λύω for the present indicative and interrogative active. Thus the form λύετε could mean "you are loosing" or "are you loosing?" This particular form of the verb also happens to be the same for a command, i.e. the imperative mode. So it can also mean, "Loose!" as an order. Usually the context makes it plain whether the meaning is indicative, interrogative, or imperative.

3.52 However, a number of ambiguous usages do exist in the Greek New Testament. For example, Jesus said, πιστεύετε εἰς τὸν θεόν, καὶ εἰς ἐμὲ πιστεύετε (John 14:1). Is he making a statement, asking a question, or telling his disciples something that they are to do? Or could it be that one πιστεύετε is indicative and the other is imperative? This would give the meaning as, "You believe in God; believe also in me." Knowing Greek will not automatically *solve* ambiguities of this kind — but it certainly will enable you to *be aware* of them and to read about them in the only place where they can really be dealt with: in a commentary on the Greek text of the New Testament.

3.6   TIME, ASPECT AND CONJUGATION

3.61 Past time is indicated in Greek by prefixing the *past time morph* (called an *augment*) to the beginning of the verb. If the verb lexal begins with a consonant, the augment is the addition of ε-, which is called the *syllabic augment* (e.g., verb lexal βαλ- becomes ἐβαλ-). If the verb lexal begins with a vowel, the augment consists of the *lengthening* of this vowel, and this *process of lengthening* is called the *temporal augment* (e.g., verbal lexal ἐλθ- becomes ἠλθ-).

3.62 There are three tenses in Greek which have the augment, i.e. which indicate past time: the aorist (pronounced air-rist), the imperfect, and the pluperfect. They all refer to the past; the difference between them is the *kind of action* which they indicate. This feature is called their *aspect*. The aorist indicates *punctiliar aspect*[18]: the whole aspect of the verb is regarded as a *point* — hence the name. The imperfect is *durative aspect*[18]: the emphasis is upon the *duration* of the activity, which is being shown to be of an ongoing, repeated, or incomplete nature. The pluperfect is *perfective aspect*[18]: the action has been brought to a completion, with consequences that have been continuing. (Further details about aspect will be given in the next Lesson.)

3.63 Greek contains three different patterns of the formation of the aorist tense (all with exactly the same meaning — this is similar to the different ways which English has of forming a past tense; consider the English past tense forms of *bake, make, take,* and *wake,* for example). What is called the "first aorist" pattern will be set out in Lesson Four, and the "third aorist" pattern in Lesson Seven. The "second aorist" pattern takes the verb lexal, adds the augment, and uses a special set of pronoun endings which are a little different from the set for the present tense. The second aorist flexions are given in #3.8 for the lexals βαλ- (the verb stem of βάλλω I throw) and ἐλθ- (which has no durative, i.e., present form — it has to make use of the durative flexions of another verb, ἔρχομαι, I come; see #3.66).

3.64 Verbs which have second aorist forms comprise the *Second Conjugation*; verbs which have third aorist forms and/or a lexical form ending in -μι comprise the *Third Conjugation*; all other verbs have first aorist forms, conjugate their flexions like λύω, and comprise the *First Conjugation*.

3.65 A verb lexal possesses *inherent aspect* — that is, a lexal always *is*, in itself, either durative or punctiliar aspect. First Conjugation verbs have durative lexals; Second and Third Conjugation verbs have punctiliar lexals.

3.66 Some Second Conjugation verbs (whose lexals therefore are inherently punctiliar) are defective and are incapable of forming a present tense (durative) form, and instead have to utilize the durative forms from another defective verb. Three such verbs to note this Lesson, all of which are very common in the Greek N.T., are:

Lexal	Second Aorist		Associated Present Tense	
ἐλθ-	ἦλθον	I came	ἔρχομαι	I come
ἰδ-	εἶδον	I saw	ὁράω	I see
εἰπ-	εἶπον	I spoke/said	λέγω	I speak/say

3.7 COMPOUND VERBS

3.71 A very large number of verbs in the Greek New Testament are *compound verbs*, that is, verbs compounded of a *simple* or *simplex verb* and a preposition that has been added to the beginning of it. The meaning of the simplex verb is then affected by the preposition. Sometimes compound verbs have meanings that are a compound of the meanings of the simplex verb and the preposition. Examples: ἐκ/ἐξ, out (of); βάλλω, I throw; ἐκβάλλω, I throw out, send/away, drive; ἦλθον, I came; ἐξῆλθον, I came out, departed. At other times, compound verbs will be found which have meanings that are quite different from those of the preposition plus original simplex verbs. Thus: ἀπο, from; ἔχω, I have; ἀπέχω, I have in full.

3.72 NOTE: When a compound verb is augmented, the augment goes *between* the preposition and the simplex verb. Thus: ἐξέβαλον, from ἐκβάλλω.

3.8 PARADIGMS FOR THE IMPERFECT OF 'EIMI AND THE SECOND AORIST ACTIVE

3.81

		IMPERFECT OF εἰμί			SECOND AORIST ACTIVE			
SING.	1	ἤμην	I was	ἔβαλον	I threw	ἦλθον	I came
	2	ἦς/ἦσθα	you were	ἔβαλες	you threw	ἦλθες	you came
	3	ἦν	he/she/it was	ἔβαλε(ν)	he threw	ἦλθε(ν)	he came
PL.	1	ἦμεν/ἤμεθα	we were	ἐβάλομεν	we threw	ἤλθομεν	we came
	2	ἦτε	you were	ἐβάλετε	you threw	ἤλθετε	you came
	3	ἦσαν	they were	ἔβαλον	they threw	ἦλθον	they came

3.82 The area of meaning for ἦλθον includes "I went" as well as "I came". Full details on second aorist verbs and their stems will be given later on. Notice that the second aorist forms for the first person singular and for the third person plural are identical. When one of these is encountered, it is therefore necessary to examine the context carefully for clues that will indicate which of these two possibilities is in fact the right one. Usually such indications will be available — otherwise the sentence will be ambiguous in the Greek.

3.9 THE VERB MORPH SLOTS

3.91 All the information about the total meaning of a particular verb form is conveyed through the morphs of which it is made up. These morphs can be thought of in various ways (READ #A3.4). It is important to be able to recognize each morph swiftly, and "read" the information that it contains.

3.92 There are altogether nine categories of morph which can occur in a verb (though no more than six will be found in any given verb form). The places where these morphs *can* occur in a verb are called *morph slots*.

3.93 The morphs of a verb can be set out so as to show which slot each occupies. Identifying the morphs of a verb form in this way is called *morphological analysis*[13] or *morphologizing*. The neutral morph occupies the aspect slot. The verbs that we have met in Lessons Two and Three have morphs which occupy either two, three, four or five of the nine available slots. They can be shown as follows (using as an example the first person plural of εἰμί, λύω, βάλλω and ἐκβάλλω):

VERB FORM	1	2 3	4	5 6	7	8	9
	PREPOSITION	PAST	LEXAL		ASPECT		ENDING
ἔσμεν			ἐσ				μεν
λύομεν			λυ		ο		μεν
ἐβάλομεν		ἐ	βαλ		ο		μεν
ἐξεβάλομεν	ἐξ	ε	βαλ		ο		μεν

3.94 Where a morph consists of the lengthening of a phoneme, this is indicated by a capital L in the column for that morph. Thus:

λύω			λυ		ο		L (="I")
ἦλθον		L	ελθ		ο		ν
ἐξήλθετε	ἐξ	L	ελθ		ε		τε

ASSIGNMENTS ON LESSON THREE

(Suggestions concerning the work of these assignments will be found in #A3.)

1. Read the Grammar section through a second time, aiming at an understanding of the points raised. **LEARN BY HEART:**
   (a) The paradigms of ἐγω and συ (1st & 2nd personal pronouns, #3.33);
   (b) The paradigms of the imperfect of εἰμι and of the second aorist form, ἔβαλον or ἦλθον (#3.81).
2. Read and translate literally the thirty Selections from the Greek New Testament. Aim to achieve an understanding of what the meaning is.
3. (OPTIONAL COMPREHENSION QUESTIONS)
   a. Both the beginning and the end of a sentence are positions of emphasis in Greek. Comment on Selections 7 and 18 in the light of this.
   b. Translate Selection 7 very literally, and then render it into idiomatic English. What do you notice about the Greek construction?
   c. Compare Selections 9 and 16 with each other and with the Old Testament passage they have in view.
   d. Discuss the possible alternative meanings of Selection 12. How could the intended meaning be ascertained?
   e. Which of the two possible meanings of Selection 15 is more likely? Why?
   f. In Selection 16 there is a small difference in one word from what you would have expected. What is the form used, and what form would you have expected? (There is a note on this in the Appendix; see #A3.36.)
   g. There are two possible ways of rendering Selection 20. Which is the more probable? How could the intended meaning be ascertained?
   h. What is the difference in emphasis between the actual wording of Selection 20 and if it had read Ἐγω υἱὸς τοῦ θεοῦ εἰμι. ?
   i. Translate Selection 22 carefully, and then compare it with the English versions that you have. Some ancient Greek manuscripts have ὅτε instead of ὅτι. What difference would this make to how the verse is to be translated? (Look up ὅτε in your Dictionary.
   j. Discuss and evaluate the various alternative translations that are possible for Selection 23.

k.   What range of meaning do you see (i) in Selections 2, 6 and 28 for γῆ; (ii) in Selections 6 and 29 for καρδία?

l.   It is common for the *complement* after the verb "to be" to be placed before it. In the Selections given, can you see occasions where this does and occasions where this does not happen?

4.   Do a quick preliminary reading of Lesson Four.

VOCABULARY

PREPOSITIONS

*ἀπό	(+ gen)	from
*εἰς	(+ acc)	into, to
*ἐν	(+ dat)	in, at, with (#2.63)
ἔναντι	(+ gen)	in the presence of
ἐντός	(+ gen)	within, in midst of
*μετά, μετ᾽	(+ acc)	after
μεθ᾽	(+ gen)	with
*παρά	(+ acc)	beside
*περί	(+ gen)	concerning

VERBS

*ἄγω	lead, bring, go
ἀπέχω	have/receive in full
*ἐκβάλλω	drive; send out, away
*πιστεύω	(+ dat) believe, trust
*εἶδον	I saw
*εἶπον	I said, spoke
*ἦλθον	I came
*ἐξῆλθον	I came (went) out

FIRST DECLENSION FEMININE NOUNS

*γῆ, ῆς, ἡ	the earth, land
*δόξα, ης, ἡ	glory
ἐρημία, ας, ἡ	deserted place
*ἡμέρα, ας, ἡ	day
*θάλασσα, ης, ἡ	sea
θύρα, ας, ἡ	door, gate
*καρδία, ας, ἡ	heart

FIRST DECLENSION MASCULINE NOUNS

Ἀνδρέας, ου, ὁ	Andrew
Ἡλίας, ου, ὁ	Elijah
Ἡσαΐας, ου, ὁ	Isaiah
*μαθητής, ου, ὁ	disciple
*προφήτης, ου, ὁ	prophet

SECOND DECLENSION NOUNS

*ἀδελφός, οῦ, ὁ	brother
ἔρημος, ου, ἡ	deserted place
λύκος, ου, ὁ	wolf
μισθός, οῦ, ὁ	wages, reward
*ὁδός, οῦ, ἡ	way, road
πραιτώριον, ου, τό	residence
πρόβατον, ου, τό	sheep

THIRD DECLENSION NOUNS

ἅλας, ατος, τό	salt
βάπτισμα, ατος, τό	baptism
*νύξ, νυκτός, ἡ	night
*ὄνομα, ατος, τό	name
*πατήρ, πατρός, ὁ	father
*πνεῦμα, ατος, τό	spirit

ADJECTIVES

*δύο	two
*τρεῖς	three
*ἐκεῖνος	that (one)
*ἐμός	my
*μέσος	middle, in the midst
οὐράνιος	heavenly
τέλειος	complete, perfect

EXPRESSIONS
not yet explained in the grammar

βοῶντος	of one crying aloud (gen.)
ἔσεσθε	you shall be (plural)
ἔσται	(he) will be
ἑτοιμάσατε	prepare (imperative)
εὐθεῖα	straight, right
εὐθύνατε	make straight (imperative)
ἔφη	(he) said
ἠνεῳγμένη	standing open
κηρύσσων	preaching
λεγόμενον	called
περιπατῶν	walking
σεαυτοῦ	yourself (gen. sing.)
συνηγμένοι	gathered together

OTHER WORDS

*ἀμήν	truly, indeed, amen
*γάρ	for, since
*ἐκεῖ	there (in that place)
*ἔξω	outside, outer
*εὐθύς	immediately
*ἤ	or
*καθώς	just as
μακράν	far/far off
οὗ	where
*πάλιν	again
*ὡς	as, like

SELECTIONS FROM THE GREEK NEW TESTAMENT

(NOTE: These are selections from the verses listed; in most cases only a part of the verse is being set for you to read at this stage.)

1. Περιπατῶν δὲ παρὰ τὴν θάλασσαν τῆς Γαλιλαίας εἶδεν δύο ἀδελφούς, Σίμωνα τὸν λεγόμενον Πέτρον καὶ Ἀνδρέαν τὸν ἀδελφὸν αὐτοῦ. (ΚΑΤΑ ΜΑΘΘΑΙΟΝ 4:18.)

2. Ὑμεῖς ἐστε τὸ ἅλας τῆς γῆς. Ὑμεῖς ἐστε τὸ φῶς τοῦ κόσμου. (ΚΑΤΑ ΜΑΘΘΑΙΟΝ 5:13-14.)

3. Ἔσεσθε οὖν ὑμεῖς τέλειοι ὡς ὁ πατὴρ ὑμῶν ὁ οὐράνιος τέλειός ἐστιν. (ΚΑΤΑ ΜΑΘΘΑΙΟΝ 5:48.)

4. ἀμὴν λέγω ὑμῖν, ἀπέχουσιν τὸν μισθὸν αὐτῶν. (ΚΑΤΑ ΜΑΘΘΑΙΟΝ 6:2.)

5. Ἰδοὺ ἐγὼ ἀποστέλλω ὑμᾶς ὡς πρόβατα ἐν μέσῳ λύκων. (ΚΑΤΑ ΜΑΘΘΑΙΟΝ 10:16.)

6. ἔσται ὁ υἱὸς τοῦ ἀνθρώπου ἐν τῇ καρδίᾳ τῆς γῆς τρεῖς ἡμέρας καὶ τρεῖς νύκτας. (ΚΑΤΑ ΜΑΘΘΑΙΟΝ 12:40.)

7. καὶ λέγουσιν αὐτῷ οἱ μαθηταί, Πόθεν ἡμῖν ἐν ἐρημίᾳ ἄρτοι; (ΚΑΤΑ ΜΑΘΘΑΙΟΝ 15:33.)

8. οὗ γάρ εἰσιν δύο ἢ τρεῖς συνηγμένοι εἰς τὸ ἐμὸν ὄνομα, ἐκεῖ εἰμι ἐν μέσῳ αὐτῶν. (ΚΑΤΑ ΜΑΘΘΑΙΟΝ 18:20.)

9. φωνὴ βοῶντος ἐν τῇ ἐρήμῳ, Ἑτοιμάσατε τὴν ὁδὸν κυρίου. (ΚΑΤΑ ΜΑΡΚΟΝ 1:3.)

10. Καὶ εὐθὺς τὸ πνεῦμα αὐτὸν ἐκβάλλει εἰς τὴν ἔρημον. (ΚΑΤΑ ΜΑΡΚΟΝ 1:12.)

11. ἦλθεν ὁ Ἰησοῦς εἰς τὴν Γαλιλαίαν κηρύσσων τὸ εὐαγγέλιον τοῦ θεοῦ. (ΚΑΤΑ ΜΑΡΚΟΝ 1:14.)

12. πιστεύετε ἐν τῷ εὐαγγελίῳ. (ΚΑΤΑ ΜΑΡΚΟΝ 1:15.)

13. τὸ βάπτισμα τὸ Ἰωάννου ἐξ οὐρανοῦ ἦν ἢ ἐξ ἀνθρώπων; (ΚΑΤΑ ΜΑΡΚΟΝ 11:30.)

14. καὶ ὁ Ἰησοῦς εἶπεν αὐτῷ, Οὐ μακρὰν εἶ ἀπὸ τῆς βασιλείας τοῦ θεοῦ. (ΚΑΤΑ ΜΑΡΚΟΝ 12:34.)

15. ἰδοὺ γὰρ ἡ βασιλεία τοῦ θεοῦ ἐντὸς ὑμῶν ἐστιν. (ΚΑΤΑ ΛΟΥΚΑΝ 17:21.)

16. Τί οὖν; Σὺ Ἠλίας εἶ; καὶ λέγει, Οὐκ εἰμί. Ὁ προφήτης εἶ σύ; Οὔ. εἶπαν οὖν αὐτῷ, Τίς εἶ; τί λέγεις περὶ σεαυτοῦ; ἔφη, Ἐγὼ φωνὴ βοῶντος ἐν τῇ ἐρήμῳ, Εὐθύνατε τὴν ὁδὸν κυρίου, καθὼς εἶπεν Ἠσαΐας ὁ προφήτης. (ΚΑΤΑ ΙΩΑΝΝΗΝ 1:21-23.)

17. Ὁ πατὴρ ἡμῶν Ἀβραάμ ἐστιν. (ΚΑΤΑ ΙΩΑΝΝΗΝ 8:39.)

18. Σὺ μαθητὴς εἶ ἐκείνου, ἡμεῖς δὲ τοῦ Μωϋσέως ἐσμὲν μαθηταί. (ΚΑΤΑ ΙΩΑΝΝΗΝ 9:28.)

19. τὰ πρόβατα τῆς φωνῆς αὐτοῦ ἀκούει.....Εἶπεν οὖν πάλιν ὁ Ἰησοῦς, Ἀμὴν ἀμὴν λέγω ὑμῖν ὅτι ἐγώ εἰμι ἡ θύρα τῶν προβάτων. (ΚΑΤΑ ΙΩΑΝΝΗΝ 10:3 καὶ 10:7.)

20. εἶπον, Υἱὸς τοῦ θεοῦ εἰμι. (ΚΑΤΑ ΙΩΑΝΝΗΝ 10:36.)

21. τίς ἐστιν οὗτος ὁ υἱὸς τοῦ ἀνθρώπου; (ΚΑΤΑ ΙΩΑΝΝΗΝ 12:34.)

22. ταῦτα εἶπεν Ἠσαΐας, ὅτι εἶδεν τὴν δόξαν αὐτοῦ. (ΚΑΤΑ ΙΩΑΝΝΗΝ 12:41.)

23. πιστεύετε εἰς τὸν θεόν, καὶ εἰς ἐμὲ πιστεύετε. (ΚΑΤΑ ΙΩΑΝΝΗΝ 14:1.)

24. ταῦτα δὲ ὑμῖν ἐξ ἀρχῆς οὐκ εἶπον, ὅτι μεθ' ὑμῶν ἤμην. (ΚΑΤΑ ΙΩΑΝΝΗΝ 16:4.)

25. Ἄγουσιν οὖν τὸν Ἰησοῦν ἀπὸ τοῦ Καϊάφα εἰς τὸ πραιτώριον. (ΚΑΤΑ ΙΩΑΝΝΗΝ 18:28.)

26. Καὶ ἐξῆλθεν πάλιν ἔξω ὁ Πιλᾶτος καὶ λέγει αὐτοῖς, Ἴδε ἄγω ὑμῖν αὐτὸν ἔξω. (ΚΑΤΑ ΙΩΑΝΝΗΝ 19:4.)

27. Θωμᾶς εἶπεν αὐτῷ, Ὁ κύριός μου καὶ ὁ θεός μου. (ΚΑΤΑ ΙΩΑΝΝΗΝ 20:28.)

28. οἱ μαθηταὶ οὐκ ἦσαν μακρὰν ἀπὸ τῆς γῆς. (ΚΑΤΑ ΙΩΑΝΝΗΝ 21:8.)

29. ἡ καρδία σου οὐκ ἔστιν εὐθεῖα ἔναντι τοῦ θεοῦ (ΠΡΑΞΕΙΣ 8:21.)

30. Μετὰ ταῦτα εἶδον, καὶ ἰδοὺ θύρα ἠνεῳγμένη ἐν τῷ οὐρανῷ. (ΑΠΟΚΑΛΥΨΙΣ ΙΩΑΝΝΟΥ 4:1.)

LESSON FOUR

THE RELATIVE; THE ACTIVE VOICE

4.1 THE RELATIVE PRONOUN

4.11 The relative pronoun is "who", "whose", "which", etc. The paradigm for this is very similar to that for the article (see #2.4) except (a) that it always has an accent (the article does not have an accent in the forms ὁ, ἡ, οἱ and αἱ); (b) that it always commences with a rough breathing and never with a "τ"; and (c) that the masculine nominative singular has the standard ending "ς" (the corresponding form of the article is ὁ).

4.12 The relative pronoun consists in fact solely of the endings for οὗτος (see #3.33), and its stem is simply the rough breathing.

4.13 Notice that the only difference between the forms ἥ, οἵ and αἵ and those for the article is that the relative pronoun has an accent (either an acute or a grave: see #1.25) while the article does not have an accent.

4.14

		m.		**f.**		**n.**	
SINGULAR	N	ὅς	who	ἥ		ὅ	which/what
	A	ὅν	whom	ἥν		ὅ	which/what
	G	οὗ	whose	ἧς		οὗ	of which/what
	D	ᾧ	to/for whom	ᾗ		ᾧ	to/for which/what
PLURAL	N	οἵ	who	αἵ		ἅ	which/what
	A	οὕς	whom	ἅς		ἅ	which/what
	G	ὧν	whose	ὧν		ὧν	of which/what
	D	οἷς	to/for whom	αἷς		οἷς	to/for which/what

4.15 The relative pronoun takes the *gender* and *number* of the word to which it refers (called its *antecedent*), and the *case* that is appropriate for its function in its own clause. However, in some sentences the writer will be found to have put the relative into the case of its antecedent. This is referred to as the "attraction of the relative".

4.16 The translation of the relative (for both singular and plural) is usually "who" etc. if personal (i.e. masculine or feminine) or "which" etc. if neuter: e.g. "The Lord whom you seek will come . . ."; "The body of which you all are members . . ." It needs to be remembered that "who" and "which" are used according to the gender of the antecedent in *English* — the gender in Greek may be different (#2.13). In many cases the relative may be best translated "that": "The words that I have spoken to you . . ."

4.2   THE REST OF THE ACTIVE VERB

4.21 So far we have been introduced to the present and second aorist of the indicative active verb (#2.81 and #3.81). Here now are the flexions for the remaining tenses and modes of the active of λύω:

INDICATIVE   **SUBJUNCTIVE**

	FUTURE	IMPERFECT	1st AORIST	PERFECT	PRESENT	AORIST
S1	λύσω	ἔλυον	ἔλυσα	λέλυκα	λύω	λύσω
2	λύσεις	ἔλυες	ἔλυσας	λέλυκας	λύῃς	λύσῃς
3	λύσει	ἔλυε(ν)	ἔλυσε(ν)	λέλυκε(ν)	λύῃ	λύσῃ
P1	λύσομεν	ἐλύομεν	ἐλύσαμεν	λελύκαμεν	λύωμεν	λύσωμεν
2	λύσετε	ἐλύετε	ἐλύσατε	λελύκατε	λύητε	λύσητε
3	λύσουσι(ν)	ἔλυον	ἔλυσαν	λελύκασι(ν)	λύωσι(ν)	λύσωσι(ν)

IMPERATIVE:		PRESENT	AORIST	PERFECT
S2	loose! (singular)	λῦε	λῦσον	(No forms
3	let him loose (something)	λυέτω	λυσάτω	occur in
				the New
P2	loose! (plural)	λύετε	λύσατε	Testament)
3	let them loose (something)	λυέτωσαν	λυσάτωσαν	

INFINITIVE	to loose	λύειν	λῦσαι	λελυκέναι to have loosed

PARTICIPLE	m.	loosing	λύων	λύσας	λελυκώς	having loosed
	f.		λύουσα	λύσασα	λελυκυῖα	
	n.		λῦον	λῦσαν	λελυκός	
	m/n gen.		λύοντος	λύσαντος	λελυκότος	

4.22 As we saw last Lesson (#3.61, 3.62), Greek indicates *past time* by adding the *past time morph*, ε-, to the beginning of a verb. Two of the above tenses, the imperfect and the first aorist, have ε- prefixed to their forms in the Indicative Mode, and thus we can see that these are past time flexions. (λύω is the model verb for the First Conjugation; that is, its aorist active indicative flexion follows the first aorist pattern.)

4.23 Greek indicates *future time* by adding the *future time morph*, -σ-, to the verb stem, in front of the present tense endings. Thus we can notice that the only difference between the forms of the present tense (#2.81) and the future tense is that the future tense forms contain the future time morph, -σ-. Thus λύσω means, "I will loose".

4.24 However, when a verb stem ends in a liquid, either oral or nasal (see #1.45, 1.47), that verb adds -ε- as its future time morph instead of -σ-. If the present stem ends in double λ, it also drops one λ. If the present stem has a diphthong in ι before the liquid, it drops the ι. The added -ε- then contracts with the vowel of the ending into a long vowel or diphthong in accordance with linguistic rules to be introduced later (#6.9).

4.25 Where the future stem ends in -ε- plus ρ, λ or ν, then it always forms its aorist by adding -ι- before the liquid, and it adds -α, not -σα, after the liquid (see #4.36); and if its stem is a monosyllable (not counting prepositions) then it changes the -ε- of the future stem into -α- in forming its perfect.

4.26 Where the future stem ends in -ιν-, the -ν- is dropped before the endings of the perfect.

4.27 The following verbs illustrate these linguistic modifications:

PRESENT	MEANING	FUTURE	1st AORIST	PERFECT
σύρω	drag	συρέω	ἔσυρα	σέσυρκα
σκύλλω	trouble	σκυλέω	ἔσκυλα	—
φαίνω	shine/appear	φανέω	ἔφανα	—
δέρω	thrash	δερέω	ἔδειρα	—
ἀγγέλλω	announce	ἀγγελέω	ἤγγειλα	ἤγγελκα
στέλλω	send	στελέω	ἔστειλα	ἔσταλκα
σπείρω	sow	σπερέω	ἔσπειρα	ἔσπαρκα
κρίνω	judge	κρινέω	ἔκρινα	κέκρικα

4.28 Fuller information about forming liquid verbs is given in #C1.81.

4.3 ASPECT

4.31 In Greek, the most important aspect of tense is the *kind of action* that is being referred to. This is called *aspect*, and it is where the major distinction between the different tenses lies.

4.32 There are three aspects which a Greek verb can have: a verb either **(a)** denotes *durative* or *linear* or *progressive* action (where the emphasis is upon the *duration* or *continuation* of the action, i.e. it refers to an *ongoing, repeated* or *incomplete* action); or **(b)** *punctiliar* action (where the reference is to a specific, completed or once-for-all action, or where an action is viewed in its totality no matter how long it lasted, or the point of commencing or completing an action is being stressed); or **(c)** *perfective* or *accomplished* action (where the present state or present consequence of a prior action are being stressed; "the meaning of the perfect is *I am in the position of having done*"[19]). These aspects can be shown diagrammatically as:

(a) Durative Aspect (Present and Imperfect Tenses):————— or · · · · · · · · · · ·
                 Linear action: ongoing action or repeated action

(b) Punctiliar Aspect (Aorist Tense):   · or °
                Point-of-time action: action viewed in its totality

(c) Perfective Aspect (Present Perfect and Pluperfect Tenses): ·—————————
                Accomplished action: action leading to a state

4.33 The present and imperfect tenses are always durative in aspect; the aorist is always punctiliar; and the perfect (sometimes called the present perfect) and pluperfect (the past tense of the perfect) are always perfective. The future tense is often durative (i.e. referring to an ongoing action in the future) but can have punctiliar significance — this usually is related to the lexical meaning of a given verb[20].

4.34 The pluperfect tense is rare in the Greek N.T., and therefore is not included here; but it is a part of the verb system available for the use of the Greek speaker/writer, and it will be found set out in Appendix C, #C1.1.

4.35 In the Paradigms of the First Conjugation, punctiliar aspect is indicated by the addition of the punctiliar morph to the stem of the verb. For Paradigm C1.1, λύω, the punctiliar morph is -σα- before consonants and form final (i.e. at the end of the word form); and -σ- before vowels (i.e. the -α- elides). There are one complete flexion (the subjunctive) and three individual forms in the above λύω paradigm (#4.21) where the endings commence with a vowel (3rd person singular indicative, -ε-; 2nd person singular imperative, -ον; and the infinitive, -αι — the -α- here is part of the ending) and in all these cases the punctiliar morph consists of -σ-. In all other cases it comes before a consonant ending and is therefore -σα-. Note very carefully that -σ- followed by a consonant could NEVER be the punctiliar morph, because the punctiliar morph is -σα- (NOT -σ-), and only loses the -α- in front of a vowel, i.e. by elision.

4.36 When the verb stem ends in a liquid, the punctiliar morph is -α- before consonants and form final; and ∅ (zero) before vowels (i.e. when a vowel ending is attached to a liquid verb, that verb will contain no aspect morph — and it is this very fact that will indicate that it is aorist).

4.37 Perfective aspect is indicated in Paradigm C1.1 (λύω) in two ways: by *reduplication* (where the first letter of the stem is added again to the front of the word with the vowel -ε-) and by the addition of the perfective active morph to the stem of the verb. This perfective morph is -κ- before vowels; -κε- in front of the infinitive morph -ναι; and -κα- in all other forms. The perfect, λέλυκα, means "I have loosed".

4.38 When a verb commences with a vowel, a ρ, an aspirate, a double letter or two consonants together, special reduplication rules apply (see #E4.3).

4.39 In the λύω Paradigm, there is no morph added to the verb to indicate durative aspect for the present or imperfect tenses. Instead, in the place where the punctiliar or perfective morph would be used (that is, in what is called the *aspect slot*, or place in the word), the *neutral morph* ε/ο (see #2.77; #A2.44, A2.45) is used. This simply fills the slot without conveying any meaning — hence the term the "neutral morph". The neutral morph is also found in the future tense, which can be either durative or punctiliar (#4.33), and in the second aorist (#3.81), which is always punctiliar.

4.4 MODE

4.41 Notice that the aorist tense only has the augment in the indicative mode, for only in the indicative does the aorist refer to past time. The aorist does not have the augment in the subjunctive, imperative, infinitive, or participle, because these do NOT refer to past time. They refer to punctiliar aspect, in contrast with the present, which designates durative aspect. The reduplication in the perfect tense is a perfective aspect morph, and quite unrelated to past time, and so is kept in all modes.

4.42 The *indicative mode* "indicates" something; i.e. it is used for making a statement (or asking a question) about what *is*. The *subjunctive mode* is used for making a statement (or asking a question) about what *might be*: the conditional, the potential, the possible, the hypothetical, etc. There are only two tenses of the subjunctive in common use: the present and aorist. (A perfect subjunctive existed, but was rarely used.) The difference between them is solely one of *aspect* i.e. type of action.

4.43 The subjunctive morph is a *process morph*[21] not an *additive morph* — it is something *done to* a word form, not something *added to* it. A comparison of the present subjunctive with the present indicative (#4.21 with #2.81) will reveal the nature of the process morph: it is the lengthening of the neutral morph. Thus the neutral morph is the *carrier* for the subjunctive process morph. Where the neutral morph is part of a diphthong with -ι- the -ι- goes subscript; where it is part of a diphthong with -υ-, the -υ- is squeezed out of the word altogether.

4.44 The aorist subjunctive flexion is formed from the present subjunctive by adding the punctiliar morph in front of the neutral morph, and as this means it always comes in front of a vowel it is always -σ-, never -$\sigma\alpha$- (#4.35).

4.45 The words $\H{\iota}\nu\alpha$ ("in order that") and $\H{\alpha}\nu$ ("ever" as in the word "whoever", indicating indefiniteness) and any words compounded with $\H{\alpha}\nu$ (such as $\e\acute{\alpha}\nu$, "if ever", from $\e\iota$, "if") always take the subjunctive after them. They therefore act as indicators that a subjunctive is coming.

4.46 The *imperative mode* is used for any form of requesting: begging, entreating, praying, exhorting, commanding. Note (#4.21) that Greek has a third person imperative, for which there is no equivalent form in English. We can approximate the meaning as "let (him/her/it/them) carry out the action of the verb". Again, the difference between the tenses is one of aspect. The present imperative implies that the action expressed in the verb is continued or repeated; the aorist imperative implies that the action is not continued or repeated. The aorist imperative is the one that is normally used unless there is some reason to indicate durative action. With the negative ($\mu\acute{\eta}$), the present imperative expresses the prohibition of an act already begun: Do not continue doing, i.e. stop doing, (the action of the verb). The prohibition of an act not yet begun — Do not begin doing (the action of the verb) — is expressed by $\mu\acute{\eta}$ with the aorist subjunctive.

4.47 The *infinitive* is used: to complete the thought or the action of the main verb; in the place of a noun (in which case it will have the definite article, and is referred to as the *articular infinitive*); in indirect speech. The infinitive can have a subject (which is put in the accusative case, not the nominative), and it can also govern an object.

4.48 The *participle* is given here (#4.21) for the masculine, feminine and neuter nominative singular, and the masculine/neuter genitive singular. It will be explained in a later Lesson. But note the participle and infinitive forms for second aorist words, which take the neutral morph and therefore have the same endings as the present, not those of the first aorist. As the aorist does not take an augment outside the indicative mode, the second aorist form for the infinitive and participle will be without the augment. Thus for ἦλθον this gives ἐλθεῖν and ἐλθών, -ουσα, -ον;

and for εἶδον this gives ἰδεῖν and ἰδών, -ουσα, -ον;

but for εἶπον we find εἰπεῖν and εἰπών, -ουσα, -ον.

Thus the second aorist infinitive ends in -ειν, as does the present infinitive, rather than -σαι, like the first aorist infinitive.

4.49 The word οὐ/οὐκ/οὐχ/οὐχί is used as the negative with verbs in the indicative mode. A completely different word, μή, is used as the negative with all other modes. Both negatives go before the word to which they refer. The two words can be used together, οὐ μή, as an emphatic negative.

4.5 LINGUISTIC MODIFICATION RULES

4.50 Most verbs modify their stems in taking the augment when the stem begins with a vowel, and in taking endings with sigma. The rules are:

4.51 Verbs beginning with a short vowel take the temporal augment, i.e. they lengthen: α- and ε- to η-, o- to ω-; and ι of a diphthong will become subscript. A small number of verbs beginning with ε- will, for particular linguistic reasons (to be explained later) lengthen to ει- instead of η- (#C8.7 has full details).

4.52 When prepositions ending in a vowel (except πρό and περί) are added to a simplex verb to make a compound verb, the final vowel *elides* completely before a vowel (including the augment). The prepositions where the vowel is elided in this way (called the *eliding prepositions*) are: ἀνα, ἀντι, ἀπο, δια, ἐπι, κατα, μετα, παρα, ὑπο.

4.53 Before the augment (as before any vowel), ἐκ becomes ἐξ.

4.54 Where a verb stem ends in a short vowel, this vowel regularly lengthens when followed by a suffix beginning with a consonant: -α into -η, -ε into -η, and -o into -ω. This can be referred to as "the Short Vowel Lengthening Rule".

4.55 When a verb stem ends in a labial, it combines with a following σ into ψ.

4.56 When a verb stem ends in a palatal, it combines with a following σ into ξ. The -σσ- ending for a verb stem is treated as being a palatal.

4.57 When a verb stem ends in a dental (τ, δ, θ or ζ), the dental drops out before a following σ. When a verb stem ends in -$\pi\tau$-, the τ drops out under this rule, and the π then combines with the σ to give ψ (per #4.55).

4.58 When a verb stem ends in an oral or nasal liquid, the verb adds ε not σ to form the future tense, and stem changes may occur (see #4.24). The verb $\theta\acute{\varepsilon}\lambda\omega$ adds a double future morph — in accordance with this rule, it adds ε to become $\theta\varepsilon\lambda\acute{\varepsilon}\omega$, and then it adds -$\sigma$- as well, and follows #4.54 to make its future $\theta\varepsilon\lambda\acute{\eta}\sigma\omega$. (The verbs that take this double future morph are listed in #C1.88.)

4.59 Some verbs exhibit various irregularities. For the present, these are used only in forms which will be recognizable by these rules.

Examples of verbs in each of these categories are given in the Vocabulary, where the category number corresponds with the nine rules above.

4.6   DOUBLE AUGMENT

4.61 A small number of verbs take a double augment. Thus $\theta\acute{\varepsilon}\lambda\omega$ becomes $\mathring{\eta}\theta\varepsilon\lambda o\nu$ (not $\mathring{\varepsilon}\theta\varepsilon\lambda o\nu$) in the imperfect and $\mathring{\eta}\theta\acute{\varepsilon}\lambda\eta\sigma\alpha$ (not $\mathring{\varepsilon}\theta\acute{\varepsilon}\lambda\eta\sigma\alpha$) in the first aorist. Others taking a double augment are $\delta\acute{\upsilon}\nu\alpha\mu\alpha\iota$, to be able, $\mu\acute{\varepsilon}\lambda\lambda\omega$, to intend, and $\acute{o}\rho\acute{\alpha}\omega$, to see.

4.62 $\acute{\alpha}\nu o\acute{\iota}\gamma\omega$ is a compound with $\acute{\alpha}\nu\alpha$ and is double augmented in the aorist to $\acute{\alpha}\nu\acute{\varepsilon}\mathord{\omega}\xi\alpha$, while the forms $\mathring{\eta}\nu o\iota\xi\alpha$ and $\mathring{\eta}\nu\acute{\varepsilon}\mathord{\omega}\xi\alpha$ (triple!) are also found.

4.7   GUIDELINES ON HOW TO DECIPHER A VERB

4.71 First, locate the verb. If it is not one you recognize at once, it can be identified **(a)** by its ending, which you know (even if you don't know the rest of it); **(b)** because of a negative in front of it; or **(c)** by a process of elimination, because you recognize the words around it as nouns etc.

4.72 Does it have a reduplication in -ε-? Then it is a present perfect, or a pluperfect if it has an augment as well and/or a suffix in -$\varepsilon\iota$-.

4.73 Does it have an augment? Remember **(a)** to look for the augment *between* the preposition and the verb stem in compound words, and **(b)** that the augment may be contained in an initial long vowel or diphthong. If it has an augment, does it also have -$\sigma\alpha$- (or -σ- before a vowel) between the verb stem and the ending? If so then it is a first aorist indicative. If not, then it is either a second or third aorist or an imperfect. Strip off the augment and ending, substitute -ω, and if it is an imperfect you should find your word now in the lexicon. If not, check it out as a second aorist: try it with the augment and the first person singular second aorist ending and see if that form is in the lexicon. If it is, it will tell you the corresponding first person singular of the present active. If you have no success with these efforts, go on to #4.74.

4.74 Does it have -σα- (or -σ- before a vowel) between the stem and the ending? If so, and it also has an augment, then it is a first aorist indicative. If it has -σ- but no augment, then it is either a future or a first aorist in a mode other than the indicative. Check to see if the endings are those of the future indicative or those of the aorist subjunctive, imperative, or infinitive. (Remember that the future and the aorist subjunctive have the same form for the first person singular; that a future -σ- will always be followed by a neutral morph; that -σα- always indicates a first aorist.) But what verb does it come from? Strip off the -σα- or -σ- and ending (and augment if any), substitute -ω, and you should be able to find your word in the lexicon. If not, the probability is that this word is a dental stem verb and the dental has dropped out before the -σ-, as per #4.57. So restore the dental. Try each dental in turn until you find a word that is listed in your lexicon. Start with ζ first (there are 211 Greek N.T. verbs with present stems ending in ζ, 8 in δ, 6 in θ; and one in τ).

4.75 It is important for deciphering a verb to be able to recognize and identify all the morphs of which it is composed. We can now add two extra morph slots — for the reduplication and the future morph — to the five we have already met in Lesson Three (#3.93). We should also note that the neutral morph (o/ε), the punctiliar morph (σα) and the perfective active morph (κα) are *alternatives* in the aspect slot — one or other of them will occur; that when the neutral morph is lengthened this indicates subjunctive mode; and that the aorist subjunctive thus requires *both* the punctiliar morph (σ in front of a vowel) *and* the lengthened neutral morph. Moreover, the *infinitive ending* is an alternative to the pronoun ending: a verb will have one or the other.

4.76 Here is the morphological analysis of a selection of forms from λύω (#4.21). Examine each form, identify what it is, and work out its meaning:

VERB FORM	1 PREP.	2 PAST	3 REDUPLICATION	4 LEXAL	5	6 FUTURE	7 ASPECT	8	9 ENDING
λύσω				λυ		σ	o		L
λύσω				λυ			σω		L
λύσουσι(ν)				λυ		σ	o		υσι(ν)
ἔλυε(ν)	ἐ			λυ			∅		ε(ν)
ἐλύομεν	ἐ			λυ			o		μεν
ἔλυσα	ἐ			λυ			σα		∅
ἐλύσαμεν	ἐ			λυ			σα		μεν
λελύκαμεν			λε	λυ			κα		μεν
λύῃ				λυ			η		ι
λύωμεν				λυ			ω		μεν
λύσωμεν				λυ			σω		μεν
λῦσαι				λυ			σ		αι
λελυκέναι			λε	λυ			κε		ναι

4.77 Slots 1, 4, 7 and 9 can be likened to multiposition switches (see #A3.47) — you can have any preposition in Slot 1, any lexal in Slot 4, one of the aspect morphs (neutral, punctiliar or perfective) in Slot 7, and a pronoun or infinitive ending in Slot 9. Slots 2, 3 and 6 are like simple on/off switches — when the morph is there, that switch is "on", and switches the word to "past time", "perfect", or "future time" respectively.

4.8 USING THE GUIDELINES TO UNDERSTAND VERBS IN THE G.N.T. SELECTIONS

4.81 ἀνῆλθεν: The beginning of the word is the preposition ἀνα, which has elided its final vowel when prefixed to a stem commencing with a vowel (see #4.52). The main verb is then seen to be -ῆλθεν. (Selection 7.)

4.82 δεδουλεύκαμεν: The reduplication indicates that this is present perfect, confirmed by the -κα- between stem and ending. The ending shows that the verb form is first person plural. Remove reduplication and ending, add -ω, and you have the lexical form, δουλεύω. (Selection 8.)

4.83 Μὴ νομίσητε: The μή alerts you that the following word is likely to be a verb, and if so it will not be indicative mode (#4.49). The -σ- of νομίσητε indicates either the future or the aorist, the -η- after the -σ- shows it to be subjunctive. As there is no future subjunctive, you check your paradigm pattern and confirm that it is first aorist subjunctive, the -τε ending identifying it as the second person plural. But of what verb? The stem before the sigma is νομι-, so the verb could be νομίω. You check your wordlist and find that there is no such word. So it is either a dental stem verb, with the dental having dropped out before sigma, or it is some irregular form. You check out the dental possibilities and discover that the verb is: νομίζω. You can now see that it is a negative second person plural aorist subjunctive, which (as per #4.46) is "The prohibition of an act not yet begun." Thus μὴ νομίσητε means, "Do not have the thought . . .", "Do not imagine for a single moment . . ." (Selection 18.)

4.9 NOTES FOR THE SELECTIONS

4.91 Verbs with stems ending in -ε- absorb it into a following long vowel or diphthong ending, and also contract with a following -ε- into the dipthong -ει-. (Other types of contraction will be explained in #6.9.)

4.92 The infinitive after ἐν τῷ expresses the time at or during which the action occurred; it can be translated "when . . ." or "while . . ." (verb action).

4.93 The article plus δέ can be used on its own as the subject of a sentence, referring to someone previously mentioned: ὁ δὲ . . ., "and he . . ."

4.94 There will be occasions when the aorist is best rendered into English by the present perfect. Ἐχθρὸς ἄνθρωπος τοῦτο ἐποίησεν — "some enemy has done this" (ἐχθρὸς ἄνθρωπος = a hostile man, an enemy).

ASSIGNMENTS ON LESSON FOUR

(Suggestions concerning the work of this Lesson will be found in #A4.)

1.   Read Lesson Four through twice. **LEARN BY HEART**: (a) the paradigm of the first aorist indicative active of λύω and (b) the forms of the present and aorist active imperative, infinitive and participle of λύω (#4.21).

2.   Read and translate literally all the Selections from the Greek N.T. Read carefully through all the new Vocabulary, which you will notice is arranged in categories: note the different words and their category. (If you need a word and cannot find it promptly in the Vocabulary, look it up in your Dictionary.) Make sure that you read all the Selections aloud, to help cultivate your "feel" for the Greek. If there are some Selections you cannot unravel, do not worry about them — further familiarity with Greek will make them clear in due course.

3.   (OPTIONAL COMPREHENSION QUESTIONS)
     a.   What is the tense used, and what is its significance, in Selections 1, 3, 4, 8, 12 and 17?
     b.   Comment upon the word order of Selection 6.
     c.   Comment upon what is unusual about the word order of the two sentences of Selection 10, and what the purpose is for this word order.
     d.   Explain the form ἀνέῳξεν in Selection 10.
     e.   What can you see regarding the meaning of ἐγγύς from its use in Selections 6, 7, 11, and 13?
     f.   What can you see regarding the meaning of κύριε from its use in Selections 1, 3, 14, and 20?
     g.   There are numbers of subjunctives used in Selection 18. Identify them. Can you account for the use of the subjunctive in these cases?
     h.   Parse (give number, gender and case of) ὅν, used twice in Selection 19.
     i.   What is unusual about the word order of ἦλθεν αὐτοῦ ὁ ἐχθρός in Selection 20 and what is its effect?
     j.   Parse (give the lexical verb and explain the person, number, tense, mode and voice of) these words from Selection 21: ἐλέησον, εἶπεν, φωνήσατε, θέλεις, ποιήσω, ἀναβλέψω, σέσωκεν, ἀνέβλεψεν, ἠκολούθει, ὑπάγετε, ποιεῖτε, εἴπατε.
4.   Do a quick preliminary reading of Lesson Five.

VOCABULARY

GENERAL WORDS

*ἄν	ever
διὰ τί	why
*ἐάν	if (ever)
ἐὰν μή, εἰ μή	except, unless
ἐγγύς (+ gen.)	near, close to
*εἷς, μία, ἕν	one (see #5.66)
*ἕως	until
*ἵνα	(in order) that
κατέναντι (+ gen.)	opposite
ναί	yes
*ὅτε	when, while
*οὕτως	thus, so
*οὐχί (interr.)	not (expects "yes")
ποτέ	once, at some time
πώποτε	at any time
*τις	any one
*τότε	then
*ὧδε	here

EXPRESSIONS

ἀνὰ μέσον	up the middle (= amongst)
ἀνέβη	(he) went up
ἀποκριθείς	answering
γένηται	happens, is accomplished
ἐκάθητο	(he) sat/was sitting (down)
ἔστη	(he) stood
ἐφάνη	(it) appeared
κληθήσεται	(he) shall be called
ὅς ἄν, ὅς ἐάν	whoever
οὐδενί	to no one
πάντα, πάντας	all, everything
πληρωθῇ	(it) might be fulfilled
τὸ ῥηθέν	what was said/spoken
σπείραντι	sowing
ὡμοιώθη	may be compared

ADJECTIVES

ἐλάχιστος, η, ον	least
ἐχθρός, ά, όν	enemy, hated
*μέγας, μεγάλη, μέγα	great
*πιστός, ή, όν	faithful
*πλείων, πλεῖον (+ gen.)	more (than)
*πολλοί	many
*τυφλός, ή, όν	blind
φανερός, ά, όν	known

VERBS

(The verbs are grouped and numbered in sequence according to the Linguistic Modification Rules — #4.5 — which affect them. Those in Category 0 do not modify stem letters in adding affixes.)

0.	δουλεύω	I am a slave, enslaved
	θεραπεύω	heal, cure
	καταλύω	do away with, destroy
	περισσεύω	exceed, overflow
1.	αἱρετίζω	choose, appoint
	*ἀκολουθέω (+ dat.)	follow
	εὐδοκέω	take delight in
2.	ἀνῆλθον	I went up
	*ἀπῆλθον	I departed
	*εἰσῆλθον	I entered
	παρῆλθον	I passed away
	*προσῆλθον	I approached
	*ὑπάγω	go (one's way)
3.	*ἐκβάλλω	drive, send away
4.	βλαστάω	sprout
	ἐλεάω	be merciful
	ἐπιτιμάω	command, order
	*πληρόω	accomplish, fulfil
	*ποιέω	do, carry out, practise
	φωνέω	call
5.	ἀναβλέπω	see again
	ἐπιστρέφω	return, turn around
6.	*ἀνοίγω	open
	*κηρύσσω	proclaim, preach
	φυλάσσω	guard, keep
7.	ἐγγίζω	come near
	καθεύδω	sleep
	νομίζω	think, suppose, consider
	στηρίζω (f. στηρίξω)	strengthen
	*σώζω	save, rescue, deliver, cure
8.	ἐπισπείρω	sow over, resow
	*θέλω	wish, want
	*σπείρω	sow
	*φέρω	bring
9.	*διδάσκω	teach
	*δίδωμι	give
	*εὑρίσκω	find

NOUNS

(The nouns are grouped and numbered by their Declension. Those in Category 4 are indeclinables.)

1. *ἀλήθεια, ας, ἡ — truth
 *δικαιοσύνη, ης, ἡ — righteousness
 *εἰρήνη, ης, ἡ — peace
 ἐλαία, ας, ἡ — olive (-tree)
 *ἐντολή, ῆς, ἡ — commandment
 ἑορτή, ῆς, ἡ — feast
 κεραία, ας, ἡ — stroke of a letter
 κώμη, ης, ἡ — village
 οἰκοδεσπότης, ου, ὁ — master
 *συναγωγή, ῆς, ἡ — synagogue
 χρεία, ας, ἡ — need

2. *δαιμόνιον, ου, τό — demon
 *δοῦλος, ου, ὁ — slave
 *καρπός, οῦ, ὁ — fruit
 *ὀφθαλμός, οῦ, ὁ — eye
 πηλός, οῦ, ὁ — clay, mud
 πῶλος, ου, ὁ — colt
 σῖτος, ου, ὁ — wheat
 χόρτος, ου, ὁ — grass

3. ἀνάστασις, εως, ἡ — resurrection
 *γραμματεύς, έως, ὁ — scribe
 Ἱεροσόλυμα, ων, τά — Jerusalem
 *ὄρος, ους, τό — mountain
 παῖς, παιδός, ὁ/ἡ — servant, child

4. ἰῶτα, τό — iota (Gk) = yod (Heb)
 πάσχα, τό — Passover
 Ραββι, Ραββουνι — Rabbi

SELECTIONS FROM THE GREEK NEW TESTAMENT

1. Κύριε, σῶσόν με. (ΚΑΤΑ ΜΑΘΘΑΙΟΝ 14:30.)

2. καὶ ἦλθον εἰς Βηθφαγὴ εἰς τὸ Ὄρος τῶν Ἐλαιῶν. (ΚΑΤΑ ΜΑΘΘΑΙΟΝ 21:1.)

3. Κύριε, κύριε, ἄνοιξον ἡμῖν. (ΚΑΤΑ ΜΑΘΘΑΙΟΝ 25:11.)

4. καὶ ἦλθεν κηρύσσων εἰς τὰς συναγωγὰς αὐτῶν εἰς ὅλην τὴν Γαλιλαίαν καὶ τὰ δαιμόνια ἐκβάλλων. (ΚΑΤΑ ΜΑΡΚΟΝ 1:39.)

5. καὶ σύ ποτε ἐπιστρέψας στήρισον τοὺς ἀδελφούς σου. (ΚΑΤΑ ΛΟΥΚΑΝ 22:32.)

6. καὶ ἐγγὺς ἦν τὸ πάσχα τῶν Ἰουδαίων, καὶ ἀνέβη εἰς Ἱεροσόλυμα ὁ Ἰησοῦς. (ΚΑΤΑ ΙΩΑΝΝΗΝ 2:13.)

7. ἀνῆλθεν δὲ εἰς τὸ ὄρος Ἰησοῦς, καὶ ἐκεῖ ἐκάθητο μετὰ τῶν μαθητῶν αὐτοῦ. ἦν δὲ ἐγγὺς τὸ πάσχα, ἡ ἑορτὴ τῶν Ἰουδαίων. (ΚΑΤΑ ΙΩΑΝΝΗΝ 6:3-4.)

8. σπέρμα Ἀβραάμ ἐσμεν καὶ οὐδενὶ δεδουλεύκαμεν πώποτε. (ΚΑΤΑ ΙΩΑΝΝΗΝ 8:33.)

9. ἐγὼ δὲ ὅτι τὴν ἀλήθειαν λέγω, οὐ πιστεύετέ μοι. εἰ ἀλήθειαν λέγω, διὰ τί ὑμεῖς οὐ πιστεύετέ μοι; (ΚΑΤΑ ΙΩΑΝΝΗΝ 8:45-46.)

10. Ἄγουσιν αὐτὸν πρὸς τοὺς Φαρισαίους τόν ποτε τυφλόν. ἦν δὲ σάββατον ἐν ᾗ ἡμέρᾳ τὸν πηλὸν ἐποίησεν ὁ Ἰησοῦς καὶ ἀνέῳξεν αὐτοῦ τοὺς ὀφθαλμούς. (ΚΑΤΑ ΙΩΑΝΝΗΝ 9:13-14.)

11. ἦν δὲ ἡ Βηθανία ἐγγὺς τῶν Ἱεροσολύμων. (ΚΑΤΑ ΙΩΑΝΝΗΝ 11:18.)

12. εἶπεν αὐτῇ ὁ Ἰησοῦς, Ἐγώ εἰμι ἡ ἀνάστασις καὶ ἡ ζωή. πιστεύεις τοῦτο; λέγει αὐτῷ, Ναί, κύριε· ἐγὼ πεπίστευκα ὅτι σὺ εἶ ὁ Χριστὸς ὁ υἱὸς τοῦ θεοῦ. (ΚΑΤΑ ΙΩΑΝΝΗΝ 11:25-27.)

13. Ἦν δὲ ἐγγὺς τὸ πάσχα τῶν Ἰουδαίων. (ΚΑΤΑ ΙΩΑΝΝΗΝ 11:55.)

14. Κύριε, θέλομεν τὸν Ἰησοῦν ἰδεῖν. (ΚΑΤΑ ΙΩΑΝΝΗΝ 12:21.)

15. εἰρήνην τὴν ἐμὴν δίδωμι ὑμῖν. (ΚΑΤΑ ΙΩΑΝΝΗΝ 14:27.)

16. ἦλθεν ὁ Ἰησοῦς καὶ ἔστη εἰς τὸ μέσον καὶ λέγει αὐτοῖς, Εἰρήνη ὑμῖν. εἶπεν οὖν αὐτοῖς πάλιν, Εἰρήνη ὑμῖν. (ΚΑΤΑ ΙΩΑΝΝΗΝ 20:19, 21.)

17. πιστὸς δέ ἐστιν ὁ κύριος, ὃς στηρίξει ὑμᾶς καὶ φυλάξει ἀπὸ τοῦ πονηροῦ. (ΠΡΟΣ ΘΕΣΣΑΛΟΝΙΚΕΙΣ Β, 3:3.)

18. Μὴ νομίσητε ὅτι ἦλθον καταλῦσαι τὸν νόμον ἢ τοὺς προφήτας· οὐκ ἦλθον καταλῦσαι ἀλλὰ πληρῶσαι. ἀμὴν γὰρ λέγω ὑμῖν, ἕως ἂν παρέλθῃ ὁ οὐρανὸς καὶ ἡ γῆ, ἰῶτα ἓν ἢ μία κεραία οὐ μὴ παρέλθῃ ἀπὸ τοῦ νόμου ἕως ἂν πάντα γένηται. ὃς ἐὰν οὖν λύσῃ μίαν τῶν ἐντολῶν τούτων τῶν ἐλαχίστων καὶ διδάξῃ οὕτως τοὺς ἀνθρώπους, ἐλάχιστος κληθήσεται ἐν τῇ βασιλείᾳ τῶν οὐρανῶν· ὃς δ᾽ ἂν ποιήσῃ καὶ διδάξῃ, οὗτος μέγας κληθήσεται ἐν τῇ βασιλείᾳ τῶν οὐρανῶν. λέγω γὰρ ὑμῖν ὅτι ἐὰν μὴ περισσεύσῃ ὑμῶν ἡ δικαιοσύνη πλεῖον τῶν γραμματέων καὶ Φαρισαίων, οὐ μὴ εἰσέλθητε εἰς τὴν βασιλείαν τῶν οὐρανῶν. (ΚΑΤΑ ΜΑΘΘΑΙΟΝ 5:17-20.)

19. καὶ ἠκολούθησαν αὐτῷ πολλοί, καὶ ἐθεράπευσεν αὐτοὺς πάντας, καὶ ἐπετίμησεν αὐτοῖς ἵνα μὴ φανερὸν αὐτὸν ποιήσωσιν· ἵνα πληρωθῇ τὸ ῥηθὲν διὰ Ἠσαΐου τοῦ προφήτου λέγοντος, Ἰδοὺ ὁ παῖς μου ὃν ᾑρέτισα, ὁ ἀγαπητός μου εἰς ὃν εὐδόκησεν ἡ ψυχή μου. (ΚΑΤΑ ΜΑΘΘΑΙΟΝ 12:15-18.)

20. Ὡμοιώθη ἡ βασιλεία τῶν οὐρανῶν ἀνθρώπῳ σπείραντι καλὸν σπέρμα ἐν τῷ ἀγρῷ αὐτοῦ. ἐν δὲ τῷ καθεύδειν τοὺς ἀνθρώπους ἦλθεν αὐτοῦ ὁ ἐχθρὸς καὶ ἐπέσπειρεν ζιζάνια ἀνὰ μέσον τοῦ σίτου καὶ ἀπῆλθεν. ὅτε δὲ ἐβλάστησεν ὁ χόρτος καὶ καρπὸν ἐποίησεν, τότε ἐφάνη καὶ τὰ ζιζάνια· προσελθόντες δὲ οἱ δοῦλοι τοῦ οἰκοδεσπότου εἶπον αὐτῷ, Κύριε, οὐχὶ καλὸν σπέρμα ἔσπειρας ἐν τῷ σῷ ἀγρῷ; πόθεν οὖν ἔχει ζιζάνια; ὁ δὲ ἔφη αὐτοῖς, Ἐχθρὸς ἄνθρωπος τοῦτο ἐποίησεν. (ΚΑΤΑ ΜΑΘΘΑΙΟΝ 13:24-28.)

21. ὁ υἱὸς Τιμαίου Βαρτιμαῖος τυφλὸς ἐκάθητο παρὰ τὴν ὁδόν· καὶ λέγει, Υἱὲ Δαυὶδ Ἰησοῦ, ἐλέησόν με. καὶ ὁ Ἰησοῦς εἶπεν, Φωνήσατε αὐτόν. ὁ δὲ ἦλθεν πρὸς τὸν Ἰησοῦν. καὶ ἀποκριθεὶς αὐτῷ ὁ Ἰησοῦς εἶπεν, Τί σοι θέλεις ποιήσω; ὁ δὲ τυφλὸς εἶπεν αὐτῷ, Ῥαββουνι, ἵνα ἀναβλέψω. καὶ ὁ Ἰησοῦς εἶπεν αὐτῷ, Ὕπαγε, ἡ πίστις σου σέσωκέν σε. καὶ εὐθὺς ἀνέβλεψεν, καὶ ἠκολούθει αὐτῷ ἐν τῇ ὁδῷ. Καὶ ὅτε ἐγγίζουσιν εἰς Ἱεροσόλυμα εἰς Βηθφαγὴ καὶ Βηθανίαν πρὸς τὸ Ὄρος τῶν Ἐλαιῶν, ἀποστέλλει δύο τῶν μαθητῶν αὐτοῦ καὶ λέγει αὐτοῖς, Ὑπάγετε εἰς τὴν κώμην τὴν κατέναντι ὑμῶν, καὶ εὐθὺς εὑρήσετε πῶλον· λύσατε αὐτὸν καὶ φέρετε. καὶ ἐάν τις ὑμῖν εἴπῃ, Τί ποιεῖτε τοῦτο; εἴπατε, Ὁ κύριος αὐτοῦ χρείαν ἔχει, καὶ εὐθὺς αὐτὸν ἀποστέλλει πάλιν ὧδε. καὶ ἀπῆλθον καὶ εὗρον πῶλον, καὶ λύουσιν αὐτόν. (ΚΑΤΑ ΜΑΡΚΟΝ 10:46-11:4.)

LESSON FIVE

THE THIRD DECLENSION

5.1   HOW TO FIND YOUR WAY THROUGH THE THIRD DECLENSION

5.11 Many students find the Third Declension to be the hardest part of Greek to be mastered. There are so many Third Declension words and they decline so differently from each other that this Declension seems to look like a grabbag of whatever is left over from the First and Second Declensions rather than an orderly pattern. The forms of many words are unexpected and their behaviour quite unpredictable. Twenty or thirty different paradigms exist, and many of them are followed by only two or three words in the New Testament — or maybe by just one word. To master the Third Declension seems like a great deal of work.

5.12 It is: if the aim is to be able to *write* in New Testament Greek. Even the Greeks themselves got lost in the Third Declension at times, and in the general Greek literature (and on occasions in the New Testament too) various alternative forms are found for some of the cases of some words.

5.13 However, our aim is a more modest one: to be able to *recognize* and *identify* words of the Third Declension when we come across them in reading the Greek New Testament. It is much easier to identify forms when we encounter them than to be able to predict what a particular case will be.

5.14 There are four basic patterns for the Third Declension, from which other paradigms can be seen as variations and irregularities. These four basic patterns differ according to gender, and whether the stem ends in a vowel or a consonant. (Some sample paradigms are given here for each type.)

5.2   THIRD DECLENSION VOWEL STEMS

5.20 Third Declension nouns with vowel stems vary in behaviour depending upon the vowel itself, and how it reacts with the endings that are added. There are five standard paradigm patterns — four for masculine/feminine nouns, and the other for neuter nouns. These are set out here, together with a listing of the endings, and of the Second Declension for comparison:

SECOND DECLEN-SION	Endings	THIRD DECLENSION — VOWEL STEMS			
		D3.1 fish ὁ ἰχθύς	D3.2 city ἡ πόλις	D3.4 king ὁ βασιλεύς	D3.5 race τὸ γένος
SN κύριος	-ς	ἰχθύς	πόλις	βασιλεύς	γένος
V κύριε	-	ἰχθύ	πόλι	βασιλεῦ	—
A κύριον	-ν	ἰχθύν	πόλιν	βασιλέα	γένος
G κυρίου	-ος	ἰχθύος	πόλεως	βασιλέως	γένους
D κυρίῳ	-ι	ἰχθύϊ	πόλει	βασιλεῖ	γένει
PN κύριοι	-ες	ἰχθύες	πόλεις	βασιλεῖς	γένη
A κυρίους	-ας	ἰχθύας	πόλεις	βασιλεῖς	γένη
G κυρίων	-ων	ἰχθύων	πόλεων	βασιλέων	γενέων/γενῶν
D κυρίοις	-σι(ν)	ἰχθύσι(ν)	πόλεσι(ν)	βασιλεῦσι(ν)	γένεσι(ν)

POINTS To be Noted:

5.21 The Second and Third Declensions have a separate form for the vocative singular. For the Third Declension, this is usually the word stem (usually minus the final consonant of a consonant stem if this is other than "ρ"). (If a dash, —, is put opposite the vocative in these paradigms it does not mean that that type can have no vocative, but that the nominative form is used as the vocative.)

5.22 The dative plural ending is -σι(ν), with a moveable nu.

5.23 The ἰχθύς paradigm retains the vowel of its stem unchanged throughout, and simply adds the endings. In all other types the basic endings have become modified through amalgamation with the vowel of the stem. The stem is usually found by removing -ος from the genitive singular.

5.24 The βασιλεύς paradigm takes the ending "-α" for the accusative singular, which is the customary ending for Third Declension consonant stems. In the accusative plural, nouns of this group can also be found with the ending "-εας" (like ἰχθύας) as an alternative to the normal "-εις" (like πόλεις).

5.25 The γένος paradigm follows the invariable pattern of all neuters in having the same form for nominative and accusative. At first sight it may appear to depart from the pattern that neuters always end in "-α" in nominative and accusative plural. In fact the "-α" is there but disguised, having contracted with the "ε" of the stem to produce "-η".

5.26 The genitive plural forms in "-εων" are often found contracted to "-ῶν", e.g. γενῶν.

5.27 Compare and contrast the Second and Third Declension forms. One potential source of confusion for students is to misread a Third Declension neuter as a Second Declension masculine and take a noun in "-ους" as accusative plural rather than genitive singular. Again, it is necessary to distinguish carefully the neuter plural form in "-η" from the First Declension nominative singular.

5.3   THIRD DECLENSION MASCULINE AND FEMININE CONSONANT STEMS

5.31 Third Declension nouns with consonant stems have the same pattern of endings as those with vowel stems, except that the masculine/feminine accusative singular ending is "-α", not "-ν". The final consonant of the stem interacts with the endings and this gives the different subgroups of masculine and feminine nouns. There is one main paradigm for neuter nouns with consonant stems. In all these paradigms the stem of the word shows up clearly in the genitive singular, which is always given in a lexicon with the nominative singular. The masculine/feminine paradigms are:

		Endings	D3.6 flesh ἡ σάρξ	D3.8 child ὁ/ἡ παῖς	D3.11 saviour ὁ σωτήρ	D3.12 star ὁ ἀστήρ	D3.16 leader ὁ ἡγεμών
S	N	-ς	σάρξ	παῖς	σωτήρ	ἀστήρ	ἡγεμών
	A	-α	σάρκα	παῖδα	σωτῆρα	ἀστέρα	ἡγεμόνα
	G	-ος	σαρκός	παιδός	σωτῆρος	ἀστέρος	ἡγεμόνος
	D	-ι	σαρκί	παιδί	σωτῆρι	ἀστέρι	ἡγεμόνι
P	N	-ες	σάρκες	παῖδες	σωτῆρες	ἀστέρες	ἡγεμόνες
	A	-ας	σάρκας	παῖδας	σωτῆρας	ἀστέρας	ἡγεμόνας
	G	-ων	σαρκῶν	παίδων	σωτήρων	ἀστέρων	ἡγεμόνων
	D	-σι(ν)	σαρξί(ν)	παισί(ν)	σωτῆρσι(ν)	ἀστέρσι(ν)	ἡγεμόσι(ν)

5.32 No separate form for the vocative is given, as occurrences of this are rare. When it does occur, it usually conforms to the principle set out in #5.21 (e.g. in Attic Greek, παῖ, σῶτερ — note the short ε).

5.33 The paradigms of this declension arise when stems and endings combine according to linguistic rules (cf. #4.5). For the other paradigms referred to here, see #D3.

5.34 A sigma ending combines with a palatal stem into ξ (example: σάρξ, Paradigm D3.6); and with a labial stem into ψ (example: λίψ, Paradigm D3.7).

5.35 When the stem ends in a dental, this drops out when a sigma ending is added. Example: παῖς (Paradigm D3.8).

5.36 When the stem ends in -ρ, this remains in the nominative singular and the -ς ending disappears. In the dative plural the -σι ending is added to the stem in the usual way. Examples: σωτήρ, χείρ (Paradigms D3.11, D3.31). If the vowel before the -ρ is short, it lengthens in the nominative singular. Examples: ἀστήρ, ἀστέρος (some irregular forms of the dative plural are found in practice); ἀλέκτωρ, ἀλέκτορος (Paradigms D3.12, D3.13).

5.37 When the stem ends in -ν, this remains in the nominative singular and the -ς ending disappears, but the -ν drops out before the -σι of the dative plural. Examples: αἰών, αἰῶνος; μήν, μηνός (Paradigms D3.14, D3.15). If the vowel before the -ν is short, it lengthens in the nominative singular. Examples: ἡγεμών, ἡγεμόνος; ποιμήν, ποιμένος (Paradigms D3.16, D3.17).

5.38 When the stem ends in a palatal plus -τ, the -τ follows #5.35 and drops out before the -ς, and the -ς then follows #5.34 and combines with the palatal to give -ξ in the nominative singular and dative plural. Examples: νύξ, νυκτός.

5.39 When the stem ends in -ντ, the -τ follows #5.35 and drops out before the -ς, and the -ν stem then follows #5.37, the -ν being retained and the -ς disappearing in the nominative singular, but the -ν dropping out before the -σι of the dative plural. However, a short vowel in the dative plural lengthens or becomes a diphthong by a rule of "compensation" for the loss of *both* -ν- and -τ-. Example: ἄρχων, ἄρχοντος; dative plural ἄρχουσιν (Paradigm D3.18 — this is the pattern followed by participles in -ων). Note the resemblance of the dative plural, with its moveable nu, to the third person plural verb ending — beware of confusing these two forms.

5.4 SLIGHTLY IRREGULAR THIRD DECLENSION MASCULINE/FEMININE NOUNS

5.41 A quite large number of Third Declension masculine and feminine nouns are slightly irregular in that they form their nominative singular (and at times, their dative plural) in a way that varies to a small extent (usually by only a single letter) from what would have been expected under the rules of linguistic modification given above. The "irregular" form is still so close to what you would expect to find that usually you would have no more than a slight hesitation in recognizing the word. The more common of these have been set out in the Vocabulary for this Lesson; you can see the irregularity by comparing the other forms with the genitive singular, which shows the stem.

5.42 Five other irregulars form what you could call "the family group": "father", "mother", "daughter", "husband", and "wife" — all of them words that are so common that they are set out in full here (Paradigms D3.26 and D3.32) for ease of identification. (Only three paradigms are needed, as "mother", μήτηρ, and "daughter", θυγάτηρ, follow "father", πατήρ, exactly.)

5.43 πατήρ, πατρός follows ἀστήρ, ἀστέρος, but is irregular in dropping the "ε" of its stem in the genitive and dative singular and in having an unexpected dative plural. "Husband, man", ἀνήρ, ἀνδρός, replaces the "δ" of its stem with an "ε" for nominative and vocative singular and conforms then to the pattern of πατήρ in these forms and in the dative plural. "Wife, woman", γυνή, γυναικός is irregular in its nominative singular, but in all other forms it conforms to the regular pattern of σάρξ, σαρκός.

5.44 D3.18 ruler D3.32 father D3.32 husband/man D3.26 wife/woman D3.9 body

	ὁ ἄρχων	ὁ πατήρ	ὁ ἀνήρ	ἡ γυνή	τὸ σῶμα
S N	ἄρχων	πατήρ	ἀνήρ	γυνή	σῶμα
V	—	πάτερ	ἄνερ	γύναι	—
A	ἄρχοντα	πατέρα	ἄνδρα	γυναῖκα	σῶμα
G	ἄρχοντος	πατρός	ἀνδρός	γυναικός	σώματος
D	ἄρχοντι	πατρί	ἀνδρί	γυναικί	σώματι
P N	ἄρχοντες	πατέρες	ἄνδρες	γυναῖκες	σώματα
A	ἄρχοντας	πατέρας	ἄνδρας	γυναῖκας	σώματα
G	ἀρχόντων	πατέρων	ἀνδρῶν	γυναικῶν	σωμάτων
D	ἄρχουσι(ν)	πατράσι(ν)	ἀνδράσι(ν)	γυναιξί(ν)	σώμασι(ν)

THIRD DECLENSION NEUTER CONSONANT STEMS

5.45 The Third Declension neuter nouns with consonant stems all conform exactly to the dental stem pattern of παῖς, παιδός (see Paradigm D3.8), but have the two characteristics of the neuter that **(a)** in the nominative singular the "-ς" that one finds in the masculine and feminine forms is dropped, thus giving the ending "-μα" (from the original stem in "-ματ"), and **(b)** the nominative plural adds "-α" to the stem, giving "-ματα". The accusative is always identical with the nominative, as is invariable for the neuter gender. Example: σῶμα, σώματος (Paradigm D3.9).

5.46 Of the 140 words that follow this paradigm, a dozen or so occur very frequently in the New Testament. In addition, there are three common words which do not have the ending "-ματ-" that is characteristic of this paradigm, and which have irregular nominative singular forms, but which in all other ways follow σῶμα. These words are: γόνυ, γόνατος, knee (#D3.29); οὖς, ὠτός, ear (#D3.30); and ὕδωρ, ὕδατος, water (#D3.13). Also neuter is πῦρ, πυρός, fire, which follows σωτήρ (Paradigm D3.11) but with the neuter characteristic that the accusative form is identical with the nominative (set out in full in Appendix, #D3.11).

5.5   LEARNING THE THIRD DECLENSION ???

5.50 It is not really necessary to learn the Third Declension paradigms — they are not given for that purpose. Learn ἰχθύς (Paradigm D3.1), which will give you the endings, and look through the remainder carefully to see how stems and endings are modified when different types are added together. Aim to be sufficiently familiar with the overall pattern that you can expect to have a good likelihood of recognizing the number and case of a Third Declension word when you encounter one. Remember, you can always refer back to these paradigms. If you *want* to learn some of the other paradigms in addition to ἰχθύς, the most useful would probably be σάρξ, βασιλεύς, γένος and σῶμα. (For the full list of all paradigms, see #D3.)

5.6   ADJECTIVES, PARTICIPLES AND PRONOUNS

5.60 Adjectives follow two basic patterns of declension, with two subgroups in each:

1.   FIRST & SECOND DECLENSION PATTERN

1a: Three-Termination Adjectives of the 1st & 2nd Declensions (#D4.1, D4.2)

5.61 In this pattern, the feminine form of the adjective will follow the First Declension paradigms (as in #3.11). The masculine and neuter forms of the adjective are declined exactly like nouns, masculine and neuter respectively, of the Second Declension. These are cited in a lexicon in the masculine form followed by the feminine and neuter endings (for examples, see "Adjectives" in the Vocabulary of Lesson Four).

1b: Two-Termination Adjectives of the Second Declension

5.62 Some adjectives have only the Second Declension terminations and no distinctive feminine form — the masculine form does duty as the feminine also. (This category comprises particularly adjectives that are compound, including those beginning with "α-", meaning "not" or "un-", e.g. ἄδικος, ον, unjust, ἀδύνατος, ον, incapable, impossible.)

5.63 Some adjectives vary between being used as two-termination and three-termination adjectives, and in these cases there are frequently variant readings in the manuscripts of the Greek, as ancient editors "corrected" the text in one direction or the other.

2.   FIRST & THIRD DECLENSION PATTERN

2a: Three-Termination Adjectives of the 1st & 3rd Declensions (#D4.4, D4.6)

5.64 In this pattern, the feminine form of the adjective usually ends in "-α": which means its stem will end either in ρ, ι, or ε (in which case it declines like καρδία, D1.1 [#3.11]; example: βαρεῖα, from βαρύς, heavy/hard), or else its stem will end in a sigma (in which case it declines like δόξα, D1.3 [#3.11]; example: πᾶσα, from πᾶς, all). Those few ending in "-η" follow φωνή, D1.2 (#3.11). The masculine form follows the same rules for the Third Declension as set out in this Lesson, and the neuter form is the same as the masculine except for the usual neuter characteristics: the nominative singular ends in a short vowel where the masculine has a long vowel, and frequently ends in "-ν" or the bare stem without any ending; the nominative plural adds "-α" to the stem; the accusative is always the same as the nominative. As in the Second Declension, the genitive and dative forms (both singular and plural) are the same for the masculine and neuter.

5.65 πᾶς, παντός, all/everything, follows Paradigm D3.18 (#5.44), with the masculine retaining the "-ς" ending in the nominative singular and dropping the "-ν" of the stem, and the neuter, by contradistinction, dropping the "-ς" ending and retaining the "-ν". All participles in "-ας" (such as λύσας, #4.21) follow πᾶς. ἑκών, ἑκόντος also follows Paradigm D3.18 (#5.44), ἄρχων, ἄρχοντος, with neuter nominative and accusative singular ἑκόν. All participles in "-ων" (such as λύων, #4.21) decline like ἑκών. There is a third type of adjective, βαρύς, -έως, heavy/hard, which follows Paradigm D3.3 (#5.20), πόλις, πόλεως. Two very common adjectives follow a mixed paradigm of Second and Third forms:

πολύς, **much, many**   μέγας, **great**

		m.	f.	n.		m.	f.	n.
S	N	πολύς	πολλή	πολύ		μέγας	μεγάλη	μέγα
	A	πολύν	πολλήν	πολύ		μέγαν	μεγάλην	μέγα
	G	πολλοῦ	πολλῆς	πολλοῦ		μεγάλου	μεγάλης	μεγάλου

Dative and plural forms are regular Second Declension with stems πολλ- and μεγαλ- respectively. These flexions are set out in full in D4.42, D4.43.

5.66 The word for "one" has these forms:

NOTE: In the nature of the case, there is no plural. The feminine uses a completely different stem. The forms εἷς and ἕν are

		m.	f.	n.
S	N	εἷς	μία	ἕν
	A	ἕνα	μίαν	ἕν
	G	ἑνός	μιᾶς	ἑνός
	D	ἑνί	μιᾷ	ἑνί

distinguished from the prepositions εἰς and ἐν by the accent and the rough breathing on each. These forms combine with οὐδέ and μηδέ to give οὐδείς, οὐδεμία, οὐδέν and μηδείς, μηδεμία, μηδέν, no-one, nothing.

2b: Two-Termination Adjectives of the Third Declension (#D4.7, D4.8)

5.67 Some adjectives have only the Third Declension terminations and no distinctive feminine form — the masculine form does duty as the feminine also. There are two main patterns for these, shown by ἄφρων (which follows Paradigm D3.16 [#5.31], ἡγεμών, ἡγεμόνος) and ἀληθής (which follows Paradigm D3.5, [#5.2], γένος, γένους). All positive adjectives in "-ων" (except ἑκών and ἄκων) and all comparative adjectives in "-ων" follow ἄφρων.

5.68 The pronoun τις, τι (genitive τινος) also has only two terminations and apart from the nominative singular follows ἡγεμών, ἡγεμόνος, Paradigm D3.16 (#5.31). When accented, this is the interrogative pronoun "who?, what?", and when unaccented it is the indefinite pronoun, "someone, a certain, something". (Given in full in the Appendix, Paradigms D6.5, D6.6.)

5.69 Because of the extent to which these various adjectives, pronouns and participles have the same endings and follow the same general patterns as the nouns of the First, Second, and Third Declensions, their case, number and gender will usually be easily recognizable, and so it has not been necessary to give paradigms for them all here. Any unusual or difficult forms will always be explained in the textual notes on the passage of the Greek New Testament that you are reading. All the paradigms, however, for the various types of adjectives and participles are given in Appendix D.

ASSIGNMENTS ON LESSON FIVE

1. Read Lesson Five through twice. **LEARN BY HEART**: ἰχθύς (Paradigm D3.1).
2. Read and translate literally all the Selections from the Greek N.T. Aim to gain such an understanding of them that, with the assistance of a wordlist, you can translate them verbally at will. In conjunction with your work on the Selections, go carefully through the Vocabulary.
3. Do a quick preliminary reading of Lesson Six.

EXPLANATORY NOTES AND VOCABULARY

NOTES AND COMMENTS
(Numbers refer to N.T. Selections)

2. φιμώθητι — Be quiet!
σπαράξαν (aor. ptc.) throwing into convulsions
3. ἐξηραμμένην — shrivelled
6. πρός — because of, to
προσκολληθήσεται (he) will be united
ἔσονται — (they) will be
οὐκέτι — no longer
συνέζευξεν
  1st aor, συζεύγνυμι — join
7. ἀπεκρίθη — (he) answered
πλησίον (indeclinable) neighbour
8. λάβετε 2nd aor. impv: take
9. εἰς — for, with a view to
11. νεώτερος, α, ον — the younger
δός 2nd sg. aor. impv: give
ἐπιβάλλον (ptc.) falling by inheritance
12. εἰ — if
ἀπεκρίθη — see Selection 7
13. *κἀγω — = καὶ ἐγω
ἀπόλωνται — (they) shall perish
εἰς τὸν αἰῶνα — to eternity, ever
δέδωκεν — perfect from δίδωμι
δύναται — (he) is able
14. ἔρχεται — (he) comes
εἰ μή — except, unless
17. ἐκλήθητε — you were called
18. εἰς τὸ στηρίξαι (εἰς plus articular infinitive expresses purpose) to strengthen
παρακαλέσαι — encourage (aor. infin. of παρακαλέω — note short -εσ-)
19. ἤγγικεν perfect
from ἐγγίζω come near
20. ἐρχομένους coming (participle)
ὑπέδειξεν 3rd sg. 1st aor. from
ὑποδείκνυμι, — warn, indicate
φυγεῖν 2nd aor, infin.
from φεύγω, — escape, flee
μελλούσης fut. ptc.of
μέλλω, to be about to
ἐγένετο — came
πατέρα for father, as our father

ἐγεῖραι (infin.) — to raise up
κεῖται 3rd Sg. from
κεῖμαι, — to lie, be laid
ποιοῦν pres. part. a., fr. ποιέω
ἐκκόπτεται — is chopped down
βάλλεται — is thrown
*μὲν...δὲ...on the one hand... on the other hand
εἰς — for, with a view to
ὀπίσω — after
διακαθαριεῖ 3rd Sg. fut. a. (irregular) of διακαθαρίζω — clean out
21. ἀποκριθείς answering (participle)
ζῶν, ζῶντος — living (participle)
βαριωνᾶ — son of John (Heb.)
22. λαβεῖν — to take (aor. infin.)
σφραγίς, ῖδος, ἡ — seal
ἐσφάγης — you (sg.) were slain
ζῷον, ου, τό — living creature
ἀριθμός, οῦ, ὁ — number
ἀρνίον, ου, τό — lamb
ἐσφαγμένον — (participle) slain
*σοφία, ας, ἡ — wisdom

NOUNS (Numbers refer to paradigms)

D1. * ἁμαρτία, ας, ἡ — sin
γλῶσσα, ης, ἡ — language
διαθήκη, ης, ἡ — covenant
* ἐξουσία, ας, ἡ — authority
μετάνοια, ας, ἡ — repentance
οὐσία, ας, ἡ — property
παρουσία, ας, ἡ — coming
σκληροκαρδία, ας, ἡ hardheartedness
τιμή, ῆς, ἡ — honour
φυλή, ῆς, ἡ — tribe
D2. ἀποστάσιον ου τό divorce notice
βιβλίον, ου, τό — scroll, book
δένδρον, ου, τό — tree
περίχωρος, ου,ἡ surrounding region
συνεργός, οῦ, ὁ fellow-worker
* λίθος, ου, ὁ — a stone
* τέκνον, ου, τό — child
D3.1 † ἰσχύς, ύος, ἡ — strength, might
ἰχθύς, ύος, ὁ — a fish

D3.2   ἄφεσις, εως, ἡ   forgiveness
    * δύναμις, εως, ἡ   power, deed
                        of power
      κλῆσις, εως, ἡ   calling
      κτίσις, εως, ἡ   creation
    * πίστις, εως, ἡ   faith
D3.3   νοῦς, νοός, ὁ   mind
D3.4   ἱερεύς, έως, ὁ   priest
D3.5   γένος, ους, τό   race
    * ἔθνος, ους, τό   nation
      μέρος, ους, τό   part
D3.6   * νύξ, νυκτός, ἡ   night
    * σάρξ, σαρκός, ἡ   flesh
D3.8   * ἐλπίς, ίδος, ἡ   hope
    † ἔρις, ιδος, ἡ   strife
    † κλείς, εῖδος, ἡ   key
      μυριάς, άδος, ἡ   myriad
      παῖς, παιδός, ὁ/ἡ   child
    * πούς, ποδός, ὁ   foot
  †* χάρις, ιτος, ἡ   grace
      χιλιάς, άδος, ἡ   thousand

    † These three take Acc. Sing. in "-ν", and
      may have Pl. Nom. and/or Acc. in
      "-εις" instead of the usual ending.

D3.9   * αἷμα, ατος, τό   blood
      βάπτισμα, ατος, τό   baptism
    * θέλημα, ατος, τό   will, wish
      κρίμα, ατος, τό   judgement
    * ὄνομα, ατος, τό   name
    * πνεῦμα, ατος, τό   spirit
    * ῥῆμα, ατος, τό   word, thing
    * σῶμα, ατος, τό   body
D3.10 * φῶς, φωτός, τό   light
D3.11 * πῦρ, πυρός, τό   fire
      σωτήρ, ῆρος, ὁ   saviour
D3.12 ἀστήρ, έρος, ὁ   star
D3.13 * ὕδωρ, ὕδατος, τό   water
D3.14 * αἰών, ῶνος, ὁ   age
D3.16 ἡγεμών, όνος, ὁ   leader
D3.17 ἄρσην, εν (ενος)   (adj.) male
      ποιμήν, ένος, ὁ   shepherd
D3.18 ἄρχων, οντος, ὁ   ruler
D3.26 * γυνή, αικός, ἡ   wife, woman
D3.30 οὖς, ὠτός, τό   ear
D3.31 * χείρ, χειρός, ἡ   hand
D3.32 θυγάτηρ, τρός, ἡ   daughter
    * μήτηρ, τρός, ἡ   mother
    * ἀνήρ, ἀνδρός, ὁ   husband, man

GENERAL WORDS

* διά, δι'   (+ gen) through, by means of
  ἕνεκεν   (+ gen) because of
* ἐπί, ἐπ')   {(+ gen) over, upon
  ἐφ'   (+ acc) for, to
* οὐδέ   and not, neither, nor
* ὑπέρ   (+ gen) for, concerning
* ὥστε   so that

VERBS

* ἀγαπάω   love
  ἀγοράζω   purchase
  ἀνακράζω   cry out
* ἀπολύω   divorce, send away
  ἁρπάζω   snatch
* βαπτίζω   baptize
  βασιλεύω   reign
* γινώσκω   know
* δοκέω   think, presume
  ἐπιτρέπω   allow, permit
  καταλείπω   leave, forsake
  μακροθυμέω   wait patiently
  οἰκοδομέω   build
* παρακαλέω   encourage, request
* πέμπω   send
* συνάγω   gather
  χωρίζω   separate, sever

THIRD DECLENSION PRONOUNS

D6.6   * τις, τι (τινος)   See #5.68
D6.7   * οὐδεις, εμία, έν}   {no one,
        (ενος)   nothing

(For full Third Declension Paradigms,
see #D3-D6.)

THIRD DECLENSION ADJECTIVES

D4.4   θῆλυς, εια, υ   female
D4.5   ἑκών, οῦσα, όν   willing
D4.6 * πᾶς, πᾶσα, πᾶν   all
D4.8   μείζων, ον   greater

OTHER ADJECTIVES

* ἅγιος, α, ον	holy
* αἰώνιος, ον	eternal
ἀκάθαρτος, ον	unclean
* ἄλλος, η, ο	(an)other
ἄξιος, α, ον	worthy of, fitting
δεύτερος α ον	second
καινός, ή, όν	new
* μακάριος, α, ον	blessed, fortunate
* πολύς, πολλή, πολύ	many, much
* πρῶτος, η, ον	first, foremost

REFLEXIVE PRONOUNS

ἐμαυτόν, ήν	1st person sing. myself
σεαυτόν, ήν	2nd person sing. yourself
ἑαυτόν, ήν, ό	3rd person sing. himself, etc.
ἑαυτούς, άς, ά	1st/2nd/3rd pl. our- selves/yourselves/themselves

NOTE: There can be no nominative. The plural has only the one form.

SELECTIONS FROM THE GREEK NEW TESTAMENT

1. ἐγὼ ἐβάπτισα ὑμᾶς ὕδατι, αὐτὸς δὲ βαπτίσει ὑμᾶς ἐν πνεύματι ἁγίῳ. (ΚΑΤΑ ΜΑΡΚΟΝ 1:8.)

2. ἦν διδάσκων αὐτοὺς ὡς ἐξουσίαν ἔχων καὶ οὐχ ὡς οἱ γραμματεῖς. καὶ εὐθὺς ἦν ἐν τῇ συναγωγῇ αὐτῶν ἄνθρωπος ἐν πνεύματι ἀκαθάρτῳ, καὶ ἀνέκραξεν ... καὶ ἐπετίμησεν αὐτῷ ὁ Ἰησοῦς λέγων, Φιμώθητι καὶ ἔξελθε ἐξ αὐτοῦ. καὶ σπαράξαν αὐτὸν τὸ πνεῦμα τὸ ἀκάθαρτον καὶ φωνῆσαν φωνῇ μεγάλῃ ἐξῆλθεν ἐξ αὐτοῦ. (ΚΑΤΑ ΜΑΡΚΟΝ 1:22-26.)

3. καὶ εἰσῆλθεν πάλιν εἰς τὴν συναγωγήν. καὶ ἦν ἐκεῖ ἄνθρωπος ἐξηραμμένην ἔχων τὴν χεῖρα. (ΚΑΤΑ ΜΑΡΚΟΝ 3:1.)

4. ἔλεγον, Πνεῦμα ἀκάθαρτον ἔχει. (ΚΑΤΑ ΜΑΡΚΟΝ 3:30.)

5. εἴ τις ἔχει ὦτα ἀκούειν ἀκουέτω. Καὶ ἔλεγεν αὐτοῖς, Βλέπετε τί ἀκούετε. (ΚΑΤΑ ΜΑΡΚΟΝ 4:23-24.)

6. οἱ δὲ εἶπαν, Ἐπέτρεψεν Μωϋσῆς βιβλίον ἀποστασίου γράψαι καὶ ἀπολῦσαι. ὁ δὲ Ἰησοῦς εἶπεν αὐτοῖς, Πρὸς τὴν σκληροκαρδίαν ὑμῶν ἔγραψεν ὑμῖν τὴν ἐντολὴν ταύτην. ἀπὸ δὲ ἀρχῆς κτίσεως ἄρσεν καὶ θῆλυ ἐποίησεν αὐτούς. ἕνεκεν τούτου καταλείψει ἄνθρωπος τὸν πατέρα αὐτοῦ καὶ τὴν μητέρα καὶ προσκολληθήσεται πρὸς τὴν γυναῖκα αὐτοῦ, καὶ ἔσονται οἱ δύο εἰς σάρκα μίαν. ὥστε οὐκέτι εἰσὶν δύο ἀλλὰ μία σάρξ. ὃ οὖν ὁ θεὸς συνέζευξεν ἄνθρωπος μὴ χωριζέτω. (ΚΑΤΑ ΜΑΡΚΟΝ 10:4-9.)

7. ἀπεκρίθη ὁ Ἰησοῦς ὅτι Πρώτη ἐστίν, Ἄκουε, Ἰσραήλ, κύριος ὁ θεὸς ἡμῶν κύριος εἷς ἐστιν, καὶ ἀγαπήσεις κύριον τὸν θεόν σου ἐξ ὅλης τῆς καρδίας σου καὶ ἐξ ὅλης τῆς ψυχῆς σου καὶ ἐξ ὅλης τῆς διανοίας σου καὶ ἐξ ὅλης τῆς ἰσχύος σου. δευτέρα αὕτη, Ἀγαπήσεις τόν πλησίον σου ὡς σεαυτόν. μείζων τούτων ἄλλη ἐντολή οὐκ ἔστιν. (ΚΑΤΑ ΜΑΡΚΟΝ 12:29-31.)

8. καὶ εἶπεν, Λάβετε, τοῦτό ἐστιν τὸ σῶμά μου ... καὶ εἶπεν αὐτοῖς, Τοῦτό ἐστιν τὸ αἷμά μου τῆς διαθήκης. (ΚΑΤΑ ΜΑΡΚΟΝ 14:22, 24.)

9. ἐγένετο ῥῆμα θεοῦ ἐπὶ Ἰωάννην τὸν Ζαχαρίου υἱὸν ἐν τῇ ἐρήμῳ. καὶ ἦλθεν εἰς πᾶσαν τὴν περίχωρον τοῦ Ἰορδάνου κηρύσσων βάπτισμα μετανοίας εἰς ἄφεσιν ἁμαρτιῶν. (ΚΑΤΑ ΛΟΥΚΑΝ 3:2-3.)

10. λέγω γὰρ ὑμῖν ὅτι πολλοὶ προφῆται καὶ βασιλεῖς ἠθέλησαν ἰδεῖν ἃ ὑμεῖς βλέπετε καὶ οὐκ εἶδαν, καὶ ἀκοῦσαι ἃ ἀκούετε καὶ οὐκ ἤκουσαν. (ΚΑΤΑ ΛΟΥΚΑΝ 10:24.)

11. Εἶπεν δέ, Ἄνθρωπός τις εἶχεν δύο υἱούς. καὶ εἶπεν ὁ νεώτερος αὐτῶν τῷ πατρί, Πάτερ, δός μοι τὸ ἐπιβάλλον μέρος τῆς οὐσίας. (ΚΑΤΑ ΛΟΥΚΑΝ 15:11-12.)

12. καὶ ἦσαν ἐκ τῶν Φαρισαίων. καὶ εἶπαν αὐτῷ, Τί οὖν βαπτίζεις εἰ σὺ οὐκ εἶ ὁ Χριστὸς οὐδὲ Ἠλίας οὐδὲ ὁ προφήτης; ἀπεκρίθη αὐτοῖς ὁ Ἰωάννης λέγων, Ἐγὼ βαπτίζω ἐν ὕδατι. (ΚΑΤΑ ΙΩΑΝΝΗΝ 1:24-26.)

13. ἀλλὰ ὑμεῖς οὐ πιστεύετε, ὅτι οὐκ ἐστὲ ἐκ τῶν προβάτων τῶν ἐμῶν. τὰ πρόβατα τὰ ἐμὰ τῆς φωνῆς μου ἀκούουσιν, κἀγὼ γινώσκω αὐτά, καὶ ἀκολουθοῦσίν μοι, κἀγὼ δίδωμι αὐτοῖς ζωὴν αἰώνιον, καὶ οὐ μὴ ἀπόλωνται εἰς τὸν αἰῶνα, καὶ οὐχ ἁρπάσει τις αὐτὰ ἐκ τῆς χειρός μου. ὁ πατήρ μου ὃ δέδωκέν μοι πάντων μεῖζόν ἐστιν, καὶ οὐδεὶς δύναται ἁρπάζειν ἐκ τῆς χειρὸς τοῦ πατρός. ἐγὼ καὶ ὁ πατὴρ ἕν ἐσμεν. (ΚΑΤΑ ΙΩΑΝΝΗΝ 10:26-30.)

14. λέγει αὐτῷ ὁ Ἰησοῦς, Ἐγώ εἰμι ἡ ὁδὸς καὶ ἡ ἀλήθεια καὶ ἡ ζωή. οὐδεὶς ἔρχεται πρὸς τὸν πατέρα εἰ μὴ δι' ἐμοῦ. (ΚΑΤΑ ΙΩΑΝΝΗΝ 14:6.)

15. πιστεύετέ μοι ὅτι ἐγὼ ἐν τῷ πατρὶ καὶ ὁ πατὴρ ἐν ἐμοί. (ΚΑΤΑ ΙΩΑΝΝΗΝ 14:11.)

16. ἡμεῖς δὲ νοῦν Χριστοῦ ἔχομεν. (ΠΡΟΣ ΚΟΡΙΝΘΙΟΥΣ Α, 2:16.)

17. ἓν σῶμα καὶ ἓν πνεῦμα, καθὼς καὶ ἐκλήθητε ἐν μιᾷ ἐλπίδι τῆς κλήσεως ὑμῶν· εἷς κύριος, μία πίστις, ἓν βάπτισμα· εἷς θεος καὶ πατὴρ πάντων, ὁ ἐπὶ πάντων καὶ διὰ πάντων καὶ ἐν πᾶσιν. (ΠΡΟΣ ΕΦΕΣΙΟΥΣ 4:4-6.)

18. καὶ ἐπέμψαμεν Τιμόθεον, τὸν ἀδελφὸν ἡμῶν καὶ συνεργὸν τοῦ θεοῦ ἐν τῷ εὐαγγελίῳ τοῦ Χριστοῦ, εἰς τὸ στηρίξαι ὑμᾶς καὶ παρακαλέσαι ὑπὲρ τῆς πίστεως ὑμῶν. (ΠΡΟΣ ΘΕΣΣΑΛΟΝΙΚΕΙΣ Α, 3:2.)

19. μακροθυμήσατε καὶ ὑμεῖς, στηρίξατε τὰς καρδίας ὑμῶν, ὅτι ἡ παρουσία τοῦ κυρίου ἤγγικεν. (ΙΑΚΩΒΟΥ 5:8.)

PASSAGES IN THE GREEK NEW TESTAMENT

You are now ready to begin reading directly from the Greek New Testament. Using your Grammatical Analysis (Zerwick and Grosvenor, or Rienecker), read the following passages:

20. ΚΑΤΑ ΜΑΘΘΑΙΟΝ 3:7-12.

21. ΚΑΤΑ ΜΑΘΘΑΙΟΝ 16:15-18.

22. ΑΠΟΚΑΛΥΨΙΣ ΙΩΑΝΝΟΥ 5:9-12.

NOTE: Use your Dictionary for any additional words that you need.

LESSON SIX

THE MIDDLE AND PASSIVE VOICE

6.1 THE PASSIVE AND MIDDLE VOICES OF THE VERB

6.11 So far we have covered only the *active* voice of the verb — where the subject of the verb is the doer of the action of the verb, i.e. where the action of the verb moves outwards from the subject. It could be described diagrammatically as:

SUBJECT ——**VERB**——➤

There are two other voices in Greek: the *passive*, and the *middle*.

6.12 The passive voice has the same meaning and operates in the same way as in English: the subject of the sentence is the person or thing upon whom the action of the verb is carried out. "Blessed are those who mourn, for they *shall be comforted*"; "The word *was spoken* by the prophet in days of old". It could be described diagrammatically as:

SUBJECT ◄——**VERB**——

6.13 The middle voice is (as its name suggests) between the active and the passive in its function. No simple explanation is possible of what the middle voice is: in fact, its function and meaning can vary from verb to verb. The middle voice can be found used in these ways:

    1. Commonly, the middle voice is used for intransitive verbs, or where the action of the verb does not carry over to an object but solely affects the subject. Often the subject of a middle voice verb is acting for himself or in his own interests.

    2. Closely related to the first use, the middle voice can have a reflexive sense — the action was done to or for the subject.

6.14 These two basic usages shade into each other. Something of the force of the middle can be seen in these examples, which you should consider:

Acts 8:32   A lamb is dumb before the one who *is shearing* it (κείρω, active), but
Acts 18:18   Paul had his head *shorn* (κείρω, this time in the middle)
John 13:14   Jesus *washed* the disciples' feet (active of νίπτω), but
Matthew 27:24   Pilate *washed* his hands (middle voice of νίπτω).
Matthew 27:31   They *put on* him his own clothes (active of ἐνδύω), but
Mark 6:9   Do not *put on* two tunics (middle of ἐνδύω).
Acts 21:24   You yourself *keep* the law (active of φυλάσσω), but
Acts 21:25   They are to *keep* themselves from idol food (middle of φυλάσσω).

However, the middle voice was falling out of use in koine Greek, and it is not always found where it might be expected. Thus Matthew and Luke use the active voice of φυλάσσω in a passage where it is appropriate for the middle to be used, whereas in this passage Mark does use the middle:

Matthew 19:20   All these I have kept (active of φυλάσσω)
Mark 10:20   All these I have kept (middle of φυλάσσω)
Luke 18:21   All these I have kept (active of φυλάσσω)

6.15 The reflexive use of the middle is seen in:

Matthew 27:5   Judas went away and *hanged himself* (middle).

But it is common to find a reflexive expressed by an active voice and the reflexive pronoun, as in:

John 17:19   I *sanctify* myself (active voice + reflexive pronoun).

6.16 Most commonly the middle voice will be rendered in English by the active voice, occasionally with the added pronoun (himself, for himself, etc.), and at times with a construction that indicates that the subject had the action carried out upon himself. The middle voice could be described diagrammatically as:

VERB

SUBJECT ⟵⟸⟩

6.17 There are two other usages of the middle voice in Greek:

3. Some verbs have developed a distinctive meaning in the middle voice which is only rather distantly related to their active meaning. Thus:

αἱρέω (active):	I take away	αἱρέομαι (middle):	I choose
ἀποδίδωμι (active):	I repay	ἀποδίδομαι (middle):	I sell
ἅπτω (active):	I light	ἅπτομαι (middle):	I touch
ἄρχω (active):	I rule/govern	ἄρχομαι (middle):	I begin
καταλαμβάνω (active):	I obtain	καταλαμβάνομαι (middle):	I realize/learn
πείθω (active):	I persuade	πείθομαι (middle):	I obey

4. A number of verbs have only a middle form, without any corresponding active voice. These verbs have an active meaning and (in accordance with the connotations of the middle voice) they are intransitive or where they do require or can have an object it will be in a case other than the accusative. These verbs are known as deponent middle verbs. (There are a small number of deponent passive verbs i.e. verbs which exist only in the passive voice but which have an active meaning; a few deponents use some middle and some passive forms.)

6.18 A comprehensive list of 59 verbs which are (always, or frequently) deponent in the N.T. is given in #C7.5. Of these, there are twenty-four which occur more than 20 times each, and which therefore are particularly to be noted. These are:

ἀποκρίνομαι	answer	δέχομαι	receive	κάθημαι	sit down
ἅπτομαι	touch	δύναμαι	be able	καυχάομαι	boast
ἀρνέομαι	deny	ἐργάζομαι	work	κεῖμαι	lie down
ἄρχομαι	begin	ἔρχομαι	come	λογίζομαι	account/reckon
ἀσπάζομαι	greet	εὐαγγελίζομαι	preach	πορεύομαι	go/proceed
βούλομαι	want	ἡγέομαι	think/lead	προσεύχομαι	pray
γίνομαι	become	θεάομαι	look at	φοβέομαι	fear
δέομαι	beseech	ἰάομαι	heal	χαρίζομαι	grant/forgive

6.19 Verbs that are deponent in the present are (almost without exception) deponent in the other tenses also. In addition, there are fourteen verbs (set out in #C7.6) which are deponent in their future tense in the N.T. and have active forms in their other tenses. These are all quite common and important verbs, and should be noted carefully. It is important to be able to recognize a deponent form, so that it can be correctly interpreted.

6.2 THE PARADIGM OF THE MIDDLE VOICE

6.21 The middle voice has its own set of endings, which are added to the same stem as for the active. The six Greek tenses fall into two groups, which are known as the *primary* and *secondary* tenses. The primary and secondary tenses have slightly different pronoun endings. They are:

	Characteristic Letter	Primary Tenses (Present, Future, Present Perfect)	Secondary Tenses (Imperfect, Aorist, Pluperfect)
S 1	μ	-μαι	-μην
2	σ	-σαι	-σο
3	τ	-ται	-το
P 1	μ	-μεθα	-μεθα
2	σ	-σθε	-σθε
3	τ	-νται	-ντο

6.22 Note that the secondary tenses are the ones that take the augment (in the indicative mode), whereas the primary tenses do not. The secondary tenses are also known as the *historic* tenses. Note the characteristic letters found for 1st, 2nd and 3rd person (μ, σ, τ) which also surface in other places — the μ and σ in the personal pronouns ἐμέ, με, σύ, etc.,and in ἐμός, σός, ἐμαυτόν, σεαυτόν; and the τ in αὐτός, οὗτος, the article.

6.23 The same procedures are used as in the active voice for adding the endings to the stem: the present tense adds the neutral morph -ε or -ο to the stem and then takes the primary endings; the future is the same as the present with the -σ- future morph inserted between the stem and the endings; the imperfect has the augment, adds the neutral morph -ε or -ο to the stem and then takes the secondary endings; the first aorist has the augment, adds the punctiliar morph -σα (σ before vowels) to the stem and then takes the secondary endings. The one difference is that the present perfect does not have the perfective morph -κα (as in the active) but adds the ending straight on to the reduplicated stem. The pluperfect is rare, and so is not set out here (it is given in #C1.1); like the present perfect middle, it adds its endings (the secondary endings) straight on to the stem, and takes the augment — thus giving the form ἐλελύμην. However, the pluperfect frequently omits the augment. Some verbs form their pluperfect middle and possibly some forms of their perfect middle as well by the use of the perfect middle participle and the imperfect tense of εἰμί, or present tense respectively. These will be covered more fully at a later time.

6.24 There is one complication: the -σ- of the second person singular is squeezed out and disappears in the present, future, imperfect, and aorist tenses, and the neutral morph -ε (or the -α in the aorist) then contracts with the vowel that follows the lost -σ into a diphthong or long vowel.

6.25 The indicative and subjunctive middle paradigm flexions for λύω are:

INDICATIVE: Primary Tenses			Secondary Tenses		SUBJUNCTIVE	
Present	**Future**	**Perfect**	**Imperfect**	**1st Aorist**	**Present**	**Aorist**
λύομαι	λύσομαι	λέλυμαι	ἐλυόμην	ἐλυσάμην	λύωμαι	λύσωμαι
λύῃ/λύει	λύσῃ	λέλυσαι	ἐλύου	ἐλύσω	λύῃ	λύσῃ
λύεται	λύσεται	λέλυται	ἐλύετο	ἐλύσατο	λύηται	λύσηται
λυόμεθα	λυσόμεθα	λελύμεθα	ἐλυόμεθα	ἐλυσάμεθα	λυώμεθα	λυσώμεθα
λύεσθε	λύσεσθε	λέλυσθε	ἐλύεσθε	ἐλύσασθε	λύησθε	λύσησθε
λύονται	λύσονται	λέλυνται	ἐλύοντο	ἐλύσαντο	λύωνται	λύσωνται

6.26 As in the active voice, there are two tenses of the subjunctive, the present and the aorist. The present subjunctive middle is the same as the indicative but with the neutral morph -ε- or -o- lengthened to -η- and -ω- respectively (and iota being subscript on -η-). That is, the subjunctive morph is not something that is *added* to the word, but a *process* which affects part of the word (the lengthening of the neutral morph). The subjunctive morph is therefore called a *process morph*. Again, as in the active, the aorist subjunctive middle is identical with the present subjunctive middle but with the aorist morph -σ- inserted between the stem and the endings. This means that in the subjunctive the aorist follows the primary pattern of endings (and has no augment) —contrast its secondary indicative pattern.

6.27 There are two possible forms of the 2nd person singular present indicative, λύῃ and λύει. Both forms are identical with others which occur elsewhere in the paradigms — λύει with the 3rd person singular present indicative active (see #2.81) and λύῃ with the 3rd person singular present subjunctive active (see #4.21) and also with the 2nd person singular present subjunctive middle (see #6.25). Usually the context will make it clear which form is intended (just as the context in English will usually make it clear, when one sees "read", "put", etc., whether the present or past tense is meant). But occasionally a form is encountered which is ambiguous.

6.28 Another pair of identical forms, to which the same comments apply, are the 2nd person singular future indicative middle and aorist subjunctive middle, both of which are λύσῃ (see #6.25).

6.29 The present, aorist and perfect middle for the imperative, infinitive and participle are:

IMPERATIVE:	Present	Aorist	Perfect
S 2	λύου	λῦσαι	λέλυσο
3	λυέσθω	λυσάσθω	λελύσθω
P 2	λύεσθε	λύσασθε	λέλυσθε
3	λυέσθωσαν	λυσάσθωσαν	λελύσθωσαν
INFINITIVE:	λύεσθαι	λύσασθαι	λελύσθαι
PARTICIPLE:	λυόμενος, η, ον	λυσάμενος, η, ον	λελυμένος, η, ον

6.3 POINTS TO NOTE

6.31 The 2nd person plural present is the same form for the imperative (see above) as for the indicative (see #6.25); this was true also for the active voice (see #3.51). In the aorist, these same forms are distinguished only by the augment — it is affixed to the aorist form in the indicative, but absent in the imperative. The forms for other persons and numbers are distinctive.

6.32 The letters -σθ- comprise the *specifier morph* for the middle imperative and infinitive; but this morph is absent from the forms for all tenses of the 2nd person singular imperative, and does not occur in the flexions of the indicative middle (except, incidentally, in the 2nd person plural forms), and these forms have to be identified as middle by the distinctive sets of middle pronoun suffixes which they have, which bear some similarities to the equivalent suffixes for the active but are distinguishably different from them. The morph -μεν- occurs in *all* middle participles and *only* in middle participles, and thus is a specifier morph: it effectively identifies any word in which it occurs as being a middle participle. It can be noted that each participle consists of the lexal (the word stem), the aspect morph (the neutral morph -o- for the present tense, -σα- for the first aorist, and prefixed reduplication for the perfect), the specifier morph for the middle participle, -μεν-, and the respective number-case endings of the First and Second Declensions. In all tenses, the middle participle declines in the pattern of the First and Second Declensions (see the complete set of paradigm flexions in Appendix D, #D5.14-D5.16). The specifier morph occupies the eighth of the verb's nine morph slots.

6.33 It needs to be kept in mind at all times that all the above-mentioned flexions are middle in *form*; those for the present/imperfect and the perfect tenses can be either middle or passive in *meaning*: see #6.50.

6.34 Another pair of identical forms needs now to be noted: the 2nd person singular aorist middle imperative, λῦσαι, is the same form as that for the aorist infinitive (see #4.21).

6.35 The same linguistic modification rules given earlier (#4.5) apply when adding -σ- and when adding the endings of the perfect tense to a consonant verb stem. (Further details of these linguistic modifications are set out in #9.75.) In almost all cases, the verb, and the effect of the -σ- or the fact that it is perfect tense (as the case may be), will be easily recognizable. Difficult and irregular cases will be explained fully in your Analysis when you encounter them in reading your Greek New Testament.

6.4   THE FUTURE INDICATIVE AND THE OTHER MODES OF EIMI

6.41 The verb εἰμί is deponent in the future indicative, and has the stem ἐ- and the endings of the middle of λύω (but note it has ἔσται, not "ἔσεται").

6.42	INDICATIVE	SUBJUNCTIVE	IMPERATIVE		INFINITIVE	PARTICIPLE
	Future	Present	Present		Present: εἶναι	ὤν οὖσα ὄν
S 1	ἔσομαι	ὦ	—		Future: ἔσεσθαι	ἐσόμενος, η, ον
2	ἔσῃ	ᾖς	ἴσθι			(The declension
3	ἔσται	ᾖ	ἔστω/ἤτω			of ὤν follows
P 1	ἐσόμεθα	ὦμεν	—			#D5.11. See
2	ἔσεσθε	ἦτε	ἔστε			#C6, Conjuga-
3	ἔσονται	ὦσι(ν)	ἔστωσαν			tion Conspectus,
						for εἰμί
						Paradigm.)

6.5   THE PARADIGM OF THE PASSIVE VOICE

6.50 The passive voice in Greek is a distinct voice different from the active and middle in sense, and yet it has only a small number of distinct forms of its own: for the future and aorist indicative, the aorist subjunctive, the aorist imperative, and the aorist infinitive. For the present and perfect tense systems the passive borrows and uses the corresponding forms of the middle voice. This will mean that there are at times middle forms used in the New Testament which could be either middle or passive in meaning, so that it becomes a question of exegesis and interpretation to say which is intended.

		INDICATIVE				SUBJUNCTIVE		IMPERATIVE	
	Present	Future	Perfect	Imperfect	Aorist	Present	Aorist	Present	Aorist
S 1	*	λυθήσομαι	*	*	ἐλύθην	*	λυθῶ	—	
2		λυθήσῃ			ἐλύθης		λυθῇς	*	λύθητι
3		λυθήσεται			ἐλύθη		λυθῇ		λυθήτω
P 1		λυθησόμεθα			ἐλύθημεν		λυθῶμεν	—	—
2		λυθήσεσθε			ἐλύθητε		λυθῆτε		λύθητε
3		λυθήσονται			ἐλύθησαν		λυθῶσι(ν)		λυθήτωσαν
Infinitive *		λυθήσεσθαι	*	—	λυθῆναι				
Participle *		λυθησόμενος	*	—	λυθείς, λυθεῖσα, λυθέν, λυθέντος				

Points to notice:

6.51 In the table, a dash (—) indicates that the form does not exist; an asterisk (*) means that there are no special passive forms for that flexion but instead in these cases the middle forms are used for the passive voice as well as for the middle voice.

6.52 The passive morph is -θε-, the -ε- of which lengthens into -η- before a consonant (except in the aorist participle), and contracts with the following vowel in the subjunctive. There is thus as a rule a very clear indication of the passive in all its special forms. The passive morph occupies the fifth of the verb's nine morph slots.

6.53 The aorist indicative passive is formed by adding the passive morph -θε- (which lengthens to -θη-) to the verb stem, and to this are then added directly the endings of the third aorist active (from which in fact the passive was developed, as described in #C3.86; see also #7.44). That is to say, like the third aorist, the aorist passive does not have an aspect morph.

6.54 The future indicative passive is formed from the aorist indicative passive by replacing the final -ν of the flexion form with -σομαι, i.e. with the endings of the future *middle* flexion. Thus the presence of the passive morph -θη- is the sole feature which distinguishes the future passive from the future middle. That is, -θη- switches the verb from middle voice to passive voice.

6.55 The aorist subjunctive passive takes the same pronoun endings as the aorist subjunctive active, adding them to the passive morph -θε-, which takes the place of the punctiliar morph -σ-. The -ε- of the passive morph then contracts with the endings (re contraction, see #6.9), and this contraction is marked by the circumflex accent over the contracted long vowels.

6.56 There are, however, some verbs which take their passive flexion without the -θ- of the passive morph (so that this flexion is called a *direct flexion* — these are fully discussed in #C4); and at times some of the forms of these verbs may not immediately be recognized as passives because of the absence of the -θ- of the usual passive morph. The future passive is always derived directly from the form of the aorist passive, so if the latter is a direct flexion, then the future passive will be a direct flexion also.

6.57 The ending of the 2nd person singular imperative is -θι, which would give the form λύθηθι. However, Greek seeks to avoid having aspirates in successive syllables, separated only by a vowel (see #E2.8). The passive morph -θε- never loses its aspiration, so the aspiration is lost from the ending, which becomes -τι, and thus the form is λύθητι. But when the imperative ending is added to any verb which has a direct flexion, that ending is -θι, because in such a case it does not follow another -θ-. The remaining forms of the imperative have the same pronoun endings as the aorist active imperative (#4.21).

6.58 The feminine participle, λυθεῖσα, having a sibilant stem, is declined like δόξα (#3.15); the masculine and neuter forms (λυθείς, λυθέν, genitive λυθέντος) follow the usual Third Declension pattern (cf. ἄρχων, ἄρχοντος, in #5.44) and are set out in full in Appendix D, #D5.17.

6.6 SELF-TESTING REVIEW

All the forms of Paradigm C1.1, λύω, have now been introduced (except the rarely-used optative, and perfect subjunctive). The flexion form for each flexion, and its meaning, will be found set out in the Meaning Synopsis of the Greek Verb, #C0.4. REVIEW the Indicative Mode (#C0.43) and satisfy yourself that you can correctly identify the tense and voice, and the meaning, of each of these forms. To do this, cover the right-hand (English meaning) part of each column with a piece of paper, exposing only the left-hand Greek forms, and write on it alongside each Greek word its tense, voice and meaning. Remove the paper and verify the correctness of your answers. To extend your knowledge further, you can do this with the other modes also.

6.7 THE SECOND AORIST AND IMPERFECT MIDDLES COMPARED

6.71 It has been seen that the first aorist active is formed (see #4.21, 4.35) by prefixing the augment to the verb stem and adding first the punctiliar morph -σα- (-σ before vowels) and then the active suffixes of the pronoun ending. Thus the 1st person plural of λύω is ἐ-λυ-σα-μεν. The second aorist active is formed in the same way, but with the neutral morph ο/ε used instead of the punctiliar morph (#3.81, 4.39). Thus the 1st person plural of βάλλω is ἐ-βαλ-ο-μεν.

6.72 This pattern is followed by the aorist in the middle voice also, the fact that the form is *middle* not *active* being indicated by the use of the middle suffixes of the pronoun ending. Thus the 1st person singular of the first aorist, as seen in λύω, is ἐ-λυ-σα-μην, and the first person singular of the second aorist, as seen in βάλλω, is ἐ-βαλ-ο-μην.

6.73 The imperfect is also formed by adding to the stem, an augment, the neutral morph, and the appropriate pronoun suffix. This means that for Second Conjugation verbs (i.e., those with a second aorist), the only difference between their imperfect and aorist flexions is in their *stem* or *lexal*. Seven Second Conjugation verbs have completely different lexals in the present (and these are set out in #7.3); most of the rest —there are only two exceptions — add an extra morph to their verb stem as a durative morph in forming their durative stem, for the present and imperfect tenses. For βάλλω this durative morph is the second -λ which is added to the verb root βαλ. Thus the Imperfect and Aorist Indicative Middle flexions, and the flexions for other modes of the second aorist middle, are:

	IMPERFECT Indicative	**AORIST** Indicative	Subjunctive	Imperative	Infinitive	**PRESENT** Infinitive
S 1	ἐβαλλόμην	ἐβαλόμην	βάλωμαι	—	βαλέσθαι	βάλλεσθαι
2	ἐβάλλου	ἐβάλου	βάλῃ	βαλοῦ	**Participle**	**Participle**
3	ἐβάλλετο	ἐβάλετο	βάληται	βαλέσθω	βαλόμενος	βαλλόμενος
P 1	ἐβαλλόμεθα	ἐβαλόμεθα	βαλώμεθα	—	βαλομένη	βαλλομένη
2	ἐβάλλεσθε	ἐβάλεσθε	βάλησθε	βάλεσθε	βαλόμενον	βαλλόμενον
3	ἐβάλλοντο	ἐβάλοντο	βάλωνται	βαλέσθωσαν	βαλομένου	βαλλομένου

6.74 Compare the forms of the Imperfect and Aorist Indicative, and note that the only difference between them is whether they do or do not have the second -λ-, the durative morph. Similarly, this is the only difference between the forms of the Present and the Aorist in the other modes (the forms of the Present Infinitive and Participle are given here alongside those of the Aorist for comparison).

6.75 The durative morph is added to or into the verb's *stem* or *lexal*, and thus in morphologizing the verb (#3.93) the durative morph will be placed with the lexal in the lexal slot (Slot 4). A morph which is placed into another morph in this way is termed an *infix*. The durative morph in the lexal is the only infix which occurs in Greek — all other morphs are prefixes or suffixes or process morphs.

6.8   COMPLETE PARADIGM OF THE VERB

The complete paradigm of the forms of λύω is set out in #C1.1. Go through this paradigm to ensure that you are familiar (except for the optative) with the verb patterns given there, and know them well enough to recognize the characteristic morphs which indicate person, number, tense, voice, and mode. **Note carefully** #A6.2 and A6.3, which set out a complete diagram of the nine morph slots of the verb and what morphs can occur in each slot.

6.9   CONTRACT VERBS

6.91 When the neutral morph o/ε used in the formation of the present and imperfect tenses is added to a stem ending in a short vowel (-α, -ε or -o), the two vowels combine and form either a long vowel or a diphthong. This *contraction* takes place in accordance with specific rules. These are given in detail in #E2.1; the common ones (which therefore need to be noted) are:
- (a) $o + \varepsilon\iota$ or $o + \eta \rightarrow o\iota$; $\varepsilon + \alpha\iota \rightarrow \eta$
- (b) Apart from as in (a), -ε- or -o- followed by a long vowel or diphthong is absorbed into it.
- (c) $\varepsilon + \varepsilon \rightarrow \varepsilon\iota$
- (d) $\varepsilon + o$ or $o + \varepsilon$ or $o + o \rightarrow ov$
- (e) $\alpha + \varepsilon$ or $\alpha + \eta \rightarrow \alpha$, and $\alpha + \varepsilon\iota$ or $\alpha + \eta \rightarrow \alpha$
- (f) $\alpha + o$ or $\alpha + ov \rightarrow \omega$
- (g) α, ε or $o + \iota$ or v makes a diphthong; e.g., $\varepsilon + \iota \rightarrow \varepsilon\iota$

6.92 Where an acute accent would fall on the short stem vowel in the uncontracted form, then the contracted vowel/diphthong will have a circumflex.

6.93 Verbs that contract in this way are called *contract verbs*. The above information should assist in enabling you to recognize a contract verb form when you encounter one. Contract verbs in -α, -ε, and -o comprise respectively Paradigms C1.2, C1.3 and C1.4 of the First Conjugation, and these paradigms, showing both the uncontracted and contracted forms, are set out in Appendix C under these references. In tenses other than the present and imperfect, the suffix that is added to the verb stem commences with a consonant, and so no contraction of vowels occurs.

6.94 All contract verbs are *listed in the lexicon* in their uncontracted form, and *used* in their contracted form. In practice you will have little difficulty in recognizing and identifying a contract verb from its features — you will at times, however, have to check on the three possibilities for the lexical form of a contract verb (with -α, -ε, and -ο), as the form used in a N.T. passage will not always reveal if the verb ends in αω, εω or οω.

6.95 As noted in #4.24, liquid verbs add -ε not -σ in forming the future tense. As the neutral morph is then added in forming the future, the future tense of liquid verbs is thus a contract flexion, following the pattern of λαλέω, C1.3. Liquid verbs comprise Paradigms C1.8 and C1.9 of the First Conjugation, and these paradigms are set out in Appendix C under those references. In addition to those mentioned there, two other contracted futures occur in the N.T.: the deponents (see #C7.6) (ἀπο)θανέομαι, from (ἀπο)θνήσκω, and πεσέομαι, from πίπτω.

6.96 Contraction will normally occur also in other verb forms where a short vowel occurs with another vowel (e.g., in the passive subjunctive). The same principles of contraction will operate in these instances.

SELECTIONS FROM THE GREEK NEW TESTAMENT

(Use the Explanatory Notes, opposite, in working on these Selections.)

1. καλέσεις τὸ ὄνομα αὐτοῦ Ἰησοῦν, αὐτὸς γὰρ σώσει τὸν λαὸν αὐτοῦ ἀπὸ τῶν ἁμαρτιῶν αὐτῶν. (ΚΑΤΑ ΜΑΘΘΑΙΟΝ 1:21.)

2. Μὴ θησαυρίζετε ὑμῖν θησαυροὺς ἐπὶ τῆς γῆς, ὅπου σὴς καὶ βρῶσις ἀφανίζει, καὶ ὅπου κλέπται διορύσσουσιν καὶ κλέπτουσιν· θησαυρίζετε δὲ ὑμῖν θησαυροὺς ἐν οὐρανῷ, ὅπου οὔτε σὴς οὔτε βρῶσις ἀφανίζει, καὶ ὅπου κλέπται οὐ διορύσσουσιν οὐδὲ κλέπτουσιν· ὅπου γάρ ἐστιν ὁ θησαυρός σου, ἐκεῖ ἔσται καὶ ἡ καρδία σου. (ΚΑΤΑ ΜΑΘΘΑΙΟΝ 6:19-21.)

3. ὁ Ἰησοῦς εἶπεν αὐτοῖς, Πορευθέντες ἀπαγγείλατε Ἰωάννῃ ἃ ἀκούετε καὶ βλέπετε· τυφλοὶ ἀναβλέπουσιν καὶ χωλοὶ περιπατοῦσιν, λεπροὶ καθαρίζονται καὶ κωφοὶ ἀκούουσιν, καὶ νεκροὶ ἐγείρονται καὶ πτωχοὶ εὐαγγελίζονται· καὶ μακάριός ἐστιν ὃς ἐὰν μὴ σκανδαλισθῇ ἐν ἐμοί. (ΚΑΤΑ ΜΑΘΘΑΙΟΝ 11:4-6.)

4. τότε ὁ Ἰησοῦς εἶπεν τοῖς μαθηταῖς αὐτοῦ, Εἴ τις θέλει ὀπίσω μου ἐλθεῖν, ἀπαρνησάσθω ἑαυτὸν καὶ ἀράτω τὸν σταυρὸν αὐτοῦ καῖ ἀκολουθείτω μοι. (ΚΑΤΑ ΜΑΘΘΑΙΟΝ 16:24.)

5. τότε δύο ἔσονται ἐν τῷ ἀγρῷ, εἷς παραλαμβάνεται καὶ εἷς ἀφίεται· δύο ἀλήθουσαι ἐν τῷ μύλῳ, μία παραλαμβάνεται καὶ μία ἀφίεται. (ΚΑΤΑ ΜΑΘΘΑΙΟΝ 24:40-41.)

Selections continue on page 82

ASSIGNMENTS ON LESSON SIX

1. Read Lesson Six through twice. **LEARN** εἰμί (#6.42) and **NOTE** λύω flexions.

2. Read and translate literally Selections 1 to 15, and also, using your Grammatical Analysis (Zerwick and Grosvenor, or Rienecker), these passages from your Greek New Testament: 16. Mark 6:1-6
                                                17. John 1:1-5

3. Do a quick preliminary reading of Lesson Seven.

EXPLANATORY NOTES

An arrow, →, indicates the word from which a form has come. A superscript number (as in aor[2]) is used to indicate a Second or Third Conjugation verb (as the case may be).

1. καλέ-σ-εις → *καλέω call (2sg fut.) — note the ε, not η, before σ: καλέω is irregular in this respect ■ σώ-σ-ει → *σῴζω save (3sg fut.) ■ *λαός οῦ ὁ a people ■ *ἁμαρτία ας ἡ sin, a sin.

2. μή θησαυρίζετε impv.; do not store up (pres. implying, do not continue with a present practice) ■ θησαυρός οῦ ὁ treasure ■ *ὅπου where ■ σής σητός ὁ (clothes-)moth ■ βρῶσ-ις -εως ἡ corrosion, rust ■ ἀφανίζω ruin, destroy ■ κλέπτης ου ὁ thief ■ δι-ορύσσω dig through, break through ■ κλέπτω steal ■*οὔτε . . . οὔτε . . . neither . . . nor . . . ■ ἔ-σ-ται → *εἰμι (3sg fut.) ■*καρδία heart.

3. πορευ-θέντες → *πορεύομαι go (aor. ptc dep.) — when followed by an impv. means, go and . . . ■ ἀπαγγείλατε → ἀπαγγέλλω announce, report (2 pl aor. impv) ■ *τυφλός blind ■ χωλός lame, crippled ■*περι-πατέω walk around, move about ■ λεπρός leper ■ καθαρίζω cleanse, make clean (3pl pass.)■ κωφός deaf; dumb ■ *νεκρός dead ■ *ἐγείρω raise (3pl pass.) ■ πτωχός poor ■ *εὐαγγελίζω proclaim, preach, bring good news (3pl pass.) ■ *μακάριος blessed, happy, fortunate ■ ὃς ἐάν whoever ■ σκανδαλι-σ-θῇ → -δαλίζω cause to stumble, give offence, anger (someone); (3sg aor. subj. pass. — in the pass., take offence, be made angry).

4. *θέλω wish, want ■ ὀπίσω after (+ gen.); with ἔρχομαι, come, means to come after or follow (someone) ■ ἀπ-αρνη-σάσθω → ἀπαρνέομαι deny, disown, utterly renounce (3sg aor. impv) ■ *ἑαυτον himself ■ ἀρ-άτω → *αἴρω take up, lift up (3sg aor. impv) ■ σταυρός cross ■ ἀκολουθ-είτω → *ἀκολουθέω follow (3sg pres. impv — notice the significance of the pres. here, aor. prev.).

5. ἔ-σονται → εἰμι (3pl fut.) ■ παρα-λαμβάνω take along, take away (3sg pass.) ■ ἀφί-εται → *ἀφίημι leave behind, forsake (3sg prs pass.) ■ ἀλήθ-ουσαι → ἀλήθω grind (fem. pl pres. ptc) ■ μύλος mill.

6. ἐ-λάλη-σεν → *λαλεω speak, talk, converse (3sg aor) ■ ἐ δό θη → *δίδωμι give (3sg aor. pass.) ■ πᾶσα → *πας ■ *ἐξουσία authority ■ πορευ-θέντες see Selection 3 ■ μαθητεύ-σατε → μαθητεύω make a disciple

6. ὁ Ἰησοῦς ἐλάλησεν αὐτοῖς λέγων, Ἐδόθη μοι πᾶσα ἐξουσία ἐν οὐρανῷ καὶ ἐπὶ γῆς. πορευθέντες οὖν μαθητεύσατε πάντα τὰ ἔθνη, βαπτίζοντες αὐτοὺς εἰς τὸ ὄνομα τοῦ πατρὸς καὶ τοῦ υἱοῦ καὶ τοῦ ἁγίου πνεύματος, διδάσκοντες αὐτοὺς τηρεῖν πάντα ὅσα ἐνετειλάμην ὑμῖν· καὶ ἰδοὺ ἐγὼ μεθ᾽ ὑμῶν εἰμι πάσας τὰς ἡμέρας ἕως τῆς συντελείας τοῦ αἰῶνος. (ΚΑΤΑ ΜΑΘΘΑΙΟΝ 28:18-20.)

7. τί δέ με καλεῖτε, Κύριε, κύριε, καὶ οὐ ποιεῖτε ἃ λέγω; (ΚΑΤΑ ΛΟΥΚΑΝ 6:46.)

8. (α) Ἄλλους ἔσωσεν, σωσάτω ἑαυτόν, εἰ οὗτός ἐστιν ὁ Χριστὸς τοῦ θεοῦ ὁ ἐκλεκτός. (ΚΑΤΑ ΛΟΥΚΑΝ 23:35.) (β) Εἰ σὺ εἶ ὁ βασιλεὺς τῶν Ἰουδαίων, σῶσον σεαυτόν. (ΚΑΤΑ ΛΟΥΚΑΝ 23:37.) (γ) Οὐχὶ σὺ εἶ ὁ Χριστός; σῶσον σεαυτὸν καὶ ἡμᾶς. (ΚΑΤΑ ΛΟΥΚΑΝ 23:39.) (δ) Ἰησοῦ, μνήσθητί μου ὅταν ἔλθῃς εἰς τὴν βασιλείαν σου. (ΚΑΤΑ ΛΟΥΚΑΝ 23:42.) (ε) Ἀμήν σοι λέγω, σήμερον μετ᾽ ἐμοῦ ἔσῃ ἐν τῷ παραδείσῳ. (ΚΑΤΑ ΛΟΥΚΑΝ 23:43.)

9. Ἰησοῦς εἶπεν αὐτῷ, Σὺ πιστεύεις εἰς τὸν υἱὸν τοῦ ἀνθρώπου; ἀπεκρίθη ἐκεῖνος καὶ εἶπεν, Καὶ τίς ἐστιν, κύριε, ἵνα πιστεύσω εἰς αὐτόν; (ΚΑΤΑ ΙΩΑΝΝΗΝ 9:35-36.)

10. ἀπεκρίθη αὐτῷ Ἰησοῦς, Ἐγὼ παρρησίᾳ λελάληκα τῷ κόσμῳ· ἐγὼ πάντοτε ἐδίδαξα ἐν συναγωγῇ καὶ ἐν τῷ ἱερῷ, ὅπου πάντες οἱ Ἰουδαῖοι συνέρχονται, καὶ ἐν κρυπτῷ ἐλάλησα οὐδέν. (ΚΑΤΑ ΙΩΑΝΝΗΝ 18:20.)

11. Ἕλλην ὁ πατὴρ αὐτοῦ ὑπῆρχεν. (ΠΡΑΞΕΙΣ 16:3.)

12. καὶ ἐλθὼν εὐηγγελίσατο εἰρήνην ὑμῖν τοῖς μακρὰν καὶ εἰρήνην τοῖς ἐγγύς. (ΠΡΟΣ ΕΦΕΣΙΟΥΣ 2:17.)

13. ἡμῶν γὰρ τὸ πολίτευμα ἐν οὐρανοῖς ὑπάρχει, ἐξ οὗ καὶ σωτῆρα ἀπεκδεχόμεθα κύριον Ἰησοῦν Χριστόν. (ΠΡΟΣ ΦΙΛΙΠΠΗΣΙΟΥΣ 3:20.)

14. Ἄξιος εἶ, ὁ κύριος καὶ ὁ θεὸς ἡμῶν,
λαβεῖν τὴν δόξαν καὶ τὴν τιμὴν καὶ τὴν δύναμιν,
ὅτι σὺ ἔκτισας τὰ πάντα,
καὶ διὰ τὸ θέλημά σου ἦσαν καὶ ἐκτίσθησαν. (ΑΠΟΚΑΛΥΨΙΣ ΙΩΑΝΝΟΥ 4:11.)

15. καὶ ἤκουσα φωνῆς μεγάλης ἐκ τοῦ θρόνου λεγούσης, Ἰδοὺ ἡ σκηνὴ τοῦ θεοῦ μετὰ τῶν ἀνθρώπων, καὶ σκηνώσει μετ᾽ αὐτῶν, καὶ αὐτοὶ λαοὶ αὐτοῦ ἔσονται, καὶ αὐτὸς ὁ θεὸς μετ᾽ αὐτῶν ἔσται, αὐτῶν θεός, καὶ ἐξαλείψει πᾶν δάκρυον ἐκ τῶν ὀφθαλμῶν αὐτῶν, καὶ ὁ θάνατος οὐκ ἔσται ἔτι, οὔτε πένθος οὔτε κραυγὴ οὔτε πόνος οὐκ ἔσται ἔτι· ὅτι τὰ πρῶτα ἀπῆλθαν. οὗτοι οἱ λόγοι πιστοὶ καὶ ἀληθινοί εἰσιν. (ΑΠΟΚΑΛΥΨΙΣ ΙΩΑΝΝΟΥ 21:3-5.)

16. Mark 6:1-6

17. John 1:1-5

(2pl aor. impv) ■ βαπτίζ-οντες → * βαπτίζω (masc. nom. pl ptc) ■ διδάσκ-οντες → *διδάσκω teach (masc. nom. pl ptc) ■ τηρ-εῖν → *τηρέω keep, observe, watch (inf.) ■ ἐν-ε-τειλ-ά-μην → ἐντελλομαι (+ dat.) enjoin, command, give orders (to someone); (1sg aor. dep.); ὅσα → *ὅσος η ον as much (many, great) as; πάντα ὅσα ἐνετειλάμην = all things as many as I commanded = everything that I have commanded ■ πάσας τὰς ἡμέρας = all the days = always (Hebraism) ■ συν-τέλεια completion, end ■ αἰῶνος → *αἰών (gen. sg) age; here, the present age, preceding His Return.

7. τί why ■ καλ-εῖτε → *καλέω (2pl pres.) ■ ποι-εῖτε → *ποιέω.

8(α) ἄλλος η ο other, another ■ ἔ-σω-σεν → σῴζω (3sg aor.) save ■ σω-σάτω (3sg aor. impv) ■ ἐκ-λεκτός elect, chosen. 8(β) σῶσον (2sg aor. impv) ■ σεαυτόν yourself (sg). 8(δ) μνήσ-θητι → μιμ-νήσκομαι (+ gen.) remember (something, someone); (2sg dep. aor. impv) ■ *ὅταν whenever (indefinite —contrast the decisiveness of Christ's reply: "today . . . ") ■ ἔλθῃς → *ἔρχομαι come (2sg aor² subj.). 8(ε) σήμερον today, this very day ■ παράδεισος paradise, garden.

9. ἀπ-ε-κρί-θη → *ἀποκρίνομαι answer (3sg aor. dep.) ■ πιστεύσω (in form could also be fut., but must be aor. subj. 1sg after ἵνα).

10. παρρησίᾳ openly/plainly/freely (dat. sg of παρρησία openness) ■ λε-λάλη-κα → λαλέω (1sg pf) see Sel. 6 ■ *κόσμος world ■ πάντοτε always ■ *συναγωγή synagogue ■ *ἱερόν temple ■ *ὅπου where ■ συνέρχομαι come together ■ κρυπτός secret ■ οὐδέν → *οὐδείς no one/nothing.

11. Ἕλλην a Greek ■ ὑπ-ῆρχ-εν → *ὑπάρχω be, continue to be, exist.

12. ἐλθών → *ἔρχομαι (pres. ptc: and coming, he preached. . .; translate as, he came and preached. . .) ■ εὐ-ηγγελί-σατο → εὐαγγελίζω preach (3sg aor., dep. in this context) ■ τοῖς μακράν, τοῖς ἐγγύς to those far away, to those nearby.

13. πολίτευμα place of citizenship ■ σωτήρ saviour ■ ἀπ-εκ-δεχ-όμεθα → ἀπεκδέχομαι await expectantly (1pl dep).

14. ἄξιος worthy, deserving ■ λαβ-εῖν → *λαμβάνω receive, take (aor² inf.) ■ τιμή honour, respect ■ ἔ-κτι-σας → κτίζω create (2sg aor.) ■ *θέλημα -ατος τό will ■ ἐ-κτί-σ-θησαν (3pl aor. pass.)

15. ἤκου-σα → *ἀκούω (1sg aor.) ■ *θρόνος throne ■ λεγ-ούσης → *λέγω (fem. sg gen. pres. ptc, agreeing with φωνῆς) ■ σκηνή dwelling ■ σκηνώ-σ-ει → σκηνόω live, dwell (3sg fut.) ■ αὐτὸς ὁ θεός God Himself (αὐτός in front of the article = self) ■ ἐξαλεί-ψ-ει → ἐξαλείφω wipe away (3sg fut.) ■ δάκρυον τό tear ■ *θάνατος death ■ *ἔτι still, yet, longer ■ πένθος ους τό sorrow, sadness, grief, mourning ■ κραυγή crying, shout ■ πόνος pain, suffering, labour ■ τὰ πρῶτα (→ *πρῶτος) the first things, the former things ■ ἀπ-ῆλθαν, for ἀπῆλθον have passed away, gone ■ λόγος word ■ πιστός trustworthy, faithful ■ ἀληθινός true, genuine.

LESSON SEVEN

ADJECTIVES, VERBS AND PARTICIPLES

7.1 CORRESPONDING ADJECTIVES/PRONOUNS

7.11 Greek contains sets of adjectives/pronouns which differ in function and are related in meaning (and often, in root). A similar system of corresponding adverbs will be introduced in #9.1. These corresponding sets are:

TYPE	INTERROGATIVE	INDEFINITE	DEMONSTRATIVE	RELATIVE
Identification	τίς; who?	τις anyone	ὁ, ὅδε, οὗτος this (one) ἐκεῖνος that, that one	ὅς who, which ὅστις who, which
Quantity	πόσος; how much/many?	ποσός of some quantity	τοσοῦτος so much/ many/great	ὅσος as great/ much/many as
Quality	ποῖος; of what kind? ποταπός of what kind?	ποιός of some kind	τοιόσδε of such kind τοιοῦτος of such kind	οἷος of what kind ὁποῖος such as
Size	πηλίκος; how large/great?	—	τηλικοῦτος so large, so great	ἡλίκος how large/great
Distribution	πότερος; which of the two?	—	ἕτερος the one or the other/ another/different ἄλλος other ἕκαστος each, each one	—

7.12 Most of these words can occur either with a noun (i.e., as an adjective), or without a noun (i.e., as a pronoun).

7.13 Note how τοσοῦτος, τοιοῦτος and τηλικοῦτος are formed by replacing the initial ʽ/τ- of οὗτος with τοσ-, τοι- and τηλικ-. The declension of the flexion of the word follows οὗτος.

7.14 ὅδε, ἥδε, τόδε is a demonstrative pronoun/adjective formed by adding the enclitic δε to the definite article. Its meaning is the same as that of οὗτος: this/these (without a noun, this/man/woman/thing). It does not often occur in the N.T., and the majority of its occurrences is in the expression τάδε λέγει plus the speaker in the nominative, as Acts 21:11, τάδε λέγει τὸ πνεῦμα τὸ ἅγιον, "These things says the Holy Spirit."

7.15 ὅστις, ἥτις, ὅ τι is a relative pronoun similar in meaning to ὅς, ἥ, ὅ, but made rather general or indefinite by the addition of τις, meaning, whoever, everyone who, etc. The neuter ὅ τι is often written that way, as two words, to distinguish it from ὅτι, that, because. Otherwise the two parts of the word are written in combination together as a single word — but *both parts* of the word are declined in the usual way, as if they were

84

separate words, to show gender, case, and number. However, the New Testament use of this common Greek word is very limited, and virtually confined to the nominative case and the neuter accusatives, singular and plural. Sometimes the indefinite particle ἄν is also used with ὅστις to stress the indefinite element in its meaning. At times, however, ὅστις is used without any real difference in meaning from the simple form, ὅς.

7.2 ATTRIBUTIVE AND PREDICATIVE USE OF ADJECTIVES

7.21 Where an adjective is used with an article and noun, the adjective goes either **(a)** between the article and noun, or **(b)** after the noun, with the article repeated before the adjective. These are the two forms of what is called the *attributive* use of the adjective, and these two positions can be described as the *Attributive Intermediate Position* (i.e., between article and noun) and the *Attributive Post Position* (i.e., immediately after the noun, with only the repeated article between them). Some examples from the Selections at the end of this Lesson (L7/5 means Lesson 7, Selection 5):

(a) Attributive Intermediate Position

Mt 27:53 (L7/5):   εἰσῆλθον εἰς   τὴν   ἁγίαν   πόλιν.
                   they entered   the   holy   city.

(b) Attributive Post Position

Rev 21:2 (L7/30):   τὴν πόλιν τὴν ἁγίαν εἶδον, I saw the holy city.

7.22 Notice that in both these forms of the attributive position, the adjective has the article immediately in front of it. Note: the possessive adjectives ἐμός, my, and σός, your (singular), take the article in the same way as any other adjective. (For examples, see L2/23 and L3/8 for the Attributive Intermediate Position, and L2/28 and L5/13 for the Attributive Post Position.) An entire adjectival phrase can be used in this way as if it were an adjective, and the article will be used in front of it (see the discussion of this in #2.97 and examples L2/8 and L2/27).

7.23 By contrast, an adjective can be used as the complement of the verb "to be", i.e. as the "completement" of the thought. Here, the adjective is the predicate, and it is placed in the *predicative position*, which may be either *prior to* the article and noun (the *Predicative Prior Position*), or *after* the article and noun (the *Predicative Post Position*). Notice that it can *never* come *between* the article and its noun, or in any circumstances have the article immediately in front of it. Examples of the two forms of the Predicative Position from the Selections in these Lessons:

(c) Predicative Prior Position (with εἰμι)

Heb 11:38 (L7/26): ὧν οὐκ ἦν ἄξιος ὁ κόσμος
                   of whom the world was not worthy

Rev 5:12 (L5/21):   ἄξιον ἐστιν τὸ ἀρνίον τὸ ἐσφαγμένον
                    worthy is   the lamb   that has been slain

(d) Predicative Post Position (with εἰμι)

I Cor 3:17 (L7/23): ὁ γὰρ ναὸς τοῦ θεοῦ ἅγιος ἐστιν
　　　　　　　　　 for the temple of God 　　is holy

7.24 As the position of the words is an adequate indication of meaning, the verb "to be" is not really necessary, and so it is often omitted:

(e) Predicative Prior Position (without εἰμι)

Lk 1:49 (L7/10): καὶ ἅγιον τὸ ὄνομα αὐτοῦ,
　　　　　　　　　and holy is his name
Luke 10:7 (L7/13): ⎰ ἄξιος ὁ ἐργάτης τοῦ μισθοῦ αὐτοῦ
I Tim 5:18 (L7/25): ⎱ 'the workman is worthy of his wages

(f) Predicative Post Position (without εἰμι)

Rom 7:12 (L7/22): ὥστε ὁ μὲν νόμος ἅγιος, καὶ ἡ 　　 ἐντολὴ ἁγία
　　　　　　　　　 so the 　　　　law is holy 　and the commandment is holy

7.25 The two uses, attributive and predicative, can be clearly seen in the following example, without the verb "to be", which is unambiguous:

Rev 20:5 (L7/29): αὕτη ἡ ἀνάστασις ἡ πρώτη
　　　　　　　　　this is the 　　　first resurrection

7.26 Note the distinction between the two positions (i.e. in the relationships of article and adjective):

　　(a) In the attributive positions, the adjective is *always* immediately preceded by the article.

　　(b) In the predicative positions, the adjective is *never* immediately preceded by the article.

　　The meaning is thus always indicated quite clearly.

7.27 There are five common words which always take the predicative position (that is, they do not ever have the article immediately preceding them) but which nonetheless have the usual adjectival sense and do not imply the verb "to be". These are: οὗτος (this), ἐκεῖνος (that), ὅλος (whole, complete, entire), πᾶς (all), and ἅπας (alternative form of πᾶς). Examples of their use:

(a) In the Predicative Prior Position

Jn 12:34 (L3/21): τίς ἐστιν οὗτος ὁ υἱὸς τοῦ ἀνθρώπου;
　　　　　　　　　who is 　 this 　 son 　of man?

Mk 12:30 (L5/7): ἐξ ὅλης τῆς καρδίας σου, (etc.)
　　　　　　　　　from your whole heart 　　(etc.)

Mt 16:18 (L5/20): ἐπὶ ταύτῃ τῇ πέτρᾳ οἰκοδομήσω...
                  upon   this   rock   I will build...

Mt 28:19 (L6/6): πάντα τὰ ἔθνη...
                  all   (the) nations...

(b) In the Predicative Post Position

Mk 10:5 (L5/6) ... τὴν ἐντολὴν ταύτην
               ... this   commandment

Mt 3:9 (L5/21):... ἐκ τῶν λίθων τούτων
               ... from   these stones

7.3 SUPPLETIVES, AND OTHER VERBS OF THE SECOND AORIST

7.31 A number of Greek verbs are incomplete, in that they cannot be used in all tenses, because in some tenses the expected forms do not exist. These verbs are referred to as "defective" in those tenses. What happens in such cases is that forms from some quite different verbs are treated as filling the gaps.

7.32 We have defective verbs in English, and we fill the gaps from other verbs in a similar way. Consider the following: "See how God has answered prayer in the past, and believe that He will answer prayer in the future also; see what wonders God has wrought in the past, and believe that He will — wonders in the future also." What is the future tense of "wrought", to be used where the dash is? There is no such future tense in use, so we have to borrow from another verb, perhaps "do", or "work" or "perform". Similarly, what are the infinitives of "can" and "will"? We have to borrow from other verbs and say, "to be able to" and "to intend to" or "to be about to". English has formed the tense system of some verbs from different roots: e.g., "go" is defective, and has taken as its past tense "went", which is actually the past tense of "wend".

7.33 Verbs which join together forms from different roots in this way are called *suppletives*. There are seven suppletives used in the New Testament:

Meaning	Present Active	Future Active	Aorist Active	Perfect Active	Perfect Midd/Passive	Aorist Passive
take/choose	αἱρέω	⎰ἐλέω ⎱αἱρήσομαι	⎰εἶλον⎱ ⎰εἶλα⎱	—	ἥρημαι	ᾑρέθην
come	ἔρχομαι	ἐλεύσομαι	ἦλθον	ἐλήλυθα	—	—
eat	ἐσθίω	φάγομαι	ἔφαγον	—	—	—
say/speak	λέγω/φημί	ἐρέω	εἶπον	εἴρηκα	εἴρημαι	ἐρρέθην
see	†ὁράω	ὄψομαι	εἶδον	†ἑώρακα	†(ἑώραμαι)	ὤφθην
run	τρέχω	(δραμέομαι)	ἔδραμον	(δεδράμηκα)	(δεδράμημαι)	—
carry/bring	φέρω	οἴσω	⎰ἤνεγκον⎱ ⎱ἤνεγκα⎰	ἐνήνοχα	(ἐνήνεγμαι)	ἠνέχθην

† Note the rough breathing on these three forms.

7.34 Both λέγω and φημί occur in the N.T. only in the present and imperfect, and φημί is found only in these forms: Present, φημί, I say; φησίν, he says; φασίν, they say; Imperfect, ἔφη, he said. (These forms occur 70 times in the N.T., ἔφη being by far the most common.) The gap for both verbs for other tenses is filled by ἐρέω, εἶπον, etc. All these words, originally different verbs, have the same root meaning of "say/speak/tell", and are used to *supplete* each other. Similarly for the other suppletives.

7.35 Note that all seven suppletives are Second Conjugation verbs (i.e., have second aorist forms, indicated by the -ον ending). Two verbs (αἱρέω and φέρω) are shown as having first aorist alternatives, and also εἶπον and εἶδον can have forms in the N.T. with first aorist endings. αἱρέω and its compounds have two alternative forms of the future used in the N.T.

7.36 For Second Conjugation verbs, their verb stem is their aorist stem, and (except for ἄγω and ἔχω) they add a durative morph to form their present stem. A fuller explanation of verb formation will be given in due course (#9.5), and all 34 Second Conjugation verbs which occur in the N.T. are listed in #C2. However, the 15 more frequent and more important of these should be noted now. The Principal Parts (#9.6) for these are:

Meaning	Present Active	Future Active	Aorist Active	Perfect Active	Perfect Midd/Passive	Aorist Passive
lead	ἄγω	ἄξω	ἤγαγον	(ἦχα)	ἦγμαι	ἤχθην
sin	ἁμαρτάνω	ἁμαρτήσω	ἥμαρτον	ἡμάρτηκα	(ἡμάρτημαι)	(ἡμαρτήθην)
throw	βάλλω	βαλέω	ἔβαλον	βέβληκα	βέβλημαι	ἐβλήθην
become	γίνομαι	γενήσομαι	ἐγενόμην	γέγονα	γεγένημαι	ἐγενήθην
find	εὑρίσκω	εὑρήσω	εὗρον	εὕρηκα	(εὕρημαι)	εὑρέθην
have	ἔχω	† ἕξω	ἔσχον	ἔσχηκα	—	—
die	(ἀπο)θνήσκω	-θανέομαι	-ἔθανον	τέθνηκα	—	—
take	λαμβάνω	λήμψομαι	ἔλαβον	εἴληφα	εἴλημμαι	ἐλήμφθην
leave	λείπω	λείψω	ἔλιπον	(λέλοιπα)	λέλειμμαι	ἐλείφθην
learn	μανθάνω	μαθήσομαι	ἔμαθον	μεμάθηκα	—	—
suffer	πάσχω	—	ἔπαθον	πέπονθα	—	—
drink	πίνω	πίομαι	ἔπιον	πέπωκα	(πέπομαι)	ἐπόθην
fall	πίπτω	πεσέομαι	ἔπεσον	πέπτωκα	—	—
bear	τίκτω	τεξόμαι	ἔτεκον	(τέτοχα)	(τέτεγμαι)	ἐτέχθην
flee	φεύγω	φεύξομαι	ἔφυγον	πέφευγα	—	—

† Note the rough breathing on this form.

The preposition ἀπο is usually prefixed to θνήσκω. In other cases, a form in brackets is one which does not occur in the N.T. but is worthy of note.

7.37 Note that where the stem of a word ends in a labial, the -κ- of the perfect active morph combines with it and gives -φ- (as in εἴληφα), and similarly the -κ- combines with a palatal at the end of the stem to give -χ- (as in ἦχα). Some perfects take the -α ending direct — see #7.5, below.

7.38 These patterns are not given for learning, but for you to look through so that you begin to become familiar with the kinds of changes that occur in a word. (When you encounter one of these forms, your Analysis will remind you of the lexical form for a word.)

7.39 Once the first person singular of a flexion (the *flexion form*) is known, the remaining forms of that flexion will all conjugate regularly.

7.4 THE THIRD AORIST, AND THE THIRD CONJUGATION

7.41 So far we have met two ways of forming and conjugating the aorist active — adding the punctiliar morph -σα, and conjugating as for ἔλυσα (#4.21) and, secondly, adding the neutral morph o/ε and conjugating as for ἔβαλον (#3.81).

7.42 There is a third aorist pattern of conjugation which is followed by a small but important group of verbs: they add a third set of endings (slightly different from the other two) directly to the verb root, lengthening the final vowel of the root if it is short. Note that the 3rd person singular pronoun ending is ∅ (zero), and that it is in fact the *absence* of any other ending that is what is significant in indicating the person and number.

7.43 Lexical form:

		ἵστημι (**stand**)	βαίνω (**go**)	γινώσκω (**know**)	δύνω (**sink**)
Root:		στα-	-βα-	γνο-	δυ-
AORIST:	**Ending**				
ACTIVE SING. 1	-ν	ἔστην	-ἔβην	ἔγνων	ἔδυν
2	-ς	ἔστης	-ἔβης	ἔγνως	ἔδυς
3	∅	ἔστη	-ἔβη	ἔγνω	ἔδυ
PLUR. 1	-μεν	ἔστημεν	-ἔβημεν	ἔγνωμεν	ἔδυμεν
2	-τε	ἔστητε	-ἔβητε	ἔγνωτε	ἔδυτε
3	-σαν	ἔστησαν	-ἔβησαν	ἔγνωσαν	ἔδυσαν

7.44 In the Middle Voice, third aorist verbs take the *same* pronoun endings as the first aorists, but once again add them directly to the verb root. In the Passive Voice third aorist verbs add the passive morph -θε- (which lengthens to -θη-) directly to their root and then again take the Third Conjugation endings. It will be noted that λύω (and all First and Second Conjugation verbs) follow the Third Conjugation pattern in the passive (compare the passive of λύω, #6.50, with the following Table). That is to say, all verbs are Third Conjugation in the Aorist Passive.

AORIST PASSIVE:					
S	1	ἐστάθην	-ἐβάθην	ἐγνώσθην*	-ἐδύην †
	2	ἐστάθης	-ἐβάθης	ἐγνώσθης	-ἐδύης
	3	ἐστάθη	-ἐβάθη	ἐγνώσθη	-ἐδύη
P	1	ἐστάθημεν	-ἐβάθημεν	ἐγνώσθημεν	-ἐδύημεν
	2	ἐστάθητε	-ἐβάθητε	ἐγνώσθητε	-ἐδύητε
	3	ἐστάθησαν	-ἐβάθησαν	ἐγνώσθησαν	-ἐδύησαν

* In this flexion (and in the perfect middle/passive and the future passive) the lexal -γνω- has the allomorph form -γνωσ-.
† This is a direct flexion passive without -θ-: see #7.5.

7.45 The third aorist is thus *a third way of conjugating the aorist*, i.e., a Third Conjugation. Third Conjugation verbs form their present stem, like the Second Conjugation, by adding a durative morph to their verb stem. But -βαίνω, γινώσκω and δύνω have then taken the First Conjugation ending -ω, and they conjugate their present tense on a First Conjugation pattern. However, ἴστημι adds -μι to its stem and follows a distinctive (i.e., Third Conjugation) pattern of conjugating its present tense.

7.46 This conjugation (shown here for five representative -μι verbs) is:

PRESENT Root: στα- **(stand)** δυνα- **(can)** θε- **(place)** δο- **(give)** δεικ- **(show)**

ACTIVE	**S** 1	ἵστημι	(none —	τίθημι	δίδωμι	δείκνυμι
	2	ἵστης	deponent	τίθης	δίδως	δείκνυς
	3	ἵστησι(ν)	verb)	τίθησι(ν)	δίδωσι(ν)	δείκνυσι(ν)
	P 1	ἵσταμεν		τίθεμεν	δίδομεν	δείκνυμεν
	2	ἵστατε		τίθετε	δίδοτε	δείκνυτε
	3	ἱστᾶσι(ν)		τιθέασι(ν)	διδόασι(ν)	δεικνύασι(ν)
MIDDLE	**S** 1	ἵσταμαι	δύναμαι	τίθεμαι	δίδομαι	δείκνυμαι
	2	ἵστασαι	δύνασαι	τίθεσαι	δίδοσαι	δείκνυσαι
	3	ἵσταται	δύναται	τίθεται	δίδοται	δείκνυται
	P 1	ἱστάμεθα	δυνάμεθα	τιθέμεθα	διδόμεθα	δεικνύμεθα
	2	ἵστασθε	δύνασθε	τίθεσθε	δίδοσθε	δείκνυσθε
	3	ἵστανται	δύνανται	τίθενται	δίδονται	δείκνυνται

7.47 δύναμαι is deponent. Its imperfect is ἐδυνάμην or ἠδυνάμην (with double augment — see #4.6), and follows ἱστάμην (see Conspectus, #C6).

7.48 Three other important Third Conjugation deponents are κάθημαι, I sit down, κεῖμαι, I lie down, and -ἵημι, I send (which conjugates like τίθημι, but only occurs in the N.T. in compounds, notably, ἀφίημι).

7.49 Many of the forms in the above flexions are never actually found in the N.T., but are included to show clearly the pattern of conjugating. A fuller explanation of verb formation will be given in due course (#9.5), and all 36 Third Conjugation verbs which occur in the N.T. are listed in #C3.

7.5 DIRECT FLEXIONS

7.51 Some Greek verbs form one of their tenses without the use of the usual consonant in the aspect or voice morph. Two verbs form their future (deponent) without a future morph: φάγομαι (from ἐσθίω — see #7.33); πίομαι (from πίνω — see #C4.2). Nine verbs form their perfect active without either aspirating the stem consonant or adding -κ-, as the case may be; e.g. γέγονα from γίνομαι (see #C4.3 for the full list). Thirty verbs can form their aorist passive without taking the -θ- of the passive morph; e.g. ἠγγέλην, not ἠγγέλθην, from ἀγγέλλω (see #C4.4 for the full list). These flexions which add the next vowel directly to the lexal without the usual consonant of the morph can be termed "direct flexions".

7.52 Among the direct flexions of the perfect, there is one which requires special comment: $οἶδα$, from the same root, $ιδ$-, as $εἶδον$, I saw. It is:

		Perfect	Pluperfect	Subjunctive	Imperative	Infinitive
SINGULAR	1	$οἶδα$	$ᾔδειν$	$εἰδῶ$		$εἰδέναι$
	2	$οἶδας$	$ᾔδεις$	$εἰδῇς$	$ἴσθι$	**Participle**
	3	$οἶδε(ν)$	$ᾔδει$	$εἰδῇ$	$ἴστω$	m. $εἰδώς$
PLURAL	1	$οἴδαμεν$	$ᾔδειμεν$	$εἰδῶμεν$		f. $εἰδυῖα$
	2	$οἴδατε$	$ᾔδειτε$	$εἰδῆτε$	$ἴστε$	n. $εἰδός$
	3	$οἴδασι(ν)$	$ᾔδεισαν$	$εἰδῶσι(ν)$	$ἴστωσαν$	g. $εἰδότος$

This perfect has the present meaning, "I know", and the pluperfect is the past tense, "I knew".

7.53 The second-last morph in the pluperfect flexion, $-ει-$, identifies the pluperfect form. Thus it is a *specifier morph*, and occupies Slot 8 of a verb's nine morph slots. (Because this specifier morph identifies the pluperfect in an unambiguous way, some writers of koine Greek considered an initial augment unnecessary for the pluperfect, and omitted it for many words in the pluperfect.)

7.54 A word very similar to $οἶδα$ (though rare, while $οἶδα$ is common) is $εἴωθα$, which is also a perfect form which has present meaning, "I am accustomed", from an original present form ($ἔθω$) which has been obsolete since Homer's time. Again like $οἶδα$, it has a pluperfect form $εἰώθειν$ (which follows $ᾔδειν$) that has simple past meaning, "I was accustomed". The neuter perfect participle $εἰωθός$ occurs with the meaning "custom" (cf. the perfect participle $εἰδός$ from $οἶδα$).

7.6 THE PARADIGM OF THE PARTICIPLE

7.61 The participle in English has two forms, active and passive: "lest *coming* unexpectedly he should find you *sleeping*" (Mark 13:36); "in order to fulfil the word *spoken* by Isaiah the prophet" (Matthew 12:17); "my body *given* for you" (Luke 22:19). We can also construct more complex forms using auxiliary words: "*having been promised* of old", etc. In Greek, the participle exhibits at times the functions of both noun and verb, and can act like an adjective or adverb. Accordingly it has different forms to correspond with the range of variations of noun/adjective and verb. That is, the forms of the Greek participle differ to indicate tense, voice, person, number, gender, and case. (All these forms are set out in full in Appendix D, #D5.)

7.62 The multiplicity of forms is daunting; in practice it is only necessary to learn four forms for a given paradigm of the participle to be able to recognize any form of that paradigm. These four forms are the masculine, feminine and neuter nominative singular, and the masculine/neuter genitive singular. All participles decline their feminine forms in accordance with the First Declension paradigms; when you know the nominative singular, you can tell, therefore, how the feminine paradigm will run. If you have the masculine and neuter nominative singular forms, and the genitive form (which is always the same for both these genders), you can see whether the particular paradigm follows the Second Declension or Third Declension pattern, and what its stem is, and therefore, how it declines.

7.63 For example, when one sees the forms λύων, λύουσα, λῦον, λύοντος (present active), one knows that λύουσα declines like δόξα (D1.3, #3.11 — First Declension stem in -σ), while the masculine/neuter genitive λύοντος has the ending -ος, indicating Third Declension, and the stem λύοντ-, showing that it declines like ἀρχων, ἀρχοντος (Paradigm D3.18, #5.44 — Third Declension stem in -ντ). Similarly λυσάμενος, λυσαμένη, λυσάμενον, λυσαμένου indicates that this paradigm — first aorist middle — follows that for the First Declension consonant stem, feminine (D1.2, #3.11) and Second Declension for the masculine and neuter (#2.4).

7.64 There are seven voice/tense patterns, which can be conveniently arranged in groups in this way:

	DURATIVE	PUNCTILIAR	PERFECTIVE
	1. Present Active	**2. 1st Aorist Active**	**3. Perfect Active**
m.	λύων	λύσας	λελυκώς
f.	λύουσα	λύσασα	λελυκυῖα
n.	λῦον	λῦσαν	λελυκός
g.	λύοντος	λύσαντος	λελυκότος
	4. Present Middle/Passive	**5. 1st Aorist Middle**	**6. Perfect Middle/Passive**
m.	λυόμενος	λυσάμενος	λελυμένος
f.	λυομένη	λυσαμένη	λελυμένη
n.	λυόμενον	λυσάμενον	λελυμένον
g.	λυομένου	λυσαμένου	λελυμένου

7. Aorist Passive
m. λυθείς
f. λυθεῖσα
n. λυθέν
g. λυθέντος

The four forms given under each heading are the singular masculine, feminine and neuter nominative and masculine/neuter genitive respectively.

7.65 When the participle forms for different voices and tenses are grouped as above, certain facts and relationships become clear:

(a) There are no separate forms for the second aorist. The second aorist participle active and middle has exactly the same endings as the present participle active and middle, these endings being added directly to the second aorist stem. All the direct flexion passives (#7.51) have exactly the same endings as the first aorist participle, these endings being added directly on to the aorist passive stem (i.e. without the linking -θ).

(b) There are three tense forms of the participle; present, first aorist, and perfect, i.e. one for each *aspect*: durative, punctiliar, and perfective. (There also exists a rarely-used future participle — see #D5.18 and D5.19.)

(c) A separate passive paradigm exists only for the aorist: the passive uses the middle paradigm forms for present and perfect participle.

(d) All feminine participles follow one or other of the three feminine First Declension paradigms, according to whether the stem ends in -σ, another consonant, or a vowel.

(e) All active masculine/neuter participles and the separate passive forms of the aorist are Third Declension; all middle masculine/neuter participles (including the present and perfect forms which are also used for the passive) are Second Declension.

(f) All middle participles have the same endings (-μενος, etc.) the difference of tense being shown by the stem (plus another difference that in the perfect the accent is always on the first syllable of the ending). The present participle consists of the verb stem, characteristic linking -ο-, and -μενος; the first aorist participle consists of the verb stem, characteristic linking -σα-, and -μενος; the perfect participle consists of the reduplication, the verb stem, and -μενος. Thus -μεν- is the *specifier* of the middle participle, and occupies Slot 8 of a verb's nine morph slots (#6.32).

7.66 A knowledge of these features is all you need to enable you, when you encounter a participle, to recognize its gender, case and number (and thus to see its grammatical function in the sentence), and to identify its tense and voice, and the verb it comes from (and thus to see its meaning).

7.67 If you do have a problem in deciphering a particular participle, you can use the full list of participle forms in Appendix D, #D5, to identify what it is. All the participles are explained in your Analysis — you can turn to this when you encounter a participle that is still troublesome.

7.7 THE USE OF THE PARTICIPLE

7.71 The participle is used in two main ways: **(a)** similarly to an adjective, and **(b)** similarly to an adverb, (or an adjectival or adverbial phrase or clause). Its various usages are best illustrated with examples — the examples given are taken from Selections already used in previous Lessons.

(a) The Adjectival Use of the Participle

Mt 13:37 (L2/24) ὁ   σπείρων   τὸ   καλὸν   σπέρμα
                 the one who sows the   good   seed

Mt 12:17 (L4/19) ἵνα   πληρωθῇ τὸ   ῥηθὲν   διὰ Ἡσαΐου τοῦ προφήτου
                  in order to   fulfil   the thing spoken through   Isaiah the prophet
                                    i.e. what was spoken

Lk 9:35 (L2/26) Οὗτός ἐστιν ὁ υἱός μου ὁ ἐκλελεγμένος
                This   is   my son whom I have chosen

Mt 13:24 (L4/20) Ὡμοιώθη ἡ βασιλεία τῶν οὐρανῶν ἀνθρώπῳ
                 the kingdom of the heavens may be compared to a man

                       σπείραντι καλὸν σπέρμα . . .
                       who sowed good   seed . . .

          (NOTICE that σπείραντι is dative, agreeing with ἀνθρώπῳ.)

Rev 5:12 (L5/21) Ἄξιόν ἐστιν τὸ ἀρνίον τὸ ἐσφαγμένον
                 Worthy is   the lamb that has been slain

7.72 Most frequently, the best way of translating the adjectival participle is by means of an adjectival clause (i.e., one beginning with "who", "what", or "that"), as in the above five examples. Sometimes however the English participle on its own is the right translation:

Mt 4:18 (L3/1) Σίμωνα τὸν λεγόμενον Πέτρον   Simon *called* Peter

Mt 3:7 (L4/19) ἀπὸ τῆς μελλούσης ὀργῆς   from the *coming* wrath (Or, this
               could be translated, from the wrath *that is coming*)

7.73 On occasions, the participle is virtually equivalent to a noun (just as we have seen the adjective used as a noun).

Acts 2:44 πάντες δὲ οἱ πιστεύοντες . . .
               and   all the *believing ones* . . . (i.e. all the believers)

Mt 22:32 (L2/15) οὐκ ἔστιν ὁ θεὸς νεκρῶν ἀλλά ζώντων
                 he is not the god of dead ones but of *living ones*

     (Here, νεκρῶν is an adjective being used as a noun, and ζώντων is a participle being used as a noun.)

7.74 Notice that most of these examples have the article with the participle: this is very common with the adjectival participle.

(b) The Adverbial Participle

7.75 In this usage, the participle does not have the article, and is best translated by an adverbial clause (or phrase), the particular type being indicated by the context. Some examples of these usages:

Mt 4:18 (L3/1) Περιπατῶν δὲ παρὰ τὴν θάλασσαν τῆς Γαλιλαίας . . .
               And *as he was walking* beside the Sea of Galilee . . .

Mt 3:7 (L5/19) ἰδὼν δὲ πολλοὺς τῶν Φαρισαίων καὶ Σαδδουκαίων
and *when he saw* many of the Pharisees and Sadducees

ἐρχομένους ἐπὶ τὸ βάπτισμα αὐτοῦ εἶπεν αὐτοῖς ...
coming   to   his baptism he said to them ...

7.76 Sometimes the Greek participle can be translated either by an English participle or by a finite verb or adjectival clause, and both translations will make good sense:

Mt 3:17 (L2/13) Ἰδοὺ φωνὴ ἐκ τῶν οὐρανῶν λέγουσα,   Οὗτός ἐστιν ...
Behold a voice out of the heavens *saying*,   This   is ...
Or: Behold a voice out of the heavens *which said*,   This   is ...

And so similarly for the following examples (you supply the alternative):

Mk 1:3 (L3/9)   φωνὴ βοῶντος ἐν τῇ ἐρήμῳ, Ἑτοιμάσατε ...
a voice *of one crying* in the desert, Prepare ...

Jn 1:23 (L3/16)   Ἐγὼ φωνὴ βοῶντος ἐν τῇ ἐρήμῳ ...
I (am) a voice *of one crying* in the desert ...

Rev 4:1 (L3/30)   εἶδον, καὶ ἰδοὺ θύρα ἠνεῳγμένη ...
I looked, and behold a door *standing open* ...

In the following examples, the alternative to the *-ing* participle is to use the word "and" and turn the participle into a full verb. (After the first example, you supply the alternative form of translation):

Mk 1:11 (L3/11) ἦλθεν ὁ Ἰησοῦς ...   κηρύσσων   τὸ εὐαγγέλιον
Jesus came   ...   *preaching*   the gospel
Jesus came   *and preached*   the gospel

Mk 1:39 (L4/5)   καὶ ἦλθεν κηρύσσων ... εἰς ὅλην τὴν Γαλιλαίαν
and he went throughout the whole of Galilee *preaching*

καὶ τὰ δαίμονια ἐκβάλλων
and   *driving out*   the demons

Mk 10:51 (L4/21) καὶ ἀποκριθεὶς αὐτῷ ὁ Ἰησοῦς εἶπεν ...
and *answering* him   Jesus   said ...

7.8   THE VOICE OF THE PARTICIPLE

7.81 In translating, it is important to bear in mind that the present middle and perfect middle participle *forms* can be either middle or passive *in meaning*, as the same *form* does duty for both *voices* — see #7.65(c). Thus, for the present participle, ὁ λύων will be: the one who looses (active); while ὁ λυόμενος can be: the one who looses for himself (middle) or else; the one who is being loosed (passive). The similar dual possibility of middle or passive exists with the perfect participle. The context will be the guide, to indicate which is the intended meaning. In the aorist, on the other hand, there

are separate forms: ὁ λύσας   will be: the one who loosed (active);
ὁ λυσάμενος will be: the one who loosed for himself (middle);
ὁ λυθείς   will be: the one who was loosed (passive).

7.82 The same considerations will apply in the other uses of the participle. Remember, however, that participles of deponent verbs will have an *active* meaning though they have a middle or passive form. Cf. the example from Mk 10:51 given above: ἀποκριθείς means *answering*, not *answered*.

7.9 THE TENSE OF THE PARTICIPLE

7.91 Note the difference in meaning between the tenses of the participle: As a general rule, the present participle indicates action taking place *at the same time as* the main verb: so, translate the present participle when adverbial by an adverbial clause introduced by "while" or "as" (cf. the example from Mt 4:18, in L3/1 — it was *while* he was walking that he saw). The aorist participle, on the other hand, is normally used when the time of the action of the participle is *prior to* the action of the main verb: so translate the adverbial aorist participle by an adverbial clause introduced by "when" or "after" (cf. the example from Mt 3:7 in L5/19: it was *after* John noticed the Pharisees and Sadducees coming — and as a result of seeing them — that he spoke to them).

7.92 The perfect participle indicates (as in other modes) that an action has taken place which has ongoing consequences, right up to the time of the main action, and it needs to be translated in some way that indicates this (cf. the example from Rev 4:1 in L3/30 — the door had been opened before John looked, and was still *standing open* when he looked).

SELECTIONS FROM THE GREEK NEW TESTAMENT

(Use the Explanatory Notes, opposite, in working on these Selections.)

1. μακάριοι οἱ καθαροὶ τῇ καρδίᾳ, ὅτι αὐτοὶ τὸν θεὸν ὄψονται. (ΚΑΤΑ ΜΑΘΘΑΙΟΝ 5:8.)

2. καὶ λέγουσιν αὐτῷ οἱ μαθηταί, Πόθεν ἡμῖν ἐν ἐρημίᾳ ἄρτοι τοσοῦτοι ὥστε χορτάσαι ὄχλον τοσοῦτον; (ΚΑΤΑ ΜΑΘΘΑΙΟΝ 15:33.)

3. ὅστις δὲ ὑψώσει ἑαυτὸν ταπεινωθήσεται, καὶ ὅστις ταπεινώσει ἑαυτὸν ὑψωθήσεται. (ΚΑΤΑ ΜΑΘΘΑΙΟΝ 23:12.)

4. πολλοὶ γὰρ ἐλεύσονται ἐπὶ τῷ ὀνόματί μου λέγοντες, Ἐγώ εἰμι ὁ Χριστός, καὶ πολλοὺς πλανήσουσιν. (ΚΑΤΑ ΜΑΘΘΑΙΟΝ 24:5.)

5. καὶ εἰσῆλθον εἰς τὴν ἁγίαν πόλιν καὶ ἐνεφανίσθησαν πολλοῖς. (ΚΑΤΑ ΜΑΘΘΑΙΟΝ 27:53.)

6. Καὶ τοιαύταις παραβολαῖς πολλαῖς ἐλάλει αὐτοῖς τὸν λόγον, καθὼς ἠδύναντο ἀκούειν· χωρὶς δὲ παραβολῆς οὐκ ἐλάλει αὐτοῖς, κατ᾽ ἰδίαν δὲ τοῖς ἰδίοις μαθηταῖς ἐπέλυεν πάντα. (ΚΑΤΑ ΜΑΡΚΟΝ 4:33-34.)

Selections continue on page 98

ASSIGNMENTS ON LESSON SEVEN

1. Read Lesson Seven through twice. **LEARN** the aorist active (#7.43) and present active and middle (#7.46) of ἵστημι, as the paradigm of the Third Declension, and **NOTE** the difference between it and the other paradigms given.

2. **LEARN** which are the seven verbs which are suppletives (#7.33), and **NOTE** the suppletive forms which are used in their other tenses.

3. **NOTE CAREFULLY** the verbs given in the list of Second Conjugation verbs, and **NOTE** their corresponding aorist and other forms (#7.36).

4. **NOTE CAREFULLY** the four key forms for each of the seven participles (see #7.64). The pattern for each voice and each tense should be noted.

5. Translate literally Selections 1 to 34 (below), using the Explanatory Notes.

6. If time permits, read a Commentary on the Greek text of Selections 31-34.

7. Do a quick preliminary reading of Lesson Eight.

EXPLANATORY NOTES

1. Absence of verb "to be": see #7.24(e) ■ καθαρός clean, pure ■ καρδίᾳ dat. meaning "at heart" or "in heart" ■ ὄψονται → *ὁράω see (3pl dep. fut. — #7.33).

2. ἐρημία a remote or deserted place ■ τοσοῦτοι, τοσοῦτον → τοσοῦτος so many, so great (#7.13) ■ *ὥστε so that, so as ■ χορτά-σαι → χορτάζω feed, satisfy with food (aor. inf.) ■ *ὄχλος (a) crowd.

3. *ὅστις whoever (#7.15) ■ ὑψώ-σ-ει → ὑψόω exalt (3sg fut.) ■ *ἑαυτόν himself ■ ταπεινω-θή-σ-εται → ταπεινόω humble (3sg fut. pass.) ■ταπεινώ-σ-ει (3sg fut.) ■ ὑψω-θή-σ-εται (3sg fut. pass.)

4. ἐλεύσονται → *ἔρχομαι come (3pl fut. dep. — #7.33) ■ *ἐπί under (my name) i.e. taking my name for themselves ■ πλανή-σ-ουσιν → πλανάω lead astray, mislead, deceive (3pl fut.).

5. *πόλις city ■ ἐν-ε-φανίσ-θη-σαν → ἐμφανίζω manifest (3pl aor. pass. — appear).

6. τοιαύταις → *τοιοῦτος of such a kind (#7.13) ■ *παραβολή parable ■ τοιαύταις παραβολαῖς πολλαῖς with many par. of this kind ■ ἐλάλει → *λαλέω speak (3sg impf) ■ καθώς to the extent that ■ ἠδύναντο for ἐδύναντο → *δύναμαι be able (3pl impf dep. of the Third Conjugation — see #7.47; note the double augment, ἠ- for ἐ-: see #4.61) ■ ἀκούειν → *ἀκούω hear, understand (inf.) ■ χωρίς (+ gen.) apart from, without ■ *ἴδιος one's own, his own; κατ' ἰδίαν on their own, privately ■ ἐπ-έ-λυεν → ἐπιλύω explain (3sg impf).

7. λέγει αὐτῷ, Ὕπαγε εἰς τὸν οἶκόν σου πρὸς τοὺς σούς, καὶ ἀπάγγειλον αὐτοῖς ὅσα ὁ κύριός σοι πεποίηκεν καὶ ἠλέησέν σε. (ΚΑΤΑ ΜΑΡΚΟΝ 5:19-20.)

8. Καὶ συνάγονται οἱ ἀπόστολοι πρὸς τὸν Ἰησοῦν, καὶ ἀπήγγειλαν αὐτῷ πάντα ὅσα ἐποίησαν καὶ ὅσα ἐδίδαξαν. (ΚΑΤΑ ΜΑΡΚΟΝ 6:30.)

9. ἀλλὰ λέγω ὑμῖν ὅτι καὶ Ἠλίας ἐλήλυθεν, καὶ ἐποίησαν αὐτῷ ὅσα ἤθελον, καθὼς γέγραπται ἐπ᾽ αὐτόν. (ΚΑΤΑ ΜΑΡΚΟΝ 9:13.)

10. ἐποίησέν μοι μεγάλα ὁ δυνατός, καὶ ἅγιον τὸ ὄνομα αὐτοῦ. (ΚΑΤΑ ΛΟΥΚΑΝ 1:49.)

11. οὐκ ἐλήλυθα καλέσαι δικαίους ἀλλὰ ἁμαρτωλοὺς εἰς μετάνοιαν. (ΚΑΤΑ ΛΟΥΚΑΝ 5:32.)

12. ἀκούσας δὲ ταῦτα ὁ Ἰησοῦς ἐθαύμασεν αὐτόν, καὶ στραφεὶς τῷ ἀκολουθοῦντι αὐτῷ ὄχλῳ εἶπεν, Λέγω ὑμῖν, οὐδὲ ἐν τῷ Ἰσραὴλ τοσαύτην πίστιν εὗρον. (ΚΑΤΑ ΛΟΥΚΑΝ 7:9.)

13. ἄξιος ὁ ἐργάτης τοῦ μισθοῦ αὐτοῦ. (ΚΑΤΑ ΛΟΥΚΑΝ 10:7.)

14. Ἀκούσας δέ τις τῶν συνανακειμένων ταῦτα εἶπεν αὐτῷ, Μακάριος ὅστις φάγεται ἄρτον ἐν τῇ βασιλείᾳ τοῦ θεοῦ. (ΚΑΤΑ ΛΟΥΚΑΝ 14:15.)

15. Εἶπεν δὲ πρὸς τοὺς μαθητάς, Ἐλεύσονται ἡμέραι ὅτε ἐπιθυμήσετε μίαν τῶν ἡμερῶν τοῦ υἱοῦ τοῦ ἀνθρώπου ἰδεῖν καὶ οὐκ ὄψεσθε. (ΚΑΤΑ ΛΟΥΚΑΝ 17:22.)

16. Καὶ ἐμαρτύρησεν Ἰωάννης λέγων ὅτι Τεθέαμαι τὸ πνεῦμα καταβαῖνον ὡς περιστερὰν ἐξ οὐρανοῦ, καὶ ἔμεινεν ἐπ᾽ αὐτόν· κἀγὼ οὐκ ᾔδειν αὐτόν, ἀλλ᾽ ὁ πέμψας με βαπτίζειν ἐν ὕδατι ἐκεῖνός μοι εἶπεν, Ἐφ᾽ ὃν ἂν ἴδῃς τὸ πνεῦμα καταβαῖνον καὶ μένον ἐπ᾽ αὐτόν, οὗτός ἐστιν ὁ βαπτίζων ἐν πνεύματι ἁγίῳ. κἀγὼ ἑώρακα, καὶ μεμαρτύρηκα ὅτι οὗτός ἐστιν ὁ υἱὸς τοῦ θεοῦ. (ΚΑΤΑ ΙΩΑΝΝΗΝ 1:32-34.)

17. λέγει ἡ μήτηρ αὐτοῦ τοῖς διακόνοις, Ὅ τι ἂν λέγῃ ὑμῖν ποιήσατε. (ΚΑΤΑ ΙΩΑΝΝΗΝ 2:5.)

18. ἐγὼ ἐλήλυθα ἐν τῷ ὀνόματι τοῦ πατρός μου καὶ οὐ λαμβάνετέ με· ἐὰν ἄλλος ἔλθῃ ἐν τῷ ὀνόματι τῷ ἰδίῳ, ἐκεῖνον λήμψεσθε. (ΚΑΤΑ ΙΩΑΝΝΗΝ 5:43.)

Selections continue on page 100

―――――――――

Continued from next page

17. *μήτηρ mother ▰ διάκονος servant ■ ὅ τι → ὅστις (neut., #7.15) ■ λέγῃ → *λέγω (3sg subj.) ■ ποιή-σατε → *ποιέω do (2pl aor. impv).

18. ἐλήλυθα: Sel. 11 ■ λαμβάνετε → *λαμβάνω receive (2pl)■ *ἐάν if ■ ἄλλος another ■ ἔλθῃ → *ἔρχομαι (3sg aor² subj.: were to come) ■ *ἴδιος his own ■ λήμψεσθε → *λαμβάνω (2pl fut., #7.36).

7. ὕπαγε → *ὑπάγω go, go back (2sg impv) ■ σός your (sg); οἱ σοί your family/friends; πρός to ■ἀπάγγειλον → ἀπαγγέλλω report (impv aor[1] — no -σ because liquid stem causes it to drop out) ■ ὅσα how many things (#7.11); i.e. all that ■ σοι dat.: to you, or, for you ■ πεποίηκεν → *ποιέω do (3sg pf) ■ ἠλέη-σεν → ἐλεέω/ἐλεάω have mercy, compassion (3sg aor.); note the significance of the aor. here and pf of ποιέω, both referring to the one act.

8. συνάγονται → *συνάγω gather together (3pl mid/pass. — come together, meet) ■ ἀπόστολος apostle ■ ἀπ-ήγγειλ-α-ν → ἀπαγγέλλω report (3pl aor.) ■ ὅσα how many things (#7.11) ■ ἐ-δίδα-ξ-αν → *διδάσκω teach (3pl aor.).

9. καί also ■ ἐλήλυθεν → *ἔρχομαι come (3sg pf, #7.33) ■ ἐποίη-σαν → *ποιέω (3pl aor.) ■ ἤθελον → *θελω wish (3pl impf, double augment #4.61) ■ γέγραπται → *γράφω write (3sg pf pass.; #6.35, #9.75).

10. ὁ δυνατός the Almighty ■ μεγάλα → *μέγας great ■ *ἅγιος holy.

11. ἐλήλυθα → *ἔρχομαι come (1sg pf) ■ καλέ-σαι → *καλέω call (aor. inf.) ■ *δίκαιος righteous ■ ἁμαρτωλός sinner ■ μετάνοια repentance.

12. ἀκούσας (masc. nom. sg aor. ptc) ■ ἐ-θαύμα-σεν → θαυμάζω marvel at (3sg aor.) ■ στραφ-είς → στρέφω turn (masc. nom. sg aor. pass. ptc, refl. meaning) ■ ἀκολουθοῦντι → *ἀκολουθέω follow (masc. dat. sg ptc, used as adj. w. ὄχλος crowd, in the attributive intermediate position, #7.21); αὐτῷ is object of ἀκολουθέω and is dat. as usual; = to the crowd following him ■ *οὐδέ not even ■τοσαύτην → τοσοῦτος such great ■ εὗρον → *εὑρίσκω find (1sg aor[2]).

13. ἐργάτης workman ■ μισθός pay, wages, reward ■ ἄξιος worthy.

14. ἀκούσας: Sel. 12 ■ συν-ανα-κει-μένων → συνανάκειμαι recline (at table) with (masc. gen. pl ptc, = table companions) ■ ταῦτα acc. pl, object of ἀκούσας ■ φάγεται → *ἐσθίω eat (3sg fut dcp: #7.33).

15. ἐλεύσονται: Sel. 4 ■ *ὅτε when ■ ἐπι-θυμή-σετε → ἐπιθυμέω desire, long (for) ■ ἰδεῖν → *ὁράω (aor[2] inf.) ■ μίαν acc. sg fem. of εἷς, object of ἰδεῖν ■ ὄψεσθε → *ὁράω see (2pl fut. dep., #7.33).

16. ἐ-μαρτύρη-σεν → *μαρτυρέω testify, bear witness (3sg aor.) ■ ὅτι = "... ■ τε-θέα-μαι → θεάομαι look at, notice, observe (1sg pf dep.; re reduplic., see #E4.33) ■ καταβαῖνον → *κατα-βαίνω come/go down (pres. ptc, neut. agreeing with πνεῦμα) ■ περιστερά dove, pigeon ■ ἔ-μειν-εν → *μένω rest, remain, abide (3sg aor[1] — no -σ, because liquid stem) ■ κἀγω = καὶ ἐγω ■ ᾔδειν → *οἶδα know, understand (1sg plpf, w. impf meaning — see #7.52) ■ ἀλλ' = ἀλλά ■ πέμψας → *πέμπω send (masc. nom. sg ptc) ■ βαπτίζειν (inf.) ■ ὕδατι → *ὕδωρ water (dat. sg) ■ ἐφ' (= ἐπί) ὃν ἄν on whomsoever ■ ἴδ-ῃς → *ὁράω (2sg aor[2] subj.) ■ μένον → *μένω (ptc) ■ βαπτίζων (ptc) ■ ἑώρακα → *ὁράω (1sg pf, #7.33) ■ με-μαρτύρη-κα → *μαρτυρέω (1sg pf).

Continued at foot of previous page

19. Ἔστιν παιδάριον ὧδε ὃς ἔχει πέντε ἄρτους κριθίνους καὶ δύο ὀψάρια·
     ἀλλὰ ταῦτα τί ἐστιν εἰς τοσούτους; (ΚΑΤΑ ΙΩΑΝΝΗΝ 6:9.)

20. οἱ πατέρες ἡμῶν τὸ μάννα ἔφαγον ἐν τῇ ἐρήμῳ, καθώς ἐστιν γεγραμμένον
     Ἄρτον ἐκ τοῦ οὐρανοῦ ἔδωκεν αὐτοῖς φαγεῖν. (ΚΑΤΑ ΙΩΑΝΝΗΝ 6:31.)

21. ἐγὼ ἐξ ἐμαυτοῦ οὐκ ἐλάλησα, ἀλλ᾽ ὁ πέμψας με πατὴρ αὐτός μοι ἐντολὴν
     δέδωκεν τί εἴπω καὶ τί λαλήσω. καὶ οἶδα ὅτι ἡ ἐντολὴ αὐτοῦ ζωὴ αἰώνιός
     ἐστιν. ἃ οὖν ἐγὼ λαλῶ, καθὼς εἴρηκέν μοι ὁ πατήρ, οὕτως λαλῶ. (ΚΑΤΑ
     ΙΩΑΝΝΗΝ 12:49-50.)

22. ὁ μὲν νόμος ἅγιος, καὶ ἡ ἐντολὴ ἁγία καὶ δικαία καὶ ἀγαθή. τὸ οὖν
     ἀγαθὸν ἐμοὶ ἐγένετο θάνατος; (ΠΡΟΣ ΡΩΜΑΙΟΥΣ 7:12-13.)

23. ὁ γὰρ ναὸς τοῦ θεοῦ ἅγιός ἐστιν, οἵτινές ἐστε ὑμεῖς. (ΠΡΟΣ
     ΚΟΡΙΝΘΙΟΥΣ Α, 3:17.)

24. τὴν δὲ δοκιμὴν αὐτοῦ γινώσκετε, ὅτι ὡς πατρὶ τέκνον σὺν ἐμοὶ ἐδούλευσεν
     εἰς τὸ εὐαγγέλιον. τοῦτον μὲν οὖν ἐλπίζω πέμψαι ὡς ἂν ἀφίδω τὰ περὶ ἐμὲ
     ἐξαυτῆς· πέποιθα δὲ ἐν κυρίῳ ὅτι καὶ αὐτὸς ταχέως ἐλεύσομαι. (ΠΡΟΣ
     ΦΙΛΙΠΠΗΣΙΟΥΣ 2:22-24.)

25. λέγει γὰρ ἡ γραφή, βοῦν ἀλοῶντα οὐ φιμώσεις· καί, Ἄξιος ὁ ἐργάτης τοῦ
     μισθοῦ αὐτοῦ. (ΠΡΟΣ ΤΙΜΟΘΕΟΝ Α, 5:18.)

26. ὧν οὐκ ἦν ἄξιος ὁ κόσμος ... (ΠΡΟΣ ΕΒΡΑΙΟΥΣ 11:38.)

27. Καὶ τῷ ἀγγέλῳ τῆς ἐν Φιλαδελφείᾳ ἐκκλησίας γράψον· Τάδε λέγει ὁ
     ἅγιος, ὁ ἀληθινός, ὁ ἔχων τὴν κλεῖν Δαυίδ, ὁ ἀνοίγων καὶ οὐδεὶς κλείσει,
     καὶ κλείων καὶ οὐδεὶς ἀνοίγει· Οἶδά σου τὰ ἔργα. (ΑΠΟΚΑΛΥΨΙΣ
     ΙΩΑΝΝΟΥ 3:7-8.)

28. Καὶ τῷ ἀγγέλῳ τῆς ἐν Λαοδικείᾳ ἐκκλησίας γράψον· Τάδε λέγει ὁ ἀμήν,
     ὁ μάρτυς ὁ πιστὸς καὶ ἀληθινός, ἡ ἀρχὴ τῆς κτίσεως τοῦ θεοῦ· Οἶδά σου
     τὰ ἔργα. (ΑΠΟΚΑΛΥΨΙΣ ΙΩΑΝΝΟΥ 3:14.)

29. οἱ λοιποὶ τῶν νεκρῶν οὐκ ἔζησαν ἄχρι τελεσθῇ τὰ χίλια ἔτη. αὕτη ἡ
     ἀνάστασις ἡ πρώτη. μακάριος καὶ ἅγιος ὁ ἔχων μέρος ἐν τῇ ἀναστάσει τῇ
     πρώτῃ. (ΑΠΟΚΑΛΥΨΙΣ ΙΩΑΝΝΟΥ 20:5-6.)

30. καὶ τὴν πόλιν τὴν ἁγίαν Ἰερουσαλὴμ καινὴν εἶδον καταβαίνουσαν ἐκ τοῦ
     οὐρανοῦ ἀπὸ τοῦ θεοῦ, ἡτοιμασμένην ὡς νύμφην κεκοσμημένην τῷ ἀνδρὶ
     αὐτῆς. (ΑΠΟΚΑΛΥΨΙΣ ΙΩΑΝΝΟΥ 21:2.)

31. John 4:39-45   Do the translation of this passage from your Greek New
                     Testament as an exercise in class, using your Analysis.

32. Matthew 18:3-5   Translate these passages from your Greek New Testament,
33. Mark 10:10-16   making the fullest use of your Analysis.
34. John 1:6-13

67362

19. παιδάριον a young boy ∎ ὧδε here ∎ πέντε five ∎ κρίθινος barley ∎ ὀψάριον fish ∎ εἰς among ∎ τοσοῦτος so much/so many (#7.13).

20. πατέρες → *πατήρ father ∎ μάννα manna ∎ ἔφαγον → *ἐσθίω eat (3pl aor², #7.33) ∎ γεγραμμένον → *γράφω write (pf midd/pass. ptc) ἐστιν γεγραμμένον, it stands written ∎ ἔ-δω-κ-εν → *δίδωμι (3sg aor) ∎ φαγεῖν → *ἐσθίω eat (aor² inf.).

21. ἐμ-αυτοῦ myself ∎ ἐ-λάλη-σα → *λαλέω (1sg aor.) ∎ πέμψας Sel. 16 ∎ αὐτός emphatic, himself ∎ ἐντολή commandment, instruction ∎ δέ-δω-κεν → *δίδωμι (3sg pf) ∎ εἴπω and λαλήσω: 1sg aor. subj. ∎ *οἶδα know (1sg) ∎ αἰώνιος eternal ∎ εἴρηκεν → *λέγω (3sg pf; #7.33).

22. νόμος law ∎ ἐντολή Sel. 21 ∎ *δίκαιος righteous ∎ *ἀγαθός good ∎ ἐγένετο → γίνομαι become (3sg aor²) ∎ θάνατος death.

23. ναός temple, sanctuary ∎ οἵτινες → *ὅστις (#7.15) ∎ ἐστε → *εἰμί.

24. δοκιμή worth ∎ γινώσκ-ετε (2pl) ∎ ὡς πατρὶ τέκνον as a child with his father ∎ σύν with ∎ ἐ-δούλευ-σεν → δουλεύω serve as (like) a slave, εἰς in ∎ μέν contrast particle, not translated ∎ ἐλπίζω hope ∎ πέμψαι → *πέμπω send ∎ ὡς ἄν ... ἐξαυτῆς as ever ... immediately, = just as soon as ∎ ἀφ-ίδω → ἀφ-οράω see (1sg aor² subj.) ∎ τὰ περὶ ἐμέ (how) things (go) concerning me ∎ πέ-ποιθα → *πείθω persuade, trust in (1sg pf, #C8.63) ∎ αὐτός self (i.e., I myself) ∎ ταχέως soon, swiftly ∎ ἐλεύσομαι → *ἔρχομαι come (1sg fut dep).

25. *γραφή scripture ∎ βοῦς ox ∎ ἀλοῶ-ντα → ἀλοάω thresh (masc. acc. sg ptc) ∎ φιμώ-σ-εις → φιμόω muzzle (2sg fut.) ∎ ἐργάτης Sel. 13.

26. ὧν of whom (from ὅς, gen. pl) ∎ *κόσμος world.

27. ἐν Φιλαδελφείᾳ adj. prep. phrase in attributive intermediate position (see #7.21) ∎ γρά-ψ-ον → *γράφω (2sg aor. impv) ∎ τάδε → ὅδε (see #7.14) ∎ ἀληθινός true, genuine ∎ κλείς key ∎ ἀνοίγων (ptc) ∎ οὐδείς no one ∎ κλεί-σ-ει → κλείω shut (3sg fut.) ∎ *ἔργον work, deed, action ∎ *οἶδα know (1sg pf in form, pres. meaning).

28. See also the vocabulary for Sel. 27 ∎ ἀμήν Amen ∎ μάρτυς witness, martyr ∎ *πιστός faithful ∎ *ἀρχή ruler, beginning (both meanings apply here) ∎ κτίσεως → κτίσις creation (gen. sg).

29. *λοιπός remainder, remaining, rest ∎ *νεκρός dead ∎ ἔ-ζη-σαν → *ζάω live (3pl aor.) ∎ ἄχρι until ∎ τελεσ-θῇ → τελέω end, complete, finish (3sg aor. pass. subj.) ∎ χιλιάς a thousand (neut. nom. pl) ∎ ἔτη → ἔτος, ους, τό year (nom. pl) ∎ αὕτη → οὗτος ∎ ἀνάστασις resurrection ∎ πρῶτος first ∎ μέρος, ους, τό a part.

30. *πόλις city ∎ καινός new ∎ καταβαίν-ουσαν → *κατα-βαίνω come down (acc. sg fem. ptc, agreeing with πόλις) ∎ ἡτοιμα-σ-μένην → ἑτοιμάζω prepare (acc. sg fem. pf pass. ptc, having been prepared) ∎ νύμφη bride ∎ κε-κοσμη-μένην → κοσμέω decorate, adorn (acc. sg fem. pf pass. ptc) ∎ ἀνδρί → *ἀνήρ husband (dat.) ∎ αὐτῆς → αὐτός he/she/it (fem. gen. sg).

LESSON EIGHT

USING NOUNS, PREPOSITIONS, AND THE ARTICLE

8.1 INVESTIGATING: THE CASE OF THE FLEXIBLE NOUN

8.11 The Greek noun is very flexible, and by its ending alone it can indicate a wide and diverse range of relationships within the sentence. This range is extended even further when a preposition is used with a noun.

8.12 For the student learning Greek, deciphering a Greek sentence is rather like working out "who dunnit" in a detective story: all the clues are there in front of you, and you have to be able to spot them and work out what they mean and what they indicate, and how you are to put them all together to get the complete picture of what happened.

8.13 The nouns (and adjectives) give you the participants in the action, and the verb tells you the nature of the action and when it occurred. Deciphering the verb correctly is important for knowing accurately the details of what happened; deciphering the nouns correctly is essential for knowing who and what were involved in what happened, and the part played by each.

8.14 The noun is so flexible that it can fit anywhere into the pattern of what happened. The case of the noun is what tells you just where the noun fits in. That is, the meaning of a sentence is contained to a large extent in the cases of the nouns, for it is the case which shows the relationship to each other of the person(s) and/or thing(s) mentioned in the sentence. Contrast this with English, where that relationship is shown by *word order*: the sentences "The man ate a large fish" and "A large fish ate the man" use exactly the same words but mean very different things — and that difference is conveyed entirely by the word order (#2.91). In Greek, the relationship of the participants in an action (the nouns/adjectives) to each other and to that action (the verb) is shown by the *case*, and so the word order can vary without affecting that basic meaning. Word order can thus be used for other purposes, particularly for conveying nuances of emphasis and shades of meaning (#2.92).

8.15 Thus the key to understanding the meaning of the average Greek sentence is the deciphering of the case of each of its nouns.

8.16 A noun consists of a *stem* which gives the lexical meaning of the word (i.e., the semantic meaning, what the noun refers to), and the *numbercase ending*, which gives the grammatical meaning of the word (i.e., number — whether one or more were involved in what happened, and, case). The ending may also indicate gender, which is sometimes important, and sometimes not.

8.17 There are three quite different patterns in Greek by means of which noun endings indicate the number and case of the noun. For convenience of reference and description

102

these are called the First, Second, and Third Declensions. Within each Declension there are subgroups exhibiting some differences of the endings according to the nature of the stem and the gender of the noun. These Declensions have been discussed in Lessons Two, Three, and Five, and the complete paradigms are set out in Appendix D.

8.18 There are eight basic case forms for each noun: four forms for the singular, and four for the plural. In addition, some nouns have an additional, ninth, form for the vocative singular (which, where it exists, is usually the stem of the word or — in the Second Declension masculine — the stem of the word plus -ε, as in κύριε).

8.2 PRONOUNS

8.21 The comments about nouns apply to pronouns also. In addition, the third person pronouns have three sets of eight case forms, one for each gender. (There are no vocative forms for pronouns.)

8.22 The case endings for pronouns need to be individually noted, though in most cases they have case endings which are the same as or recognizably similar to the usual endings of the Declensions.

8.23 The comments which follow about case meanings apply to both noun and pronoun alike.

8.3 SELF-TESTING REVIEW

8.31 Turn to the paradigms for the three Declensions in Appendix D, and go through them. Check that you are able to recognize and identify each of the noun case endings. If necessary, return to Lessons Two, Three, or Five, and revise the grammar given there.

8.32 Similarly, check that you are able to recognize and identify the cases of all the pronouns.

8.33 NOTE CAREFULLY the endings which are not decisive but which occur with different case meanings in the different paradigms (e.g. -ους can be accusative plural, Second Declension, or genitive singular, Third Declension neuter, vowel stem). These case ambiguities will be resolved in a great many instances by the form of the article used with the noun; identifying the word in a lexicon or vocabulary will give you its nominative and genitive forms, and this will clarify what paradigm it follows and thus what its various case endings will be.

8.4 THE MEANING AND USE OF THE CASES

8.41 THE NOMINATIVE CASE

The nominative case will be found used in these ways:

(a) The subject of the verb (i.e., the person or thing concerning which the verb is making a statement, whether the verb is active or passive).

Thus: *I* went out.   *I* was cleansed.   *I* am the one.
(But note: when an infinitive has a subject, this is in the accusative.)

(b) The complement of the verb

Certain verbs take a noun after them which refers not to some other person or thing, but to the verb's subject, concerning which it gives further information. These include: verbs of being, becoming, being made, being named or called. This noun is thus the "complete-ment", or *complement* of the thought of the subject and verb. Examples:

Mk 2:28 (L2/25) κύριός ἐστιν ὁ υἱὸς τοῦ ἀνθρώπου The son of man is Lord

Lk 23:12 (L8/6) ἐγένοντο δὲ φίλοι ὅ τε Ἡρῴδης καὶ ὁ Πιλᾶτος . . .
                and Herod and Pilate became friends . . .

Mt 5:9 (L8/2) . . οἱ εἰρηνοποιοί, ὅτι αὐτοὶ υἱοὶ θεοῦ κληθήσονται
              the peacemakers, for they shall be called sons of God

(c) Independent Nominative

At times a noun may be treated as independent of its place in the sentence structure, and have the nominative case instead of its appropriate case. Example:

Jn 13:13 (L8/9) φωνεῖτέ με ὁ διδάσκαλος καὶ ὁ κύριος
                you call me   teacher   and   lord

The "correct" case here would be accusative after "call", agreeing with (in apposition with) με.

A nominative can also be left hanging on its own (so, sometimes called a "hanging nominative") at the beginning of a sentence where the grammatical construction changes. Example:

Rev 3:21 (L8/12) ὁ νικῶν δώσω αὐτῷ καθίσαι μετ᾽ ἐμοῦ . . .
                The one who overcomes, to him I will give to sit with me . . .

(d) Appellation

When a name is being introduced or indicated, it may be given in the nominative case even though, grammatically, it should be in another case:

Rev 9:11 ὄνομα ἔχει Ἀπολλύων he has the name Apollyon

This occurrence of the nominative is called "appellation".

(e) Nominative For Vocative

Sometimes a nominative case is used for a vocative — see below.

8.42 THE VOCATIVE CASE

The vocative case is the case used when addressing someone. Consequently, words in the vocative are not grammatically related to the rest of the sentence. Sometimes a vocative is preceded by ὦ, O, and sometimes not. Except in Luke, the inclusion of ὦ usually indicates strong emotion.

A separate form exists for the vocative in:
  (i)   the singular of the First Declension masculine (μαθητά, νεανία);
  (ii) the singular of the Second Declension (κύριε, ἄνθρωπε, υἱέ, etc.);
  (iii) the singular of some Third Declension nouns (πάτερ, γύναι, etc.).

For most other words (including all plurals) the nominative form is used for the vocative. In addition, the nominative is sometimes used even where a vocative form does exist. This reflects a tendency for the vocative to be dropping out of use in the colloquial koine Greek usage in New Testament times. Compare:

Mk 15:34   Ὁ θεός μου ὁ θεός μου, εἰς τί ἐγκατέλιπές με;
Mt 27:46   Θεέ μου   θεέ μου, ἱνατί με ἐγκατέλιπες;
                my God   my God, why have you forsaken me?

As there is no vocative of the article, when the article is needed it forces the following noun into the nominative. An interesting case arises in John 20:28 (L3/27). In the gospels, κύριε is used very lightly at times, as no more than "Sir" (e.g., see L4/14). Thomas, in his proclamation of faith, uses the article and the nominative (instead of the vocative) of κύριος to indicate the definiteness of "Lord":

Ὁ κύριός μου καὶ ὁ θεός μου   My lord and my God

OBLIQUE CASES

The accusative, genitive and dative cases are referred to by grammarians as the *oblique* cases. They may be used after (called being "governed by") a verb or a preposition. Their use with prepositions is discussed below; in this Section we consider their use without a preposition.

8.43 THE ACCUSATIVE CASE (WITHOUT PREPOSITION)

There are three main ways in which the accusative case is used: as the object of a verb, for a word indicating the extent of something, and as the subject of an infinitive.

(a) The Objective Accusative

The accusative case is used for the direct object of the verb, i.e. the person or thing to which the action of the verb carries directly. The direct object of the verb usually follows it closely in English and can be identified by asking "whom" or "what" after the verb.

Mk 1:8 (L5/1)   ἐγὼ ἐβάπτισα ὑμᾶς   ὕδατι
                 I baptized *you* with water

Jn 6:31 (L7/20) Ἄρτον ἐκ τοῦ οὐρανοῦ ἔδωκεν αὐτοῖς φαγεῖν.
                 bread from the heaven he gave them to eat.

(b) The Extentive Accusative (or, Accusative of Extent)

The intrinsic idea of the accusative could be said to be, motion towards, or, extension towards. The accusative is used at times with this implication of the extent of something.

This may be *the extent of* the time involved (so that it answers the question, How long?); e.g.:

Mt 28:20 (L6/6) ἐγὼ μεθ' ὑμῶν εἰμι   πάσας τὰς ἡμέρας
                 I   am with you during (for) all the days

Jn 4:40 (L8/8)   καὶ ἔμεινεν ἐκεῖ δύο ἡμέρας
                 and he remained there for (during) two days

The accusative can also be used for *the extent of* distance involved (so that it answers the question, How far?); e.g.:

Lk 24:13 (L8/7) εἰς κώμην ἀπέχουσαν σταδίους ἐξήκοντα ἀπὸ Ἰερουσαλήμ.
                 to a village *which was distant sixty stades*   from Jerusalem.

(c) The Accusative and Infinitive

The infinitive is frequently used in Greek with a subject, that is, a word which says who it is who is to do the action of the infinitive. This is one way of setting out indirect speech, and it is found in various other constructions as well. The subject of the infinitive is regularly put into the accusative case. Examples:

Mk 12:18 (L8/5) Καὶ ἔρχονται Σαδδουκαῖοι πρὸς αὐτόν, οἵτινες
                 And there came Sadducees   to   him,   who

                 λέγουσιν   ἀνάστασιν μὴ εἶναι.
                 say   *a resurrection* there not to be.

(What the Sadducees would have said in direct speech would have been, "There is no resurrection".)

Mt 17:4 (L8/3)   Κύριε, καλόν ἐστιν ἡμᾶς ὧδε εἶναι.
                 Lord, good it is *us* here to be.
                 (Lord, it is good that *we* are here.)

8.44 THE GENITIVE CASE (WITHOUT PREPOSITION)

There are two different relationships which both have the same, genitive, case endings. To distinguish them, these two relationships or functions can be called the "True Genitive" (the term of N. Turner in "A Grammar of N.T. Greek, Vol III, p. 231), and the Ablative. Most true genitives are the equivalent of "of" in English, and ablatives have the sense "from".

(i) The True Genitive

The word "genitive" means the case showing the *genus* or kind of thing being discussed. It is thus the case used to define or describe or specify. It limits the generality of a word to a more specific case. Words in the genitive case are therefore most commonly used with nouns, and usually follow the noun to which they refer.

(ii) The Ablative

The word "ablative" means "that which is carried away or separated". It indicates the derivation, source, or origin of something, from which that something is now separated. The ablative is the meaning of the genitive form used with many prepositions, especially ἀπό and ἐκ.

A wide range of differing relationships can be set out through the genitive case. A word will be in the genitive case because either it comes after (i.e. is governed by) a preposition or a verb which requires the genitive case, or because it expresses a relationship to a noun. Prepositions which require the genitive case are covered below, in #8.5. Verbs taking the genitive case are for the most part verbs of touching or grasping (e.g., ἅπτομαι I touch); of perception and feeling (e.g., ἀκούω I hear: takes genitive of the *person* heard and accusative of the *thing* heard); of remembering and forgetting; of emotion and accusation; or ruling and surpassing (e.g., ἄρχω I rule). Thus:

Jn 10:27 (L5/13) τὰ πρόβατα τὰ ἐμὰ τῆς φωνῆς μου ἀκούουσιν (so also L3/19)
            my sheep   my *voice*   hear

Rev 21:3 (L6/12) καὶ ἤκουσα φωνῆς μεγάλης
           and I heard   *a loud voice*

Mk 10:42 (L9/7)   οἱ δοκοῦντες ἄρχειν τῶν ἐθνῶν ...
           those who seem to rule *over the gentiles/nations*...

The most important relationships with a noun that a genitive expresses are:

(a) Possessive Genitive

This genitive means "belonging to", and indicates ownership or close relationship. Examples:

Mt 13:24 (L4/20)   ... ἐν τῷ ἀγρῷ αὐτοῦ
           in   *his* field

Mk 14:22-24 (L5/8) τοῦτό ἐστιν τὸ σῶμά μου/τοῦτό ἐστιν τὸ αἷμά μου
           this is   *my* body / this is   *my* blood

Mk 10:46 (L4/21)   ὁ υἱὸς Τιμαίου
           the son *of Timaios*

The genitive of this type can be used alone, without the noun expressing the relationship actually being stated, so that this has to be supplied from the context or from prior knowledge. Thus:

Mk 1:19   Ἰάκωβον τὸν τοῦ Ζεβεδαίου
          James   the(-)   *of Zebedee*   (supply, "son")

Jn 19:25 Μαριὰ   ἡ   τοῦ Κλωπᾶ
          Mary   the(-) *of Clopas*   (supply, "wife")

I Cor 15:23   οἱ τοῦ Χριστοῦ
              the(-)   *of Christ*   (i.e., those who are *Christ's*)

(b) Subjective Genitive

In this use, the genitive is the *subject* of the idea in the noun (a noun of action) to which it refers. Examples:

Mk 10:6 (L5/6) ἀπὸ δὲ ἀρχῆς κτίσεως ...
                but from the beginning *of creation*   (when *creation* began . .)

Rom 5:5   ἡ ἀγάπη τοῦ θεοῦ ἐκκέχυται ἐν ταῖς καρδίαις ἡμῶν
          the love *of God* is poured out in   our hearts
          (i.e. *God's* love for us ...)

I Thess 2:13   λόγον   θεοῦ
               the word *of God*   (i.e. what *God* has said, not just, what is said
                                    about God — see the whole of this verse)

(c) Objective Genitive

In this use, the genitive is the *object* of the idea in the noun of action to which it refers. Thus:

Jn 6:48 (L2/9)   Ἐγώ εἰμι τὸ φῶς τοῦ κοσμοῦ
                 I   am the light *of the world*
                 (i.e., I light up *the world*, I give light to *the world*)

The meaning of the objective genitive is often well brought out by the use of the word "for" or "about" instead of "of":

Rom 10:2   ζῆλος θεοῦ   zeal *for God*
Mt 5:13   Ὑμεῖς ἐστε τὸ ἅλας τῆς γῆς   you are salt *for the earth*
Mk 1:1   τοῦ εὐαγγελίου Ἰησοῦ Χριστοῦ the gospel *about Jesus Christ*

(d) Durative Genitive

This expresses "time-within-which", that is, time during which something else happened. Examples:

Mt 24:20=Mk 13:18 χειμῶνος   *during the winter*

Mt 2:14 (L8/1)   ὁ δὲ ἐγερθεὶς   παρέλαβεν τὸ παιδίον καὶ τὴν
                 and he arose and   took   the   child and

                 μητέρα αὐτοῦ νυκτὸς καὶ ἀνεχώρησεν εἰς Αἴγυπτον.
                 his mother *during the night* and departed to   Egypt.

(e) Comparative Genitive

Adjectives and adverbs of comparison take the genitive after them, with the meaning "than". Examples:

Mk 12:31 (L5/7) *μείζων τούτων   ἄλλα ἐντολὴ οὐκ ἔστιν.*
                greater *than these* other commandment there is not.

Mk 1:7   *Ἔρχεται ὁ ἰσχυρότερός μου ὀπίσω μου*
                There comes one *stronger than me* after me

(f) Definitive Genitive (also known as Epexegitical or Appositive Genitive)

In this use, the genitive defines further the noun to which it refers — that is, both words are referring to the one person or thing, the genitive thus really being (in sense) in apposition to the first noun. Examples:

Phil 2:1   ... if any comfort of love (love *is* the comfort)
Acts 2:38   You will receive the gift of the Holy Spirit (the gift *is* the Holy Spirit)
Mt 12:39   the sign of Jonah (the sign *is* Jonah himself)
2 Cor 1:22; 5:5 the downpayment of the Spirit (the downpayment *is* the Spirit)
Rev 2:10   I will give you the crown of life (the crown *is* life)

(g) Adjectival Genitive (also known as Qualitative or Attributive Genitive)

Sometimes the genitive has a simple adjectival force. Examples:

Mt 4:18 (L3/1) *παρὰ τὴν θάλασσαν τῆς Γαλιλαίας*
              beside the   sea   *of Galilee*   (= the Galilean sea)

2 Thess 1:8   *ἐν πυρὶ φλογός*
              in fire *of flame*   (= in flaming fire)

Lk 4:22   *οἱ λόγοι τῆς χάριτος*
              the words   *of grace*   (= gracious words)

James 1:25   *ἀκροατὴς ἐπιλησμονῆς*
              a hearer *of forgetfulness* (= a forgetful hearer)

(h) Partitive Genitive

In this use, the genitive indicates the whole category while the noun to which the genitive refers gives the part of that category under discussion. Examples:

Mk 11:1 (L4/21) *ἀποστέλλει δύο τῶν μαθητῶν αὐτοῦ*
                he sends   two   *of his disciples*

Lk 14:15 (L7/14) *τις τῶν συνανακειμένων*
                one *of his table companions*

Lk 17:22 (L7/15) *μίαν τῶν ἡμερῶν*   one *of the days*

Rev 20:5 (L7/29) *οἱ λοιποὶ τῶν νεκρῶν*   the rest *of the dead*

(i) Genitive of Content

In this construction the genitive states the content of the noun to which the genitive refers. Examples:

Jn 2:7   γεμίσατε τὰς ὑδρίας ὕδατος
                   fill   the waterpots *(full) of water*

Jn 21:8 (L8/10)   τὸ δίκτυον   τῶν ἰχθύων
                 the   net   *of (containing) fishes*

(j) Genitive Absolute

This is a construction consisting of a participle and noun (or pronoun) which agree in number and gender and are both in the genitive case, the expression being grammatically independent of the rest of the sentence. The genitive absolute is common in the Greek N.T., and is used to provide some extra item of information relating to the sentence, usually a reference to time, place or circumstance. It will usually be translated into English by the equivalent conjunction and adverbial clause:

Mk 6:2 (L6/13)   καὶ γενομένου σαββάτου ἤρξατο διδάσκειν ...
                 and *when the Sabbath came* he began to teach ...

In accordance with #7.9, a present participle will usually indicate simultaneous action, and be translated with a clause beginning with *while* or *as*, and an aorist participle will usually indicate an action *prior in sequence* to the action of the main verb, and be rendered with *when* or *after*. The genitive absolute construction is appropriate when the noun (or pronoun) in it does not have any relation to the main verb of the sentence; if such a relationship did exist (subject, direct or indirect object), then that relationship would dictate the case which that noun (or pronoun) should take.

NOTE: It is important for exegesis and interpretation to be aware of these different types of relationships expressed by the genitive so that in considering the meaning of a passage one is able to weigh and choose between the range of possibilities that exist. For example, to regard "the sign of Jonah" or "the gift of the Holy Spirit" as Subjective Genitives and not recognize them as Definitive (Epexegetic) Genitives would be to seriously misinterpret the whole passage in which each occurs. On the other hand, some genitive usages overflow the boundaries of such a grammatical system of classification. Thus, "the love of Christ" (2 Cor 5:14) means Christ's love for us and, also, our love for Christ. Similarly, "the gospel of Jesus Christ" (Mk 1:1) means: the gospel which Jesus Christ himself proclaimed (e.g. Mk 1:14); the gospel *about* Jesus Christ; and also, the gospel which Jesus Christ personifies — i.e., in himself he *is* the gospel, the good news, the Word of God to mankind.

8.45 THE DATIVE CASE (WITHOUT PREPOSITION)

Three different cases in Greek have come, historically, to have the same case ending, traditionally called the "dative". These are described as: the True Dative (or, Dative Proper), the Instrumental, and the Locative.

(a) The True Dative

The word "dative" derives from a form of the Latin verb for "to give"; it is the "giving" case, and has the primary idea of personal interest or reference, designating personal relations or involvement. There are various types of dative relationship, a number of which can be categorized together as "the dative of the person involved". This includes what is often called in English the "indirect object", the idea of "to" or "for" someone. Verbs like "say", "write", or "give" take the direct object (accusative) of the *thing* (what was said or written or given, etc.) and the indirect object (dative) of the *person* (to whom it was said or written or given, etc.). Examples:

Jn 16:4 (L3/24)   ταῦτα δὲ ὑμῖν   ἐξ ἀρχῆς οὐκ εἶπον . . .
                    I did not say *these things to you* from the beginning . . .

Mk 10:5 (L5/6) ἔγραψεν ὑμῖν τὴν ἐντολὴν ταύτην
                    he wrote   *this commandment to you* (or, *for you*)

Jn 14:27 (L4/15)   εἰρήνην τὴν ἐμὴν δίδωμι ὑμῖν
                    I give   *my peace*   *to you*

With numerous other verbs also, "the person involved" is put into the dative in Greek, even where it could be the direct object in English: for example, after ἀκολουθέω (follow), ἀποκρίνομαι (answer), δουλεύω (serve), προσεύχομαι (pray), πιστεύω (believe), and so on.

Another type of dative of personal involvement is when something is done *for a person*; and yet another type of dative is the dative of reference, which explains *in what respect* a previous word is applicable. Some examples of these various kinds of dative usages include:

Mt 5:8 (L7/1) μακάριοι οἱ καθαροὶ   τῇ καρδίᾳ
                    blessed are the pure *in reference to their heart*

Mt 6:19 (L6/2) Μὴ θησαυρίζετε ὑμῖν θησαυροὺς ἐπὶ τῆς γῆς
                    Do not store up *for yourselves* treasures upon the earth

Mt 15:33 (L3/7) Πόθεν   ἡμῖν ἐν ἐρημίᾳ ἄρτοι;
                    Whence is there *for us*   bread in a desert place?

Mt 25:11 (L4/3) Κύριε, κύριε, ἄνοιξον ἡμῖν
                    Lord, lord,   open up *for us*

Lk 24:13 (L8/7) δύο ἐξ αὐτῶν ἦσαν πορευόμενοι εἰς κώμην ᾗ ὄνομα Ἐμμαοῦς
                    two of them were going to a village *to which* the name Emmaus

Phil 1:21 (L8/11) ἐμοὶ γὰρ τὸ ζῆν Χριστός
                    for, *for me*, to live is Christ (i.e., Christ is my life)

Jn 20:21 (L4/16) εἶπεν οὖν αὐτοῖς πάλιν, Εἰρήνη ὑμῖν.
                    he said then *to them* again, Peace *to you*.

(b) The Instrumental

Frequently the means by which or with which the action of the verb is carried out is put into the dative case, sometimes without a preposition, and often with the preposition ἐν. Examples without a preposition:

Mk 1:8 (L5/1)   ἐγω ἐβάπτισα ὑμᾶς   ὕδατι
                  I   baptized you *with water*

Mk 1:26 (L5/2)   καὶ φωνῆσαν φωνῇ μεγάλῃ . . .
               and calling out *with a loud voice* . . .

Mk 5:4   πολλάκις   πέδαις   καὶ ἀλύσεσιν   δεδέσθαι
         often   *with fetters* and *with chains* to have been bound

(c) The Locative

The locative (from the Latin for "place") indicates "rest at" a particular place; it is the case used for "position". Frequently ἐν or some other preposition is also used; occasionally it is without a preposition:

Jn 21:8 (L8/10)   οἱ δὲ ἄλλοι μαθηταὶ τῷ πλοιαρίῳ ἦλθον
               and the other disciples came *in the small boat*

A corresponding temporal use is the locative of point of time:

Mt 17:23 (L8/4)   καὶ τῇ τρίτῃ ἡμέρᾳ ἐγερθήσεται
               and *on the third day* he will be raised

8.5   THE INS AND OUTS OF PREPOSITIONS

8.51 Originally, in the history of the Greek language, the case of the noun was the means of expressing all the relationships within a sentence. As the language developed, a number of adverbs were placed in front of nouns in various cases, to make possible greater precision in stating relationships. This usage became fixed, and the adverbs that were used in this way were called "prepositions" (i.e. in the "pre-position", from the Latin *praeponere*, "to place before").

8.52 In the further development of the language from "Classical Greek" to "Hellenistic Greek" (the koine Greek of the New Testament), three particular developments can be noted:

(a) The increasing use of prepositions, upon which (rather than upon case itself) now rests the major responsibility of expressing relationships clearly, and case functions began to be transferred to prepositions (e.g., "say to . . ." is frequently found in Luke/Acts as πρός plus the accusative, instead of the use of the dative case);

(b) The decrease in the number of cases with which some prepositions would be used — there is a tendency towards using a preposition with only one or, at most, two, cases;

(c) Greek speakers felt free to press additional adverbs into service as prepositions when they wanted them.

8.53 Several prepositions in New Testament Greek can be used with two or with all three of the oblique cases: it is helpful to remember that strictly speaking it is the *case of the noun* which indicates the meaning of the preposition, and not the other way round (though it is still convenient to speak of a preposition governing a noun in the accusative case, etc.).

8.6   THE CASES, MEANINGS, AND FREQUENCIES OF THE PREPOSITIONS

8.61 PREPOSITIONS GOVERNING ALL THREE CASES

1. ἐπί (878 occurrences — 4th in frequency in the New Testament)
    (a) With Accusative (50% of use): across, to, against, on, upon, with
    (b) With Genitive (25%): upon, over, at/in the time of, before
    (c) With Dative (25%): at, by, on, upon, on the basis of

2. παρά (191 — 12th in New Testament frequency)
    Basic meaning: beside. This is then influenced by each case:
    (a) With Accusative (60 times): motion to beside, alongside, near
    (b) With Genitive (79 times): motion from the side of, away from
    (c) With Dative (52 times): rest at, alongside, in the presence of

3. πρός (696 — 5th in New Testament frequency)
    (a) With Accusative (689 times): to, towards, for, with, against
    (b) With Genitive (1 only — Acts 27:34) for, to the advantage of
    (c) With Dative (6 times): nearby, at, beside, on
    (For practical purposes, πρός can virtually be regarded as a preposition governing one case.)

8.62 PREPOSITIONS GOVERNING ACCUSATIVE & GENITIVE CASES

4. διά (666 — 6th in New Testament frequency)
    (a) With Accusative (280 times): because of, on account of
    (b) With Genitive (386 times): through (of place, and of agent)

5. κατά (471 — 8th in New Testament frequency)
    (a) With Accusative (398 times): according to (throughout, during)
    (b) With Genitive (73 times): against, down from

6. μετά (467 — 9th in New Testament frequency)
    (a) With Accusative (103 times): after (of time)
    (b) With Genitive (364 times): with, together with, in company with

7. περί (331 — 10th in New Testament frequency)
    (a) With Accusative (less common): about, around (of place and time)
    (b) With Genitive (extremely common): about, concerning

8. ὑπό (217 — 11th in New Testament frequency)
    (a) With Accusative (50 times): under, underneath, below
    (b) With Genitive (167 times): by (personal agent), at the hands of

9. ὑπέρ (149 — 13th in New Testament frequency)
    (a) With Accusative (19 times): over and above, beyond, more than
    (b) With Genitive (130 times): on behalf of, for the sake of

8.63 PREPOSITIONS GOVERNING THE ACCUSATIVE CASE ONLY

10. εἰς (1753 — 2nd in N.T. frequency): into (to), for (with a view to)

11. ἀνά (13 — 17th in N.T.): up; to each one; between; one at a time

8.64 PREPOSITIONS GOVERNING THE GENITIVE CASE ONLY

12. ἐκ (915 — 3rd in N.T. frequency): out, out of, from within (from)

13. ἀπό (645 — 7th in N.T. frequency): from, away from

14. πρό (47 — 15th in N.T. frequency): before, prior to (usually of time)

15. ἀντί (22 — 16th in N.T. frequency): instead of, in place of, because

16. ἀμφί (-) Not in N.T. as a word, but in compounds: about, on both sides

8.65 PREPOSITIONS GOVERNING THE DATIVE CASE ONLY

17. ἐν (2713 — 1st in N.T. frequency): in, within, among, by means of, with (instrumental)

18. σύν (127 — 14th in N.T. frequency): with, together with, in company with (means the same as μετά with the genitive)

All the above eighteen prepositions can be prefixed to a verb, in the Preposition slot (Slot 1) (#E4.11).

8.66 ADVERBS USED AS PREPOSITIONS (GOVERNING THE GENITIVE)

1. ἐνώπιον (93 times): in front of, in the presence of, before

2. ἔξω (62 times): outside, out of

3. ἔμπροσθεν (48 times): in front of, in the presence of, before

4. χωρίς (41 times): without, apart from

5. ὀπίσω (35 times): after, behind.

6. ἐγγύς (31 times, 10 as preposition): near, close to

8.67 CONJUNCTIONS USED AS PREPOSITIONS (GOVERNING THE GENITIVE)

1. ἕως (145): up to, until, as far as

2. ἄχρι (48): up to, until, as far as

3. μέχρι (20): up to, until, as far as

8.68 There are a dozen or so other words (mostly adverbs) which are used a small number of times each in the New Testament as prepositions, almost always taking the genitive case. These can be noted when encountered.

8.69 CHANGES BEFORE VOWELS

When a preposition that ends in a vowel (other than περί or πρό) occurs before a word commencing with a vowel or is prefixed to a verb commencing with a vowel, the final vowel of that preposition *elides*, and if the final consonant of that preposition is a stop consonant, it will aspirate in front of a following rough breathing (in a compound verb, it will absorb the rough breathing). Where the preposition is a separate word, the elision is marked by an apostrophe, but there is no mark for an elision of a preposition that is part of a compound verb. Thus:

before a:		when a separate preposition smooth breathing	rough breathing	in a compound verb smooth breathing	rough breathing
ἀνά	elides to	ἀν᾽	ἀν᾽	ἀν	ἀν
ἀντί	″	ἀντ᾽	ἀνθ᾽	ἀντ	ἀνθ
ἀπό	″	ἀπ᾽	ἀφ᾽	ἀπ	ἀφ
διά	″	δι᾽	δι᾽	δι	δι
ἐπί	″	ἐπ᾽	ἐφ᾽	ἐπ	ἐφ
κατά	″	κατ᾽	καθ᾽	κατ	καθ
μετά	″	μετ᾽	μεθ᾽	μετ	μεθ
παρά	″	παρ᾽	παρ᾽	παρ	παρ
ὑπό	″	ὑπ᾽	ὑφ᾽	ὑπ	ὑφ
ALSO: ἐκ becomes	ἐξ	ἐξ	ἐξ	ἐξ	ἐξ
BUT περί remains	περί	περί	περι	περι	
AND πρό remains	πρό	πρό	προ	προ	

NOTE that the form of the preposition in a compound is determined according to these rules for each individual form of the verb. Thus ἀπό + ἵστημι becomes ἀφίστημι (Luke 8:13), and in the aorist of this verb ἀπό + ἔστην becomes ἀπέστην (Luke 4:13); and when in this verb ἀπό is followed by an aorist form other than the indicative (i.e., a form which does not begin with a vowel), the elided -o- will reappear: ἀποστῇ (subjunctive, 2 Corinthians 12:8); ἀπόστητε (imperative, Luke 13:27); ἀποστῆναι (infinitive, Hebrews 3:12); ἀποστάς (participle, Acts 19:9).

8.7　INTERRELATIONSHIPS AND USAGES OF THE PREPOSITIONS

8.71 These may be illustrated diagrammatically, thus:

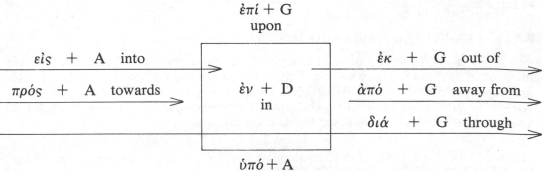

8.72 Instrument, Agent, and Intermediary

Note that: By (= by means of — instrumental) is dative alone or ἐν + dative
By (= the personal agent)　　　　　is ὑπό + genitive
By (= the intermediary)　　　　　　is διά + genitive.

As: Mt 2:15 ἵνα　　πληρωθῇ　τὸ ῥηθεν　　ὑπό κυρίου διὰ τοῦ προφήτου
(L8/1)　in order to fulfil　what was spoken *by* the lord *through* the prophet.

8.73 Time and Case

Length of (extent of) time　　　　　　is expressed by the accusative case.
Time during which (something happened) is expressed by the genitive case.
Point of time when or at which (something happened) is expressed by the dative
case.

8.74 Hellenistic Blurring of Distinctions

It should be noted that the distinction of the basic meaning of the cases (accusative, motion towards or around; genitive, motion through or away from; dative, rest at) was becoming blurred in Hellenistic times, with, in consequence, less precision in the use of some prepositions (e.g., εἰς was sometimes used in the place of ἐν). Additionally, the distinction between πρός and εἰς, and ἀπό and ἐκ respectively, was also less carefully observed in Hellenistic Greek and (in consequence) in some New Testament passages which reflect these Hellenistic blurrings (see also #A4.2).

8.8 THE USE OF THE ARTICLE

8.80 The article ὁ, ἡ, τό has a wide range of usages some of which are similar to English, and some of which have no parallel in English. The most frequent ways in which the article is used are:

8.81 To Indicate That A Noun Is Definite

ὁ ἄνθρωπος is "the man", i.e. a particular man, a man who has already been mentioned or who is already known. This usage parallels the normal English use of the article *the*. It contrasts with the indefinite usage, i.e. a noun without any article (as in John 4:29, Δεῦτε ἴδετε ἄνθρωπον ὃς εἶπέν μοι πάντα ὅσα ἐποίησα, "Come see *a man* who told me everything that I have done"); and with a noun used with τις (as in Luke 10:30, Ἄνθρωπός τις κατέβαινεν ἀπὸ Ἰερουσαλὴμ εἰς Ἰεριχώ, "A (certain) man went down from Jerusalem to Jericho", which is equivalent to, "There was once a man who went down", etc.).

The article is used with a noun when a genitive pronoun is also used on occasions when the noun is definite. Contrast:

ὁ δοῦλός σου "your slave", where this is definite (i.e., "the slave whom you know I mean", or, "the only slave you have")

δοῦλός σου   "a slave of yours", "one of your slaves".

It is quite common for the article before a noun to have the force of a personal pronoun without the latter having to be stated, especially when the noun in question refers to something closely related to one such as a part of the body. See Luke 15:11 (L5/10), where τῷ πατρί = to his father; and Mark 6:5 (L6/13), where τὰς χεῖρας = his hands.

8.82(a) To Indicate A Class

οἱ ἄνθρωποι means *man* as a class, as distinct from the beasts, from angels, or from God.

8.82(b) With Abstract Nouns and Nouns Indicating Qualities

Greek frequently (but not always) uses the article with nouns such as "grace", "greed", "sin", "law", "flesh", "life", "death" etc. In most cases this article is not translated into English, but in some instances the English will require it, e.g. "the grace given to me" (Romans 12:3, 6, etc.), "the life of God" (Ephesians 4:18). On occasions, in an expression with a genitive the Greek omits the article where English requires it: e.g. Luke 5:17, καὶ δύναμις κυρίου ἦν εἰς τὸ ἰᾶσθαι αὐτόν, "and *the* power of *the* Lord was with him to heal" — it does not mean "*a* power of *a* lord"; Romans 15:13, ἐν δυνάμει πνεύματος ἁγίου, "by *the* power of *the* Holy Spirit".

8.82(c) With Names

Sometimes the article with a name has the same meaning as it has with a common noun: ὁ Ἰωάννης, the John who has previously been mentioned. Usually the use or absence of the article with a name appears, however, to be a matter of the author's stylistic preference.

8.83(a) With μέν and δέ

The article without a noun but followed by μέν and then subsequently repeated followed by δέ, means "the one . . . the other . . .", or "one . . . another . . .". I Corinthians 7:7, ("Each person has his own gift from God), one has this gift, another has that" (NIV): ὁ μὲν οὕτως, ὁ δὲ οὕτως. The plural οἱ μέν . . . οἱ δέ . . . means "some . . ., and others . . .". Acts 14:4, καὶ οἱ μὲν ἦσαν σὺν τοῖς Ἰουδαίοις οἱ δὲ σὺν τοῖς ἀποστόλοις, "and some were with the Jews and others with the apostles".

(This same type of construction with μέν and δέ is found with the relative pronoun as an alternative to the article.)

8.83(b) With δέ

The article in the nominative with δέ is used for the continuation of a narrative (and thus commonly indicates the end of direct speech). This use means that ὁ δέ frequently denotes a change of speaker. It will normally be translated, "And he . . ." An excellent example of this usage is the conversation between Jesus and the lawyer in Luke 10:25-37, where most of the changes of speaker are indicated by ὁ δὲ εἶπεν, "and the other man said . . ." Similarly, ἡ δέ means "and she", τὸ δέ "and it", τὰ δέ "and the things", etc.

8.84(a) With Adjective and Noun

The details of this use and its meaning have already been discussed in Lesson Seven (see #7.2).

8.84(b) With Adjectives

The article may be used in front of an adjective, and gives that adjective the force of a noun: I Peter 4:18, ὁ δίκαιος, the righteous man; Matthew 13:38 (L2/24), οἱ υἱοὶ τοῦ πονηροῦ, the sons of the Evil One (the devil); Philemon 14, τὸ ἀγαθόν σου, your good deed; James 2:6, οἱ πλούσιοι, the rich; Revelation 20:5 (L7/29), οἱ λοιποὶ τῶν νεκρῶν, the remainder of the dead (both words are adjectives used as nouns).

8.84(c) With Adverbs

The article may be used with an adverb in a way similar to its use with an adjective, so that the adverb is then acting as a noun. Ephesians 2:17 (L6/10), . . . εἰρήνην ὑμῖν τοῖς μακρὰν καὶ εἰρήνην τοῖς ἐγγύς — literally, ". . . peace to you the far away, and peace to the near", that is, ". . . peace to you who were far away, and peace to those who were near".

8.85 With Genitives

In this construction, usually plural, it means "the people of" (e.g. I Corinthians 15:23, οἱ τοῦ Χριστοῦ, "the people of Christ", those who belong to Christ) or, according to gender, "the things of" (e.g. Luke 20:25, τὰ Καίσαρος . . ., τὰ τοῦ θεοῦ, "the things of Caesar . . ., the things of God"). Often the article used in this way (and either singular or plural, according to the sense required) can mean "the wife/daughter/son of . . .", with the reader left to supply the correct relationship: e.g. John 19:25; 21:2; Luke 3:23-38. (See also #8.44a.)

8.86 With Prepositional Phrases

In this construction, the article will usually be translated as "those", as in Luke 9:32, Πέτρος καὶ οἱ σὺν αὐτῷ, Peter and those with him, and Mark 1:36, Σίμων καὶ οἱ μετ' αὐτοῦ, Simon and those with him.

8.87 With the Infinitive

The article may be used before an infinitive, treating it as a noun. Often this is used as a way of indicating the case that the infinitive is to be regarded as having. This is called the "articular infinitive". There are a number of special uses of the articular infinitive, which should be noted when encountered. (They are covered in the set readings of the Intermediate Course.)

8.88 With The Participle

This construction means, if active, "the one who (does or suffers the action of the verb)" or (if neuter) "the thing that is/was (doing the action); if passive, it means the thing that was done or the person to whom it was done. Thus Mt. 13:37 (L2/24) ὁ σπείρων τὸ καλὸν σπέρμα, "The one who sows the good seed"; Mt. 2:17 (L4/19) τὸ ῥηθὲν διὰ Ἡσαΐου τοῦ προφήτου, "the thing spoken by Isaiah the prophet", i.e., "what was spoken by Isaiah the prophet".

8.89 With A Quotation or Thought

A group of words which are a single entity in some way (such as a quotation, a proverb, a saying) can be introduced by the neuter article and treated as a connected whole. So Mark 9:23, τὸ Εἰ δύνῃ, "the (idea or thought of saying), 'If you can!'"

8.9 THE RECIPROCAL PRONOUN

8.91 The reciprocal pronoun means: "one another". In the nature of the case it has no nominative, and is only found in the plural.

8.92 There are no feminine or neuter forms in the New Testament, only the masculine forms, which are:

Acc. ἀλλήλους
Gen. ἀλλήλων
Dat. ἀλλήλοις

ASSIGNMENTS ON LESSON EIGHT

1. There are no new forms to be learnt this Lesson. **(a)** Reread the grammar, and revise the case endings for the Declensions; **(b)** Note the various prepositions in use, and the cases they take, and the differences in meaning.

2. Read and translate literally Selections 1 to 20 (below).

3. If time permits, read a Commentary on the Greek text of Selections 17-20.

4. Do a quick preliminary reading of Lesson Nine.

SELECTIONS FROM THE GREEK NEW TESTAMENT

1. ὁ δὲ ἐγερθεὶς παρέλαβεν τὸ παιδίον καὶ τὴν μητέρα αὐτοῦ νυκτὸς καὶ ἀνεχώρησεν εἰς Αἴγυπτον, καὶ ἦν ἐκεῖ ἕως τῆς τελευτῆς Ἡρῴδου· ἵνα πληρωθῇ τὸ ῥηθὲν ὑπὸ κυρίου διὰ τοῦ προφήτου λέγοντος, Ἐξ Αἰγύπτου ἐκάλεσα τόν υἱόν μου. (ΚΑΤΑ ΜΑΘΘΑΙΟΝ 2:14-15.)

2. μακάριοι οἱ εἰρηνοποιοί, ὅτι αὐτοὶ υἱοὶ θεοῦ κληθήσονται. (ΚΑΤΑ ΜΑΘΘΑΙΟΝ 5:9.)

3. Καὶ μεθ' ἡμέρας ἓξ παραλαμβάνει ὁ Ἰησοῦς τὸν Πέτρον καὶ Ἰάκωβον καὶ Ἰωάννην τὸν ἀδελφὸν αὐτοῦ, καὶ ἀναφέρει αὐτοὺς εἰς ὄρος ὑψηλὸν κατ' ἰδίαν. καὶ μετεμορφώθη ἔμπροσθεν αὐτῶν, καὶ ἔλαμψεν τὸ πρόσωπον αὐτοῦ ὡς ὁ ἥλιος, τὰ δὲ ἱμάτια αὐτοῦ ἐγένετο λευκὰ ὡς τὸ φῶς. καὶ ἰδοὺ ὤφθη αὐτοῖς Μωϋσῆς καὶ Ἡλίας συλλαλοῦντες μετ' αὐτοῦ. ἀποκριθεὶς δὲ ὁ Πέτρος εἶπεν τῷ Ἰησοῦ, Κύριε, καλόν ἐστιν ἡμᾶς ὧδε εἶναι. (ΚΑΤΑ ΜΑΘΘΑΙΟΝ 17:1-4.)

4. Συστρεφομένων δὲ αὐτῶν ἐν τῇ Γαλιλαίᾳ εἶπεν αὐτοῖς ὁ Ἰησοῦς, Μέλλει ὁ υἱὸς τοῦ ἀνθρώπου παραδίδοσθαι εἰς χεῖρας ἀνθρώπων, καὶ ἀποκτενοῦσιν αὐτόν, καὶ τῇ τρίτῃ ἡμέρᾳ ἐγερθήσεται. (ΚΑΤΑ ΜΑΘΘΑΙΟΝ 17:22-23.)

5. Καὶ ἔρχονται Σαδδουκαῖοι πρὸς αὐτόν, οἵτινες λέγουσιν ἀνάστασιν μὴ εἶναι, καὶ ἐπηρώτων αὐτὸν λέγοντες, Διδάσκαλε, Μωϋσῆς ἔγραψεν ἡμῖν ὅτι ἐάν τινος ἀδελφὸς ἀποθάνῃ καὶ καταλίπῃ γυναῖκα καὶ μὴ ἀφῇ τέκνον, ἵνα λάβῃ ὁ ἀδελφὸς αὐτοῦ τὴν γυναῖκα καὶ ἐξαναστήσῃ σπέρμα τῷ ἀδελφῷ. (ΚΑΤΑ ΜΑΡΚΟΝ 12:18-19.)

Selections continue on page 122

EXPLANATORY NOTES

MAKE A TRANSLATION of each Selection on your own, first of all, and then use these Explanatory Notes and your other tools to fill in the gaps.

1. ὁ δέ = "and he": see #8.83(b) ■ ἐγερθείς → *ἐγείρω raise up (aor. ptc pass., because intrans.: get up) ■ παρ-έ-λαβ-εν → παραλαμβάνω take (with one) (3sg aor²) ■ *παιδίον child ■ νυκτός → *νύξ gen. of time within which: by night ■ ἀν-ε-χώρη-σεν → ἀναχωρέω go away ■ Αἴγυπτος Egypt ■ τελευτή end (=death) ■ πληρωθῇ → *πληρόω fulfil (3sg aor. pass. subj.) ■ ῥηθέν → *λέγω (nom. neut. sg aor. ptc pass.: see #8.88) ■ ἐ-κάλε-σα → *καλέω call (1sg aor.).

2. εἰρηνο-ποιός peacemaker ■ κλη-θή-σονται → *καλέω (3pl fut. pass).

3. ἕξ six ■ παραλαμβάνω Sel. 1 ■ ἀνα-φέρω lead up ■ ὑψηλός high ■ κατ᾽ ἰδίαν on their own, privately ■ μετ-ε-μορφώ-θη → μεταμορφόομαι be transformed (3sg aor. pass.) ■ ἔμπροσθεν in front of ■ ἔλαμψεν → λάμπω shine (3sg aor.) ■ ἥλιος sun ■ *ἱμάτιον garment, clothing ■ λευκός white, shining ■ ἐγένετο → *γίνομαι (3sg aor²; re sg, see #A3.67) ■ ὤφθη → *ὁράω (3sg aor. pass. = appear) ■ συλ-λαλέω (=συν-λαλέω) talk with ■ καλόν etc.: #8.43(c).

4. συ-στρεφο-μένων → συστρέφω gather around, together (pres ptc pass — with αὐτῶν, gen. absolute, = while they were gathered together) ■ *μέλλω to be about to ■ παρα-δίδοσθαι → *παραδίδωμι deliver up, hand over, pass on (pres. inf. pass.) ■ ἀπο-κτεν-οῦσιν → *ἀποκτείνω kill (3pl fut.) ■ τρίτος third ■ ἐγερ-θήσεται → *ἐγείρω raise up (3sg fut. pass., = will be raised up, or, rise again).

5. ὅστις who (used rather than ὅς because antecedent Σαδδουκαῖοι is without an article) ■ ἀνάστασις resurrection; see #8.43(c) ■ ἐπ-ηρώτων → *ἐπ-ερωτάω ask (a question) (3pl impf - contract verb) ■ *διδάσκαλος teacher ■ ἔγραψεν → *γράφω (3sg aor.) ■ *ἐάν if ■ ἀπο-θάνῃ → *ἀποθνῄσκω die (3sg aor² sub.) ■ κατα-λίπῃ → καταλείπω leave (behind) (3sg aor² subj.) ■ γυναῖκα → *γυνή (acc. sg) ■ ἀφ-ῇ → *ἀφίημι leave (3sg aor³ subj.) ■ *τέκνον child ■ ἵνα λάβῃ (→ *λαμβάνω) = let him take (3sg aor² subj.) ■ ἐξ-ανα-στήσῃ → ἐξανίστημι raise up (3sg aor³ subj.) ■ σπέρμα seed = offspring.

6. ἐγένοντο δὲ φίλοι ὅ τε Ἡρῴδης καὶ ὁ Πιλᾶτος ἐν αὐτῇ τῇ ἡμέρᾳ μετ᾽ ἀλλήλων. (ΚΑΤΑ ΛΟΥΚΑΝ 23:12.)

7. Καὶ ἰδοὺ δύο ἐξ αὐτῶν ἐν αὐτῇ τῇ ἡμέρᾳ ἦσαν πορευόμενοι εἰς κώμην ἀπέχουσαν σταδίους ἐξήκοντα ἀπὸ Ἰερουσαλήμ, ᾗ ὄνομα Ἐμμαοῦς, καὶ αὐτοὶ ὡμίλουν πρὸς ἀλλήλους περὶ πάντων τῶν συμβεβηκότων τούτων. καὶ ἐγένετο ἐν τῷ ὁμιλεῖν αὐτοὺς καὶ συζητεῖν καὶ αὐτὸς Ἰησοῦς ἐγγίσας συνεπορεύετο αὐτοῖς. (ΚΑΤΑ ΛΟΥΚΑΝ 24:13-15.)

8. ὡς οὖν ἦλθον πρὸς αὐτὸν οἱ Σαμαρῖται, ἠρώτων αὐτὸν μεῖναι παρ᾽ αὐτοῖς· καὶ ἔμεινεν ἐκεῖ δύο ἡμέρας. (ΚΑΤΑ ΙΩΑΝΝΗΝ 4:40.)

9. Ὅτε οὖν ἔνιψεν τοὺς πόδας αὐτῶν ἔλαβεν τὰ ἱμάτια αὐτοῦ καὶ ἀνέπεσεν πάλιν, εἶπεν αὐτοῖς, Γινώσκετε τί πεποίηκα ὑμῖν; ὑμεῖς φωνεῖτέ με Ὁ διδάσκαλος καὶ Ὁ κύριος, καὶ καλῶς λέγετε, εἰμὶ γάρ. εἰ οὖν ἐγὼ ἔνιψα ὑμῶν τοὺς πόδας ὁ κύριος καὶ ὁ διδάσκαλος, καὶ ὑμεῖς ὀφείλετε ἀλλήλων νίπτειν τοὺς πόδας. (ΚΑΤΑ ΙΩΑΝΝΗΝ 13:12-14.)

10. οἱ δὲ ἄλλοι μαθηταὶ τῷ πλοιαρίῳ ἦλθον, οὐ γὰρ ἦσαν μακρὰν ἀπὸ τῆς γῆς ἀλλὰ ὡς ἀπὸ πηχῶν διακοσίων, σύροντες τὸ δίκτυον τῶν ἰχθύων. (ΚΑΤΑ ΙΩΑΝΝΗΝ 21:8.)

11. ὡς πάντοτε καὶ νῦν μεγαλυνθήσεται Χριστὸς ἐν τῷ σώματί μου, εἴτε διὰ ζωῆς εἴτε διὰ θανάτου. ἐμοὶ γὰρ τὸ ζῆν Χριστὸς καὶ τὸ ἀποθανεῖν κέρδος. (ΠΡΟΣ ΦΙΛΙΠΠΗΣΙΟΥΣ 1:20-21.)

12. ὁ νικῶν δώσω αὐτῷ καθίσαι μετ᾽ ἐμοῦ ἐν τῷ θρόνῳ μου, ὡς κἀγὼ ἐνίκησα καὶ ἐκάθισα μετὰ τοῦ πατρός μου ἐν τῷ θρόνῳ αὐτοῦ. (ΑΠΟΚΑΛΥΨΙΣ ΙΩΑΝΝΟΥ 3:21.)

13. καὶ οἱ πρεσβύτεροι ἔπεσαν καὶ προσεκύνησαν. (ΑΠΟΚΑΛΥΨΙΣ ΙΩΑΝΝΟΥ 5:14.)

14. καὶ ἤκουσαν φωνῆς μεγάλης ἐκ τοῦ οὐρανοῦ λεγούσης αὐτοῖς, Ἀνάβατε ὧδε· καὶ ἀνέβησαν εἰς τὸν οὐρανὸν ἐν τῇ νεφέλῃ, καὶ ἐθεώρησαν αὐτοὺς οἱ ἐχθροὶ αὐτῶν. (ΑΠΟΚΑΛΥΨΙΣ ΙΩΑΝΝΟΥ 11:12.)

15. τίς οὐ μὴ φοβηθῇ, κύριε, καὶ δοξάσει τὸ ὄνομά σου; ὅτι μόνος ὅσιος, ὅτι πάντα τὰ ἔθνη ἥξουσιν καὶ προσκυνήσουσιν ἐνώπιόν σου. (ΑΠΟΚΑΛΥΨΙΣ ΙΩΑΝΝΟΥ 15:4.)

16. Κἀγὼ Ἰωάννης ὁ ἀκούων καὶ βλέπων ταῦτα. καὶ ὅτε ἤκουσα καὶ ἔβλεψα, ἔπεσα προσκυνῆσαι ... Ὁ καιρὸς γὰρ ἐγγύς ἐστιν ... Ἰδοὺ ἔρχομαι ταχύ, καὶ ὁ μισθός μου μετ᾽ ἐμοῦ, ἀποδοῦναι ἑκάστῳ ὡς τὸ ἔργον ἐστιν αὐτοῦ. ἐγὼ τὸ Ἄλφα καὶ τὸ Ὦ, ὁ πρῶτος καὶ ὁ ἔσχατος, ἡ ἀρχὴ καὶ τὸ τέλος. (ΑΠΟΚΑΛΥΨΙΣ ΙΩΑΝΝΟΥ 22:8-13.)

17. Matthew 10:34-39
18. Matthew 14:13-21
19. Mark 3:20-35
20. John 1:14-18

Translate these passages from your Greek New Testament, making the fullest use of your Analysis.

6. αὐτὸς ὁ = that very ■ ἐγένοντο → *γίνομαι (3pl aor²) ■ φίλος friend ■ *τε both/and (sometimes left untranslated).

7. ἦσαν πορευόμενοι were walking (pres. ptc, → πορεύομαι, + impf εἰμι) ■ κώμη village ■ ἀπ-έχουσαν → ἀπέχω be distant ■ στάδιοι stades (a measure of distance) ■ ἐξήκοντα sixty ■ ᾗ to which (dative of giving a name, = which was called) ■ ὡμίλουν → ὁμιλέω converse ■ συμ-βε-βη-κ-ότων → συμβαίνω happen (gen. pl pf ptc = things that had happened) ■ ἐν τῷ + inf. = while ■ ὁμιλεῖν → ὁμιλέω (inf.) ■ συ-ζητεῖν → συ-ζητέω discuss (inf.) ■ αὐτός self ■ ἐγγίσας → ἐγγίζω come up to (aor. ptc) ■ συν-ε-πορεύετο → συμ-πορεύομαι walk with (impf).

8. ἠρώτων → *ἐρωτάω ask (3pl impf) ■ μεῖναι → *μένω remain (aor. inf.).

9. ἔνιψεν → νίπτω wash ■ πόδας → *πούς foot ■ ἀν-έ-πεσεν → ἀναπίπτω sit at table ■ πε-ποίη-κα → *ποιέω ■ καλῶς well ■ εἰ if ■ ὀφείλω ought ■ *ἀλλήλους one another.

10. πλοιάριον boat ■ πῆχυς cubit ■ διακόσιοι two hundred ■ σύροντες → σύρω drag (ptc) ■ δίκτυον net ■ ἰχθύς a fish.

11. πάντοτε always ■ *νῦν now ■ μεγαλυν-θήσεται → μεγαλύνω magnify (3sg fut. pass.) ■ *εἴτε . . . εἴτε . . . whether . . . or . . . ■ κέρδος gain.

12. νικάω overcome ■ δώσω → δίδωμι ■ καθίζω sit (down).

13. *πρεσβύτερος elder ■ ἔπεσαν → *πίπτω fall (3pl, aor¹ variant of aor² verb) ■ προσ-ε-κύνη-σαν → *προσκυνέω worship (3pl aorist).

14. ἀνά-βα-τε → *ἀναβαίνω come up (2 pl aor³ impv) ■ ἐ-θεώρη-σαν → *θεωρέω watch (3 pl aor) ■ ἐχθρός enemy.

15. φοβη-θῇ → *φοβέομαι fear (3sg aor dep. pass. subj) ■ δοξά-σ-ει → *δοκάζω glorify (3sg fut) ■ *μόνος only ■ ὅσιος holy ■ ἥξουσιν → ἥκω come (3pl fut) ■ ἐνώπιον before.

16. *ὅτε when ■ ἔπεσα → *πίπτω (1sg) see Sel 13 ■ *καιρός time ■ ταχύ soon ■ μισθός reward, pay ■ ἀπο-δοῦ-ναι → ἀποδίδωμι render (aor³ inf) ■ *ἕκαστος each ■ *ἔσχατος last ■ τέλος end.

LESSON NINE

ADVERBS; COMPARISON; VERB CONJUGATION

9.1 CORRESPONDING ADVERBS

9.11 Just as Greek had a system of corresponding adjectives/pronouns (see #7.1) so also it had a system of corresponding adverbs. This had been more complete in classical times, but some of the parts had fallen out of colloquial use in Hellenistic Greek (much as our English patterns "where, whence, whither", "there, thence, thither" and "here, hence, hither" have contracted down to just "where", "there" and "here" and the other forms, if used at all, have a somewhat archaic flavour).

9.12 In particular there is less use of the indefinite forms (which are enclitic — that is, they throw their accent on the word preceding them: see #E6.3).

9.13 The corresponding adverbs are:

TYPE	INTERROGATIVE	INDEFINITE	DEMONSTRATIVE	RELATIVE
Time	πότε; when?	ποτέ at some time	τότε then	ὅτε when ὁπότε when
Place	ποῦ where?	πού somewhere	ἐκεῖ there ἐνθάδε here	οὗ where ὅπου where
Source	πόθεν; whence?	ποθέν from some place	ἐκεῖθεν thence ἐνθέν from here ἐντεῦθεν from here	ὅθεν from where (ὁπόθεν) from where
Manner	πῶς; how?	πώς somehow	οὕτως thus, in this way	ὡς as, in which way ὅπως in order that
Frequency	ποσάκις; how often?	—	πολλάκις often, frequently	ὁσάκις whenever, as often as

9.2 FORMATION OF ADVERBS: THE REGULAR PATTERN

9.21 Most of the common adverbs of the New Testament are the same in form as the corresponding adjective in the genitive plural, but with -ς instead of -ν.

9.22

Adjective		Its Genitive Plural	Adverb	
ἀληθής	true	ἀληθῶν	ἀληθῶς	truly
δίκαιος	righteous, just	δικαίων	δικαίως	justly
κακός	bad	κακῶν	κακῶς	badly
καλός	good	καλῶν	καλῶς	well
ὅμοιος	like	ὁμοίων	ὁμοίως	similarly

124

9.23 But also note these forms:

οὗτος	this	τούτων		οὕτως	thus
πρῶτος	first	πρώτων		πρῶτον	firstly
ἐκεῖνος	that	ἐκείνων		ἐκεῖ	there
ἐκ/ἐξ	out of (preposition)	—		ἔξω	outside

9.3 COMPARISON OF ADJECTIVES AND ADVERBS

9.31 The standard or basic form of an adjective or adverb is referred to as the *positive degree*. There are two other forms which it can have: it can be used in the *comparative degree* (strictly speaking, comparison of two instances or examples), and the *superlative degree* (strictly speaking, used of an instance or example that exceeds two or more others). These correspond with the sequence *great, greater, greatest; short, shorter, shortest* in English, where the comparative and superlative forms are made by the addition of the suffixes *-er* and *-est*. For some English words, however, a change in the word is made: cf. *good, better, best; bad, worse, worst; little, less, least.*

9.32 There are the same two types of comparatives and superlatives in Greek: those formed by adding a suffix to the positive stem (the more common), and those formed by a change in the form of the word itself.

9.33 The comparative suffix is -τερος, and the superlative suffix is -τατος. If the second-last vowel of the word is short, then the last vowel will become long in the comparative and superlative stem, before the ending.

> Thus: ὑψηλός, ὑψηλότερος, ὑψηλότατος high, higher, highest
> σοφός, σοφώτερος, σοφώτατος wise, wiser, wisest

9.34 The forms in -τερος decline like ἅγιος, the forms in -τατος decline like καλός (see Appendix D, #D4.1 and D4.2).

9.35 These are the adjectives which use different word forms (those in brackets are not found in the New Testament):

Positive		Comparative		Superlative	
ἀγαθός	good	(βελτίων)		(βέλτιστος)	
,,	,,	κρείσσων	better	κράτιστος	most excellent
κακός	bad	χείρων	worse	—	
,,	,,	ἥσσων	worse, less	—	
μέγας	great	μείζων	greater	μέγιστος	greatest
μικρός	little	μικρότερος	less	—	
,,	,,	ἐλάσσων	less	ἐλάχιστος	least
πολύς	much, many	πλείων	more	πλεῖστος	most
—		—		ἔσχατος	last

Comparatives in -ων decline like ἄφρων (see Appendix D, #D4.8).

9.36 The comparative of an adverb is the *neuter singular* of the corresponding comparative adjective. The superlative of an adverb is the *neuter plural* of the corresponding superlative adjective.

9.37 These are the adverbs which use different forms in the comparative and superlative degrees (those in brackets are not in the New Testament):

ἐγγύς	near	ἐγγύτερον	nearer	ἔγγιστα	nearest
εὖ	well	βέλτιον	very well	(βέλτιστα)	
”	”	κρεῖσσον	better	—	
ἡδέως	gladly	(ἥδιον)		ἥδιστα	most gladly
κακῶς	badly	ἧσσον	worse, less	(ἥκιστα)	
καλῶς	well	κάλλιον	better	(κάλλιστα)	
(μάλα)		μᾶλλον	more	μάλιστα	most of all
πέραν	across	περαιτέρω	further	—	
πολύ	much	πλεῖον	more	(πλεῖστα)	
ταχέως	quickly	τάχιον	more quickly	τάχιστα	most quickly

9.38 A comparative may be followed by a genitive of comparison, or by ἤ, "than", in which instance the things being compared will have the same case.

9.39 The superlative forms of adjective and adverb are rarely used in the New Testament, and when they do occur they are more likely to have what is called an "elative" sense, i.e., they mean "very" (or something similar), than they are to have a strict superlative sense. Often, when the superlative is meant, the comparative form is used; and on frequent occasions when a comparative meaning is intended, the positive form is used. E.g.:

Mk 9:45 καλόν ἐστίν σε εἰσελθεῖν εἰς τὴν ζωὴν χωλὸν ἤ ... κτλ.*
better it is for you to enter into   life lame than ... etc.

Mk 14:21 (L9/9)καλὸν αὐτῷ εἰ οὐκ ἐγεννήθη ὁ ἄνθρωπος ἐκεῖνος.
better for him if not   born   that man.

Clearly here καλόν has the comparative sense, "better", rather than "good", so that these sentences do not mean, "It is good for you to enter into life lame than ... (etc.)", or "It would be good for that man if he had not been born." It is wise to bear this type of usage in mind when translating.

9.4 GREEK VERB CONJUGATIONS

9.41 In the course of the previous Lessons we have encountered most of the Greek verb system. In this Lesson we will complete the building of the framework, and fill in more fully some of the details.

9.42 A *conjugation* is a group of verbs which share the common feature that they *conjugate* one or more of their tenses in the same way (allowing for phonemic changes due to the last letter of the stem interacting with the suffix). On the basis of this

*κτλ is the abbreviation for καὶ τὰ λοιπά, = "and the rest", equivalent to English "etc."

definition, there are three conjugations in Greek, as there are three different patterns of conjugation for the aorist active, and the choice of pattern of conjugation that a given verb will follow is not predictable upon the basis of any *phonemic* features such as what the final letter of the stem is, but simply happens to be a function of that particular verb.

9.43 The three conjugations which can be recognized on this basis are:

First Conjugation: Those verbs which in the aorist active add -α-, either alone or with another letter, to their stem (these aorists are called "first aorists"). For paradigm, see #4.21.

Second Conjugation: Those verbs which in the aorist active add -ο- (before nasals) and -ε- (otherwise) to their stem (these aorists are called "second aorists"). For paradigm, see #3.81.

Third Conjugation: Those verbs which in the aorist active add their pronoun (person/number) endings directly to the verb stem (these verbs are sometimes called "-μι verbs" as most of them have their lexical form ending in -μι rather than in -ω, but it is clearer, and therefore preferable, to refer to them as "third aorists"). For paradigm, see #7.43.

9.44 First and Second Conjugation verbs both have lexical forms in -ω, and all but four Third Conjugation words have lexical forms in -μι, so that there is only a two-way contrast of conjugation in the present tense. This has led some scholars to classify Greek verbs into only two conjugations, an -ω conjugation and an -μι conjugation. However this not only fails to take account of the difference in conjugation between first and second aorists but also obscures the important distinction relating to how the verbs of these two conjugations are formed: First Conjugation verbs build their verb system upon their present stem while Second Conjugations verbs build their verb system upon their aorist stem. Other scholars yet again do not accept the classification of the Greek verb into conjugations at all, but regard all Greek verbs as belonging to a single or unitary conjugation. This view must involve a redefining of "conjugation", because if it means "a pattern of conjugating", then it simply is not true that all Greek verbs belong to the one conjugation, because they do NOT all follow the one pattern of conjugating.

9.45 The situation is further complicated by the fact that a number of -μι verbs (i.e. verbs which are Third Conjugation in the present tense) change over and follow the first system of conjugation in the aorist. On top of that, some verbs are found in the New Testament (and koine Greek generally) with both First and Second Conjugation forms in use side by side, while others are found with both First and Third (-μι) Conjugation forms in use: this being due to a tendency in the language for both second aorists and -μι forms to drop out of use and give way to First Conjugation (-ω) forms.

9.46 The clearest way of handling a complex (and changing) language situation of this kind — and the way that is followed here — is to give full recognition to the different conjugation patterns that do exist, illustrate them by means of selected verbs which follow in a regular way those different conjugation patterns, and describe the departures from these regular patterns that are to be observed.

9.47 The great majority of Greek verbs belong to the First Conjugation, and those which follow the Second or Third Conjugation in the New Testament are only a small — though important — minority: in the New Testament there are just 34 verbs (counting each simplex verb and its compounds as a single verb) which have second aorists and are thus to be classified as Second Conjugation, and a total of only 36 verbs which have Third Conjugation forms, 32 of which have -$\mu\iota$ in the present tense (or, if deponent, come from an -$\mu\iota$ root) and four of which have -ω in the present tense but follow the Third Conjugation in the aorist. A number of these Second and Third Conjugation verbs occur only once or twice altogether in the New Testament. Many of the more frequently-occurring ones have forms that vary between or are selected from both the Second Conjugation and the First Conjugation, or the Third Conjugation and the First Conjugation.

9.48 Apart from these 70 verbs in the Second and Third Conjugations, the remainder of the 1000 New Testament verbs take regular First Conjugation endings throughout. Many First Conjugation verbs are irregular in that they do not form their stems for their different tenses in a way that is predictable from the phonemic rules; however, once the stem of a tense is known, they conjugate that tense in a completely regular manner.

9.49 First Conjugation verbs fall into nine different classes, with separate paradigms, as a result of the influence of the final letter of their stem upon the endings which are added. (These are set out in #9.7.)

9.5   THE FORMATION OF THE TENSE STEMS

9.51 A Greek verb is constructed of *a lexal* (the *lexical morph*, which contains the verb's basic semantic information i.e. its *lexical meaning*) together with various *affixes* (*prefixes, infixes* and *suffixes*) which are *grammatical morphs* and which indicate the *grammatical meaning* of the verb for the particular sentence in which it is being used, i.e. they indicate person, number, tense, mode, and voice.

9.52 For some Greek verbs the *root* or *basic stem* upon which it constructs its inflectional system is the *durative verb stem* (i.e. the verb system is constructed upon the basis of the present tense forms, and a punctiliar morph is added in forming the aorist). For other verbs the basic stem is the *punctiliar verb stem* (i.e. the verb system is constructed upon the basis of the aorist tense forms, and a durative morph is added in forming the present).

9.53 There are some verbs which add to their basic stem both a durative morph to form the present, and a punctiliar morph to form the aorist; but most verbs add only one or the other.

9.54 The stem for each tense is known as the *tense stem*. There are three patterns which underlie the formation of the tense stem systems of Greek verbs. These patterns (and examples of each) are:

9.55 PATTERN 1: The present stem consists of the verb stem together with the neutral morph (and sometimes with an additional phoneme or so in it as a durative morph), and the aorist stem is formed from the verb stem by adding the punctiliar morph, that is **(a)** -$\iota.\alpha$ for a basic stem ending in -ε- plus a liquid, **(b)** -α for other liquids, and **(c)** -$\sigma\alpha$ in all other cases (see #4.25, 4.35, 4.36). The resultant aorist is known as a *first aorist*, and follows the first pattern of aorist conjugation. The verbs which follow this pattern of aorist conjugation comprise the **First Conjugation.**

9.56 PATTERN 2: The aorist stem consists of the verb stem together with the neutral morph, and the resultant aorist is known as a *second aorist* and follows the second pattern of aorist conjugation The verbs which follow this pattern of aorist conjugation comprise the **Second Conjugation.** The present stem is formed by the addition of one or more phonemes as a durative morph. In most cases the future stem is formed from the basic (aorist) stem in the regular way in accordance with the rules (see #4.23, 4.24) by adding -ε- to liquid stems and -σ- to other stems, but some irregularities can be found. The additions to the verb stem to form the present stem require to be individually noted.

9.57 PATTERN 3: The aorist stem consists of the verb stem without addition, to which the **Third Conjugation** aorist endings are added directly (if the stem ends in a short vowel, this is usually lengthened when the endings are added — cf. #4.54). The present stem is formed by the affixing of a durative morph, and to this stem the Third Conjugation present and imperfect endings are then added. The Third Conjugation lexical-form ending is -$\mu\iota$ and therefore this conjugation is frequently known as the -$\mu\iota$ Conjugation. It is to be noted that some verbs are Third Conjugation in the present/imperfect tense flexions, and First Conjugation in the aorist (i.e., take -$\sigma\alpha$), while four verbs (-$\beta\alpha\acute{\iota}\nu\omega$, $\gamma\iota\nu\acute{\omega}\sigma\kappa\omega$, $\delta\acute{\upsilon}\nu\omega$, $\phi\acute{\upsilon}\omega$) are First Conjugation in the present/imperfect and Third Conjugation in the aorist.

9.58 The clearest way of identifying the verb stem (and thus finding the basic form of a verb) is to compare the second person plural of the present and aorist active imperatives. The derived tense will be seen to contain the verb stem together with the durative or punctiliar aspect morph (as the case may be) and, where, appropriate, the neutral morph.

9.59 Examples of the different verb categories (durative and punctiliar aspect morphs underlined):

FIRST CONJUGATION	Lexical Form	Meaning	PRESENT Impv.	AORIST Impv.
liquid: add -α	$\sigma\acute{\upsilon}\rho\omega$	drag	$\sigma\acute{\upsilon}\rho$-$\varepsilon$-$\tau\varepsilon$	$\sigma\acute{\upsilon}\rho$-$\underline{\alpha}$-$\tau\varepsilon$
-ε- + liquid: add -$\iota.\alpha$	$\mu\acute{\varepsilon}\nu\omega$	remain	$\mu\acute{\varepsilon}\nu$-$\varepsilon$-$\tau\varepsilon$	$\mu\varepsilon\acute{\iota}\nu$-$\underline{\alpha}$-$\tau\varepsilon$
other cases: add -$\sigma\alpha$	$\lambda\acute{\upsilon}\omega$	loose	$\lambda\acute{\upsilon}$-ε-$\tau\varepsilon$	$\lambda\acute{\upsilon}$-$\underline{\sigma\alpha}$-$\tau\varepsilon$

SECOND CONJUGATION				
doubling λ	$\beta\acute{\alpha}\lambda\lambda\omega$	throw	$\beta\acute{\alpha}\lambda$-$\underline{\lambda}$-$\varepsilon\tau\varepsilon$	$\beta\acute{\alpha}\lambda$-$\varepsilon$-$\tau\varepsilon$
adding -$\iota\sigma\kappa$-	$\varepsilon\dot{\upsilon}\rho\acute{\iota}\sigma\kappa\omega$	find	$\varepsilon\dot{\upsilon}\rho$-$\underline{\iota\sigma\kappa}$-$\varepsilon$-$\tau\varepsilon$	$\varepsilon\ddot{\upsilon}\rho$-$\varepsilon$-$\tau\varepsilon$
adding -$\mu.\alpha\nu$-	$\lambda\alpha\mu\beta\acute{\alpha}\nu\omega$	take	$\lambda\alpha\underline{\mu}\beta$-$\underline{\alpha\nu}$-$\varepsilon$-$\tau\varepsilon$	$\lambda\acute{\alpha}\beta$-$\varepsilon$-$\tau\varepsilon$

THIRD CONJUGATION

reduplicating with -ι-	δίδωμι	give	δί-δο-τε	δό-τε
	τίθημι	place	τί-θε-τε	θέ-τε
adding -ιν-	-βαίνω	go	-βαίν-ε-τε	-βῆ-τε
adding -ι.σκ-	γινώσκω	know	γινώ-σκ-ε-τε	γνῶ-τε

9.6   THE PRINCIPAL PARTS OF THE VERB

9.61 A large number of Greek verbs form some of their tenses in ways that could not be predicted from their lexical form (the first person singular present indicative active). The entire scheme of a verb's paradigms can be known, however, if one knows six of that verb's forms. As the *endings* of a paradigm follow regularly, given the 1st person singular of that tense, it follows that all the forms of a verb can be obtained by adding the appropriate ending to the stem for a given tense.

9.62 These six forms, which are all in the indicative mode, are therefore known as the "principal parts of the verb", as all other tenses and modes are formed from them. The Principal Parts (in the order in which it is standard for them to be given), and other tenses formed from them, are:

PRINCIPAL PART	FORMED FROM THEM	MIDDLE FORMS
1. Present Active	Imperfect	Other than as
2. Future Active		indicated, middle
3. Aorist Active		forms are derived
4. Perfect Active	Pluperfect Active	from the stem of
5. Perfect Middle/Passive	Pluperfect Middle/Passive	the corresponding
6. Aorist Passive	Future Passive	active form.

Other modes are derived from the corresponding indicative stem.

9.63 Not all verbs have all these parts, and the absence or non-existence of a Principal Part is usually indicated within a table of Principal Parts by a dash. Such verbs are said to be *defective*. A verb can be defective to a greater or less extent, i.e. can have one or several parts lacking.

9.64 Seven verbs found in the New Testament (set out in #7.33, C2.8) draw elements from more than one verb root to supplement each other, and thus make up a more complete frame of Principal Parts. These are called *suppletives*.

9.65 The paradigm of λύω is given in full in Appendix C, together with particular flexions for some other verbs where these differ from that for λύω, or else present difficulties or unusual features. However, for many words other paradigms and conjugations differ only in relation to how their tense stems are formed, and the flexion for each particular tense then follows λύω exactly. In such cases it is therefore only necessary to set out the six Principal Parts, and every form of that verb can be known.

9.7   THE PARADIGMS OF THE FIRST CONJUGATION

9.71 The nine paradigms of the First Conjugation are as follows:
1.1 Long Vowel Verbs (λύω)	(70 in ευ, 30 other)
1.2 Short Vowel Verbs in -α (τιμάω)	(78 verbs)
1.3 Short Vowel Verbs in -ε (λαλέω)	(235 verbs)
1.4 Short Vowel Verbs in -ο (πληρόω)	(91 verbs)
1.5 Labial Verbs (βλέπω, θλίβω, γράφω, καλύπτω)	(18 in πτ, 19 other)
1.6 Palatal Verbs (ἄγω, διώκω, ἄρχω, κηρύσσω)	(35 verbs)
1.7 Dental Verbs (σπεύδω, δοξάζω)	(206 in ζ, 15 other)
1.8a Polysyllabic Oral Liquid Verbs (ἀγγέλλω, ἐγείρω)	(4 verbs)
1.8b Monosyllabic Oral Liquid Verbs (ἀνατέλλω, φθείρω)	(17 verbs)
1.9a Polysyllabic Nasal Liquid Verbs (ξηραίνω)	(27 verbs)
1.9b Monosyllabic Nasal Liquid Verbs (ἀποκτείνω)	(6 verbs)
1.9c Nasal Liquid Verbs in -ιν (κρίνω)	(3 verbs)

9.72 The numbers after each paradigm indicate the number of New Testament verbs (simplex and compound forms counted as one) that there are in each category. But it must be noted that many of these occur only a very small number of times and therefore (as least as far as the New Testament is concerned) are very defective i.e. have forms representing only one or two or three of the Principal Parts.

9.73 The paradigm for λύω is given in full in Appendix C, #C1.1.

9.74 The Short Vowel paradigms are of considerable importance, containing between them more than four hundred verbs, or 47% of all First Conjugation verbs in the New Testament. They have two specific characteristics: **(a)** In all modes and both tenses of the durative aspect they combine their stem final vowel with the initial vowel of the suffix according to the rules of contraction (#6.9); and **(b)** Before a consonant affix they lengthen their stem final vowel (#4.54). Apart from the flexions of the durative aspect, the verbs of these paradigms have the same forms as Paradigm C1.1. The durative aspect flexions and the first form of the other flexions are given in Appendix C, #C1.2 — C1.48.

9.75 The Consonant paradigms (1.5 to 1.9) are quite regular for the most part, their Principal Parts being formed in accordance with the application of the Rules of Amalgamation and Assimilation (touched on at times in the Lessons, and set out in detail in #E2.4 and #E2.5). In particular :

Labials (π β ϕ $\pi\tau$) $+ \sigma = \psi$ $+ \kappa = \phi$ $+ \mu = \mu\mu$ $+ \tau = \pi\tau$ $+ \theta = \phi\theta$
Palatals (κ γ χ $\sigma\sigma$) $+ \sigma = \xi$ $+ \kappa = \chi$ $+ \mu = \gamma\mu$ $+ \tau = \kappa\tau$ $+ \theta = \chi\theta$
Dentals (τ δ θ ζ) $+ \sigma = \sigma$ $+ \kappa = \kappa$ $+ \mu = \sigma\mu$ $+ \tau = \sigma\tau$ $+ \theta = \sigma\theta$
Oral Liquids (λ ρ) $+ \sigma = \varepsilon$ after the oral liquid;
                                    no change before other consonants.

Nasal Liquids —
    in -αινω, -εινω, -υνω: $+ \sigma = \varepsilon$* $+ \kappa = \gamma\kappa$ $+\mu =\sigma\mu$ $+\tau =\nu\tau$ $+ \theta = \nu\theta$
    in other vowel $+$ -νω: $+ \sigma = \varepsilon$ $+ \kappa = \kappa$ $+\mu = \mu$ $+\tau = \tau$ $+ \theta = \theta$

*But in the perfect, $+ \sigma = \nu$. ·

9.8   THE OPTATIVE MODE

9.81 An earlier Lesson (#4.4) has introduced the concept of *mode*. This feature of the verb is referred to by some grammarians as "mood", but as it deals with the type of statement being made about an action and not with overtones of feelings, "mode" is a more appropriate and much preferable designation.

9.82 A.T. Robertson[22] says "Mode (Latin, *modus*) deals with the *manner* of the *affirmation.* Voice and tense deal with the *action*, not the affirmation . . . The modes, like the tenses, deal with the *statement*, not with the facts in the case."

9.83 In addition to the modes mentioned in #4.4, there is a further mode in Greek called the *optative*, from the Latin *opto*, I wish. This mode was never common in Greek. "It was always a luxury of the language and was used more by Xenophon and Plato than other writers. κοινή writers like Strabo and Polybius use it sparingly."[23] Its use was declining in New Testament times — Robertson notes that it is used 67 times in the New Testament, including 28 times in Luke and 31 in Paul, but never in John, Matthew or James[24]. Turner, who counts 68 uses in the New Testament, gives quite a comprehensive discussion of the optative in Hellenistic Greek generally as well as in the New Testament[25].

9.84 The main New Testament use of the optative is in the expression of a wish (hence its name — #9.83), especially in a few set phrases. The most common of these is "may it never be", μὴ γένοιτο, used fifteen times in the New Testament, fourteen of them in Paul (once in I Corinthians, thrice in Galatians, and ten times in Romans), and the other instance in Luke (20:16). Other examples are Mark 11:14, "May no-one eat . . .", and I Thessalonians 5:23, "and may the God of peace himself sanctify you . . ."

9.85 The optative was also used in a potential sense as a kind of softened future (e.g. Acts 26:29, "I could wish . . .") and in a deliberative sense (e.g. Luke 1:62, "as to what he would wish . . ."; Luke 6:11, "what they would do . . ."). Some usages combine the potential and deliberative connotations (e.g. Acts 8:31, "how could I . . .?"; Acts 17:18, "What would/might he wish to say . . .?").

9.86 It is hard to state a clear distinction between the use of the optative and that of the subjunctive. Thus Turner[26] says that the optative "was declining during the three centuries B.C. . . . It was probably never used much in conversation, even in Athens . . . The reason for the decline probably lies in the 'syntactical weakness' . . . of the optative. No one can or could quite define its essential function. The two chief functions, volitive and potential, were too dissimilar to give a unity to the mood, and the subjunctive was always at hand for a substitute for either."

9.87 The volitional (volitive, i.e. "wish") use of the optative will usually be rendered "may . . .", and the other uses by means of the same kinds of expressions as the subjunctive, "could", "would", "might", etc. The particular shade of meaning for an optative in a given context is a matter for discussion in a commentary on the Greek text.

9.88 The optative is found in the New Testament only in two tenses, the present and the aorist. (In classical Greek the optative also occurs in future and perfect flexions.)

9.89 The optative mode morph is -ι- added to the aspect morph (in the passive, -ιη- is added to the passive morph; in the Third Conjugation aorist, -ι- is added directly to the stem and when this has lengthened, is subscript — thus: δῷη, 3rd singular, from δίδωμι; δυναίμην, 1st singular middle, from δύναμαι). This always results in a diphthong: in the present (and in the second aorist) this produces -οι-; in the first aorist active and middle, -σαι-; and in the aorist passive, -θειη-. The flexions for the optative are set out in Paradigm C1.1, λύω, in Appendix C. The optative morph is a *specifier morph*, and occupies Slot 8 of a verb's nine morph slots.

9.9   OTHER VERB TERMINOLOGY

9.91 Periphrastic Tenses: A *periphrastic tense* is one that is formed by the use of a participle of the main verb and a part of εἰμι. This was a required construction for some forms because of the difficulty of pronouncing the form if it were a single word — this particularly applied to the third person plural of the perfect middle, where it was difficult to add the ending -νται to consonant stems. Thus we find forms such as πεπεισμένοι εἰσιν, "they have been persuaded". Some complete tense flexions were formed on a periphrastic basis for this reason (e.g. the perfect subjunctive λελυμένος ὦ, and so forth, and the pluperfect of many verbs).

9.92 However, there are a considerable number of examples in the New Testament of periphrastic forms for the present, imperfect, future, and perfect tenses where the usual single-word forms are also in regular use. For example, see L3/8: οὗ γάρ εἰσιν δύο ἢ τρεῖς συνηγμένοι... Sometimes the use of the periphrastic form may emphasize the continuity of the action, but in most cases it probably simply reflects the kind of colloquial Greek spoken at the time (some scholars would suggest that this is under the influence of Aramaic and the Septuagint, which used quite numerous periphrastics in its translation of the Old Testament; but these periphrastic forms were quite common in Hellenistic Greek generally). No difference in meaning is detectable for example between ἐπεγέγραπτο (Acts 17:23) and ἦν γεγραμμένον (John 19:19). In fact within a few lines we find both forms: ἔστιν γεγραμμένα (John 20:30) and ταῦτα δέ γέγραπται (John 20:31). The most frequent New Testament users of periphrastics are Mark and Luke.

9.93 The periphrastic:

present	is formed with the present of εἰμι and the present participle
imperfect	is formed with the imperfect ,, ,, ,, ,, ,, ,,
future	is formed with the future ,, ,, ,, ,, ,, ,,
perfect	is formed with the present ,, ,, ,, ,, perfect participle
pluperfect	is formed with the imperfect ,, ,, ,, ,, ,, ,,

9.94 The Impersonal Verb: An *impersonal verb* is one which does not have a personal or specific subject. The clearest example is, "It is raining." It does not make sense to ask, "What is raining?" The term is also on occasions extended more widely to include verbs without a particular subject in a given context. The subject may be people in general — "they say"; i.e., "Rumour has it that . . ." At time the subject that is understood may be "God". In a few instances the word "it says" is used, and the implied meaning is, "the Scripture says".

9.95 In English, as in "It is raining", "it" is used as a pseudo-subject. In such a usage, Greek has the verb alone. The two most common impersonal verbs are δεῖ (past tense ἔδει), meaning "it is necessary", and also used with the meaning "you ought to", "it would be a good idea to"; and ἔξεστιν, "it is permitted", "it is lawful". Another is μέλει, "it matters". The infinitive used in conjunction with such verbs is in fact their subject. Consider these examples:

Mt 17:10 (L9/5) Τί οὖν οἱ γραμματεῖς λέγουσιν ὅτι Ἡλίαν δεῖ
Why then do the scribes say that it is necessary for Elijah

ἐλθεῖν πρῶτον;
to come first of all?

Here Ἡλίαν is the subject of ἐλθεῖν (the subject of an infinitive is put in the accusative — see #8.43 (c)), and ἐλθεῖν is the subject of δεῖ — Elijah is the one who is to come, and his coming is what is necessary. The sentence could be translated, "Elijah must come first of all".

Acts 5:29 (L9/23) Πειθαρχεῖν δεῖ θεῷ μᾶλλον ἢ ἀνθρώποις.
It is necessary to obey God rather than men.

Here "God" is the indirect object of "to obey", and "to obey" is the subject of δεῖ, i.e. what it is that is necessary. The subject of "to obey" is unstated and could be "we", "you", "everyone". Similarly:

Mt 22:17 ἔξεστιν δοῦναι κῆνσον Καίσαρι ἢ οὔ;
Is it lawful to give tribute to Caesar or not?

9.96 Direct Flexions: We have seen that it is customary for a Greek verb to indicate aspect and voice by appropriate morphs added to the stem. Some verbs have flexions where the expected morph (or the consonant part of it) is omitted — e.g. a perfect active without the -κ-, an aorist passive without the -θ-. Sometimes these are referred to as "second" tenses (second perfect, second aorist passive, etc.) on the basis of a supposed analogy with the second aorist active. This is in fact a particularly misleading manner of reference, as the analogy does not hold. The second aorist active flexion is not simply the first aorist active with a phoneme missing — it is a completely different pattern of conjugation (see #3.81 and 4.21). It therefore genuinely deserves the designation of *second* aorist. But all the other so-called second tenses are in fact conjugated *exactly the same* as the corresponding flexion of λύω: they simply omit a consonant phoneme of the aspect or voice morph in forming the appropriate tense stem. That is, they are formed by the adding of the endings (including the vowel of the aspect or voice morph) directly to the stem. They are therefore more appropriately called *direct flexions*. They are fully listed and discussed in Appendix C, #C4.

9.97 Strong Verbs: This term is sometimes used to designate flexions that are formed by *changing the stem* (e.g., second aorist active forms) or by *adding endings directly* to the same stem without using the usual aspect or voice morph (i.e. direct flexions). By contrast, verbs that add such a morph are called "weak" verbs. The rationale for these terms is that the strong verbs do not need "outside help" in forming other tenses/modes/voices (i.e. the appropriate morphs), while the weak verbs are weak because they do need such "outside help". This seems a very tenuous and far-fetched basis for a term, and it is terminology which is not self-explanatory. It therefore has not been used in this book. When, however, you encounter it in other books that you consult, you will readily recognize that it refers to Second (or perhaps Third) Conjugation forms, or direct flexions.

9.98 Thematic and Athematic Verbs: The o/ε vowel of the durative flexions, the future, the second aorist, and the subjunctive flexions, which in this book has been classified (on linguistic grounds) as the *neutral morph* is referred to in other grammars as the *thematic vowel.* By contrast, the -$\mu\iota$ flexions which lack the o/ε vowel are called *athematic.* This particular way of making a distinction does not appear particularly helpful or linguistically intelligible, and therefore these terms have not been used in this book. The o/ε occupies the slot which is filled by the punctiliar or perfective active aspect morphs -$\sigma\alpha$- and -$\kappa\alpha$- when these occur, and never occurs together with them (except in the special instance of the aorist subjunctive) so that it is said (in linguistic terminology) to be in complementary distribution with them. This indicates that, on the basis of synchronic linguistic description (which means, discussing the language as it actually operates at a particular point in time), o/ε is an aspect morph without specific meaning of its own but is used when neither of the other aspect morphs appears. Hence the basis for the description of it in this book as the *neutral (aspect) morph.*

9.99 A concluding word about verbs: Appendix C gives detailed and comprehensive information about Greek verb conjugation, and Appendix E gives explanations in phonemic modification and morphology. Familiarize yourself with these Appendices, so that you can refer to them when you encounter verb forms you need to check on. Whenever you come across unrecognized forms as you read the Greek N.T., always check them out in these conjugation paradigms if the Grammatical Analysis explanation does not remind you of them.

ASSIGNMENTS ON LESSON NINE

1. Read Lesson Nine through twice.

2. **LEARN** the *names* and the *order* of the six Principal Parts (# 9.62) — these will apply to the columns of verb parts given throughout Appendix C.

3. In Appendix G, Greek Vocabulary, read through the list of the most common New Testament words. You have met all of these at one time or another in the course of these nine Lessons. How many of them can you remember? Seek now to learn the others — but remember that the meanings given here represent only *a part* of the range of meaning of each word, and that you must seek to expand your understanding of a word each time you encounter it.

4.   Read and translate literally all the Selections from the Greek N.T.

5.   Familiarize yourself with the contents of the Appendices C, D and E, so that you are aware of what they contain, and can make use of them whenever they can be of assistance to you.

6.   Do a preliminary reading of the Outline of Lesson Ten.

7.   (Optional, or as directed by your teacher.) Answer the questions given at the end of each explanation for a Selection, in the Notes (below).

SELECTIONS FROM THE GREEK NEW TESTAMENT

1. Αἰτεῖτε, καὶ δοθήσεται ὑμῖν· ζητεῖτε, καὶ εὑρήσετε· κρούετε, καὶ ἀνοιγήσεται ὑμῖν. (ΚΑΤΑ ΜΑΘΘΑΙΟΝ 7:7.)

2. εἰσερχόμενοι δὲ εἰς τὴν οἰκίαν ἀσπάσασθε αὐτήν. (ΚΑΤΑ ΜΑΘΘΑΙΟΝ 10:12.)

3. τότε πορεύεται καὶ παραλαμβάνει μεθ᾽ ἑαυτοῦ ἑπτὰ ἕτερα πνεύματα πονηρότερα ἑαυτοῦ, καὶ εἰσελθόντα κατοικεῖ ἐκεῖ· καὶ γίνεται τὰ ἔσχατα τοῦ ἀνθρώπου ἐκείνου χείρονα τῶν πρώτων. οὕτως ἔσται καὶ τῇ γενεᾷ ταύτῃ τῇ πονηρᾷ. (ΚΑΤΑ ΜΑΘΘΑΙΟΝ 12:45.)

4. τὸ μὲν πρόσωπον τοῦ οὐρανοῦ γινώσκετε διακρίνειν, τὰ δὲ σημεῖα τῶν καιρῶν οὐ δύνασθε. Γενεὰ πονηρὰ καὶ μοιχαλὶς σημεῖον ἐπιζητεῖ, καὶ σημεῖον οὐ δοθήσεται αὐτῇ εἰ μὴ τὸ σημεῖον Ἰωνᾶ. καὶ καταλιπὼν αὐτοὺς ἀπῆλθεν. (ΚΑΤΑ ΜΑΘΘΑΙΟΝ 16:3-4.)

5. καὶ ἐπηρώτησαν αὐτὸν οἱ μαθηταὶ λέγοντες, Τί οὖν οἱ γραμματεῖς λέγουσιν ὅτι Ἠλίαν δεῖ ἐλθεῖν πρῶτον; ὁ δὲ ἀποκριθεὶς εἶπεν, Ἠλίας μὲν ἔρχεται καὶ ἀποκαταστήσει πάντα· λέγω δὲ ὑμῖν ὅτι Ἠλίας ἤδη ἦλθεν, καὶ οὐκ ἐπέγνωσαν αὐτὸν ἀλλὰ ἐποίησαν ἐν αὐτῷ ὅσα ἠθέλησαν· οὕτως καὶ ὁ υἱὸς τοῦ ἀνθρώπου μέλλει πάσχειν ὑπ᾽ αὐτῶν. (ΚΑΤΑ ΜΑΘΘΑΙΟΝ 17:10-12.)

6. Καὶ ἔτι αὐτοῦ λαλοῦντος ἰδοὺ Ἰούδας εἷς τῶν δώδεκα ἦλθεν καὶ μετ᾽ αὐτοῦ ὄχλος πολὺς μετὰ μαχαιρῶν καὶ ξύλων ἀπὸ τῶν ἀρχιερέων καὶ πρεσβυτέρων τοῦ λαοῦ. ὁ δὲ παραδιδοὺς αὐτὸν ἔδωκεν αὐτοῖς σημεῖον λέγων, Ὃν ἂν φιλήσω αὐτός ἐστιν· κρατήσατε αὐτόν. (ΚΑΤΑ ΜΑΘΘΑΙΟΝ 26:47-48.)

7. Καὶ ἀκούσαντες οἱ δέκα ἤρξαντο ἀγανακτεῖν περὶ Ἰακώβου καὶ Ἰωάννου. καὶ προσκαλεσάμενος αὐτοὺς ὁ Ἰησοῦς λέγει αὐτοῖς, Οἴδατε ὅτι οἱ δοκοῦντες ἄρχειν τῶν ἐθνῶν κατακυριεύουσιν αὐτῶν καὶ οἱ μεγάλοι αὐτῶν κατεξουσιάζουσιν αὐτῶν. οὐχ οὕτως δέ ἐστιν ἐν ὑμῖν· ἀλλ᾽ ὃς ἂν θέλῃ μέγας γενέσθαι ἐν ὑμῖν, ἔσται ὑμῶν διάκονος, καὶ ὃς ἂν θέλῃ ἐν ὑμῖν εἶναι πρῶτος, ἔσται πάντων δοῦλος· καὶ γὰρ ὁ υἱὸς τοῦ ἀνθρώπου

Selections continue on page 138

EXPLANATORY NOTES

MAKE A TRANSLATION of each Selection on your own, first of all. Then use these Explanatory Notes and your other tools to fill in any gaps in your work.

1. αἰτεῖτε: impv of *αἰτέω ask ■ δο-θή-σ-εται → *δίδωμι give (3sg fut pass) ■ ζητεῖτε: impv of *ζητέω seek ■ εὑρή-σ-ετε → *εὑρίσκω find (2pl fut) ■ κρούετε: impv of κρούω knock ■ ἀν-οιγ-ή-σ-εται → *ἀν-οίγω open (3sg fut pass — direct flexion, no -θ-). (What is the significance of the tense of the three imperatives?)

2. εἰσ-ερχ-ό-μεν-οι → *εἰσέρχομαι enter (pres ptc) ■ ἀσπά-σα-σθ-ε → *ἀσπάζομαι greet (aor impv) ■ *οἰκία house/those who live in a house, household. (What is the significance of the tense of the participle?)

3. *πορεύομαι go ■ παραλαμβάνω take along with (oneself) ■ *ἑαυτόν oneself ■ *ἑπτά seven ■ *ἕτερος other (different) ■ πονηρό-τερος (#9.33) more evil (than) ■ εἰσ-ελθ-ό-ντ-α → *εἰσέρχομαι (aor² ptc) ■ κατοικέω settle down/dwell ■ ἔσχατα → *ἔσχατος last (n pl neut) ■ *ἐκεῖνος that ■ χείρονα → χείρων worse (#9.35) ■ πρώτων → *πρῶτος first (g pl neut) ■ *οὕτως thus ■ καί also/even ■ γενεά generation ■ *πονηρός evil. (What is the meaning of the dative case for the words in the last sentence?)

4. *μὲν ... *δὲ ... on the one hand ... (but) on the other hand ... ■ *γινώσκω know how to ■ διακρίνω evaluate/judge/discern/distinguish ■ δύνασθε → *δύναμαι be able to (2pl pres³ dep) ■ *σημεῖον sign ■ *καιρός season/(appointed) time ■ μοιχαλίς adulterous/unfaithful ■ ἐπι-ζητέω seek/desire/want/search for/look for ■ δοθήσεται see Sel 1 ■ εἰ μή except ■ Ἰωνᾶ → Ἰωνᾶς ᾶ ὁ Jonah (gen. sg) ■ κατα-λιπών → καταλείπω leave (behind) (n. sg masc aor² ptc act) ■ ἀπῆλθεν → *ἀπέρχομαι depart. (What is the significance of μοιχαλίς?)

5. ἐπ-ηρώτη-σα-ν → *ἐπερωτάω ask (a question) (3pl aor) ■ *δεῖ it is necessary for (= must) ■ *πρῶτον firstly/first of all ■ *μέν indeed ■ ἀπο-κατα-στή-σ-ει → ἀποκαθίστημι restore again (3sg fut) ■ *ἤδη already ■ ἐπ-έ-γνω-σαν → ἐπιγινώσκω know, recognize (3pl aor³) ■ ὅσα → *ὅσος (see #7.11) ■ ἠ-θέλη-σα-ν → *θέλω (note double augment; cf #4.61) ■ *μέλλω be about to, be going to, be destined to ■ πάσχω suffer. (In this Selection, what are the two ways in which ὅτι could be taken?)

6. *ἔτι still ■ αὐτοῦ λαλοῦντος genitive absolute, indicating the time factor for the main clause ■ *δώδεκα twelve ■ μάχαιρα sword ■ ξύλον tree/wood/piece of wood/club/the cross ■ *ἀρχιερεύς high priest/chief priest ■ *λαός a people ■ παρα-δι-δούς → *παραδίδωμι hand over/deliver up/betray (n. sg masc pres³ ptc) ■ ἔ-δω-κεν → *δίδωμι (3sg aor in -κα) ■ φιλήσω → φιλέω have affection for/kiss (1sg aor subj after ἄν) ■ κρατή-σα-τε → κρατέω take hold of/seize/arrest (2pl aor impv). (What is the significance of the tense of παραδιδούς?)

οὐκ ἦλθεν διακονηθῆναι ἀλλὰ διακονῆσαι καὶ δοῦναι τὴν ψυχὴν αὐτοῦ
λύτρον ἀντὶ πολλῶν. (ΚΑΤΑ ΜΑΡΚΟΝ 10:41-45.)

8. καὶ ἤκουσαν οἱ ἀρχιερεῖς καὶ οἱ γραμματεῖς, καὶ ἐζήτουν πῶς αὐτὸν
ἀπολέσωσιν· ἐφοβοῦντο γὰρ αὐτόν, πᾶς γὰρ ὁ ὄχλος ἐξεπλήσσετο ἐπὶ τῇ
διδαχῇ αὐτοῦ. (ΚΑΤΑ ΜΑΡΚΟΝ 11:18.)

9. ὁ μὲν υἱὸς τοῦ ἀνθρώπου ὑπάγει καθὼς γέγραπται περὶ αὐτοῦ, οὐαὶ δὲ τῷ
ἀνθρώπῳ ἐκείνῳ δι᾽ οὗ ὁ υἱὸς τοῦ ἀνθρώπου παραδίδοται· καλὸν αὐτῷ εἰ
οὐκ ἐγεννήθη ὁ ἄνθρωπος ἐκεῖνος. (ΚΑΤΑ ΜΑΡΚΟΝ 14:21.)

10. ἡ γυνή σου Ἐλισάβετ γεννήσει υἱόν σοι, καὶ καλέσεις τὸ ὄνομα αὐτοῦ
Ἰωάννην. καὶ ἔσται χαρά σοι καὶ ἀγαλλίασις, καὶ πολλοὶ ἐπὶ τῇ γενέσει
αὐτοῦ χαρήσονται. (ΚΑΤΑ ΛΟΥΚΑΝ 1:13-14.)

11. ἐλήλυθεν γὰρ Ἰωάννης ὁ βαπτιστὴς μὴ ἐσθίων ἄρτον μήτε πίνων οἶνον,
καὶ λέγετε, Δαιμόνιον ἔχει· ἐλήλυθεν ὁ υἱὸς τοῦ ἀνθρώπου ἐσθίων καὶ
πίνων, καὶ λέγετε, Ἰδοὺ ἄνθρωπος φάγος καὶ οἰνοπότης, φίλος τελωνῶν
καὶ ἁμαρτωλῶν. (ΚΑΤΑ ΛΟΥΚΑΝ 7:33.)

12. Ἄνθρωποι δύο ἀνέβησαν εἰς τὸ ἱερὸν προσεύξασθαι, ὁ εἷς Φαρισαῖος καὶ
ὁ ἕτερος τελώνης. (ΚΑΤΑ ΛΟΥΚΑΝ 18:10.)

13. ἀμὴν λέγω ὑμῖν, ὃς ἂν μὴ δέξηται τὴν βασιλείαν τοῦ θεοῦ ὡς παιδίον, οὐ
μὴ εἰσέλθῃ εἰς αὐτήν. (ΚΑΤΑ ΛΟΥΚΑΝ 18:17.)

14. λέγει αὐτῷ, Ἐκ τοῦ στόματός σου κρινῶ σε, πονηρὲ δοῦλε. (ΚΑΤΑ
ΛΟΥΚΑΝ 19:22.)

15. καὶ θρὶξ ἐκ τῆς κεφαλῆς ὑμῶν οὐ μὴ ἀπόληται. (ΚΑΤΑ ΛΟΥΚΑΝ 21:18.)

16. καὶ εἱστήκει ὁ λαὸς θεωρῶν. (ΚΑΤΑ ΛΟΥΚΑΝ 23:35.)

17. ὁ δὲ Ἰησοῦς ἀπεκρίνατο αὐτούς, Ὁ πατήρ μου ἕως ἄρτι ἐργάζεται, κἀγὼ
ἐργάζομαι. διὰ τοῦτο οὖν μᾶλλον ἐζήτουν αὐτὸν οἱ Ἰουδαῖοι ἀποκτεῖναι,
ὅτι οὐ μόνον ἔλυεν τὸ σάββατον ἀλλὰ καὶ πατέρα ἴδιον ἔλεγεν τὸν θεόν,
ἴσον ἑαυτὸν ποιῶν τῷ θεῷ. (ΚΑΤΑ ΙΩΑΝΝΗΝ 5:17-18.)

18. ἠκολούθει δὲ αὐτῷ ὄχλος πολύς, ὅτι ἐθεώρουν τὰ σημεῖα ἃ ἐποίει ἐπὶ τῶν
ἀσθενούντων. (ΚΑΤΑ ΙΩΑΝΝΗΝ 6:2.)

Selections continue on page 140

Continued from next page

     κτεῖν-αι → *ἀποκτείνω kill (aor inf act) ■ *μόνος only/alone ■ ἔλυεν
→ λύω loose/relax (here: break/set aside) (3sg impf) ■ *ἴδιος one's own
■ ἔλεγεν → *λέγω say/tell (here: saying (someone) to be (something)/
call) (3sg impf) ■ ἴσος equal ■ ἑαυτόν himself/oneself. (What exactly
was it that made the Jews seek to kill Jesus?)

18. ἠκολούθει → *ἀκολουθέω follow (3sg impf) ■ *σημεῖον sign/miracle ■
ἀσθενούντων → ἀσθενέω I am weak/sick (g. pl pres ptc). (What is being
indicated by the use of the word σημεῖον in this verse?)

7. δέκα ten ■ ἤρξαντο → *ἄρχομαι begin (3pl aor mid) ■ ἀγανακτέω I am indignant/angry at/with ■ προσ-καλε-σά-μεν-ος → προσκαλέω call to oneself (n. sg masc aor ptc mid) ■ δοκοῦντες → *δοκέω be thought/seem (n. pl masc pres ptc) ■ *ἄρχω rule over (+ gen) ■ *ἔθνος nation (pl: gentiles) ■ κατακυριεύω lord it over (+ gen) ■ μεγάλοι → *μέγας great ■ κατεξουσιάζω exercise authority over (+ gen) ■ θέλη → *θέλω want/wish (3sg pres subj) ■ *ἐν amongst ■ διάκονος servant ■ *δοῦλος slave ■ διακονη-θῆ-ναι → διακονέω serve (aor inf pass) ■ διακονή-σ-αι (aor inf act) ■ δοῦ-ναι → *δίδωμι (aor³ inf) ■ λύτρον ransom (price of freedom; from λύω) ■ ἀντί in place of/instead of. (What is the significance of λύτρον ἀντί?)

8. *πῶς how ■ ἀπ-ολέ-σ-ω-σιν → *ἀπόλλυμι destroy (3pl aor subj) ■ ἐ-φοβοῦντο → *φοβέομαι fear (3pl impf) ■ ἐξ-ε-πλήσσ-ετο → ἐκπλήσσω astound/astonish (3sg impf pass) ■ διδαχή teaching. (What is the significance of the tense of ἐφοβοῦντο and ἐξεπλήσσετο?)

9. *ὑπάγω go/go away ■ *καθώς just as ■ οὐαί woe to/alas for ■ *διά (+ gen) through ■ παρα-δί-δο-ται → *παραδίδωμι (Sel 6) (3sg pres³ pass) ■ *καλός good (here, = comp., i.e. better; cf. #9.39 ■ ἐ-γεννή-θη → *γεννάω beget/bear (pass: be born) (3sg aor pass). (What is the significance of the tense of γέγραπται?)

10. γεννή-σ-ει → *γεννάω (3sg fut) ■ *χαρά joy ■ ἀγαλλίασις exultation ■ γένεσις birth ■ χαρή-σ-ονται → *χαίρω rejoice (3 pl fut dep). (What is irregular in the form καλέσεις?)

11. ἐλήλυθεν → *ἔρχομαι (3sg pf) ■ βαπτιστής baptist ■ ἐσθίων → *ἐσθίω eat (pres ptc) ■ μήτε nor■ πίνων → *πίνω drink (pres ptc) ■ οἶνος wine ■ *δαιμόνιον demon ■ φάγος glutton ■ οἰνοπότης drinker/drunkard ■ φίλος friend ■ τελώνης tax-collector ■ ἁμαρτωλός sinner. (What is the significance of the tense of ἐλήλυθεν?)

12. ἀν-έ-βη-σαν → *ἀναβαίνω go up (3pl aor³) ■ *ἱερόν temple ■ προσ-εύξ-α-σθ-αι → *προσεύχομαι pray (aor inf dep) ■ *ἕτερος another/different. (What is the significance of the tense of προσεύξασθαι?)

13. δέξ-η-ται → *δέχομαι receive (3sg aor subj dep) ■ *παιδίον child ■ εἰσ-έλθ-ῃ → *εἰσέρχομαι (3sg aor² subj act). (What is the gender of αὐτήν, and why?)

14. στόματος → *στόμα mouth ■ κρινῶ = κριν-έ-ω → *κρίνω judge (1sg fut). (What is the case of πονηρέ, and why?)

15. θρίξ a hair ■ *κεφαλή head ■ ἀπ-όλη-ται → *ἀπόλλυμι destroy (mid: perish) (3sg aor³ subj mid). (Why is ἀπόλλυμι put into the subjunctive?)

16. εἰ-στή-κ-ει → *ἵστημι stand (3sg plpf, with sense of impf) ■ θεωρῶν → *θεωρέω watch (pres ptc). (What is the force of the tenses of the verbs?)

17. ἀπ-ε-κρίν-α-το → *ἀποκρίνομαι answer (3sg aor dep) ■ ἐργάζομαι work ■ *μᾶλλον more/rather ■ ἐζήτουν → *ζητέω seek (3pl impf) ■ ἀπο-

Continued at foot of previous page

19. θεωροῦσιν τὸν Ἰησοῦν περιπατοῦντα ἐπὶ τῆς θαλάσσης καὶ ἐγγὺς τοῦ πλοίου γινόμενον, καὶ ἐφοβήθησαν. ὁ δὲ λέγει αὐτοῖς, Ἐγώ εἰμι, μὴ φοβεῖσθε. (ΚΑΤΑ ΙΩΑΝΝΗΝ 6:19-20.)

20. Ἐν δὲ τῇ ἐσχάτῃ ἡμέρᾳ τῇ μεγάλῃ τῆς ἑορτῆς εἱστήκει ὁ Ἰησοῦς καὶ ἔκραξεν λέγων, Ἐάν τις διψᾷ ἐρχέσθω πρός με καὶ πινέτω. (ΚΑΤΑ ΙΩΑΝΝΗΝ 7:37.)

21. Ἐλθὼν οὖν ὁ Ἰησοῦς εὗρεν αὐτὸν τέσσαρας ἤδη ἡμέρας ἔχοντα ἐν τῷ μνημείῳ. εἶπεν οὖν ἡ Μάρθα πρὸς τὸν Ἰησοῦν, Κύριε, εἰ ἦς ὧδε οὐκ ἂν ἀπέθανεν ὁ ἀδελφός μου· ἀλλὰ καὶ νῦν οἶδα ὅτι ὅσα ἂν αἰτήσῃ τὸν θεὸν δώσει σοι ὁ θεός. λέγει αὐτῇ ὁ Ἰησοῦς, Ἀναστήσεται ὁ ἀδελφός σου. λέγει αὐτῷ ἡ Μάρθα, Οἶδα ὅτι ἀναστήσεται ἐν τῇ ἀναστάσει ἐν τῇ ἐσχάτῃ ἡμέρᾳ. εἶπεν αὐτῇ ὁ Ἰησοῦς, Ἐγώ εἰμι ἡ ἀνάστασις καὶ ἡ ζωή. (ΚΑΤΑ ΙΩΑΝΝΗΝ 11:17, 21-25.)

22. καὶ ὑμεῖς οὖν νῦν μὲν λύπην ἔχετε· πάλιν δὲ ὄψομαι ὑμᾶς, καὶ χαρήσεται ὑμῶν ἡ καρδία, καὶ τὴν χαρὰν ὑμῶν οὐδεὶς αἴρει ἀφ' ὑμῶν. (ΚΑΤΑ ΙΩΑΝΝΗΝ 16:22.)

23. Πειθαρχεῖν δεῖ θεῷ μᾶλλον ἢ ἀνθρώποις. (ΠΡΑΞΕΙΣ 5:29.)

24. Οὐδὲν κακὸν εὑρίσκομεν ἐν τῷ ἀνθρώπῳ τούτῳ. (ΠΡΑΞΕΙΣ 23:9.)

25. ἡ ἀγάπη τῷ πλησίον κακὸν οὐκ ἐργάζεται· πλήρωμα οὖν νόμου ἡ ἀγάπη. (ΠΡΟΣ ΡΩΜΑΙΟΥΣ 13:10.)

26. Διὸ ἀποθέμενοι τὸ ψεῦδος λαλεῖτε ἀλήθειαν ἕκαστος μετὰ τοῦ πλησίον αὐτοῦ, ὅτι ἐσμὲν ἀλλήλων μέλη. (ΠΡΟΣ ΕΦΕΣΙΟΥΣ 4:25.)

27. καὶ αὐτός ἐστιν πρὸ πάντων καὶ τὰ πάντα ἐν αὐτῷ συνέστηκεν. καὶ αὐτός ἐστιν ἡ κεφαλὴ τοῦ σώματος, τῆς ἐκκλησίας. (ΠΡΟΣ ΚΟΛΟΣΣΑΕΙΣ 1:17-18.)

28. εἴ τις οὐ θέλει ἐργάζεσθαι μηδὲ ἐσθιέτω. (ΠΡΟΣ ΘΕΣΣΑΛΟΝΙΚΕΙΣ Β 3:10.)

29. εὔχεσθε ὑπὲρ ἀλλήλων, ὅπως ἰαθῆτε. (ΙΑΚΩΒΟΥ 5:16.)

30. καὶ αὕτη ἐστὶν ἡ ἐπαγγελία ἣν αὐτὸς ἐπηγγείλατο ἡμῖν, τὴν ζωὴν τὴν αἰώνιον. (ΙΩΑΝΝΟΥ Α 2:25.)

31. Καὶ ὅτε εἶδον αὐτόν, ἔπεσα πρὸς τοὺς πόδας αὐτοῦ ὡς νεκρός· καὶ ἔθηκεν τὴν δεξιὰν αὐτοῦ ἐπ' ἐμὲ λέγων, Μὴ φοβοῦ· ἐγώ εἰμι ὁ πρῶτος καὶ ὁ ἔσχατος. (ΑΠΟΚΑΛΥΨΙΣ ΙΩΑΝΝΟΥ 1:17.)

Continued from next page

31. ἔπεσα → *πίπτω fall (1sg aor, C1 from an original C2 flexion) ■ ἔ-θη-κ-εν → *τίθημι place (3sg aor) ■ δεξιάν (understand, χεῖρα) right (hand), → *δεξιός. (What is the significance of the tense of φοβοῦ?)

19. περι-πατοῦντα → *περιπατέω walk (about)/stroll (a. sg masc pres ptc) ■
*πλοῖον boat ■ ἐ-φοβή-θη-σαν → *φοβέομαι fear (3pl aor pass) ■
φοβεῖ-σθ-ε (2pl pres impv). (What is the significance of the tense of
ἐφοβήθησαν and of φοβεῖσθε?)

20. ἔσχατος last ■ ἑορτή feast ■ εἱστήκει (Sel 16) ■ ἔ-κρα-ξ-εν → κράζω (3sg
aor, from √ κραγ-) ■ διψᾷ → διψάω (3sg pres indic or subj; here: subj, =
διψά-η, #C1.2) ■ ἐρχέσθω → *ἔρχομαι come (3sg pres impv) ■ πινέτω
→ *πίνω drink (3sg pres impv). (What is the significance of the tense of
two imperatives?)

21. εὑρ-εν → *εὑρίσκω find (3sg aor) ■ τέσσαρες four ■ μνημεῖον tomb ■ ἦς →
*εἰμί (2sg impf) ■*ὧδε here ■*ἄν particle, here following upon the
previous "if" and giving the sense of "would have" to the next verb ■ ἀπ-
ἐ-θαν-εν → *ἀποθνήσκω die (3sg aor²) ■ *νῦν now ■ ὅσα ἄν (→ *ὅσος;
cf. #7.11) however many things as, = whatever things ■ αἰτή-σ-η →
*αἰτέω ask for/request (2sg aor subj mid) ■ δώ-σ-ει → *δίδωμι give (3sg fut)
■ ἀνα-στή-σ-εται → *ἀνίστημι raise, rise (3sg fut midd) ■ ἀνάστασις
resurrection ■*ἔσχατος last. (Explain how the form ἀναστήσεται is built
up.)

22. λύπη grief/sorrow/pain ■ ὄψομαι from root ὀπ-; suppletive of ὁράω (1sg fut
dep) ■ χαρ-ή-σ-εται → *χαίρω rejoice (3sg fut pass, direct flexion
#C4.4) ■ *χαρά joy ■ αἴρει → *αἴρω remove/take up (3sg pres). (Why
is καρδία singular?)

23. πειθαρχεῖν → πειθαρχέω give the obedience due to one in authority (pres inf)
■*δεῖ it is necessary (= one must) ■ *μᾶλλον rather/more ■*ἤ than.
(What is the relevance of the meaning of πειθαρχέω here?)

24. *κακός evil/wrong ■ εὑρίσκομεν → *εὑρίσκω find (1pl pres) ■ οὐδέν →
*οὐδείς (a. sg neut). (What is the significance of the gender of οὐδέν?)

25. *ἀγάπη love ■ πλησίον neighbour (indecl) ■ πλήρωμα fulfilling/completeness.
(How is ἀγάπη the πλήρωμα of νόμος?)

26. *διό therefore ■ ἀπο-θέ-μεν-οι → ἀποτίθημι put away/cast off (n. pl masc
aor³ ptc mid) ■ ψεῦδος falsehood/lying/lie ■ *ἀλήθεια truth ■
*ἕκαστος each ■ ἀλλήλων → *ἀλλήλους one another ■ μέλος
part/limb.

27. συν-έ-στη-κ-εν → συνίστημι hold together/cohere/be established (3sg pf act;
with the idea of an ongoing state of affairs) ■ *κεφαλή head ■ *σῶμα
body ■ *ἐκκλησία church. (Why is συνέστηκεν singular?)

28. *εἰ if ■ *μηδέ neither/and not ■ ἐσθιέτω → *ἐσθίω eat (3sg impv act). (Why
here do we find εἰ with the indic., not ἐάν with the subj.?)

29. εὔχεσθε → εὔχομαι pray (simplex of *προσεύχομαι) (2pl pres impv) ■ *ὑπέρ
(+ gen) on behalf of/for ■ *ὅπως so that/in order that ■ ἰα-θ-ῆ-τε →
ἰάομαι heal/cure (2pl aor subj pass).

30. *ἐπαγγελία promise ■ ἐπ-ηγγείλ-α-το → ἐπαγγέλλομαι promise (aor).

Continued at foot of previous page

THE WAY AHEAD

You have now completed your Beginner's Course, Stage I of your work in Learning to Read the Greek New Testament.

You have been introduced to all the basic grammar of the Greek New Testament. (Your work from here on will be directed towards consolidating, clarifying, and reinforcing this grammar, and refining, sharpening, and deepening your knowledge of its various ramifications.)

You have worked your way through almost 200 Greek New Testament Selections, of various lengths. You have encountered a great many Greek words (including the 300 words of the "common N.T. vocabulary" — see Appendix G).

You have (it is sincerely to be hoped) put a considerable amount of effort into your studies, and already you have begun (it is also to be hoped) to see fruit from this work from the N.T. passages you have been working on. Now you are at the point where your labours can really begin to repay you, as you commence reading the Greek New Testament itself.

At the present moment, remember: in this (as in all language study) you face the inexorable operation of a basic rule: "Use it, or lose it."

If you now have a vacation in your studies, utilize the opportunity to read swiftly through the entire Beginner's Course again. And read quickly through the Greek N.T. Selections at the end of each Lesson, without stopping to check every word for grammar or vocabulary meaning, to see how much you already know, and to aid in consolidating that knowledge.

You are now ready for Stage II, the Intermediate Course (Lessons 10 to 27). This will involve the systematic presentation of Conjugation, Declension, and various Explanations, which will have the multiple purpose of revising and systematizing your existing knowledge, filling in the gaps, and giving you some "behind-the-scenes" comments about what is going on in the language. Simultaneously, you will have commenced the actual study of a book of the New Testament in Greek. And this, after all, is the purpose of everything you have been doing.

STAGE II

INTERMEDIATE GREEK COURSE

Stage II consists of 18 units-of-work (or, Lessons), divided into two equal Parts, Part I and Part II. For convenience, the Lessons are numbered 10 to 18 and 19 to 27 respectively, but in fact Part I and Part II may be taken in either order. It is possible, for example, to conduct an ongoing Stage II Class which has two possible entry points for Intermediate students — at Lesson 10 and again at Lesson 19. Those who entered at Lesson 19 would thus do Part II (Lessons 19 to 27) before Part I (Lessons 10 to 18).

The outline of Lessons 10 to 27 is given below. The work of Stage II is set out in Appendices, C, D, and E, and also includes the reading of *Biblical Greek* by Max Zerwick (Biblical Institute Press, Rome, 1964-1977). The work on these Lessons is intended to proceed *in parallel with* the actual reading and study of the Greek text of a book of the N.T. (normally Mark, or possibly John) — this work should be proceeding throughout the whole of Stage II and in fact constitutes the primary reason for the Course: that the student should be brought to, and set to work on, and given maximum exposure in, the Greek N.T. itself. (Unless a particular syllabus is requiring the use of another set text, the 27 sections from Mark — or as many of them as may be required — can be used, as given below at the end of the Lesson Outlines.)

PART I: CONJUGATION

LESSON TEN

STUDY: The Paradigm of λύω, #C0.1 to #C1.14. Ensure that you have in your mind an overview of the First Paradigm (λύω) in its various aspects, modes and voices (#C0.2), and that you understand the meaning of the flexions (#C0.4). Seek to improve your familiarity with the forms of each flexion (#C1.1).
READ *Biblical Greek*: Voice (§225-§236) and Aspect (§240-§241).

LESSON ELEVEN

STUDY: The Short Vowel and Stop Consonant Paradigms, #C1.2 to #C1.7. Notice that they differ in the interaction of the final stem phoneme with the ending.
READ *Biblical Greek*: The Aorist (§242-§269).

LESSON TWELVE

STUDY: The Liquid Paradigms, #C1.8 and #C1.9.
READ *Biblical Greek*: The Imperfect, Future, Perfect and Pluperfect (§270-§291).

LESSON THIRTEEN

STUDY: The Second Conjugation, #C2.
READ *Biblical Greek*: The Moods (Part I) (§295-§312).

LESSON FOURTEEN

STUDY: The Third Conjugation, #C3.
READ *Biblical Greek*: The Moods (Part II) (§313-§339).

LESSON FIFTEEN

STUDY: Verbs with Direct Flexions; Verbs with Two Aspect Morphs, #C4 & #C5.
READ *Biblical Greek*: The Moods (Part III) (§340-§358).

LESSON SIXTEEN

STUDY: Conspectus of the Three Conjugations, #C6.
READ *Biblical Greek*: The Participle (§360-§377).

LESSON SEVENTEEN

STUDY: Deponent Verbs, and Irregular Verbs (Part I), #C7- #C8.64.
READ *Biblical Greek*: The Infinitive (§380-§395) and The Negatives (§440-§447).

LESSON EIGHTEEN

STUDY: Irregular Verbs (Part II), #C8.7-#C9.3.
READ *Biblical Greek*: Conjunctions (§400-§429).

PART II: DECLENSION AND EXPLANATIONS

LESSON NINETEEN

STUDY: The First and Second Declensions, #D0.1-#D2.45.
READ *Biblical Greek*: Concord (§1-§21).

LESSON TWENTY

STUDY: The Third Declension (Part I), #D3.0-#D3.11.
READ *Biblical Greek*: The Cases — Nominative, Vocative, Genitive (§25-§50).

LESSON TWENTY-ONE

STUDY: The Third Declension (Part II), #D3.12-#D3.40.
READ *Biblical Greek*: The Cases — Dative and Accusative (§51-§74).

LESSON TWENTY-TWO

STUDY: Adjectives, #D4.
READ *Biblical Greek*: Adjectives, Numerals, The Article (§ 140- § 192).

LESSON TWENTY-THREE

STUDY: Participles and Pronouns, #D5 and #D6.
READ *Biblical Greek*: The Pronoun (§ 195- § 223).

LESSON TWENTY-FOUR

STUDY: Explanations: Introduction, and Phonemics (Part I), #E1-#E2.46.
READ *Biblical Greek*: Prepositions (Part I) — In General; Rival Prepositions (§ 78- § 111).

LESSON TWENTY-FIVE

STUDY: Phonemics (Part II), and Morphology, #E2.5-#E3.38.
READ *Biblical Greek*: Prepositions (Part II) — Some Individual Prepositions (§ 112- § 135).

LESSON TWENTY-SIX

STUDY: The Morphology of the Greek Verb, #E4.
READ *Biblical Greek*: Particles (§ 450- § 477).

LESSON TWENTY-SEVEN

STUDY: Morphological Analysis, and Accents, #E5 and #E6. (Do #E5.6.)
READ *Biblical Greek*: Conclusions (§ 480- § 494).

UNITS OF THE TEXT OF MARK

Ideally, the whole of Mark's Gospel should be read in Greek at this Stage. It divides conveniently into three sections:

First Term	: Early Ministry	Chapters 1-5
Second Term	: The Central Period	Chapters 6-10
Third Term	: Passion Week	Chapters 11-16

(For a two-semester Course, half the Gospel would be read each semester.)

Where the availability of tuition time does not allow the entire Gospel to be covered, a selection of representative passages should be made. Twenty-seven selections are recommended below, nine from each part of the Gospel, each one approximately 15 verses, or 30 lines, in length. Some additional optional selections, marked with an asterisk instead of a unit number, are also included for reading in classes where time permits more than nine sections per term to be covered.

1.	1:1-13	John the Baptist/The Temptation
2.	1:14-28	Jesus Begins His Ministry
3.	1:29-45	Healings, and First Tour of Galilee
4.	2:1-14	Healing the Paralytic/Calling Levi
*	2:15-28	Controversies With the Pharisees
5.	3:1-15	Healing and Teaching
6.	3:20-35	Jesus and Beelzebul/Jesus's Family
*	4:1-20	The Parable of the Sower, and Its Explanation
7.	4:35-5:10	Confronting A Storm and A Demoniac
8.	5:11-24a	Healing the Demoniac/Jairus's Request
9.	5:24b-43	Healing the Sick Woman/Raising the Dead Girl
10.	6:1-13	Rejection At Nazareth/Sending Out the Twelve
11.	6:14-29	The Death of John the Baptist
*	6:30-44	Feeding the Five Thousand
12.	7:1-15	The Tradition of the Elders
*	7:17-30	Explaining to the Disciples/The Syrophoenician Woman
13.	8:27-9:1	Peter's Declaration About Jesus/Jesus's Prediction
14.	9:2-13	The Transfiguration
15.	9:14-29	The Boy With An Unclean Spirit
16.	10:1-16	Marriage and Divorce/Blessing The Children
17.	10:17-31	The Rich Man Who Went Away Sadly
18.	10:32-45	Third Passion Prediction/The Request of James and John
19.	11:1-14	The Triumphal Entry/The Cursing of the Fig Tree
*	11:15-33	Temple Cleansing/Lesson From Fig Tree/Authority Question
20.	12:1-12	Parable of the Vineyard and its Tenants
21.	12:13-27	Questions About Paying Tax and About the Resurrection
22.	12:28-40	The Great Commandment/David's Son/Denouncing the Scribes
23.	14:12-26	The Last Passover
*	14:27-31, 66-72	Peter's Denial: Prediction and Fulfilment
*	14:32-50	Gethsemane
24.	14:51-65	The Young Man Who Fled/Jesus Before the Council
25.	15:1-15	Jesus Before Pilate
26.	15:16-32	Mocking and Crucifixion
27.	15:33-47	Death and Burial
*	16	Resurrection

APPENDIX A

A STUDENT'S GUIDE TO THE USE OF THIS BOOK

AO. SOME GENERAL EXPLANATIONS AND COMMENTS

AO.1 APPENDIX PURPOSE

AO.11 This Appendix aims to provide additional material which may prove helpful for those who are studying on their own and also for those who are part of a Greek class but who would find it useful to have further explanations and comments on some of the steps being taken in the main Lessons.

AO.12 Those students who prefer lesson material to be broken up into smaller steps will find this Appendix of especial help. It gives additional comments on the first five Lessons (after Lesson Five this is not necessary). However, a diagram of Greek morph slots is provided at #A6, for use with Lesson Six. The comments on each Lesson should be read in conjunction with that Lesson, and the indicated Grammar learnt.

AO.13 In general, material of continuing reference value is given in the Lessons, and this Appendix contains additional explanatory material and comments which once noted will probably not need to be referred to again.

AO.14 Because of individual differences between all of us, the rate at which you personally will progress, and your speed and understanding and retentivity, will be different from that of others. However, it will help you to attain the maximum of which you are capable in these areas if you note some positive and negative factors that will affect language learning.

AO.15 Eugene Nida, in writing *Learning A Foreign Language — A Handbook For Missionaries*, begins on page 1 to analyze why missionaries find they have great difficulties in learning a language, and his comments will apply equally well to your learning N.T. Greek. He says:

> "There is no valid reason for tragic failure in language learning, for languages can be learned. Children of six years of age in all cultures are able to speak their mother-tongue intelligibly and to discuss many things which missionaries seem never able to talk about. Naturally, we may then ask ourselves, 'Why do we not learn a language as well as a child?' The reasons for our deficiencies are not difficult to discover. In the first place, as adult missionaries we have already acquired a set of language habits, and we have practised them for fully twenty years, until they have become thoroughly a part of us. In the second place, we shelter our ego with all types of inhibitions and restraints. We are afraid of exposing our ignorance and of being laughed at, and as a result our speech becomes ridiculous. Of course, it is also true that we do not have native parents who fondly try to teach us, who never seem to tire of repeating words, and who praise us for our feeble efforts. Furthermore, we are not exposed to the taunting of other children who cruelly force conformity upon their playmates. In reality, we do not have many of the advantages afforded children."

AO.16 F.L. Billows (*The Techniques of Language Teaching*, page 38) makes a comment on rather similar lines: "Opinionated, over-confident people have not the flexibility of mind to learn languages easily." The extent to which we can put aside our inhibitions and self-consciousness, and risk making ridiculous mistakes and take them in our stride, is the extent to which we will make good progress in language learning.

AO.17 And Nida adds three other comments which are relevant: "On the other hand, we have other advantages which come from analytical training and mature mental faculties." (p.2.) "Lack of time is the most common reason for failure in language learning." (p.8.) "Some of the failure to learn a language results from the wrong approach." (p.9.)

AO.18 From what Nida and Billows have said, one can draw the observation, regarding participation and learning in class: "The smaller the pride, the greater the progress: I will learn lots of Greek from participation in class — unless my pride and dignity get in the way."

AO.19 On page 26, Nida stresses that "Language learning means language using". We can see then that a second major principle in the learning of Greek is, in effect, "Use it, or lose it".

AO.2   THE PHILOSOPHY OF "FRAMEWORK" LEARNING

AO.21 The major problem for many students in this Course is one of attitude and expectation. They expect to be able to memorize and master everything they are told the first time they are told it. This is the approach to learning which has been customary in other subjects they have studied, and so they come to Greek with the intention of mastering it in the same way. They believe this is what is expected of them. Then they find that the material is presented to them faster than they can absorb it, and that they are becoming overwhelmed by an avalanche of information which they cannot keep up with.

AO.22 If you *are* able to assimilate thoroughly everything in the lessons as they are presented, this is excellent; but it is also exceptional. You are *not* expected to master all the contents of a lesson when you go through it.

AO.23 What is happening during this Stage I Course is that you are being introduced swiftly and systematically to the entire range of Greek grammar that is needed for beginning to read and understand the New Testament. The more fundamental paradigms and constructions are set for learning; the rest are provided at this stage as information. What you are asked to do is to *become aware of them* without necessarily learning them (e.g., to know that there is such a thing as the perfect tense without necessarily memorizing the flexion). Then, when these words and forms are encountered in New Testament sentences, you will begin to get practice in recognizing them, and your teacher (if you are a member of a class) will explain the forms and their use, in the contexts in which they are actually used in the New Testament — and you will be able to follow and to understand the explanation.

AO.24 This does not mean that you are now being told not to try too hard to learn your work. Not at all. But it *does* mean that you are not being asked to do all your learning on your own account, by rote, in isolation from actual use situations: you are being asked to *become aware* of the total framework of work to be learnt, and then progressively to flesh out that skeleton with knowledge and understanding as you gain experience with actual sentences from the Greek New Testament.

AO.25 Your learning acquisition is thus to be a steady progress on a broad base, so that you are gradually developing an increasing awareness of the way in which Greek words and forms and constructions are actually used, from encountering them in use.

AO.26 For most people this is a completely new approach to learning a subject, though it is in fact akin to how you progressively learned your own mother tongue in the first place.

AO.27 This all means that you should indeed learn as much as you can by means of each of the learning opportunities (as set out below), concentrating particularly upon those sections of a Lesson that are indicated as most important: but you should not be dismayed or even surprised when you are taken on to a new Lesson before you have fully grasped the last one. You should proceed at your own pace (that is, irrespective of whether others are ahead of you or behind) without being concerned that your pace is not faster. Be content to build your knowledge of Greek gradually; do not be discouraged if you do not remember everything at the first or second hearing: you are not expected to. Your knowledge of the different aspects of Greek will fill out as you are exposed to more and more of the language in extracts from the New Testament during Stage I (the Beginner's Course) and, in Stage II, in progressing through Mark (or some other N.T. book) and in using Appendices C, D, and E. The Grammar that you do need to remember from each Lesson is set out for you in this Appendix at the end of the Notes on each Lesson.

AO.3   LEARNING OPPORTUNITIES

AO.30 For those who are part of a class (students studying privately, there will be comments for your situation later on), there are several "learning points" for each Lesson which provide "learning opportunities" that will contribute cumulatively to the growth of your knowledge of Greek:

AO.31 Student's Preliminary Reading of the Lesson: The final Assignment set at the end of each Lesson is to do a quick preliminary reading of the following Lesson. The purpose of this is to provide you with a sense of direction — an awareness, in a general way, of the work that is to be tackled next, and an overview of that work. This Preliminary Reading enables you to see the whole of the next work unit in its totality, to get an idea of its scope, and thus to prepare yourself for its presentation in detail.

AO.32 The Introduction of the Lesson by the Teacher: In the following Session, the teacher introduces the grammar content of the new Lesson, going through each section and explaining it, giving drilling in the new paradigms, and discussing any questions raised by the class. This provides you with the opportunity of becoming familiar with the new material, seeing its interrelationships, and gaining an initial understanding of its use.

AO.33 Second Reading By the Student: The first Assignment which is set for the student on that Lesson will be a complete rereading of the Lesson material. This is to consolidate your overall understanding of the Lesson.

AO.34 Specific Memorization: In each Lesson, one (or more) of the paradigms or flexions or other material is set for memorization. A specific effort is now to be made by the student to memorize this particular material.

AO.35 Sentence Translation: Next, the work of the Lesson is to be put to immediate use in translating sentences from the Greek N.T. which utilize the grammatical content of the Lesson. The aim of the translation is to reflect an understanding of the meaning of the Greek text, and therefore it must be as literal as it can be (a full explanation of the approach to your translation will be given in #A2.5). In seeking to understand the meaning of the Greek, you will need to refer back frequently to the grammatical content of the Lesson, and to use other aids available: paradigm and vocabulary lists, and your Dictionary, and (in later Lessons) the Sentence Analysis that is given. This point in your work, at which you make use of the Lesson material in gaining an understanding of a Greek sentence, is a major learning opportunity: seek therefore to gain an adequate grasp of the grammar that is needed to understand the sentence, and of how the sentence uses that grammar to express its meaning. There will be words, expressions, or constructions, that you cannot readily decipher: do not spend time on these (see #A2.7) but make a note of the problem for classroom discussion.

AO.36 Revision and Recapitulation: Your next Classroom Session will commence with a brief recapitulation of the previous Lesson, and drills in that Lesson's flexions (or the most important ones, at least). Use this as a check on your overall understanding of that Lesson and of your work in memorizing the set flexions, and in your general understanding of the other flexions and your ability to recognize forms from them.

AO.37 Classroom Consideration of Sentences: After the recapitulation and drills, the class will consider in detail the Greek sentences given in the set Assignments. Avail yourself of every opportunity of translating a sentence in class and having it commented upon. Note differences between how you have rendered each of the sentences and the renderings of others given in class, and ask questions about all the points that are not clear to you. It is important for the learning process that you should come to the point where you can understand the explanations that are given, and the form and meaning of the words in the sentences (apart of course from those words in the early Lessons given under "Expressions" that are not explained as yet).

AO.38 Review and Reference Back: In the work on subsequent Lessons, matters will arise which require you to refer back to points of grammar in earlier Lessons. Use these references back to earlier material as an opportunity to review and consolidate your knowledge of that work. Additionally, use any break between the conclusion of your Stage I (Beginner's) Course and the commencement of Stage II to work through all the Lessons again, in sequence. You will find that the Greek sentences will now be considerably easier, and that many matters not quite clear when you went through the book the first time will have now fallen into place, and you will be able to have a much better "feel" for the overall functioning of Greek. In your Review of Stage I in this way, attempt to translate the sentences accurately at sight, without writing down a translation. The greater the extent to which you can do this, the better the extent to which you have grasped your work. But however well (or badly) you fare in this Review, the next stage in your learning, studying a Gospel in Greek, will help you progress further.

AO.4   SELF STUDY SUGGESTIONS

AO.41 If you are not a member of a Greek class, why not form a class of your own to work with you? In your church or Christian fellowship or circle of friends, there are sure to be several people who would like to learn to read the Greek New Testament, given the opportunity and a little encouragement. You can provide both of these. Gather together those interested, and plan a suitable meeting night and venue. Read through the Basic Principles For Teachers (Appendix B) and you can teach yourselves, even though none of you has done Greek before. Amongst the many advantages of working together in this way: you can give help and encouragement to each other in the work; you can verify each other's pronunciations of the Greek; one member of a group will often spot an error that another has made and not noticed; you can test each other's memorizing of the paradigms and flexions; a co-operative attack on the translation of the Greek sentences will produce better results than if you are working alone; often a small group working together will persevere with the Course through the hard and the tedious parts where a lone student will be tempted to give up; and so on.

AO.42 A small group working together can provide an environment for learning that is not far below that of a formal class, if the group has made up its mind that its members intend to have fun and fellowship together in their Greek, while simultaneously taking their work seriously.

AO.43 If joining a class or forming your own group are both out of the question, you can certainly do this Course successfully on your own. But you need to realize that to do this *is* more difficult, and that you will have to accept the discipline of putting time aside for Greek on a regular basis a few days every week, and keeping that time sacrosanct — or there will always be something "more important" that will arise and claim it. Make it your aim to progress through this book at the fastest rate you can, and follow as far as possible in your personal study all the guidelines for classroom situations that are given in this Appendix and Appendix B — adapt these according to circumstances and apply them to your own situation.

AO.44 There will of course be problems you encounter where you (or your group) will need to consult someone with a greater knowledge of Greek. A minister or some other person who has studied Greek may be your answer here. Alternatively, you yourself may be that person at a later stage of your own Course — you yourself will then have a greater knowledge of Greek, and you will find that many of your earlier problems simply resolve themselves.

A1. LESSON ONE

A1.1 LESSON GOAL

The initial goal for this Lesson is to become fluent in reading the Greek letters accurately. The following graduated pronunciation exercises will help you with the alphabet (#1.27).

A1.2 ATTAINING FLUENCY

A1.21 First, read through the notes in Lesson One about the alphabet, and note the letters of the alphabet — their appearance, both capitals and cursive, and the English guidewords which contain their pronunciations.

A1.22 Secondly, learn the "nonsense sentence" (#1.51) which contains all the English guide words — this is a valuable standby during the early days, when you may hesitate at the pronunciation of a new word, and recollecting the English guide word containing the particular letter or diphthong is of help.

A1.23 Next, practise the pronunciation of the sample words given below (in #A1.4 to A1.8). The first section uses only those letters which in Greek have an appearance and pronunciation similar to English — you can pronounce these as if they were new English words you had come across. The following sections introduce progressively the Greek letters which look something like English letters but are in fact quite different, and then those which do not look anything like English letters. Then there are notes on a special nasal letter, and the pronunciation of Greek diphthongs.

A1.24 When each new letter is introduced in its turn, you are given several words which use that letter together with the letters that you already know. Make sure that you correctly understand the pronunciation of the new letter, and then read out aloud all the words given for that letter, pronouncing them several times each until you are sure that you can say them fluently. Then move on to the next line and the next letter.

A1.25 After completing this exercise, go back to the charts of the alphabet and diphthongs (#1.27, 1.33) and read out the Greek words in the Greek Examples list. You should now be able to read these fluently; if not, repeat the exercises that are given here until you can readily recognize and pronounce the Greek letters, and thus read out these Greek words fluently.

A1.3 BREATHING AND ACCENTS

A1.31 As the Greek cursive (lower case) letters are much more common than the capitals, these exercises concentrate on them.

A1.32 Every Greek word beginning with a vowel or a diphthong has a sign over it (over the second vowel of a diphthong) called a *breathing*.

A1.33 If it is curled to the right, like an opening inverted comma, ', then it is called a *rough breathing* and it is pronounced as an "h" in front of the word.

A1.34 If the breathing is curled to the left, like a closing inverted comma, ', then it is called a *smooth breathing* and it simply indicates that the word is not pronounced with an "h" in front of it.

A1.35 Thus ὃς is pronounced "os", but ὃς is pronounced "hos"; ἐκ is pronounced "ek", but ἑκ is pronounced "hek".

A1.36 Automatically note the breathing when you come to words beginning with a vowel and be sure that you never drop your aitches but always pronounce a rough breathing when it occurs.

A1.37 The other signs on words, ' ` and ~, are accents, which can be ignored at this stage.

A1.4   LETTERS SIMILAR TO ENGLISH IN APPEARANCE AND PRONUNCIATION

A1.41 Almost half the letters of the Greek alphabet — ten out of twenty-four — are sufficiently close to their English counterparts for them to be readily recognizable. Nine of the ten can also be pronounced similarly to English (the tenth, υ, will be discussed a little later).

A1.42 The ten letters are: α β δ ε ι κ ο ς τ and υ.
Their English equivalents are: a b d e i k o s t and u.

A1.43 Note: α can be pronounced as in "along", or "father", and ι as in "in" or "kiosk" (i.e., either short or long — in pronouncing a Greek word, make them short unless it "feels" best to you to pronounce them long). But ε can only be short, as in "penguin", and ο can only be short, as in "kiosk".

A1.44 The following fifty Greek words use only these letters (not including υ). Practice reading them out aloud a few times.

ἀββα, βία, δέκα, διά, κατά, κακός, τάς, βάτος, βίος, διαβάς, καταβάς, δέ, δίς, δοκός, δέος, δέδεκος, ἰδέ, τε, ἐκ, ἔτι, τίς, ἔτεκες, ἔκδικος, τίκτετε, ἴδιος, ἀδικία, διότι, κακία, ἀκακός, ἄδικος, κόκκος, κόκκε, ἔκδοτος, ὁ, ὅς, ὅτι, ὅτε, ὅδε, τόδε, ἔτος, ὁδός, τότε, ἐδίδοτε, ἕκτος, δεκτός, δέκατος, τακτός, ἄτακτος, διδακτός, διδακτικός.

A1.5   LETTERS SIMILAR IN APPEARANCE BUT DIFFERENT FROM ENGLISH

Half a dozen Greek letters look something like English letters but are in fact quite different — and so they need to be carefully noted.

A1.51 γ is not "y", but "g" as in "got". Practise reading these words — and remember to *pronounce each letter separately — there are no pairs of vowels here that are pronounced together as one sound (a diphthong).*

ἅγιος, γέ, διάγετε, διαταγάς, ὄγδοος, ἀγάγετε

A1.52 η is not "n", but long ε̄, pronounced as in "there", "where".

ἤ, ἥ, γῆ, δή, βοή, δίκη, γόης, ἀκοή, ἤδη, δεκάτη, διετής, ἀκήκοα

(Take care to get this pronunciation right. Note that the word ἤ is pronounced exactly the same as the English word "hair", and δή is pronounced exactly the same as "dare", but without any pronunciation of the "r" in these English words.)

A1.53 ν is not "v", but "n" as in "in".

ἔν, ἕν, ἀνά, ἵνα, ὅταν, ναός, τέκνον, γένος, ἤγαγον, ἱκανός, ἐγένετο, ἀγνήν

A1.54 ρ is not "p", but "r" as in "throw", "rope".

ἀγρός, ὄρος, ὅρος, ἕτερος, τρίτος, νεκρός, γὰρ, ἄρτος, καρδία, ἔργον.

A1.55 χ is not "x", but "ch" (sometimes written "kh") as in "loch" or "Bach" (or if you cannot make this aspirated palatal sound, pronounce it as in "chemist").

χρόνος, χάρις, χαρά, χόρτος, ἀρχή, ἔχιδνα, δοχή, διδαχή, ἔνοχος.

A1.56 ω is not "w", but long ō ("ow"), pronounced as in "throw", "rope".

ἐγώ, ἔχω, ἄρχω, ἕως, ὧδε, ὥρα, κρίνω, ὁράω, δώδεκα, ἐρωτάω, ἀγωγή

A1.57 υ is indeed "u", but it is NEVER pronounced like the English "u" in "but". It can be short (in which case it is pronounced like the "u" in "put") or long (in which case it is pronounced like the "u" in "lute"). A student will not usually know whether it is short or long — adopt the general rule-of-thumb of pronouncing it short as in "put" unless it seems in a particular word to need to be pronounced as long.

νῦν, γυνή, ὕβρις, ὕδωρ, δυνατός, ἔτυχον, κύριος, τέτυχα, ὑγιές

A1.6   LETTERS DIFFERENT IN APPEARANCE FROM ENGLISH

The remaining eight Greek letters are different in appearance from any English letters, and there is, in addition, another form of the letter "s" which is used initially or medially in a word.

A1.61 ζ is "dz" (a double letter), as in "adze". Be careful to pronounce both sounds, even when this letter stands first in a word.

γάζα, ἔζην, κράζω, ῥίζα, βιάζω, ἀγιάζω, ζωή, ζάω, ζητέω, ζυγός.

A1.62 θ is "th" as in "think" or "throw", NEVER as in "this" or "though".

θεός, θύρα, θρόνος, ἔθνος, καθώς, ἐχθές, ἀγαθός, θάνατος, θεωρέω.

A1.63 λ is "l" as in "lute", "glimpse".

λέγω, λόγος, βάλλω, ἀλλά, καλός, λίθος, ὅλος, λαός, ὄχλος, λαλέω, βιβλίον

A1.64 μ is "m", as in "chemist", "glimpse".

μόνος, νόμος, ἅμα, ἐμός, ῥῆμα, μετά, μένω, μήτηρ, ὄνομα, τίθημι, ἡμέρα, ἔρημος, μαρτυρέω.

A1.65 ξ is "x" (a double letter), as in "six", "locks".

νύξ, δόξα, ἔξω, ἔξω, ἔξοδος, ἐξάγω, ἄξιος, δεξιός, δοξάζω, ἀξίνη, ἐδέξατο, ξένος, ξύλον.

A1.66 π is "p", as in "put", "soup".

πᾶς, πρός, ὑπό, ἐπί, ἑπτά, τόπος, πόλις, πάλιν, πίπτω, ἄνθρωπος.

A1.67 σ is "s" when used elsewhere than at the end of a word.

σύ, σύν, σάρξ, σώζω, ὥστε, ὅσος, μέσος, κόσμος, ὅστις, χριστός.

A1.68 φ is "ph", as in "photograph" (pronounced as the "f" in "feuding").

φῶς, φωνή, φημί, τυφλός, γράφω, σοφία, ἔφαγον, ἔφυγον, κεφαλή, ἀδελφός, προφήτης, ὀφθαλμός.

A1.69 ψ is "ps" (a double letter), as in "glimpse", "steps".

ἄψας, ὀψία, διψάω, ὑψόω, θλῖψις, ψυχή, ψηφίζω, ἀποκάλυψις, ψαλμός, ψαλλέτω.

A1.7   PRONUNCIATION OF NASAL GAMMA

It should be noted that γ is enga (i.e., pronounced as "ng") before a palatal (κ, γ, χ, ξ). Examples:

ἐγγύς, ὄγκος, ἄγγελος, ἀγκάλη, ἄγκυρα, ἐγγίζω, ἐγχρίω, ἐγκρίνω, τυγχάνω, ἐγγράφω, ἐγκακέω, ἐγκαλέω, ἐγκάθετος, σάλπιγξ, φάραγξ.

A1.8   PRONUNCIATION OF THE DIPHTHONGS

A1.81 In addition, Greek has seven diphthongs, or vowel pairs pronounced together.

These are combinations of the short vowels α, ε and ο with ι and υ respectively, and ι and υ with each other: αι ει οι υι αυ ευ ου: αι as in "aisle", ει as in "eight", οι as in "boiling", υι as in "penguin" (if ι is short) or "suite" (if ι is long), αυ as in "Strauss", "Mau Mau", "Faust", and "kauri", ευ as in "feuding", and ου as in "soup", "you". Practise your pronunciation of the diphthongs with these Greek words:

A1.82 καί, ναί, παῖς, καιρός, καινός, χαίρω, δίκαιος, παιδίον, δαιμόνιον, αἰών, αἷμα, αἰτέω.

A1.83 εἰ, εἰς, εἷς, δεῖ, εἴτε, εἶδον, εἶπον, εἰμί, τρεῖς, ἡμεῖς, πλείων, πείθω, σπείρω, εἰρήνη, ἐκεῖνος, ἀλήθεια.

A1.84 οἶδα, οἶκος, οἰκία, λοιπός, ποιμήν, πλοῖον, κατοικέω, ποιέω, ὅμοιος, ἀνοίγω.

A1.85 υἱός, λελυκυῖα *(This diphthong is not at all common.)*

A1.86 αὐτός, αὐτή, αὕτη, αὐταί, αὗται, αὐγή, αὐλός, αὔριον, αὐξάνω, σεαυτοῦ, σταυρόω, θησαυρός.

A1.87 εὖ, εὐθύς, πιστεύω, βασιλεύς, εὐαγγέλιον, δεύτερος, ψεῦδος, εὐλογέω, εὐχαριστέω, εὑρίσκω, εὐαγγελίζω, πνεῦμα, γραμματεύς.

A1.88 οὐ, οὐκ, οὐχ, οὐχί, οὖν, οὐδέ, οὐκέτι, οὐρανός, οὗτος, οὔτε, ποῦ, πούς, νοῦς, ἰδού, ὅπου, δοῦλος, ἀκούω, ἐξουσία.

A1.9 PRONOUNCING THE GREEK EXAMPLES AND LETTER NAMES

A1.91 When you have satisfied yourself with the pronunciation of these words, read out aloud the "Greek Examples" (#1.27 and 1.33) and the names of the letters of the Greek alphabet as set out in #1.27, giving them their pronunciation in accordance with what you have learned.

A1.92 Unlike in English, the pronunciation system you have just learned for Greek is largely phonemic — each letter has only one sound, and each sound is represented by only one letter (or diphthong). (The two exceptions are that υ when long — which is not so very common — is pronounced the same as ου, and English speakers find it difficult to pronounce χ as an aspirate — as in Scottish "loch", German "Bach" — and sometimes pronounce it indistinguishably from κ.) This means that, in general, if you can pronounce a Greek word correctly, you can spell it.

A1.93 When going through the Vocabulary list of each new Lesson, always carefully pronounce each word aloud. When commencing work on each Selection from the Greek N.T., read it aloud in Greek first of all.

A1.94 This care about pronunciation, and practising reading out aloud, is exceedingly important. An incorrect pronunciation will very easily mislead you into an incorrect spelling and possible confusion about words and forms. On the other hand, if you harness your eye and ear together, so that they operate in conjunction, each will aid and reinforce the other in the learning process. In consequence you will learn your work more quickly, more effectively, and more permanently.

A1.95 These are questions that you need to be able to answer completely correctly from the reading of Lesson One:
1.1   What are the three occasions in Greek when a capital letter is used?
1.2   Name these ten signs: ´ ` ~ ’ ‘ , . · ; ¨
1.3   From memory, write out in Greek the names of the letters of the Greek alphabet, correctly spelt and in the right order.
1.4   What are the seven Greek diphthongs?
1.5   What are the English keywords which contain each of the seven Greek vowels and seven diphthongs with the pronunciation that these vowels and diphthongs have in Greek?
1.6   (a) What are the two different pronunciations for Greek γ? (b) When does the less common one occur? (c) What are the two names for this letter, for its two pronunciations?
1.7   In what circumstances does ἐκ ("out of") become ἐξ?
1.8   What is the meaning of *inflection?*
1.9   What is a morph?

A2.   LESSON TWO

A2.1   STEMS AND SUFFIXES

A2.11 The first goal for Lesson Two is understanding the concept of an inflected word. As a rough and ready rule-of-thumb you can take it that, in a given flexion, the part of a word that does not change is the stem, and the part that changes in the different forms in the flexion is the suffix.

A2.12 Exercise: Apply this to κύριος and ἔργον (#2.4): what is the stem of each?

A2.13 Answer: The stem of κύριος is κυρι-, which is the lexical morph carrying the meaning "lord". The various morphs added to κυρι- are the suffixes meaning "nominative singular", "genitive plural", and so on as the case may require. Similarly the stem of ἔργον is ἐργ-, and the morphs that are added indicate number and case.

A2.14 Exercise: Apply this to λύω (#2.81): what is its stem and suffixes?

A2.15 Answer: The stem of λύω is λυ-, which is the lexical morph carrying the meaning "loose", and the morphs added to λυ- can for practical purposes be treated as suffixed pronouns meaning "I", "you", "they", etc.

A2.16 This rough rule-of-thumb sometimes needs to be elastic enough to take account of the fact that a stem *can* change. Thus, **Exercise:** What is the stem of the Article (#2.4) and of εἰμί (#2.81)?

A2.17 Answer: The stem of the Article is τ-, and the rest of each form of the Article consists of the person/number/gender suffix; but in the nominative singular and plural of both masculine and feminine, the stem is the rough breathing only. The stem of $\varepsilon\dot{\iota}\mu\dot{\iota}$ is really $\dot{\varepsilon}\sigma$-, but in three forms the -σ- has become a -ι- (the reason for this will be explained in due course).

A2.2 THE REASON FOR THE MANY FORMS OF THE ARTICLE

A2.21 The second goal is to understand the reason for the twenty-four forms of the Article. Why so many?

A2.22 The explanation is: the noun *selects* the form of the Article that must be used with it, and the form of the Article selected will be the one that agrees with it in gender, number, and case.

A2.23 A noun has an inherent gender: $\check{\varepsilon}\rho\gamma o\nu$, for example, is always neuter. This means that only the neuter forms of the Article can be used with it. In a particular sentence, if $\check{\varepsilon}\rho\gamma o\nu$ is being used as a subject, and in the plural (as for example, "The works of the flesh . . .", Galatians 5:19), then the form of $\check{\varepsilon}\rho\gamma o\nu$ used will need to be the nominative plural, $\check{\varepsilon}\rho\gamma\alpha$, and this will select to accompany it the form of the neuter Article which is nominative plural, $\tau\acute{\alpha}$.

A2.24 Similarly, if one wished to say "of the lord", $\kappa\acute{\upsilon}\rho\iota o\varsigma$ will need to be in the genitive singular, $\kappa\upsilon\rho\acute{\iota}o\upsilon$, and being masculine will select the form of the Article that is masculine genitive singular, i.e. $\tau o\bar{\upsilon}$.

A2.25 The converse of this is that the Article is frequently a useful guide to the gender, number, and case of the noun with which it is used — something which becomes quite important with the Third Declension (see #5).

A2.3 MEMORIZATION

At this point, memorize the set paradigms (see Assignment 1).

A2.4 USING A PARADIGM TO FIND THE MEANING OF OTHER WORDS

A2.41 The next goal is understanding how the paradigm of one word applies as a pattern for other words.

A2.42 If the stem of $\kappa\acute{\upsilon}\rho\iota o\varsigma$ is $\kappa\upsilon\rho\iota$-, and -$o\varsigma$ is the suffix, then we can tell that the stem of $\nu\acute{o}\mu o\varsigma$ is $\nu o\mu$-, for -$o\varsigma$ is its suffix. From the paradigm of $\kappa\acute{\upsilon}\rho\iota o\varsigma$ we see that -$o\iota\varsigma$ is the dative plural suffix, having the meaning "to (the) —" or "for (the) —", so that $\tau o\bar{\iota}\varsigma$ $\kappa\upsilon\rho\acute{\iota}o\iota\varsigma$ means "to the lords" or "for the lords". Therefore if we put this same ending on to the stem $\nu o\mu$- (which means "law" — see #1.27), then we get $\tau o\bar{\iota}\varsigma$ $\nu\acute{o}\mu o\iota\varsigma$, which thus means "to the laws" or "for the laws" (which of these two possible meanings is intended would be indicated by the context of use).

A2.43 So when you come across a Greek noun (say, θεοῦ), the first step towards understanding its meaning is to break it into stem and suffix, then locate the lexical meaning of the word in the Vocabulary/Dictionary, and work out the meaning of the suffix from the parallel form in a paradigm (i.e. the form that has the same suffix). The lexical form of θεοῦ is θεός, "God", and so the appropriate paradigm is the one for κύριος, and the parallel form is κυρίου, which is genitive singular. Thus we arrive at the meaning of θεοῦ as "of God", "God's".

A2.44 The same approach is followed with verbs, using the paradigm for λύω: λυ- is the stem (the lexal, carrying the verb's meaning) and the balance of the word consists of two grammatical morphs that are closely joined together. The first of these is the *neutral morph* and the second is the *pronoun morph* or *pronominal morph*, a cut-down version of an unemphasized personal pronoun added to the word, meaning "I", "you", "they", and the like.

A2.45 The neutral morph is always -o- or -ε-: -o- when the pronoun morph commences with a nasal or with -υ-, or consists of lengthening the neutral morph (as in λύ-ομεν, λύ-ουσιν, and λύ-ω); -ε- in all other cases. The role of the neutral morph will be explained later. It does not affect us at present and so for convenience it can be taken with the pronoun morph.

A2.46 Thus we can divide the forms of the flexion of λύω in this way:

			loose
SINGULAR	1	λύ - ω	I
	2	λύ - εις	you (sing.)
	3	λύ - ει	he/she/it
PLURAL	1	λύ - ομεν	we
	2	λύ - ετε	you (pl.)
	3	λύ - ουσι(ν)	they

A2.47 The same flexion can be constructed for any other verb:

			see
SINGULAR	1	βλέπ - ω	I
	2	βλέπ - εις	you (sing.)
	3	βλέπ - ει	he/she/it
PLURAL	1	βλέπ - ομεν	we
	2	βλέπ - ετε	you (pl.)
	3	βλέπ - ουσι(ν)	they

A2.48 For the verbs that follow λύω in their present tense (the great majority of New Testament verbs), you can divide them in the same way that has been done for βλέπω and substitute the appropriate pronoun suffix for the -ω of the lexical form, and thus obtain whatever form is required. Thus to form "they say", take the lexical form, λέγω, "I say", and substitute -ουσι(ν) ("they") for -ω ("I") to get the correct form λέγουσι(ν).

A2.49 Test yourself: from ἔχω, "I have", construct the form "we have".

A2.5 PRINCIPLES OF TRANSLATION

A2.51 The various explanations and ideas that have been given so far can now be put together and used as the translation techniques for deciphering Greek sentences. The section which follows next will show how that is to be done.

A2.52 First of all, however: reflect for a moment upon the question of what kind of translation you should aim to produce. There is a temptation for a student to attempt to give the best, smoothest, and most idiomatic English translation of the Greek sentences he is working on. This attempt is in fact misguided and unhelpful. Do not allow yourself to fall into this trap.

A2.53 When you translate Greek material into English, this is not the ultimate purpose of your study in Greek at all. It is simply a means to an end. Your goal is to be able to read the Greek New Testament with understanding; when you translate from Greek into English, this is done as a stage in the process of developing your own understanding of the Greek, and it is also to enable your teacher to assess the level of your progress. Do not try, therefore, to put the passage into a kind of smooth-flowing, natural language that the inspired author may have used if he had in fact been writing in English. On the contrary: render the Greek into equivalent English so that the English shows what the author actually wrote in Greek.

A2.54 Your aim therefore must be absolute accuracy in your translation into English. The Greek grammatical form must be expressed in its precise English equivalent: you must render a plural in Greek by a plural in English; if the Greek verb is present tense you must express it by a present tense in English; and so on. Translate what is there, without omitting material that is in the Greek or adding extra material into the English. This will very definitely mean that at times you are producing English that is stilted, jerky, and even perhaps unnatural, but the test is, Is it conveying accurately exactly what is being said in the Greek?

A2.55 However, it is important to translate not only the words of the Greek into English, but also the other features of Greek syntax — word order, special constructions and ways of expressing an idea, etc. There is a difference, that is, between a word-for-word translation and a literal translation. A word-for-word translation renders each word by its English equivalent but does not take due notice of units of expression larger than the word. A literal translation (and this is your aim) expresses in English exactly what is in the Greek but in doing so translates the other features of the Greek in addition to the words as such.

A2.56 The features of Greek syntax that have been referred to are ones that will be explained in subsequent lessons, but to anticipate a little, we can note these examples: **(a)** Greek names of people often have the Article; this Article would not usually be rendered in English; **(b)** Greek word position can indicate special emphasis, and it may be desirable at times to find a way of indicating this emphasis in English; **(c)** you will learn later (#A3.56) that it is a Greek idiom that a neuter plural subject can have a singular verb — you would render this verb into English in the plural; **(d)** When Greek reports indirect speech, it retains the tense that the speaker would have used whereas English requires that in indirect speech the verb be put into the past.

A2.57 At times the Greek will be found to be ambiguous, being capable of having two (or more) interpretations. So far as possible, retain this ambiguity in your English rendering, so that you show an awareness of both possibilities; do not shut out, in your English version, part of the range of meaning that is present in the Greek.

A2.58 The ultimate goal towards which you are aiming in Stage I of your Course is to be able to read the selections from the Greek New Testament in Greek and *understand the meaning of what the Greek is saying* without actually translating them into English. Now this goal may prove to be beyond the reach of many who do the Course: but a slightly lower goal which should be well within the range of most students is to be able to reach the capability of reading through the sentences in this Course and translating them *orally at sight.* You may well fall short of this at the time of doing each Lesson (though some will be able to attain it), but after you have gone through all nine Lessons and return to the earlier Lessons to revise them (#AO.38), you should find yourself increasingly able to do this.

A2.59 Always write your translation of sentences on a separate piece of paper. **NEVER** write a translation on the pages of this book itself. If you were to do that, you would see it each time you revised your earlier sentences, and your understanding would thus become limited to what it had been at the time your translation was first written out. To translate afresh each time you revise is to improve your competence in understanding the meaning of the Greek.

A2.6   TRANSLATION TECHNIQUES

A2.61 Before attempting the translation of a Greek sentence, read it over aloud in Greek one or more times, being careful to use the correct pronunciation. Try to get a "feel" for how the sentence operates (this will become easier as your familiarity with Greek improves). Associating the *sound* of Greek in word and sentence with the *appearance* of the Greek is a very valuable aid to learning which should not be neglected — it is reinforcing learning by familiarizing you with the sight and sound of Greek simultaneously.

A2.62 The first step to take in commencing the work of translation is to check whether or not the sentence is a question. This will be indicated in your edition of the Greek N.T. by a question mark (;) at the end — as your familiarity with Greek increases, you will also learn that there are also a number of Greek words which indicate that a question is being asked. If it *is* a question, you may possibly find it easier to translate it first of all as if it were a statement, and then transform it into a question in English as a second step.

A2.63 Look for the verb in the sentence (or, if it is a long sentence, joined by conjunctions such as καί, δέ, ἀλλά, γάρ, οὖν, or others that you will learn, work on the first section of the sentence first). At this stage you will be able to recognize the verb by its form: either it will be one of the forms from the flexion of εἰμί that you have learned

(#2.81) or it will consist of the stem of a verb plus one of the endings of λύω (see #2.81, #A2.46 and A2.47). If you have learned λύω thoroughly, you should be able to spot a verb quite quickly. In subsequent lessons you will be introduced to more of the varied forms that a verb can take — each time you are presented with a new verb flexion it is important for you to note the features that will enable you to recognize each of its forms as being a verb.

A2.64 If it is a first or second person form, then the subject is an *internal* one, i.e. within the verb: "I", "we" or "you" (singular or plural) as the case may be. There may also be an *external* subject, which will be the nominative case of the separate pronoun with the same meaning, and this will thus have an emphatic effect. The degree of emphasis will vary according to the style of the author and his intention in a particular context, and can range from slight to very emphatic: the context will be your guide.

A2.65 If the verb is third person, then the next step is to look for an *external* subject. If there is one, it will have three features which will aid you in locating it: **(a)** it will be in the nominative case (which you will recognize by noting the nominative case endings for the different paradigms); **(b)** it will very frequently have the definite article in front of it (and the forms of the article are ones that you have learnt, and are very easy to recognize); and **(c)** it will customarily be either just after or sometimes just in front of the verb of which it is the subject — occasionally it may be separated from its verb by other words. If there is no *external* subject to be found, then you will make use of the verb's *internal* subject: "he" (or sometimes "she" or "it") if the verb is singular, and "they" if it is plural.

A2.66 Look next for other words which are linked to subject and verb — an adjective referring to the subject (which will be either in front of the noun, or after the noun with the noun's article repeated in front of it; such an adjective will have the same gender, number and case as the noun), or a word — such as a negative — referring to the verb. Another common type of word to look for is a noun or pronoun in the genitive case referring to the subject. The usual position for such a genitive is immediately after the word to which it refers.

A2.67 Now see if there are words in front of, after, or fairly close to the verb which are accusative case and are *not* preceded by a preposition. Apart from a few special idioms that you will meet in due course, these accusatives will normally form the object of the verb, i.e. in English you will translate such a word or words immediately after the verb.

A2.68 Finally, translate any prepositional phrases (a preposition followed by a noun, either with or without an article between them) and any other words which remain. Use your Vocabulary and Dictionary for any words you do not know.

A2.69 Assemble your translation, putting the Greek word order into correct English order: any introductory words (such as "and" or "for" or "behold", etc.), the subject, the verb (noting if it is negative or interrogative), the object, if any, and any other expressions in the sentence, putting these with the words to which they refer. If a sentence is in two (or more) parts, the division will usually be marked by punctuation and/or "and" or "but" or similar word, and each part of the sentence is best handled separately. Do not take words out of one part of a sentence and put them into another part in your translation.

A2.7   TACKLING PROBLEMS

A2.71 The foregoing procedures can be used for the Sentences of Lesson Two and subsequent Lessons, and will enable you to decipher most of them. But what should you do when you meet problems: a word or a sentence that you simply cannot work out?

A2.72 The best advice for such a situation is, Give up on it. Don't worry about that particular Selection — leave it altogether, and go on to the next one. **Never feel obliged to solve each Sentence before you can leave it for another one**: if you keep wrestling with one that you find difficult you could waste a great deal of your valuable time which could be more profitably used in doing the other Selections. The problem which has temporarily defeated you will invariably solve itself as the range of your exposure to Greek material increases. If however you do wish to pursue the problem further when you first encounter it, the following may be of help.

A2.73 Reread the Course Lesson, and if necessary the previous Lessons as well. Chances are that you have overlooked some comment or explanation which will give you the key to the point that is unclear, or unlock the right approach to the meaning. (If there is not a comment or explanation in any of the previous Lesson material, write and tell me — it means I have omitted including one, and it would be helpful to have you point this out to me.)

A2.74 Consult (according to the nature of the problem) a lexicon or dictionary, the appropriate Appendix at the end of this book, a detailed grammar book, or a commentary on the Greek text of the New Testament.

A2.75 Check out the particular passage in an Interlinear Greek N.T. or one of the more literal English translations (R.V. or N.A.S.B.), and see if this clears up the difficulty. (This is most likely to be helpful if the problem is getting the right English order for the Greek words.)

A2.76 If you are a member of a Greek class, discuss the problem with other members of your class. This is always a good practice for your Greek work generally — two or three students working together can often help each other to understand the full meaning of a Sentence, for one will see what another misses.

A2.77 Make a note of the problem that you have met, and raise it in class for discussion and clarification.

A2.78 But remember: don't be at all concerned at finding in practice that your knowledge of Greek is only partial and incomplete, even for dealing with these Selections from the Greek N.T. Reading and more reading from the Greek N.T. is the best way of filling the gaps in one's knowledge (and also the most enjoyable way).

A2.8 GRAMMAR FROM LESSON TWO THAT YOU NEED TO KNOW

2.1 What is meant by the *subject* of a sentence?

2.2 What is the meaning of each of the five Greek cases, Nominative, Vocative, Accusative, Genitive, Dative?

2.3 What is meant by the term *declension* in Greek?

2.4 When the Greek definite article is used, what does it indicate?

2.5 When the vocabulary entry for a noun appears as (e.g.) πρόσωπον ου τό, or, ἀρχή ῆς ἡ, what is the meaning of what is written after the noun itself?

2.6 (a) Only the *oblique* cases in Greek can be governed by a preposition. Which cases are called the oblique cases? (b) A preposition must always be read together with the noun or pronoun which follows it. Why?

2.7 What is meant by the terms (a) *flexion*? (b) *paradigm*? (c) *conjugation*?

2.8 Explain the idea of the *internal subject* and the *external subject* of a Greek verb.

2.9 In the following N.T. sentences, all the Greek words for the English are given, but in *English* word order. Rearrange the Greek words into the standard *Greek* word order.

(a) And the passover of the Jews was near ...
καὶ τὸ πάσχα τῶν Ἰουδαίων ἦν ἐγγὺς ...

(b) The son of man has power to forgive
ὁ υἱὸς τοῦ ἀνθρώπου ἔχει ἐξουσίαν ἀφιέναι

(c) and the flow of her blood immediately dried up
καὶ ἡ πηγὴ αὐτῆς τοῦ αἵματος εὐθὺς ἐξηράνθη

(d) Jesus's mother says to him, They have no wine.
τοῦ Ἰησοῦ ἡ μήτηρ λέγει πρὸς αὐτόν, ἔχουσιν οὐκ οἶνον.

A3. LESSON THREE

A3.1 POINTS TO NOTE RE THE FIRST DECLENSION

A3.11 Paradigm D1.2, φωνή, is made up of stem φων- and ending -η, and the ending is identical with that of the feminine article (#2.4) — in fact the feminine article consists simply of stem τ- or rough breathing, and the same endings.

A3.12 Paradigm D1.1, καρδία, is the same as φωνή except that -η (which only occurs in the singular) is replaced by -α.

A3.13 Paradigm D1.3, δόξα, has -α in its first two forms, like καρδία, and -η in its next two forms, like φωνή.

A3.14 The masculine Paradigms D1.4 and D1.5 are identical with their feminine counterparts except: **(a)** The nominative singular has an additional -ς, which is a morph indicating the masculine form; **(b)** the genitive singular follows the Second Declension in having its ending -ου; **(c)** it has a vocative form, ending in -α.

A3.15 All plural forms of the First Declension are the same as the flexion of the Article.

A3.2 PRONOUNS

A3.21 The English equivalents for the personal pronouns should be carefully noted. They are as follows:

ἐγώ	I	σύ	you	αὐτός	he	αὐτή	she	αὐτό	it
ἐμέ/με	me	σέ	you	αὐτόν	him	αὐτήν	her	αὐτό	it
ἐμοῦ/μου	my	σοῦ	your	αὐτοῦ	his	αὐτῆς	her	αὐτοῦ	its
ἐμοί/μοι	to me / for me	σοί	to you / for you	αὐτῷ	to him / for him	αὐτῇ	to her / for her	αὐτῷ	to it / for it

ἡμεῖς	we	ὑμεῖς	you	αὐτοί	αὐταί	αὐτά		they
ἡμᾶς	us	ὑμᾶς	you	αὐτούς	αὐτάς	αὐτά		them
ἡμῶν	our	ὑμῶν	your	αὐτῶν	αὐτῶν	αὐτῶν		their
ἡμῖν	to us / for us	ὑμῖν	to you / for you	αὐτοῖς	αὐταῖς	αὐτοῖς		to them / for them

A3.22 The longer forms of the first person singular pronoun (ἐμέ, etc.) are usually the emphatic forms, and the shorter forms (με, etc.) are usually unemphatic, but sometimes this distinction does not seem to hold. The second person singular forms are emphatic if accented, unemphatic if not.

A3.23 If you tend to confuse the respective meanings of ἡμεῖς and ὑμεῖς, remember that the *last* letter of the English word is the *first* letter of its Greek equivalent:

we — long e — ἡμεῖς

you — u — ὑμεῖς

A3.24 αὐτός, αὐτή, αὐτόν means he/she/it, but "it" refers to some other word and should take the gender of the word that it refers to. Thus if αὐτός refers to (say) "kingdom" or "cloud" (which are feminine in Greek — see Lesson Two Vocabulary), then it will need to be feminine in form, though the English translation would be "it" (i.e. neuter in English).

A3.25 The plural forms of αὐτός all are equivalent to English "they", but: the masculine plural covers masculine or combined masculine and feminine units; the feminine plural covers a group of units all of which are feminine; the neuter plural covers units which are neuter. "Unit" here means whatever the word refers to, whether person or thing, and masculine, feminine and neuter refers to its/their grammatical gender in Greek.

A3.26 The singular of οὗτος (see #3.33) means "this" and the plural means "these"; the same case meanings apply as usual, and the same features about gender apply as in #A3.25. Note that when a form of this word is used as a pronoun (i.e. without referring to another noun) it means "this one", and the gender indicates "this man", "this woman", "this thing" (#3.35).

A3.3 THE PAST TENSE OF THE VERB

A3.31 Note (#3.62) that ἐ- at the beginning of a verb form is the *augment*, the past time indicator or morph. Thus every verb that is referring to past time will commence with an ἐ-; e.g. ἔβαλον, second aorist (note the single -λ-) from βάλλω; and εἶδον, from verb stem ἰδ-. But there are some verbs which have a verb stem commencing with ἐ- (e.g., ἔχω, which we met in Lesson Two). Therefore whenever we come across a verb form which commences with ἐ-, we need to check in our Vocabulary or Dictionary to see whether the ἐ- is part of the verb stem (i.e. part of the lexical form of the verb) or whether it is the past time morph added to the verb stem.

A3.32 When the verb stem begins with ἐ-, the past time morph is the change of this ἐ- into ἠ-. Thus the verb stem ἐλθ- becomes ἠλθ- when it is augmented (second aorist, ἠλθον). Whenever therefore we come across a verb form which commences with ἠ-, we have to bear in mind that this may conceal an augment and thus the word may be a past time form of the verb.

A3.33 There are some verb stems which already begin with a long vowel or diphthong and are not changed by the addition of an augment. Thus the verb stem εἰπ- remains εἰπ- when augmented (second aorist, εἶπον).

A3.34 There are three different patterns of the aorist active tense in Greek. This is to say, there are three *conjugations* in Greek (see #9.4) which may be distinguished in the aorist active flexion. The one being introduced this Lesson is the second aorist, i.e. the aorist active flexion of the Second Conjugation. The first aorist will be introduced in Lesson Four, and the third aorist in Lesson Seven. (εἰμί is from the Third Conjugation, but the flexion from it which is given in Lesson Three is the imperfect — it has no aorist flexion.)

A3.35 The second aorist active indicative is formed by prefixing the augment and adding to the verb stem a two-part ending. The first part of this ending consists of a vowel which is called the *neutral morph* (see #2.77, A2.45). As in the present tense (see #A2.44) this two-part ending consists of the neutral morph followed by the pronoun morph. In the third person singular the ending is just -ε, however. This is the pronoun morph — the neutral morph, -ε-, *elides* (i.e., *slides* off or *hides* from view) when a vowel suffix is added. (Elision will be further explained later on.) Some of the pronoun morphs are the same as they were in the present tense (#A2.46), and some are different.

A3.36 Sometimes a second aorist form replaces the neutral morph with the vowel -α-, which is the vowel of the punctiliar morph which is used by the first aorist. Thus we can come across εἶπαν for the third person plural instead of εἶπον. An example of this is given in Selection 16. It is a stylistic variation, and makes no difference in meaning.

A3.37 Note the moveable nu (#1.65) in the second aorist third person singular.

A3.4   WAYS OF THINKING ABOUT GREEK VERB MORPHS

A3.41 Understanding the functioning of the Greek verb is crucial for understanding the meaning of a Greek sentence. And a Greek verb is made up of many morphs each containing a unit of meaning, which together give the total meaning of the verb form in any particular sentence.

A3.42 Like a freight train loaded with valuable merchandise, a Greek verb form is loaded with meaning. Just as a freight train consists of a number of "units" — trucks — each carrying valuable goods of different kinds, so a verb form consists of a number of "units" — morphs — each of which brings you a different piece of information.

A3.43 To get the total value of your freight-train-load of goods, you have to unload all the trucks. Similarly, to get the value out of all the morphs in a Greek verb form, you must be sure to "unload" the meaning out of each individual morph, for every morph in the verb form is carrying its own piece of information for you.

A3.44 Alternatively, a verb form can be viewed as a key to a lock, the morphs being the various bumps and indentations on the key. The exact form of these determines the particular meaning "unlocked" by a given verb form.

A3.45 Or, a verb form can be likened to a jigsaw puzzle, the morphs being the different pieces, each of which has to be identified and put in its right place to build up the total picture.

A3.46 Again, the meaning of a verb form is a mystery, and the morphs of the verb are the clues — work out the meaning of the clues, put everything all together, and you solve the mystery of what happened (the action described by that verb form).

A3.47 One of the most helpful ways of viewing the verb morphs is as being like a set of electrical switches — some are simple on/off switches, and some are multiposition switches. The augment is the past time on/off switch: when the augment is present in a word, this switch is "on", and switches the meaning of that particular form of the verb to "past time position". The ending is a multiposition switch: when this switch reads "μεν", this "position" indicates the meaning "we"; when this switch reads "τε", however, this "position" switches the meaning of the verb form to "you plural". And so on.

A3.48 Keeping in your imagination these different ways of viewing the nature and function of the morphs in a verb form can help you in your approach to it to unscramble its meaning.

A3.5   CASE AFTER VERBS

A3.51 Most verbs require accusative case in the noun which follows them. Thus: εἶδεν δύο ἀδελφούς, where δύο ἀδελφούς ("two brothers") is the object of εἶδεν ("he saw"), and thus accusative.

A3.52 Some verbs take the genitive case instead of or as an alternative to the accusative. Thus ἀκούω "I hear" is sometimes followed by the accusative case and on other occasions by the genitive (as in Selection 19). Different shades of meaning can sometimes be intended (see for example the standard commentaries on φωνή in the genitive in Acts 9:7 and 22:7, but in the accusative in Acts 22:9, in the accounts of Paul's conversion).

A3.53 Some verbs take the dative case instead of the accusative case, especially where the noun refers to the person to whom the action of the verb applies. Thus πιστεύω ("I believe") is often followed by the person who is to be believed, in the dative case. Alternatively, it can be followed by εἰς plus the accusative (as in Selection 23) or ἐν plus the dative (as in Selection 12).

A3.6   COMMENTS ON THE ASSIGNMENTS

A3.61 Make sure that you memorize the flexions set in the first assignment — and that you understand the meaning of each of the forms you memorize.

A3.62 Read through the Vocabulary aloud, and pronounce each word, taking care to get it correct. There is no need to *learn* these words at this stage; just aim at a general familiarity with what is included. Note that in this Vocabulary the words are grouped according to word class, to assist you in knowing how each of them can be expected to function. Note particularly the Prepositions and the fact that each takes or *selects* a particular case (μετά has *two* possible cases, each with a different meaning). Note also the "Expressions" — forms used in the Selections which have not yet been explained in the Grammar.

A3.63 When you commence your work on the Selections, remember to read each Selection aloud carefully and correctly before attempting to translate it (#A2.61). Then translate the Selections, not so as to produce smooth-flowing idiomatic English, but so as to bring out the exact meaning of the Greek. Read again #A2.54 re your aims in this regard.

A3.64 Note that δέ *never* comes first in the Greek, but is virtually *always* put first in the English rendering. It can be translated either "and" or "but" (use your judgement from the context as to which is preferable).

A3.65 Some common expressions, especially with prepositions, are regarded as definite even though they do not use the definite article. Thus ἐν μέσῳ (Selections 5 and 8) means "in the middle/midst". Conversely, watch for places where the Greek article would not be translated into English (cf. Selection 21).

A3.66 If you need to find the meaning of a word for understanding a particular Selection and cannot see it immediately in the Vocabulary, look it up in your Dictionary, which is alphabetical. (The Vocabulary is not intended as a substitute for your Dictionary.)

A3.67 Contrary to the normal rules of agreement, Greek grammar allows a *singular* verb to be used after a *neuter plural* subject (see Selection 19).

A3.68 Assignment 3 is provided so that it can be done when instructed by your teacher, or as an optional exercise.

A3.7 GRAMMAR FROM LESSON THREE THAT YOU NEED TO KNOW

3.1 How do the masculine nouns of the First Declension differ from the corresponding feminine nouns of the First Declension?

3.2 Both ὁδός ("way") and ἔρημος ("desert") are Second Declension feminine nouns. Write out the Greek for "the way" and "the desert" (nominative singular only).

3.3 Some forms of the flexion of οὗτος ("this") have the diphthong αυ- in place of ου-. Under what circumstances does this happen? (That is, give the rule that explains when αυ- occurs.)

3.4 The second person plural ("you") form of a verb — and ONLY this form — has three possible ways in which it can be translated. What are these three possible meanings for πιστεύετε (from πιστεύω, "I believe")?

3.5 What is the meaning of the term "past time morph" in Greek, and what is this morph? (In your answer, be sure to explain "syllabic augment" and "temporal augment".)

3.6 What is the inherent aspect of the lexals of verbs which are (a) First Conjugation? (b) Second Conjugation? (c) Third Conjugation?

3.7 (a) What is a compound verb? (b) What happens to the augment in a compound verb?

3.8 What is meant by the "verb morph slots" for Greek?

A4.   LESSON FOUR

A4.1 PARADIGM OF THE ACTIVE OF λύω

A4.11 Note carefully the indicative flexions of this Paradigm: that the future is the same as the present, with the future time morph, -σ-, added between stem and endings; that the imperfect has the augment and exactly the same set of endings as the second aorist (see #3.81); that the first aorist is marked by having -σα- throughout, except only for the third person singular where the punctiliar morph is -σ-, the -α- eliding when a vowel suffix (-ε-) is added; that the perfect has the same suffixes as the first aorist (with -κα- instead of -σα-) except only for the third person plural (which is -σι(ν) not -ν).

A4.12 Note carefully the subjunctive flexions: that the present is the same as for the indicative but with the neutral morph lengthened, and that the -ι- of a diphthong goes subscript and the -υ- of a diphthong drops out; that the aorist subjunctive is the same as the present subjunctive, with the punctiliar morph, -σ-, added between stem and endings (the -α- of the full morph -σα- eliding before the vowel suffixes).

A4.13 Note carefully the other forms of the active Paradigm, and especially the differences between the corresponding forms of present and aorist.

A4.14 Note that the aorist only has the augment in the indicative mode, which means that the aorist has past time signification only in the indicative mode.

A4.15 Note the three pairs of forms which have the same spelling: the 1st person singular and 3rd person plural of the imperfect (we saw this also last Lesson for the second aorist, #3.82); the 1st person singular present of the indicative and the subjunctive (both are λύω); the 1st person singular future indicative and aorist subjunctive (both are λύσω). When these "ambiguous" forms are used, usually some factor in the context will enable you to know which of the pair is intended in any given instance.

A4.2   THE DISTINCTION BETWEEN εἰς/πρός AND ἐκ/ἀπό

A4.21 The core meaning of εἰς is "into" — something/someone is outside an environment, and enters it. Thus Jesus was driven by the Spirit εἰς τήν ἔρημον (L3/10). The core meaning of πρός is "towards" — it means to go to someone/something, but does not include entering it. The English sentence "They came to the town" does not itself indicate whether they entered it or stopped outside. Greek is able to resolve this ambiguity: if it uses εἰς for "to", then they entered the town; if it uses πρός then it implies they reached the town but does not *in itself* imply that they entered it.

A4.22 Part of the extended meaning of εἰς is "right up on to". Thus if they came πρός the mountain, they arrived at it; if they came εἰς the mountain, they went right up on to it. (See Selections 2 and 7.) Both πρός and εἰς imply motion, but εἰς indicates that the motion continued right into the sphere indicated by the word which follows it.

A4.23 Sometimes the sense of εἰς is "throughout", as in Selection 5, εἰς ὅλην τὴν Γαλιλαίαν, "throughout the whole of Galilee".

A4.24 An extended meaning of εἰς is "for, with a view to". Thus L5/9, εἰς ἄφεσιν ἁματιῶν, "for the forgiveness of sins".

A4.25 There is an exactly parallel distinction between ἐκ and ἀπό. ἐκ indicates the source or origin out of which something has come. It was inside, and now it has come from there. Thus L3/13, "Did the baptism of John arise out of heaven or out of men?" (ἐξ οὐρανοῦ ἤ ἐξ ἀνθρώπων) — this is a question about its origin or source. Similarly in L2/25.

A4.26 An extended meaning of ἐκ is that something started right at the point mentioned. Thus L3/24, ἐξ ἀρχῆς, "right at the beginning, or at any point after that".

A4.27 In contrast, ἀπό can be used of being distant from something without implying having or not having come from that something. Thus in L3/28 the disciples in the boat were not far ἀπό τῆς γῆς, "from the land". Had they come from that shore or not? The wording does not indicate. Again in L3/14 Jesus tells a man that he is not far ἀπό τῆς βασιλείας, "from the kingdom". It is obvious that this does not mean that he had been in the kingdom and had left it; on the contrary, he was coming close to the kingdom, but he was still some distance ἀπό it.

A4.28 Another extended meaning of ἐκ is to indicate the connection of someone with a group. Thus L5/12, ἐστὲ ἐκ τῶν προβάτων τῶν ἐμῶν, "you are out of my sheep", i.e. "you are part of my sheep, you belong to my flock". It does NOT mean, "you have left my flock".

A4.3   GRAMMAR FROM LESSON FOUR THAT YOU NEED TO KNOW

4.1   (a) What is the stem of the relative pronoun paradigm? (b) What other paradigm does its ending follow?

4.2   What are the morphs in a word which allow you to recognize that a word is: (a) future time, for a liquid verb? (b) future time, for other verbs? (c) punctiliar aspect, first aorist? (d) perfective aspect?

4.3   (a) Explain what *aspect* means. (b) Name the three aspects in Greek and explain what each of them indicates.

4.4   Give the aspect of these tenses: (a) present; (b) imperfect; (c) aorist; (d) present perfect; (e) pluperfect; (f) future.

4.5   (a) Explain the meaning of the indicative mode and of the subjunctive mode. (b) The subjunctive morph, which indicates that a verb is subjunctive, is unusual — describe what it is.

4.6   State the "Short Vowel Lengthening Rule".

A5.   LESSON FIVE

A5.1   GRAMMAR AND VOCABULARY

A5.11 Learn ἰχθύς first, as your basic Third Declension pattern paradigm, and note how the other vowel stem paradigms (#5.2) vary from it. Next, compare it with σάρξ, and then note how the other consonant stem paradigms vary from σάρξ, and the explanations of these variations (#5.31-5.44).

A5.12 The most important of the Third Declension noun paradigms are set out in Lesson Five. For all the others, including adjectives, see Appendix D.

A5.13 Note particularly πολύς and μέγας (#5.65), which change from Third to Second Declension after the first two forms; and εἷς, μία, ἕν (#5.66) — students often confuse the masculine and neuter forms with prepositions through not noting the rough breathing, and totally fail to recognize a feminine flexion form when they encounter it. Be sure that you are also able to identify the compound forms οὐδείς and μηδείς.

A5.14 The Vocabulary for this Lesson is given in two parts. The first columns contain words and expressions needed for the various Selections (the number in front of them is the number of the Selection where that word appears). Then follow nouns (listed in Paradigm order), and various verbs, adjectives, pronouns, and other words. Read through this Vocabulary a couple of times before you tackle the Selections; say each word out loud, and take care that you get the right pronunciation for it.

A5.15 Do not overlook the Reflexive Pronoun given at the end of the Vocabulary (it is set out in full in Appendix D, #D6.8). The 1st person singular means "myself", the 2nd person singular "yourself", the 3rd person singular "himself/herself/itself" (depending upon gender). Note that the plural means "ourselves/yourselves/themselves".

A5.2   NOTES RE THE GREEK N.T. SELECTIONS

A5.21 The dative case can be used to indicate the means with which something was done or the instrument that was used. This is called the *instrumental dative*. It is usually best translated into English as "by means of . . ." or "with . . .". Thus L5/1, ὕδατι, means "with water". Sometimes ἐν (plus dative) is used with this same sense, the *instrumental ἐν*. Thus ἐν πνεύματι ἁγίῳ means "with the Holy Spirit" in this context, not "in the Holy spirit". That is, the meaning of ἐν here is not *positional*, where the baptism takes place, but *instrumental*, what the baptism is with. Whether a particular use of the dative or the dative-plus-ἐν is instrumental or has some other meaning must be decided from the context in each particular case.

A5.22 Note the difference between ἔλυσαν and λύσαν. Both contain the punctiliar morph -σα- and are therefore first aorist tense. The ἐ- is the past time morph and this factor in itself indicates *indicative* (because the aorist only takes the past time morph in the indicative — #3.62, #4.41, #A4.14). The form is thus seen as 3rd person plural aorist indicative. However, λύσαν is the neuter aorist nominative singular of λύσας and means "loosing" or "having loosed", with reference to a word that is neuter. This should be borne in mind in tackling L5/2.

A5.3   LEVEL OF DIFFICULTY

A5.31 At this point you have reached the maximum level of difficulty which you will find in this Course.

A5.32 Lesson Six is about as demanding as Lesson Five; Lessons Seven to Nine do not present very many completely new areas of grammar but, rather, build upon what has already been introduced, and further expand it, explain it, illustrate it and consolidate it.

A5.33 Explanatory Notes are given for the Selections in the Lessons themselves from Lesson Six onwards, and (apart from the verb morph chart which follows) no further supplementary students' notes are provided here.

A5.4   GRAMMAR FROM LESSON FIVE THAT YOU NEED TO KNOW

5.1   There is a rule for finding the stem of a Third Declension noun that works for almost all words. What is it?

5.2   What is the difference between the set of Third Declension endings for vowel stem nouns and those for consonant stem nouns?

5.3   State the rules that account for the forms of each of the following paradigms: (a) παῖς, παιδός (b) ἀστήρ, ἀστέρος (c) ἡγεμών, ἡγεμόνος (d) ἄρχων, ἄρχοντος.

5.4   Explain what is unusual about the way the adjectives πολύς and μέγας decline.
5.5   What are the feminine and neuter nominative forms for εῖς, one?

A6.   LESSON SIX

A6.1   GRAMMAR FROM LESSON SIX THAT YOU NEED TO KNOW

6.1   What is the meaning of the (a) *active voice*? (b) *middle voice*? (c) *passive voice*?
6.2   What is meant by the term "deponent verb"?
6.3   The aorist tense has the augment in the indicative mode and not in the other modes. What is the significance of this fact?
6.4   Of the four tense systems in Greek (Present/Imperfect; Future; Perfect/Pluperfect; Aorist), only two have special forms for the passive voice. (a) Which two? (b) What happens in the other two tense systems when you want to convey passive meaning?
6.5   What is meant by saying that contract verbs are listed in the lexicon in their uncontracted form and used in their contracted form?

A6.2   THE NINE MORPH SLOTS OF THE VERB

A6.21 The nine morph slots of the verb can be likened to switches each of which "switches" the meaning of the verb to a particular alternative.

A6.22 In a compound verb, four slots are always filled, that is, always contain a morph, each of which will be one of a range of alternatives (with different meanings) which can occur in that slot. Each of these four slots is thus like a multiposition selection switch — it selects for that slot a particular meaning out of the range of alternatives available. These four slots are Preposition, Lexal, Aspect, and Ending, and they thus provide the basic framework for the structure of every verb form. They are represented in the diagram that follows as circular switches.

A6.23 In between these four framework slots are five other slots, all of which can be likened to on/off switches. They are represented in the diagram as rectangular switches. Four of the five are simple on/off switches — for these slots there is no range of alternative morphemes. Rather, there is only one morpheme (or unit of meaning) which can occur in a given slot, though it can have different *allomorphs* or alternative morphs — that is, it can have different forms, with the same meaning (e.g., the future morph, which is -ε- after liquids and -σ- otherwise). If this morpheme is present in its slot it switches the verb to have that particular meaning. Thus these are all optional slots — slots which may contain a morph, or may not.

A6.24 The fifth optional slot, Slot 8, is also an on/off switch, but if it is "on" — that is, if it is filled by a morph — it can have in it any one of six different possible morphemes, and the verb will then be "switched" to the meaning given by that particular morpheme. Only one of these six morphemes can occur in any given verb form; or Slot 8 may have no morpheme in it at all.

A6.3 THE GREEK VERB MORPH SLOT DIAGRAM

The Greek verb has nine morph slots, which can be viewed as being a mixture of on/off and multi-position switches.

#E4.1 SLOT 1	#E4.2 SLOT 2	#E4.3 SLOT 3	#E4.4 SLOT 4	#E4.5 SLOT 5	#E4.6 SLOT 6	#E4.7 SLOT 7	#E4.8 SLOT 8	#E4.9 SLOT 9
PREPOSITION	PAST-TIME	REDUP-LICATION	LEXAL	VOICE	FUTURE TIME	ASPECT	SPECIFIER	ENDING

PREPOSITION

20-position switch for:
No preposition (simplex)
18 prepositions
Special prefix (#E4.14)

PAST-TIME

On/Off

REDUP-LICATION

On/Off

(Fourteen N.T. verbs take a durative reduplication in -ι-: see #E4.39.)

LEXAL

The lexal will be one of the one thousand that occur in the New Testament.

PASSIVE VOICE

On/Off

FUTURE TIME

On/Off

ASPECT

3-position switch

(Absent in Third Conjugation flexions.)

SPECIFIER

On/Off switch — but when it is on, it will specify one or other of six pieces of information:

1. pluperfect active
2. perfect active participle
3. other active participle
4. middle participle
5. middle imperative/ infinitive
6. optative mode

ENDING

3-position switch

When switched to one of these three positions, the verb will then take one of the range of endings for that position.

A7. LESSON SEVEN

GRAMMAR FROM LESSON SEVEN THAT YOU NEED TO KNOW

7.1   (a) What is the "attributive use of adjectives"? (b) Describe the two attributive positions.

7.2   (a) What is the "predicative use of adjectives"? (b) Describe the two predicative positions. (c) What are the five words which always take the predicative position but which do not imply the verb "to be"?

7.3   There are seven suppletive verbs in the Greek New Testament. What is the present active form for each of these seven verbs?

7.4   In Greek, what is a *conjugation*?

7.5   What is meant by the term "direct flexion"?

7.6   There are only four forms that need to be known in order to recognize any form from a participle paradigm. Name the four forms that need to be known.

7.7   Describe the type of action indicated by each of the participles — the present, the aorist, and the perfect.

A8. LESSON EIGHT

GRAMMAR FROM LESSON EIGHT THAT YOU NEED TO KNOW

8.1   The subject of a verb is almost always in the nominative case. There is one exception. (a) What is the form of a verb which has its subject in another case instead of the nominative? (b) What is the case that it is in?

8.2   What is the case used when addressing or speaking to someone?

8.3   What is meant by the "accusative of extent" (of time or distance)?

8.4   What is the "genitive absolute", and what is it used for?

8.5   What is the "instrumental dative"?

8.6   Which is the Greek case used to express these? (a) Length of (or, extent of) time; (b) Time during which (something happened); (c) Point of time when or at which (something happened).

A9. LESSON NINE

GRAMMAR FROM LESSON NINE THAT YOU NEED TO KNOW

9.1   What are the various characteristics on the basis of which you can recognize the verbs that are (a) First Conjugation? (b) Second Conjugation? (c) Third Conjugation?

9.2   The formation of a verb's tense system is based upon its root, which is either durative (present) or punctiliar (aorist). (a) Which stem is the First Conjugation pattern built upon? (b) Which stem for the Second Conjugation? (c) Which for the Third?

9.3   (a) What is meant by "the Principal Parts of a verb"? (b) What are the names of the six Principal Parts of a verb?

9.4   What is meant by a "periphrastic tense"?

9.5   What is an "impersonal verb"?

APPENDIX B

BASIC PRINCIPLES FOR TEACHERS USING THIS BOOK

B1. A PERSONAL WORD FROM AUTHOR TO TEACHER

B1.1 This book provides an initial Course of instruction for those who wish to learn to read the Greek New Testament. The Course differs from others in the principles upon which it is based. If it is to be used to best advantage, it needs to be taught by a teaching approach which is in harmony with those principles.

B1.2 The purpose of this Appendix is to explain those principles (some of them theoretical, some of them practical) and the teaching methods which are recommended for teachers using this book.

B1.3 These recommendations have three sources:

B1.31 General educational theory about how people learn (and the recognition that what works well for one person is not necessarily the most effective means of learning for another).

B1.32 Modern linguistic principles developed for use in the teaching of a foreign language, which is almost invariably envisaged as a living, spoken language in today's world, which I am seeking to apply to learning to read documents written in a language that is not spoken today[27].

B1.33 My own practical experience in teaching this Course to classes of students, and the immensely valuable feedback that I have received from them.

B1.4 This book is a pioneering venture, therefore, in language teaching, and it will be subject to all the weaknesses and shortcomings of any pioneering effort. I have taken the fullest possible account of all the books on teaching N.T. Greek that I have been able to find, together with the standard works on modern linguistic science, especially as these apply to questions of language analysis. But so far as I know, in my particular approach I am breaking new ground[28].

B1.5 There are two consequences of this that will be relevant for other teachers interested in using this approach to teaching N.T. Greek:

B1.51 First of all, the suggestions outlined in this Appendix arise out of my own experience, and I share them with you because I am able to say of them: they work. I have taught classes both of theological students and of others by means of what I might call (without any intended disparagement) the "traditional" approach, and I have now taught similar groups using my new approach, and I have found very significant differences all along the line — from initial motivation, to the speed with which they are

176

able to enter into meaningful encounter with a book of the N.T. in Greek, to the extent to which subsequently they use the knowledge they have acquired. Perhaps this may encourage you to make the experiment of joining me in teaching on the basis of this new method.

B1.52 Secondly, because my method is a new one, and based largely on my own experience so far, there can be no doubt that further refinement and improvement will be possible. Thus the suggestions which follow should be recognized as being only suggestions. Therefore they should be assessed on their merits, implemented tentatively, and adapted where improvements can be made or adopted as they are when they are confirmed in practice.

B1.6   Please feel free to write to me and tell me about your experiences in following this new approach, and how you have found these ideas working out in practice for you in teaching people to read their Greek New Testament.

B2.   COURSE TEACHING PATTERNS

B2.1   THE FUNDAMENTAL PROPOSITION, AND COURSE TIMING

B2.11 This Course is premissed upon one fundamental proposition: that the most effective, most efficient, and most helpful way of learning to read the Greek N.T. is by practising reading the Greek N.T.

B2.12 The Course therefore introduces the student to all of the grammar that is necessary for him to be able to do this. It does not require him to *learn* all the grammar before he starts studying from a part of the N.T., but to *be aware* of it. Then, when the student begins working directly from the Greek N.T., normally from Mark (or John), the teacher will describe the grammatical points as they arise, and refer students back to the relevant sections of this book for the explanation. Thus the major ongoing work of learning the meaning of the Greek N.T. comes through the actual reading of Mark.

B2.13 Therefore the aim, under this method, is to bring the student as quickly as possible to the place where he can begin working from Mark.

B2.14 Stage 1 is structured for use as, first, an initial orientation session (at which the alphabet is taught) followed by nine weeks of student work on sentences from the Greek N.T., each week's work culminating in a class session when the class goes through the assignments of one Lesson and is then introduced to the grammar of the next Lesson.

B2.15 This Course is planned on the basis of requiring 2½ hours per Lesson, i.e. 25 hours of face-to-face class time for the ten sessions needed. A teacher may be tempted to allow himself to be discursive and take double that time per Lesson, in order "to cover it more thoroughly". HE MUST NOT TOO READILY ALLOW HIMSELF TO DO SO. If he takes five hours per Lesson, then instead of 25 hours it will require 50 hours of session time before his students begin Stage II, Mark's Gospel in Greek. If (as is often the case) there are a total of 75 tuition hours available in the academic year, then the result of this would be that only 25 of them would be spent in Mark whereas it should be 50.

B2.16 Each Lesson CAN be covered in 2½ hours, given that the teacher is disciplined and adequately prepared, and that the class is co-operative.

B2.2   FOUR ALTERNATIVE TEACHING PATTERNS

B2.21 Depending upon timetabling exigencies, etc., there have been two ways in which I have had the 2½ hours for each Lesson: three periods of 50 minutes each, on different days, or one slab of 2½ hours as a single block, either in the morning or (in Courses conducted for members for the Christian public who work during the day) in the evening, from 7.00 to 9.30 p.m. Of these alternatives, I have found by far the better to be the Lesson given in a Session of 2½ hours as a single block, which I therefore would designate as the *Normal Teaching Pattern*. It allows the students to become thoroughly immersed in the Greek, and thus make better progress.

B2.22 The composition of such a 2½-hour Session of the Normal Teaching Pattern would be:

(a) "Limbering-up": drilling in the paradigms of the Lesson of the previous Session; class "chorus-reading" of the vocabulary (Greek only) of that Session;

(b) Teacher quickly revises the main points of the grammar introduced in the previous Session, invites and answers questions on any difficulties;

(c) Translation of the N.T. Selections set as the week's assignment (for how this translation is to be done, see #B4.4 and A2.5; for the approach to handling classroom translation, see #B5.23, B5.75-B5.76);

(d) Short break (approximately 10 minutes):

(e) Introduction and presentation of the content of the next Lesson — explanation of the grammar — drawing attention to and drilling in the important paradigms in the Lesson — answering questions from the class — class "chorus-reading" in the Greek of the vocabulary for the Lesson.

B2.23 Note: In some Lessons, more sentences and passages are provided than can usually be covered in the planned 2½ hours of class time per week — these are provided for use by the class that is making quicker progress than average, or which has more than 2½ hours of class time available per week.

B2.24 In the case of a *Subdivided Teaching Pattern*, i.e. where the time per Lesson is broken up into three periods of 50 minutes, then I would suggest that a few minutes at the beginning of each of the three periods of the cycle be spent in "limbering-up" exercises — drilling in the paradigms; that Period One of the cycle of three commence with a short review of the previous Lesson and then proceed quickly to the work on the Greek Selections; that Period Two (after brief initial drilling) proceed to work on the remaining Selections; that Period Three be used for the presentation of the content of the next Lesson. From the following period the cycle is repeated.

B2.25 In most teaching situations it is envisaged that the Course would progress at the rate of one Leson in this book per week. Where more class time is available per week than 2½ hours, the additional time can be utilized in an *Intensive Teaching Pattern*, i.e. for additional drills, a slower coverage of the Selections (with more time allowed for explanation of the grammatical points, more student participation in the class translation) and translation of additional Selections and Passages.

B2.26 This book is also suitable for use in an *Accelerated Teaching Pattern* for a concentrated two-week Course held before the start of the academic year, with class time from (say) 9.00 to 11.30 a.m. each weekday, and afternoons and evenings spent by the students on the assignments. If this initial Accelerated Teaching Pattern is used, then students can study Mark in Greek from the first day of the normal academic year.

B3.   GENERAL APPROACH TO COURSE TEACHING

B3.0   NATURAL LANGUAGE ACQUISITION

B3.01 Any child can learn any language and in fact any number of different languages, if given adequate exposure to them before the age of six. After this age, the child has learnt the fundamentals of his mother tongue(s) and has attained a level of quite sophisticated linguistic maturity. It will never again be quite as easy for him to learn a new language.

B3.02 Why is this so? There are numerous reasons, including the fact that he has learnt to discriminate all the sounds that are meaningful in his language (i.e., as phonemes), and to reject those that are not. It is always much more difficult for him later in life to learn *then* to make sounds which he discarded in childhood as not required for his native tongue, when these sounds are needed for a language he is seeking to acquire. But there is another factor which is more directly relevant to our present considerations.

B3.03 A small child is much less self-conscious, and is much more willing to give something a try, to be corrected, to accept this correction, to try again, and to keep on trying until he gets it right.

B3.04 He is highly motivated, because he wants to understand others, and be understood by them.

B3.05 Moreover, he responds to praise and encouragement, and he will normally get individual encouragement from his parents to learn how to speak, to formulate what he wants into words, and to continue expanding his vocabulary. When he errs, he will be corrected — he knows this, he takes it in his stride without resentment, and he improves as a consequence.

B3.06 The contrast between this situation and that of most adult-learning situations for a foreign language is very considerable. Adults are sensitive, do not relish being corrected, expect to master everything as they go, and are reluctant to "give it a try" unless they already believe that they can do it quite well[29].

B3.07 There are many things from the child-learning situation which can help adults learn also: in particular, those factors which now follow.

B3.1 MOTIVATION

B3.11 Adequate and sustained motivation is the key to student success. And the motivation must be directed towards the best goals. The motivation for many students of Greek has been, in the past, merely to pass an examination which was requisite (for ordination, or for a university degree, or similarly). Consequently, when that goal was attained — or abandoned — they discarded their work on Greek, for attaining competence in Greek for its own sake, irrespective of examinations, had never been a personal goal for them. There are innumerable people today, on both sides of the pulpit, who in years past spent a considerable time in studying New Testament Greek but who now would never seek to make any real use of it in studying their Bible.

B3.12 Make it your aim so to motivate the members of your class that this will not be true of them in the years to come. This means that, while accepting the role and value of examinations as intermediate goals, your class members must view their work in Greek as being the acquiring of a skill, the fashioning of a tool that they will go on using with increasing skill for the rest of their life — and they must of course get adequate practice during the Course at using it for its ultimate purpose: which is, giving them an increased understanding of the meaning of the New Testament.

B3.13 Use to the full the motivational opportunities which this book provides: stimulate interest with the initial material which points out what a student can achieve through the Course (see the Preface and Introduction); be alert in each Lesson to draw attention to shades of meaning which can be perceived in the Greek but which do not readily translate into English; guide your students to recognize ways in which their increasing knowledge of Greek can aid them to have a richer appreciation and understanding of the sentences and passages of Scripture set in the Lessons.

B3.14 Three simple examples of the kinds of things which can be used in this way: **(a)** shades of emphasis in the Greek text due to the position of words, or to the use of emphatic pronouns; **(b)** delicate nuances of meaning conveyed by the use of a present or aorist or perfect tense in a particular context; **(c)** the precise thought conveyed by the use of one word in the Greek instead of another close synonym.

B3.15 When a student is putting his growing knowledge of Greek to practical use during the Course, and gaining benefit from it, he will be encouraged to persevere with his work in Greek, and will have a positive attitude towards it which will facilitate his learning.

B3.2 PARTICIPATION

B3.21 Encourage, and provide opportunities for, maximum class participation by each student, without "putting him on the spot". Suggested ways of doing this which are described more fully below include: chorus repetition, when he can get used to hearing his own voice in class speaking Greek words; reading Greek sentences aloud (in Greek); giving a literal translation of a Greek sentence (at times on a volunteer basis, and at other times on a teacher-selected basis); asking and answering questions about points of grammar, translation, or meaning.

B3.22 But when calling upon students to participate, allow them without blame to opt out of a particular situation where they feel inadequate, so that they are not compelled to expose their shortcomings to their peers and thus (in their own eyes) "lose face". Perhaps if they are unable to respond when called upon, they can simply reply "I pass", and someone else is asked instead.

B3.23 If a student is made to feel foolish or ridiculous or unsuccessful, this will hinder — not aid — his future learning potential in your Course.

B3.3 ENCOURAGEMENT AND RECOGNITION

B3.31 Do not criticize, blame, embarrass, scold, or shame a student for a mistake or anything he has done, or for what he did not do or has not done — remember at all times that different individuals have different levels of ability and learning spans, and that they acquire language, like other skills and abilities, at different rates of progress.

B3.32 Instead, they should be given full recognition for whatever they *have* learnt, and positive encouragement to persevere. More than anything else, what a student needs for success is the grace of perseverance.

B3.4 MAKING USE OF AIDS AND HELPS

B3.41 Be sure that you NEVER tie the ability of a student to progress with his work in N.T. Greek to his facility at remembering things or mastering the intricacies of grammar. Some teachers do this as an established policy by requiring their students to memorize pages of vocabulary or reams of paradigms, frowning on the use of wordlists and the consultation of grammatical analysis books by their students, and demanding that they pass an examination or reach a certain standard in one area of their language study before they can proceed to the next.

B3.42 If you do this kind of thing, you are limiting the progress your students can make with the language to the level of success that they can attain in your chosen method of approach (which may not be the best for them), in aspects of ability which are peripheral to their task.

B3.43 A person with an atrocious memory can still learn to read his Greek N.T. so long as he is not compelled to attempt to memorize everything but is encouraged to look up any vocabulary or paradigms that he needs — he will just be a bit slower than those with better memories, that is all.

B3.44 Innumerable people who go from their homeland to another country learn to use a foreign language even if they have a poor memory and are hopeless at grammar. Though at first they will misunderstand words and get their grammar mixed up, they are able to understand most of what they hear and read, and mastery of the rest will come through getting practice in using what they do know. And they are always able to look up or ask about a word or an expression without being made to feel that their need to learn something further is somehow blameworthy.

B3.45 Therefore *never* imply that a student should wait until he has mastered all the rules before he can work on his Greek N.T., using the language knowledge that he has gained; *always* make it easy for him to look up or ask about anything he does not know or has forgotten; and *always* encourage him to make use of whatever he does know while you unobtrusively fill in for him anything that he doesn't know. As this is done time and time again in one passage after another, the gaps in his knowledge will gradually fill up as his familiarity with the language increases.

B3.5 COMPETITION AND CO-OPERATION

B3.51 Some competition can perhaps be allowed (maybe even encouraged) amongst the more able students, but should not extend to the point of making the less able student feel incompetent or embarrassed.

B3.52 Many students are more greatly helped by co-operation — by working together in two's and three's: one student can often pick up a wrong pronunciation or a slip of grammar made by another, and thus help him.

B3.53 Each student needs to be reminded that whatever he learns of N.T. Greek, be it much or little, can be of value to him. I have had numbers of class members whose performance was quite mediocre in comparison with the best in the group but who themselves were thrilled with their accomplishment and the insights into the meaning of the Greek that it gave them. If they had been studying under a system by which they were required to master each section as they went and maybe pass an examination in it, they would never have reached the point where they could open a Greek N.T. and attempt to understand it — they would have dropped out along the way.

B3.6 PROGRESSION

B3.61 Do not hold back the rate of progress of the more able students to that of their "weaker brethren", nor require of the latter that they pass some test of competence before being able to continue with the class to the next area of study. (Can you imagine someone doing this for a very young child, learning his language?!)

B3.62 It is better that the slower students keep up with the rest of the class in the rate of the introduction of new material. Some will have a less complete grasp of the earlier material than others — but then, will not this be true no matter what the class, what the language, what the method, what the intensity of teaching, or who the teacher?

B3.7   GROW TALL POPPIES

B3.71 Many students will be able to obtain a quite astonishing mastery of N.T. Greek in the ten weeks of Stage I on the Normal Teaching Pattern. This is especially likely to be the case where they have studied Latin (or some other language) beforehand, or if they prove to have a natural ability.

B3.72 Encourage such students to use this advantage of theirs to master each Lesson to a more thorough extent than you would ask of the average student. Thus, where the class as a whole is given an absolute minimum of paradigm material to learn by rote, the "tall poppies" could be encouraged to learn more than the rest. They can tackle the sentences and passages that you may not deal with in class (for the sake of such people, and for the particularly bright class that you might happen to have, more material is provided for some Lessons than you will always have time to cover in full — see #B3.23).

B3.73 Moreover, these students can be encouraged to make the fullest use of the Appendices during the progress of their Course, some of which will assist them in getting a better "feel" for the language, and an overall understanding of how it works, and why certain things are so.

B3.74 It can be noticed at times that some teachers are uneasy about their tall poppies, and attempt to cut them down, to hold them back to the class average.

B3.75 Never do that. The God of Creation delights in diversity and variety. Welcome it whenever you find it in your Greek class.

B3.8   CONFIDENCE AND THE BANE OF PERFECTIONISM

B3.81 People respond to the confident leader. Make yourself conversant with this book so that you understand where it is going, and whereabouts in the overall plan you and your class are at any point in time.

B3.82 Then you can approach each Lesson with confidence, and your class will have confidence in your leadership.

B3.83 This is important, because for many students it will only be their confidence in you, that you know what you are doing, which will keep them going. This is because the basic principles of this Course are so different from those that they are used to in other work they do. And the bane of your Course, and the biggest hurdle that you will have to overcome, will be student perfectionism.

B3.84 There will be students who want you to proceed at half the pace (or a quarter the pace) because they know they have not mastered everything so far to perfection.

B3.85 You will have to reassure them that you know this, you expect it to be the case, and it does not matter at all. Tell them that the gaps in their knowledge will be filled up progressively as they work their way through Mark — the aim of the Course in this book is to introduce the student to the entire range of koine grammar that he will need in order to read a book like Mark, and to give him some preliminary experience and basic facility in handling sentences from the Greek N.T., so that when he is taken through Mark by his teacher and the points of grammar that arise are explained to him, *he can understand the explanation* — and he can be referred by the teacher to the appropriate section of this book, where the details for that explanation are set out.

B3.86 The intention is to cover Stage I in the shortest possible time (a fortnight, if circumstances permit — see #B2.26), so that the students can begin working from Mark itself.

B3.87 The best, the clearest, the most obvious, and the most logical way of getting to understand the meaning of the Greek New Testament is to begin reading the Greek New Testament.

B3.88 Some minimal basic foundations are necessary as a preliminary for this goal. The present book is intended to supply that base — to construct a scaffolding, build a framework. Thereafter, it can be used for reference as the student works from Mark. But do not allow this book to be a *substitute* for studying the Greek N.T. itself. For *that* is the purpose of it all.

B3.9   ENJOYMENT

B3.91 An aim in Lesson presentation should be enjoyment: that is, that both teacher and students enjoy their class time together. A class session which teacher and students hate (or to which they are indifferent) is not a good learning environment.

B3.92 This aim can be assisted if the teacher is well-prepared, cheerful with his students, and cultivates a light touch. The studies in which we are engaged are serious, but the presentation does not need to be.

B3.93 A similar comment applies to examinations (see #B7.16). A well-presented lesson and a well-structured examination paper should leave both teacher and student with a feeling of fulfilment and satisfaction, and a sense of accomplishment.

B3.94 Where a Course has been presented with a light touch and in a pleasant way, where a student has been able in that Course to show the progess he has made, and where it has been an enjoyable and satisfying experience, as well as a challenging one, then it can be expected that that student will learn well, will use what he has learnt, and will go on to expand his knowledge further in the future.

B4.   COURSE TEACHING AIMS

B4.1   OVERALL AIM

The Stage I Course aims to bring people to the place where they are able to begin reading, and understanding, the simpler parts of the Greek N.T.

B4.2   EXPECTED MAXIMUM AND MINIMUM ATTAINMENT LEVELS

B4.21 This book is planned so as to allow the highly motivated, gifted, or linguistically experienced student to make the maximum progress of which he is capable, whilst simultaneously allowing the less able student to achieve a level of attainment which he will find satisfying and valuable.

B4.22 Maximum and minimum levels of attainment can be stated as a guide to the expected range of student performance in the Course. This will be subject to exceptions, like all generalizations, but may be of interest as a guide. These levels refer to the student's attainment at the end of Stage I.

B4.23 The maximum level should be attainable by a reasonably able student with adequate time for study and good motivation. The maximum level is: that the student will be able to read, and understand the meaning of, a Gospel passage previously unseen if he is told the meaning of all words he does not know, and if the less straight-forward grammatical constructions and word-formations (such as irregular verbs in the passage) are explained as they are encountered. He will be able to recognize the case of declined words (except some of the more difficult or unusual Third Declension forms) and the person, number, tense, mode and voice, and thus the grammatical meaning, of most of the regular verb forms and many of the more common irregular verb forms. He will be familiar with the normal sentence structure.

B4.24 The minimum level should be attainable by a below-average student with a fair amount of time for study and adequate motivation, or an average student with inadequate time for study but reasonable motivation.

B4.25 The minimum level of attainment is: that the student will recognize the more frequently-used words and expressions, and the number and case of the easier of the declined words and the more common forms of verbs, and — which is the important point — can understand the meaning of the explanation when the words that he does not know are explained to him.

B4.26 Thus the minimum level of attainment really means that if you, as teacher, take your student through the first chapter of Mark or John and explain to him the form and meaning of the words that he does not know, he is able to understand the meaning of the verse in question in the Greek after your explanation, because he has learnt enough from the Course for your explanation to make sense. A student who has reached this level can proceed with the study of the Greek text of Mark or John, and learn his Greek from it as the work proceeds during the year.

B4.27 You will encourage as many students as possible to be near the maximum rather than the minimum level, of course: but those who only reach the minimum level have nonetheless reached the point where they can make use of their knowledge of Greek in understanding the New Testament if they are helped and encouraged to do so; and it is far better for them to have reached this point than not to have done the Course at all. We must expect that there will be different levels of achievement and performance in any group, and not discourage the less successful by criticizing them for not being better but encourage them by showing them how to get good value out of what they do know. Thus we can motivate them to persevere with reading their Greek N.T., and thereby improve their knowledge of Greek.

B4.28 There is a "language threshold" which is important in language study and which will vary according to a number of factors including the method of study used. Up till that threshold, a student cannot make any use of the study he has done. After he crosses that threshold, although he still has much to learn he can nonetheless start putting to use what he has already learned. That is by far the greatest motivation to further learning.

B4.29 Where that threshold is, is largely up to the teacher. So teach, that you keep the threshold low, and aim to help your students across it at the earliest possible point in their Course with you.

B4.3 VOCABULARY AIMS

Students should be encouraged not to learn vocabulary as the Greek equivalents of particular English words, but rather to add Greek words to their existing vocabulary as they would a new English word they encountered.[30].

B4.4 TRANSLATION AIMS

B4.41 It should at all times be remembered that the aim of the Course is not primarily to train an army of translators who can produce smooth, polished English translations of the Greek text, but to train people in having a clear and accurate understanding of the meaning of the Greek text.

B4.42 It is important for this to be reflected in the type of translating at which the student should be encouraged to aim, which should be literal and precise even to the point of being pedantic. A clumsy English translation is better than a smooth and idiomatic one, if the clumsy one conveys more accurately exactly what the author wrote in Greek, with its overtones and shades of meaning. The aim is thus to be for the student to give a very literal English translation which brings out precisely what is being said in the Greek.

B4.43 It should be noted however that a literal translation is not necessarily the same as a word-for-word translation. Not merely the words but syntactical features such as word order must be translated from Greek into English.

B4.44 This concept is further discussed in #A2.5.

B4.5 EXAMINATION AIMS

B4.51 If (as is customary) a student is to be examined in his work, then clearly his approach to study must include as one of its aims to be successful in his examinations, and the teacher's program must include having the aim of facilitating his students' success.

B4.52 A detailed discussion of the question of examinations is found in #B.7.

B4.6   UTILIZATION AIMS

B4.61 It is a great loss at every level when a student spends a considerable time in the study of Greek and then fails to make any further use of it subsequently.

B4.62 The nine Lessons of the Beginner's Course (Stage I) lead into the eighteen Lessons of the Intermediate Course (Stage II), during which the student's knowledge of grammar is consolidated and he also works on the text of Mark (or John) in Greek. This goal of commencing to read a Gospel in Greek should be kept clearly before the student during Stage I, especially in those situations (such as voluntary classes held on a term-by-term basis) where the student decides term by term whether or not to continue.

B4.63 When he finishes his formal study of N.T. Greek, over whatever period of time, what use he thereafter makes of it will be closely related to whether he has in fact been taught how to use it, and how useful he perceives his study to have been.

B4.64 Aim therefore to show the student how to make use of his knowledge of Greek at each stage of the process of acquiring it, during his Stage I Course. And aim to lay a good foundation of preparation for him to use it more fully as he advances at the completion of Stage I into Stage II, and the study of a Gospel in Greek.

B4.65 Further, seek to show your student that he is engaged in acquiring a skill which will be a valuable asset for the rest of his life.

B4.66 If it is your aim during the Stage I Course to inculcate these attitudes, to prepare your students to use the skill they acquire, and to motivate them to want to do so, then they themselves will gain substantial lasting benefit from this Course (and so will those to whom they minister in any way in the years to come) and they will move forward eagerly into Stage II.

B5.   COURSE TEACHING METHODS

B5.0   USE OF A RANGE OF METHODS

B5.01 There are wide individual differences in the ways in which people learn, and therefore in the methods that will prove most effective in teaching them. Most people, moreover, learn better when the subject material is presented to them by means of different methods in succession.

B5.02 This book has been planned so as to facilitate teachers employing a wide range of complementary methods in teaching the Course.

B5.03 It is suggested that students will gain greatest benefit from the Course if a teaching routine is set up for each Session which includes the use of the various teaching methods which are given here.

B5.1   LISTENING PRACTICE

B5.11 The class listens while following the Greek text as the teacher reads out sentences in Greek. This trains the student in associating the written word with its aural representation.

B5.12 This is particularly valuable because the pronunciation system used in this book means that if a student remembers the sound of a word he should be able to spell it. A wide range of students find it a strong aid to learning when they can see and hear something simultaneously.

B5.13 Listening practice is especially vital in the early Lessons of the Course, when students are still growing in fluency in reading the Greek text and in pronouncing it correctly.

B5.2   ORAL PRACTICE

B5.21 The class practises reading Greek sentences aloud, to foster increased reading fluency and comprehension.

B5.22 Some oral practice will include chorus reading, where the whole class reads a section of Greek in chorus. This gives the poorer reader who is unsure of himself an opportunity to participate to the extent that he can without being conspicuous, and to correct himself by the stronger members of the class around him. Is is especially useful in the early Lessons of a Course to enable the teacher to verify that the class taken as a whole has mastered Greek pronunciation.

B5.23 Oral practice will also include individual reading — whenever a student is about to translate a Greek sentence in class, he should always read it out aloud first of all. This should be a permanent, invariable part of the class routine, not only in the Stage I Course, but subsequently as well, when students in Stage II are reading verses from their Greek New Testaments.

B5.24 Individual oral practice is an important opportunity for you to monitor this aspect of the progress of individual class members, and correct errors. Incorrect pronunciation indicates one or more of: inability to recognize exactly what the Greek says; a careless attitude towards the need for accuracy and precision, an attitude which needs to be changed; a misunderstanding about one or more letters and the phonemes they represent; probable future trouble in relation to word recognition, correct spelling, and/or recognition of the significance of inflections. Be careful and consistent yourself in using the pronunciations given in this book, and require your class to adopt the same standards of care and consistency as yourself.

B5.3 DRILLS

B5.31 Drills consist of the systematic repetition of a pattern of material, either while reading the material or by reciting it from memory. They are thus a specific type of oral practice, but their purpose is not primarily to achieve correct pronunciation. Rather, it is to foster familiarization with material, and to aid rote learning.

B5.32 Drills are normally by chorus repetition, with the whole class reciting the material together.

B5.33 A common — and useful — drill pattern is to combine it with Listening Practice: the teacher reads out a word or the flexion of a paradigm while the class listens; secondly the teacher repeats it and the class says it with him; thirdly the class repeats it on their own and the teacher monitors them. This is especially useful in the early Lessons, with the list of Greek words in #1.27 and 1.33, the paradigms in Lessons Two and Three, and so on. Later either the first or second of the three elements of this drill could be omitted thereafter, so that it becomes a two-part exercise.

B5.34 One of the uses for drills is with vocabulary. The Greek words of the vocabulary for each Lesson can be helpfully introduced by means of a drill. (This is suggested for the *Greek* words, to familiarize the class with them and their pronunciation, not for the *English* equivalents. It is not recommended that these be learned in this way, but that an understanding of the area of meaning of a word should be built up by encountering the word in use.)

B5.35 A second major use for drills is with paradigms. Regular class drills in these are an aid to familiarization and memorization.

B5.4 MEMORIZATION

B5.41 A small number of paradigm flexions (indicated in each Lesson) are set for memorization. These are deliberately kept to a minimum, which has been chosen for maximum usefulness, so that the student who lacks the ability to memorize things easily is not held back and disadvantaged by a Course that is arranged so as to depend heavily upon him doing so.

B5.42 For the very reason that there are so few of them, it becomes all the more important for this basic set of core paradigms to be memorized thoroughly. Students should be pressed to commit them to memory, to go over them regularly, to work with a friend to help in learning them, and so on.

B5.43 While those set for learning by heart constitute the *minimum* requirements in this regard, there is of course no maximum. Those students who find that they have the capacity, the time, and the inclination, for a greater amount of memorization, should be encouraged to memorize further paradigms.

B5.44 Vocabulary (especially the "common New Testament words", Appendix G) can also profitably be memorized, so long as the student is careful to remember in doing so that the English meaning he is learning is one meaning of the word, and would not represent its *whole* area of meaning.

B5.45 The drills which are recommended for inclusion in the class routine for the purpose of *familiarization* of the students with words and forms will for some students be an opportunity and an incentive for *memorization*. But this memorization should not be required of all the students in the class.

B5.5   CUE PRACTICE

B5.51 Cue Practice exercises the students in flexibility in the use of the word forms. It can be introduced into class routines as time and opportunity allows, in those situations where it appears it will be helpful.

B5.52 In Cue Practice, a pattern is set up, and then the teacher provides a cue and the class (together, or a selected individual member) responds with the correct form of the cue word.

B5.53 For example, the pattern may be a particular preposition plus article and a noun. The teacher will then give another noun (nominative singular or plural) as the cue and the class puts this word and its article into the correct case with that preposition. At first the words will all be the same gender, and then, later, words of other genders would be given so that the cue word has to be given the correct number, case and gender.

B5.54 Cue practice can also be used with the forms of verbs after a particular nominative pronoun, and so on.

B5.6   BASE SENTENCE AND SUBSTITUTION DRILLS

B5.61 In this exercise, a base sentence is set up, and then class members suggest alternative words (in their proper form) which can be used in place of one or other of the words of the sentence.

B5.62 Numerous permutations of this are possible, according to what is helpful to the class. The purpose is for the class to become used to the "word-slots" in a typical Greek sentence, and to seeing what words can fill them, and what form those words take when they do fill those slots.

B5.63 When a class is following an Intensive Teaching Pattern (see #B2.25), some of the additional time available can very profitably be used this way.

B5.7   ASSIGNMENTS AND EXERCISES

B5.71 These terms refer particularly to the work which is set for students which involves them in utilizing what they have been covering in class.

B5.72 The usual form that this takes is the translation of Greek into English, or comprehension and discussion questions.

B5.73 Ideally, the student should prepare his work in advance to such a standard that he is able, in class, to give a direct oral rendering of the Greek into English when called upon. In practice, most students will write out their translations during their preparations during the week. This is probably unavoidable, but it has the disadvantage that when they read out their work in class and have it commented upon, they have forgotten the issues and alternatives they wrestled with at the point of their translation.

B5.74 Written student assignments can be handed in and marked, and this may be desirable from time to time. But apart from the additional burden that this places on the teacher, it causes a further lapse in time between when the student did the work and when he receives his teacher's comments on it — by then, it is often a matter of ancient history to him.

B5.75 The recommended procedure is that students take it in turn to read out to the class their translations of a Greek sentence, and the teacher comments upon this at once. Other students are then able to ask questions about differences they had in their translations, or points of difficulty.

B5.76 The procedure can be varied: sometimes the teacher will call for a volunteer for each sentence in turn (if a student has only succeeded in working out a number of the Selections, this enables him to opt for one that he can do); and at times the teacher will go around the class and nominate the student to translate the next Selection (with the selected student always being free to say "I pass" — #B3.22).

B5.77 Further possible variations are: that the teacher himself does the reading out of the Greek of some sentences and their translation (much faster, if time is short); that the teacher reads out the Greek a word or phrase at a time and the class as a whole calls out the translation of it.

B5.8   WRITING PRACTICE

B5.81 Some form of practice in writing Greek needs to be incorporated into the Course on a few occasions at least. The teacher can choose when and how this is to be done, according to circumstances.

B5.82 The purpose of this is to give the students supervised practice in writing Greek characters, and to provide the teacher with an opportunity of monitoring their progress and correcting their writing style as necessary.

B5.83 A convenient way of introducing this may be to include within the class lesson a time when the students are asked to write down from memory a paradigm they were set to learn, correcting their work themselves from this book. You can move amongst them and see which ones need guidance with their writing. Other points to check are that they are exercising care about spelling, particularly in regard to the perennial indicators of the careless student: breathings and iota subscripts. Apart from occasions when they serve to distinguish words, accents can be ignored.

B6.   COURSE PRESENTATION

B6.1   PRESENTATION

B6.11 The presentation outline for the Stage One Course is as follows:

Session	Presentation
1	Present Lesson 1 (also using material in #A1); set the assignments.
2	Revise L1 and go through the assignments; present L2 & assignments.
3	Revise L2 and go through the assignments; present L3 & assignments. (And similarly for Sessions 4 to 8.)
9	Revise L8 and go through the assignments; present L9 & assignments.
10	Revise L9 and go through the assignments; revise chosen sections of the Course; discuss the format of the examination paper (if the Course is being examined); present the Vacation Work (till Stage Two).
11	Examination (if the Course is being examined).

B6.12 It will be seen that the procedure being followed in the recommended pattern of presentation is: A Lesson is introduced in one Session, and the class is taken through that Lesson up to the assignments, which are set for the class. During the interval between Sessions the students work on the assignments, and at the next Session these are presented in class and discussed. The work of the following Lesson is then introduced. The class thus meets for ten Sessions, engaging in nine weeks of work in between them.

B6.13 The outline that is suggested here is for the Normal Teaching Pattern, and will be adapted for other Teaching Patterns — see #B2.2.

B6.14 The Course is planned so as to facilitate the use of the widest range of teaching methods. The presentation of each Session should be built up as a routine which incorporates the elements listed below.

B6.2   DRILLING

The class is drilled (see #B5.3) in all key sections of the work (including paradigms and vocabulary) so as to establish a recognition pattern of the sight and sound of words and word forms. The emphasis is more on becoming well familiar with the Greek words as such rather than on their English meanings.

B6.3   EXPLANATION

All grammatical points, word forms, paradigm comparisons, syntactical usage, etc., are explained Lesson by Lesson. This is particularly aimed at those who learn best through gaining an understanding of why something is so.

B6.4   COMPARISON

To the greatest extent possible, paradigms are presented side by side for ease of comparison, because a great deal of learning consists of recognizing the ways in which like things are different and similar. Paradigm-by-paradigm comparison allows these points of difference and similarity to be noted, and this in turn aids the recognition of forms when encountered in the Greek N.T. It facilitates, also, an understanding of *why* paradigm differences occur. In particular, the large-scale exposure simultaneously to extensive areas of a language enables the student to obtain an *overview* of that entire area — he can come back later and fill in more of the details.

B6.5   SATURATION

From the opening Lessons the student is immersed in the language itself. He reads and rereads sentences of Greek in Greek, so that he begins to develop an awareness of how Greek sentences are constructed, and how a Greek sentence *sounds*. This is separate from the question of what it *means* (essential though this obviously is). It has similarities with how a young baby is at first engulfed in a sea of meaningless noise, from which gradually he learns to detect and recognize meaningful patterns and combinations of sounds as words.

B6.6   IMPLEMENTATION

After being introduced to each new Lesson in class Session, the student rises to a new level of learning as he begins to implement what he has learnt by seeking to understand the meaning of the Selections from the Greek N.T. given in the assignments at the end of each Lesson.

B6.7   REINFORCEMENT AND REVISION

At the beginning of each Session, the new work introduced in the latter part of the previous Session is briefly revised. Points that were unclear previously can be raised by students, as a result of their own revision during the week, and these are then clarified by the teacher.

B6.8   RECOGNITION AND SATISFACTION

Students are able to take their turn at explaining a sentence in class, thus applying and demonstrating their knowledge, and gaining recognition for it from their peers, and the satisfaction of having succeeded in their work.

B6.9   DEMONSTRATION AND UTILIZATION

The teacher answers all points of difficulty which students have encountered as they have sought to understand the meaning of the sentences, and he himself translates some of these sentences in class, in each one drawing attention to overtones and aspects of the meaning of the Greek text which may not easily translate into English. The student himself is to be encouraged to look for such insights into the meaning of the original text of the N.T. and to seek to grasp exactly what it is saying. It is as he learns to draw out the sense of the Greek N.T. in this way that he is taking the knowledge he has gained and utilizing it in accordance with the aims of this Course.

B7.   COURSE EXAMINATIONS

B7.1   EXAMINATIONS: TYPES AND ATTITUDES

B7.11 Students of this Course may be preparing for internal or external examinations, or both. An *internal* examination is one that is set by you, as the teacher of this Course, or by someone else familiar with the work of your students, so that it tests them upon what they are actually doing, and can be drawn up so as to relate directly to their Course. An *external* examination is one that is set by an external examining authority and/or conforms to an external syllabus, so that the teaching of the Course must be directed towards preparing students for that examination.

B7.12 The difference between the two could be summarized: In the case of the internal examination, the examination is determined by the nature of the students' course; in the case of the external examination, the students' course is determined by the nature of the examination.

B7.13 It is a matter of regret that often some examining bodies can test candidates (and thus cause candidates to concentrate their preparation upon) fine points of grammar, feats of memory (such as a detailed knowledge of the forms of irregular verbs, which in practice a person could easily look up when the need arose), or inconsequential minutiae such as the exact positioning of the correct accent on the oblique cases of the Third Declension. But often teachers have to prepare students for examinations they did not set.

B7.14 This section discusses both examination situations. (Some of these remarks apply to any examination on any course of study.)

B7.15 It is traditional for students to fear or hate examinations. But this ought not to be so. When a student has such a negative attitude towards an examination, something is wrong. The fault may be in the form in which the examination paper itself is drawn up, in the course of preparation for the examination, in the teacher (his ability, the adequacy of his lesson preparation or his coverage of the course) or in the student himself (if he is lazy or for some reason has not prepared himself adequately).

B7.16 When an examination paper is correctly constructed so as to be a good test of the student's work in his subject (this is discussed in #B7.2), and the course of study is correctly related to the examination, and the teacher has done his work well, and the student has been attentive and diligent, then the examination can be the fitting climax to the course of study, and a joyful and satisfying and constructive and creative experience, where the student can demonstrate (to himself and to his teacher) the extent of his mastery of his subject and the success of his efforts during the course; and the teacher can be encouraged by seeing the fruitful outcome of *his* work.

B7.17 If students have a negative attitude towards their examinations, then this is an indication that there is something wrong somewhere that needs to be identified and corrected.

B7.2   INTERNAL EXAMINATIONS

B7.21 When you have a part in the setting of an examination paper (either setting it yourself or participating on an examining panel), give full attention to the question of the *philosophy of examination* that your paper will reflect, and to its effect upon the form of preparation that it will encourage students to follow.

B7.22 The basic "philosophy of examination" reflected by your examination paper should be: **(a)** to concentrate upon the more important aspects of the course; **(b)** to encourage students to direct their attention to the course in the most profitable way (because the examination paper of one year will influence the direction of study of the students of subsequent years); **(c)** to allow students to show the examiner the work that they *have* done in the subject — that is, it must provide adequate opportunity to show what they know (there is nothing more frustrating for a student than to have done a considerable amount of work in an important section of the syllabus and to find this section entirely ignored in the examination paper); **(d)** to take adequate account of the range of ability and attainment amongst the examinees, so that this range will be fairly reflected in the results that your examination paper will produce.

B7.23 The main aim of the present Course is to develop in students a progressively increasing ability to understand the Greek N.T. This ability, then, should be the main factor tested by the examination. The major part of the paper will consist of representative Selections taken from those at the end of each Lesson. The candidate will be required **(a)** to translate these in such a way as to show his understanding of the Greek (as distinct from his ability to memorize parts of the N.T. from an English translation), and **(b)** to comment upon points that are significant to meaning, such as: emphatic pronouns in a Selection, word order, use of a particular synonym, significance of the tense used, and so on. If a student is capable of understanding adequately the N.T. Selections in this book, then the examination paper should allow him to get a correspondingly high mark.

B7.24 An understanding of the grammar of Greek is very relevant to an understanding of the meaning of Greek sentences. Therefore the examination paper will require the candidate to show a knowledge of the grammar relevant to particular N.T. Selections, and these will be chosen on the basis that they illustrate grammatical points of importance.

B7.25 Other questions in the paper will ask candidates to show their understanding of such matters as the difference in meaning and function between (say) the three verb aspects, the indicative and subjunctive, and so on. These can be essay-type questions, or can be related to particular N.T. Selections.

B7.26 A small part of the paper can be given to such matters as **(a)** writing out the flexion of a word that is regular but not one normally used in a paradigm, **(b)** explaining the basis for the construction of the various Third Declension paradigms or the Greek verbal system, etc., **(c)** discussing the "area of meaning" of various selected vocabulary words.

B7.27 The paper should be structured so that an average-ability student who has done his work satisfactorily during the period of the Course and has prepared himself adequately for the examination can achieve a high mark. It should also include a small number of the more difficult Selections and harder questions so as to spread out the candidates in their performance and allow for the differences to show up between the students who are good and those who are very good. Thus the candidate who has worked especially diligently at the Course will be able to see this reflected in the fact that he can accept a harder challenge in the examination paper, and do well.

B7.28 A proposal worthy of consideration is to provide in the examination paper a "credit" section which is optional, and which will enable the more able students to aim for a higher goal, a credit level pass. This section of the paper will include **(a)** more difficult Selections to translate than in the "pass" section, and more difficult word forms to analyze and comment on; **(b)** more difficult grammatical and/or linguistic points to explain; and **(c)** an unseen passage from a Gospel to be translated.

B7.29 Marking will normally proceed on the basis of allocating a number of marks to each part of a question and deducting marks for errors: half a mark off for a minor error (e.g. translating a verb correctly but putting past tense when it is present; omitting a breathing or a iota subscript from a Greek word) and a full mark off for a more significant error (such as a completely wrong word or word form).

B7.3   AIDS IN THE EXAMINATION ROOM

B7.31 There is a good case to be made for setting an "open book" examination, where the candidate takes into the examination room with him a copy of this present book, his N.T. Analysis book, and his Greek N.T. and Dictionary.

B7.32 In a "closed book" examination, the candidate is being tested, inevitably, upon the extent of his memory rather than primarily upon his knowledge of Greek and his ability to use it.

B7.33 In an "open book" examination, the candidate is being tested on his ability to correlate all his existing knowledge, including his ability to use aids, to refer to paradigms, to consult a Greek Dictionary, to transfer learning from one application to another, and to make use of reference materials at speed under pressure of time.

B7.34 Preparing for an "open book" examination will encourage the student to refine all these useful skills, not just to learn up paradigms and vocabulary (which is NOT the main aim of this Course). It is also a much more realistic preparation for his "real-life" use of his Greek skills, when all these aids will be available to him, and when he ought to be making full use of them. Thus preparing for an "open book" examination runs directly parallel with the aims of the Course in the way that preparing for a "closed book" examination does not.

B7.35 Only the student who has done adequate work beforehand and has prepared himself properly will be able to do well in an "open book" examination — the inadequately prepared student will not be able to compensate for all that he does not know by attempting to find his way around the Course book while the examination is in progress.

B7.36 The "open book" policy would not extend, of course, to permitting use of a student's own prior translations of the Selections, to an Interlinear N.T. or to any English N.T. translation.

B7.4   EXTERNAL EXAMINATIONS

B7.41 When students are being prepared as candidates for an external examination in New Testament Greek, then the dominant factor in the situation is the syllabus for that examination, and the way it is actually examined.

B7.42 The first stage in any program of preparation for an external examination is still to take the students through this Course in the way already outlined in this Appendix. Usually a minimum of a year is allocated for the preparation for such an external examination — use the First Term to take your students through the whole of Stage I, and your Second and Third Terms to give them plenty of experience in reading the Gospel of Mark (or John) from their Greek N.T., together with taking them through Stage II (or as much of it as time allows) to help them in consolidating their grammar.

B7.43 At the appropriate point in time, change the class over to working on the other Greek N.T. book/books required by the examination syllabus.

B7.44 During the course of the term prior to the examination, give the students additional instruction in any areas which may be required for that examination and which are not covered in this Course or the Appendices.

B7.45 One of these areas may be translation from English into Greek. Set English renderings of Selections in this book to be translated back into Greek. The Selections themselves will then act as the "key" for students checking their own work. Then, progress from this to setting other passages from a literal English version of the N.T. (such as the N.A.S.B.), for which their Greek N.T. itself provides a means for them to check their work.

B7.46 Another possible requirement for an external examination is the ability to provide accents for Greek words. The ability to understand Greek accents is NOT a beginner's-level skill. It is dealt with in reasonable detail at the end of the Intermediate Course (#E6), which provides sufficient information to cover most situations. If your candidates know these things, the inaccuracies with accents that they may then still display in an examination will not be enough materially to affect their results, and a more thorough mastery of all the idiosyncracies of Greek accentuation is NOT a justifiable use of study time for a student.

B7.47 It is possible that candidates will need to memorize additional paradigms beyond those set as requisite in this Course. This is best done during the term prior to the examination, when it is likely that the extra work that this entails will prove to be minimal, as most of the forms will be found to be already known to the candidates through comparison and understanding rather than through the effort of deliberate rote learning.

B7.48 Attention must also be given to vocabulary. Students should ensure, as a general foundation, that they are familiar with the three hundred "common N.T. words" in Appendix G, and then proceed to the particular words required for the books or passages set by the examination syllabus.

B7.49 The best foundation for any examination in New Testament Greek is to be familiar with the whole framework of grammar, and with some part of the text of the Greek New Testament itself. That is precisely what this Course will provide, and to this foundation can then be added preparation in any specific requirements of a specific examination syllabus.

B7.5   TESTS AND LEARNING GOALS

B7.51 Compare and contrast what has been said about examinations with the idea of tests given on what ought to be thoroughly known by heart.

B7.52 In Appendix A, the Notes on each Lesson end with a set of questions which represent the minimum that ought to be known (in addition to the set paradigms) of the work of that Lesson. These questions can be used as class tests, done from memory. They are not examinations in the ordinary sense — they are the setting-out of the learning goals for each Lesson and thus can be used by each student as a guide to what he ought to come to know from memory. The "pass mark" (if you like) for these tests is 100%: complete familiarity with what is set out here is desirable — if possible, as each Lesson is completed, and certainly by the end of the Beginner's Course.

APPENDIX C

CONJUGATION

C0. THE GREEK VERB

C0.1 THE GREEK CONJUGATION SYSTEM

C0.11 There are three conjugations in Greek (#9.42). Their distinctive features may be seen in the following table:

Conjugation: Feature:	FIRST	SECOND	THIRD
Ending of lexical form:	-ω	-ω	-μι
Aorist active, when adding endings, takes the morph:	punctiliar morph -σα-	neutral morph -o/ε-	no morph — adds endings directly
Builds verb system upon:	present stem	aorist stem	aorist stem
In forming of the present stem, requires to add a durative morph?	no	yes	yes
No. of verbs in the N.T. following this conjugation:	930	34	36

(counting each simplex verb and its compounds as a single verb)

C0.12 Numbers of the Second and Third Conjugation verbs have forms and flexions which follow the First Conjugation.

C0.13 For a discussion of these Conjugations, see #9.4 and 9.5

C0.14 The Greek verb system in all its ramifications will be presented in full for the regular First Conjugation verb, λύω, for which there will be given a **Paradigm Synopsis,** setting out the first person singular form for all the flexions of the paradigm of λύω, followed by a **Meaning Synopsis** of the meanings of the various flexions. The other paradigms of the First Conjugation are then given, followed by the Second and Third Conjugations (#C2 and C3), and sections discussing Verbs With Direct Flexions (#C4), and Verbs Which Add a Durative Aspect Morph (#C5). Finally a Conspectus is given for the three Conjugations (#C6), and details of Deponent Verbs (#C7), Irregular Verbs (#C8) and Verb Groups (#C9).

C0.15 The form from a flexion given in the Paradigm Synopsis (always the first person singular where it exists, but the second person singular for the imperative and the masculine nominative singular for the participle) is called the *flexion form*. It consists of the *tense stem* (see #9.5) and the *pronoun suffix* (see #2.76).

C0.2   PARADIGM SYNOPSIS OF THE GREEK VERB

(For explanations, see the Notes which follow in #C0.3.)

ASPECT:		DURATIVE		PUNCTILIAR	PERFECTIVE	
TIME:			FUTURE			(FUTURE)
TENSE:		PRESENT/ IMPERFECT	FUTURE	AORIST	PRESENT PERFECT/ PLUPERFECT	FUTURE PERFECT
MODE:						
Primary	**A**	λύω	λύσω		λέλυκα	λελυκὼς ἔσομαι
Indicative	**M**	λύομαι	λύσομαι	none	λέλυμαι	λελύσομαι
(6 each)	**P**	*	λυθήσομαι		*	?
Secondary	**A**	ἔλυον		ἔλυσα	ἐλελύκειν	
Indicative	**M**	ἐλυόμην	none	ἐλυσάμην	ἐλελύμην	none
(6 each)	**P**	*		ἐλύθην	*	
	A	λύω		λύσω	λελυκὼς ὦ	
Subjunctive	**M**	λύωμαι	none	λύσωμαι	λελυμένος ὦ	none
(6 each)	**P**	*		λυθῶ	*	
Optative	**A**	λύοιμι	λύσοιμι	λύσαιμι	λελυκὼς εἴην	lacking
(6 each)	**M**	λυοίμην	λυσοίμην	λυσαίμην	λελυμένος εἴην	λελυσοίμην
	P	*	λυθησοίμην	λυθείην	*	?
Imperative	**A**	λῦε		λῦσον	λελυκὼς ἴσθι	
(4 each)	**M**	λύου	none	λῦσαι	λέλυσο	none
	P	*		λύθητι	*	
Infinitive	**A**	λύειν	λύσειν	λῦσαι	λελυκέναι	lacking
(1 each)	**M**	λύεσθαι	λύσεσθαι	λύσασθαι	λελύσθαι	λελύσεσθαι
	P	*	λυθήσεσθαι	λυθῆναι	*	?
Participle	**A**	λύων	λύσων	λύσας	λελυκώς	lacking
(24 each)	**M**	λυόμενος	λυσόμενος	λυσάμενος	λελυμένος	λελυσομένος
	P	*	λυθησόμενος	λυθείς	*	?
No. of forms in the column:		106	111	141	106	43 = 507

C0.3   NOTES ON THE PARADIGM SYNOPSIS

C0.31 This shows the flexion form (the first person singular, apart from the Imperative, where it is the second person singular, and the Participle, for which it is the masculine nominative singular) for all the possible flexions of a single Greek verb. Some categories do not exist at all, and these are indicated by the word "none". Some forms *could* exist but are not found in Hellenistic literature, and are indicated by the word "lacking". Some of the verb forms illustrated in this Synopsis are not found in the New Testament but *can* occur in Hellenistic Greek; that is to say, they were available to the New Testament writers had they had occasion to use them. Other forms illustrated in the Synopsis are very rare in the New Testament. (See further, #C0.33.)

C0.32 In the Synopsis, **A** = Active, **M** = Middle, and **P** = Passive. Separate forms exist for the passive only in the Future and Aorist systems; in the Present and Perfect systems the middle forms are found used with passive meaning as well as being used with middle meaning. The places in the Synopsis where a middle flexion is used with passive as well as middle meanings are indicated by *.

C0.33 Some forms were rare even in Classical times, primarily because the circumstances for their use would arise so infrequently. In Hellenistic times a number of categories had become virtually obsolete or, if used, usually had something of an archaic connotation. These were: The Optative Mode, the Future Perfect, the Perfect Imperative, and the Future Infinitive and Participle. Nonetheless, all these verb categories were available for use to the Hellenistic writer if he wished to call upon them[31]. In fact some examples of forms from all of these categories are found in the pages of the New Testament, amounting to several dozen instances in all. Some forms, though possible, are so conjectural as to be omitted from the Synopsis — e.g. such a form as the future perfect passive participle, which would be λελυθησομένος, if it were ever needed.

C0.34 The numbers that are given under the name of the Mode indicate the number of forms which there are in each of the flexions for which the flexion form has been given, and the totals for each aspect are given at the foot of each column. It can be seen that the number of forms of a verb available to a Greek writer was 507. (It was greater still in Classical times, when a Dual number was in use for second and third person of each flexion, in addition to Singular and Plural.) If one deducts the 107 forms in the rarely-used flexions (#C0.33), this leaves 400 forms in the frequently-used flexions of a verb — though in the nature of the case some of these would be used less frequently and others more frequently.

C0.35 Some verbs would not have any passive forms in consequence of their meaning (e.g., φεύγω, I flee). Many verbs were *defective*, i.e., they did not have a full range of flexions in use (and various verbs would of course be defective to varying degrees). There are seven verbs which are actually "verb sets", where two or three defective verbs were used in association, one supplying flexions which the other lacked. These are called *suppletives* (see #7.33 and #C2.8).

C0.36 In the Indicative Mode, the present, future, present perfect and future perfect tenses are sometimes called the *Primary Tenses*. They have in common that they do not refer to past time, and they take similar pronoun suffixes in the middle flexions. The imperfect, aorist and pluperfect tenses are sometimes called the *Secondary Tenses* or *Historic Tenses*. They have in common that they *do* refer to past time, and their middle pronoun suffixes are similar to each other and differ in some forms from those of the Primary Tenses. The middle forms of the subjunctive have pronoun suffixes similar to those of the Primary Tenses, while those for the optative have pronoun suffixes similar to the Secondary Tenses.

C0.37 It should be noted that the Greek verb has four tense systems, one for each of the three *aspects* in Greek, *durative, punctiliar,* and *perfective*, and the fourth is the *future* system. Each of the three aspect tense systems has a *Secondary Indicative* or *past time* flexion (the Imperfect, Aorist, and Pluperfect), and two of the three have a *Primary Indicative* or *present* flexion (the Present and the Present Perfect). The aorist has no present or Primary Indicative form, but outside the Indicative Mode it indicates only punctiliar aspect and not past time (and accordingly has no past time morph). The perfective aspect system also has future time flexions, the Future Perfect flexions, which are used in referring to something having been completed (and thus inaugurating a new state of affairs) at some time in the future. In the nature of the case, the occasions for the use of this tense are few.

C0.38 The future forms have no inherent aspect, but can be either durative or punctiliar — and this will be related to the lexical meaning of a particular verb, or, according to circumstances, indicated by the context in which a verb is used.

C0.4 MEANING SYNOPSIS OF THE GREEK VERB

C0.41 This Synopsis gives the nearest English approximation of the meaning of the flexion form of each of the Greek verb flexions, for most contexts.

C0.42 Some of these English renderings are cumbersome, to say the least, and are not necessarily intended to represent how that verb ought to be translated in English, but rather to give an approximation of the force of the Greek. The meaning of the less common, more difficult forms (including those like the optative, which have not been given in this Synopsis) is best grasped by noting them in the context where they occur at the time when they are encountered.

C0.43 INDICATIVE

	PRESENT			**FUTURE**
A	λύω	I am loosing	λύσω	I will loose/be loosing
M	λύομαι	I am loosing for myself	λύσομαι	I will loose/be loosing for myself
P	λύομαι	I am (being) loosed	λυθήσομαι	I will be loosed

	IMPERFECT			**AORIST**
A	ἔλυον	I was loosing	ἔλυσα	I loosed
M	ἐλυόμην	I was loosing for myself	ἐλυσάμην	I loosed for myself
P	ἐλυόμην	I was being loosed	ἐλύθην	I was loosed

	PRESENT PERFECT			**FUTURE PERFECT**
A	λέλυκα	I have loosed	λελυκὼς ἔσομαι	I will have loosed
M	λέλυμαι	I have loosed for myself	λελύσομαι	I will have loosed for myself
P	λέλυμαι	I have been loosed	λελύσομαι	I will have been loosed

	PLUPERFECT	
A	(ἐ) λελύκειν	I had loosed
M	(ἐ) λελύμην	I had loosed for myself
P	(ἐ) λελύμην	I had been loosed

C0.44 SUBJUNCTIVE

PRESENT (Durative)   **AORIST (Punctiliar)**

A λύω   I would/might be loosing   λύσω   I would/might loose
M λύωμαι   I would/   λύσωμαι I would/
                      might be loosing for myself   might loose for myself
P λύωμαι   I would/might be being loosed λυθῶ   I would/might be loosed

PRESENT PERFECT

A λελυκὼς ὦ   I would/might have been loosing
M λελυμένος ὦ I would/might have been loosing for myself
P λελυμένος ὦ I would/might have been loosed

C0.45 IMPERATIVE

PRESENT (Durative)   **AORIST (Punctiliar)**

A λῦε   loose!   λῦσον   loose!
M λύου   loose for yourself!   λῦσαι   loose for yourself!
P λύου   be loosed!   λύθητι   be loosed!

PRESENT PERFECT

A λελυκὼς ἴσθι   be having been loosing!
M λέλυσο   be having been loosing for yourself!
P λέλυσο   be having been loosed!

C0.46 INFINITIVE

PRESENT (Durative)   **FUTURE**

A λύειν   to be loosing   λύσειν   to be about to loose
M λύεσθαι   to be loosing for oneself λύσεσθαι   to be about to loose for oneself
P λύεσθαι   to be being loosed   λυθήσεσθαι to be about to be loosed

PRESENT PERFECT   **AORIST (Punctiliar)**

A λελυκέναι   to have loosed   λῦσαι   to loose
M λελύσθαι   to have loosed for oneself λύσασθαι   to loose for oneself
P λελύσθαι   to have been loosed   λυθῆναι   to be loosed

C0.47 PARTICIPLE

PRESENT (Durative)   **FUTURE**

A λύων   (while) loosing   λύσων   being about to loose
M λυόμενος (while) loosing for oneself λυσόμενος   being about to loose for oneself
P λυόμενος (while being) loosed   λυθησόμενος being about to be loosed

PRESENT PERFECT   **AORIST (Punctiliar)**

A λελυκώς   having loosed   λύσας   having loosed/after loosing
M λελυμένος having loosed for oneself   λυσάμενος having loosed/after loosing for oneself
P λελυμένος having been loosed   λυθείς   having been loosed/after being loosed

C1. THE FIRST CONJUGATION

There are nine paradigms of the First Conjugation.

C1.1 LONG VOWEL STEM PARADIGM (λύω, I loose, untie, release)

The Principal Parts for λύω are: λύω, λύσω, ἔλυσα, λέλυκα, λέλυμαι, ἐλύθην.

This paradigm is followed by approximately 100 N.T. verbs (70 of which end in -ευ).

C1.11 ACTIVE:

		PRESENT	FUTURE	AORIST	PERFECT
INDICATIVE					
Singular	1	λύω	λύσω	none	λέλυκα
	2	λύεις	λύσεις		λέλυκας
	3	λύει	λύσει		λέλυκε(ν)
Plural	1	λύομεν	λύσομεν		λελύκαμεν
	2	λύετε	λύσετε		λελύκατε
	3	λύουσι(ν)	λύσουσι(ν)		λελύκασι(ν)
		Imperfect			**Pluperfect**
Singular	1	ἔλυον	none	ἔλυσα	(ἐ) λελύκειν
	2	ἔλυες		ἔλυσας	(ἐ) λελύκεις
	3	ἔλυε(ν)		ἔλυσε(ν)	(ἐ) λελύκει
Plural	1	ἐλύομεν		ἐλύσαμεν	(ἐ) λελύκειμεν
	2	ἐλύετε		ἐλύσατε	(ἐ) λελύκειτε
	3	ἔλυον		ἔλυσαν	(ἐ) λελύκεισαν

		PRESENT	FUTURE	AORIST	PERFECT
SUBJUNCTIVE					
Singular	1	λύω	none	λύσω	λελυκὼς ὦ
	2	λύῃς		λύσῃς	λελυκὼς ᾖς
	3	λύῃ		λύσῃ	λελυκὼς ᾖ
Plural	1	λύωμεν		λύσωμεν	λελυκότες ὦμεν
	2	λύητε		λύσητε	λελυκότες ἦτε
	3	λύωσι(ν)		λύσωσι(ν)	λελυκότες ὦσι(ν)

		PRESENT	FUTURE	AORIST	PERFECT
OPTATIVE					
Singular	1	λύοιμι	λύσοιμι	λύσαιμι	λελυκὼς εἴην
	2	λύοις	(No forms	λύσαις	(No forms
	3	λύοι	occur	λύσαι	occur
Plural	1	λύοιμεν	in the	λύσαιμεν	in the
	2	λύοιτε	New	λύσαιτε	New
	3	λύοιεν	Testament)	λύσαιεν	Testament)

		PRESENT	FUTURE	AORIST	PERFECT
IMPERATIVE					
Singular	2	λῦε	none	λῦσον	λελυκὼς ἴσθι
	3	λυέτω		λυσάτω	(No forms occur
Plural	2	λύετε		λύσατε	in the New
	3	λυέτωσαν		λυσάτωσαν	Testament)
INFINITIVE		λύειν	λύσειν	λῦσαι	λελυκέναι

		PRESENT	FUTURE	AORIST	PERFECT
PARTICIPLE					
Nom S	M	λύων	λύσων	λύσας	λελυκώς
	F	λύουσα	λύσουσα	λύσασα	λελυκυῖα
	N	λῦον	λῦσον	λύσαν	λελυκός
Gen S	M/N	λύοντος	λύσοντος	λύσαντος	λελυκότος

C1.12 MIDDLE AND PASSIVE:

PRESENT INDICATIVE MIDDLE & PASSIVE	FUTURE		AORIST		PERFECT
	MIDDLE	PASSIVE	MIDDLE	PASSIVE	MIDDLE & PASSIVE
S1 λύομαι	λύσομαι	λυθήσομαι	none	none	λέλυμαι
2 λύῃ	λύσῃ	λυθήσῃ			λέλυσαι
3 λύεται	λύσεται	λυθήσεται			λέλυται
P1 λυόμεθα	λυσόμεθα	λυθήσομεθα			λελύμεθα
2 λύεσθε	λύσεσθε	λυθήσεσθε			λέλυσθε
3 λύονται	λύσονται	λυθήσονται			λέλυνται

Imperfect					Pluperfect
S1 ἐλυόμην	none	none	ἐλυσάμην	ἐλύθην	(ἐ) λελύμην
2 ἐλύου			ἐλύσω	ἐλύθης	(ἐ) λέλυσο
3 ἐλύετο			ἐλύσατο	ἐλύθη	(ἐ) λέλυτο
P1 ἐλυόμεθα			ἐλυσάμεθα	ἐλύθημεν	(ἐ) λελύμεθα
2 ἐλύεσθε			ἐλύσασθε	ἐλύθητε	(ἐ) λέλυσθε
3 ἐλύοντο			ἐλύσαντο	ἐλύθησαν	(ἐ) λέλυντο

SUBJUNCTIVE

S1 λύωμαι	none	none	λύσωμαι	λυθῶ	λελυμένος ὦ
2 λύῃ			λύσῃ	λυθῇς	λελυμένος ῇς
3 λύηται			λύσηται	λυθῇ	λελυμένος ῇ
P1 λυώμεθα			λυσώμεθα	λυθῶμεν	λελυμένοι ὦμεν
2 λύησθε			λύσησθε	λυθῆτε	λελυμένοι ἦτε
3 λύωνται			λύσωνται	λυθῶσι(ν)	λελυμένοι ὦσι(ν)

OPTATIVE

S1 λυοίμην	λυσοίμην	λυθησοίμην	λυσαίμην	λυθείην	λελυμένος εἴην
2 λύοιο	(No forms	(No forms	λύσαιο	λυθείης	(No forms
3 λύοιτο	occur	occur	λύσαιτο	λυθείη	occur
P1 λυοίμεθα	in the	in the	λυσαίμεθα	λυθείημεν	in the
2 λύοισθε	New	New	λύσαισθε	λυθείητε	New
3 λύοιντο	Testament)	Testament)	λύσαιντο	λυθείησαν	Testament)

IMPERATIVE

S2 λύου	none	none	λῦσαι	λύθητι	λέλυσο
3 λυέσθω			λυσάσθω	λυθήτω	λελύσθω
P2 λύεσθε			λύσασθε	λύθητε	λέλυσθε
3 λυέσθωσαν			λυσάσθωσαν	λυθήτωσαν	λελύσθωσαν

INFINITIVE

λύεσθαι	λύσεσθαι	λυθήσεσθαι	λύσασθαι	λυθῆναι	λελύσθαι

PARTICIPLE

NSM	λυόμενος	λυσόμενος	λυθησόμενος	λυσάμενος	λυθείς	λελυμένος
F	λυομένη	λυσομένη	λυθησομένη	λυσαμένη	λυθεῖσα	λελυμένη
N	λυόμενον	λυσόμενον	λυθησόμενον	λυσάμενον	λυθέν	λελυμένον
GSM/N	λυομένου	λυσομένου	λυθησομένου	λυσαμένου	λυθέντος	λελυμένου

C1.13 For many of the forms given in this paradigm, variant forms will be encountered in the New Testament at times. When these occur in the Greek text, they will usually be mentioned in commentaries or grammatical analyses on the text. They can be noted when encountered, but there is no need to give all these possible variant forms in the standard paradigm.

C1.14 It will be noticed that the augment on the forms in the two pluperfect flexions (for Active and Middle-Passive) is placed in brackets. This augment is "correct" in that the pluperfect is a past tense and therefore "should" have the augment, but because the pluperfect forms are adequately identifiable by reduplication, the pluperfect active specifier (-ει-) in Slot 8, and distinctive endings, the augment was often omitted.

C1.2   SHORT VOWEL STEM IN -α (τιμάω, I honour)

C1.21 The Principal Parts for τιμάω are:

τιμάω, τιμήσω, ἐτίμησα, τετίμηκα, τετίμημαι, ἐτιμήθην.

C1.22 In those flexions where the neutral morph is added to the stem (i.e. in all flexions of the durative aspect), the short -α of the stem combines with the -ε- to give long -α- (and with -ει- to give -ᾳ-); with the -ο- (and -ω- and -ου-) to give -ω-. There are 78 N.T. verbs which follow this paradigm.

C1.3   SHORT VOWEL STEM IN -ε (λαλέω, I speak, chat, converse)

C1.31 The Principal Parts for λαλέω are:

λαλέω, λαλήσω, ἐλάλησα, λελάληκα, λελάλημαι, ἐλαλήθην.

C1.32 In all flexions of the durative aspect, the short -ε of the stem combines with -ε- to give -ει-, with -ο- to give -ου-, and is absorbed into a long vowel/diphthong. There are 235 N.T. verbs which follow this paradigm.

C1.4   SHORT VOWEL STEM IN -ο (πληρόω, I fulfil, make come true, accomplish)

C1.41 The principal Parts for πληρόω are:

πληρόω, πληρώσω, ἐπλήρωσα, πεπλήρωκα, πεπλήρωμαι, ἐπληρώθην.

C1.42 In all flexions of the durative aspect, the short -ο of the stem combines with -ε- or -ο- to give -ου-, with -η- to give -ω-, with -ει- or -η- to give -οι-, and is absorbed into -ω- and -ου-. There are 91 N.T. verbs which follow this paradigm.

C1.43 There are two apparent exceptions to the above contraction rules for these verbs: for τιμάω and πληρόω in the active infinitive, when taking -ειν. But the infinitive ending was originally -σεν, from which the -σ- was lost by syncopation (#E2.5) between two vowels. The process was:

τιμά-ε-σεν contracts to τιμᾶ-σεν, thence τιμᾶ-εν and finally τιμᾶν;
πληρό-ε-σεν contracts to πληροῦ-σεν, thence πληροῦ-εν and finally πληροῦν.

C1.44 Because short vowel stem verbs contract in the durative flexions, they are frequently referred to as *contracted* or *contract* verbs.

C1.45 The following conspectus gives the contracted form of each paradigm verb, and then in brackets shows the short vowel and ending which have contracted together. The N.T. does not contain any form of the optative of a contract verb, so the optative is not given in this paradigm conspectus.

		C1.2 τιμάω	Contraction	**C1.3** λαλέω	Contraction	**C1.4** πληρόω	Contraction
DURATIVE ACTIVE:							
INDICATIVE							
Present							
S	1	τιμῶ	(-ά-ω)	λαλῶ	(-έ-ω)	πληρῶ	(-ό-ω)
	2	τιμᾷς	(-ά-εις)	λαλεῖς	(-έ-εις)	πληροῖς	(-ό-εις)
	3	τιμᾷ	(-ά-ει)	λαλεῖ	(-έ-ει)	πληροῖ	(-ό-ει)
P	1	τιμῶμεν	(-ά-ομεν)	λαλοῦμεν	(-έ-ομεν)	πληροῦμεν	(-ό-ομεν)
	2	τιμᾶτε	(-ά-ετε)	λαλεῖτε	(-έ-ετε)	πληροῦτε	(-ό-ετε)
	3	τιμῶσι(ν)	(-ά-ουσιν)	λαλοῦσι(ν)	(-έ-ουσιν)	πληροῦσι(ν)	(-ό-ουσιν)
Imperfect							
S	1	ἐτίμων	(-α-ον)	ἐλάλουν	(-ε-ον)	ἐπλήρουν	(-ο-ον)
	2	ἐτίμας	(-α-ες)	ἐλάλεις	(-ε-ες)	ἐπλήρους	(-ο-ες)
	3	ἐτίμα	(-α-ε)	ἐλάλει	(-ε-ε)	ἐπλήρου	(-ο-ε)
P	1	ἐτιμῶμεν	(-ά-ομεν)	ἐλαλοῦμεν	(-έ-ομεν)	ἐπληροῦμεν	(-ό-ομεν)
	2	ἐτιμᾶτε	(-ά-ετε)	ἐλαλεῖτε	(-έ-ετε)	ἐπληροῦτε	(-ό-ετε)
	3	ἐτίμων	(-α-ον)	ἐλάλουν	(-ε-ον)	ἐπλήρουν	(-ο-ον)
SUBJUNCTIVE							
S	1	τιμῶ	(-ά-ω)	λαλῶ	(-έ-ω)	πληρῶ	(-ό-ω)
	2	τιμᾷς	(-ά-ῃς)	λαλῇς	(-έ-ῃς)	πληροῖς	(-ό-ῃς)
	3	τιμᾷ	(-ά-ῃ)	λαλῇ	(-έ-ῃ)	πληροῖ	(-ό-ῃ)
P	1	τιμῶμεν	(-ά-ωμεν)	λαλῶμεν	(-έ-ωμεν)	πληρῶμεν	(-ό-ωμεν)
	2	τιμᾶτε	(-ά-ητε)	λαλῆτε	(-έ-ητε)	πληρῶτε	(-ό-ητε)
	3	τιμῶσι(ν)	(-ά-ωσιν)	λαλῶσι(ν)	(-έ-ωσιν)	πληρῶσι(ν)	(-ό-ωσιν)
INFINITIVE							
		τιμᾶν	(-ά-ε-εν)	λαλεῖν	(-έ-ε-εν)	πληροῦν	(-ό-ε-εν)
IMPERATIVE							
S	2	τίμα	(-α-ε)	λάλει	(-ε-ε)	πλήρου	(-ο-ε)
	3	τιμάτω	(-α-έτω)	λαλείτω	(-ε-έτω)	πληρούτω	(-ο-έτω)
P	2	τιμᾶτε	(-ά-ετε)	λαλεῖτε	(-έ-ετε)	πληροῦτε	(-ό-ετε)
	3	τιμάτωσαν	(-α-έτωσαν)	λαλείτωσαν	(-ε-έτωσαν)	πληρούτωσαν	(-ο-έτωσαν)
PARTICIPLE							
NSM		τιμῶν	(-ά-ων)	λαλῶν	(-έ-ων)	πληρῶν	(-ό-ων)
F		τιμῶσα	(-ά-ουσα)	λαλοῦσα	(-έ-ουσα)	πληροῦσα	(-ό-ουσα)
N		τιμῶν	(-ά-ον)	λαλοῦν	(-έ-ον)	πληροῦν	(-ό-ον)
GSM/N		τιμῶντος	(-ά-οντος)	λαλοῦντος	(-έ-οντος)	πληροῦντος	(-ό-οντος)

	C1.2 τιμάω	Contraction	**C1.3** λαλέω	Contraction	**C1.4** πληρόω	Contraction

DURATIVE MIDDLE AND PASSIVE: INDICATIVE

Present

S 1	τιμῶμαι	(-ά-ομαι)	λαλοῦμαι	(-έ-ομαι)	πληροῦμαι	(-ό-ομαι)
2	τιμᾷ	(-ά-η)	λαλῇ	(-έ-η)	πληροῖ	(-ό-η)
3	τιμᾶται	(-ά-εται)	λαλεῖται	(-έ-εται)	πληροῦται	(-ό-εται)
P 1	τιμώμεθα	(-α-όμεθα)	λαλούμεθα	(-ε-όμεθα)	πληρούμεθα	(-ο-όμεθα)
2	τιμᾶσθε	(-ά-εσθε)	λαλεῖσθε	(-έ-εσθε)	πληροῦσθε	(-ό-εσθε)
3	τιμῶνται	(-ά-ονται)	λαλοῦνται	(-έ-ονται)	πληροῦνται	(-ό-ονται)

Imperfect

S 1	ἐτιμώμην	(-α-όμην)	ἐλαλούμην	(-ε-όμην)	ἐπληρούμην	(-ο-όμην)
2	ἐτιμῶ	(-ά-ου)	ἐλαλοῦ	(-έ-ου)	ἐπληροῦ	(-ό-ου)
3	ἐτιμᾶτο	(-ά-ετο)	ἐλαλεῖτο	(-έ-ετο)	ἐπληροῦτο	(-ό-ετο)
P 1	ἐτιμώμεθα	(-α-όμεθα)	ἐλαλούμεθα	(-ε-όμεθα)	ἐπληρούμεθα	(-ο-όμεθα)
2	ἐτιμᾶσθε	(-ά-εσθε)	ἐλαλεῖσθε	(-έ-εσθε)	ἐπληροῦσθε	(-ό-εσθε)
3	ἐτιμῶντο	(-ά-οντο)	ἐλαλοῦοντο	(-έ-οντο)	ἐπληροῦντο	(-ό-οντο)

SUBJUNCTIVE

S 1	τιμῶμαι	(-ά-ωμαι)	λαλῶμαι	(-έ-ωμαι)	πληρῶμαι	(-ό-ωμαι)
2	τιμᾷ	(-ά-η)	λαλῇ	(-έ-η)	πληροῖ	(-ό-η)
3	τιμᾶται	(-ά-ηται)	λαλῆται	(-έ-ηται)	πληρῶται	(-ό-νται)
P 1	τιμώμεθα	(-α-ώμεθα)	λαλώμεθα	(-ε-ώμεθα)	πληρώμεθα	(-ο-ώμεθα)
2	τιμᾶσθε	(-ά-ησθε)	λαλῆσθε	(-έ-ησθε)	πληρῶσθε	(-ό-ησθε)
3	τιμῶνται	(-ά-ωνται)	λαλῶνται	(-έ-ωνται)	πληρῶνται	(-ό-ωνται)

INFINITIVE

	τιμᾶσθαι	(-ά-εσθαι)	λαλεῖσθαι	(-έ-εσθαι)	πληροῦσθαι	(-ό-εσθαι)

IMPERATIVE

S 2	τιμῶ	(-ά-ου)	λαλοῦ	(-έ-ου)	πληροῦ	(-ό ιυ)
3	τιμάσθω	(-α-έσθω)	λαλείσθω	(-ε-έσθω)	πληρούσθω	(-ο-έσθω)
P 2	τιμᾶσθε	(-ά-εσθε)	λαλεῖσθε	(-έ-εσθε)	πληροῦσθε	(-ό-εσθε)
3	τιμάσθωσαν	(-α-έσθωσαν)	λαλείσθωσαν	(-ε-έσθωσαν)	πληρούσθωσαν	(-ο-έσθωσαν)

PARTICIPLE

NSM	τιμώμενος	(-α-όμενος)	λαλούμενος	(-ε-όμενος)	πληρούμενος	(-ο-όμενος)
F	τιμωμένη	(-α-ομένη)	λαλουμένη	(-ε-ομένη)	πληρουμένη	(-ο-ομένη)
N	τιμώμενον	(-α-όμενον)	λαλούμενον	(-ε-όμενον)	πληρούμενον	(-ο-όμενον)
GSM/N	τιμωμένου	(-α-ομένου)	λαλουμένου	(-ε-ομένου)	πληρουμένου	(-ο-ομένου)

C1.46 In the foregoing conspectus it can be observed that whenever the *first* vowel of those contracting (i.e., the short stem vowel) has the verb accent, then the contracted vowel/diphthong carries a circumflex accent (˜); whenever the *second* vowel of those contracting has the verb accent, then the contracted vowel/diphthong carries that accent (′). If neither of the contracting vowels has the accent, then the contracted vowel/diphthong will not be accented.

C1.47 In the short vowel verb flexions other than in the durative (present-tense) system, the suffix that is added to the stem always begins with a consonant (i.e., in the case of all of the future time morph, the punctiliar and perfective aspect morphs, the pronoun morphs added directly for the perfect middle/passive, and the aorist passive morph). Thus no contraction of vowels takes place in any of these flexions. Rather, in accordance with the rule in #E2.31, the short stem vowel lengthens before the consonant: α to η, ε to η, and o to ω. Thus the flexion forms for these flexions (from which the rest of each flexion, and the other modes, are conjugated as for $\lambda\acute{v}\omega$) are:

TENSE		C1.2	C1.3	C1.4
FUTURE	**ACTIVE**	τιμήσω	λαλήσω	πληρώσω
	MIDDLE	τιμήσομαι	λαλήσομαι	πληρώσομαι
	PASSIVE	τιμηθήσομαι	λαληθήσομαι	πληρωθήσομαι
AORIST	**ACTIVE**	ἐτίμησα	ἐλάλησα	ἐπλήρωσα
	MIDDLE	ἐτιμησάμην	ἐλαλησάμην	ἐπληρωσάμην
	PASSIVE	ἐτιμήθην	ἐλαλήθην	ἐπληρώθην
PERFECT	**ACTIVE**	τετίμηκα	λελάληκα	πεπλήρωκα
	MIDDLE	τετίμημαι	λελάλημαι	πεπλήρωμαι
	PASSIVE	τετίμημαι	λελάλημαι	πεπλήρωμαι

C1.48 There are a number of verbs in -α and -ε which do not follow the rule in #E2.31 but which retain these vowels in front of a consonant (in the case of -ε, sometimes not in all flexions). Not all of the forms below necessarily occur in the N.T. but they are given here to show the verb's patterns. The verbs are:

(a) In all cases where -α follows -ρ, -ι, or -ε (called "α pure") — these six verbs:

ἀγαλλιάω	rejoice	(ἀγαλλιάσομαι)	ἠγαλλίασα	—	—	ἠγαλλιάθην
ἐάω	allow	ἐάσω	εἴασα	(εἴακα)	(εἴαμαι)	εἰάθην
θεάομαι	look at	(θεάσομαι)	ἐθεασάμην	—	τεθέαμαι	ἐθεάθην
ἰάομαι	heal	(ἰάσομαι)	ἰασάμην	—	ἴαμαι	ἰάθην
καταράομαι	curse	(καταράσομαι)	κατηρασάμην	—	(κατήραμαι)	(κατηράθην)
κοπιάω	toil	(κοπιάσω)	ἐκοπίασα	κεκοπίακα	—	—

(b) In the following five -α verbs:

γελάω	laugh	γελάσω	ἐγέλασα	—	γεγέλαμαι	ἐγελάσθην
κλάω	break	κλάσω	ἔκλασα	—	κέκλασμαι	ἐκλάσθην
πεινάω	be hungry	πεινάσω	ἐπείνασα	πεπείνηκα	—	—
σπάω	draw, pull	σπάσω	ἔσπασα	ἔυπακα	ἔσπασμαι	ἐσπάσθην
χαλάω	let down	χαλάσω	ἐχάλασα	κεχάλακα	κεχάλασμαι	ἐχαλάσθην

(c) In the following seven -ε verbs:

αἰνέω	praise	αἰνέσω	ἤνεσα	ἤνεκα	ἤνημαι	ἠνέθην
ἀρκέω	be sufficient	ἀρκέσω	ἤρκεσα	—	—	ἠρκέσθην
δέω	bind, tie	δήσω	ἔδησα	δέδεκα	δέδεμαι	ἐδέθην
ἐμέω	vomit	(ἐμέσω)	ἤμεσα	—	—	—
καλέω	call	καλέσω	ἐκάλεσα	κέκληκα	κέκλημαι	ἐκλήθην
τελέω	finish	τελέσω	ἐτέλεσα	τετέλεκα	τετέλεσμαι	ἐτελέσθην
φορέω	wear	φορέσω	ἐφόρεσα	—	—	—

C1.5 LABIAL STEM PARADIGM (followed by 18 verbs in πτ, and 19 others)

The Principal Parts for representative verbs of this paradigm are:

βλέπω	see	βλέψω	ἔβλεψα	βέβλεφα	βέβλεμμαι	ἐβλέφθην
θλίβω	press hard	θλίψω	ἔθλιψα	τέθλιφα	τέθλιμμαι	ἐθλίφθην
γράφω	write	γράψω	ἔγραψα	γέγραφα	γέγραμμαι	ἐγράφθην*
καλύπτω†	cover	καλύψω	ἐκάλυψα	κεκάλυφα	κεκάλυμμαι	ἐκαλύφθην

* The direct flexion form ἐγράφην (#C4.53) is common in the New Testament.
† The τ is a durative morph added in the present system only (see #C5.7), and in all other tenses the flexions are formed from the stem καλυπ-.

C1.6 PALATAL STEM PARADIGM (followed by 35 verbs)

The Principal Parts for representative verbs of this paradigm are:

ἄγω	lead, bring	ἄξω	-ῆξα*	ἦχα	(ἦγμαι)	ἤχθην
διώκω	persecute	διώξω	ἐδίωξα	(δεδίωχα)	δεδίωγμαι	ἐδιώχθην
ἄρχω	rule	ἄρξω	ἦρξα	ἦρχα	ἦργμαι	(ἤρχθην)
κηρύσσω	proclaim	κηρύξω	ἐκήρυξα	κεκήρυχα	κεκήρυγμαι	ἐκηρύχθην

* This First Conjugation form is found in the New Testament only in the compound verb; the aorist of the simplex verb is the Second Conjugation form, ἤγαγον (see Second Conjugation, #C2.7).

C1.7 DENTAL STEM PARADIGM (followed by 206 verbs in ζ, and 15 others)

The Principal Parts for representative verbs of this paradigm are:

σπεύδω	hasten	σπεύσω	ἔσπευσα	ἔσπευκα	ἔσπευσμαι	—
δοξάζω	glorify	δοξάσω	ἐδόξασα	δεδόξακα	δεδόξασμαι	ἐδοξάσθην

C1.8a POLYSYLLABIC ORAL LIQUID VERBS (4 verbs)*

The Principal Parts for representative verbs of this paradigm are:

ἀγγέλλω	announce	ἀγγελέω	ἤγγειλα	ἤγγελκα	ἤγγελμαι	ἠγγέλθην
ἐγείρω	raise	ἐγερέω	ἤγειρα	ἐγήγερκα	ἐγήγερμαι	ἠγέρθην

C1.8b MONOSYLLABIC ORAL LIQUID VERBS (17 verbs)*

The Principal Parts for representative verbs of this paradigm are:

ἀνατέλλω	rise	ἀνατελέω	ἀνέτειλα	ἀνατέταλκα	ἀνατέταλμαι	—
φθείρω	ruin	φθερέω	ἔφθειρα	ἔφθαρκα	ἔφθαρμαι	ἐφθάρην†

C1.9a POLYSYLLABIC NASAL LIQUID VERBS (27 verbs)*

The Principal Parts for a representative verb of this paradigm are:

ξηραίνω	dry up	ξηρανέω	ἐξήρανα	ἐξήραγκα	ἐξήρασμαι	ἐξηράνθην

C1.9b MONOSYLLABIC NASAL LIQUID VERBS (6 verbs)*

The principal Parts for a representative verb of this paradigm are:

ἀποκτείνω kill ἀποκτενέω ἀπέκτεινα   —   —   ἀπεκτάνθην

C1.9c NASAL LIQUID VERBS IN -ιν (3 verbs)*

The Principal Parts for a representative verb of this paradigm are:

κρίνω   judge   κρινέω   ἔκρινα   κέκρικα   κέκριμαι   ἐκρίθην

* Liquid verbs are an important (and rather troublesome) subsection of the First Conjugation, so a detailed coverage of these paradigms is given below, following the Conspectus of the Consonant Paradigms.

† ἐφθάρην is a *direct flexion* form, that is, it lacks the -θ- which is to be expected in the aorist passive flexion (if it had this -θ-, its form would be ἐφθάρθην) — see Verbs With Direct Flexions, #C4.

NOTE: Once the flexion form (the first person singular) of each flexion has been determined, that flexion will conjugate regularly, taking exactly the same endings as λύω for that flexion. But there are two special kinds of changes which need to be carefully noted. First of all, the effects of the Linguistic Modification Rules (see #4.5) in the formation of the flexion form for the future tense — especially for liquid verbs, which add -ε-, not -σ-, as the future morphs, and thereupon contract and then conjugate like the *present* tense of λαλέω (see #C1.3). Secondly, numbers of phonemic changes occur in the Perfect Middle/Passive which need to be noted; these are summarized in #9.75 and set out more fully in #E2.6 and E2.7. The following CONSPECTUS OF THE CONSONANT PARADIGMS gives the flexions of the Future Indicative Active and Middle, and of the Perfect (and Pluperfect) Middle/Passive for the paradigms of the consonant stem verbs.

FUTURE

	C1.5 καλύπτω	**C1.6** ἄγω	**C1.7** δοξάζω	**C1.8** ἀγγέλλω	**C1.9** κρίνω

FUTURE ACTIVE:
INDICATIVE

		C1.5	C1.6	C1.7	C1.8	C1.9
S	1	καλύψω	ἄξω	δοξάσω	ἀγγελῶ	κρινῶ
	2	καλύψεις	ἄξεις	δοξάσεις	ἀγγελεῖς	κρινεῖς
	3	καλύψει	ἄξει	δοξάσει	ἀγγελεῖ	κρινεῖ
P	1	καλύψομεν	ἄξομεν	δοξάσομεν	ἀγγελοῦμεν	κρινοῦμεν
	2	καλύψετε	ἄξετε	δοξάσετε	ἀγγελεῖτε	κρινεῖτε
	3	καλύψουσι(ν)	ἄξουσι(ν)	δοξάσουσι(ν)	ἀγγελοῦσι(ν)	κρινοῦσι(ν)

INFINITIVE

	καλύψειν	ἄξειν	δοξάσειν	ἀγγελεῖν	κρινεῖν

PARTICIPLE

	καλύπτω	ἄγω	δοξάζω	ἀγγέλλω	κρίνω
NSM	καλύψων	ἄξων	δοξάσων	ἀγγελῶν	κρινῶν
F	καλύψουσα	ἄξουσα	δοξάσουσα	ἀγγελοῦσα	κρινοῦσα
N	καλύψον	ἄξον	δοξάσον	ἀγγελοῦν	κρινοῦν
GSM/N	καλύψοντος	ἄξοντος	δοξάσοντος	ἀγγελοῦντος	κρινοῦντος

FUTURE MIDDLE:
INDICATIVE

S	1	καλύψομαι	ἄξομαι	δοξάσομαι	ἀγγελοῦμαι	κρινοῦμαι
	2	καλύψῃ	ἄξῃ	δοξάσῃ	ἀγγελῇ	κρινῇ
	3	καλύψεται	ἄξεται	δοξάσεται	ἀγγελεῖται	κρινεῖται
P	1	καλυψόμεθα	ἀξόμεθα	δοξασόμεθα	ἀγγελούμεθα	κρινούμεθα
	2	καλύψεσθε	ἄξεσθε	δοξάσεσθε	ἀγγελεῖσθε	κρινεῖσθε
	3	καλύψονται	ἄξονται	δοξάσονται	ἀγγελοῦνται	κρινοῦνται

INFINITIVE

καλύψεσθαι	ἄξεσθαι	δοξάσεσθαι	ἀγγελεῖσθαι	κρινεῖσθαι

PARTICIPLE

NSM	καλυψόμενος	ἀξόμενος	δοξασόμενος	ἀγγελούμενος	κρινούμενος
F	καλυψομένη	ἀξομένη	δοξασομένη	ἀγγελουμένη	κρινουμέμη
N	καλυψόμενον	ἀξόμενον	δοξασόμενον	ἀγγελούμενον	κρινούμενον
GSM/N	καλυψομένου	ἀξομένου	δοξασομένου	ἀγγελουμένου	κρινουμένου

FUTURE PASSIVE

This is formed from the sixth Principal Part, the aorist passive, in completely regular fashion. Thus from Paradigm C1.5, ἐκαλύφθην, is derived the flexion form καλυφθήσομαι; and similarly for each other paradigm.

PERFECT (AND PLUPERFECT) MIDDLE/PASSIVE:

C1.5 καλύπτω **C1.6** ἄγω **C1.7** δοξάζω **C1.8** ἀγγέλλω **C1.9** ξηραίνω **C1.9** κρίνω

INDICATIVE
Present Perfect

κεκάλυμμαι	ἦγμαι	δεδόξασμαι	ἤγγελμαι	ἐξήραμμαι	κέκριμαι
κεκάλυψαι	ἦξαι	δεδόξασαι	ἤγγελσαι	ἐξήρανσαι	κέκρισαι
κεκάλυπται	ἦκται	δεδόξασται	ἤγγελται	ἐξήρανται	κέκριται
κεκαλύμμεθα	ἤγμεθα	δεδοξάσμεθα	ἠγγέλμεθα	ἐξηράμμεθα	κεκρίμεθα
κεκάλυφθε	ἦχθε	δεδόξασθε	ἤγγελθε	ἐξήρανθε	κέκρισθε
κεκαλυμμένοι	ἠγμένοι	δεδοξασμένοι	ἠγγελμένοι	ἐξηραμμένοι	κέκρινται
εἰσί(ν)	εἰσί(ν)	εἰσί(ν)	εἰσί(ν)	εἰσί(ν)	

Pluperfect

(ἐ)κεκαλύμμην	ἤγμην	(ἐ)δεδοξάσμην	No pluperfect
(ἐ)κεκάλυψο	ἦξο	(ἐ)δεδόξασο	oral or nasal
(ἐ)κεκάλυπτο	ἦκτο	(ἐ)δεδόξαστο	liquid forms
(ἐ)κεκαλύμμεθα	ἤγμεθα	(ἐ)δεδοξάσμεθα	occur in the
(ἐ)κεκάλυφθε	ἦχθε	(ἐ)δεδόξασθε	New
κεκαλυμμένοι	ἠγμένοι	δεδοξασμένοι	Testament
ἦσαν	ἦσαν	ἦσαν	

OPTATIVE

No forms occur in the New Testament.

IMPERATIVE

No forms from consonant verbs occur in the New Testament.

C1.5 καλύπτω   **C1.6** ἄγω   **C1.7** δοξάζω   **C1.8** ἀγγέλλω   **C1.9** ξηραίνω   **C1.9** κρίνω

SUBJUNCTIVE

κεκαλυμμένος ὦ ἠγμένος ὦ δεδοξασμένος ὦ ἠγγελμένος ὦ ἐξηραμμένος ὦ κεκριμένος ὦ
κεκαλυμμένος ᾖς   etc.   etc.   etc.   etc.   etc.
κεκαλυμμένος ᾖ
κεκαλυμμένοι ὦμεν
κεκαλυμμένοι ἦτε
κεκαλυμμένοι ὦσι(ν)

C1.5 καλύπτω **C1.6** ἄγω **C1.7** δοξάζω **C1.8** ἀγγέλλω **C1.9** ξηραίνω **C1.9** κρίνω

INFINITIVE

κεκαλύφθαι   ἦχθαι   δεδοξάσθαι   ἠγγέλθαι   ἐξηράνθαι   κεκρίσθαι

PARTICIPLE

κεκαλυμμένος ἠγμένος δεδοξασμένος ἠγγελμένος ἐξηραμμένος κεκριμένος
κεκαλυμμένη ἠγμένη δεδοξασμένη ἠγγελμένη ἐξηραμμένη κεκριμένη
κεκαλυμμένον ἠγμένον δεδοξασμένον ἠγγελμένον ἐμηραμμένον κεκριμένον
κεκαλυμμένου ἠγμένου δεδοξασμένου ἠγγελμένου ἐμηραμμένου κεκριμένου

For the phonemic rules which are reflected in the above flexions of the Consonant Stem Paradigms, see #9.75 and #E2.6 and E2.7.

C1.8   ORAL LIQUID VERBS; C1.9 NASAL LIQUID VERBS

C1.81 The verb stem of a liquid verb is often somewhat disguised in the present and aorist tenses by the addition of other morphs; it can be seen most clearly in the future tense, by deleting the future morph and pronoun ending from the flexion form for the future.

C1.82 The general rule for obtaining the Principal Parts of a liquid verb is: **(a)** The future is formed from the verb stem by adding -ε- as the future morph instead of -σ-; **(b)** The aorist is formed by adding the augment ἐ- and the punctiliar morph -α to the verb stem, **(c)** The perfect forms are obtained by adding the reduplication and -κα and -μαι respectively for active and middle flexions, but -ν- changes to -γ- (enga[11]) before -κα, and to -μ- (occasionally to -σ-) before -μαι.

C1.83 Where the verb stem ends in a single vowel plus -λ, the -λ doubles in the present stem. There are twelve N.T. verbs with stems in -λ (nine of the First Conjugation, three of the Second Conjugation) which conform to this rule. The rule does not apply to the one N.T. verb with a stem in a diphthong plus -λ (nor the five irregular -λ verbs in #C1.88). These thirteen verbs are:

FIRST CONJUGATION:

Stem	Present	Meaning
ἀγγελ-	ἀγγέλλω	announce
ἀλ-	ἄλλομαι	leap
ἀνατελ-	ἀνατέλλω	rise
ἐντελ-	ἐντέλλομαι	command
ἐπικελ-	ἐπικέλλω	run aground
σκυλ-	σκύλλω	trouble
στελ-	στέλλω	send
τιλ-	τίλλω	pluck
ψαλ-	ψάλλω	sing

SECOND CONJUGATION:

Stem	Present	Meaning
ἀναθαλ-	ἀναθάλλω	revive
βαλ-	βάλλω	throw
ἐφαλ-	ἐφάλλομαι	jump on

DIPHTHONG-λ STEM:

ὀφειλ-	ὀφείλω	owe

C1.84 Where the lexical form of a verb ends in -αιρ, -ειρ, -αιν, or -ειν, the verb has inserted -ι-before the liquid in forming the present stem, and the verb stem lacks this -ι-. There are 26 N.T. verbs in this category, seven with stems in -ρ, and nineteen with stems in -ν. They are:

STEMS IN -ρ

Stem	Present	Meaning
ἀρ-	αἴρω	take up
ἐγερ	ἐγείρω	raise
καθαρ	καθαίρω	clean
κερ-	κείρω	shear
σπερ-	σπείρω	sow
φθερ-	φθείρω	ruin
χαρ-	χαίρω	rejoice

STEMS IN -ν

Stem	Present	Meaning
ἀποκτεν-	ἀποκτείνω	kill
βασκαν-	βασκαίνω	bewitch
εὐφραν-	εὐφραίνω	make glad
θερμαν-	θερμαίνομαι	warm
λευκαν-	λευκαίνω	whiten
λυμαν-	λυμαίνομαι	harass
μαν-	μαίνομαι	be insane
μαραν-	μαραίνω	wither away
μιαν-	μιαίνω	defile
μωραν-	μωραίνω	make foolish
ξηραν-	ξηραίνω	dry up
πικραν-	πικραίνω	make bitter
ποιμαν-	ποιμαίνω	shepherd
ρυπαν-	ρυπαίνομαι	be impure
σαν-	σαίνομαι	be disturbed
σημαν-	σημαίνω	indicate
-τεν-	-τείνω	stretch
ὑγιαν-	ὑγιαίνω	be healthy
φαν-	φαίνω	shine/appear

Two verbs in -ερ and one in -εν do not add -ι- in forming the present stem:

δερ-	δέρω	thrash	μεν-	μένω	remain.
φερ-	φέρω	carry			

C1.85 Where the verb stem ends in -ε- plus -ρ, -λ, or -ν, then: **(a)** That verb always forms its aorist active from the verb stem by adding -ι- before the liquid as well as -α after it. **(b)** Where the stem is a monosyllable (not counting the preposition in compound forms), it forms its perfect and its aorist passive flexions from the verb stem by changing the -ε- to -α- (see Paradigm C1.8b: of the nine -ε- monosyllabic oral liquid verbs which follow this paradigm in the N.T., only six have forms occurring in the perfect and/or aorist passive in the N.T. or related literature: ἀνατέλλω, δέρω, ἐντέλλομαι, σπείρω, στέλλω, φθείρω; see also Paradigm C1.9b: of the six monosyllabic nasal liquid verbs which follow this paradigm in the N.T., only one — ἀποκτείνω — occurs in the perfect and/or aorist passive and has -ε- as its stem vowel). **(c)** Where the stem is polysyllabic it retains the -ε- throughout all its flexions (see Paradigms C1.8a and C1.9a: of the four verbs which follow C1.8a, only two, ἀγγέλλω and ἐγείρω, have stems in -ε-, and none of the twenty-seven verbs of C1.9a have stems in -ε-). The vowel change from -ε- to -α- is the only difference between the Paradigms C1.8a and C1.8b, and between C1.9a and C1.9b. (The Principal Parts for these seven verbs which are used in the N.T. are set out in #C8.61.)

C1.86 Where the verb stem ends in -ιν, the -ν- is dropped before the endings of the perfect and of the aorist passive. The three N.T. verbs which have stems in -ιν are κλίνω, κρίνω, and ὠδίνω.

C1.87 Verbs with stems in -ν add -θην to form the aorist passive (exception: φαίνω, which adds -ην, i.e. has a direct flexion); while verbs with stems in oral liquids (-λ and -ρ) add -ην (i.e., have direct flexion aorist passives; exceptions: αἴρω and ἐγείρω, which take -θην). Verbs with direct flexions are discussed in #C4.

C1.88 Nine liquid verbs in the N.T. add -ε- to their stem in forming the future or the perfect, and then function as if they were -ε- stem verbs like λαλέω (lengthening the -ε- to -η- before suffixes, as per #E2.31). Of these nine verbs, seven add -ε- to the stem in forming the future, then -σ-, in effect taking a double future morph. These seven verbs are:

ἀπόλλυμι	destroy	ἀπολέσω} ἀπολέω	ἀπώλεσα	ἀπόλωλα	—	—
βούλομαι	want	βουλήσομαι	—	—	βεβούλημαι	ἐβουλήθην
γίνομαι	become	γενήσομαι	ἐγενόμην	γέγονα	γεγένημαι	ἐγενήθην
θέλω	wish	θελήσω	ἠθέλησα	—	—	—
μέλλω	intend	μελλήσω	(ἐμέλλησα)	—	—	—
μέλω	concern	-μελήσω	—	—	—	-ἐμελήθην
οἰκτίρω	compassion	οἰκτιρήσω	—	—	—	—

The other two verbs add -ε- to the stem in forming their perfect and their aorist passive. They are:

διανέμω	spread	διανεμέω	διένειμα	διανενέμηκα	διανενέμημαι	διενεμήθην
μένω	remain	μενέω	ἔμεινα	μεμένηκα	—	—

Actually, one of these nine verbs is Second Conjugation (γίνομαι, which can be seen to have second aorist forms), and one is Third Conjugation (ἀπόλλυμι), but it is convenient to include them here with those of the First Conjugation with which they share in common the addition of the -ε-.

C1.89 The following Synopsis is a complete listing of the 75 liquid verbs of the First and Second Conjugations found in the N.T., and gives their Principal Parts (see #9.6). Second Conjugation forms are marked [2] against the second aorist Principal Part; direct flexions are marked [†] against the Principal Part. As a general rule, only those Principal Parts are given from which forms found in the N.T. are derived; occasionally forms not found in the N.T. are included where it assists in some way to have this information (e.g. in seeing how another part is derived). A hyphen in front of a form (e.g., -τείνω) indicates that this is the simplex form of the verb, but that it is only found in the N.T. in compounds.

ἀγγέλλω	announce	ἀγγελέω	ἤγγειλα	ἤγγελκα	ἤγγελμαι	[†] ἠγγέλην
αἴρω	take up	ἀρέω	ἦρα	ἦρκα	ἦρμαι	ἤρθην
αἰσχύνομαι	be ashamed	αἰσχυνθήσομαι	—	—	—	ἠσχύνθην
ἅλλομαι	leap	ἀλέομαι	ἡλάμην	—	—	—
ἀμύνομαι	help	ἀμυνέομαι	ἡμυνάμην	—	—	—
ἀναθάλλω	revive	ἀναθαλέω	[2]ἀνέθαλον	—	—	—
ἀνατέλλω	rise	ἀνατελέω	ἀνέτειλα	ἀνατέταλκα	ἀνατέταλμαι	—
ἀποκτείνω	kill	ἀποκτενέω	ἀπέκτεινα	—	—	ἀπεκτάνθην
ἀπονέμω	render	(ἀπονεμέω)	(ἀπένειμα)	—	—	—
βαθύνω	go deep	βαθυνέω	—	—	—	—
βάλλω	throw	βαλέω	[2]ἔβαλον	βέβληκα	βέβλημαι	ἐβλήθην
βασκαίνω	bewitch	βασκανέω	ἐβάσκανα	—	—	—
βούλομαι	want	βουλήσομαι	—	—	βεβούλημαι	ἐβουλήθην
βραδύνω	be delayed	βραδυνέω	ἐβραδυνα	—	—	—
γίνομαι	become	γενήσομαι	[2]ἐγενόμην	[†]γέγονα	γεγένημαι	ἐγενήθην
δέρω	thrash	(δερέω)	ἔδειρα	—	(δέδαρμαι)	[†]ἐδάρην
διανέμω	spread	διανεμέω	διένειμα	διανενέμηκα	διανενέμημαι	διενεμήθην
ἐγείρω	raise	ἐγερέω	ἤγειρα	ἐγήγερκα	ἐγήγερμαι	ἠγέρθην
ἐντέλλομαι	command	ἐντελέομαι	ἐνετειλάμην	—	ἐντέταλμαι	—
ἐπικέλλω	run aground	ἐπικελέω	ἐπέκειλα	—	—	—
εὐθύνω	make straight	εὐθυνέω	εὔθυνα	—	—	—
εὐφραίνω	make glad	εὐφρανέω	εὔφρανα	—	—	εὐφράνθην
ἐφάλλομαι	jump on	ἐφαλέομαι	[2]ἐφαλόμην	—	—	—
θέλω	wish	θελήσω	ἠθέλησα	—	—	—
θερμαίνω	warm	θερμανέω	—	—	—	—
καθαίρω	clean	καθαρέω	ἐκάθαρα	—	—	—
καταβαρύνω	weigh down	καταβαρυνέω	—	—	—	—
κείρω	shear	κερέω	ἔκειρα	—	—	—
κλίνω	incline	κλινέω	ἔκλινα	κέκλικα	κέκλιμαι	ἐκλίθην
κρίνω	judge	κρινέω	ἔκρινα	κέκρικα	κέκριμαι	ἐκρίθην
λευκαίνω	whiten	λευκανέω	ἐλεύκανα	—	—	—
λυμαίνομαι	harass	λυμανέομαι	ἐλυμηνάμην	—	—	—
μαίνομαι	be insane	μανέομαι	ἐμηνάμην	—	—	—
μαραίνω	wither away	μαρανέω	ἐμάρανα	—	μεμάραμμαι	ἐμαράνθην
μαρτύρομαι	testify	μαρτυρέομαι	ἐμαρτυράμην	—	—	—
μεγαλύνω	magnify	μεγαλυνέω	—	—	—	ἐμεγαλύνθην
μέλλω	intend	μελλήσω	(ἐμέλλησα)	—	—	—
(μέλω) μέλει	concern	-μελήσω	ἐμέλησεν (3rd sg.; impersonal)	—	—	-ἐμελήθην
μένω	remain	μενέω	ἔμεινα	μεμένηκα	—	—
μεταμέλομαι	regret	μεταμελήσομαι	—	—	—	μετεμελήθην
μηκύνω	grow	μηκυνέω	—	—	—	—
μιαίνω	defile	μιανέω	ἐμίανα	μεμίαγκα	μεμίασμαι	ἐμιάνθην
μολύνω	defile	μολυνέω	ἐμόλυνα	—	—	ἐμολύνθην
μωραίνω	make foolish	μωρανέω	ἐμώρανα	—	—	ἐμωράνθην
ξηραίνω	dry up	ξηρανέω	ἐξήρανα	ἐξήραγκα	ἐξήραμμαι	ἐξηράνθην

οἰκτίρω	compassion	οἰκτιρήσω	–	–	–	–
ὀμείρομαι	yearn for	–	–	–	–	–
ὀφείλω	owe	–	–	–	–	–
παροξύνω	irritate	παροξυνέω	παρώξυνα	–	–	παρωξύνθην
παροτρύνω	incite	παροτρυνέω	παρώτρυνα	–	–	–
πικραίνω	make bitter	πικρανέω	ἐπίκρανα	–	–	ἐπικράνθην
πλατύνω	enlarge	πλατυνέω	ἐπλάτυνα	–	πεπλάτυμμαι	ἐπλατύνθην
πληθύνω	increase	πληθυνέω	ἐπλήθυνα	–	–	ἐπληθύνθην
πλύνω	wash	πλυνέω	ἔπλυνα	–	–	ἐπλύνθην
ποιμαίνω	shepherd	ποιμανέω	ἐποίμανα	–	–	–
πτύρω	frighten	πτυρέω	–	–	–	–
ῥυπαίνομαι	be impure	ῥυπανέομαι	–	–	–	ἐρρυπάνθην
σαίνομαι	be disturbed	–	–	–	–	–
σημαίνω	indicate	σημανέω	ἐσήμανα	–	–	ἐσημάνθην
σκληρύνω	harden	σκληρυνέω	ἐσκλήρυνα	–	–	ἐσκληρύνθην
σκύλλω	trouble	σκυλέω	ἔσκυλα	–	ἔσκυλμαι	–
σπείρω	sow	(σπερέω)	ἔσπειρα	(ἔσπαρκα)	ἔσπαρμαι	†ἐσπάρην
στέλλω	send	στελέω	ἔστειλα	ἔσταλκα	ἔσταλμαι	†ἐστάλην
σύρω	drag	(συρέω)	ἔσυρα	(σέσυρκα)	(σέσυρμαι)	(†ἐσύρην)
-τείνω	stretch	-τενέω	-έτεινα	–	–	–
-τέμνω	cut	-τεμέω	²-ἔτεμον	-τέτμηκα	-τέτμημαι	-ετμήθην
τίλλω	pluck	τιλέω	ἔτιλα	–	–	–
τρέμω	tremble	–	–	–	–	–
ὑγιαίνω	be healthy	ὑγιανέω	ὕγιανα	–	–	–
φαίνω	shine/appear	φανέομαι	ἔφανα	–	–	†ἐφάνην
φέρω	carry	–	–	–	–	–
φθείρω	ruin	φθερέω	ἔφθειρα	(ἔφθαρκα)	ἔφθαρμαι	†ἐφθάρην
χαίρω	rejoice	χαρήσομαι	(ἐχάρην)	–	–	†ἐχάρην
ψάλλω	sing	ψαλέω	–	–	–	–
ὠδίνω	be in pain	ὠδινέω	–	–	–	–

This list contains only two verbs with -μ stems which are used in the N.T. outside the present/imperfect tense system (διανέμω and -τέμνω, in the compound περιτέμνω). That is, all other verbs with -μ stems occur in the N.T. only with forms of the present stem.

The future forms are all given in their uncontracted form with -ε-; but note that they *always* contract in use, according to the normal rules of contraction (see Paradigms C1.8 and C1.9 for their flexions).

C2.   THE SECOND CONJUGATION

C2.0   FEATURES OF THE SECOND CONJUGATION

C2.01 Verbs of the Second Conjugation are those which have the following two features: **(a)** The verb stem is the aorist stem, to which affixes are added to form all the other tenses; and **(b)** The Indicative active aorist is formed from the verb stem by adding the augment, the neutral morph (ο/ε) and the secondary endings as the pronoun morphs; that is, the indicative active aorist of Second Conjugation verbs is formed in exactly the same way as the indicative active past durative (i.e., the imperfect) is formed for First Conjugation verbs from the durative (i.e., present) stem of those verbs.

C2.02 The conjugation of Second Conjugation verbs is shown in the Conjugation Conspectus, #C6. It will be seen that, as the aorist and imperfect indicative active have the same pronominal endings, and as, both being past tense flexions, they each have the augment, they differ only in their *stem*: the aorist flexion is built directly on the verb stem, while the imperfect is built on the present (durative) stem — which for the Second Conjugation is always longer than the aorist (verb) stem. (There are two exceptions — see #C2.7; in these two verbs the aorist and present stems differ in other ways.)

C2.03 For a comparison of the formation of the flexions for the three Conjugations, see #9.5.

C2.04 The following Synopsis contains the thirty-four Second Conjugation verbs occurring in the N.T., i.e., verbs for which second aorist forms occur in the N.T. Some verbs had both first aorist and second aorist forms simultaneously in existence in Hellenistic Greek usage; these circulated side by side as it were, and which form a writer used was a matter of style or personal preference — though during the New Testament period the first aorist forms were tending to supplant the second aorist alternatives. In some verbs this had reached the point where, for a given verb, only first aorist forms are found in the N.T. although the second aorist forms were still also in use, or had been in use in Classical Greek. In such cases, and in the case of any other verbs which take second aorist forms but no such forms actually occur in the N.T., the verb is not listed here as Second Conjugation — there is no reason to distinguish it from First Conjugation in learning to read the Greek N.T.

C2.05 The main feature subdividing the Second Conjugation verbs is that of the manner in which they form their durative (present) stem from their verbal (aorist) stem, and they are categorized here on this basis. It will be seen that they subdivide into eight groups.

C2.1   REDUPLICATE IN -ι-

γίνομαι	become	γενήσομαι	ἐγενόμην	γέγονα	γεγένημαι	ἐγενήθην
πίπτω	fall	πεσέομαι	{ἔπεσον / ἔπεσα}	πέπτωκα	—	—
τίκτω	bear	τέξομαι	ἔτεκον	(τέτοχα)	(τέτεγμαι)	ἐτέχθην

C2.2   DOUBLE THE -λ

ἀναθάλλω	revive	ἀναθαλέω	ἀνέθαλον	—	—	—
βάλλω	throw	βαλέω	ἔβαλον	βέβληκα	βέβλημαι	ἐβλήθην
ἐφάλλομαι	jump on	ἐφαλέομαι	ἐφαλόμην	—	—	—

C2.3   ADD -ν (alone, or with other letters)

C2.31   ADD -ν

κάμνω	be ill	—	ἔκαμον	—	—	—
περιτέμνω	circumcize	περιτεμέω	περιέτεμον	περιτέτμηκα	περιτέτμημαι	περιετμήθην
πίνω	drink	πίομαι	ἔπιον	πέπωκα	(πέπομαι)	ἐπόθην

C2.32 ADD -νε

ἀφικνέομαι reach   (ἀφίξομαι) ἀφικόμην   –   –   –

C2.33 ADD -αν

αἰσθάνομαι understand αἰσθήσομαι ᾐσθόμην   –   –   –

ἁμαρτάνω   sin   ἁμαρτήσω {ἥμαρτον / ἡμάρτησα} ἡμάρτηκα (ἡμάρτημαι) (ἡμαρτήθην)

C2.34 ADD -ν.αν

θιγγάνω	touch	(θίξω)	ἔθιγον	–	–	–
λαγχάνω	obtain	(λήξομαι)	ἔλαχον	–	–	–
λαμβάνω	take	λήμψομαι	ἔλαβον	εἴληφα	εἴλημμαι	ἐλήμφθην
λανθάνω	be hidden	(λήσω)	ἔλαθον	(λέληθα)	λέλησμαι	–
μανθάνω	learn	(μαθήσομαι)	ἔμαθον	μεμάθηκα	–	–
πυνθάνομαι	inquire	–	ἐπυθόμην	–	–	–
τυγχάνω	happen	–	ἔτυχον	τέτυχα	–	–

C2.4 ADD -ισκ (after a consonant) OR -σκ (after a vowel)

εὑρίσκω   find   εὑρήσω   {εὗρον / εὕρησα} εὕρηκα (εὕρημαι) εὑρέθην

-θνήσκω   die   -θανέομαι -ἔθανον   τέθνηκα   –   –

πάσχω   suffer   –   ἔπαθον   πέπονθα   –   –

C2.5 ADD -ε- TO FORM A DIPHTHONG

λείπω   leave   λείψω   {ἔλιπον / ἔλειψα} (λέλοιπα) λέλειμμαι ἐλείφθην

φεύγω   flee   φεύξομαι ἔφυγον   πέφευγα   –   –

C2.6 CHANGE -γ- INTO -ζ-

ἀνακράζω   cry out   ἀνακράξω {ἀνέκραγον / ἀνέκραξα} ἀνακέκραγα – –

C2.7 SUBTRACTION OF INITIAL SEGMENT OF STEM

ἔχω   have   ἕξω   ἔσχον   ἔσχηκα   –   –

ἄγω   bring   ἄξω   {ἤγαγον / -ῆξα} (ἦχα) ἦγμαι ἤχθην

C2.8 SUPPLETIVES

αἱρέω   take away {ἑλέω / αἱρήσομαι} {εἷλον / εἷλα} – ᾕρημαι ᾑρέθην

ἔρχομαι   come   ἐλεύσομαι ἦλθον   ἐλήλυθα   –   –

ἐσθίω   eat   φάγομαι ἔφαγον   –   –   –

λέγω/φημί say   ἐρέω   {εἶπον / εἶπα} εἴρηκα εἴρημαι ἐρρέθην

ὁράω   see   ὄψομαι   {εἶδον / εἶδα} {ἑώρακα / ἑόρακα} (ἑώραμαι) ὤφθην

τρέχω   run   (δραμέομαι) ἔδραμον (δεδράμηκα) (δεδράμημαι) –

φέρω   carry   οἴσω   {ἤνεγκον / ἤνεγκα} ἐνήνοχα (ἐνήνεγμαι) ἠνέχθην

C2.9   CONCERNING THE FEATURES OF VERBS OF THE SECOND CONJUGATION

C2.91 This is the complete list of all verbs which have a second aorist active form in the N.T. Where a dash occurs in this Synopsis, it indicates that no form derived from that particular Principal Part occurs in the Third Edition of United Bible Societies' New Testament, either for the simplex or compound form of that verb. Other tenses and forms may be found in variant readings or in koine Greek outside the N.T., but it is not necessary to give them here. However, some forms are given in this Synopsis even though no derived forms from them occur in the N.T., where these are of interest or of help in understanding the pattern of the verb — brackets indicate such a form.

C2.92 Usually the simplex form of a verb is given in the Synopsis. It must be remembered that many of these verbs also take initial prepositions to form compound verbs. These comments apply to the compound as well as to the simplex form of these verbs.

C2.93   Of these thirty-four verbs, ten also have first aorist forms which are found in Hellenistic (and New Testament) Greek. These ten are: πίπτω, ἁμαρτάνω, εὑρίσκω, ἀνακράζω, ἄγω, αἱρέομαι, λέγω, λείπω, ὁράω, φέρω. For some words, it is the first aorist form which is the more common, and for others the second aorist form is the usual one. For example: ἤγαγον is the usual aorist for ἄγω, and ἦξα is much less common and found only in compounds; but the first aorist ἤνεγκα is the usual one for φέρω and the second aorist ἤνεγκον is rare and limited to the infinitive. The tendency to form first aorists in place of second aorists (see #C2.04) can be seen in the forms εἶπα (for εἶπον) and εἶδα (for εἶδον), where the second aorist set of endings for the flexion are replaced by the first aorist endings — but without the use of the -σ- with the -α-, although the sigma is otherwise absent only in the case of the liquid stem verbs.

C2.94 The endings of the second aorist active are identical with those of the imperfect active, and the endings of the second aorist middle are identical with those of the imperfect middle. Thus the forms of a Second Conjugation verb in the aorist and imperfect flexions differ only in stem. The flexions for the Second Conjugation are set out in the Conjugation Conspectus, #C6. (For a comparison of second aorist and imperfect flexions, see #6.73.)

C2.95 Apart from their aorist active and middle flexions, Second Conjugation verbs are declined identically with First Conjugation verbs, once the Principal Parts are known — but the formation of the Principal Parts for Second Conjugation verbs is unpredictable from the stem (i.e. they are classified as irregular verbs) and these need to be noted individually.

C2.96 Five Second Conjugation verbs display *metathesis* (the transposing of two letters of their stem). The metathesis for these verbs can be seen:

(a) βάλλω: stem βαλ → βλα → βλη (as in βέβληκα)
(b) τίκτω: stem τεκ, with reduplication in -ι- (#C2.1) τιτεκ → τιτκ (by
                 syncopation, #C2.97) → τικτ (as in τίκτω)
(c) θνῄσκω: stem θαν → τεθανκα → τεθνακα → τέθνηκα

(d) περιτέμνω: stem (περι)τεμ → τετεμκα → τετμεκα → (περι)τέτμηκα
(e) ἔχω: stem σεχ → σχε → ἔσχεκα → ἔσχηκα

C2.97 Six verbs have lost a short vowel between consonants (this feature is called *syncopation*) and/or a consonant; and have also had the stem vowel change to -*o*- in the perfect:

(a) γίνομαι: stem γεν → γιγενομαι (#C2.1) → γίγνομαι → γίνομαι
                   stem γεν → γεγενα → γέγονα
(b) ἔχω: stem σεχ → σεχω → ἔχω → ἔχω
                   stem σεχ → ἐσεχον → ἔσχον
(c) πίπτω: stem πετσ → πιπετσω (#C2.1) → πιπετω → πίπτω
                   stem πετσ → πεπετ → πεπτε (#C2.96) → πεπτοκα → πέπτωκα
(d) φέρω: stem (ἐν)ενεκ → ἠνενκον → ἤνεγκον
                   stem   ἐνεκ → ἐνηνεχα → ἐνήνοχα
(e) πάσχω: stem πα(ν)θ → παθσκω (#C2.4) → πάσχω
                   stem πα(ν)θ → πεπανθα → πέπονθα
(f) πίνω: stem πι → πεπικα → πεποκα → πέπωκα

The arrows indicate changes that have taken place (or that are hypothesized to have taken place), most of them in the pre-history of the language, before we have any record of it, to account for the forms that do occur.

C2.98 Seven verbs (set out in #C2.34) add to the lexal of the word a two-part or *discontinuous* infix : -ν- between the final vowel of the stem and the final consonant, plus -αν after the final consonant. This is written as the infix -ν.αν, where the point (.) indicates the final consonant of the stem. This -ν- then assimilates (see #E2.77) to the place of articulation (see #1.42-1.47) of the consonant which follows, becoming -μ- in front of a labial, and -γ- (enga, "ng") in front of a palatal.

C2.99 Seven verbs (as in #C2.8) are *suppletives*, that is, they are defective, and supplement their missing tenses (to some extent, at least) by drawing upon flexions from one or two other roots with similar lexical meanings. These seven are the only suppletive verb systems which occur in the N.T. (Some have identified τύπτω/παίω/πατάσσω/πλήσσω as an eighth, but as these verbs all have a present form and overlap in distribution and usage, they are better to be regarded simply as synonyms.)

C3.   THE THIRD CONJUGATION

C3.0   FEATURES OF THE THIRD CONJUGATION

C3.01 For Third Conjugation verbs, as for Second Conjugation verbs, the verb stem is the aorist stem, to which affixes are added to form the various other tenses. Verbs of the Third Conjugation are those which have one or both of the following two features: **(a)** They lack the neutral morph (*o*/ε) which is used by the Second Conjugation in adding the aorist endings to the stem, and which is used in both the First and Second Conjugations in adding the present and imperfect endings to the durative stem; and/or **(b)** They have their lexical form ending in -μι.

C3.02 The conjugation of Third Conjugation verbs is shown in the Conjugation Conspectus, #C6.

C3.03 For a comparison of the formation of the flexions of the three Conjugations, see #9.5.

C3.04 There are altogether 36 Third Conjugation verbs occurring in the N.T., 32 of which have lexical forms ending in -μι, and four verbs in -ω which are Third Conjugation in the aorist. A number of those which have forms in -μι also have First Conjugation forms which circulated in Hellenistic Greek and which can at times be found in the New Testament. For many verbs, the First Conjugation forms were, in New Testament times, in the process of supplanting the Third Conjugation forms.

C3.05 The main feature subdividing the Third Conjugation verbs is that of the manner in which they form their durative (present) stem from their verb stem, which is usually also the aorist stem; and they are categorized here primarily on that basis. Other differences may be noted from a comparison of their Principal Parts.

C3.1   REDUPLICATE IN -ι-

δίδωμι	give	(√ δο)	δώσω	ἔδωκα	δέδωκα	δέδομαι	ἐδόθην
-ἵημι	send	(√ ἑ)	-ἥσω	-ἧκα	-εἷκα	-εἷμαι	-ἔθην
ἵστημι	stand	(√ στα)	στήσω	ἔστην	ἔστηκα	ἔσταμαι	ἐστάθην
κίχρημι	lend	(√ χρα)	(χρήσω)	ἔχρησα	(κέχρηκα)	(κέχρημαι)	
ὀνίνημι	benefit	(√ ὀνα)	(ὀνήσω)	ὠνάμην	–	–	(ὠνήθην)
πίμπλημι	fill	(√ πλα)	(πλήσω)	ἔπλησα	(πέπληκα)	(πέπλησμαι)	ἐπλήσθην
πίμπρημι	burn	(√ πρα)	(πρήσω)	(ἔπρησα)	–	(πέπρησμαι)	(ἐπρήσθην)
τίθημι	place	(√ θε)	θήσω	ἔθηκα	τέθεικα	τέθειμαι	ἐτέθην

C3.2   ADD -λυ (after λ), -νυ (after other consonant) or -ννυ (after vowel)

ἀμφιέννυμι	clothe	(√ ἑ)	(ἀμφιέσω)	(ἠμφίεσα)	–	ἠμφίεσμαι	(ἠμφιέσθην)
ἀπόλλυμι	destroy	(√ ὀλ)	ἀπολέσω} ἀπολέω	ἀπώλεσα	(ἀπολώλεκα)	ἀπόλωλα	–
δείκνυμι	show	(√ δεικ)	δείξω	ἔδειξα	(δέδειχα)	δέδειγμαι	ἐδείχθην
ἐκπετάννυμι	hold out	(√ πετα)	(ἐκπετάσω)	ἐξεπέτασα	–	–	–
ζώννυμι	gird	(√ ζω)	ζώσω	ἔζωσα	–	ἔζωσμαι	–
κατάγνυμι	break	(√ ἀγ)	κατεάξω	κατέαξα	–	–	κατεάγην
κεράννυμι	mix	(√ κερα)	–	ἐκέρασα	(κεκέρακα)	κεκέρασμαι	–
κορέννυμι	fill	(√ κορε)	–	(ἐκόρεσα)	–	κεκόρεσμαι	ἐκορέσθην
κρεμάννυμι	hang	(√ κρεμα)	–	ἐκρέμασα	–	–	ἐκρεμάσθην
μίγνυμι	mix	(√ μιγ)	(μίξω)	ἔμιξα	–	μέμιγμαι	(ἐμίγην)
ὄμνυμι	vow	(√ ὀμ)	(ὀμόσω)	ὤμοσα	(ὀμώμοκα)	(ὀμώμοσμαι)	–
πήγνυμι	fasten	(√ πηγ)	(πήξω)	ἔπηξα	–	–	–
ῥήγνυμι	break up	(√ ῥηγ)	ῥήξω	ἔρρηξα	–	–	–
ῥώννυμι	strengthen	(√ ῥω)	(ῥώσω)	ἔρρωσα	–	ἔρρωμαι	(ἐρρώσθην)
σβέννυμι	extinguish	(√ σβε)	σβέσω	ἔσβεσα	–	–	(ἐσβέσθην)
στρώννυμι	spread	(√ στρω)	(στρώσω)	ἔστρωσα	–	ἔστρωμαι	–
συζεύγνυμι	join	(√ ζευγ)	–	συνέζευξα	–	–	–

C3.3   ADD ENDINGS DIRECT TO STEM (SOMETIMES WITH VOWEL LENGTHENING)

δύναμαι	be able	(√ δυνα)	δυνήσομαι	–	–	(δεδύνημαι)	ἠδυνήθην
εἰμί	be	(√ ἐσ)	ἔσομαι	–	–	–	–
-εἶμι	go	(√ ἰ)	–	–	–	–	–
ἐπίσταμαι	understand	(√ στα)	–	–	–	–	–
κάθημαι	sit down	(√ ἡσ)	καθήσομαι	–	–	–	–
κεῖμαι	lie down	(√ κει)	(κείσομαι)	–	–	–	–
φημί	say	(√ φα)	–	–	–	–	–

C3.4-C3.7   TAKE -ω NOT -μι IN THE PRESENT TENSE, AND:

C3.4   ADD -ιν

-βαίνω	go	(√ βα)	-βήσομαι	-ἔβην	-βέβηκα	(-βέβαμαι)	(-ἐβάθην)

C3.5   REDUPLICATE IN -ι AND ADD -σκ-

γινώσκω	know	(√ γνο)	γνώσομαι	ἔγνων	ἔγνωκα	ἔγνωσμαι	ἐγνώσθην

C3.6   ADD -ν

δύνω	sink	(√ δυ)	(δύσω)	ἔδυν	–	–	–

C3.7   ADD ENDINGS DIRECT TO THE STEM

φύω	grow up	(√ φυ)	(φύσω)	(ἔφυν)	–	–	ἐφύην

C3.8   CONCERNING THE FEATURES OF THE VERBS OF THE THIRD CONJUGATION

C3.81 A hyphen in front of a word (e.g., -βαίνω) indicates that this is the simplex form of the verb, but that it is only found in the N.T. in compounds. Where a dash occurs in this Synopsis, it indicates that no form derived from that particular Principal Part occurs in the Third Edition of the United Bible Societies' New Testament, either for the simplex or compound form of that verb. However, some forms are given in this synopsis even though no derived forms from them occur in the N.T., where these are of interest or of help in understanding the pattern of the verb — brackets indicate such a form. (The root is also given in brackets and indicated by the sign √ — see #C3.84.)

C3.82 This is a Synopsis of all the verbs found in the N.T. which have a lexical form ending in -μι and/or which form their aorist active by adding the Third Conjugation endings directly to the verb stem or root. As it was, however, this Conjugation was breaking down in N.T. times and assimilating to the First Conjugation, so that it can be seen from the Synopsis that there were only five verbs which followed the aorist pattern of the Third Conjugation: ἵστημι, -βαίνω, δύνω, γινώσκω, and φύω. Of these, φύω is a verb with a Third Conjugation aorist active, but no forms from this flexion actually occur in the N.T.; and there is only one occurrence (in Mark 1:32) of a form from the aorist of δύνω. This means that the aorist indicative active of the Third Declension is represented in the N.T. by only three verbs, ἵστημι, -βαίνω, and γινώσκω, together with the occurrence of one third aorist form from δίδωμι (παρέδοσαν in Luke 1:2, where Luke is very consciously using the classical form in his Prologue). As shown in the Conspectus, #C6, the Third Conjugation aorist active does occur for some verbs in other modes. All other Third Conjugation verbs in the N.T. follow the First Conjugation pattern of λύω for their aorist indicative active. These words come to be included in the Third Conjugation list only by virtue of having a lexical form in -μι, and in the case of many of these words, they only occur in the N.T. a very small number of times, and none of these occurrences may necessarily be from the distinctive Third Conjugation flexions. Moreover, a number of these words had parallel -ω forms in use in Hellenistic (and N.T.) Greek alongside their -μι forms. But all these words are included here in order that this Synopsis constitutes a complete listing of all the -μι words used in the N.T.

C3.83 On the other hand, some of these words are of very frequent occurrence, both in their simplex forms and also compounded with a wide range of prepositions.

C3.84 The root of each verb is given in brackets after its lexical form, with the sign √. Thus it is usually easy to see how the particular durative morph has been added to the verb stem to form the present stem. A number of the verbs are deponent, so their endings are -μαι, not -μι.

C3.85 It is noteworthy that three verbs — δίδωμι, -ἵημι, and τίθημι (and only these three) — form their aorist active forms (which are first aorist active flexions that follow λύω) by adding -κα, not -σα, to their stem. These forms are nonetheless easily distinguished from their perfects.

C3.86 The flexions of the Third Conjugation are set out in the Conjugation Conspectus, #C6. In this it will be noted that the third aorist endings (seen in ἵστημι, -βαίνω, γινώσκω and δύνω) are identical with those of the aorist passive, where they are added to the passive morph. A.T. Robertson, commenting on the voices in Greek, explains[32]: "Originally there was no passive voice, but only active and middle ... The passive voice is a later development ... In fact, in Greek only two tenses developed separate passive forms (the aorist and the future) ... The active and middle had separate endings all through, while the passive had no separate endings at all, but even in the aorist and future had to borrow the active endings for the aorist and the middle for the future, added to a special suffix for these tenses." That is to say, the aorist passive is formed from the active by adding the passive morph -θε- to the stem and then suffixing to this morph (which thereupon lengthens to -θη-) the endings of the third aorist (respectively, -ν, -ς, -∅, -μεν, -τε, -σαν). Thus the passive aorist and third aorist endings correspond because the passive was built upon the model of the third aorist paradigm, with the addition of the passive morph. Third Conjugation endings will also be noted on: the pluperfect active; the aorist optative passive.

C3.87 It will be noted from the Conspectus that the verbs τίθημι and δίδωμι had third aorist forms in the plural, though these had become almost entirely superseded in N.T. times by the first aorist flexions ἔθηκα and ἔδωκα — as mentioned (#C3.82), a third aorist form from δίδωμι occurs only once in the N.T., and there are no third aorist forms in the N.T. from τίθημι. ἵστημι, "I stand", is unique in possessing both first aorist and third aorist forms in active use, with divergent meanings. The third aorist indicative active flexion ἔστην, and the other aorist modes and forms, subjunctive, imperative, infinitive and participle, are all *intransitive*, and refer to the subject taking his stand himself. Thus ἔστην is used in the passage where Jesus stood on a level place (Luke 6:17), and in the statement that after the resurrection, Jesus stood in their midst (Luke 24:36). In contrast, the first aorist indicative active flexion ἔστησα, together with the entire durative system (present and imperfect indicative active, present subjunctive, imperative, infinitive and participle) are all *transitive*, so that the action carries over to an object. Thus ἔστησα is used with the meaning "I made to stand, I caused to stand, I set up, I placed in position", with reference to a specific person or thing. In the RSV this use is often translated "set" or "put" — thus the devil set Jesus on the pinnacle of the temple (Matthew 4:5; Luke 4:9); Jesus put a child in the midst of them (Matthew 18:2): the NIV translates respectively, "the devil . . . made him stand on the highest point of the temple"; "Jesus called a child and had him stand among them".

C3.88 There are 34 Second Conjugation verbs and 36 Third Conjugation verbs (a total of 70) in the New Testament. Of the 1,000 different verbs used in the N.T., the remaining 930 (93%) can be treated as First Conjugation.

C4.   VERBS WITH DIRECT FLEXIONS

C4.1   THE SO-CALLED "SECOND TENSES"

C4.11 The tense stem for a flexion of certain verbs is formed without the morph consonant which is normally used for that tense. As we have seen (#C1.82), this always happens in the case of the aorist active of liquid verbs, which take -α and not -σα as their punctiliar morph. It also occurs in a number of consonant-stem verbs (and one with a vowel stem) in the future middle (deponent), the perfect active and middle/passive, and the aorist passive (and thus in the future passive which is formed from it).

C4.12 No special name seems to have been given to this characteristic when it occurs in the aorist active of liquid verbs or of such other verbs as εἶπα and εἶδα (#C2.93), but in the other tenses it is said (on the supposed analogy of the second aorist active) to be a second future, second perfect, or a second aorist passive. This is a misleading and confusing choice of terminology, as the true second aorist has *a completely different set of endings* from the first aorist, whereas these so-called other second tenses simply lack the consonant part of the morph which identifies their aspect or voice (i.e. they contain a shorter *alternative morph* or *allomorph* of the usual aspect and/or voice morph) and in respect of their *endings* it can be seen that *they do not differ in any way* from the regular paradigms of the First Conjugation.

C4.13 A more accurate approach is to note that these verbs add their endings *more directly* to the tense stem, i.e. without the usual intervening consonant, and a more appropriate descriptive term for them is therefore *direct verbs* or verbs with a *direct tense* or *direct flexion.*

C4.14 As noted, all liquid verbs take a direct flexion in the aorist active and middle; and direct flexions may also be found in the future middle (lacking -σ-); in the perfect active (lacking the aspiration of the consonant if the stem ends in a labial, palatal or dental, or the -κ- in other cases); or in the aorist passive/future passive (lacking the -θ-).

C4.15 The following Synopsis gives the complete list of all direct flexions of verbs found in the N.T. (other than the first aorist for liquid verbs, for which see #C1.89). Verb roots are given in brackets with the sign √.

C4.2   DIRECT FLEXION FUTURE MIDDLE (DEPONENT)

ἐσθίω	eat	(√ φαγ)	φάγομαι	ἔφαγον	–	–	–
πίνω	drink	(√ πι)	πίομαι	ἔπιον	πέπωκα	–	–

C4.3   DIRECT FLEXION PERFECT ACTIVE

ἀκούω	hear	(√ ἀκου)	ἀκούσω	ἤκουσα	ἀκήκοα	(ἤκουσμαι)	ἠκούσθην
*ἀνοίγω	open	(√ οιγ)	ἀνοίξω	ἀνέῳξα	ἀνέῳγα	ἀνέῳγμαι	ἀνεῴχθην
ἀπόλλυμι	destroy	(√ ολ)	ἀπολέσω	ἀπώλεσα	ἀπόλωλα	–	–
γίνομαι	become	(√ γεν)	γενήσομαι	ἐγενόμην	γέγονα	γεγένημαι	ἐγενήθην
ἥκω	be present	(√ ἡκ)	ἥξω	ἦξα	ἥκα	–	–
κράζω	cry out	(√ κραγ)	κράξω	ἔκραξα/ον	κέκραγα	–	–
–	know	(√ εἰδ)	–	–	οἶδα	–	–
σήπω	decay	(√ σηπ)	(σήψω)	(ἔσηψα)	σέσηπα	–	–
φεύγω	flee	(√ φυγ)	φεύξομαι	ἔφυγον	πέφευγα	–	–

* Variant forms occur for this verb: see #4.62, and Matthew 7:7, etc.

C4.4   DIRECT FLEXION AORIST/FUTURE PASSIVE

ἀγγέλλω	announce	(√ ἀγγελ)	ἀγγελέω	ἤγγειλα	ἤγγελκα	ἤγγελμαι	ἠγγέλην
ἀλλάσσω	change	(√ ἀλλαγ)	ἀλλάξω	ἤλλαξα	(ἤλλαχα)	ἤλλαγμαι	ἠλλάγην
ἁρπάζω	snatch	(√ ἁρπαζ)	ἁρπάσω	ἥρπασα	ἥρπακα	(ἥρπασμαι)	ἡρπάγην
γράφω	write	(√ γραφ)	γράψω	ἔγραψα	γέγραφα	γέγραμμαι	ἐγράφην
δέρω	thrash	(√ δερ)	(δερέω)	ἔδειρα	–	(δέδαρμαι)	ἐδάρην
θάπτω	bury	(√ θαφ)	(θάψω)	ἔθαψα	–	(τέθαμμαι)	ἐτάφην
καίω	burn	(√ καυ)	καύσω	ἔκαυσα	–	κέκαυμαι	ἐκάην
κατάγνυμι	break	(√ αγ)	κατεάξω	κατέαξα	–	–	κατεάγην
κόπτω	cut	(√ κοπ)	κόψω	ἔκοψα	(κέκοφα)	(κέκομμαι)	ἐκόπην
κρύπτω	conceal	(√ κρυβ)	(κρύψω)	ἔκρυψα	(κέκρυφα)	κέκρυμμαι	ἐκρύβην
νύσσω	prick	(√ νυγ)	–	ἔνυξα	–	–	ἐνύγην
πλέκω	weave	(√ πλεκ)	(πλέξω)	ἔπλεξα	(πέπλεχα)	πέπλεγμαι	ἐπλάκην
πλήσσω	strike	(√ πληγ)	(πλήξω)	ἔπληξα			{ ἐπλήγην ‾επλάγην
πνίγω	choke	(√ πνιγ)	(πνίξω)	ἔπνιξα	–	–	ἐπνίγην
ῥέω	flow	(√ ρευ)	ῥεύσω	–	(ἐρρύηκα)	–	ἐρρύην
σπείρω	sow	(√ σπερ)	σπερέω	ἔσπειρα	(ἔσπαρκα)	ἔσπαρμαι	ἐσπάρην
στέλλω	send	(√ στελ)	στελέω	ἔστειλα	ἔσταλκα	ἔσταλμαι	ἐστάλην
στρέφω	turn	(√ στρεφ)	στρέψω	ἔστρεψα	–	ἔστραμμαι	ἐστράφην
σφάζω	slaughter	(√ σφαγ)	σφάξω	ἔσφαξα	–	ἔσφαγμαι	ἐσφάγην
τάσσω	appoint	(√ ταγ)	τάξω	ἔταξα	τέταχα	τέταγμαι	ἐτάγην
-τρέπω	turn	(√ τρεπ)	(τρέψω)	-ἔτρεψα	–	(τέτραμμαι)	-ἐτράπην
τρέφω	nourish	(√ θρεφ)	(θρέψω)	ἔθρεψα	–	τέθραμμαι	ἐτράφην
-τρίβω	rub	(√ τριβ)	-τρίψω	-ἔτριψα	(τέτριφα)	-τέτριμμαι	-ἐτρίβην
φαίνω	shine/appear	(√ φαν)	φανέομαι	ἔφανα	–	–	ἐφάνην
φθείρω	ruin	(√ φθερ)	φθερέω	ἔφθειρα	(ἔφθαρκα)	ἔφθαρμαι	ἐφθάρην
φράσσω	close up	(√ φραγ)	(φράξω)	ἔφραξα	–	–	ἐφράγην
φύω	grow up	(√ φυ)	(φύσω)	(ἔφυν)	–	–	ἐφύην
χαίρω	rejoice	(√ χαρ)	χαρήσομαι	–	–	–	ἐχάρην
ψύχω	cool down	(√ ψυχ)	(ψύξω)	ἔψυξα	–	–	ἐψύγην

C4.5   CONCERNING VERBS WITH DIRECT FLEXIONS

C4.51 A direct flexion form is an irregular verb form because it is not possible to predict from the verb's lexical form that it will occur.

C4.52 The above is a complete list of all the direct flexions which actually occur in the N.T. There are numbers of other verbs used in the N.T. which have direct flexions but which are not included here because no form from such a direct flexion appears in the N.T. (Examples of such verbs are: with direct perfect active, ἀποκτείνω/ἀπέκτονα, λάμπω/λέλαμπα, λείπω/λέλοιπα; with direct aorist passive, μίγνυμι/ἐμίγην, σύρω/ἐσύρην.)

C4.53 Several of the words with an aorist passive direct flexion are also found with the regular forms in use as well. Thus for ἁρπάζω both ἡρπάγην and ἡρπάσθην were in use; and similarly for γράφω (ἐγράφην/ἐγράφθην); δέρω (ἐδάρην/ἐδάρθην); τάσσω (-ετάγην/-ετάχθην); -τρίβω (-ετρίβην/-ετρίφθην).

C4.54 Numbers of verbs do not take -κα in the perfect active, but instead aspirate the final stem consonant. Grammarians have frequently grouped these with the direct flexion perfects and also called them "second perfects". This is a misclassification, and arises from a failure in phonemic analysis of the language. The phoneme, "aspiration plus -α" as an allomorph of -κα as the perfect active morph, is completely regular. It is in accordance with simple, straightforward phonemic rules (see #9.75 and #E2.6) and thus is predictable for all regular verbs. There is therefore no basis for classifying verbs of this kind with irregular (i.e., unpredictable) verbs forms. Examples of verbs with this completely regular perfect active can be seen from #C4.4 (which lists those with a direct flexion — and thus, irregular — aorist passive): a labial plus -κα aspirates to -φα, as in γράφω → γέγραφα, κόπτω → κέκοφα, κρύπτω → κέκρυφα, τρίβω → τέτιφα; a palatal (including -σσ) plus -κα aspirates to -χα, as in ἀλλάσσω → ἤλλαχα, πλέκω → πέπλεχα, τάσσω → τέταχα. Similarly if the stem ends in -χ: ἄρχω → ἦρχα. (See the paradigms for labial stem and palatal stem verbs, #C1.5 and #C1.6.)

C5.   VERBS WHICH TAKE TWO ASPECT MORPHS

C5.0   FEATURES OF THIS GROUP OF VERBS

C5.01 Greek contains a number of verbs which are conjugational hybrids: like verbs of the Second and Third Conjugations (#C2 and #C3), they add a durative aspect morph in the formation of their present/imperfect tense system, and in addition, like verbs of the First Conjugation (#C1), they add the punctiliar aspect morph -σα (-α for liquids) in forming the aorist.

C5.02 Because their aorist thus formed is a first aorist, they are to be classified as verbs of the First Conjugation.

C5.03 The durative morphs that they add are similar to those used by Second and/or Third Conjugation verbs in the same way.

C5.04 Those with verb stems in -λ double the -λ in accordance with the regular rule for liquids (#C1.83), and those with present stems in -αιρ, -ειρ, -αιν, and -ειν have added the infix -ι- in the formation of the present stem (#C1.84). This -λ- or -ι- (as the case may be) is a durative morph in the verb in which it occurs, indicating a verb form from that verb's durative aspect system. This -ι- in the present/imperfect is to be distinguished from the -ι- which occurs together with -α (the -ι- before the liquid and the -α after it) as the punctiliar morph in liquid verbs which have -ε- as the stem vowel before the liquid: see #C1.85. This aorist change when ε becomes ει is *compensatory lengthening* for the loss of the -σ- (#E2.43).

C5.05 All the verbs occurring in the New Testament which take both a durative and a punctiliar aspect morph are given in the following Synopsis, grouped according to the particular durative aspect morph they take.

C5.1   REDUPLICATE IN -ι-

βιβρώσκω	consume	(√ βρω)	—	—	βέβρωκα	—	—
μιμνήσκω	remember	(√ μνη)	μνήσω	ἔμνησα	—	μέμνημαι	ἐμνήσθην
πιπράσκω	sell	(√ πρα)	—	—	πέπρακα	πέπραμαι	ἐπράθην

(These have also added -σκ, and so are listed again in #C5.4.)

C5.2   DOUBLE THE -λ

(The nine verbs in this category are listed under First Conjugation in #C1.83, and their Principal Parts are given in the list of liquid verbs in #C1.89.)

C5.3   ADD -ν (alone, or with other letters)

C5.31   ADD -ν

αὐξάνω	increase	(√ αὐξα)	αὐξήσω	ηὔξησα	(ηὔξηκα)	(ηὔξημαι)	ηὐξήθην
βλαστάνω	sprout	(√ βλαστα)	(βλαστήσω)	ἐβλάστησα	(βεβλάστηκα)	—	—
τίνω	pay	(√ τι)	τίσω	—	—	—	—
φθάνω	precede	(√ φθα)	(φθάσω)	ἔφθασα	ἔφθακα	—	—

C5.32   ADD -νν

-χύννω	pour	(√ χυ)	—	—	-κέχυκα	-κέχυμαι	-ἐχύθην

C5.33   ADD -ιν

κερδαίνω	gain	(√ κερδα)	κερδήσω	ἐκέρδησα	—	—	ἐκερδήθην

C5.34 ADD -νν

ἐλαύνω	drive	(√ ἐλα)	ἐλάσω	ἤλασα	ἐλήλακα	–	–

C5.4 ADD -ε

-ωθέω	thrust	(√ ὠθ)	(-ώσω)	-ῶσα	–	–	–

C5.5 ADD -ισκ (after a consonant) OR -σκ (after a vowel)

ἀναλίσκω	destroy	(√ ἀναλο)	ἀναλώσω	ἀνήλωσα	–	–	ἀνηλώθην
ἀρέσκω	please	(√ ἀρε)	ἀρέσω	ἤρεσα	–	–	–
βιβρώσκω	consume	(√ βρω)	–	–	βέβρωκα	–	–
βόσκω	feed	(√ βο)	–	–	–	–	–
γαμίσκω	marry	(√ γαμ)	–	–	–	–	–
γηράσκω	grow old	(√ γηρα)	(γηράσω)	ἐγήρασα	–	–	–
διδάσκω	teach	(√ διδακ)	διδάξω	ἐδίδαξα	–	–	ἐδιδάχθην
ἐνδιδύσκω	clothe in	(√ ἐνδυ)	–	–	–	–	–
ἐπιφαύσκω	shine upon	(√ ἐπιφαυ)	ἐπιφαύσω	–	–	–	–
ἐπιφώσκω	dawn	(√ ἐπιφω)	–	–	–	–	–
ἱλάσκομαι	propitiate	(√ ἱλα)	–	–	–	–	ἱλάσθην
μεθύσκομαι	get drunk	(√ μεθυ)	–	–	–	–	ἐμεθύσθην
μιμνήσκω	remember	(√ μνη)	μνήσω	ἔμνησα	–	μέμνημαι	ἐμνήσθην
πιπράσκω	sell	(√ πρα)	–	–	πέπρακα	πέπραμαι	ἐπράθην
φάσκω	assert	(√ φα)	–	–	–	–	–

C5.6 ADD INFIX -ι- TO THE STEM

The 26 verbs in this category are all listed in #C1.84, and their Principal Parts are given in the list of liquid verbs in #C1.89.)

C5.7 ADD -τ TO VERB IN -π-

These verbs have the same form as καλύπτω, and follow its paradigm (see #C1.5), losing the -τ outside the durative system and following the usual pattern of labial stem verbs. Three (θάπτω, κόπτω, κρύπτω) have direct flexions in the aorist passive, and are included in the list in #C4.4. The eighteen verbs which add -τ as a durative morph are:

ἅπτω	light	θάπτω	bury	κύπτω	stoop
ἀστράπτω	flash	καλύπτω	cover	νίπτω	wash
βάπτω	dip	κάμπτω	bend	ῥίπτω	cast down
βλάπτω	harm	κλέπτω	steal	σκάπτω	dig
ἐπιράπτω	sew on	κόπτω	cut	συνθρύπτω	break
ἐπισκέπτομαι	visit	κρύπτω	conceal	τύπτω	strike/hit

C6.   CONSPECTUS OF THE THREE CONJUGATIONS

C6.0   CONSPECTUS COVERAGE

C6.01 This Conspectus shows in parallel columns the various conjugations (and paradigms within a Conjugation, to the extent that they exhibit differences) for each tense.

C6.02 At the top of each of the two main sections of the Conspectus is given the Paradigm Number for each paradigm set out there, and the Paradigm Number is followed by the root for the exemplar verb of that paradigm.

C6.03 Numbers of forms are given in this Conspectus which do not occur in the New Testament. These forms are included here for two main reasons: Firstly, the most effective way of mastering these paradigms is, for many students, not by rote learning but by gaining an overall appreciation of the pattern of word formation, and this is more easily seen when all the forms are set out. Secondly, where a student is analyzing a form in the N.T. text and trying to track it down, frequently the easiest way he can rule out some of the possibilities that he is considering is for him to be able to look up what those forms would be and thus confirm that (and how) they differ from the one on which he is working.

C6.1   PRESENT TENSE PARADIGMS

C6.11 Those set out are:

First Conjugation	Second Conjugation	Third Conjugation
C1.1 λύω	(C2 follows λύω	C3.1a ἵστημι
C1.2 τιμάω	exactly and therefore	C3.1b τίθημι
C1.3 λαλέω	does not need to be	C3.1c δίδωμι
C1.4 πληρόω	set out.)	C3.2 δείκνυμι
(C1.5 to C1.9 follow		C3.3 εἰμί
λύω exactly and		(C3.4 to C3.6 follow λύω
therefore do not need		exactly and therefore do
to be set out.)		not need to be set out.)

C6.12 After the Present Indicative for both Active and Middle Voice is set out the Imperfect, which differs from it only in having past time reference.

C6.13 The First Conjugation form consists, in each instance, of the Present stem (in the verbs given in C1.1 to C1.4, this corresponds with the verb root), to which is added the neutral morph o/ε and the pronoun suffix. Where the stem ends in a short vowel (-α, -ε, -o) this short vowel contracts with the neutral morph according to the rules of contraction.

C6.14 Note the similarities and differences in the forms of the Infinitive. All these forms can be explained on the basis of these rules: **(a)** When the verb takes the neutral morph (i.e. in the First and Second Conjugations), this is added to the stem first, and contracts with it if it ends in a short vowel. **(b)** For Middle forms, add the Middle Voice morph, -σθ-. **(c)** Now add the Infinitive morph: if being added directly to the neutral morph (whether this has contracted or not), this Infinitive morph is -σεν, which then loses the -σ- by syncopation (#E2.5), after which the -ε- of -εν contracts with the vowel which precedes it; in all other instances add -ναι to a vowel or -αι to a consonant.

C6.15 The following generalizations concerning the Third Conjugation only apply in part to εἰμί, which exists only in the Present, Imperfect, and Future Tenses, and which has numerous irregular forms.

C6.16 The Third Conjugation form consists, in each instance, of the verb root, to which the pronoun suffix is added directly, and the durative morph. For δείκνυμι, this consists of -νυ, and for ἵστημι, τίθημι and δίδωμι it consists of reduplication in -ι-. (For ἵστημι, this is not σίστημι, but the initial σ- has been lost and replaced by a rough breathing.)

C6.17 In the Third Conjugation Indicative Active singular of both Present and Imperfect, the stem vowel has been lengthened to either the equivalent long vowel or to a diphthong. In all Middle forms the stem vowel remains, and the pronoun endings have not affected it.

C6.18 In the Third Conjugation Subjunctive Mode (both Active and Middle), the short stem vowel has contracted with the long vowel of the Subjunctive endings (cf. the uncontracted forms in δείκνυμι, which does not contract since the -υ- is long). Allowing for the effect of this contraction (cf. δίδωμι), Third Conjugation Present Subjunctives have the same endings as λύω.

C6.19 Note that the Present Active Optative of εἰμί is εἴην. This follows the conjugation of ἔστην (the Aorist Indicative Active of ἵστημι), though on occasions the -η- in the plural is lost through contraction.

C6.2   AORIST TENSE PARADIGMS

C6.21 Those set out are:

First Conjugation	Second Conjugation	Third Conjugation
C1.1 λύω	C2 βάλλω	C3.1a ἵστημι
(C1.2 to C1.7 follow the	(All second aorists	C3.1b τίθημι
conjugation of λύω	follow the conjugation	C3.1c δίδωμι
exactly and therefore do	of βάλλω.)	C3.2 δείκνυμι
not need to be set out.		C3.4 βαίνω
C1.8 and C1.9 follow		C3.5 γινώσκω
λύω but with -α not -σα		C3.6 δύνω
as the punctiliar morph —		(There is no aorist
see Liquid Verbs,		for C3.3, εἰμί.)
#C1.82.)		

C6.22 Note that the Second Conjugation adds the neutral morph to its stem before taking its distinctive endings. In the Second Conjugation Indicative, the same endings are taken by the Imperfect and the Aorist, so that the only difference between the two flexions for a Second Conjugation verb is the durative morph which these verbs add in forming their Present stem. For $\beta\acute{\alpha}\lambda\lambda\omega$ this is the second-λ which is added to the verb root $\beta\alpha\lambda$, so that the Imperfect and Aorist Active flexions for this verb are:

Imperfect	Aorist
ἔβαλλον	ἔβαλον
ἔβαλλες	ἔβαλες
ἔβαλλε(ν)	ἔβαλε(ν)
ἐβάλλομεν	ἐβάλομεν
ἐβάλλετε	ἐβάλετε
ἔβαλλον	ἔβαλον

Similarly, the second -λ is the only difference between the Imperfect and Aorist Middle flexions. (For the Second Aorist verbs, see #C2.)

C6.23 Only the plural forms of the third aorist flexions of $\tau\acute{\iota}\theta\eta\mu\iota$ and $\delta\acute{\iota}\delta\omega\mu\iota$ were in use, and these were rare in N.T. times. Instead, the usual aorist forms of these verbs were first aorists, $\ddot{\epsilon}\theta\eta\kappa\alpha$ and $\ddot{\epsilon}\delta\omega\kappa\alpha$. Moreover, $\delta\epsilon\acute{\iota}\kappa\nu\upsilon\mu\iota$ has only a first aorist form, $\ddot{\epsilon}\delta\epsilon\iota\xi\alpha$. But $\ddot{\iota}\sigma\tau\eta\mu\iota$ has both the third aorist flexion $\ddot{\epsilon}\sigma\tau\eta\nu$ and the first aorist flexion $\ddot{\epsilon}\sigma\tau\eta\sigma\alpha$, with different meanings. (For a fuller discussion, see #C3.82 and C3.87.) There are also two forms of the Perfect Participle of $\ddot{\iota}\sigma\tau\eta\mu\iota$: $\dot{\epsilon}\sigma\tau\acute{\omega}\varsigma$ (given in the Conspectus), and $\dot{\epsilon}\sigma\tau\eta\kappa\acute{\omega}\varsigma$ (follows $\lambda\epsilon\lambda\upsilon\kappa\acute{\omega}\varsigma$, from $\lambda\acute{\upsilon}\omega$), and there are thus two forms of the Perfect Subjunctive Active, using these two participles respectively; both participles have the same meaning, "standing" (intransitive) (#D5.33).

C6.24 The rules for the formation of the Present Infinitives (#C6.14) also explain the Aorist Infinitives. Note that in the Active, the second aorist takes the neutral morph and then the infinitive ending, and thus in accordance with Rule (c) this is -$\epsilon\nu$, giving (after contraction) $\beta\alpha\lambda\epsilon\tilde{\iota}\nu$. In no other instance in the aorist is the infinitive morph added to the neutral morph, so it is always -$\nu\alpha\iota$ (if added to a vowel) or -$\alpha\iota$ (if added to a consonant).

C6.25 Two forms of the 2nd Singular Aorist Active Imperative are found for both $\ddot{\iota}\sigma\tau\eta\mu\iota$ and $\beta\alpha\acute{\iota}\nu\omega$. Both are given in the Conspectus.

C6.26 Greek tends to avoid having two aspirates in successive syllables, separated only by a vowel: hence in the Aorist Passive $\tau\acute{\iota}\theta\eta\mu\iota$ does not become (as would be expected) $\dot{\epsilon}\theta\acute{\epsilon}\theta\eta\nu$ but $\dot{\epsilon}\tau\acute{\epsilon}\theta\eta\nu$. So also $\theta\acute{\alpha}\pi\tau\omega$ (#C4.4). See #E2.8.

C6.27 Second and Third Conjugation aorists differ from the First Conjugation only in the Active and Middle. Verbs of all three Conjugations are Third Conjugation in the Aorist Passive — that is, they take the passive morph and then add the third aorist endings directly (without an aspect morph). (Re "second aorist passives", see #C4.12.)

C6.28 It will be noted that frequently Third Conjugation forms do not follow the Short Vowel Lengthening Rule (#E2.31), the stem vowel remaining short instead.

C6.3   CONSPECTUS OF THE THREE CONJUGATIONS

	C1.1 √λυ-	C1.2 √τιμα-	C1.3 √λαλε-	C1.4 √πληρο-	C3.1a √στα-	C3.1b √θε-	C3.1c √δο-	C3.2 √δεικ-	C3.3 √ἐσ-
PRESENT ACTIVE: INDICATIVE									
	λύω	τιμῶ	λαλῶ	πληρῶ	ἵστημι	τίθημι	δίδωμι	δείκνυμι	εἰμί
	λύεις	τιμᾷς	λαλεῖς	πληροῖς	ἵστης	τίθης	δίδως	δείκνυς	εἶ
	λύει	τιμᾷ	λαλεῖ	πληροῖ	ἵστησι(ν)	τίθησι(ν)	δίδωσι(ν)	δείκνυσι(ν)	ἐστί(ν)
	λύομεν	τιμῶμεν	λαλοῦμεν	πληροῦμεν	ἵσταμεν	τίθεμεν	δίδομεν	δείκνυμεν	ἐσμέν
	λύετε	τιμᾶτε	λαλεῖτε	πληροῦτε	ἵστατε	τίθετε	δίδοτε	δείκνυτε	ἐστέ
	λύουσι(ν)	τιμῶσι(ν)	λαλοῦσι(ν)	πληροῦσι(ν)	ἱστᾶσι(ν)	τιθέασι(ν)	διδόασι(ν)	δεικνύασι(ν)	εἰσί(ν)
Imperfect									
	ἔλυον	ἐτίμων	ἐλάλουν	ἐπλήρουν	ἵστην	ἐτίθην	ἐδίδουν	ἐδείκνυν	ἤμην
	ἔλυες	ἐτίμας	ἐλάλεις	ἐπλήρους	ἵστης	ἐτίθεις	ἐδίδους	ἐδείκνυς	ἦς
	ἔλυε(ν)	ἐτίμα	ἐλάλει	ἐπλήρου	ἵστη	ἐτίθει	ἐδίδου	ἐδείκνυ	ἦν
	ἐλύομεν	ἐτιμῶμεν	ἐλαλοῦμεν	ἐπληροῦμεν	ἵσταμεν	ἐτίθεμεν	ἐδίδομεν	ἐδείκνυμεν	ἦμεν
	ἐλύετε	ἐτιμᾶτε	ἐλαλεῖτε	ἐπληροῦτε	ἵστατε	ἐτίθετε	ἐδίδοτε	ἐδείκνυτε	ἦτε
	ἔλυον	ἐτίμων	ἐλάλουν	ἐπλήρουν	ἵστασαν	ἐτίθεσαν	ἐδίδοσαν	ἐδείκνυσαν	ἦσαν
PRESENT ACTIVE: SUBJUNCTIVE									
	λύω	τιμῶ	λαλῶ	πληρῶ	ἱστῶ	τιθῶ	διδῶ	δεικνύω	ὦ
	λύῃς	τιμᾷς	λαλῇς	πληροῖς	ἱστῇς	τιθῇς	διδῷς	δεικνύῃς	ᾖς
	λύῃ	τιμᾷ	λαλῇ	πληροῖ	ἱστῇ	τιθῇ	διδῷ/διδοῖ	δεικνύῃ	ᾖ
	λύωμεν	τιμῶμεν	λαλῶμεν	πληρῶμεν	ἱστῶμεν	τιθῶμεν	διδῶμεν	δεικνύωμεν	ὦμεν
	λύητε	τιμᾶτε	λαλῆτε	πληρῶτε	ἱστῆτε	τιθῆτε	διδῶτε	δεικνύητε	ἦτε
	λύωσι(ν)	τιμῶσι(ν)	λαλῶσι(ν)	πληρῶσι(ν)	ἱστῶσι(ν)	τιθῶσι(ν)	διδῶσι(ν)	δεικνύωσι(ν)	ὦσι(ν)

PRESENT ACTIVE: OPTATIVE
Only λύω and εἰμί have any forms of the Present Active Optative in the New Testament: λύοιμι ... εἴην

PRESENT ACTIVE: IMPERATIVE

λῦε	τίμα	λάλει	πλήρου	ἵστη	τίθει	δίδου	δείκνυ	ἴσθι
λυέτω	τιμάτω	λαλείτω	πληρούτω	ἱστάτω	τιθέτω	διδότω	δεικνύτω	ἔστω
λύετε	τιμᾶτε	λαλεῖτε	πληροῦτε	ἵστατε	τίθετε	δίδοτε	δείκνυτε	ἔστε
λυέτωσαν	τιμάτωσαν	λαλείτωσαν	πληρούτωσαν	ἱστάτωσαν	τιθέτωσαν	διδότωσαν	δεικνύτωσαν	ἔστωσαν

PRESENT ACTIVE: INFINITIVE

λύειν	τιμᾶν	λαλεῖν	πληροῦν	ἱστάναι	τιθέναι	διδόναι	δεικνύναι	εἶναι

PRESENT ACTIVE: PARTICIPLE

λύων	τιμῶν	λαλῶν	πληρῶν	ἱστάς	τιθείς	διδούς	δεικνύς	ὤν
λύουσα	τιμῶσα	λαλοῦσα	πληροῦσα	ἱστᾶσα	τιθεῖσα	διδοῦσα	δεικνῦσα	οὖσα
λῦον	τιμῶν	λαλοῦν	πληροῦν	ἱστάν	τιθέν	διδόν	δεικνύν	ὄν
λύοντος (D5.11)	τιμῶντος	λαλοῦντος	πληροῦντος	ἱστάντος	τιθέντος (D5.31)	διδόντος	δεικνύντος	ὄντος

PRESENT MIDDLE: INDICATIVE

λύομαι	τιμῶμαι	λαλοῦμαι	πληροῦμαι	ἵσταμαι	τίθεμαι	δίδομαι	δείκνυμαι
λύῃ	τιμᾷ	λαλῇ	πληροῖ	ἵστασαι	τίθεσαι	δίδοσαι	δείκνυσαι
λύεται	τιμᾶται	λαλεῖται	πληροῦται	ἵσταται	τίθεται	δίδοται	δείκνυται
λυόμεθα	τιμώμεθα	λαλούμεθα	πληρούμεθα	ἱστάμεθα	τιθέμεθα	διδόμεθα	δεικνύμεθα
λύεσθε	τιμᾶσθε	λαλεῖσθε	πληροῦσθε	ἵστασθε	τίθεσθε	δίδοσθε	δείκνυσθε
λύονται	τιμῶνται	λαλοῦνται	πληροῦνται	ἵστανται	τίθενται	δίδονται	δείκνυνται

Imperfect

ἐλυόμην	ἐτιμώμην	ἐλαλούμην	ἐπληρούμην	ἱστάμην	ἐτιθέμην	ἐδιδόμην	ἐδεικνύμην
ἐλύου	ἐτιμῶ	ἐλαλοῦ	ἐπληροῦ	ἵστασο	ἐτίθεσο	ἐδίδοσο	ἐδείκνυσο
ἐλύετο	ἐτιμᾶτο	ἐλαλεῖτο	ἐπληροῦτο	ἵστατο	ἐτίθετο	ἐδίδοτο	ἐδείκνυτο
ἐλυόμεθα	ἐτιμώμεθα	ἐλαλούμεθα	ἐπληρούμεθα	ἱστάμεθα	ἐτιθέμεθα	ἐδιδόμεθα	ἐδεικνύμεθα
ἐλύεσθε	ἐτιμᾶσθε	ἐλαλεῖσθε	ἐπληροῦσθε	ἵστασθε	ἐτίθεσθε	ἐδίδοσθε	ἐδείκνυσθε
ἐλύοντο	ἐτιμῶντο	ἐλαλοῦντο	ἐπληροῦντο	ἵσταντο	ἐτίθεντο	ἐδίδοντο	ἐδείκνυντο

PRESENT MIDDLE: SUBJUNCTIVE

λύωμαι	τιμῶμαι	λαλῶμαι	πληρῶμαι	ἱστῶμαι	τιθῶμαι	διδῶμαι	δεικνύωμαι
λύῃ	τιμᾷ	λαλῇ	πληροῖ	ἱστῇ	τιθῇ	διδῷ	δεικνύῃ
λύηται	τιμᾶται	λαλῆται	πληρῶται	ἱστῆται	τιθῆται	διδῶται	δεικνύηται
λυώμεθα	τιμώμεθα	λαλώμεθα	πληρώμεθα	ἱστώμεθα	τιθώμεθα	διδώμεθα	δεικνυώμεθα
λύησθε	τιμᾶσθε	λαλῆσθε	πληρῶσθε	ἱστῆσθε	τιθῆσθε	διδῶσθε	δεικνύησθε
λύωνται	τιμῶνται	λαλῶνται	πληρῶνται	ἱστῶνται	τιθῶνται	διδῶνται	δεικνύωνται
(D5.14)							

PRESENT MIDDLE: OPTATIVE

Apart from verbs following Paradigm C1.1, λύω, no Present Middle/Passive Optatives occur in the N.T., except two forms from δύναμαι (deponent, following the Middle of ἵστημι). These forms (and the λύω equivalents — see #C1.12) are: 1st Sing. λυοίμην δυναίμην
3rd Plural λύοιντο δύναιντο

PRESENT MIDDLE: IMPERATIVE

λύου	τιμῶ	λαλοῦ	πληροῦ	ἵστασο	τίθεσο	δίδοσο	δείκνυσο
λυέσθω	τιμάσθω	λαλείσθω	πληρούσθω	ἱστάσθω	τιθέσθω	διδόσθω	δεικνύσθω
λύεσθε	τιμᾶσθε	λαλεῖσθε	πληροῦσθε	ἵστασθε	τίθεσθε	δίδοσθε	δείκνυσθε
λυέσθωσαν	τιμάσθωσαν	λαλείσθωσαν	πληρούσθωσαν	ἱστάσθωσαν	τιθέσθωσαν	διδόσθωσαν	δεικνύσθωσαν

PRESENT MIDDLE: INFINITIVE

λύεσθαι	τιμᾶσθαι	λαλεῖσθαι	πληροῦσθαι	ἵστασθαι	τίθεσθαι	δίδοσθαι	δείκνυσθαι

PRESENT MIDDLE: PARTICIPLE

λυόμενος	τιμώμενος	λαλούμενος	πληρούμενος	ἱστάμενος	τιθέμενος	διδόμενος	δεικνύμενος
λυομένη	τιμωμένη	λαλουμένη	πληρουμένη	ἱσταμένη	τιθεμένη	διδομένη	δεικνυμένη
λυόμενον	τιμώμενον	λαλούμενον	πληρούμενον	ἱστάμενον	τιθέμενον	διδόμενον	δεικνύμενον
λυομένου	τιμωμένου	λαλουμένου	πληρουμένου	ἱσταμένου	τιθεμένου	διδομένου	δεικνυμένου
(D5.14)						(D5.34)	

AORIST ACTIVE: INDICATIVE

	C1.1 √λυ-	C2 √βαλ-	C3.1a √στα-	C3.1b √θε-	C3.1c √δο-	C3.2 √δεικ-	C3.4 √βα-	C3.5 √γνο-	C3.6 √δυ-
	ἔλυσα	ἔβαλον	ἔστην	—	—	ἔδειξα	-ἔβην	ἔγνων	ἔδυν
	ἔλυσας	ἔβαλες	ἔστης	—	—	ἔδειξας	-ἔβης	ἔγνως	ἔδυς
	ἔλυσε(ν)	ἔβαλε(ν)	ἔστη	—	—	ἔδειξε(ν)	-ἔβη	ἔγνω	ἔδυ
	ἐλύσαμεν	ἐβάλομεν	ἔστημεν	ἔθεμεν	ἔδομεν	ἐδείξαμεν	-ἔβημεν	ἔγνωμεν	ἔδυμεν
	ἐλύσατε	ἐβάλετε	ἔστητε	ἔθετε	ἔδοτε	ἐδείξατε	-ἔβητε	ἔγνωτε	ἔδυτε
	ἔλυσαν	ἔβαλον	ἔστησαν	ἔθεσαν	ἔδοσαν	ἔδειξαν	-ἔβησαν	ἔγνωσαν	ἔδυσαν

AORIST ACTIVE: SUBJUNCTIVE

	C1.1 √λυ-	C2 √βαλ-	C3.1a √στα-	C3.1b √θε-	C3.1c √δο-	C3.2 √δεικ-	C3.4 √βα-	C3.5 √γνο-	C3.6 √δυ-
	λύσω	βάλω	στῶ	θῶ	δῶ	δείξω	-βῶ	γνῶ	δύω
	λύσῃς	βάλῃς	στῇς	θῇς	δῷς/δοῖς	δείξῃς	-βῇς	γνῷς	δύῃς
	λύσῃ	βάλῃ	στῇ	θῇ	δῷ/δοῖ	δείξῃ	-βῇ	γνῷ/γνοῖ	δύῃ
	λύσωμεν	βάλωμεν	στῶμεν	θῶμεν	δῶμεν	δείξωμεν	-βῶμεν	γνῶμεν	δύωμεν
	λύσητε	βάλητε	στῆτε	θῆτε	δῶτε	δείξητε	-βῆτε	γνῶτε	δύητε
	λύσωσι(ν)	βάλωσι(ν)	στῶσι(ν)	θῶσι(ν)	δῶσι(ν)	δείξωσι(ν)	-βῶσι(ν)	γνῶσι(ν)	δύωσι(ν)

AORIST ACTIVE: OPTATIVE

Apart from verbs following λύω, the only N.T. Aorist Active Optative is δῴη (δίδωμι, 3rd sing.).

AORIST ACTIVE: IMPERATIVE

	C1.1 √λυ-	C2 √βαλ-	C3.1a √στα-	C3.1b √θε-	C3.1c √δο-	C3.2 √δεικ-	C3.4 √βα-	C3.5 √γνο-	C3.6 √δυ-
	λῦσον	βάλε	στῆθι/-στα	θές	δός	δεῖξον	-βηθι/-βα	γνῶθι	δῦθι
	λυσάτω	βαλέτω	στήτω	θέτω	δότω	δειξάτω	-βάτω	γνώτω	δύτω
	λύσατε	βάλετε	στῆτε	θέτε	δότε	δείξατε	΄-βατε	γνῶτε	δῦτε
	λυσάτωσαν	βαλέτωσαν	στήτωσαν	θέτωσαν	δότωσαν	δειξάτωσαν	-βάτωσαν	γνώτωσαν	δύτωσαν

AORIST ACTIVE: INFINITIVE

	C1.1 √λυ-	C2 √βαλ-	C3.1a √στα-	C3.1b √θε-	C3.1c √δο-	C3.2 √δεικ-	C3.4 √βα-	C3.5 √γνο-	C3.6 √δυ-
	λῦσαι	βαλεῖν	στῆναι	θεῖναι	δοῦναι	δεῖξαι	-βῆναι	γνῶναι	δῦναι

AORIST ACTIVE: PARTICIPLE

	C1.1 √λυ-	C2 √βαλ-	C3.1a √στα-	C3.1b √θε-	C3.1c √δο-	C3.2 √δεικ-	C3.4 √βα-	C3.5 √γνο-	C3.6 √δυ-
	λύσας	βαλών	στάς	θείς	δούς	δείξας	-βάς	γνούς	δύς
	λύσασα	βαλοῦσα	στᾶσα	θεῖσα	δοῦσα	δείξασα	-βᾶσα	γνοῦσα	δῦσα
	λῦσαν	βαλόν	στάν	θέν	δόν	δεῖξαν	-βάν	γνόν	δύν
	λύσαντος	βαλόντος	στάντος	θέντος	δόντος	δείξαντος	-βάντος	γνόντος	δύντος
	(D5.12)			(D5.32)					

AORIST MIDDLE: INDICATIVE

ἐλυσάμην	ἐβαλόμην	lacking	ἐθέμην	ἐδόμην	ἐδειξάμην	lacking	lacking	lacking
ἐλύσω	ἐβάλου		ἔθου	ἔδου	ἐδείξω			
ἐλύσατο	ἐβάλετο		ἔθετο	ἔδοτο	ἐδείξατο			
ἐλυσάμεθα	ἐβαλόμεθα		ἐθέμεθα	ἐδόμεθα	ἐδειξάμεθα			
ἐλύσασθε	ἐβάλεσθε		ἔθεσθε	ἔδοσθε	ἐδείξασθε			
ἐλύσαντο	ἐβάλοντο		ἔθεντο	ἔδοντο	ἐδείξαντο			

AORIST MIDDLE: SUBJUNCTIVE

λύσωμαι	βάλωμαι	θῶμαι	δῶμαι	δείξωμαι
λύσῃ	βάλῃ	θῇ	δῷ	δείξῃ
λύσηται	βάληται	θῆται	δῶται	δείξηται
λυσώμεθα	βαλώμεθα	θώμεθα	δώμεθα	δειξώμεθα
λύσησθε	βάλησθε	θῆσθε	δῶσθε	δείξησθε
λύσωνται	βάλωνται	θῶνται	δῶνται	δείξωνται

AORIST MIDDLE: OPTATIVE

The only Second or Third Conjugation Aorist Middle Optatives in the N.T. are respectively from γίνομαι (root γεν, Second Conjugation), and from ὀνίνημι (root ὀνα, Third Conjugation, this Middle Optative being the one occurrence of this verb in the N.T.). These forms (and the λύω equivalents — see #C1.12) are:

1st Singular λυσαίμην   —   ὀναίμην   —
3rd Singular λύσαιτο   γένοιτο   —

AORIST MIDDLE: IMPERATIVE

λῦσαι	βαλοῦ	θοῦ	δοῦ	δεῖξαι
λυσάσθω	βαλέσθω	θέσθω	δόσθω	δειξάσθω
λύσασθε	βάλεσθε	θέσθε	δόσθε	δείξασθε
λυσάσθωσαν	βαλέσθωσαν	θέσθωσαν	δόσθωσαν	δειξάσθωσαν

AORIST MIDDLE: INFINITIVE

λύσασθαι	βαλέσθαι	θέσθαι	δόσθαι	δείξασθαι

AORIST MIDDLE: PARTICIPLE

λύω	βάλλω	τίθημι	δίδωμι	δείκνυμι
λυσάμενος	βαλόμενος	θέμενος	δόμενος	δειξάμενος
λυσαμένη	βαλομένη	θεμένη	δομένη	δειξαμένη
λυσάμενον	βαλόμενον	θέμενον	δόμενον	δειξάμενον
λυσαμένου	βαλομένου	θεμένου	δομένου	δειξάμενου
(D5.15)				(D5.35)

AORIST PASSIVE: INDICATIVE

λύω	βάλλω	ἵστημι	τίθημι	δίδωμι	δείκνυμι	βαίνω	γινώσκω	δύω
ἐλύθην	ἐβλήθην	ἐστάθην	ἐτέθην	ἐδόθην	ἐδείχθην	-εβάθην	ἐγνώσθην	-εδύθην
ἐλύθης	ἐβλήθης	ἐστάθης	ἐτέθης	ἐδόθης	ἐδείχθης	-εβάθης	ἐγνώσθης	-εδύθης
ἐλύθη	ἐβλήθη	ἐστάθη	ἐτέθη	ἐδόθη	ἐδείχθη	-εβάθη	ἐγνώσθη	-εδύθη
ἐλύθημεν	ἐβλήθημεν	ἐστάθημεν	ἐτέθημεν	ἐδόθημεν	ἐδείχθημεν	-εβάθημεν	ἐγνώσθημεν	-εδύθημεν
ἐλύθητε	ἐβλήθητε	ἐστάθητε	ἐτέθητε	ἐδόθητε	ἐδείχθητε	-εβάθητε	ἐγνώσθητε	-εδύθητε
ἐλύθησαν	ἐβλήθησαν	ἐστάθησαν	ἐτέθησαν	ἐδόθησαν	ἐδείχθησαν	-εβάθησαν	ἐγνώσθησαν	-εδύθησαν

FUTURE ACTIVE: INDICATIVE

λύω	βάλλω	ἵστημι	τίθημι	δίδωμι	δείκνυμι	βαίνω	γινώσκω	δύω
λύσω	βαλῶ	στήσω	θήσω	δώσω	δείξω	-βήσομαι	γνώσομαι	δύσω

FUTURE PASSIVE: INDICATIVE

λύω	βάλλω	ἵστημι	τίθημι	δίδωμι	δείκνυμι	βαίνω	γινώσκω	δύω
λυθήσομαι	βληθήσομαι	σταθήσομαι	-τεθήσομαι	δοθήσομαι	δειχθήσομαι	-βηθήσομαι	γνωσθήσομαι	-δυθήσομαι

PERFECT ACTIVE: INDICATIVE

λύω	βάλλω	ἵστημι	τίθημι	δίδωμι	δείκνυμι	βαίνω	γινώσκω	δύω
λέλυκα	βέβληκα	ἕστηκα	τέθεικα	δέδωκα	δέδειχα	-βέβηκα	ἔγνωκα	—

PERFECT ACTIVE: INFINITIVE

λύω	βάλλω	ἵστημι	τίθημι	δίδωμι	δείκνυμι	βαίνω	γινώσκω	δύω
λελυκέναι	βεβληκέναι	ἑστάναι	τεθεικέναι	δεδωκέναι	δεδειχέναι	-βεβηκέναι	ἐγνωκέναι	—

PERFECT ACTIVE: PARTICIPLE

λύω	βάλλω	ἵστημι	τίθημι	δίδωμι	δείκνυμι	βαίνω	γινώσκω	δύω
λελυκώς	βεβληκώς	ἑστώς	τεθεικώς	δεδωκώς	δεδειχώς	-βεβηκώς	ἐγνωκώς	—
λελυκυῖα	βεβληκυῖα	ἑστῶσα	τεθεικυῖα	δεδωκυῖα	δεδειχυῖα	-βεβηκυῖα	ἐγνωκυῖα	—
λελυκός	βεβληκός	ἑστός	τεθεικός	δεδωκός	δεδειχός	-βεβηκός	ἐγνωκός	—
λελυκότος	βεβληκότος	ἑστῶτος	τεθεικότος	δεδωκότος	δεδειχότος	-βεβηκότος	ἐγνωκότος	—
(D5.13)		(D5.33)						

C7.   DEPONENT VERBS

C7.1   A number of Greek verbs do not have active forms in use and are found only in the middle and/or passive, but with active meaning. These are called *deponent verbs* (meaning "set aside", the active being no longer used).

C7.2   With these are usually classified a number of verbs that are frequently deponent (i.e., used in the middle or passive, but with active meaning) but which may also be found used in the active (e.g., εὐαγγελίζομαι), and others which are not found in the active but which have a "middle"-type meaning (e.g. ἀπολογέομαι, defend oneself) or a passive sense (δαιμονίζομαι, be demon-possessed), and also others that do exist in the active but with a different meaning (e.g. ἅπτω light/ἅπτομαι touch; ἄρχω rule/ἄρχομαι begin; cf. #6.17).

C7.3   It is important for a reader of the Greek N.T. to be able to recognize a deponent verb, especially one with active meaning, so that he can take account of this meaning when he encounters one.

C7.4   When a verb is deponent in the present tense, it will normally be deponent in all tenses and modes. An exception is γίνομαι, which has an active perfect (γέγονα); and the suppletive ἔρχομαι has aorist and perfect forms from ἐλθ- (ἦλθον, ἐλήλυθα) which are active in form.

C7.5   The following list contains all the deponents which occur in the N.T. ten times or more, apart from those that are compounds where the simplex verb is not deponent. Some verbs occurring less than ten times are also included where they are of interest for some other reason. Second and Third Conjugation verbs are indicated by the figures [2] and [3] respectively. A cross reference is given for verbs listed elsewhere in this Appendix as well (where the Principal Parts are given).

[2]αἰσθάνομαι	(#C2.33)	understand	ἐμβριμάομαι		be moved with anger
αἰσχύνομαι	(#C1.89)	be ashamed	ἐντέλλομαι	(#C1.89)	command
ἅλλομαι	(#C1.89)	leap/spring	ἐπαγγέλλομαι	(#C1.8a)	promise
ἀμύνομαι	(#C1.89)	come to help	ἐπισκέπτομαι	(#C5.7)	care for/visit
ἀποκρίνομαι	(#C1.9c)	answer	[3]ἐπίσταμαι	(#C3.3)	understand
ἀπολογέομαι		defend oneself	ἐργάζομαι	(#C8.74)	work
ἅπτομαι	(#C5.7)	touch	[2]ἔρχομαι	(#C2.8)	come
ἀρνέομαι		deny	εὐαγγελίζομαι		preach the gospel
ἄρχομαι	(#6.17)	begin	εὔχομαι		pray
ἀσπάζομαι		greet	[2]ἐφάλλομαι	(#C2.2)	jump on
[2]ἀφικνέομαι	(#C2.32)	reach	ἡγέομαι		think/lead
βούλομαι	(#C1.89)	want	θεάομαι	(#C1.48)	look at
γεύομαι		taste	ἰάομαι	(#C1.48)	heal
[2]γίνομαι	(#C2.1)	become	ἱλάσκομαι	(#C5.5)	propitiate
δαιμονίζομαι		be demon-possessed	[2]κάθημαι	(#C3.3)	sit down
δέομαι	(#C8.76)	entreat/beseech	καταράομαι	(#C1.48)	curse
δέχομαι		receive	καυχάομαι		boast
[3]δύναμαι	(#C3.3)	be able	[3]κεῖμαι	(#C3.3)	lie down

κοιμάομαι	sleep	²πυνθάνομαι (#C2.34)	inquire
κολλάομαι	join/cleave to	ῥύομαι	rescue/deliver
λογίζομαι	account/reckon	ῥυπαίνομαι (#C1.89)	be impure
λυμαίνομαι (#C1.89)	harass/destroy	σαίνομαι (#C1.89)	be disturbed
μαίνομαι (#C1.89)	be insane	σέβομαι	worship
μαρτύρομαι (#C1.89)	testify	σπλαγχνίζομαι	have compassion
μεθύσκομαι (#C5.5)	get drunk	φείδομαι	spare
μεταμέλομαι (#C1.89)	regret	φοβέομαι	fear
μοιχάομαι	commit adultery	χαρίζομαι	grant/forgive
ὁμείρομαι (#C1.89)	yearn for	χράομαι	use
ὀρχέομαι	dance	ψεύδομαι	deceive/lie
πορεύομαι	go/come/proceed		

C7.6　There are a number of verbs which are deponent only in their future tense, and have active forms in the present and the other tenses. Because of this special feature, these verbs need to be carefully noted. There are fourteen verbs which have deponent future forms in the N.T. (A number of other verbs which occur in the N.T. but not in the future are not included, though they have deponent futures in literature outside the N.T.)

αἱρέω	αἱρήσομαι(#C2.8)	take away	ὁράω	ὄψομαι	(#C2.8)	see
-βαίνω	-βήσομαι (#C3.41)	go	πίνω	πίομαι	(#C2.31)	drink
γινώσκω	γνώσομαι (#C3.5)	know	πίπτω	πεσέομαι	(#C2.1)	fall
εἰμί	ἔσομαι (#C3.3)	be	τίκτω	τέξομαι	(#C2.1)	bear
ἐσθίω	φάγομαι (#C2.8)	eat	φαίνω	φανέομαι	(#C1.89)	shine/appear
θνήσκω	θανέομαι (#C2.4)	die	φεύγω	φεύξομαι	(#C2.5)	flee
λαμβάνω	λήμψομαι (#C2.34)	take	χαίρω	χαρήσομαι	(#C1.89)	rejoice

C7.7　Rarely, one encounters a *reverse deponent* — an *active* form with *passive* meaning. One such is ἀπόλωλα, the direct flexion perfect active from ἀπόλλυμι (#C4.3), meaning "I have been destroyed", i.e. passive (cf. #C3.2).

C8.　IRREGULAR VERBS

C8.0　REGULARITY AND IRREGULARITY IN VERBS

C8.01　A general description can be given of how the Greek verb behaves in constructing all its forms. The behaviour of most verbs can be covered by such a description, and a verb is said to be *regular* if all its forms are derived from its lexical form with complete regularity in accordance with such a general description of verb behaviour.

C8.02　Such a general description includes *descriptive phonemic rules*[33]. These are rules which describe the effect upon a particular tense or form which results because the verb's stem ends in one *phoneme* (or *sound*, represented by a letter) rather than another. Thus the descriptive rules can be stated to cover all the different phoneme groups of a language. An example of such a rule is the Short Vowel Stem Rule, in its two parts: "A short vowel stem verb **(a)** lengthens this short vowel when it adds an ending that begins with a consonant, and **(b)** contracts this short vowel with the following vowel when it adds an ending that begins with a vowel" (see #E2.11, E2.31). Another descriptive rule will cover the pattern of this vowel contraction. Similarly, the Labial Amalgamation Rule states, "A final labial amalgamates **(a)** with a following -σ- to form -ψ-; **(b)** with a following rough breathing or -κ- to form -φ-" (see #E2.61). And so on. All these descriptive rules have been set out in their appropriate places.

C8.03 It can be seen that all the nine paradigms of the First Conjugation are regular, because the differences between them are entirely related to the particular phonemes with which their verb stems end, and can be stated in terms of those phonemes. Thus upon the basis of these descriptive rules, it is possible to know what the form will be for any part of any tense of any regular verb, when you are given the lexical form of that verb.

C8.04 This can be summed up by saying that, upon the basis of the descriptive rules, all the forms of all the tenses of a regular verb are *entirely and accurately predictable.*

C8.05 An *irregular verb* is a verb which has some forms that are *not predictable* from its lexical form, on the basis of the descriptive rules[34].

C8.06 The extent of the irregularity can vary from very small (e.g. in the verb αἰνέω, for which the irregularity is only that it does not lengthen its short stem vowel -ε- to -η- in forming its various tenses — see #C1.48) to very extensive (e.g., in the case of the suppletives — see #C2.8).

C8.07 The irregularities of irregular verbs occur in the formation of the *tense stem* for each of its Principal Parts (see #9.6). Once a particular Principal Part is known, all the forms and flexions derived from that Principal Part will follow regularly, according to the paradigm of the verb's particular Conjugation. Exceptions to this are almost non-existent; the only one of any consequence is the durative aspect of ζάω, live/be alive.

C8.08 The regular durative forms of τιμάω and the forms of ζάω are:

PRESENT INDICATIVE		IMPERFECT INDICATIVE			INFINITIVE	
					τιμᾶν	ζῆν
τιμῶ	ζῶ	ἐτίμων	ἔζων (ἔζην)			
τιμᾷς	ζῇς	ἐτίμας	ἔζης		**PARTICIPLE**	
τιμᾷ	ζῇ	ἐτίμα	ἔζη	NSM	τιμῶν	ζῶν
τιμῶμεν	ζῶμεν	ἐτιμῶμεν	ἐζῶμεν	F	τιμῶσα	ζῶσα
τιμᾶτε	ζῆτε	ἐτιμᾶτε	ἐζῆτε	N	τιμῶν	ζῶν
τιμῶσι(ν)	ζῶσι(ν)	ἐτίμων	ἔζων	GSM/N	τιμῶντος	ζῶντος

For both τιμάω and ζάω, the present subjunctive of each verb is identical with its respective present indicative flexion. No forms of the optative or imperative of ζάω occur in the N.T. It will be noticed that the "irregularity" of ζάω is that it has -η- in its ending wherever τιμάω has -α-. This arises because the root of the verb is in fact ζη- rather than ζα-.

C8.09 Irregular verbs can be classified according to the nature of the irregularity. Many of the various categories or groups of irregular verbs have already been discussed in this Appendix.

C8.1   SHORT VOWEL STEM VERBS WHICH DO NOT LENGTHEN THE VOWEL

These have been discussed in #C1.48.

C8.2   VERBS WHICH ADD -ε- IN FORMING THE FUTURE AND/OR PERFECT STEM

These have been discussed in #C1.88.

C8.3   VERBS OF THE SECOND AND THIRD CONJUGATIONS

C8.31 Although most verbs of the Second and Third Conjugations follow regular patterns in the formation of their other tense stems from their aorist root, what the Principal Parts will be cannot be predicted in advance, either from the lexical form or from the aorist of a verb. That is, the Principal Parts need to be separately noted for each verb of these Conjugations. Thus, as they have Principal Parts which are unpredictable, these verbs must all be classified as irregular.

C8.32 The verbs of the Second and Third Conjugations found in the N.T. are listed and discussed in C2 and C3.

C8.4   VERBS WITH DIRECT FLEXIONS/TWO ASPECT MORPHS

Verbs in these two categories have been discussed in #C4 and #C5 respectively.

C8.5   DEPONENT VERBS

C8.51 Many of these verbs are regular in their forms; their irregularity consists of the fact that they take a middle or passive form with active meaning, instead of an active form. It could be argued however that *merely* being deponent does not mean that a verb is irregular, as the fact of its being deponent is indicated by the lexical form being middle, not active.

C8.52 Some deponent verbs, though, are irregular in other ways. Certainly the verbs that are deponent only in their future (#C7.6) are to be classified as irregular, because this feature is unpredictable from their lexical forms.

C8.53 The deponents found in the N.T. are listed and discussed in #C7.

C8.6   VERBS WHICH CHANGE THEIR STEM VOWEL TO *o/α* IN THE PERFECT

C8.61 Monosyllabic liquid verbs in -ε- regularly change this vowel to -α- in the perfect and/or aorist passive. The seven monosyllabic liquid verbs which occur in the N.T. — and all of which follow this pattern (see #C1.85) — are:

ἀνατέλλω	rise	ἀνατελέω	ἀνέτειλα	ἀνατέταλκα	ἀνατέταλμαι	—
ἀποκτείνω	kill	ἀποκτενέω	ἀπέκτεινα	—	—	ἀπεκτάνθην
δέρω	thrash	(δερέω)	ἔδειρα	—	(δέδαρμαι)	ἐδάρθην
ἐντέλλομαι	command	ἐντελέομαι	ἐνετειλάμην	—	ἐντέταλμαι	—
σπείρω	sow	(σπερέω)	ἔσπειρα	(ἔσπαρκα)	ἔσπαρμαι	ἐσπάρην
στέλλω	send	στελέω	ἔστειλα	ἔσταλκα	ἔσταλμαι	ἐστάλην
φθείρω	ruin	φθερέω	ἔφθειρα	(ἔφθαρκα)	ἔφθαρμαι	ἐφθάρην

C8.62 Quite a number of other verbs change their stem vowel to -*o*- in the perfect active and/or to -α- in the perfect passive (and, usually, aorist passive). Where the -*o*- is followed by the -κα of the perfect active, it lengthens to -ω- in accordance with the Short Vowel Lengthening Rule (#E2.31).

C8.63 There are eleven such verbs which occur in the N.T. in a form affected by one or both of these changes, and three other N.T. words (λείπω, πέμπω and τίκτω) the perfect active of which does not actually occur in the N.T. but which are included here for their usefulness in illustrating the change and/or because the perfect is found in other Christian writings of the Hellenistic period. In addition there are two other N.T. words (given in square brackets) which in Hellenistic Greek are found only in the perfect, the present being obsolete.

γίνομαι	become	γενήσομαι	ἐγενόμην	γέγονα	γεγένημαι	ἐγενήθην
[ἔθω]	be accustomed	—	—	εἴωθα	—	—
[εἴκω]	be like	—	—	ἔοικα	—	—
λείπω	leave	λείψω	ἔλιπον} ἔλειψα}	(λέλοιπα)	λέλειμμαι	ἐλείφθην
πάσχω	suffer	—	ἔπαθον	πέπονθα	—	—
πείθω	persuade	πείσω	ἔπεισα	πέποιθα	πέπεισμαι	ἐπείσθην
πέμπω	send	πέμψω	ἔπεμψα	(πέπομφα)	(πέπεμμαι)	ἐπέμφθην
πίνω	drink	πίομαι	ἔπιον	πέπωκα	—	ἐπόθην
πίπτω	fall	πεσέομαι	ἔπεσον} ἔπεσα}	πέπτωκα	—	—
πλέκω	weave	(πλέξω)	ἔπλεξα	(πέπλεχα)	(πέπλεγμαι)	ἐπλάκην
πλήσσω	strike	(πλήξω)	ἔπληξα	—	—	-επλάγην
στρέφω	turn	στρέψω	ἔστρεψα	(ἔστροφα)	ἔστραμμαι	ἐστράφην
τίκτω	bear	τέξω	ἔτεκον	(τέτοκα)	—	ἐτέχθη
-τρέπω	turn	(τρέψω)	-έτρεψα	(τέτροφα)	(τέτραμμαι)	ἐτράπην
τρέφω	nourish	(θρέψω)	ἔθρεψα	—	(τέθραμμαι)	ἐτράφην
φέρω	carry	οἴσω	ἤνεγκον} ἤνεγκα}	ἐνήθοχα	—	ἠνέχθην

C8.64 When nouns are formed from verbs which have -ε- as their vowel, it is common for such nouns to have -ο- in place of the -ε-. Some examples:

ἀνατολή (ἀνατέλλω); ἀποδοχή (ἀποδέχομαι); ἀπόστολος (ἀποστέλλω); ἐντολή (ἐντέλλομαι); ἐπιστολή (ἐπιστέλλω); λόγος (λέγω); συνοχή (συνέχω); τροφή (τρέφω); ὑπομονή (ὑπομένω).

C8.7 DIGAMMA VERBS

C8.71 In ancient times, a number of Greek words had contained a letter digamma, Ϝ (see Footnotes #4 and #5) which dropped out of use well before the period of Hellenistic Greek. When the digamma had been the first letter of a verb its disappearance meant that in the past tenses (the imperfect and aorist) the augment was brought next to the first vowel of the stem. When the first vowel of the stem was -ε- or -ι-, the two vowels then contracted in accordance with the regular rules. Similarly, when the perfect flexion lost the reduplicated and initial digamma, the -ε- of the reduplication contracted with the first vowel of the stem, if -ε- or -ι-.

C8.72 There are also verbs with original roots commencing with sigma from which this sigma has been lost: thus an original σέχω became ἔχω. This situation is similar to that of the loss of a digamma — in such a word as this, the augment in the past tense was also brought next to the -ε- of the stem, and contracted with it. (For two words — given below — the evidence indicates that they commenced with σϜ, with both consonants being lost.)

C8.73 Thus words to which this has happened will have imperfect, aorist, and perfect flexions commencing with ει- (due to the contraction of ε+ε or ε+ι) instead of η- (the augmented ε-) or long ι- (the augmented short ι-). However, when a digamma has dropped out between ε- and a vowel other than -ε- or -ι-, the two vowels do not contract but remain distinct. Thus, in the one verb where the first vowel of the stem was -ο- (Ϝορα-), this has not contracted with the prefixed ε- but each has continued as a separate syllable in both of the alternative forms that occur, ἑόρακα and ἑώρακα.

C8.74 The ten verbs found in the N.T. with forms affected in this way are:

			imperfect	future	aorist	perfect	perfect mid/pass	aorist passive
ἐάω	allow	(√Ϝεαω?)	εἶων	ἐάσω	εἶασα	—	—	—
ἐθίζω	accustom	(√σϝεθιζ)	—	—	—	—	εἴθισμαι	—
[ἔθω]	be accustomed	(√σϝεθ)	—	—	—	εἴωθα	—	—
ἑλκόομαι	be covered with sores	(√Ϝελκο?)	—	—	—	—	εἵλκωμαι	—
ἕλκω	pull/drag	(√Ϝελκ)	εἷλκον	ἑλκύσω	εἵλκυσα	—	—	—
ἐργάζομαι	work	(√Ϝεργαζ)	εἰργαζόμην	—	εἰργασάμην	—	εἴργασμαι	εἰργάσθην
[ἔρω]	speak	(√Ϝερ)	—	ἐρέω	—	εἴρηκα	εἴρημαι	ἐρρέθην
ἔχω	have	(√σεχ)	εἶχον	ἕξω	ἔσχον	ἔσχηκα	—	—
[ἴδω]	see	(√Ϝιδ)	—	—	εἶδον	—	—	—
ὁράω	watch	(√Ϝορα)	—	—	—	ἑώρακα / ἑόρακα	—	—

(It will be noted that in three of these verbs the present form, given in square brackets, is obsolete, and is not found in Classical/Hellenistic Greek.) In this table, if the verb has an imperfect, this is given immediately after the root, before the future. For two verbs the root is conjectural, and it is therefore followed by a question mark. In three verbs the dropped digamma has been replaced by a rough breathing; the others however commence with a smooth breathing.

C8.75 Verbs which had stems *ending* in a digamma became modified when the digamma dropped out of Greek. These descriptive rules tell what happened:
(a) Before *vowel endings* the digamma was simply omitted, but the vowels thus brought together only contracted in the case of ε+ε and ε+ι (to ει), i.e. not with α, η, ο, ω, οι, or ου; and this applies also to all flexion forms.
(b) Before *consonant endings* the digamma was replaced by upsilon.
(c) Where the stem has -α- before the digamma, then in the present tense this -α- added -ι- as a durative morph in the same way as liquids (#C5.04). These modifications can all be seen clearly exemplified in the verb καίω — note especially that it has two alternative forms of the aorist passive, one a regular form with -θ-, and the other a direct flexion (#C4.4), and that where the digamma used to occur in the regular form it was before a -θ- and thus has been replaced by -υ- (ἐκαύθην), and where the digamma used to occur in the direct flexion form it was before a vowel, -η-, and thus simply dropped out but without contraction occurring (ἐκάην).

C8.76 The nine verbs of this kind found in the N.T. are:

ἀκούω	hear	(√ ἀκοϜ)	ἀκούσω	ἤκουσα	ἀκήκοα	(ἤκουσμαι)	ἠκούσθην
δέομαι	entreat	(√ δεϜ)	—	—	—	—	ἐδεήθην
ζέω	boil	(√ ζεϜ)	—	—	—	—	
καίω	burn	(√ καϜ)	καύσω	ἔκαυσα	—	κέκαυμαι	{ἐκαύθην / ἐκάην
κλαίω	weep	(√ κλαϜ)	κλαύσω	ἔκλαυσα	—	—	—
πλέω	sail	(√ πλεϜ)	(πλεύσω)	ἔπλευσα	—	—	—
πνέω	breathe	(√ πνεϜ)	(πνεύσω)	ἔπνευσα	—	—	—
ῥέω	flow	(√ ῥεϜ)	ρεύσω	—	—	—	ἐρρύην
-χέω	pour	(√ χεϜ)	-χεέω	-ἔχεα	—	—	—
-χύννω	pour	(√ χυ)	—	—	(-κέχυκα)	-κέχυμαι	-ἐχύθην

C8.77 It will be seen that -χέω differs from the others in this list by taking the Attic future (see #C8.85); i.e. instead of adding -σ- to form the future it adds -ε- as its future morph, like a liquid. Similarly it rejects -σ- (again like a liquid) in the aorist, giving the form -ἔχεϜα and thence -ἔχεα (instead of -ἔχεϜσα and thence -ἔχευσα). It does not contract even ε and ε.   -χύννω is a parallel verb supplying the other flexions.

C8.78 For ἀκούω, the perfect form ἀκήκοα, with reduplication of the initial syllable, has resulted from loss of the original digamma from a primitive ἀκήκοϜα, the -ο- and -α- continuing as separate syllables, in accordance with the digamma-vowel rule, #C8.75(a), that (except ε+ε and ε+ι), vowels brought together by the disappearance of digamma do not contract. In accordance with the digamma-consonant rule, the digamma was replaced by -υ- before a consonant, i.e. in the future, aorist active and aorist passive. Contrary to these rules, the -υ- was then also retained in the present form, ἀκούω.

C8.79 As digamma is not present in the documents which have come down to us from the ancient world, its original occurrence in a word is hypothetical. In many cases, that digamma used to be part of a word is postulated upon strong evidence: e.g., occasional inscriptions that are very ancient and contain it; the scanning of a word in a line of verse from Homer which can only be explained on the basis of digamma having originally been present; or a parallel word in Latin which possess the equivalent "v", such as *vidē* for Greek ιδ-, see. It needs to be mentioned that in some cases, however, the evidence is less certain, and is based on analogy from similar or parallel words, or simply that an original digamma provides a clear logical explanation for word forms that would be difficult to account for on any other basis.

C8.8   IRREGULAR ζητα VERBS

C8.81 Several -ζ verbs in the N.T. do not follow the usual rule (#4.57, #C1.7) of taking -σ- as their future morph and dropping the -ζ of their stem. There are two groups of these irregular -ζ verbs: those which comprise the first group behave like palatals in how they form their other tenses; those in the second group behave like liquids in the formation of their future.

C8.82 Some -ζ stem verbs are present tense forms which have arisen from an original palatal verb root, and outside the present system they behave like palatal verbs, forming their future and aorist active in -ξ, and aorist passive in -χ- before -θ-, or in -γ- if a direct flexion.

C8.83 There are five verbs which have these palatal forms in the N.T., one of which also has parallel forms in the future and aorist which are formed in the regular way for a dental stem verb.

C8.84 These five verbs are:

κράζω cry out (√ κραγ)	κράξω	ἔκραξα ⎰ ἔκραγον ⎱	κέκραγα	—	—
παίζω dance, play (√ παιγ)	παίξω	ἔπαιξα	—	—	ἐπαίχθην
στενάζω groan, sigh (√ στεναγ)	στενάξω	ἐστέναξα	—	—	
στηρίζω strengthen (√ στηριγ)	στηρίξω στηρίσω	ἐστήριξα ἐστήρισα ⎱	—	ἐστήριγμαι	ἐστηρίχθην
σφάζω slaughter (√ σφαγ)	σφάξω	ἔσφαξα	—	ἔσφαγμαι	ἐσφάγην

C8.85 In the Attic dialect, verbs in -ζ did not always indicate the future by adding -σ- as the future morph. To quote from Section 665 of Goodwin's "Greek Grammar" of Classical Greek: "Futures in ισω and ισομαι from verbs in ιζω of more than two syllables regularly drop σ and insert ε; then ιέω and ιέομαι are contracted to ιῶ and ιοῦμαι; as κομίζω, carry, κομίσω, (κομιέω,) κομιῶ; κομίσομαι, (κομιέομαι,) κομιοῦμαι, inflected like φιλῶ, φιλοῦμαι. These forms of future are called *Attic*, because the pure Attic seldom uses any others in these tenses; but they are found also in other dialects and even in Homer."[35] That is to say, these particular verbs behave as if they had, not a dental stem, but a liquid stem.

C8.86 The Attic future is usual in the Septuagint, and is found in the N.T. for a number of these verbs, especially (but not exclusively) in quotations from or allusions to the Septuagint, or passages such as Luke 1:48, in a hymn in the Old Testament style.

C8.87 There is one other N.T. verb, -χέω (found only in compounds), which also behaves like a liquid and takes -ε- as its future morph instead of -σ-, and this future morph -ε- then similarly contracts with the neutral morph which is added in the suffix (the contraction being marked by the circumflex accent). Thus the full (uncontracted) future is -χεέω, which contracts to -χεῶ (Acts 2:17 and 18). This contrasts with the way in which the -ε- of the *stem* resists contracting with endings, even those commencing with -ε- (see #C8.77).

C8.88 The ten N.T. verbs which are not liquids but which nonetheless are found with -ε- as their future morph, are set out below. Note that (except for the non-ζητα verb -χέω) they all take -σα- as their punctiliar morph. For the two verbs marked † the regular dental future form is also found in the N.T.: ἀφορίσω in Matthew 25:32 and κομίσω in Ephesians 6:8 and Colossians 3:25.

ἀφορίζω†	separate	¹ἀφοριέω	ἀφώρισα	—	ἀφώρισμαι	ἀφωρίσθην
ἐγγίζω	draw near	²ἐγγιέω	ἤγγισα	ἤγγικα	—	—
ἐδαφίζω	raze totally	³ἐδαφιέω	—	—	—	—
ἐλπίζω	hope, expect	⁴ἐλπιέω	ἤλπισα	ἤλπικα	—	—
καθαρίζω	make clean	⁵καθαριέω	ἐκαθάρισα	—	κεκαθάρισμαι	ἐκαθαρίσθην
κομίζω†	bring, get	⁶κομιέω	ἐκόμισα	—	—	—
μακαρίζω	consider happy	⁷μακαριέω	ἐμακάρισα	—	—	—
μετοικίζω	make to move	⁸μετοικιέω	μετῴκισα	—	—	—
παροργίζω	make angry	⁹παροργιέω	παρώργισα	—	—	—
-χέω	pour	¹⁰-χεέω	-ἔχεα	—	—	—

¹Mt 13:49; ²James 4:8; ³Lk 19:44; ⁴Mt 12:21 and Rom 15:12; ⁵Hebrews 9:14; ⁶I Peter 5:4; ⁷Lk 1:48; ⁸Acts 7:43; ⁹Romans 10:19; ¹⁰Acts 2:17 and 18.

C8.89 In some manuscripts, the Attic future is also found for: γνωρίζω (Col 4:9), καταρτίζω (I Peter 5:10), φωτίζω (Revelation 22:5), and χρονίζω (Hebrews 10:37).

C8.9   OTHER IRREGULAR VERBS

C8.91 Some verbs may take (either as a general rule, or as a stylistic preference of particular authors) a sigma before the suffix of the perfect middle/passive and/or aorist passive (e.g. κλείω has κέκλεισμαι instead of κέκλειμαι and ἐκλείσθην instead of ἐκλείθην). The presence of this sigma would not affect the recognizability of such forms, and so it has not been judged necessary to list verbs of this kind.

C8.92 Some writers sometimes use rare or archaic or unusual forms of particular verbs (e.g. ἔγημα, a variant aorist form of γαμέω, found three times in the N.T. as an alternative to the regular aorist, ἐγάμησα). Where such irregular forms are the only ones that occur in the N.T., they have been covered in this Appendix. Where they are stylistic variants of the regular or usual forms, they are usually not included in this Appendix, but are regarded as a matter for discussion in commentaries on the Greek text.

C8.93 It happened on occasions that a new present tense was formed from an aorist or a perfect form. Thus the perfect of ἵστημι is ἕστηκα, and a new present flexion was formed to correspond with this perfect: στήκω. This new form of the verb was then used in the present and imperfect flexions.

C8.94 Apart from the abovementioned cases, all the verbs which are irregular in the N.T. are dealt with in this Appendix. A number of verbs which exhibit more than one irregularity are referred to in relation to each irregular feature. To find a particular verb, look it up in the Greek Index, which gives the cross reference(s) to the place(s) where that verb is described and/or its Principal Parts are set out.

C9. VERB GROUPS FOR NEW TESTAMENT VERBS

C9.1   It will be of interest to see the relative numbers of N.T. verbs in the different verb groups (classified according to stem and conjugation).

C9.2   The figure that is given for the number of verbs in the N.T. will vary depending upon the N.T. text that is used and how verbs are counted and classified. The text used here is that of the United Bible Societies Third Edition. This summary treats compound verbs as being, morphologically, forms of the simplex verb, and does not count them separately unless the simplex form is unused and the compounds are unrelated in their usage. Where separate and distinct forms of a verb are found in the N.T. belonging to different conjugations (e.g. ἱστάνω and ἵστημι) or to different subgroups within the one conjugation (e.g. -χέω and -χύννω), the two verbs are treated separately and each is counted in its appropriate group. Verbs are listed as Second or Third Conjugation if (and only if) such a form occurs in the N.T., and under First Conjugation otherwise (even if Second or Third Conjugation forms are found *outside* the New Testament).

C9.3   Using this basis for classification, there will be found to be one thousand verbs in the Greek N.T., distributed into verb groups as follows:

CONSONANT STEMS	LABIALS ππ	TΛ	Sub	PALATALS ζ	σκ	σσ	TΛ	Sub	DENTALS ζ	TΛ	Sub	LIQUIDS λ	μ	ν	+ν	ρ	Sub	Consonant σ	F	Total
1st Conj.	18	19	37	5	15	24	21	65	206	17	223	16	4	40	10	14	84	-	9	418
2nd Conj.	1	3	4	1	3	-	10	14	-	7	7	4	3	1	-	-	8	-	-	33
3rd Conj.	-	-	-	-	-	-	6	6	-	-	-	1	1	-	-	-	2	2	-	10

VOWEL STEMS	LONG VOWEL STEMS ι	υ	ω	αι	ει	οι	αυ	ευ	ου	Sub	SHORT VOWELS α	ε	ο	Sub	Vowel Total	No Pres	Cons. Total	TOTAL
1st Conj.	4	21	-	2	2	1	3	70	2	105	78	235	91	404	509	3	418	930
2nd Conj.	1	-	-	-	-	-	-	-	-	1	-	-	-	-	1	(7)	33	34
3rd Conj.	1	2	3	-	1	-	-	-	-	7	12	5	2	19	26	-	10	36

TΛ = Tὰ Λοιπά, the remainder (of the category). Sub = Subtotal (of that category). +ν = words with ν added to stem. No Pres = No Present Stem.

APPENDIX D

DECLENSION

D0. THE GREEK DECLENSION SYSTEM

D0.1 THE NATURE OF DECLENSION

D0.11 There are two types of inflection in Greek: the addition to the stem of **(a)** suffixes with person and number — the *pronoun suffixes* of the verb (which are dealt with in Appendix C); and **(b)** suffixes with number and case, the *numbercase suffixes*. Each numbercase suffix is a single morph which cannot be further subdivided and which simultaneously indicates both the number and the case of the word.

D0.12 The words which take numbercase suffixes are: nouns, adjectives, pronouns, participles, and the article. The *number* aspect of the suffix indicates either singular or plural. The *case* aspect of the suffix indicates the relationship of the word to the rest of the sentence (see #2.2ff. and #8.1ff.).

D0.13 To set out the range of numbercase forms for a word is to *decline* it. A group of words which all follow the same basic pattern of declining their forms comprise a *declension*. There are three declensions in Greek (which for convenience can be designated D1, D2, and D3). A set of the forms for a word, with the different numbercase suffixes, is called a *flexion*. Where a particular flexion provides a pattern for the way in which the numbercase suffixes are added to a particular stem phoneme, this is called a *paradigm*. Usually a particular paradigm will be followed by a number of words, but in some instances it can happen (especially with the Third Declension) that in the New Testament only a small number of words — perhaps only a single word — will occur which ends in a particular phoneme or phoneme group. Thus paradigms occur which are followed by a very few N.T. words, perhaps by only one.

D0.14 There are two different orders which are found for setting out the forms of a flexion. Some grammar books use the order: nominative, vocative, accusative, genitive, dative; others prefer: nominative, genitive, dative, accusative, vocative. The preponderance of reasons favours the first of these alternatives, as the footnote explains[36]. This therefore is the order in which the forms of a flexion are given in this book. It is suggested that students will find it advantageous to use this order for learning them.

D0.2 THE FORMATION OF DECLENSION FLEXIONS

D0.21 There are two ways in which Greek adds the numbercase suffixes to produce the forms of the Declension flexions: either **(a)** directly to the noun root, or word-base; or **(b)** with a "linking" vowel.

D0.22 This *linking vowel* or *link vowel* may be either -α- or -o-. Thus for words which use a linking vowel, the *stem* consists of the *root* plus the *linking vowel*, which may therefore also be described as the *stem vowel*. In contrast, when the root itself ends in a vowel, this vowel can be referred to as the *root vowel*. (The link vowel is not itself a morph — see #E3.36.)

D0.23 A number of nouns take -α- as their stem vowel and these together comprise the First Declension. All those which take -o- as their stem vowel comprise the Second Declension. Those which have no stem vowel, adding the numbercase suffixes directly to their root, comprise the Third Declension.

D0.24 The stem vowel undergoes some modification as follows:
(a) The -α- stem vowel lengthens to -η- in the *singular* of all words except those with the root ending in ρ, ι, ε, a sibilant, or some specific words;
(b) The -o- stem vowel shortens further to -ε- in the vocative.

D0.25 It is interesting to compare these delineating features of the three Declensions with the form of the aspect morph which is added in the formation of the aorist active and middle of the three verb Conjugations:

Declension/Conjugation:	First	Second	Third
Nouns: stem vowel added to noun root:	-α-	-o-(-ε-)	none
Aorist of verbs: aspect morph added to verb root:	-σα-	-o/ε-	none

D0.26 The numbercase suffixes added to the noun stem to give its forms are:

SUFFIX	VARIANTS FOR MASC. & FEM. WORDS	VARIANTS FOR NEUTER WORDS
SN ς V ∅* A ν	But ∅* in D1 feminine. Last vowel shortens if possible Consonant stems (D3) take -α-.	In place of ς, take ν or ∅* Identical with nominative. Identical with nominative.
G ς or o or oς D ι	D1 takes -ς, D2 takes -o, and D3 takes -oς. D1 & D2: Stem v. lengthens; ι subscript; D3: Root v. stays as is.	
PNV ι or ες A ας	D1 & D2 take -ι, D3 take -ες. But -ες after a vowel.	Always add -α to root. Identical with nominative.
G ων D ις or σι	Stem vowel (but not usually root vowel) contracts with -ων. D1 and D2 take ις, but D3 takes σι.	

* ∅ indicates zero, the absence of any phoneme, where this absence of a phoneme is itself of significance and thus is a morph. (This is known as a *zero morph*.[37])

D0.27 Contraction of vowels will take place when the numbercase suffix as above is added to a stem or root vowel. Thus:

SG κυριο+o → κυρίου; γενε(σ)+ος → γένους; but πολε+ος → πόλεως
D καρδια+ι → καρδίᾳ; κυριω+ι → κυρίῳ; πολε+ι → πόλει
PN φωνα+ι → φωναί; κυριο+ι → κύριοι; πολε+ες → πόλεις
A καρδια+ες → καρδίας; κυριο+ες → κυρίους; βασιλε+ες → βασιλεῖς
G φωνά+ων → φωνῶν; κυριο+ων → κυρίων; but βασιλε+ων → βασιλέων

However, only limited contraction occurs when vowels are brought together by the disappearance of digamma (see #D3.4).

D0.28 The genitive singular of D1 masculine words takes the D2 ending (stem vowel -*o*- plus numbercase suffix -*o*, → *ου*, as in *μαθητοῦ*), thus differentiating this form from the nominative singular (*μαθητής*) with which it would be identical if it were to have taken the usual D1 genitive singular ending.

D0.29 These factors give rise to the various paradigms within each of the three Declensions.

D1.   THE FIRST DECLENSION

There are five paradigms of the First Declension:

	FEMININE NOUNS			**MASCULINE NOUNS**	
	D1.1 *ριε* **root**	**D1.2 c. root**	**D1.3** *σ* **root**	**D1.4** *ριε* **root**	**D1.5 c. root**
	"heart"	"voice"	"glory"	"young man"	"disciple"
STEM:	*καρδι+α*	*φων+α*	*δοξ+α*	*νεανι+α*	*μαθητ+α*
SN	*καρδία*	*φωνή*	*δόξα*	*νεανίας*	*μαθητής*
V	—	—	—	*νεανία*	*μαθητά*
A	*καρδίαν*	*φωνήν*	*δόξαν*	*νεανίαν*	*μαθητήν*
G	*καρδίας*	*φωνῆς*	*δόξης*	*νεανίου*	*μαθητοῦ*
D	*καρδίᾳ*	*φωνῇ*	*δόξῃ*	*νεανίᾳ*	*μαθητῇ*
PN	*καρδίαι*	*φωναί*	*δόξαι*	*νεανίαι*	*μαθηταί*
A	*καρδίας*	*φωνάς*	*δόξας*	*νεανίας*	*μαθητάς*
G	*καρδιῶν*	*φωνῶν*	*δοξῶν*	*νεανιῶν*	*μαθητῶν*
D	*καρδίαις*	*φωναῖς*	*δόξαις*	*νεανίαις*	*μαθηταῖς*

D1.6   NOTES ON THE FIRST DECLENSION

D1.61 First Declension nouns have the characteristic that they all add the *linking vowel* -*α*- to the noun *root* to form their *stem*, before taking their numbercase suffixes. But (as explained below) some words lengthen this vowel to -*η*- throughout the singular, and a few lengthen the -*α*- to -*η*- in the genitive and dative singular only. There are also some differences between masculine and feminine forms. These factors produce the five paradigms of the singular — there is only one pattern for the plural of the First Declension.

root	ending		root	ending		root	ending
φων-η-∅			*καρδι-α-ν*			*μαθητ-α-ς*	
stem	numbercase suffix		stem	numbercase suffix		stem	numbercase suffix

D1.62 The numbercase suffix for the nominative singular of the feminine paradigms is ∅, the zero morph. That is, it is the fact that *there is nothing added to the stem* which indicates that the form is nominative singular. There is no separate feminine form of the vocative, and the nominative form is used for vocative when required. The numbercase suffix for the dative singular is ι, which in the First Declension is always written subscript. In the genitive plural the linking vowel -α- plus the numbercase suffix -ων have contracted into -ῶν, and thus in this Declension the -ῶν always carries the circumflex accent. It is at times useful to note that a genitive plural in -ων (i.e., without the circumflex) therefore cannot be First Declension and must be either Second or Third Declension, while a genitive plural in -ῶν could be First, Second, or Third Declension.

D1.63 When the root of a First Declension feminine noun ends in ρ, ι or ε, then the linking vowel is -α- throughout, as for καρδία, D1.1. (-α following ρ, ι or ε is often referred to by grammarians as "-α pure". The nouns with roots ending in ρ, ι or ε can be collectively categorized as "ριε nouns", and their paradigm, D1.1, called the "ριε paradigm".) There are 310 N.T. words which follow this paradigm (including one word, στοά, which is irregular in that it takes -α- after a root letter that is not ρ, ι or ε[38]).

D1.64 When the root of a First Declension feminine noun ends in a consonant or a vowel other than ρ, ι or ε, then (unless it follows the σ paradigm D1.3) the linking vowel -α- lengthens to -η- in all forms of the singular. This paradigm (D1.2, c. root) is followed by 191 N.T. words, 185 of them with a consonant root, four ending in -οη (ἀκοή and its compounds; ἀλόη, βοή, and πνοή), one in -ωη (ζωή), and one in -ευη (παρασκευή). It is therefore referred to as the "feminine Consonant Stem Paradigm".

D1.65 When the root of a First Declension feminine noun ends in a sibilant (ζ, σ, or a double letter containing σ), then the linking vowel -α- is retained in the nominative and accusative singular, but lengthens to -η- in the genitive and dative singular, as for δόξα. This paradigm (D1.3) is therefore referred to as the "Sigma Stem Paradigm" or "Sibilant Paradigm". There are also four nouns in -ρα which are irregular in that instead of following καρδία (the ριε Paradigm) they decline like δόξα (see below). Further, there are ten nouns in the N.T. which are irregular in taking -α- as their linking vowel in their lexical form (the nominative singular) when they have a root ending in a consonant; all of these nouns follow δόξα. There are in the N.T. a total of 22 nouns which follow δόξα:

SIBILANT ROOT (8 nouns)		ριε ROOT (4 nouns)		CONSONANT ROOT (10 nouns)	
βασίλισσα	(4) queen	μάχαιρα	(29) sword	ἄκανθα	(14) thornplant
γάζα	(1) treasury	πλήμμυρα	(1) flood	γάγγραινα	(1) gangrene
γλῶσσα	(50) tongue	πρῷρα	(2) prow	γέεννα	(12) gehenna
δόξα	(165) glory	σπεῖρα	(7) cohort	ἔχιδνα	(5) snake
θάλασσα	(91) sea			θύελλα	(1) whirlwind
ῥίζα	(16) root			μεμβράνα	(1) parchment
τράπεζα	(15) table			μέριμνα	(6) concern
χάλαζα	(4) hail			πρύμνα	(3) stern (of boat)
(The number after each word indicates the number of times it occurs in the N.T.)				πτέρνα	(1) heel
				σμύρνα	(2) myrrh

D1.66 When a First Declension noun is masculine, then it also takes -α- as its linking vowel after ριε roots, and lengthens this to -η- after other roots. It has four masculine distinctive characteristics: **(a)** There is no equivalent to the δόξα Paradigm; **(b)** It adds the characteristic masculine -ς in the nominative singular: **(c)** It takes -ου as its genitive singular ending (stem vowel -o- contracted with numbercase suffix -o); **(d)** It has a separate vocative singular form, in -α (occasionally, in -η for some masculine names in -ης). (Note that in features (b) and (c) the First Declension masculines parallel the Second Declension.) Apart from these features, D1 masculine nouns follow the same pattern of declension as the feminines.

D1.67 Some proper names have forms that differ slightly from those given in the above five paradigms. These differences usually affect only one letter in a single numbercase form and are thus not likely to prevent recognition of the word, and forms containing these differences occur very rarely in the N.T., so it is not considered necessary to list them all here.

D1.68 Of the 635 First Declension nouns in the N.T. (excluding names), 82% (523) are feminine, and 18% (112) are masculine. There are no neuters of the First Declension in Greek.

D2.   THE SECOND DECLENSION

There are two paradigms of the Second Declension found in the N.T., together with the special flexion for Ἰησοῦς, Jesus. For convenience of understanding and learning, they are given here with the article, and meanings.

D2.1 MASCULINE NOUNS			**D2.2 NEUTER NOUNS**			**D2.3**
	ὁ λόγος			τὸ ἔργον		Ἰησοῦς
	"the word"			"the work"		"Jesus"
STEM:	λογ+ο			ἐργ+ο		Ἰησο+ο
SN ὁ	λόγος	the word (subject)	τὸ	ἔργον	the work (subject)	Ἰησοῦς
V	λόγε	O word!		ἔργον	O work!	Ἰησοῦ
A τὸν	λόγον	the word (object)	τὸ	ἔργον	the work (object)	Ἰησοῦν
G τοῦ	λόγου	of the word	τοῦ	ἔργου	of the work	Ἰησοῦ
D τῷ	λόγῳ	to/for the word	τῷ	ἔργῳ	to/for the work	Ἰησοῦ
PN οἱ	λόγοι	the words (subject)	τὰ	ἔργα	the works (subject)	
A τοὺς	λόγους	the words (object)	τὰ	ἔργα	the works (object)	
G τῶν	λόγων	of the words	τῶν	ἔργων	of the works	
D τοῖς	λόγοις	to/for the words	τοῖς	ἔργοις	to/for the works	

D2.4   NOTES ON THE SECOND DECLENSION

D2.41 The N.T. also contains a very small number of forms from other Second Declension paradigms: the contracted neuter noun ὀστοῦν, bone (nominative and accusative plural, ὀστέα), and Ἀπολλῶς, Appollos, with lengthened stem vowel, and a negligible number of other words. A Greek commentary will comment on these words when they are encountered.

D2.42 Second Declension nouns have the characteristic that they all add the *linking vowel -o-* to the noun *root* to form their *stem* before taking their numbercase suffixes. In the vocative singular the linking or *stem vowel* shortens further to -ε, and in the dative singular and genitive plural it lengthens to -ω. Where the word's accent falls on the final syllable the genitive plural will carry the circumflex, -ῶν, and where the accent falls on an earlier syllable the genitive plural will have an acute on the syllable before last, -´ων.

D2.43 Counting simplex and compound forms of a noun as one noun, and omitting names, there are 595 Second Declension nouns in the N.T., 58% (347) of which are masculine in -ος, and 33% (196) of which are neuter in -ον. In addition there are 5% (28) which are feminine, 2% (11) which can be either masculine or feminine and indicate a sex difference for the word (as for example, ὁ θυρωρός, male doorkeeper; ἡ θυρωρός, female doorkeeper), and 2% (11) which may be either masculine or feminine without indicating any difference of meaning of any kind; all these 50 words which either *are* or *can be* feminine end in -ος and follow the paradigm of λόγος exactly but, being feminine (or, when feminine) take the feminine, not masculine, article.

D2.44 These 28 feminine nouns (and the times each of them occurs) are:

ἄβυσσος	(9)	the abyss	ὁδός	(101)	way, road
ἀγριέλαιος	(2)	wild olive	διέξοδος	(1)	thoroughfare
ἀμέθυστος	(1)	amethyst	εἴσοδος	(5)	entrance
ἄμμος	(5)	sand	ἔξοδος	(3)	departure
ἄμπελος	(9)	vine	πάροδος	(1)	passage
βάσανος	(3)	torment	παράλιος	(1)	seacoast
βίβλος	(10)	book	ῥάβδος	(12)	rod, staff
βύσσος	(1)	fine linen	Ῥόδος	(1)	Rhodes
διάλεκτος	(6)	a language	σάπφειρος	(1)	sapphire
δοκός	(6)	log, beam	σορός	(1)	coffin
ἔρημος	(34)	a desert	σποδός	(3)	ashes
καλλιέλαιος	(1)	cultivated olive	στάμνος	(1)	a jar
κάμινος	(4)	furnace	συκάμινος	(1)	mulberry tree
κιβωτός	(6)	box, ark	τρίβος	(3)	beaten path
νάρδος	(2)	oil of nard	τροφός	(1)	a nurse
νῆσος	(9)	island	ψῆφος	(3)	pebble, vote
νόσος	(11)	illness			

(This list includes Ῥόδος, a name, and four compounds of ὁδός; these are not included in the tally of 28 feminine Second Declension nouns.) In addition, περίχωρος, -ον, "neighbouring", a compound two-termination adjective (#5.62, #D4.03) occurring 9 times in the N.T., is used with the feminine article (ἡ περίχωρος, with γῆ understood) for "the surrounding region", thus functioning as if a Second Declension feminine noun.

D2.45 The 22 nouns which can vary in gender (and the times they occur) are:

Can Be Either Masculine or Feminine Indicating Sex of the Person/Animal		Can Be Either Masculine or Feminine With No Difference in Word Meaning	
ἄρκος	(1) bear	*ἀλάβαστρος	(4) alabaster flask
διάκονος	(29) servant, deacon	ἄψινθος	(2) wormwood
ἔριφος	(2) kid, goat	βάτος	(5) thornbush
θεός	(1314) god, goddess	βήρυλλος	(1) beryl
θυρωρός	(4) doorkeeper	ληνός	(5) winepress
κάμηλος	(6) camel	λίβανος	(2) frankincense
κληρονόμος	(15) heir	λιμός	(12) hunger, famine
συγκληρονόμος	(4) fellowheir	μάρμαρος	(1) marble
μόσχος	(6) calf, young bull, ox	σμάραγδος	(1) emerald
νεωκόρος	(1) templekeeper	*ὕσσωπος	(2) hyssop
ὄνος	(6) donkey, ass	*χαλκολίβανος	(2) burnished bronze
παρθένος	(15) virgin		

συγκληρονόμος is a compond of κληρονόμος.

* These three words can also be Second Declension neuter, with a neuter article (again, without there being any difference in their meaning).

D3.   THE THIRD DECLENSION

D3.0   GENERAL RULES FOR THIRD DECLENSION WORDS

D3.01 The Third Declension consists of those words for which the numbercase suffixes are added directly to the word root, without any linking vowel. Their noun root thus also becomes their stem. The flexion patterns of these words are determined by two main factors: their gender, and their stem phonemes. Gender makes a difference to the numbercase suffixes. Also, the words fall into different categories according to whether the stem ends in a vowel or a consonant (and are further subdivided into paradigms by the nature of the last phoneme of the stem — there are different paradigms for labials, palatals, dentals, liquids, and so on). Accordingly the behaviour of these words can be described by means of rules relating to their gender and their stem phonemes. Most of the paradigms of Third Declension words are regular i.e. the forms of the flexions can be predicted on the basis of these descriptive rules (given below); in a small number of words, alternative ways are used for handling the conjunction of stem and suffix. Some stems originally ended in digamma, and when this dropped out of Greek (#1.21) this left some complications for the digamma words. In addition, there are several words which have unexpected ways of forming their nominative singular form from their stem and are therefore to be classed as irregular; and there are a few which are irregular in other forms.

D3.02 Some Third Declension adjectives do not have separate masculine and feminine forms, but have a flexion which is common to both masculine and feminine. Such a flexion can be said to be *common gender*, or (more informatively), *personal gender*, in contradistinction from the neuter gender.

D3.03 The stem of a word is obtained by removing the genitive singular suffix (usually -ος, but in a small number of paradigms it has lengthened to -ως); but account must also be taken of some words which use *two* stems in deriving the full range of forms for their flexion, and of other words which have lost the final digamma or sigma of their stems and then contracted.

D3.04 The masculine nominative singular (or the personal nominative singular, where there is no separate feminine gender) is formed by adding the numbercase suffix -ς to the stem; this suffix is *never* added by the *neuter* nominative singular, but there are some neuter words which have their *stem* ending in -ς, and for this reason these will have their nominative singular form ending in -ς.

D3.05 To form the Third Declension masculine or feminine accusative singular, words with a vowel stem add -ν, and words with a consonant stem add -α. For all other flexion forms, both vowel- and consonant-stem words take the same numbercase suffixes.

D3.06 As is universally the case in Greek declension, Third Declension neuter nominative, vocative and accusative forms are the same as each other, within both the singular and the plural; and in the plural the form for these three cases always adds -α to its stem as its numbercase suffix.

D3.07 As a Greek word can only end (#1.64) in a vowel or in -ν, -ρ or -ς (including -ψ and -ξ) then whenever the form of a word ends in one of the other consonants this consonant will drop off. This situation will occur in particular when a stem ends in a "not-permitted-as-final" phoneme and the word form consists of the stem only (e.g., numbers of Third Declension vocatives, and the neuter nominative-vocative-accusative singular of many Third Declension words).

D3.08 In general, the phonemic modification rules which apply to verbs operate for nouns also: a labial plus -σ becomes -ψ, a palatal plus -σ becomes -ξ, a dental drops out before -σ, and -σ drops off when added to a liquid. -σ is *usually* incompatible with an oral liquid, though some rare instances exist where -λς and -ρσ- occur together. In most words where -ν- and -ς are brought together, the -ς simply slides off the nasal liquid; in a few forms the -ς forces the -ν- out of the word; at no time can -ν- and -ς coexist together in the sequence -νς in a word (except in some words of foreign origin).

D3.09 In Third Declension consonant-stem words, a short vowel can stand as the last vowel of the nominative singular form only **(a)** when followed by a double consonant (e.g., φλόξ, flame); or **(b)** when the word is neuter (e.g., ἔν, one thing): but not otherwise. In a word from which no stem consonant has been lost, the last vowel if -ε- will lengthen to -η-, and if -o- will lengthen to -ω- (e.g., ἀστερ- to ἀστήρ; ἡγεμον- to ἡγεμών; αἰδοσ- to αἰδώς). Where a stem consonant has been lost through the addition of a suffix, then *compensatory lengthening* occurs: -ε- to -ει- and -o- to -ου- (e.g. ποδ- takes the -ς suffix of the nominative singular and becomes ποδς and thence (when the -δ- drops out in front of the -ς) πούς; ἔν takes the -ς suffix and becomes ἔνς, the -ν- drops out and the form becomes εἶς). In the dative plural the rule is slightly different: As the last vowel of the stem is always followed by a full syllable, -σι(ν), it can always remain short, and will do so even if one stem consonant is lost (e.g., ἡγεμον-σιν becomes ἡγεμόσιν; ποιμεν-σιν becomes ποιμέσιν). However, when *two* stem consonants have been lost, then compensatory lengthening occurs (ἀρχοντ-σιν loses first -τ- and then -ν- and becomes ἄρχουσιν; λυθεντ-σιν loses τ and ν and becomes λυθεῖσιν).

NOTE: The widest range of paradigms for different stem phonemes is found for nouns, and these are now given: the regular paradigms first (D3.1-D3.20) followed by the irregular nouns in each of these categories (D3.21-D3.40).

D3.1-5 VOWEL STEM NOUNS

		STEMS IN υ AND ι		STEMS IN A CONSONANT WHICH DROPS OUT		
		D3.1 fish	**D3.2** city	**D3.3** ox	**D3.4** king	**D3.5** race
		ὁ ἰχθύς	ἡ πόλις	ὁ βοῦς	ὁ βασιλεύς	τὸ γένος
	STEM	ἰχθυ-	πολι-/ε-	βοϝ-	βασιλεϝ-	γενεσ-
	ENDING:					
SN	-ς	ἰχθύς	πόλις	βοῦς	βασιλεύς	γένος
V	-	ἰχθύ	πόλι	βοῦ	βασιλεῦ	-
A	-ν	ἰχθύν	πόλιν	βοῦν	βασιλέα	γένος
G	-ος	ἰχθύος	πόλεως	βοός	βασιλέως	γένους
D	-ι	ἰχθύϊ	πόλει	βοΐ	βασιλεῖ	γένει
PN	-ες	ἰχθύες	πόλεις	βόες	βασιλεῖς	γένη
A	-ας	ἰχθύας	πόλεις	βόας	βασιλεῖς	γένη
G	-ων	ἰχθύων	πόλεων	βοῶν	βασιλέων	γενῶν
D	-σι(ν)	ἰχθύσι(ν)	πόλεσι(ν)	βουσί(ν)	βασιλεῦσι(ν)	γένεσι(ν)

D3.1 ἰχθύς (stem in -υ) adds the numbercase suffixes to its stem in completely regular fashion throughout. There is one neuter word that is found in the N.T. which has its stem in -υ; δάκρυ, a tear, dative plural δάκρυσιν (note that the neuter does not add the suffix -ς in the nominative singular — #D3.04): but most of the few occurrences of this word in the N.T. overlap with forms from the Second Declension neuter noun with identical meaning, δάκρυον. There are nine nouns of Paradigm D3.1 in the N.T.

D3.2 πόλις has two stems, πολι- in the nominative, vocative and accusative singular, and πολε- in all its other forms. The usual -ος genitive singular suffix has lengthened to -ως after the short -ε- of the stem (as happens also in D3.4, βασιλεύς): it can be noted that the suffix -ος *always* lengthens to -ως after -ε-, and *only* after -ε-, not after any other phoneme. In the nominative plural πολε- has contracted with -ες into πόλεις, and this form is also used for the accusative plural. There are 131 nouns of Paradigm D3.2 in the N.T., 130 of them feminine and one of then neuter (σίναπι, σινάπεως, mustard — note that it does not add -ς); together with πῆχυς, πήχεως, ὁ, cubit, which has a -υ stem in the nominative-vocative-accusative singular and in all other forms follows πόλις.

D3.3 The paradigm of βοῦς has derived from the original form of the word with a digamma stem, but it becomes a vowel-stem noun with the loss of digamma (#1.21). Wherever the digamma occurred before a consonant suffix or in form final position (the vocative), it has been replaced by upsilon; and wherever it occurred before a vowel suffix it has simply dropped out. Paradigm D3.3 is followed in the N.T. by five words of rather infrequent occurrence: βοῦς, ox (8); νοῦς, mind (24); πλοῦς, voyage (3); χοῦς, dust (2), and ναῦς, ship (1) (but not other words in -ους which are irregulars from other paradigms).   νοῦς, πλοῦς and χοῦς had been Second Declension contracted nouns in Classical Greek, and ναῦς had been variously declined in the different Greek dialects (#1.11), but in koine Greek they had all come to conform to the paradigm of βοῦς.

D3.4 Similarly βασιλεύς was originally a consonantal-stem noun. It has come from βασιλεϜς, the digamma dropping out before vowels, and being replaced by upsilon before consonants and when form final (the vocative). In this paradigm however the digamma has had the effect of a consonant in the accusative singular, in causing the word to take the consonant suffix -α, thus (after digamma was lost) giving the form βασιλέα (*not* "βασιλευν") — contrast βοῦν. For both βοῦς and βασιλεύς, the vowels brought together by the dropping of digamma only contracted in the following cases: ε+ε and ε+ι (to ει), ε+υ (to ευ) and ο+υ (to ου), i.e. not in the case of ε- or ο- followed by α, ο or ω, or ο- followed by ε or ι. Thus in regard to contraction the behaviour of digamma-stem nouns is identical with that of digamma verbs (see #C8.75). There are nineteen N.T. words which follow Paradigm D3.4, including the names of five towns and cities.

D3.5 The stem of γένος is γενεσ-, but when -σ- comes between two short vowels, syncopation occurs: the -σ- is squeezed out and the two short vowels then contract. In the genitive plural, also, the -σ- is syncopated and the ε-ων is usually contracted into -ῶν, but may at times be written uncontracted as -έων. When a suffix commencing with σ- is added to a stem in -σ, the two *simplify* into a single -σ-. Thus the dative plural γενεσ-σι(ν) is simplified to γένεσι(ν). The neuter nominative singular would usually be the stem form, i.e. γένες; but instead (for reasons that are not very clear) this has become γένος. There are 47 N.T. words which follow Paradigm D3.5, together with two rare neuters in -ας (γῆρας, old age: found in the N.T. only in Luke 1:36, in the dative singular, γήρει; and κρέας, in the N.T. only in Romans 14:21 and I Corinthians 8:13, both times in the nominative plural, κρέα, uncontracted), and one rare feminine in stem -ος (αἰδώς, modesty, found only in I Timothy 2:9 in the genitive singular, αἰδοῦς).

D3.6-13 CONSONANT STEM NOUNS:
STOP CONSONANTS AND ORAL LIQUID CONSONANTS

STOP CONSONANTS

ORAL LIQUID CONSONANTS

D3.6 Palatal D3.7 Labial D3.8 Dental   D3.11 Long E D3.12 Short E D3.13 Short O

	ἡ σάρξ flesh	ὁ λίψ S.W. wind	ὁ πούς foot	ὁ σωτήρ saviour	ὁ ἀστήρ star	ὁ ἀλέκτωρ cock
STEM:	σαρκ-	λιβ-	ποδ-	σωτηρ-	ἀστερ-	ἀλεκτορ-
SN	σάρξ	λίψ	πούς	σωτήρ	ἀστήρ	ἀλέκτωρ
A	σάρκα	λίβα	πόδα	σωτῆρα	ἀστέρα	ἀλέκτορα
G	σαρκός	λιβός	ποδός	σωτῆρος	ἀστέρος	ἀλέκτορος
D	σαρκί	λιβί	ποδί	σωτῆρι	ἀστέρι	ἀλέκτορι
PN	σάρκες	λίβες	πόδες	σωτῆρες	ἀστέρες	ἀλέκτορες
A	σάρκας	λίβας	πόδας	σωτῆρας	ἀστέρας	ἀλέκτορας
G	σαρκῶν	λιβῶν	ποδῶν	σωτήρων	ἀστέρων	ἀλεκτόρων
D	σαρξί(ν)	λιψί(ν)	ποσί(ν)	[σωτῆρσι(ν)]	[ἀστράσι(ν)]	[ἀλέκτορσι(ν)]

NEUTER NOUNS

	τὸ γάλα milk	none	τὸ μέλι honey	τὸ πῦρ fire	none	τὸ ὕδωρ water
STEM:	γαλακτ-		μελιτ-	πυρ-		ὑδωρ-/ὑδατ-
SN	γάλα		μέλι	πῦρ		ὕδωρ
A	γάλα		μέλι	πῦρ		ὕδωρ
G	γάλακτος		μέλιτος	πυρός		ὕδατος
D	γάλακτι		μέλιτι	πυρί		ὕδατι
PN	γάλακτα		not	not		ὕδατα
A	γάλακτα		found	found		ὕδατα
G	γαλάκτων		in the	in the		ὑδάτων
D	γάλαξι(ν)		plural	plural		ὕδασι(ν)

D3.6   A palatal stem consonant amalgamates with -σ into -ξ. Paradigm D3.6 is followed by 24 N.T. nouns, 23 of personal (masculine or feminine) gender and one that is neuter. This neuter noun is γάλα, γάλακτος, milk (5 times in the N.T.; stem γαλακτ- — compare νύξ, νυκτός ἡ, night). The neuter does not add the suffix -ς of the nominative singular (#D3.04), so the nominative singular form of this word becomes γαλακτ and then progressively γαλακ and γαλα, because neither -τ nor κ can stand at the end of a word (#D3.07). In the dative plural the -τ drops out before the -σι(ν) suffix, giving γάλαξι(ν). Thus this word is completely regular in its forms, being predictable in accordance with the phonemic rules of Greek.

D3.7   A labial stem consonant amalgamates with -σ into -ψ. Nouns with a labial stem are very rare in Greek, and there are only seven of them in the N.T. which between them only occur on a total of nine occasions. These nouns (and their frequency) are: Αἰθίοψ, Αἰθίοπος, ὁ, Ethiopian (1); Ἄραψ, Ἄραβος, ὁ, Arabian (1); κώνωψ, κώνωπος, ὁ, gnat, mosquito (1); λαῖλαψ, λαίλαπος, ἡ, storm, squall (3); λίψ, λιβός, ὁ, south-west wind, facing south-west (1); μώλωψ, μώλωπος, ὁ, wound, (1); σκόλοψ, σκόλοπος, ὁ, splinter, thorn (1). There are none that are neuter.

D3.8   A dental stem consonant drops out before a sigma suffix. This means that the nominative singular will end in a vowel plus -ς; if that vowel is ε or ο, it will take *compensatory lengthening*, -ε- into -ει- and -ο- into -ου-, in "compensation" for the loss (see #D3.09). In this paradigm there is no compensatory lengthening for the same loss of the dental in the dative plural; it occurs in the nominative singular so that that form *always* contains a long vowel or diphthong when it ends in a single consonant. Thus stem ποδ- gives the nominative singular πος, which then lengthens to πούς in accordance with this rule, while the dative plural is ποσί(ν), unlengthened. Paradigm D3.8 is followed by 74 nouns in the N.T.: 34 of them (all feminine) in -θης, -θητος (1) or -της, -τητος (33; this is an ending by which an abstract noun is made, such as "holiness", "likeness", "kindness", "stubbornness", "oldness", "brightness" — the Greek equivalents of all of these being included in this group); 31 of them (all feminine) ending in -ις, -ιδος (25) or -ας, -αδος (5) or -υς, -υδος (1); one in -ις, -ιθος, one in -ις, -ιτος (both feminine); five in -ης, -ητος (2) or -ως, -ωτος (3) (all masculine); one in -αις (παῖς, παιδός) which is both masculine and feminine, and one which is neuter (μέλι, μέλιτος). The neuter does not add the suffix -ς of the nominative singular (#D3.04), so this form becomes μελιτ and then μέλι, because τ cannot stand at the end of a word (#D3.07). This word is thus completely regular in its forms, being fully predictable. It occurs only four times in the N.T. There are two neuter paradigms which have dental stems and which are sub-paradigms of D3.8:

D3.9 body	**D3.10** horn
τὸ σῶμα	τὸ κέρας
STEM: σωματ-	⎰κερας / ⎱κερατ-

SN	σῶμα	κέρας
A	σῶμα	κέρας
G	σώματος	κέρατος
D	σώματι	κέρατι
PN	σώματα	κέρατα
A	σώματα	κέρατα
G	σωμάτων	κεράτων
D	σώμασι(ν)	κέρασι(ν)

D3.9   This paradigm is in fact identical with μέλι, μέλιτος, τό (the neuter of D3.8), but has the distinctive feature that the stems of all the words of this paradigm end in -ματ. It is completely regular in accordance with the rules. Paradigm D3.9 is the most common Third Declension neuter category, being followed by 140 N.T. nouns. (The one irregular noun of this paradigm is given at #D3.29.)

D3.10   This paradigm consists of neuter words which have two stems, -ας in the nominative-vocative-accusative singular, and -ατ in all other forms. Paradigm D3.10 is followed by four N.T. nouns: ἅλας, ἅλατος, τό, salt (7); κέρας, κέρατος, τό, horn (11); πέρας, πέρατος, τό, end (4); and τέρας, τέρατος, τό, wonder, marvel (16). Declined similarly are φῶς, φωτός, τό, light (73), and perfect active participles in -ως, -οτος (#D5.13, #D5.33). (The one irregular noun of this paradigm is set out at #D3.30.)

D3.11 There are two oral liquid consonants: λ and ρ. Only one noun exists in Greek with stem in λ, ἅλς, ἁλός, ὁ, salt, and this is found only once in the N.T., in the accusative singular form ἅλα in Mark 9:50 (and it occurs a second time in the preceding verse in some manuscripts in the dative singular form, ἁλί). There was a strong tendency in Greek to avoid having a liquid followed by ς, as in ἅλς, and in koine Greek this word has virtually been replaced by a newer word, ἅλας, ἅλατος, τό, which follows Paradigm D3.10. All other oral liquid nouns have stems ending in -ρ. Paradigm D3.11 comprises those with stems ending in a long vowel and -ρ. The seven such nouns in the N.T. (and their frequency) are: five in -ηρ (all masculine): νιπτήρ, -ῆρος, ὁ, washbasin (1); στατήρ, -ῆρος, ὁ, stater (a coin) (2); σωτήρ, -ῆρος, ὁ, saviour (24); φωστήρ, -ῆρος, ὁ, radiance (2); χαρακτήρ, -ῆρος, ὁ, exact likeness (1); and one feminine: χείρ, χειρός, ἡ, hand (176; this flexion has one irregular form and will be discussed under Irregular Nouns, #D3.31); and one neuter: πῦρ, πυρός, τό, fire (71). The masculine nouns in -ηρ are all completely regular; but it should be noted that because the nominative singular suffix -ς will not hold on a liquid but slides off, in consequence the nominative singular of these words ends in their stem phonemes, -ηρ, and the numbercase suffix is ∅ (the zero morph). The neuter noun πῦρ is completely regular. (It is not found in the plural.) Further, it can be noted that there are no nouns with stems in -ωρ. The dative plural form in the paradigm is given in brackets because it is somewhat uncertain. No instance of it occurs in the N.T. and it is rare in other koine writing — unlike the nominative singular -ς, the dative plural ending -σι(ν) can succeed in holding its position on the oral liquid stem, but nonetheless there seems perhaps to be something of a tendency to avoid the form.

D3.12 As with all other stems in -ρ, nouns with -ερ stems cannot hold the -ς of the nominative singular, but this -ς slides off the liquid. A short vowel cannot stand in the nominative singular when followed only by a single consonant and therefore in that form the -ερ lengthens to -ηρ in conformity with Rule #D3.09. The dative plural form in the paradigm is given in brackets because it is somewhat uncertain. No instance of it occurs in the N.T. and it is not found at all in any other koine writings or inscriptions. The form given in brackets, ἀστράσιν is the form from Attic Greek, and it can be seen that this avoids the undesired conjunction of -ρ and σ- by dropping the -ε- before the -ρ and separating the -ρ- and -σ- with an -α. It is interesting that in the one place in the N.T. where a dative plural of ἀστήρ could be used — Luke 21:25 — we find instead, ἄστροις, from the parallel but much rarer Second Declension neuter noun ἄστρον, with the same meaning (used only four times in the N.T., against the 24 occurrences of ἀστήρ). In all forms of this paradigm other than the nominative singular and dative plural, the -ερ of the stem remains unchanged. There are only two regular nouns of Paradigm D3.12: ἀστήρ, ἀστέρος, ὁ, star (24), and ἀήρ, ἀέρος, ὁ, air (7), both masculine; there are no feminines or neuters. (The irregular nouns of this paradigm are given at #D3.32.)

D3.13 When a noun stem ends in -*ορ*, it follows the same pattern as for Paradigm D3.12: the nominative singular suffix -ς slides off the liquid, and the requirement to have a long vowel in the nominative singular when followed by a single consonant means that the -*ορ* of the stem lengthens to -*ωρ*. The dative plural form is given in brackets because it is somewhat uncertain. No instance of it occurs in the N.T. and it is almost non-existent in other koine writings. The eight nouns, all masculine, of Paradigm D3.13 which occur in the N.T. (and their frequency) are: ἀλέκτωρ, -οροϛ, ὁ, cock (12); κατήγωρ, -οροϛ, ὁ, accuser (1); κοσμοκράτωρ, -οροϛ, ὁ, world ruler (1); κτήτωρ, -οροϛ, ὁ, possessor (1); παντοκράτωρ, -οροϛ, ὁ, the Almighty (used of God) (10); πράκτωρ, -οροϛ, ὁ, court officer (2); ῥήτωρ, -οροϛ, ὁ, spokesman (1); σπεκουλάτωρ, -οροϛ, ὁ, executioner (1). There are no feminines of this paradigm. There is one common neuter noun which can be classified with this paradigm but which has two stems: ὕδωρ, ὕδατοϛ, τό, water (76) has the stem -ωρ in the nominative-vocative-accusative singular, and then (like πόλιϛ, D3.2) a different stem in the remaining forms, which are taken from ὕδατ-. Like ὕδωρ, but with the first stem in -αρ, are φρέαρ, φρέατοϛ, τό, well (7); and ὄναρ, -, τό, dream (6 — but this word is defective and used only in the nominative and accusative).

D3.14-20 CONSONANT STEM NOUNS: NASAL LIQUID CONSONANTS

NOTE: The phonemes ν and ς are incompatible in Greek, that is, they cannot occur together in the sequence νς in a word. Therefore, when a stem ends in -ν and a sigma suffix is added, either the ς slides off the ν and disappears, or the -ς dislodges the -ν (#D3.08). When a noun stem ends in a long vowel plus -ν, the nominative singular suffix -ς always slides off; when a noun stem ends in -αν, -εν, -ον, -αντ, -εντ, -οντ or -υντ, the -ς *usually* slides off the -ν but in certain words the -ς pushes the -ν out of the stem altogether. In the dative plural, the suffix -σι(ν) *always* dislodges the -ν.

	STEMS IN -ν			STEMS IN -ντ		
	Vowel Unchanged		Vowel Alters		Vowel: Alters		Unchanged
	D3.14	D3.15	D3.16	D3.17	D3.18	D3.19	D3.20
	age	month	leader	shepherd	ruler	tooth	strap
	ὁ αἰών	ὁ μήν	ὁ ἡγεμών	ὁ ποιμήν	ὁ ἄρχων	ὁ ὀδούϛ	ὁ ἱμάϛ
STEM:	αἰων-	μην-	ἡγεμον-	ποιμεν-	ἀρχοντ-	ὀδοντ-	ἱμαντ-
SN	αἰών	μήν	ἡγεμών	ποιμήν	ἄρχων	ὀδούϛ	ἱμάϛ
A	αἰῶνα	μῆνα	ἡγεμόνα	ποιμένα	ἄρχοντα	ὀδόντα	ἱμάντα
G	αἰῶνοϛ	μηνόϛ	ἡγεμόνοϛ	ποιμένοϛ	ἄρχοντοϛ	ὀδόντοϛ	ἱμάντοϛ
D	αἰῶνι	μηνί	ἡγεμόνι	ποιμένι	ἄρχοντι	ὀδόντι	ἱμάντι
PN	αἰῶνεϛ	μῆνεϛ	ἡγεμόνεϛ	ποιμένεϛ	ἄρχοντεϛ	ὀδόντεϛ	ἱμάντεϛ
A	αἰῶναϛ	μῆναϛ	ἡγεμόναϛ	ποιμέναϛ	ἄρχονταϛ	ὀδόνταϛ	ἱμάνταϛ
G	αἰώνων	μηνῶν	ἡγεμόνων	ποιμένων	ἀρχόντων	ὀδόντων	ἱμάντων
D	αἰῶσι(ν)	μησί(ν)	ἡγεμόσι(ν)	ποιμέσι(ν)	ἄρχουσι(ν)	ὀδοῦσι(ν)	ἱμᾶσι(ν)

D3.14/D3.15 When a stem ends in a long vowel plus -ν, the nominative singular suffix -ς slides off the liquid. The dative plural suffix -σι(ν) dislodges -ν. Paradigm D3.14 is followed by 17 N.T. nouns (15 masculine, 2 feminine, none neuter). Paradigm D3.15 is followed by two N.T. nouns, μήν, μηνός, ὁ, month (18) and Ἕλλην, Ἕλληνος, ὁ, Greek (26); and also by one word each in -ιν and -αν: ὠδίν, ὠδῖνος, ἡ, birth-pains (4), and μεγιστάν, μεγιστᾶνος, ὁ, person of high status (3).

D3.16/D3.17 When a stem ends in -ον or -εν, the nominative singular suffix -ς slides off the liquid, and the short vowel, being followed by a single consonant, -ν, then lengthens (into -ων and -ην respectively — #D3.09). The dative plural suffix -σι(ν) dislodges -ν, but as the short vowel (-ο- or -ε-) is followed by another syllable, not by a single consonant, it remains unlengthened. Paradigm D3.16 is followed by 13 N.T. nouns and by all N.T. adjectives in -ων (#D4.8) except ἄκων and ἑκών (#D4.5). Paradigm D3.17 is followed by four N.T. words, and there is a fifth word in which (as can sometimes be found) the nominative singular suffix -ς pushes the -ν out of the word, the -ενς thus first of all giving -ες and then, by compensatory lengthening for the loss of the stem consonant (#D3.09), becoming -εις. The word in which this occurs is the masculine flexion of εἷς, ἑνός, one. In the neuter, no -ς suffix is added in forming the nominative singular (#D3.04), and therefore the form is ἕν, and being neuter the short vowel in this form does not lengthen in any way (#D3.09).

D3.18 When a stem ends in -οντ, the -τ drops out before a sigma suffix, giving -ονς, and then the -ς slides off the -ν, leaving -ον, and the short vowel followed by a single consonant lengthens, becoming -ων. In the dative plural, -οντ-σιν becomes first -ον-σιν and then (as in Paradigm D3.16) the suffix -σιν dislodges the -ν to give -οσιν. But two phonemes (-ν and -τ) have now been lost from the stem and therefore compensatory lengthening occurs (#D3.09) to produce -ουσιν. This Paradigm is thus completely in accord with the rules, and therefore is to be classified as regular. Paradigm D3.18 is followed by five N.T. nouns, the adjectives ἄκων and ἑκών (#D4.5), and all participles in -ων (#D5.11).

D3.19 There are a small number of words with stem in -οντ which follow the alternative phonemic pattern: the -τ drops out before a sigma suffix, and then the nominative singular -ς dislodges the -ν, giving -ος, and as a stem consonant has been lost from the nominative singular, compensatory lengthening occurs, giving -ους (#D3.09). This phonemic pattern is followed by one noun, ὀδούς, ὀδόντος, ὁ, tooth (12), and participles in -ους (#D5.31, #D5.32). Furthermore, it is followed by participles in -εις: as these have their stem in -εντ, the -ν and -τ drop out in the manner of this Paradigm and the -ε- of the stem becomes -ει- before sigma by compensatory lengthening.

D3.20 Some words with stem in -αντ and -υντ follow the same phonemic pattern as for Paradigm D3.19. However, as in the case of ἱμάς, ἱμάντος, ὁ, strap (4), the stem vowel -α or -υ lengthens but does not change its form before sigma. Paradigm D3.20 is followed by this one noun, the adjectives πᾶς and ἅπας (#D4.6), participles in -ας (#D5.31, #D5.32), and participles in -υς (#D5.31).

D3.21-D3.40 IRREGULAR NOUNS

Many of Paradigms D3.1 to D3.20 contain nouns which are irregular in one or more forms. These are discussed here, in relation to the particular Paradigm which they follow, each irregular flexion carrying a paradigm number which is higher by 20 than the corresponding regular Paradigm.

	D3.26 hair ἡ θρίξ	**D3.26** wife/woman ἡ γυνή	**D3.28** strife ἡ ἔρις	**D3.30** ear τὸ οὖς	**D3.31** hand ἡ χείρ	**D3.32** father ὁ πατήρ	**D3.32** husband/man ὁ ἀνήρ
STEM:	θριχ-	γυναικ-	ἐριδ-	{οὖς- / ὠτ-	χειρ-	πατερ-	{ἀνερ- / ἀνδρ-
SN	θρίξ	γυνή	ἔρις	οὖς	χείρ	πατήρ	ἀνήρ
V	θρίξ	γύναι	ἔρις	οὖς	χείρ	πάτερ	ἄνερ
A	τρίχα	γυναῖκα	ἔριν	οὖς	χεῖρα	πατέρα	ἄνδρα
G	τριχός	γυναικός	ἔριδος	ὠτός	χειρός	πατρός	ἀνδρός
D	τριχί	γυναικί	ἔριδι	ὠτί	χειρί	πατρί	ἀνδρί
PN	τρίχες	γυναῖκες	ἔρεις	ὦτα	χεῖρες	πατέρες	ἄνδρες
A	τριχάς	γυναῖκας	ἔρεις	ὦτα	χεῖρας	πατέρας	ἄνδρας
G	τριχῶν	γυναικῶν	ἐρίδων	ὤτων	χειρῶν	πατέρων	ἀνδρῶν
D	θριξί(ν)	γυναιξί(ν)	ἔρισι(ν)	ὠσί(ν)	χερσί(ν)	πατράσι(ν)	ἀνδράσι(ν)

D3.26 θρίξ, τριχός ἡ, hair (15) has word stem θριχ-, but Greek avoids having a word with two successive syllables commencing with an aspirate, this usually being done by the first such aspirate losing its aspiration (#E2.8). Thus the stem becomes τριχ- in all forms of the flexion except where the -χ amalgamates with sigma to become -ξ; in these two forms there is nothing to prevent the first consonant being θ. Thus the flexion of θρίξ is in fact in accord with regular phonemic rules, and follows D3.6. and is not actually irregular (though it certainly looks as if it is!). γυνή, γυναικός, ἡ, wife/woman (209) has its stem, γυναικ, as the vocative, and then loses the -κ in accordance with #D3.07. The flexion follows D3.6 but has one irregular form, the nominative singular γυνή (instead of the non-existent regular form, "γυναίξ").

D3.28 Four N.T. words with stems in -ι- plus a dental have experienced "interference" from Paradigm D3.2 (πόλις), resulting in their being found at times with accusative singular and nominative-accusative plural forms as if from that paradigm (as given for ἔρις in the flexion here). Their regular dental-stem constructions for these forms (following D3.8) were in use as well, and also occur in the N.T. These four words are: ἔρις, ἔριδος, ἡ, strife (9); κλείς, κλειδός, ἡ, key (6); προφῆτις, προφήτιδος, ἡ, prophetess (2); and χάρις, χάριτος, ἡ, grace (155).

D3.29 γόνυ, γόνατος, τό, knee (12) has two stems: in the nominative-vocative-accusative singular γονυ (not "γονα"), and γονατ- in all its other forms, in which it thus follows Paradigm D3.9 (σῶμα). The Second Declension noun σάββατον, σάββατου, τό, sabbath (68) always takes its dative plural form as σάββασιν, from

Paradigm D3.9 (instead of the expected Second Declension form "σαββατοις", which does not occur).

D3.30 οὖς, ὠτός, τό, ear (36) follows Paradigm D3.10 in having its stem in -ς in the nominative-vocative-accusative singular and in -τ in all other forms of its flexion, but is irregular in having -ου as its stem vowel in these -ς forms instead of -ω.

D3.31 χείρ, χειρός, ἡ, hand (176) follows Paradigm D3.11 (σωτήρ) and has one irregular form: the dative plural is χερσίν (not "χειρσίν"). μάρτυς, μάρτυρος, ὁ, witness (35) also follows Paradigm D3.11, and has two irregular forms. These have both resulted from the sigma suffixes of the nominative singular and dative plural dislodging the -ρ of the stem in both forms and giving respectively μάρτυς (instead of "μάρτυρ") and μάρτυσιν (instead of "μάρτυρσιν").

D3.32 πατήρ, πατρός, ὁ, father (415) follows Paradigm D3.12 (ἀστήρ) but loses the short -ε- of its stem in some of its forms. Like πατήρ are declined μήτηρ, μητρός, ἡ, mother (84); θυγάτηρ, θυγατρός, ἡ, daughter (28); and γαστήρ, γαστρός, ἡ, womb (9). ἀνήρ, ἀνδρός, ὁ, husband/man (216) has two stems, ἀνδρ- in all forms except the nominative and vocative singular, where it is ἀνερ-. Allowing for this, its flexion is very similar to that for πατήρ.

D3.35 κύων, κυνός, ὁ, dog (5) follows Paradigm D3.15, but has two stems, κυων in the nominative singular and κυν- in all other forms of its flexion (its dative plural thus being κυσίν).

D3.37 ἀρήν, ἀρνός, ὁ, lamb (1) has an original stem ἀρεν- (like ποιμεν-, D3.17) but has lost the -ε-. It occurs only once in the N.T. (Luke 10:3), in the accusative plural, ἄρνας, the Second Declension diminutive form ἀρνίον, ἀρνίου, τό (30), or ἀμνός, ἀμνοῦ, ὁ (4) being preferred.

D3.38-D3.40 There are no irregular N.T. nouns in these categories.

D4.   ADJECTIVES

D4.0   THE DECLENSION OF ADJECTIVES

D4.01 The vast majority of Greek adjectives have twenty-four forms, since an adjective takes the gender, number and case of the word to which it refers. These adjectives are referred to as "adjectives of three terminations", i.e. they have a flexion of terminations for masculine, feminine and neuter genders. A smaller number are "adjectives of two terminations", which have no separate forms for the feminine but use the masculine forms as the *personal gender*, i.e. as being for both masculine and feminine gender.

D4.02 The greater number of adjectives (546, or 85%) are First/Second Declension adjectives: the masculine and neuter gender flexions follow the Second Declension Paradigms D2.1 and D2.2, and the feminine gender flexion follows the First

Declension Paradigms: D1.1 if the adjective has an ριε stem, and D1.2 otherwise. However, of these there are eight adjectives which are contracted in -εος or οος.

D4.03 Some of these adjectives have no separate feminine forms, using the masculine form as personal gender, and thus they lie entirely within the Second Declension. These two-termination Second Declension adjectives are, in general, those that are compounds (including those that commence with "α- privative", which makes a word negative: e.g. πιστός, believing, and ἄπιστος, unbelieving). But this is not an invariable rule: some compound adjectives are used in the N.T. (and in koine generally) with feminine forms i.e. as three-termination adjectives, and some simplex adjectives, especially if ending in -ιος, are used as two-termination adjectives.

D4.04 There are 21 adjectives (or 3% of the 640 which occur in the N.T.) which are First/Third Declension adjectives, having Third Declension forms (from three paradigms) in the masculine and neuter flexions, and First Declension forms (from Paradigms D1.1 and D1.3) in the feminine. The remaining 73 adjectives (11%) are two-termination adjectives, and thus they lie entirely within the Third Declension (from three paradigms) — they have no separate feminine flexion, and thus their two genders are personal and neuter.

D4.05 A Greek adjective will frequently be found used with an article but without a noun, and then it implies "man", "woman", or "thing", according to gender. Thus ὁ καλός, the good man; αἱ πτωχαί, the poor women; τὸ μέλαν, the black thing (used for referring to ink).

D4.06 The adjectives which occur in the N.T. can be classified by paradigm as follows:

PARADIGM		NUMBER		PERCENT
D4.1 ἅγιος, ἁγία, ἅγιον holy	}	538		84%
D4.2 καλός, καλή, καλόν good				
D4.3 { ἀργυροῦς, ἀργυρᾶ, ἀργυροῦν silvern χρυσοῦς, χρυσῆ, χρυσοῦν golden	}	8	546	1%
		—		
D4.4 βαρύς, βαρεῖα, βαρύ heavy/hard		16		2%
D4.5 ἑκών, ἑκοῦσα, ἑκόν willing		2		*
D4.6 πᾶς, πᾶσα, πᾶν every, each, all		3	21	*
		—		
D4.7 ἀληθής, ἀληθές true		58		9%
D4.8 ἄφρων, ἄφρον foolish		13		2%
D4.9 ἀμήτωρ, ἀμῆτορ motherless		2	73	*
		—	—	—
TOTAL N.T. ADJECTIVES:		640		100%

* indicates a percentage of less than one.

D4.1-D4.3 FIRST/SECOND DECL. THREE-TERMINATION ADJECTIVES

D4.1 ριε- STEM ADJECTIVES

	Masculine	Feminine	Neuter
SN	ἅγιος	ἁγία	ἅγιον
V	ἅγιε	ἁγία	ἅγιον
A	ἅγιον	ἁγίαν	ἅγιον
G	ἁγίου	ἁγίας	ἁγίου
D	ἁγίῳ	ἁγίᾳ	ἁγίῳ
PN	ἅγιοι	ἅγιαι	ἅγια
A	ἁγίους	ἁγίας	ἅγια
G	ἁγίων	ἁγίων	ἁγίων
D	ἁγίοις	ἁγίαις	ἁγίοις

D4.2 CONSONANT-STEM

	Masculine	Feminine	Neuter
SN	καλός	καλή	καλόν
V	καλέ	καλή	καλόν
A	καλόν	καλήν	καλόν
G	καλοῦ	καλῆς	καλοῦ
D	καλῷ	καλῇ	καλῷ
PN	καλοί	καλαί	καλά
A	καλούς	καλάς	καλά
G	καλῶν	καλῶν	καλῶν
D	καλοῖς	καλαῖς	καλοῖς

D4.3 CONTRACTED ADJECTIVES:

ριε- STEM

SN	ἀργυροῦς	ἀργυρᾶ	ἀργυροῦν
A	ἀργυροῦν	ἀργυρᾶν	ἀργυροῦν
G	ἀργυροῦ	ἀργυρᾶς	ἀργυροῦ
D	ἀργυρῷ	ἀργυρᾷ	ἀργυρῷ
PN	ἀργυροῖ	ἀργυραῖ	ἀργυρᾶ
A	ἀργυροῦς	ἀργυρᾶς	ἀργυρᾶ
G	ἀργυρῶν	ἀργυρῶν	ἀργυρῶν
D	ἀργυροῖς	ἀργυραῖς	ἀργυροῖς

CONSONANT STEM

SN	χρυσοῦς	χρυσῆ	χρυσοῦν
A	χρυσοῦν	χρυσῆν	χρυσοῦν
G	χρυσοῦ	χρυσῆς	χρυσοῦ
D	χρυσῷ	χρυσῇ	χρυσῷ
PN	χρυσοῖ	χρυσαῖ	χρυσᾶ
A	χρυσοῦς	χρυσᾶς	χρυσᾶ
G	χρυσῶν	χρυσῶν	χρυσῶν
D	χρυσοῖς	χρυσαῖς	χρυσοῖς

D4.4-D4.6 FIRST/THIRD DECL. THREE-TERMINATION ADJECTIVES

D4.4 STEM -υ/-ει

SN	βαρύς	βαρεῖα	βαρύ
A	βαρύν	βαρεῖαν	βαρύ
G	βαρέως	βαρείας	βαρέως
D	βαρεῖ	βαρείᾳ	βαρεῖ
PN	βαρεῖς	βαρεῖαι	βαρέα
A	βαρεῖς	βαρείας	βαρέα
G	βαρέων	βαρειῶν	βαρέων
D	βαρέσι(ν)	βαρείαις	βαρέσι(ν)

D4.6 STEM -αντ/-ασ

SN	πᾶς	πᾶσα	πᾶν
A	πάντα	πᾶσαν	πᾶν
G	παντός	πάσης	παντός
D	παντί	πάσῃ	παντί
PN	πάντες	πᾶσαι	πάντα
A	πάντας	πάσας	πάντα
G	πάντων	πασῶν	πάντων
D	πᾶσι(ν)	πάσαις	πᾶσι(ν)

D4.7-D4.9 THIRD DECLENSION TWO-TERMINATION ADJECTIVES

D4.7 STEM -ες

	Personal	Neuter
SN	ἀληθής	ἀληθές
A	ἀληθῆ	ἀληθές
G	ἀληθοῦς	ἀληθοῦς
D	ἀληθεῖ	ἀληθεῖ
PN	ἀληθεῖς	ἀληθῆ
A	ἀληθεῖς	ἀληθῆ
G	ἀληθῶν	ἀληθῶν
D	ἀληθέσι(ν)	ἀληθέσι(ν)

D4.8 STEM -ον

	Personal	Neuter
SN	ἄφρων	ἄφρον
A	ἄφρονα	ἄφρον
G	ἄφρονος	ἄφρονος
D	ἄφρονι	ἄφρονι
PN	ἄφρονες	ἄφρονα
A	ἄφρονας	ἄφρονα
G	ἀφρόνων	ἀφρόνων
D	ἄφροσι(ν)	ἄφροσι(ν)

D4.9 STEM -ορ

	Personal	Neuter
SN	ἀμήτωρ	ἀμῆτορ
A	ἀμήτορα	ἀμῆτορ
G	ἀμήτορος	ἀμήτορυς
D	ἀμήτορι	ἀμήτορι
PN	ἀμήτορες	ἀμήτορα
A	ἀμήτορας	ἀμήτορα
G	ἀμητόρων	ἀμητόρων
D	?	?

D4.3 χρυσοῦς (occurring 18 times) is contracted from χρύσεος, and follows καλός. The other four adjectives of this paradigm, contracted in -εος or -οος (and their frequency in the N.T.) are: ἁπλοῦς, healthy (contracted from ἁπλόος; 2); διπλοῦς, double (from διπλόος; 4); τετραπλοῦς, fourfold (from τετραπλόος: 1) and χαλκοῦς, made of copper/brass/bronze (from χάλκεος; 1). There are a further three contracted adjectives with a stem in -ρεος, and these consequently have -ᾱ- throughout the singular (following ἅγιος) instead of -ῆ-. They are: ἀργυροῦς, -ᾶ, -οῦν, silvern (from ἀργύρεος; 3); πορφυροῦς, -ᾶ, -οῦν, purple (from πορφύρεος; 4) and σιδηροῦς, -ᾶ, -οῦν iron (from σιδήρεος; 5). There are four adjectives in -εος/-οος which do not contract: νέος, -α, -ον, young, new (23); ὄγδοος, -η, -ον, eighth (5); στερεός, -ά, -όν, solid (4) and ὑπήκοος, -ον, obedient (3).

D4.4 The masculine and neuter flexions of βαρύς are Third Declension, and exactly follow πῆχυς (D3.2) i.e. they decline as πόλις but with -υ- not -ι- as the stem vowel in the nominative, vocative and accusative singular. The neuter does not take the nominative singular -ς suffix (#D3.04). The feminine flexion is formed from the stem βαρε-, with compensatory lengthening of the -ε- to -ει, as if for the loss of a stem phoneme (these words are thought to have come from an original stem in -εϝ-). The feminine flexion declines as καρδία (Paradigm D1.1; cf. ἁγία, D4.1). Paradigm D4.4 is followed by 13 N.T. adjectives, and together with these there can be classified three irregular adjectives. One of these, ἥμισυς, ἡμίσεια, ἥμισυ, half, was declined regularly in accordance with this paradigm in Classical Greek; but in the N.T. (in its five occurrences) it is found only in the neuter, ἥμισυ, and has the irregular forms: genitive singular ἡμίσους (cf. Paradigm D3.5), and nominative-accusative plural ἡμίσια. The other two irregular adjectives follow the paradigm of βαρύς only in the nominative and accusative singular of the masculine and neuter, and change their stem and their Declension from the genitive singular onwards, and become Second Declension. As usual, the feminine flexion is formed from the stem derived from the genitive singular, and is regular First Declension throughout. These two irregular, mixed-declension adjectives, which are very frequent in use, are: πολύς, πολλή, πολύ, much, many (353), and μέγας, μεγάλη, μέγα, great, large, loud (of a noise), high (of a mountain), etc. (194). These are declined as follows:

IRREGULAR ADJECTIVES OF PARADIGM D4.4

	D4.41 half	**D4.42** much, many			**D4.43** great, large		
STEM:	ἥμισυ- ἥμισι-	πολυ- πολλ-			μεγα- μεγαλ-		

	Neuter	Masculine	Feminine	Neuter	Masculine	Feminine	Neuter
SN	ἥμισυ	πολύς	πολλή	πολύ	μέγας	μεγάλη	μέγα
A	ἥμισυ	πολύν	πολλήν	πολύ	μέγαν	μεγάλην	μέγα
G	ἡμίσους	πολλοῦ	πολλῆς	πολλοῦ	μεγάλου	μεγάλης	μεγάλου
D	ἡμίσει	πολλῷ	πολλῇ	πολλῷ	μεγάλῳ	μεγάλῃ	μεγάλῳ
PN	ἡμίσια	πολλοί	πολλαί	πολλά	μεγάλοι	μεγάλαι	μεγάλα
A	ἡμίσια	πολλούς	πολλάς	πολλά	μεγάλους	μεγάλας	μεγάλα
G	–	πολλῶν	πολλῶν	πολλῶν	μεγάλων	μεγάλων	μεγάλων
D	–	πολλοῖς	πολλαῖς	πολλοῖς	μεγάλοις	μεγάλαις	μεγάλοις

D4.5   ἑκών, ἑκοῦσα, ἑκόν, willing (2) and ἄκων, ἄκουσα, ἆκον, unwilling (1), which are the only two adjectives in Paradigm D4.5, were originally participles and decline like participles, following the declension of λύων, λύουσα, λῦον (see #D5.11).

D4.6   It can be seen that πᾶς, all (1226) exactly follows Paradigm D3.20 — in the nominative singular of the masculine, when the suffix -ς has been added to the stem παντ- first the -τ and then the -ν have given way before the sibilant, thus producing the form πᾶς (with long α). No -ς suffix is added in the neuter nominative singular, so the form is derived from the stem, being first παντ and then (as τ cannot stand as the final letter of a word, #D3.07) it becomes πᾶν. The feminine ending is -σα, and when this is added to the stem παντ the -τ and the -ν are lost and the form πᾶσα results. The *feminine* stem is thus πασ-, and therefore it follows the sibilant-stem First Declension Paradigm D1.3, with -η- in genitive and dative singular. The only other regular adjective of Paradigm D4.6 is ἅπας (35), also meaning "all"; and in addition the Paradigm of πᾶς is followed by all participles in -ας (#D5.12, #D5.31 and #D5.32). Another adjective, μέλας, μέλαινα, μέλαν, black (6), is similar to πᾶς in the masculine and neuter flexions, but from the stem μελαν- (genitive μέλανος), and it has the irregularly-formed feminine μέλαινα, which declines like δόξα, Paradigm D1.3.

D4.7   ἀληθής, ἀληθές, true (26) is a two-termination adjective, i.e. the form ἀληθής is personal gender, serving for both masculine and feminine. This adjective is of the same paradigm type as γένος, γένους (D3.5) — the stem is ἀληθεσ- and in the nominative singular this takes the usual -ς suffix to become first of all ἀληθεσς, and then the two sigmas simplify to one, giving ἀληθες, and the final vowel (being followed by a single consonant only, #D3.09), lengthens to produce ἀληθής. The neuter nominative singular is the stem ἀληθές, without taking any -ς suffix, and without the lengthening of the final vowel. However, it is to be noted that in the case of an adjective in stem -ες, this final vowel remains -ε- in the nominative-vocative-accusative singular (in contrast with the noun, where it is transformed into -ο-, giving the nominative singular form γένος, not "γενες"). As in the case of γένος, the -σ- of the adjective stem is syncopated (i.e. squeezed out) when it falls between two vowels, and these vowels then contract, giving ἀληθῆ (for ἀληθέα), and so forth. The adjective συγγενής, kindred (11), is worthy of special note: in the N.T. it is used only in the masculine (i.e., personal gender with masculine article) meaning "kinsman", "relative"; and it has, as well as its usual regular dative plural συγγενέσιν, an irregular alternative συγγενεῦσιν, formed as if from συγγενεῦς. There are 58 adjectives of Paradigm D4.7 in the N.T.

D4.8   ἄφρων, ἄφρον, foolish (11) is a two-termination adjective with stem in -ον, i.e. of the same paradigm type as ἡγεμῶν, ἡγεμόνος (D3.16). The nominative singular suffix -ς of the personal gender does not hold on the liquid of the stem ἄφρον- and the final vowel (being followed by a single consonant only, #D3.09), lengthens to produce ἄφρων. This lengthening does not occur in the neuter nominative singular. There are thirteen adjectives of Paradigm D4.8 in the N.T.

D4.9   ἀμήτωρ, ἀμῆτορ, motherless (1) and ἀπάτωρ, ἀπᾶτορ, fatherless (1), the only two adjectives of Paradigm D4.9 in the N.T., follow the declension of ἀλέκτωρ, D3.13. Each occurs only once, in the personal nominative singular (in Hebrews 7:3).

D5. PARTICIPLES

D5.0 THE DECLENSION OF PARTICIPLES

D5.01 A participle can be formed for each Greek aspect and each voice (and also for the future tense — though future participles are very infrequent in the N.T.). The participle is formed from the appropriate tense stem by the addition of the appropriate participle morph and numbercase ending.

D5.02 The participle morphs, and their Declensions, are:

VOICE	TENSE	MASC. & NEUT.	FEMININE
Active:	Present, future, and aorist	-ντ (D3)	-σα (D1)
	Perfect	-ος/-οτ (D3)	-υια (D1)
Middle:	All tenses	-μεν-ο (D2)	-μεν-η (D1)
Passive:	The aorist takes the active morphs:	-ντ (D3)	-σα (D1)
	The future takes the middle morphs:	-μεν-ο (D2)	-μεν-η (D1)

The usual phonemic modifications then occur.

D5.03 All participles have 24 forms, like three-termination adjectives, to permit agreement of number, case, and gender. The active voice participles and the aorist passive participle follow the Third Declension for their masculine and neuter flexions, and follow the First Declension for their feminine flexion. The middle voice participles and the future passive participle follow the Second Declension for their masculine and neuter flexions, and follow the First Declension for their feminine flexion.

D5.04 As would be expected (see #9.56; #C2.01), Second Conjugation verbs form their aorist active participles by adding their participle morph, -ντ, to the neutral morph. Thus for example the active participle from the second aorist εἶδον is ἰδών, ἰδοῦσα, ἰδόν, masculine/neuter genitive ἰδόντος, and it declines in accordance with the paradigm of λύων, λύουσα, λῦον, D5.11.

D5.05 Third Conjugation verbs form their participles by adding the participle morph directly to their tense stem (see #9.57; #C3.01). Third Conjugation participles differ from others in that the -ς of the nominative singular ending always dislodges the -ν of the stem, instead of sliding off it. Thus the present active participle from δίδωμι has the stem διδο-ντ-, and in the masculine nominative singular this becomes διδοντς → διδονς → διδος → διδους, not "διδων" (see the compensatory lengthening rule in #D3.09). The verb εἰμί is the exception to this rule for Third Conjugation participles: its participles are ὤν, οὖσα, ὄν, and follow λύων.

D5.06 The paradigms of the declension of First and Third Conjugation participles are given in parallel columns for each tense, to facilitate comparison. There are no Second Conjugation paradigms set out here as the second aorist active and middle adds the neutral morph and the participle morph to the verb stem and then exactly follows the paradigm of the present participle of λύω (active or middle as the case may be); and the other tenses of the Second Conjugation follow the First Conjugation in forming and declining their participles.

D5.1 FIRST CONJUGATION PARADIGMS

	Masculine	Feminine	Neuter

D5.11 PRESENT ACTIVE (λύω)

	Masculine	Feminine	Neuter
SN	λύων	λύουσα	λῦον
A	λύοντα	λύουσαν	λῦον
G	λύοντος	λυούσης	λύοντος
D	λύοντι	λυούσῃ	λύοντι
PN	λύοντες	λύουσαι	λύοντα
A	λύοντας	λυούσας	λύοντα
G	λυόντων	λυουσῶν	λυόντων
D	λύουσι(ν)	λυούσαις	λύουσι(ν)

NOTE THAT the masculine and neuter flexions follow Paradigm D3.18, ἄρχων. The feminine flexion follows Paradigm D1.3, δόξα. Paradigm D5.11 is followed by: the present active of all C1 and C2 verbs, and the aorist active of C2 verbs.

D5.3 THIRD CONJUGATION PARADIGMS

	Masculine	Feminine	Neuter

D5.31 PRESENT ACTIVE (τίθημι)

	Masculine	Feminine	Neuter
	τιθείς	τιθεῖσα	τιθέν
	τιθέντα	τιθεῖσαν	τιθέν
	τιθέντος	τιθείσης	τιθέντος
	τιθέντι	τιθείσῃ	τιθέντι
	τιθέντες	τιθεῖσαι	τιθέντα
	τιθέντας	τιθείσας	τιθέντα
	τιθέντων	τιθεισῶν	τιθέντων
	τιθεῖσι(ν)	τιθείσαις	τιθεῖσι(ν)

THIS PARADIGM is followed by διδούς. The masculine and neuter flexions are identical with noun Paradigm D3.19; the feminine flexion follows Paradigm D1.3, δόξα. Declined similarly are ἱστάς and δεικνύς (in accordance with Paradigm D3.20).

D5.12 AORIST ACTIVE (λύω)

	Masculine	Feminine	Neuter
SN	λύσας	λύσασα	λῦσαν
A	λύσαντα	λύσασαν	λῦσαν
G	λύσαντος	λυσάσης	λύσαντος
D	λύσαντι	λυσάσῃ	λύσαντι
PN	λύσαντες	λύσασαι	λύσαντα
A	λύσαντας	λυσάσας	λύσαντα
G	λυσάντων	λυσασῶν	λυσάντων
D	λύσασι(ν)	λυσάσαις	λύσασι(ν)

NOTE THAT this Paradigm is identical with that for πᾶς (D4.6) and with those for Third Conjugation verbs with participles in -ας (D5.31; D5.32): ἱστάς and στάς (ἵστημι), and -βάς (-βαίνω). All First Conjugation aorist active participles follow λύσας.

D5.32 AORIST ACTIVE (τίθημι)

	Masculine	Feminine	Neuter
	θείς	θεῖσα	θέν
	θέντα	θεῖσαν	θέν
	θέντος	θείσης	θέντος
	θέντι	θείσῃ	θέντι
	θέντες	θεῖσαι	θέντα
	θέντας	θείσας	θέντα
	θέντων	θεισῶν	θέντων
	θεῖσι(ν)	θείσαις	θεῖσι(ν)

THIS PARADIGM is followed by ἀφείς (ἀφίημι), δούς (δίδωμι), στάς (ἵστημι), -βάς (-βαίνω), γνούς (γινώσκω), and other C3 aorist participles. The present participle differs from the aorist only in having the durative morph (but note that -βαίνω and γινώσκω are First Conjugation in the present tense).

D5.13 PERFECT ACTIVE (λύω)

SN	λελυκώς	λελυκυῖα	λελυκός
A	λελυκότα	λελυκυῖαν	λελυκός
G	λελυκότος	λελυκυίας	λελυκότος
D	λελυκότι	λελυκυίᾳ	λελυκότι
PN	λελυκότες	λελυκυῖαι	λελυκότα
A	λελυκότας	λελυκυίας	λελυκότα
G	λελυκότων	λελυκυιῶν	λελυκότων
D	λελυκόσι(ν)	λελυκυίαις	λελυκόσι(ν)

NOTE THAT the masculine and neuter flexions correspond with Paradigm D3.10, φῶς (but with short -o-stem). The feminine flexion follows Paradigm D.1, καρδία. The stem is -ος in the masc. SN, neut. SN & A, and thereafter is -οτ.

D5.33 PERFECT ACTIVE (ἵστημι)

ἐστώς	ἐστῶσα	ἐστός
ἐστῶτα	ἐστῶσαν	ἐστός
ἐστῶτος	ἐστώσης	ἐστῶτος
ἐστῶτι	ἐστώσῃ	ἐστῶτι
ἐστῶτες	ἐστῶσαι	ἐστῶτα
ἐστῶτας	ἐστώσας	ἐστῶτα
ἐστώτων	ἐστωσῶν	ἐστώτων
ἐστῶσι(ν)	ἐστώσαις	ἐστῶσι(ν)

NOTE: ἵστημι has two perfect participles, both with identical meaning, "standing" (intransitive): ἐστώς (as above; 57 or more occurrences), and ἐστηκώς (follows D5.13; 18 or more occurrences): in some places the mss are divided between the two.

D5.14 PRESENT MIDDLE AND PASSIVE (λύω)

SN	λυόμενος	λυομένη	λυόμενον
A	λυόμενον	λυομένην	λυόμενον
G	λυομένου	λυομένης	λυομένου
D	λυομένῳ	λυομένῃ	λυομένῳ
PN	λυόμενοι	λυόμεναι	λυόμενα
A	λυομένους	λυομένας	λυόμενα
G	λυομένων	λυομένων	λυομένων
D	λυομένοις	λυομέναις	λυομένοις

THIS PARADIGM is identical with D4.2.

D5.34 PRESENT MIDDLE AND PASSIVE (δίδωμι)

διδόμενος	διδομένη	διδόμενον
διδόμενον	διδομένην	διδόμενον
διδομένου	διδομένης	διδομένου
διδομένῳ	διδομένῃ	διδομένῳ
διδόμενοι	διδόμεναι	διδόμενα
διδομένους	διδομένας	διδόμενα
διδομένων	διδομένων	διδομένων
διδομένοις	διδομέναις	διδομένοις

SO ALSO the other C3 verbs.

D5.15 AORIST MIDDLE (λύω)

SN	λυσάμενος	λυσαμένη	λυσάμενον
A	λυσάμενον	λυσαμένην	λυσάμενον
G	λυσαμένου	λυσαμένης	λυσαμένου
D	λυσαμένῳ	λυσαμένη	λυσαμένῳ
PN	λυσάμενοι	λυσάμεναι	λυσάμενα
A	λυσαμένους	λυσαμένας	λυσάμενα
G	λυσαμένων	λυσαμένων	λυσαμένων
D	λυσαμένοις	λυσαμέναις	λυσαμένοις

D5.35 AORIST MIDDLE (τίθημι)

θέμενος	θεμένη	θέμενον
θέμενον	θεμένην	θέμενον
θεμένου	θεμένης	θεμένου
θεμένῳ	θεμένη	θεμένῳ
θέμενοι	θέμεναι	θέμενα
θεμένους	θεμένας	θέμενα
θεμένων	θεμένων	θεμένων
θεμένοις	θεμέναις	θεμένοις

D5.16 PERFECT MIDDLE AND PASSIVE (λύω)

SN	λελυμένος	λελυμένη	λελυμένον
A	λελυμένον	λελυμένην	λελυμένον
G	λελυμένου	λελυμένης	λελυμένου
D	λελυμένῳ	λελυμένῃ	λελυμένῳ

PN	λελυμένοι	λελυμέναι	λελυμένα
A	λελυμένους	λελυμένας	λελυμένα
G	λελυμένων	λελυμένων	λελυμένων
D	λελυμένοις	λελυμέναις	λελυμένοις

D5.36 PERFECT MIDDLE AND PASSIVE

NO THIRD CONJUGATION

FORMS ARE FOUND

IN THE N.T.

D5.17 AORIST PASSIVE (λύω)

SN	λυθείς	λυθεῖσα	λυθέν
A	λυθέντα	λυθεῖσαν	λυθέν
G	λυθέντος	λυθείσης	λυθέντος
D	λυθέντι	λυθείσῃ	λυθέντι

PN	λυθέντες	λυθεῖσαι	λυθέντα
A	λυθέντας	λυθείσας	λυθέντα
G	λυθέντων	λυθεισῶν	λυθέντων
D	λυθεῖσι(ν)	λυθείσαις	λυθεῖσι(ν)

THE PASSIVE PARTICIPLE adds -θεντ to the verb stem, and then declines in accordance with C3 participle θείς (D5.32). Direct flexion verbs (#D4.4) take -εντ and decline similarly (but without -θ-): thus σταλείς from ἐστάλην (στέλλω).

D5.37 AORIST PASSIVE (ἵστημι)

σταθείς	σταθεῖσα	σταθέν
σταθέντα	σταθεῖσαν	σταθέν
σταθέντος	σταθείσης	σταθέντος
σταθέντι	σταθείσῃ	σταθέντι

σταθέντες	σταθεῖσαι	σταθέντα
σταθέντας	σταθείσας	σταθέντα
σταθέντων	σταθεισῶν	σταθέντων
σταθεῖσι(ν)	σταθείσαις	σταθεῖσι(ν)

THE PASSIVE PARTICIPLE of Third Declension verbs is formed in the same way as for First Declension verbs: by adding -θεντ to the verb stem. It then declines in accordance with θείς (D5.32).

D5.18 FUTURE ACTIVE (λύω)

SN	λύσων	λύσουσα	λῦσον

Formed by adding the future morph between the stem and the neutral morph. This participle differs in form from the Present Active participle (D5.11) only in that it contains the future morph. It is rare in the N.T.

D5.19 FUTURE MIDDLE AND PASSIVE (λύω)

Middle: SN λυσόμενος   λυσομένη   λυσόμενον
Passive: SN λυθησόμενος   λυθησομένη   λυθησόμενον

The Middle is formed by adding the future morph between the stem and the neutral morph; it differs in form from the Present Middle participle (D5.14) only in that it contains the future morph. It is rare in the N.T. The Passive is formed by adding the passive morph plus future morph, θησ, between the stem and the neutral morph; it differs in form from the Present Middle/Passive participle (D5.14) only in that it contains the passive and future morphs. It is found only once in the N.T. (Hebrews 3:5).

D6. PRONOUNS

D6.1 THE ARTICLE   D6.2 THE RELATIVE

SN	ὁ	ἡ	τό	ὅς	ἥ	ὅ
A	τόν	τήν	τό	ὅν	ἥν	ὅ
G	τοῦ	τῆς	τοῦ	οὗ	ἧς	οὗ
D	τῷ	τῇ	τῷ	ᾧ	ᾗ	ᾧ
PN	οἱ	αἱ	τά	οἵ	αἵ	ἅ
A	τούς	τάς	τά	οὕς	ἅς	ἅ
G	τῶν	τῶν	τῶν	ὧν	ὧν	ὧν
D	τοῖς	ταῖς	τοῖς	οἷς	αἷς	οἷς

D6.1 The article was originally a Demonstrative Pronoun. Notice that the article has the rough breathing as its root in the masculine and feminine nominatives, singular and plural, and "τ" elsewhere.

D6.2 Note that the root of the Relative Pronoun is the rough breathing throughout.

Both the article and the relative pronoun add the *linking vowel* (see #D0.22) to their root, -*o*- for the masculine and neuter, and -*α*- (lengthening to -*η*- in accordance with #D0.24a) for the feminine. They both then take the usual endings of the First Declension (for the feminine) and Second Declension (for the masculine and neuter), except that: the article does not add the usual -ς suffix of the masculine nominative singular; neither of them adds the usual -ν suffix of the neuter nominative-accusative singular. Note also the accent: absent where the article lacks τ, always on the relative. Like ὅς, ἥ, ὅ are declined ἄλλος, η, ο, another, and ἐκεῖνος, η, ο, that (one), those.

D6.3 PERSONAL PRONOUNS PERSON:

	1st	2nd	3rd m.	3rd f.	3rd n.
S N	ἐγώ	σύ	αὐτός	αὐτή	αὐτό
A	ἐμέ /με	σέ	αὐτόν	αὐτήν	αὐτό
G	ἐμοῦ/μου	σοῦ	αὐτοῦ	αὐτῆς	αὐτοῦ
D	ἐμοί/μοι	σοί	αὐτῷ	αὐτῇ	αὐτῷ
P N	ἡμεῖς	ὑμεῖς	αὐτοί	αὐταί	αὐτά
A	ἡμᾶς	ὑμᾶς	αὐτούς	αὐτάς	αὐτά
G	ἡμῶν	ὑμῶν	αὐτῶν	αὐτῶν	αὐτῶν
D	ἡμῖν	ὑμῖν	αὐτοῖς	αὐταῖς	αὐτοῖς

See #3.31-34; #A3.21-25.

D6.4 DEMONSTRATIVE PRONOUN

	m.	f.	n.
	οὗτος	αὕτη	τοῦτο
	τοῦτον	ταύτην	τοῦτο
	τούτου	ταύτης	τούτου
	τούτῳ	ταύτῃ	τούτῳ
	οὗτοι	αὗται	ταῦτα
	τούτους	ταύτας	ταῦτα
	τούτων	τούτων	τούτων
	τούτοις	ταύταις	τούτοις

See #3.32-36; #A3.26.

THE INTENSIVE PRONOUN

This has the same 24 forms as αὐτός, but has the meaning "-self" in all persons. It precedes the article.

THE SPECIFIC PRONOUN

This has the same 24 forms as αὐτός, but has the meaning "same". In this use it is preceded by the article.

D6.5
THE INTERROGATIVE

	Personal	Neuter
SN	τίς	τί
A	τίνα	τί
G	τίνος	τίνος
D	τίνι	τίνι

PN	τίνες	τίνα
A	τίνας	τίνα
G	τίνων	τίνων
D	τίσι(ν)	τίσι(ν)

D6.6
THE INDEFINITE

	Personal	Neuter
SN	τις	τι
A	τινά	τι
G	τινός	τινός
D	τινί	τινί

PN	τινές	τινά
A	τινάς	τινά
G	τινῶν	τινῶν
D	τισί(ν)	τισί(ν)

The Interrogative Pronoun, "who?" and the Indefinite Pronoun "some", "any", differ only in their accent.

D6.7 THE NUMERICALS:
ONE

	Masculine	Feminine	Neuter
SN	εἷς	μία	ἕν
A	ἕνα	μίαν	ἕν
G	ἑνός	μιᾶς	ἑνός
D	ἑνί	μιᾷ	ἑνί

	TWO m/f/n	THREE Personal	Neuter
PN	δύο	τρεῖς	τρία
A	δύο	τρεῖς	τρία
G	δύο	τριῶν	τριῶν
D	δυσί(ν)	τρισί(ν)	τρισί(ν)

Like εἷς are declined: οὐδείς, οὐδεμία, οὐδέν, and μηδείς, μηδεμία, μηδέν no-one.

D6.8 THE REFLEXIVE:
SINGULAR

	himself	herself	itself
A	ἑαυτόν	ἑαυτήν	ἑαυτό
G	ἑαυτοῦ	ἑαυτῆς	ἑαυτοῦ
D	ἑαυτῷ	ἑαυτῇ	ἑαυτῷ

Similarly: ἐμαυτόν, myself
σεαυτόν, yourself

PLURAL

	-selves	-selves	-selves
A	ἑαυτούς	ἑαυτάς	ἑαυτά
G	ἑαυτῶν	ἑαυτῶν	ἑαυτῶν
D	ἑαυτοῖς	ἑαυταῖς	ἑαυτοῖς

Note that in the plural the same word is used for all three persons — ourselves, yourselves, themselves.

D6.9 THE RECIPROCAL

one another

PA	ἀλλήλους
G	ἀλλήλων
D	ἀλλήλοις

Plural only.

APPENDIX E

EXPLANATIONS IN PHONEMICS AND MORPHOLOGY

E1. THE COMPONENT ELEMENTS OF LANGUAGE

E1.1   The smallest unit of language is a single sound. This is called a *phone*, and is represented in writing by a *letter*. Where a sound is sufficiently different from other similar sounds as to distinguish meaning, then that sound is called a *phoneme*, i.e. a meaningful phone. For example, the words "pig" and "big" have different meanings from each other, and this indicates that in English "p" and "b" are separate phonemes, though the difference between them in pronunciation is very small: they are both made in the same way, but the vocal chords are activated for the "b".

E1.2   There can be many ways of pronouncing the one "sound", but when these differences are not intended to affect meaning, they are *allophones*, different phones of the one phoneme. Consider for example the varieties of pronunciation of the same English word that one would hear from a Londoner, a Scotsman, an American, an Australian, an Indian, a German, and a Frenchman, all speaking English. This difference in pronunciation we usually call *accent*, and we refer to "an Australian accent", "a German accent", etc.

E1.3   Differences of pronunciation only involve different *phonemes* when the speaker intends one sound to be distinguished from the other. Thus in Greek "κ" and "χ" are different phonemes (i.e. the difference between them is *phonemic*) because they affect meaning: e.g., ἐκει means "there", "in that place", and ἐχει means "he has".

E1.4   But sounds do not occur in isolation; they occur in combinations. An utterance complete in itself is called a *sentence*, and the units of speech of which it is composed — and which can be changed for other similar units, or put into a different order — are called *words*.

E1.5   A word may convey one single piece of information, or it in turn may be composed of a number of smaller units of meaning which can also be found, with the same meaning, in other words. E.g., -s can be attached to large numbers of English words with the meaning, "plural"; "-ing" can be added to many verbs with the meaning, "action in progress", the nature of the action being indicated by the word to which it is attached, such as in "walking", "sailing", "eating", etc. A word may contain several meaningful units, such as in "help-ful; "horse-man-ship"; "un-will-ing-ly". Each such unit of meaning, whether a word in itself or a part of a word, is called a *morph*. All the morphs in a language which have exactly the same meaning are collectively called a *morpheme*. Thus all the ways in which English makes a word plural will constitute together "the English plural morpheme".

E1.6   The study of the ways in which sounds (phones) are made, and their nature, is

276

called *phonetics*. The study of phonemes, and how they are used in distinguishing one word from another, and how they interact, is called *phonemics* or *phonology* (sometimes these terms are used interchangeably by scholars, and sometimes with a slight shade of difference between them — this difference will not be of concern to us). The study of morphs and morphemes, the meaning they carry, and how they constitute words, is called *morphemics* or *morphology* (again, we will not be concerned with the shade of difference that some scholars make between these two terms). The study of how words are assembled in utterances — i.e., when and how words are used, and the order of their use, and the purpose behind their use in a particular way — is called *syntax*.

E1.7   We are not directly concerned in this Course with the question of the pronunciation of Greek (except to the extent of consistently using an agreed conventional pronunciation so that we can *say* the words, and so that our pronunciation will help us remember them). As a result, this book contains only minimal material about phonetics. Our prime concerns are with phonemes (because these distinguish words), morphs (because these convey meaning), and syntax (because this assembles individual units of meaning into a total meaningful utterance). Some further specific explanations are now to be made in the areas of phonemic modification and morphology.

E2.   PHONEMIC MODIFICATION

E2.0   THE NATURE OF PHONEMIC MODIFICATION

E2.01   Whenever two sounds (phonemes) come together, either in the one word or in two consecutive words, they affect each other. This affect is greatest when the two phonemes in question are both vowels or both consonants. One of the two phonemes, or both, may be altered, or *modified*. Where a phoneme becomes modified solely because of the juxtaposition of another phoneme, this is called *phonemic modification*.

E2.02   The phenomenon of phonemic modification occurs in all languages, especially in the speaking of the language, but on most occasions the speaker of a language is so completely used to it that he is not consciously aware that it is happening.

E2.03   Numbers of the changes which occur only affect speaking, not spelling. For example, if two stop consonants come together, only the second is pronounced: "lost tribe" is pronounced like "loss tribe"; similarly in "grab bag", "weak camel", and even in "last page", etc. Often a phoneme is modified to the one which follows it — thus in the expression "bank pass-sheet" most speakers will not pronounce the "s" phoneme of "pass" but will say "pash-sheet" or "pa-sheet".

E2.04   Some phonemic modification is not a matter of individual pronunciation but is universal in the language. Thus the English "n" phoneme is normally modified to the "ng" phoneme when it is followed by a palatal (k, g, x, and similar phonemes), even though it will not be written differently. Compare the pronunciation of "n" in "ant", "and", "anthem", "answer", with its pronunciation in "ankle", "anchor", "anger", "anxious", "anxiety".

E2.05 Some phonemic modification does affect spelling. Thus when the prefix "in-", meaning "not", is added to a word beginning with a labial or a liquid it changes accordingly: "impolite", "imbalance", "immobile", "illegal", "irregular", etc. Phonemes can be squeezed out of a word in popular usage: for most people, "cannot" becomes "can't", and so on.

E2.06 Greek displays a full range of linguistic modification. A gamma followed by a palatal is enga[11], and pronounced as "ng"; thus ἐγγύς — this is not an original gamma phoneme, but a "ν" phoneme the pronunciation of which has been modified in the same way as in English: ἐν + γράφω becomes ἐγγράφω. So also a nu followed by a labial will be pronounced as a mu: ἐνβάλλω is pronounced (and may be spelt as) ἐμβάλλω, συνβαίνω as συμβαίνω. The spelling of words like these may or may not be changed, as the writer chooses.

E2.07 It is important to note that phonemic modification does not affect the *meaning* of the word. Thus phonemic modification frequently brings into existence slightly different forms of a morph, all having exactly the same meaning. These are known as *allomorphs* (#E3.2).

E2.08 There are nine major types of phonemic modification where spelling is affected which occur in Greek on a regular basis. These are: contraction, elision, vowel lengthening, compensation, syncopation, amalgamation (including simplification), assimilation, de-aspiration, and crasis.

E2.1   CONTRACTION

E2.11 Where any morph in a verb other than an elision morph ends in a short vowel, that vowel regularly contracts with the initial vowel of any contiguous following morph that commences with a vowel or diphthong, whether short or long. **This is the Short Vowel Contraction Rule.**

E2.12 An elision morph is a morph which undergoes elision not contraction when followed by a morph commencing with a vowel. The elision morphs are described in #E2.22.

E2.13 Frequently η, though a long vowel, also contracts with certain vowels which follow it.

E2.14 The pattern of contraction is as follows:

α + α, ε, η	→ α	ε + α	→ η (or α)	η + ε	→ η
α + ει, η	→ ᾳ (or α)	ε + αι	→ ῃ (or αι)	η + ει, ι	→ ῃ
α + ι	→ αι or ᾳ	ε + ε, ι, ει	→ ει	η + οι	→ ῳ
α + ο, ου	→ ω	ε + η	→ η	ι + ι, ε	→ ι
α + οι	→ ῳ	ε + ο, ου	→ ου	ο + α, η, ω	→ ω
		ε + οι	→ οι	ο + ε, ο, ου	→ ου
		ε + υ	→ ευ	ο + ει, η, ι, οι	→ οι
		ε + ω	→ ω	υ + ε	→ υ

E2.15 This schedule gives the standard pattern of contraction. The less usual alternatives are given in brackets. Exceptions to this pattern will sometimes be found.

E2.16 Where before contraction a ι subscript occurs on the second vowel, this ι subscript remains after contraction. Thus $\varepsilon + \omega = \omega$. But sometimes, irregularly, $o + \eta$ or $\omega = o\iota$; e.g. the aorist subjunctive active will be found with such forms as $\delta o\widehat{\iota}$ (instead of $\delta\widehat{\omega}$; from $\delta\acute{\iota}\delta\omega\mu\iota$), $\gamma\nu o\widehat{\iota}$ (instead of $\gamma\nu\widehat{\omega}$; from $\gamma\iota\nu\acute{\omega}\sigma\kappa\omega$).

E2.17 On some occasions contraction does not occur when it would have been expected. The two most common such occasions are: **(a)** verbs with monosyllabic stems ending in ε ($\chi\acute{\varepsilon}\omega$, $\delta\acute{\varepsilon}o\mu\alpha\iota$, etc.) and **(b)** nouns with a short vowel in their stems (e.g. such forms as $\pi\acute{o}\lambda\varepsilon\omega\varsigma$, $\beta\alpha\sigma\iota\lambda\acute{\varepsilon}\alpha$) — especially when these forms have resulted from the loss of digamma (#C8.7; #D3.4).

E2.18 A verb is to be regarded as having a grave accent (`) on the vowels not carrying the verb accent (´ or ˜). Where the uncontracted form of a verb has an acute accent on the first vowel of those being contracted, this accent and the notional grave accent on the second vowel being contracted will come together upon the contracted vowel and the two accents will combine into a circumflex. Thus: $\tau\grave{\iota}\mu\acute{\alpha}\grave{\omega} \rightarrow \tau\iota\mu\widehat{\omega}$ (i.e., $\tau\iota\mu\widehat{\omega}$). Often this circumflex is the only indication of the contraction. Thus the present of "I judge" is $\kappa\rho\acute{\iota}\nu\omega$ and the future is $\kappa\rho\iota\nu\widehat{\omega}$ (contracted from $\kappa\rho\iota\nu\acute{\varepsilon}\omega$). At times only this accent enables it to be known what has happened. Thus the passive morph $-\theta\varepsilon-$ contracts with the aorist subjunctive endings $-\omega$, $-\eta\varsigma$, $-\eta$, etc. to give $\lambda\upsilon\theta\widehat{\omega}$, $\lambda\upsilon\theta\widehat{\eta}\varsigma$, $\lambda\upsilon\theta\widehat{\eta}$, etc. — the circumflex making known the contraction. Note: if in the uncontracted form the acute accent falls on the *second* of the contracting vowels (e.g. $\lambda\alpha\lambda\varepsilon$-$\acute{\varepsilon}\tau\omega$), the contracted vowel carries an acute ($\lambda\alpha\lambda\varepsilon\acute{\iota}\tau\omega$); if the accent does not fall on either of the contracting vowels, the contracted vowel will not be accented ($\grave{\varepsilon}\tau\acute{\iota}\mu\alpha$-$o\nu \rightarrow \grave{\varepsilon}\tau\acute{\iota}\mu\omega\nu$). (For a fuller discussion of accents, see #E6.)

E2.2   ELISION

E2.21 Where an elision morph is followed by a morph commencing with a vowel, then the final vowel of the elision morph elides before the vowel of the following morph. **This is the Short Vowel Elision Rule.**

E2.22 An *elision morph* is a morph in which elision occurs in accordance with this rule. The elision morphs are:
(a) **aspect morphs:** the punctiliar, perfective-active, and neutral morphs.
(b) **prepositions prefixed to a verb** (except $\pi\rho\acute{o}$ and $\pi\varepsilon\rho\acute{\iota}$).
(c) **prepositions which can be prefixed to a verb** (i.e., those for (b) above) when standing in front of some other word which commences with a vowel.
(d) **certain conjunctions and other words,** according to the style of the author (i.e. with some words, sometimes elision occurs, sometimes not).

E2.23 Elision means that the short vowel with which an elision morph ends *elides* (or "hides") before a following morph commencing with a vowel. The elided vowel is not totally lost, and can be regarded as "waiting behind the scenes" for an opportunity to reappear, i.e. in a verb form which lacks the vowel that caused the elision. Thus ἀπο-ΐστημι becomes ἀφίστημι; but the aorist participle is ἀποστάς (Acts 19:9), with the elided vowel restored.

E2.24 The aspect morphs (-ε-, -σα-, -κα-) elide their vowel when followed by a suffix commencing w:th a vowel. This can be recognized by a comparison of these active forms:

IMPERFECT	AORIST	PERFECT
S1 ἐλυο + ν → ἔλυον	ἐλυσα + ∅ → ἔλυσα	λελυκα + ∅ → λέλυκα
2 ἐλυε + ς → ἔλυες	ἐλυσα + ς → ἔλυσας	λελυκα + ς → λέλυκας
3 ἐλυε + ε → ἔλυε	ἐλυσα + ε → ἔλυσε	λελυκα + ε → λέλυκε
Pluperfect		ἐλελυκα + ειν → ἐλελύκειν
Subjunctive	λυσα + ητε → λύσητε	
Infinitive	λυσα + αι → λῦσαι	
Participle		λελυκα + ως → λελυκώς

EXCEPTION: The present infinitive stem λυε- adds the infinitive ending -εν and contracts to λύειν instead of eliding to "λῦεν"; and similarly the second aorist ἰδε + εν gives ἰδεῖν; and τιμαε+εν gives first τιμα+εν and then τιμᾶν, by the progressive contraction of α and ε to α. Moreover, the perfect active infinitive takes the allomorph -κε- (#E4.78) instead of -κα-, and then takes the infinitive ending for a vowel stem, -ναι (#E4.94), to give λελυκέναι.

E2.25 A preposition (other than πρό or περί) which ends in a vowel and which is followed by a word commencing with a vowel will elide its final vowel, and the elision will be marked by an apostrophe. When the following word commences with a rough breathing, the preposition will aspirate its last consonant if that is a stop consonant. (See #8.69 for fuller details.)

E2.26 A preposition (other than πρό or περί) which ends in a vowel and which is prefixed to a verb form commencing with a vowel (irrespective of whether that vowel is part of the verb stem or the augment) will elide its final vowel. The elision will not be marked in any way. When the following morph commences with a rough breathing, the preposition will absorb that breathing into its last consonant and aspirate it, if that consonant is a stop consonant; in other cases the rough breathing is simply lost (#8.69).

E2.27 Elision is occasionally found with conjunctions, in particular with δέ before ἄν (and not otherwise, as a rule) and often with ἀλλά and οὐδέ, and very rarely with any other words. Often the manuscripts have variant readings, with and without the elision (as is also the situation for preposition elision).

E2.3   VOWEL LENGTHENING

E2.31 Where a verb stem ends in a short vowel, this vowel regularly lengthens when followed by a suffix beginning with a consonant, -α into -η, -ε into -η, and -o into -ω. **This is the Short Vowel Lengthening Rule.**

E2.32 This lengthening can be seen in the Principal Parts of the short vowel stem verbs:

τιμάω	τιμήσω	ἐτίμησα	τετίμηκα	τετίμημαι	ἐτιμήθην
λαλέω	λαλήσω	ἐλάλησα	λελάληκα	λελάλημαι	ἐλαλήθην
πληρόω	πληρώσω	ἐπλήρωσα	πεπλήρωκα	πεπλήρωμαι	ἐπληρώθην

E2.33 There are a small number of exceptions to verb vowel lengthening: where -α occurs after a ρ, ι, or ε root, and in some specific verbs (see #C1.48).

E2.34 Third Conjugation verbs lengthen in the singular present active (see C3.1a, C3.1b, C3.1c in the Conspectus, #C6); and in some other active forms. The reason for this lengthening is not clear. On the other hand, they do not lengthen their stem vowel in the middle or passive flexions at all.

E2.35 The passive morph -θε- lengthens its vowel to give -θη- in front of a single consonant suffix or in form-final position, but remains as -θε- before the two-consonant suffix -ντ- of the participle (the participle stem is thus λυθεντ-). It also remains short in front of, and then contracts with, a following vowel (as in the subjunctive, and with the ι of the optative, giving the diphthong ει), in accordance with #E2.11.

E2.36 Third Declension nouns, adjectives and participles lengthen ε into η and o into ω in the nominative singular masculine (or personal) gender when the vowel is followed by a single consonant, when the stem consonant(s) has/have not been replaced by the -ς suffix. Thus: stem ἀστερ → ἀστηρ (#D3.12); stem ἡγεμον → ἡγεμων (#D3.16); stem ἀρχοντ → ἀρχων (# D3.18). But see #E2.4 re stem ποδ → πους, ἐν → εἰς, etc.

E2.4   COMPENSATORY LENGTHENING

E2.41 Where a stem consonant has been lost from a word stem as the result of adding a particular suffix, then the final vowel of the stem, if short, will undergo compensatory lengthening: short α, ι, and υ will lengthen without the spelling being affected; ε lengthens to ει; and o lengthens to ου. **This is the Short Vowel Compensatory Lengthening Rule.**

E2.42 Thus: ἐν + ς → ἐς → εἷς (nominative masculine singular of "one")
         ποδ + ς → πος → πους (nominative singular of "foot")
ὀδοντ + ς → ὀδονς → ὀδος → ὀδους (nominative singular of "tooth")
λυθεντ + ς → λυθενς → λυθες → λυθεις (passive participle of λύω)
BUT: ἀρχοντ + ς → ἀρχονς → ἀρχον → ἀρχων (*not* "ἀρχουν"; #E2.36).

E2.43 Where the -σ- of the punctiliar morph is lost when it is added to a liquid verb, compensatory lengthening occurs:
μένω (I remain): ἐμεν + σα → ἐμενα → ἔμεινα
δέρω (I thrash): ἐδερ + σα → ἐδερα → ἔδειρα
σπείρω (I sow): ἐσπερ + σα → ἐσπερα → ἔσπειρα
BUT ALSO, in accordance with this rule (#E2.41),
καθαίρω (I clean/prune): ἐκαθαρ + σα → ἐκάθαρα
σημαίνω (I indicate) : ἐσημαν + σα → ἐσήμανα
κρίνω (I judge) : ἐκριν + σα → ἔκρινα
σύρω (I drag) : ἐσυρ + σα → ἔσυρα

E2.44 In the dative plural of Third Declension words, compensatory lengthening occurs upon the loss of *two* stem consonants, but not upon the loss of one only. Thus:

ἄρχων: ἀρχοντ + σιν → ἀρχονσιν → ἀρχοσιν → ἄρχουσιν (#D3.18)

τιθείς : τιθεντ + σιν → τιθενσιν → τιθεσιν → τιθεῖσιν (#D5.31)

BUT: ἡγεμών: ἡγεμον + σιν → ἡγεμόσιν (#D3.16)

ποιμήν : ποιμεν + σιν → ποιμέσιν (#D3.17)

E2.45 The form of the third person plural active is the result of compensatory lengthening: originally this was λυοντσιν — compare the dative plural; and in the same way, it became λύουσιν. The λυοντ- form of the third person plural can still be seen in the middle flexions, where it is preserved because followed by a vowel: λύονται, ἐλύοντο.

E2.46 Numerous other Greek forms are most readily explained on the basis of compensatory lengthening. Thus the stem of the verb εἰμί is ἐσ-, and the sigma is easily dislodged: but everywhere in the present flexion where the -ς has been lost the -ε has lengthened to ει. In the imperfect the ἐ- had taken the tempora! augment and had become ἠ-, which was unaffected by the loss of the stem sigma when it occurred. Grammarians find it difficult to account for the singular forms -εις and -ει in the present active indicative of the verb; possibly it is compensatory lengthening, though the reason for it is now quite unknown to us. Perhaps also compensatory lengthening may be the explanation of the final vowel -ει- in the pluperfect flexion (#E4.83), though again it is unclear what the reason for this would be.

E2.5 SYNCOPATION

E2.51 Syncopation refers to the situation where a short vowel coming between two consonants is squeezed out, or where a sigma or other consonant coming between two vowels is squeezed out.

E2.52 The genitive singular of πατήρ, father, which should "correctly" be "πατερος", has lost its -ε- by syncopation and has become πατρός.

E2.53 The original (theoretical) present tense "πιπετω" (from the verb stem πεσ-, as found in the aorist, with added -τ- as durative morph) has become πίπτω, I fall.

E2.54 The original present tense γιγνώσκω (used in Classical Greek; from the root γνο-) became γινώσκω, I know.

E2.55 The original present tense "γιγενομαι" (from the root γεν-) became first γίγνομαι (used in Classical Greek) and then γίνομαι, I become.

E2.56 The second person singular middle endings -σαι and -σο when added to aspect morphs -ε or -σα lost the sigma and the vowels contracted. Thus:

λυεσαι (present) syncopated to λυεαι and contracted to λύῃ

ἐλυεσο (imperfect) syncopated to ἐλυεο and contracted to ἐλύου

ἐλυσασο (aorist) syncopated to ἐλυσαο and contracted to ἐλύσω.

E2.57 ἔχω derives from the root σεχ, so that the imperfect was originally ἔσεχον. The -σ- was lost, and the resulting form ἔεχον then contracted into εἶχον (compare digamma verbs, #C8.71-72). In contradistinction, in the aorist the original form ἔσεχον has lost the stem -ε-, becoming ἔσχον.

E2.6   AMALGAMATION

E2.61 The final labial of a morph amalgamates **(a)** with a following -σ- to form -ψ-; and **(b)** with a following rough breathing or -κ- to form -φ-. **This is the Labial Amalgamation Rule.** Examples: the aorist active of θλίβω, ἔθλιβ- + -σα → ἔθλιψα (#C1.5); ἀπό + ἵημι → ἀφίημι (see #8.69; #E2.23); the perfect active of βλέπω, βεβλεπ- + κα → βέβλεφα (#C1.5).

E2.62 The final palatal of a morph amalgamates **(a)** with a following -σ- to form -ξ-; and **(b)** with a following -κ- to form -χ-. **This is the Palatal Amalgamation Rule.** Examples: the future active of ἄρχω, ἀρχ- + -σω → ἄρξω; the perfect active of κηρύσσω, κεκηρυσσ- + -κα → κεκήρυχα (#C1.6).

E2.63 The final dental of a morph amalgamates with a following rough breathing to form -θ-. **This is the Dental Amalgamation Rule.** Examples: κατά + ὧς → καθώς; μετά + ἵστημι → μεθίστημι (#8.69; #E2.23).

E2.64 The final dental of a morph drops out before a following -σ- or -κ-. **This is the Dental Drop-out Rule.** Examples: the future active of σπεύδω, σπευδ- + -σω → σπεύσω; the perfect active of δοξάζω, δεδοξαζ- + -κα → δεδόξακα (#C1.7). Thus in the case of a dental followed by -σ- or -κ-, the "amalgamation" of the dental effectively amounts to its "annihilation". However, a small number of verbs in -θ, when they add -κα, have -θα; thus λανθάνω (root λαθ) → perfect λέληθα (#C2.34); πάσχω (root παθ) → perfect πέπονθα (#C2.4; #C8.63); ἦλθον (root ελθ) → perfect ἐλήλυθα (#C2.8); πείθω (root πειθ) → perfect πέποιθα (#C8.63).

E2.65 These rules can be summarized thus: Labials, palatals and dentals follow a pattern of amalgamation when a morph commencing with a sigma, kappa or rough breathing is added to them, thus:

Labials (π, β or φ)   + rough breathing or κ → φ; + σ → ψ (#C1.5; cf. #C4.54)
Palatals (κ, γ, χ or σσ) +   κ → χ; + σ → ξ (#C1.6; cf. #C4.54)
Dentals (τ, δ, θ, or ζ) + rough breathing   → θ}; + σ → σ (#C1.7)
                      + κ   → κ (or θ)

E2.66 These rules apply to nouns and adjectives as well as verbs. Thus σαρκ- + -ς → σάρξ (#D3.6); λιβ- + -ς → λίψ (#D3.7); παιδ- + -ς → παῖς (#D3.8).

E2.67 Where two sigmas are brought together by adding a sigma suffix to a sigma stem, they amalgamate into a single sigma. This particular instance of amalgamation is sometimes called *simplification*. Example: stem ἀληθεσ-, true, takes the nominative singular suffix -ς and becomes ἀληθεσς, and this simplifies to ἀληθες (and then lengthens to ἀληθής, #E2.36). This does not apply when the stem ends in a double sigma, -σσ, which behaves as a single palatal phoneme (see #E2.65).

E2.7   ASSIMILATION

E2.71 Wherever a labial or palatal consonant of a particular manner of articulation (see #1.47) is followed by a morph commencing with a consonant of a different manner of articulation, the first consonant changes so as to become *similar in manner* to (hence the term as*simila*tion) the one that follows. **This is the Consonant Assimilation Rule.** The consonant still remains in its original *place* of articulation, i.e. labial or palatal as the case may be. What changes is its *manner* of articulation, i.e. whether it is unvoiced, voiced, or aspirated.

E2.72 Wherever a nasal liquid consonant is followed by a morph commencing with a consonant of a different *place* of articulation, the nasal changes its place of articulation to correspond with that of the consonant which follows it.

E2.73 Wherever a dental consonant is followed by a morph commencing with a stop or nasal consonant, it becomes -σ-.

E2.74 The pattern of assimilation can be shown in a table, thus: Where a consonant comes before another consonant that is **UNVOICED VOICED ASPIRATE** μ,

	UNVOICED	VOICED	ASPIRATE	μ
If a labial (π, β, ϕ or $\pi\tau$) it becomes respectively	π	β	ϕ	μ
If a palatal (κ, γ, χ or $\sigma\sigma$) it becomes respectively	κ	γ	χ	γ
If a dental (τ, δ, θ or ζ) then it is replaced by	σ	σ	σ	σ

E2.75 This assimilation can be seen clearly illustrated in the changes that occur in the conjugation of the perfect middle flexion of stop consonant verbs — see these flexions for Paradigms #C1.5, #C1.6, and #C1.7.

E2.76 The above pattern of assimilation is quite consistently carried out.

E2.77 Similarly, -ν- before a **LABIAL OR** μ **PALATAL DENTAL OR** ν becomes, respectively: μ γ(enga) ν

Thus: $\dot{\epsilon}\nu + \beta\alpha\dot{\iota}\nu\omega \rightarrow \dot{\epsilon}\mu\beta\alpha\dot{\iota}\nu\omega$ (but note, with augment, $\dot{\epsilon}\nu\dot{\epsilon}\beta\eta$, Mt 15:39)

$\dot{\epsilon}\nu + \mu\dot{\epsilon}\nu\omega \rightarrow \dot{\epsilon}\mu\mu\dot{\epsilon}\nu\omega$ (but note, with augment, $\dot{\epsilon}\nu\dot{\epsilon}\mu\epsilon\iota\nu\epsilon\nu$, Acts 28:30)

$\dot{\epsilon}\nu + \gamma\rho\dot{\alpha}\phi\omega \rightarrow \dot{\epsilon}\gamma\gamma\rho\dot{\alpha}\phi\omega$

$\dot{\epsilon}\nu + \kappa\alpha\lambda\dot{\epsilon}\omega \rightarrow \dot{\epsilon}\gamma\kappa\alpha\lambda\dot{\epsilon}\omega$ (but note, with augment, $\dot{\epsilon}\nu\epsilon\kappa\dot{\alpha}\lambda\upsilon\nu$, Acts 23:28)

$\dot{\epsilon}\nu + \tau\rho\dot{\epsilon}\pi\omega \rightarrow \dot{\epsilon}\nu\tau\rho\dot{\epsilon}\pi\omega$

$\dot{\epsilon}\nu + \nu\epsilon\dot{\upsilon}\omega \rightarrow \dot{\epsilon}\nu\nu\epsilon\dot{\upsilon}\omega$

Similarly with $\sigma\upsilon\nu$.

E2.78 When the augment intervenes between the preposition and the following consonant, then the two phonemes are no longer contiguous and therefore the -ν-returns (as in the forms from the passages quoted above).

E2.79 The assimilation of -ν- to -μ- or -γ- was not always consistently carried out, so forms like $\dot{\epsilon}\nu\gamma\rho\dot{\alpha}\phi\omega$, $\dot{\epsilon}\nu\kappa\dot{\delta}\pi\tau\omega$, etc., will be found.

E2.8   DE-ASPIRATION

E2.81 An aspirate with which a syllable commences becomes de-aspirated when the next syllable commences with an aspirate. This is known as "Grassman's Law" (Allen, p. 13).

E2.82 Thus the reduplication added to a word commencing with an aspirated consonant is the unaspirated equivalent (see #E4.33).

E2.83 Even a root will lose its aspiration before the -θ- of the passive. The aorist passive indicative of τίθημι would (apart from this rule) be "ἐθέθην", but instead by this rule it has become ἐτέθην, and the aorist passive subjunctive is τεθῶ (thus the third person singular τεθῇ in Mk 4:21 and the future passive προστεθήσεται in Mk 4:24). So also from θύω comes ἐτύθη, not "ἐθύθη" (I Corinthians 5:7). But θύεσθαι (Luke 22:7) is permissible because the aspirates are not commencing successive syllables.

E2.84 In one form, it is the suffix which is de-aspirated. The second person singular aorist imperative passive suffix is -θι, as in the direct flexion form διαλλάγηθι (Matthew 5:24, from διαλλάσσω, reconcile), this ending coming from the ending of the Third Conjugation aorist imperative active as seen in στῆθι, ‑βηθι, γνῶθι and δῦθι (see #C6, the Conjugation Conspectus). But when this suffix is added to the regular form of the passive, with passive morph-θε-, it is de-aspirated and becomes-τι. Thus the form is λύθητι (#C0.45; #C1.12), not "λύθηθι".

E2.85 Some word roots have an aspirate at the beginning and end of the root, and lose the initial aspiration in a word form except where the second aspiration is lost through amalgamation. Thus:
Root θριχ-, nominative singular θρίξ, genitive singular τριχός (#D3.26)
  θρεφ-, present tense τρέφω, aorist tense ἔθρεψα (#C4.4)
  ἐχ ,   present tense ἔχω, future tense ἕξω (note rough breathing) (#C2.7)

E2.86 Although de-aspiration is a standard rule it is not an invariable one, and examples can be found where two aspirates occur at the beginning of successive syllables, if they are not the same letter (e.g., ἐξεχύθη, Acts 1:18).

E2.9   CRASIS

E2.91 Sometimes two words are "crashed" together into one. These are known as instances of *crasis*.

E2.92 Crasis is not common in the N.T. It only occurred in a number of specific combinations, the most usual being κἀγώ (for καὶ ἐγώ), κἀμέ (for καὶ ἐμέ), κἀκεῖνος (καὶ ἐκεῖνος), κἀκεῖ (καὶ ἐκεῖ), κἄν (καὶ ἄν), τοὔνομα (τὸ ὄνομα), τοὐναντίον (τὸ ἐναντίον), plus a few others.

E2.93 In all occasions where crasis can occur, the first word ends and the second word commences with a vowel (or diphthong); a final -ι of the first word is lost; the vowels contract according to the normal rules of contraction (#E2.14); the breathing of the second word is retained over the contracted vowel; the accent of the first word is ignored and the combined word has the accent of the second word on the same syllable as before.

E2.94 There are similarities between crasis in Greek and such forms in English as "aren't", "can't", "don't", "won't", "I'm", "you're", "he's", etc.: the form is a combination of two words; its use is optional and colloquial; only a small, fixed number of words can be combined in this way; the combination is marked by the use of '.

E3   MORPHOLOGY

E3.1   MORPHS

E3.11 The smallest element of language which conveys a distinct and independent detail or unit of meaningful information for the understanding of an utterance is called a *morph*. Every word contains a basic morph which carries the fundamental meaning of the word, the meaning which is given in dictionary or lexicon. This is the *lexical morph or lexal*[39]. Some words consist only in this single morph — these are usually simple connectives such as conjuctions (καί, γάρ, etc.), or prepositions (ἐν, εἰς, πρό, etc.) or adverbs (ἀεί, εὖ, νῦν, οὐ, πάλιν, and so forth). Most words contain one or more other morphs which convey grammatical information about the word in its particular use in a given sentence — number, gender and case in an adjective; tense, aspect, voice, mode, etc. in a verb. These morphs are therefore called *grammatical morphs*.

E3.12 A lexal (lexical morph) always consists of phonemes, and may contain one phoneme or several. If it is capable of standing as a word on its own, a lexal is called a *free morph*. If it must always have another morph attached to it in order to form a complete word, it is called a *bound morph*. Thus ἐν, "in", is a free morph because it is a word on its own, though it can join with other morphs in forming words: ἐντός, "within", ἔνειμι, "I am in", etc. The lexal of a noun, adjective or verb is always (exceptions are negligible) a bound morph because such words cannot exist without grammatical morphs attached to them. Thus λύομεν consists of three morphs, λυ-ο-μεν, and the lexal λυ- cannot exist as a separate word on its own.

E3.13 Grammatical morphs can never be free morphs, as they must be attached to a word to have meaning. In fact, it is the *place* and *circumstances* of their attachment that give them their meaning. Thus -ε- is a grammatical morph, but the meaning that it has will depend upon *the word to which* it is attached (if added to the noun stem, e.g. κυρι-, its meaning is different from when it is used in a verb), and *where in a word* it is affixed (there are seven places in which it can be found in a verb, according to circumstances, in which it will mean respectively: past time, perfective aspect, lexal, passive voice, future time, neutral morph, or he/she/it). In this respect it is like a numeral — e.g., the numeral 2 can have an unlimited range of meaning above or below its basic meaning of "two", depending upon what other figures, and how many, are used with it in the complete number, and whether or not there is a decimal point in front of it.

E3.14 A grammatical morph can be a phoneme or group of phonemes added to the lexal (i.e., it can be an *additive morph* or *affix*), or it can be a *process of change* applied to another phoneme in the word (i.e., a *process morph*[40]) or even the *absence of a morph* from where a morph is expected to be, where that absence is itself significant (a *zero morph*, written as ∅).

E3.15 In English, "let" is a lexal and "-s" is an affix in "he lets me come". Compare this sentence with "he let me come". It is in fact the *absence* of an "-s" on "let", where one could have been expected, which indicates that the verb is past tense, not present tense. Thus the information that the verb is past tense is said to be indicated by the *zero morph* after "let" — the fact that there is nothing there when there could have been. In non-technical language this is simply to say that what is not there in a word can be as important in conveying meaning as what *is* there[41].

E3.16 Further, consider the pair "man/men" — it is not the phoneme "e" that indicates that "men" is plural ("pen", for example, is not plural), but the change made to the word; that is, the plural is indicated by the fact of the *process of change* from -a- in "man" to -e- in "men", i.e. by a *process morph*.

E3.17 Most Greek grammatical morphs are *affixes*, and may be added *in front of* the lexal (*prefixes*), *into* the lexal (*infixes*) or *after* it (*suffixes*). The augment added in front of a verb is a prefix. A durative morph added into a lexal is an infix — thus the lexal of σημαίνω (I indicate) is σημαν-, and the -ι- inserted into the present and imperfect tenses is a durative morph. All the morphs added after a lexal are suffixes.

E3.18 There are four common process morphs in Greek verbs: **(a)** the subjunctive morph, which consists of the lengthening of the neutral morph (#2.77; #4.43) — if there is not a neutral morph already in the form of a word (as for example in the first aorist) then it involves both adding it and lengthening it (additive morph plus process morph); **(b)** the lengthening of the neutral morph in the first person singular active (the *lengthening* of the neutral morph in the present stem λυο is what produces the form λύω and it indicates first person singular in the same way as the additive morph -μεν is what indicates first person plural in λύομεν); **(c)** the temporal augment (lengthening the initial vowel of a verb commencing with a vowel); **(d)** reduplication: the doubling of the first phoneme of a word, and then between the two of them inserting -ε- in the perfective active reduplication morph (as in λέλυμαι), or -ι- in the durative aspect reduplication morph (as in δίδωμι) — this involves both a process and the addition of phonemes to the word, so it also is a combined additive morph and process morph.

E3.19 A zero morph exists where an affix *could* occur, and where it is the absence of such a morph that is meaningful. For example, the form ἔλυσα is recognized as first person singular active of the aorist because in the first person singular middle an appropriate pronoun morph is added (giving the form ἐλυσάμην); and similarly there is an appropriate pronoun morph to add for all other persons and numbers of the active and middle voice. Thus it is the fact that *nothing* comes after the aspect morph -σα that indicates the person, number and voice of *this* form. Therefore the pronoun ending of this form is said to be the zero morph. Obviously there can only be *one* zero morph pronoun in a flexion; but if there is only the one, then the meaning can be quite clear. Thus: there is a zero morph pronoun also in the Third Conjugation aorist active, but here the absence of an additive pronoun morph indicates the *third* person singular (ἔγνω, with zero as its pronoun morph, means "he knew"; every other form of the flexion has an affix pronoun morph added to the stem -γνω-). The pluperfect active and the aorist passive of all conjugations are identical with the Third Conjugation aorist active in having a zero pronoun morph for the third person singular. The present imperative active comprises only the lexal and the neutral morph (λῦε) — the pronoun morph is a zero morph. Other zero morphs will also be found.

E3.2 ALLOMORPHS AND MORPHEMES

E3.21 A morph may have more than one phonemic shape. Thus in English "a" and "an" have exactly the same meaning and so are not different morphs (which, by definition, convey differences of meaning) — they are *phonemically* different versions of the same morph, one for use in front of vowels and the other for use in front of consonants. Similarly in Greek "out of" is ἐκ before consonants and ἐξ before vowels: these two forms convey no difference whatsoever in meaning, and therefore *they* are not two different morphs; they are two forms of the one morph. These two forms are called *alternative morphs* or *allomorphs* (from ἄλλος, "another of the same kind"). The whole group of allomorphs (morphs with identical meaning or function — in the case of ἐκ/ἐξ there are only the two) are said to constitute a *morpheme*, while a morpheme is said to be represented by its constituent allomorphs.

E3.22 Thus οὐ, οὐκ, οὐχ and μή are allomorphs and together constitute a morpheme (the Greek negative adverb) because they all have identical meaning and differ only in regard to the occasions when they are used. Similarly ἐν has the allomorphs ἐμ (in front of verbs beginning with a labial or a mu, as ἐμβαίνω, I embark) and ἐγ (pronounced "eng" — in front of verbs beginning with a palatal, as ἐγχρίω, I rub on). Many other prepositions have allomorphs: ἀπό, ἀπ, and ἀφ are the allomorphs of the one morpheme.

E3.23 The use of moveable nu means that numbers of verb forms have two allomorph forms: ἐστι and ἐστιν contain allomorphs (-τι and -τιν) as these two forms are identical in meaning. So also for all other moveable ν forms.

E3.24 Many other examples will be found: the syllabic and temporal augments (#E4.23) are allomorphs; the punctiliar morph σα has allomorphs (#E4.77); etc.

E3.25 For practical purposes it suffices to note that allomorphs of a morpheme are variant forms that a morph will take (without its meaning being affected) depending, usually, upon which phonemes precede or follow it.

E3.26 In this Course, morphs, allomorphs and morphemes are all referred to (for the sake of simplicity and clarity) as *morphs* unless some purpose is to be served by distinguishing between them.

E3.27 By definition, a morph is the smallest element of language which conveys a unit of information. But there are numbers of morphs which convey two (or more) units of information simultaneously and which are nonetheless a single morph because they cannot be further subdivided into sections which are able to be separately identified with each of those units of information. Thus a pronoun morph can indicate simultaneously person, number, and voice: -μεν indicates first person plural active voice while -μεθα indicates first person plural middle voice; and so on. Some pronouns also indicate past or non-past time: -ντο is past time, and -νται is non-past (present or future) time. Again, -κα- indicates perfective aspect, active voice. And so on. A morph which conveys multiple information is a *multiple morph* or *multimorph*; but in practice it is rarely necessary to distinguish multimorphs from other (simple) morphs, so the term is not often used.

E3.28 If a morph (as is often the case) only ever has the one form (i.e., there are no allomorphs), then that particular morpheme comprises only the one morph.

E3.3   ROOT, STEM AND ENDING

E3.31 The basic form from which a word is derived is called its *root*, for which often the symbol $\sqrt{}$ is used. The root may have the same form for different related words (cf. ἀρχ- in ἀρχή, ruling power; ἄρχων, ruler; ἄρχω, I rule), in which case it can be called the *word root* or *basic root*. It may have a different form in different related words (cf. λεγ- in λέγω, I say, and λογ- in λόγος, something said), in which case one would speak of the *verb root* and the *noun root* (or whatever the case may require). The verb root would be the original lexical morph from which all the forms of a verb have derived. The *root* may not appear in the verb itself, or it may only appear in certain flexions or forms. The form in which the root does occur in a verb (whether this form is identical with the verb root, or is modified) is called the *verb stem* — the *verb stem* thus corresponds with the *lexal*.

E3.32 In most First Conjugation verbs, the verb stem is seen in the present indicative active (e.g. the verb stem in λύω is λυ-, and this is also the root). In First Conjugation verbs with two aspect morphs (see #C5), the present tense contains a durative aspect morph, and the verb stem can best be seen in the future forms (thus the verb stem of μιμνήσκω, I remember, is μνη-, seen in the future μνήσω).

E3.33 The verb stem for Second and Third Conjugation verbs is seen in the aorist active. Thus the verb stem of λαμβάνω is λαβ-, seen in ἔλαβον; of γινώσκω is γνω-, seen in ἔγνων.

E3.34 The appropriate morphs are added to the verb stem to form the stem for each of the other tense flexions. Thus ἐλυσα- is the aorist active/middle stem of λύω; and ἐλυθη- is the aorist passive stem; and λελυκα- is the perfect active stem. Similarly βαιν- is the present stem from the root βα-, which has the verb stem βη- (as seen in the third aorist, ἔβην).

E3.35 To the *tense stem* is then added the required form of the pronoun suffix or other ending (see #E4.9). Sometimes the neutral morph may, for convenience, be treated as part of the ending (e.g. λυ-, stem; -ω, ending).

E3.36 Nouns of the First and Second Declensions add respectively the linking vowels -α- and -o- to their root (#D0.21-22) to form their stem when taking their numbercase suffixes: νεανίας consists of νεανι-, lexal; -α-, linking vowel of the First Declension; and -ς-, numbercase suffix. The linking vowel is not a separate morph, as it does not in any word convey on its own any distinct meaning. The noun therefore contains only two morphs, the lexal and the numbercase morph. The linking vowel may be taken with whichever of these is more convenient; it is usually taken in conjunction with the numbercase suffix, the two together constituting the ending for a noun: κύριος is thus κυρι-, root (word stem); -ος, ending.

E3.37 In summary: as a rough working rule of thumb it could be said that the stem is that part of a word which does not change in a given flexion, and the ending is the part of the word form that *changes* or *inflects* in that given flexion.

E3.38 The morphology of declined words is straightforward, and is covered adequately in Appendix D. The morphology of verbs is considerably more complex, and needs further explanation and summary here.

E4.   THE MORPHOLOGY OF THE GREEK VERB

E4.0   MORPH SLOTS OF THE VERB

E4.01 Each form of a verb is constructed upon the basis of that verb's lexal (which is, or is derived from, the root), to which are added the other morphs that are required in order to indicate each relevant detail of information about it in a given use.

E4.02 A Greek verb may have a preposition prefixed to it. A verb without a prefixed preposition is called a *simplex* verb (i.e., "single lexal", or, "simple lexal"); a verb which has a prefixed preposition is known as a *complex* verb or a *compound* verb (i.e., "combined lexals").

E4.03 A simplex verb contains a minimum of three morphs and (usually) a maximum of five morphs; a compound verb thus has a minimum of four morphs and (usually) a maximum of six morphs.

E4.04 The three morphs always to be found in a verb form are: the lexal, the aspect morph, and the ending. The ending will be: the pronoun, if the verb is indicative, subjunctive, optative or imperative mode; the infinitive morph, if it is infinitive mode; or the numbercase morph, if it is a participle. A compound verb will have a fourth morph: the prefixed preposition.

E4.05 These four morphs always occur in the fixed order: preposition, lexal, aspect, ending. Each position where a morph can occur is called a *slot*, and these morphs thus can be described as providing four slots for verb information. Each of these four slots will be filled by one particular morph out of a range of alternatives — a particular preposition (out of those available), a particular lexal, a particular aspect morph, a particular ending. Each of them is thus like a selection switch — it selects for that slot a particular meaning out of the range of alternatives available[42].

E4.06 These four morph slots provide the basic framework for the structure of the verb. In between them there are five other slots, four of which are like simple on/off switches — for these slots there is no range of alternatives. Rather, there is only one morph which can be placed into a given slot, and if that morph is present it switches the verb to have that particular meaning. These five are optional morph slots — they may or may not contain a morph. They are, in order: past time, reduplication, passive voice, future time, and specifier (whose function will be described in #E4.8). In the nature of the case these five morphs cannot all be used at the same time in a word. In fact, in normal use only one or perhaps two of these five morphs will be present simultaneously, though some rare forms could extend this to three of the five.

E4.07 The order for the nine slots (with framework slots in italics, and optional slots in standard type) is: *Preposition,* past, reduplication, *lexal,* passive, future, *aspect,* specifier, *ending*[43].

E4.08 The information jointly supplied by the morphs which occupy these slots will define the six variables for a particular form of a verb: the basic lexical meaning of the verb, and the person, number, tense (time and aspect), mode and voice of the verb in the given usage. To state each of these variables for a particular verb form is to *parse* it, and the five elements of grammatical information should be stated first in the order given here, followed by the lexical form and the meaning of the word. It will be noted that the first two grammatical variables mentioned (person and number) locate the form within its flexion, and the next three (tense, mode and voice) identify the flexion in question[44]. Thus λυσώμεθα is parsed as: 1st person plural, aorist subjunctive middle of λύω, I loose. Note that in regard to tense, the important factor for the Greeks was not so much the *time* when the action was placed by the verb, but the *type* of action that it was, i.e. its aspect, and therefore it is wise for the student to draw attention to this by putting these both in brackets after the name of the tense. Thus for ἐλύετε: 2nd person plural, imperfect (past time, durative aspect), indicative active of λύω, I loose.

E4.09 In parsing a participle, the information given will be: case, number, gender, tense (aspect), voice, followed by the fact that it is a participle and the lexical form and meaning of the word. Thus λυομένοις is parsed as: dative plural masculine/neuter of the present (durative) middle/passive participle of λύω, I loose; θέντος is parsed as: genitive singular masculine/ neuter of the aorist (punctiliar) active participle of τίθημι, I place.

E4.1   SLOT 1: THE PREPOSITION

E4.11 There are eighteen prepositions and a small number of other words which can fill this slot. These prepositions are the eighteen in #8.6. There can be two prepositions prefixed together to a verb (e.g. συν-ανά-κειμαι, I recline at table together with others). A double preposition before a verb is treated as a single morph[45].

E4.12 Large numbers of N.T. verbs are always simplex, but on the other hand compound verbs are common. The simplex form is not found in the N.T. for some verbs (most notably -βαίνω, -βιβάζω, -ἵημι, -τείνω, -τέμνω, -τρέπω, -τρίβω, -χέω, and -χύννω).

E4.13 A particular verb may be found with a large variety of prepositional prefixes: in the N.T., λαμβάνω is used in 13 different compounds with prepositions, ἔχω and φέρω are each used in 14 compounds, ἔρχομαι and -βαίνω in 15 compounds, τίθημι in 16 compounds, βάλλω in 17 compounds, ἄγω in 18 compounds, and ἵστημι in 19 compounds. Writers were free to coin new words by prefixing prepositions to verbs in new combinations, and numbers of such neologisms occur for the first time in literature in the pages of the N.T.[46]

E4.14 Some nouns, adjectives and adverbs are capable of being prefixed to appropriate verbs like prepositions: e.g. ὄχλος in ὀχλοποιέω, I gather together a crowd; ζωή in ζωοποιέω, I make alive; κακός in κακολογέω, I speak evil of; εὖ in εὐαγγελίζω, I announce good news; and so on. These prefixes can be compounded together with a preposition, as for example in συνεζωοποίησεν (Ephesians 2:5 and Colossians 2:13) — notice that in such a compound the augment comes *after* the preposition and *in front of* the other prefix being added. As these non-prepositional prefixes usually function as part of the lexal of the particular word (i.e., taking preposition, augment and reduplication in front of them), they are to be regarded as included within the lexal (Slot 4). However, where a non-prepositional prefix takes an augment *after* it, this prefix is to be viewed as filling Slot 1. Example: εὐαγγελίζω (εὐ + ἀγγελίζω), aorist εὐηγγέλισα.

E4.15 Both prepositions and also these other less common prefixes have *lexical* as distinct from *grammatical* meaning, so that a compound word contains two (or, as the case may be, three) lexals. The prefixed lexal interacts with the verb lexal to produce the lexical meaning of the compound — sometimes this is a recognizable combination of the lexal meanings, and sometimes it is a new meaning quite distinct from that of its components.

E4.16 As two prepositions prefixed to a verb do not retain their separate and distinct meaning but fuse together in meaning (in combination with the meaning of the verb's lexical morph), it is therefore appropriate (and most convenient) for two prefixed prepositions to be viewed as and treated as a single, combined prefix (though separately noted in analysis of the verb).

E4.17 Sometimes a preposition is so closely viewed as an integral part of a particular verb that its origin as a preposition is lost and it is treated as being a section of the verb's lexical morph. In consequence the augment is put in front of the erstwhile preposition: e.g., ἐκάθητο (Luke 18:35 and other passages), from κάθημαι, I sit; ἤφιεν (Mark 1:34) from ἄφίημι, I allow.

E4.18 On the other hand, sometimes a verb which begins with preposition-like phonemes is treated as a compound verb even though the phonemes are in fact really part of the verb's lexical morph. Thus throughout the N.T. and in koine Greek generally διακονέω is always treated as a compound verb (and augmented as in διηκόνει, Mark 1:31, etc.), although it is not.

E4.19 For prepositional allomorphs in front of a vowel, see #8.69; #E3.22.

E4.2   SLOT 2: PAST TIME

E4.21 There is only one morpheme which can fill this slot, and when it is present in a verb form it indicates that the action of that verb refers to past time. This morpheme, which is known as the *past time morph* or *augment*, is only found in the indicative flexions of a verb, as only the indicative mode can contain indications of time (except future participles/infinitive).

E4.22 The three tenses which are augmented are the imperfect, the aorist, and the pluperfect; but the pluperfect may be found without the augment as it can indicate its identity (and its past time) in another way (see #E4.81).

E4.23 The augment has a number of allomorphs, as set out here.

E4.24 Where a verb commences with a consonant, it indicates past time by adding the prefix ε-, called the *syllabic augment*. **This is the Syllabic Augment Rule.**

E4.25 Where a verb commences with a short vowel (including a vowel in a short diphthong), the augment for that verb consists of a process morph (called the *temporal augment*), the lengthening of that short vowel to the corresponding long vowel:

The vowel:	α	ε	ο	αι	αυ	οι
lengthens to:	η	η	ω	ῃ	ηυ	ῳ.

This is the Short Vowel Augment Rule, or the Temporal Augment Rule.

E4.26 A verb has a *zero morph augment* where it commences with a long vowel (η-, ι-, υ- or ω-) or long diphthong (ει-, ευ- or ου-; though some examples are found of verbs in ευ- lengthening to ηυ-).

E4.27 Some verbs which could have been expected to conform to the appropriate rule of the foregoing take, instead, a double augment, both an affix and the process augment[47]. Not many verbs do this, but many of those that do are very common ones. Thus: ἄγω reduplicates its first syllable and then takes the temporal augment, producing the form ἤγαγον as its aorist. Similarly the suppletive aorist of φέρω, with root ἐγκ- (i.e., from ἐνκ-) produces the form ἤνεγκον. ἀνοίγω has the form ἀνέῳξα as an aorist (as well as some other variants). θέλω and δύναμαι take first the syllabic augment and then the temporal augment to give the imperfect forms ἤθελον and ἠδυνάμην; some others also follow this pattern. (Cf. also #4.6.)

E4.3   SLOT 3: REDUPLICATION

E4.31 For the vast majority of verbs, there is only one morpheme which can fill this slot, and when it is present this morpheme indicates that the verb is perfective aspect. In addition, a limited number of specific verbs are able to take a morph in this slot which indicates durative aspect. Reduplication (of either type), being an aspect morph, is retained in all modes of a verb; contrast the past time morph, which can appear only in the indicative. Reduplication is a combination of process morph and affix. In its basic form it consists of: double the first consonant, and then separate these two consonants by -ε- (perfective reduplication) or -ι- (durative reduplication) as the case may be. But there are complications which derive from the phonemic characteristics of the first phoneme or phonemes of the verb. The following paragraphs describe *perfective reduplication*.

E4.32 Where a verb commences with the semi-vowel ρ-, the verb reduplicates with ἐρ- instead of ρε. Example: ῥίπτω → ἔρριφα.

E4.33 Where a verb commences with a single aspirated consonant or with an aspirated consonant followed by a liquid, then (cf. #E2.82) the verb will be reduplicated with the unaspirated voiceless equivalent of that initial consonant followed by the letter -ε-. Examples: φορέω → πεφόρηκα; χρίω → κέχρικα; θλίβω → τέθλιφα; θνήσκω → τέθνηκα.

E4.34 Where a verb commences with any single consonant other than an aspirate or ρ-, or where it commences with a stop consonant followed by a liquid, then that initial consonant is reduplicated with the phoneme -ε-. Examples: λύω → λέλυκα; νικάω → νενίκηκα; πνέω → πέπνευκα.

E4.35 Where a verb commences with two consonants the second of which is not a liquid, or with a double consonant, the reduplication takes the form of the syllabic augment, -ε- (which, being an aspect morph when functioning as reduplication, is retained in all modes of the perfect). Examples: πταίω → ἔπταικα; σκάπτω → ἔσκαφα; ζητέω → ἐζήτηκα; ψηφίζω → ἐψήφικα.

E4.36 Where a verb commences with a short vowel or a short diphthong (αι-, αυ-, οι-), the reduplication takes the form of the temporal augment (which, being an aspect morph when functioning as reduplication, is retained in all modes of the perfect). Examples: ἐλπίζω → ἤλπικα; αἰτέω → ᾔτηκα; αὐξάνω → ηὔξηκα; οἰκοδομέω → ᾠκοδόμηκα.

E4.37 When a verb commences with a long vowel (including ι- and υ-) or a long diphthong (ει-, ευ-, ου-), the verb has the zero morph for perfect reduplication morph. Examples: ὑστερέω → ὑστερηκα; εὑρίσκω → εὕρηκα; ἰάομαι → ἴαμαι; ἐξουθενέω → ἐξουθένημαι.

E4.38 There are verbs with morphemic allomorphs as reduplication which are exceptions to the above general statements. There are three main groups: **(a)** Certain verbs commencing with a short vowel reduplicate the entire first syllable in addition to taking the temporal augment on the original initial vowel. These include: ἐγείρω → ἐγήγερκα; ἐλαύνω → ἐλήλακα; ὀρύσσω → ὀρώρυχα; ἦλθον → ἐλήλυθα; ἐλέγχω → ἐλήλεγμαι; φέρω → ἐνήνοχα. **(b)** Certain verbs commencing with a short vowel take both the temporal augment and the syllabic augment as their reduplication. Thus: ἀνοίγω → ἀνέῳγα; ὁράω → ἑώρακα (sometimes also ἐόρακα occurs; never "ὤρακα"). **(c)** Certain verbs take -ο- as their central vowel in the perfect (either in addition to or in place of reduplication), usually using it to replace another vowel; and some others take -α-. See complete list, #C8.6.

E4.39 Fourteen N.T. verbs form their present/imperfect tenses by taking a durative allomorph in this slot, known as the *durative reduplication.* It is formed in the same manner as the perfective reduplication, but using -ι- rather than -ε- as the reduplication vowel. Examples:

stem δο-; present indicative active, δίδωμι; imperfect (past durative), ἐδίδουν;
stem θε-; present, τίθημι (not "θίθημι");
stem στα-; present ἵστημι (not "σίστημι"), imperfect, ἵστην.

These verbs are listed in #C2.1, #C3.1 and #C5.1.

E4.4   SLOT 4: THE LEXAL

E4.41 This slot will be filled in every verb form. There are one thousand morphemes in the N.T. which can fill this slot; i.e. there are one thousand verbs used in the N.T. (#C9.3) and this is the slot for the verb's lexical morph or *lexal.*

E4.42 Each verb's lexal is capable of having a number of different allomorphs as determined by phonemic (and other) factors: e.g., λαλε- has the allomorph λαλη- in front of a suffix commencing with a consonant. (These are covered in #E2.) Some verbs have individual lexal allomorphs in particular flexions: e.g. βαλ- (the lexal of βάλλω) has, by metathesis, #C2.96, βλα- in the perfect flexion, which then becomes βλη- by the Short Vowel Lengthening Rule (#E2.31). These allomorphs will be noted when encountered.

E4.43 Some verb lexals take infixes — affixes inserted into them within this slot. These infixes are durative morphs and are either inserted within the lexal (e.g. the -ι- of σημαίνω, I indicate, the lexal of which is σημαν-, #E3.17), or are attached immediately to the end of the lexal (e.g. the -σκ- of ἀρέσκω, I please, the lexal of which is ἀρε-), or both (e.g. the -ν- and -αν- of μανθάνω, I learn, the lexal of which is μαθ-). Each verb of the three Conjugations which takes a durative morph infix will be found listed by Conjugation in #C2.2-C2.5; #C3.2-C3.4; and #C5.2-C5.7.

E4.5   SLOT 5: PASSIVE VOICE

E4.51 There is only one morpheme which can fill this slot, and when it is present in a verb form it indicates that the verb is passive voice.

E4.52 Furthermore, when the following slot is not filled by a future morph, the presence of a passive morph also indicates that the verb form is aorist. That is, the passive morph is inherently aorist, but is "switched" to future passive if followed by the future morph.

E4.53 This morpheme is represented by these allomorphs:

VERB CATEGORY:	IN THE PARTICIPLE, SUBJUNCTIVE, OPTATIVE	IN OTHER MODES
Verbs with direct flexion passives (#C4.4):	-ε-	-η-
All other verbs, all Conjugations:	-θε-	-θη-

E4.54 In the subjunctive, the -ε- is in all verbs contracted with the subjunctive vowel which follows it. The contraction is marked by a circumflex.

E4.6 SLOT 6: FUTURE TIME

E4.61 There is only one morpheme which can fill this slot, and when it is present in a verb form it indicates that the action of the verb refers to future time.

E4.62 This morpheme is represented by these allomorphs:

VERB CATEGORY:	ALLOMORPH
After a liquid:	-ε-
In certain specific verbs in -ιζ- (#C8.88):	-ε-
In the two direct-flexion futures (#C4.2):	∅
In all other circumstances, all Conjugations:	-σ-

E4.63 The future morph always collocates with the neutral morph; that is, it always takes the neutral morph after it. For practical purposes this means the same as saying that it must have the equivalent present tense endings after it. (Note that -σ- followed by another vowel in a verb form would not be the future morph but the punctiliar morph of the aorist — see #E4.77.)

E4.64 When the future morph is -ε-, it always contracts with the neutral morph which follows it.

E4.7 SLOT 7: ASPECT

E4.71 This slot will be filled in every verb form, with these exceptions: in the aorist passive indicative and the perfect and pluperfect middle/passive of all Conjugations; in Third Conjugation verbs in the durative (present and imperfect) and in the third aorist. These thus have the zero morph.

E4.72 There are three morphemes which can fill this slot: the neutral morph, the punctiliar morph, and the perfective active morph. The aspect morph slot is thus a three-way switch, which has the positions "neutral", "punctiliar", and "perfective active".

E4.73 Each Greek verb possesses a "basic" aspect which is already inherent in its lexal and which can therefore be referred to as its *inherent aspect*. When the aspect "switch" is in the neutral position, the inherent aspect of the verb's lexal is allowed to flow through into the meaning of the verb form, unmodified or "unswitched" by the aspect morph. That is, the neutral morph has a neutral affect on the nature of the verb — a durative lexal plus the neutral morph leaves the aspect of the verb still durative, a punctiliar lexal plus the neutral morph leaves the aspect of the verb still punctiliar. When the aspect "switch" is in the punctiliar position, the aspect of the verb is "switched" to punctiliar (i.e., the action of the verb stated as completed, or viewed in its entirety). When the aspect "switch" is in the perfective position, the aspect of the verb is "switched" to perfective (i.e. the action of the verb is seen as completed and its effects continuing to the writer's time, or as initiating a new state of affairs that is continuing).

E4.74 The perfective morph is only used in the active voice, and thus it indicates voice as well as aspect, i.e. it is the perfective *active* morph, a multimorph. In the middle/passive flexion this slot is empty (i.e. has a zero morph) and perfective aspect is indicated by perfective reduplication alone (#E4.31).

E4.75 There is no durative morph for use in this aspect slot; if the verb is inherently punctiliar and a durative form is required, then either durative reduplication in -ι- will be added (#E4.39), or a durative infix will be inserted into the lexal slot itself (#E4.43).

E4.76 The neutral morpheme has these allomorphs:

CIRCUMSTANCES	ALLOMORPH
Form final, or before upsilon or a nasal:	-o-
In the indicative, before a morph commencing with -ε-:	∅
In the optative:	-o-
In other circumstances:	-ε-

For the subjunctive, -o- lengthens to -ω- and -ε- to -η-.

E4.77 The punctiliar morpheme has these allomorphs:

CIRCUMSTANCES	BEFORE: A CONSONANT	A VOWEL
Lexals with -ε- plus a liquid (see below):	-ι.α-	-ι.∅-
Lexals with a liquid that does not come after -ε-:	-α-	∅
In δίδωμι, τίθημι and -ἵημι:	-κα-	-κ-
For all other lexals:	-σα-	-σ-

The apparent adding of -ι- to lexals with -ε- plus a liquid is in fact the occurrence of compensatory lengthening upon the loss of the sigma of the full punctiliar morph (see #E2.43).

E4.78 The perfective active morpheme has these allomorphs:

CIRCUMSTANCES	BEFORE: INFINITIVE	A CONSONANT	A VOWEL
Lexals with labial or palatal stem:	Aspiration + ε	Aspiration + α	Aspiration
Direct flexion perfects (#C4.3):	-ε-	-α-	∅
For all other lexals:	-κε-	-κα-	-κ-

For labial or palatal plus -κ- becoming the equivalent aspirate, see #E2.61, E2.62.

E4.79 The subjunctive is a process morph, the lengthening of the neutral morph. Therefore in any form in which the neutral morph would not otherwise be found, then in the formation of the subjunctive mode it must of necessity be inserted, so that it *can* be lengthened. Thus the punctiliar morph and the (lengthened) neutral morph will occur together in the aorist subjunctive active and middle flexions.

E4.8   SLOT 8: THE SPECIFIER

E4.81 Certain other information may need to be specified about a verb, and if so it will be specified here, which is, as it were, the "last chance" before the ending of the word is added.

E4.82 The information which can be specified here is that the verb form is one of the following:

E4.83 Pluperfect tense active: insert -$\varepsilon\iota$-. (As *this* specifies the pluperfect tense, the augment in Slot 2 is not absolutely essential for the purpose of indicating past time for a pluperfect active form, and Greek writers often chose to omit it.)

E4.84 A perfect active participle: insert-$\upsilon\iota\alpha$- in feminine gender flexion
                                    -$o\varsigma$ in nominative singular masc/neuter
                                    -$o\tau$- otherwise.

E4.85 An active participle other than the perfect: insert -$\nu\tau$-, which becomes -ι- in front of -ς or -σ, by phonemic modification (see #E2.42). (The aorist passive participle also uses this specifier.)

E4.86 A middle participle: insert -$\mu\varepsilon\nu$-. (The future passive participle also uses this specifier, as it forms the passive by inserting the passive morph into the future middle forms.)

E4.87 Middle voice of the imperative or infinitive mode: insert -$\sigma\theta$-. (This specifier has been lost from the second person singular imperative forms, where the ending -σo appears to have dislodged it, -$\sigma\theta\sigma o$ not being easy to pronounce.)

E4.88 Optative mode: insert -$\iota\eta$- in the aorist passive, -ι- otherwise, forming a diphthong with whichever vowel precedes it in the word.

E4.89 Each of these specifier morphs is mutually exclusive — by their nature, only one of them will be used in any given word. Each of them thus functions as an "on/off switch", and when the particular morph is present it "switches" the word form to the particular tense, mode and voice specified.

E4.9   SLOT 9: ENDING

E4.91 This slot will be filled in every verb form. (If the slot is not overtly filled, the form will be considered to have a zero morph.)

E4.92 The slot will be filled with one of three possible endings:
    For the participle: the numbercase morph;
    For the infinitive: the infinitive morph;
    For all other modes: the pronoun morph.

E4.93 The numbercase morph used in a form will be the appropriate morph from the participle declension paradigms, #D5.

E4.94 The infinitive morpheme has three allomorphs:

When added to the neutral morph: -σεν (which then loses its -σ by syncopation, and the -ε contracts with the vowel preceding it);

When added to any other vowel: -ναι;

When added to a consonant: -αι.

For detailed rules, see #C6.14.

E4.95 The pronoun morph has the range of forms and allomorphs as set out in the paradigms of Appendix C. Pronouns normally also indicate voice, and some pronoun morphs indicate past time or non-past time as well (cf. *multimorphs*, #E3.27).

E5.   MORPHOLOGICAL ANALYSIS OF THE GREEK VERB FORM

E5.1 The identifying of the morphs of any given form of a Greek verb is called *morphological analysis* or *morphologizing*. It enables the reader to obtain the information-input of each morph and thus, by interrelating them, to understand the total significance of the word.

E5.2 The most helpful way of understanding the process of morphological analysis is to work one's way through a number of examples to verify for oneself what is being done. The following list (#E5.6) of more than 50 examples provides an opportunity for this.

E5.3 Phonemic modification which has affected the morphology needs to be "unscrambled" — e.g., where there has been amalgamation, when -ι- has gone subscript, when contraction or elision has occurred. This is indicated in these examples, as required, by placing the contracted or elided vowel in brackets.

E5.4 Where there is morphemic lengthening (i.e. lengthening which is a process morph, and conveys meaning), then in the case of the subjunctive the neutral morph as lengthened is given in the aspect slot column, and in other cases the letter L is placed in the column of the slot for which the lengthening is morphemically significant.

E5.5 The first one of these examples is the only N.T. seven-morph verb which I have been able to find, and I believe it is the only one in the N.T. It occurs (in some manuscripts only) in Mark 15:10. (If you come across any other seven-morph verbs, I would be glad to learn of them.) The other examples are given in N.T. order.

E5.6 Work your way through the following examples. First of all, cover up the page except for the reference and word columns and do your own analysis of the verb forms into the nine morphological slots; then uncover the page and check your work against the worked examples.

REFERENCE	VERB FORM	1 PREP	2 PAST	3 REDUP	4 LEXAL	5 PASS	6 FUT	7 ASP	8 SPEC	9 ENDING
Mk 15:10	παρεδεδώκεισαν	παρ(α)	ε	δε	δω			κ(α)	ει	σαν
Mt 5:17	καταλῦσαι	κατα			λυ			σ(α)		αι
Mt 5:32	ἀπολελυμένην	ἀπο		λε	λυ			∅	μεν	ην
Mt 5:33	ἀποδώσεις	ἀπο			δω		σ	ε		ις
Mt 7:7	ἀνοιγήσετε	ἀν(α)			οιγ	η	σ	ε		τε
Mt 7:22	ἐξεβάλομεν	ἐξ	ε		βαλ			ο		μεν
Mt 17:11	ἀποκαταστήσει	ἀποκατα			στη		σ	ε		ι
Mt 17:22	παραδίδοσθαι	παρα		δι	δο			∅	σθ	αι
Mt 18:28	ἀπόδος	ἀπο			δο			∅		ς
Mk 3:11	προσέπιπτον	προσ	ε	πι	πτ			ο		ν
Mk 4:34	ἐπέλυεν	ἐπ(ι)	ε		λυ			(ε)		εν
Mk 8:3	ἐκλυθήσονται	ἐκ			λυ	θη	σ	ο		νται
Mk 8:6	παρέθηκαν	παρ(α)	ε		θη			κα		ν
Mk 8:7	παρατιθέναι	παρα		τι	θε			∅		ναι
Mk 8:9	ἀπέλυσεν	ἀπ(ο)	ε		λυ			σ(α)		εν
Mk 9:1	ἑστηκότων			ἑ	στη			κ(α)	οτ	ων
Mk 9:6	ἤδει			ἤ	ιδ			∅	ει	∅
Mk 9:42	βέβληται			βε	βλη			∅		ται
Mk 10:7	καταλείψει	κατα			λειπ		σ	ε		ι
Mk 10:21	ἠγάπησεν		L		ἀγαπη			σ(α)		εν
Mk 10:33	παραδοθήσεται	παρα			δο	θη	σ	ε		ται
Mk 10:33	κατακρινοῦσιν	κατα			κριν		(ε)	ο		υσιν
Mk 10:34	ἐμπαίξουσιν	ἐμ			παιζ		σ	ο		υσιν
Mk 10:48	ἐπετίμων	ἐπ(ι)	ε		τιμ(α)			(ο)		ν
Mk 12:4	ἀπέστειλεν	ἀπ(ο)	ε		στε.λ			ι.(σα)		εν
Mk 12:25	ἀνάστωσιν	ἀνα			στ(α)			ω		σιν
Mk 12:33	ἀγαπᾶν				ἀγαπ(α)			(ε)		(ε)ν
Mk 12:36	θῶ				θ(ε)			ω		∅
Mk 14:58	καταλύσω	κατα			λυ		σ	ο		L
Lk 1:38	γένοιτο				γεν			ο	ι	το
Lk 9:12	καταλύσωσιν	κατα			λυ			σ(α)/ω		σιν
Lk 14:14	ἀνταποδοθήσεται	ἀνταπο			δο	θη	σ	ε		ται
Lk 22:68	ἀποκριθῆτε	ἀπο			κρι	θ(ε)		η		τε
Lk 23:18	ἀπόλυσον	ἀπο			λυ			σ(α)		ον
Jn 14:28	ἠγάπατε		L		ἀγαπ(α)			(ε)		τε
Jn 15:13	θῇ				θ(ε)			η		ι
Jn 19:26	παρεστῶτα	παρ(α)	ε		στ(α)			(ο)τ		α
Ac 3:13	ἀπολύειν	ἀπο			λυ			(ε)		(ε)ν
Ac 5:8	ἀπόδοσθε	ἀπο			δο			∅		σθε
Ac 5:36	διελύθησαν	δι(α)	ε		λυ	θη		∅		σαν
Ac 8:7	παραλελυμένοι	παρα		λε	λυ			∅	μεν	οι
Ac 15:26	παραδεδωκόσι	παρα		δε	δω			κ(α)	ο(τ)	σι
Ac 15:30	ἀποθέντες	ἀπο			θε			∅	ντ	ες
Ac 16:36	ἀπέσταλκαν	ἀπ(ο)			σταλ		ε	κα		ν
Ac 16:36	ἀπολυθῆτε	ἀπο			λυ	θ(ε)		η		τε
Ac 26:32	ἀπολελύσθαι	ἀπο		λε	λυ			∅	σθ	αι
Ac 26:32	ἐπεκέκλητο	ἐπ(ι)	ε	κε	κλη			∅		το
Ac 28:25	ἀπελύοντο	ἀπ(ο)	ε		λυ			ο		ντο

I C 7:3	ἀποδιδότω	ἀπο		δι	δο		∅	τω
II C 5:1	καταλυθῇ	κατα			λυ	θ(ε)	η	ι
II C 7:15	ἀναμιμνησκομένου	ἀνα		μι	μνησκ		ο μεν	ου
Gal 2:18	κατέλυσα	κατ(α)	ε		λυ		σα	∅
Eph 1:6	ἠγαπημένῳ			L	ἀγαπη		∅ μεν	ῳ
Heb 3:5	λαληθησομένων				λαλη	θη σ	ο μεν	ων
I P 4:19	παρατιθέσθωσαν	παρα		τι	θε		∅ σθ	ωσαν
I J 4:10	ἠγαπήκαμεν			L	ἀγαπη		κα	μεν
Jude 2	πληθυνθείη				πληθυν θε		∅ ιη	∅

E6.   ACCENTS

E6.1   GENERAL PRINCIPLES

E6.11 A brief acquaintance with the basic principles of accentuation can enable the student to profit from time to time from the information they provide. A fuller treatment will be found in any advanced Greek grammar.

E6.12 The accent was not intended to mark stress or emphasis (unlike English), but tone. The acute accent (´) marked a rising tone, the grave accent (`) a falling tone, and the circumflex (ˆ or ˜) a rising and then falling tone (a combination of acute and grave).

E6.13 Under normal circumstances, every Greek word carries an accent, except for clitics (#E6.3), which function as part of an adjoining word.

E6.14 The position of an accent is determined in relation to the end of a word. Whereabouts on a word that an accent can stand will depend upon whether the last vowel of the word is short or long. Short vowels (including diphthongs) are: α, ι, and υ (when short); αι and οι when final (except in the optative); ε and ο (always). Long vowels are: α, ι, and υ (when long); η, ω, and other diphthongs.

E6.15 No accent can be placed earlier in a word than the third last syllable, or the second last syllable if the last vowel is long.

E6.16 A circumflex can stand only on a diphthong or a long vowel (thus indicating it *is* long); an acute or grave can stand on any vowel or diphthong, long or short.

E6.17 When the last vowel of a word is short and the second last vowel is long, the latter *must* carry a circumflex. Thus: λῦε, ὦδε, λῦσαι, αἶρε, ἦραν, λῦσον; but ὥρα, ἄρας, δύο, ἄγε.

E6.2   ACCENT AND POSITION

When the accent falls on:	If last vowel is long:	If last vowel is short:
E6.21 The last vowel,	it may be ˜ or ´ (`)	it must be ´ (`)
E6.22 Short 2nd last vowel,	it must be ´	it must be ´
E6.23 Long 2nd last vowel,	it must be ´	it must be ˜ (#E6.17)
E6.24 The third last vowel,	(syllable cannot have it)	it must be ´

Exception: πόλεως πόλεων.

E6.25 When the acute (´) falls on the last syllable of a word, if that word is followed by another accented word without any punctuation intervening, the acute changes to the grave (`). Thus: λέγω γὰρ ὑμῖν (L5/10), but εἰμὶ γάρ. (L8/9); and: τὸν νόμον (L4/18), but τόν ποτε (see #E6.32; L4/10). Exception: interrogative τίς, τί (who, what) does not change its acute to a grave. The only time a grave accent is written is when it replaces an acute in accordance with this rule; but a grave accent is regarded as notionally present upon every vowel not bearing another accent.

E6.26 When contraction occurs, if the first of the contracting vowels carried an acute, then this ´ combines with the notional ` on the second of the contracting vowels to form ^ (i.e. ˜, a circumflex) on the contracted vowel. Thus: λαλέετε contracts to λαλεῖτε, and κρινέω to κρινῶ (the future active — only distinguishable by this accent from κρίνω, the present active).

E6.27 Nouns and adjectives have *constant accents*: in all the various cases the accent remains upon the same syllable as in the nominative singular, unless it is pulled towards the end of the word by a long vowel or affected by contraction. Thus: ἄνθρωπος, ἄνθρωπον, but ἀνθρώπων (because of #E6.24); καρδία, καρδίαις, but καρδιῶν (contraction of καρδιάων, in accordance with #E6.26).

E6.28 Verbs have *regressive accents*: the accent goes back as early in the word as the rules allow. Thus: λύω, ἐλύομεν, ἔλυον, ἀπόλυσον, ἄπαγε. But the accent cannot go back beyond an augment or reduplication: ἦλθον and ἐξῆλθον (not "ἔξηλθον"); ἦρκεν and ἐπῆρκεν (not "ἔπηρκεν"). Exceptions to the regressive accent rule: the infinitive, participle, imperative.

E6.3 CLITICS

E6.31 A *proclitic* is a monosyllable without an accent which is closely associated with the word which follows it. Proclitics are: ὁ, ἡ, οἱ, αἱ, εἰς, ἐκ, ἐξ, ἐν, οὐ, οὐκ, οὐχ, εἰ, ὡς. A proclitic is accented when it is followed by an enclitic.

E6.32 An *enclitic* is a word which is pronounced as if it were a part of the word which precedes it (with the consequence that an acute on the final vowel of that word does not become a grave), and which throws its accent back on to that word (which may therefore have two accents, but cannot have two acutes on successive syllables). Enclitics are: τε, με, μου, μοι, σε, σου, σοι, indefinite τις (all forms), the present flexion of εἰμι (except εἶ), indefinite adverbs (#9.12). Thus: ἀγαπητός μου, and παῖς μου (L4/19); σῶσόν με (L4/1); πίστις σου, and σέσωκέν με (L4/21); ὁ κύριός μου καὶ ὁ θεός μου (L3/27).

E6.33 A dissyllabic enclitic retains its accent (on the second syllable) in some circumstances.

E6.34 When an enclitic is emphatic it will be accented. Thus: ὁ προφήτης εἶ σύ; Οὔ. (L3/16).

APPENDIX F

FOOTNOTES AND BIBLIOGRAPHY

The bibliography of books referred to in these footnotes is as follows:

ALLEN W S, 1968/1981: Vox Graeca — The Pronunciation of Classical Greek (Cambridge University Press)

ARNDT & GINGRICH, 1957- : A Greek-English Lexicon of the NT (University of Chicago)

BILLOWS F L, 1961: The Techniques of Language Teaching (Longmans, London)

BLACK Max, 1968: The Labyrinth of Language (Pall Mall Press, London)

BLASS-DEBRUNNER-FUNK, 1964/74: A Greek Grammar of the NT (University of Chicago)

BRUCE F F, 1950/1971: The Books & The Parchments (Pickering and Inglis, London)

CATFORD J C, 1965: A Linguistic Theory of Translation (Oxford University Press)

COWGILL W, 1961: *A Search for Universals in Indo-European Diachronic Morphology* (Article in Greenberg.)

DAVIS W H, 1923: Beginner's Grammar of the Greek NT (Harper and Row, New York)

DIAMOND A S, 1959: The History & Origin of Language (Methuen, London)

FRIES C C, 1962: Linguistics & Reading (Holt, Rinehart & Winston, New York)

FRIES C C, 1945: Teaching & Learning English (University of Michigan, Ann Arbor)

GOODWIN W W, 1879/1959: A Greek Grammar (Macmillan and Co., London)

GREENBERG J H (Ed), 1963/1966: Universals of Language (MIT, Cambridge USA)

HARRIS Z S, 1944: *Yokuts Structure & Newmans's Grammar* (IJAL 10, pp 196-211)

HOCKETT C F, 1958: A Course in Modern Linguistics (Macmillan, New York)

JOOS M (Ed), 1957/68: Readings in Linguistics I (University of Chicago)

KUBO S, 1975/1978: A Reader's Greek-English Lexicon of the NT (Andrews University Press/Zondervan, Grand Rapids)

LADO R, 1957: Linguistics Across Cultures — Applied Linguistics For Language Teachers (University of Michigan, Ann Arbor)

LIDDELL & SCOTT (Var. Edns): Greek-English Lexicon (Clarendon Press, Oxford)

LYONS J, 1968: Introduction to Theoretical Linguistics (Cambridge University Press)

LOUNSBURY F G, 1953: *The Method of Descriptive Morphology* (Article in Joos)

McKAY K L, 1977: Greek Grammar For Students (Aust. National University, Canberra)

METZGER B M, 1964/1968: The Text of the NT (Clarendon Press, Oxford)

MOULTON J H, 1908/1968: A Grammar of NT Greek I & II (T&T Clark, Edinburgh)

MUSSIES G, 1971: The Morphology of Koine Greek As Used in The Apocalypse of St. John (E J Brill, Leiden, Netherlands)

NIDA E A, 1950: Learning a Foreign Language (National Council of the Churches of Christ in the USA, New York)

NIDA E A, 1946/1967: Morphology — the Descriptive Analysis of Words (University of Michigan Press, Ann Arbor)

PALMER F, 1971: Grammar (Penguin Books, Harmondsworth, UK)

RIENECKER F, 1976-1981: A Linguistic Key to the Greek NT (Zondervan, Grand Rapids)

ROBERTS A, 1888: Greek The Language of Christ and His Apostles

ROBERTSON A T, 1914/1934/?: A Grammar of the GNT in the Light of Historical Research (Broadman, Nashville)

ROBERTSON A T & DAVIS W H, 1908/1977: A New Short Grammar of the Greek NT (Harper & Brothers/Baker Book House, Grand Rapids)

SEVENSTER J N, 1968: Do You Know Greek? (E J Brill, Leiden, Netherlands)

TURNER N, 1963: A Grammar of NT Greek Vol III Syntax (T & T Clark, Edinburgh)

ZERWICK M, 1963/1979: Biblical Greek (Pontificio Istituto Biblico, Rome, Italy)

ZERWICK M & GROSVENOR M, 1974/80: An Analysis of the Greek NT (Pontificio Istituto Biblico, Rome, Italy)

1 **PREFACE:** "We must learn that each word in every language has its own special meaning and that we cannot assume that two languages ever fully agree in any detail . . . We are entirely too accustomed to thinking of words as having precise points of meaning, while we should regard them as having areas of meaning. Some areas are very extensive and others very restricted, but all are areas, even though their limits may be difficult to define . . . In certain instances it is very valuable to be able to define such areas of meaning in terms of a central meaning and several peripheral meanings . . . Furthermore, words only have meanings in terms of the environments in which they occur . . . The person who memorizes words but does not know when and how to use them is in a hopeless predicament." (Nida, *Learning A Foreign Language*, pp. 213, 216-7, 227, 228.) "The 'same meaning' or 'meaning transference' fallacy is seen in the view that translation is a 'transcoding' process, a well-known example being Weaver's remark: 'When I look at an article in Russian, I say: "This is really written in English, but it has been coded in some strange symbols. I will now proceed to decode".' This implies either that there is a one-to-one relationship between English and Russian grammatical/lexical items and their contextual meanings, or that there is some pre-existent 'message' with an independent meaning of its own which can be presented or expounded now in one 'code' (Russian), now in another 'code' (English). But this is to ignore the fact that each 'code' (i.e., each language) carries with it its own particular meaning, since meaning . . . is a property of a language." (Catford, p. 41.) "Words are understood, not in isolation, but in interrelationship with other words." (Black, p. 40.) "It is also important to note that although certain meanings of a word in one language are sometimes translatable into a word in another language there are very few if any words in two languages that are the same for all their meanings." (Lado, pp. 84-85; similarly pp. 77-78.) "One must let the foreign words have their own meanings and let them begin to 'ring the bell' in one's thoughts." (Nida, *Learning A Foreign Language*, p. 26.)

2 **#1.12:** "There are . . . wide differences between the various dialects of Greek, and between the various periods of ancient and modern Greek . . . Classical Attic (is) the dialect used in Athens in the classical period, the fifth and fourth centuries BC. Attic was the dialect in which most of the literature of the classical period was written, and the one which most influenced the Greek of subsequent ages . . . Other writers of this period include Herodotus, who wrote in Ionic, a dialect closely related to Attic, and Pindar, who used a conventionalised Doric. At earlier periods Alcaeus and Sappho wrote in Aeolic, while Homer (c. 1000 BC) used the traditional epic dialect, an early form of Ionic mixed with some Aeolic and other features." (McKay, p. 1.) "Much remains to be learned about the primitive Greek before Homer. The Mycenaean Age from 1500 to 1000 BC covers this period in which the obscure origin of the Greek language takes root in the Cretan civilization. The age of the Dialects runs from 1000 BC to 300 BC, from Homer to Alexander's conquest of the oriental world and a bit beyond. The age of the κοινή is roughly from 300 BC after Alexander's death to 330 AD, the time when the seat of government was set up in Constantinople instead of Rome. During this period Greek was . . . the language of the Mediterranean world, a language common (κοινή) to all instead of just a dialect. From 330 to 1453 (the year when the Turks captured Constantinople) may be called Byzantine Greek. Modern Greek runs from 1453 to the present day." (Robertson, *Short G.*, p. 8.)

3 **#1.13:** It is important to recognize the extent to which Greek was known and used in the first century AD. "The κοινή was a world speech and meant to be understood by merchants, travellers, statesmen, soldiers all over the Graeco-Roman world . . . It was a providential circumstance that Paul could carry the message of Christ in one language and be understood wherever he went. Those who held on to their local language as in Lycaonia, Palestine, Egypt, Italy, would know Greek. So Paul wrote to the church in Rome in Greek . . . Christianity arose in its very century when the κοινή reached its height as a world speech." (Robertson, *Short G.*, pp. 13-14.) It would be very surprising in these circumstances if Jesus himself, who spent much of his ministry in "Galilee of the Gentiles" (Matthew 4:15), did not have frequent occasion to speak in Greek. Mark for example tells (7:26) of the woman who was Syrophoenician by race and a Greek i.e. whose language and culture was Greek. It would thus be in this language that she conversed with Jesus — there is no point in Mark drawing attention to her being a "Hellenis" if the subsequent conversation took place in Aramaic. Similarly, we have no grounds for believing that Pilate spoke Aramaic, or that Jesus spoke Latin; when therefore in the Passion narratives we have the record of them conversing, we may take it that the language used was Greek. The most detailed examination of the evidence for recognizing that Jesus frequently taught in Greek has been made in a series of related books by Alexander Roberts, notably in *Greek The Language of Christ and His Apostles* (1888). A very useful recent consideration of this question is *Do You Know Greek?* by J. N. Sevenster (1968).

4 **#1.21** It is something of an oversimplification to say that there were once twenty-eight letters in the Greek alphabet (though it will serve as a generalization). The position was actually much more fluid, and more complex. "The traditional Greek ascription of their alphabet to the Phoenicians is confirmed by the actual facts of the case. The earliest form of the Greek alphabet *is* the Phoenician alphabet, with a few adaptations to the necessities of the Greek language, which was a totally different language from the Semitic tongue of the Phoenicians. The most important of these adaptations was the use of five Phoenician letters . . . to indicate Greek vowels. All twenty-two letters of the Phoenician alphabet represented consonants", whereas the representation of vowels was essential for writing Greek. So the Greeks used: aleph as alpha, hê as epsilon, yôd as iota, and ayin as omicron. One Phoenician letter, sadê (an "*s*" sound) was not taken over at all (except as a numeral, 900). "There were numerous varieties of the Greek alphabet in use all over the Greek world, from Asia Minor to Marseilles. One of these was the 'West Greek' alphabet, from which the Roman alphabet was derived through Etruscan intermediation. Another was the 'East Greek' or 'Ionic' alphabet . . . One of the chief differences between the West Greek and the Ionic alphabet is that in the former H represents an aspirate sound while in the latter (since most of the Ionic Greeks dropped their aitches) there was no need of a letter to indicate the aspirate sound, and so H (*eta*) was used to represent a long open *e* sound, similar to the *ea* in English *bear*. In this as in some other respects, such as its retention of the letters *digamma* (whence F) and *koppa* (whence Q), and its giving to X the value of *ks* and not *kh*, the West Greek alphabet, along with the Roman alphabet, was nearer to the original Greek alphabet than the Ionic alphabet was." (Bruce, p. 18) The Ionians gave to one Phoenician letter, *samek* (an "*s*" sound — the Phoenician alphabet contained three varieties of *s*) the value of *ks*, as ξ. They also added at the end of the Phoenician alphabet the five further letters υ, φ, χ, ψ and ω, and they dropped the letters digamma and koppa. However, these two letters were retained as numerals, and the letter *san* (or *sam* or *sampi* — the Phoenician sadê), which apparently had never been part of any actual Greek alphabet, was also pressed into service for this purpose: "The three letters omitted from the Ionic Greek alphabet were retained in use to denote certain numerals, *digamma* to denote 6, *san* or *sampi* to denote 900 (for which purpose it was placed after *omega*, the sign for 800), and *koppa* to denote 90. Twenty-seven letters instead of the normal twenty-four of the Ionic alphabet were required to denote the numerals, the units from 1 to 9, the tens from 10 to 90, and the hundreds from 100 to 900; hence these three letters, otherwise jettisoned, were still used in this way." (Bruce, p. 18.) One other complication is that a twenty-eighth letter, *stigma* (representing στ and written as a combination of final ς plus τ without the vertical stroke) was used as the sign for the numeral 6 in place of the *digamma* sign (which had the appearance of an italic capital *F*).

5 **#1.21:** The Ionic alphabet won out at Athens, and then throughout all Greece. "Only since 403 BC has the Greek alphabet regularly had 24 letters . . . (This) was the result of a law passed (403 BC) in Attica prescribing the use of the Ionic alphabet in the schools." (Robertson, *Short G.*, pp. 23-24.) The alphabet changes occurred in the archonship of Euclides (Moulton II, p. 43).

6 **#1.22:** "In antiquity two styles of Greek handwriting were in general use. The cursive or 'running' hand, which could be written rapidly, was employed for non-literary, everyday documents, such as letters, accounts, receipts, petitions, deeds, and the like. Contractions and abbreviations of frequently recurring words (such as the definite article and certain prepositions) were common. Literary works, on the other hand, were written in a more formal style of handwriting, called uncials. This 'book-hand' was characterized by more deliberate and carefully executed letters, each one separate from the others, somewhat like our capital letters. Some of the most beautiful specimens of Greek handwriting are certain classical and Biblical manuscripts dating from the third to the sixth century. In the course of time, however, the style of the book-hand began to deteriorate, and uncials became thick and clumsy. Then, about the beginning of the ninth century, a reform in handwriting was initiated, and a script of smaller letters in a running hand, called minuscules, was created for the production of books. This modified form of the cursive script became popular at once throughout the Greek world, though some liturgical books continued for one or two centuries to be written in uncial script. Thus manuscripts fall into two rather well-defined groups, the earlier being written in uncial letters . . . and the later in minuscules." (Metzger, pp. 8-10.)

7 **#1.23:** "In many respects it is not certain what exactly was the Ancient Greek pronunciation. The pronunciation of Ancient Greek varied with time and place. For the classical period we can only approximate the true pronunciation. The pronunciation of Greek in the κοινή period is a difficult

problem" (Robertson, *Short G.*, p. 28.) Two significant disagreements at the present time about the pronunciation of ancient Greek centre around ω and ζ. Some Greek scholars advocate pronouncing ω as "*or*" as in *saw* or *sore*; others prefer the pronunciation, long "*o*" as in *so* or *show*. Allen (*Vox Graeca — The Pronunciation of Classical Greek*, pp. 71ff.), while himself advocating the *saw* pronunciation, shows that the vowel had had variant pronunciations in the development of the language prior to and in the Classical period. The two pronunciations (in *saw* and *so*) both have some claim to acceptance, though the evidence indicates that *aw* in *saw* is more representative of the ancient pronunciation. However, this is not the final consideration for us today, where our primary aim is swift recognition of pronunciation from seeing the word, and clear differentiation between sounds. The case for the "*so*" pronunciation is:

(a) The history of the development of the language indicates that this is a legitimate alternative pronunciation.

(b) In English the "*aw*" or "*or*" sound always needs to be represented by two letters (or more, as in *more*), whereas the long "*o*" sound, while frequently represented by two letters (as in *foe, low, boat,* etc.), is also frequently represented by one letter, *o* (as in *bogus, coincidence, donate, go, only, told,* etc. etc.). Therefore, of the two alternatives, this sound is the more appropriate for the single letter ω of Greek.

(c) The Greek combination -oρ- can be readily — and legitimately — pronounced as "*or*" in the reading of Greek (as for example in ὀρφανός, orphan; Δορκάς, Dorcas; Κορβᾶν, Corban; μορφή. form; πορνεία, immorality; etc.). If ω is also pronounced in the same way, then the sound "*or*" can represent both ω and oρ, and this has departed from the phonemic goal for the pronunciation system.

(d) There is no other Greek letter or combination of letters which can be pronounced "*o*" as in "*so*", so this pronunciation for ω is never ambiguous or unclear.

As there are no identifiable advantages for today in pronouncing ω as "*aw/or*", and as there are some advantages in using the alternative pronunciation "*o*" as in "*so*", this is the one adopted and recommended in this book.

The second pronunciation disagreement relates to zeta, ζ, for which some scholars advocate the pronunciation "*zd*" and some prefer "*dz*". Allen sets out the evidence showing (p. 54) that "Prehistorically the combination represented by ζ derives in some cases from an Indo-European *sd* (*zd*) . . . But more often ζ derives from an original *dy* or *gy* . . . and these original groups must first have developed through an affricate stage, e.g. *dj* (as in *edge*) → *dz* as in *adze* (cf. Latin *medius* → Italian *mezzo*)." In the course of time, during the koine era, these two pronunciations *zd* and *dz* both simplified down to the single phoneme *z*. Allen (p. 54) postulates — and produces some analogies but no hard evidence for — an intermediate stage when ζ had come to be pronounced only as *zd*, as in *wisdom*, and then argues strongly for this to be the pronunciation used today for Classical Greek (pp. 134, 172).

But his evidence hardly leads to his conclusion. He acknowledges, for example (p. 57), the probable origin of ξ and ψ as "after the analogy of the other combination of plosive and fricative, viz. ζ for *dz*", but postulates that the words in which ζ was pronounced as *dz* changed to pronouncing the ζ as *zd*, while ξ and ψ remained as *ks* and *ps*. He records how the ancient grammarian Dionysius Thrax, in *Ars Grammatica* p. 11, groups ζ, ξ and ψ together as continuants rather than placing ζ with the plosive (stop) consonants, but he draws no significance from this for seeing ζ as having the continuant pronunciation *dz* rather than the terminating pronunciation *zd*. The Hebrew letter sadê, *ts*, is transliterated into Greek by ζ in Ναζαρέθ and related words. In John 5:2 the G.N.T. manuscripts have a range of variant readings for the Hebrew name of the pool. The majority of Greek manuscripts read Βηθεσδά, "Bethesda" — but none of them have the reading "Βηθεζά", which would be the expected transliteration into Greek if indeed "sd" equals ζ. Thus there are several different lines of evidence supporting the pronunciation of ζ as *dz*. We are therefore able to choose between *dz* and *zd* as the pronunciation to be used today. The one recommended in this book (as also in the vast majority of the other Greek grammars on the market) is *dz*. It is favoured because:

(a) It represents the original pronunciation of ζ in most words;

(b) It is appropriate as the pronunciation for the letter which was the model for ξ and ψ;

(c) It allows ζ to be recognized as taking its place with ξ and ψ in the pattern of affricate consonants (stop plus sibilant) in Greek;

(d) There appear to be no well-founded arguments for changing now to adopt the alternative pronunciation of *zd*.

8 **#1.24:** "The pronunciation of Greek in the Hellenistic period raises a great many difficult questions . . . it is probable that considerable differences existed between the Greek of Rome and Asia, Hellas and Egypt . . . Pronunciation had greatly changed since the classical period . . . many of the processes had already started which reach their full effect in Modern Greek. It does not follow that to pronounce Hellenistic as if it were Modern Greek would compensate in accuracy for the inconvenience it would cause. For pronouncing Attic of the classical period, the Modern Greek system is almost as wide of the mark as our English system of reading Greek as if it were English — a system which pretends to no advantage but convenience." (Moulton II, pp. 41-42.) But, notwithstanding the differences of pronunciation in different places, a Greek speaker would have been understood throughout the entire Hellenistic area: "Dialectic differences there must have been in a language spoken over so large an area. But they need not theoretically be greater than those between British and American English." (Moulton I, p. 39.)

9 **#1.25:** "The accents with which Greek has been written since the Hellenistic age are the invention of the great grammarians who tried to preserve a record of the classical language when it was in danger of obscuration. In their time the character of the accent was changing from pitch to stress . . . In classical Greek there was a 'musical' accent, the tone involving a higher note but no sort of stress . . . the tone was tied to the word or word-group, and was capable of no variation. It was a fixed element, almost as much as a similar but more elaborated tone-system is in Chinese . . . Our specific information for the accentuation of the NT text comes necessarily from later authorities . . . The earliest uncial manuscripts on vellum have no accents at all: we have to wait till the seventh century AD." (Moulton II, pp. 51-52, 55-56.) Moulton (II, p. 56) continues, "Soon after the date AD — a period when the κοινή began its first new period — the old musical accent developed into a pure stress; and we may assume that the N.T. documents were from the first pronounced with the accentual conditions familiar in Modern Greek." The problem with any efforts on our part to imitate this practice is (as Moulton immediately goes on to state) that "If we read the words aloud with a stress upon the syllables written with an accent — all three accents now being equivalent — we shall be practically compelled to reduce to a minimum the difference between long and short vowels, imparting the quality of length to the stressed syllable alone." The preferred method of pronunciation is: **(a)** ensure that the distinction between long and short vowels is always maintained, and always stress each long vowel and diphthong in a word; and **(b)** to the extent that this is possible consistent with (a), stress an accented vowel. Short vowels should be pronounced as short, but still differentiated and articulated clearly — unaccented short vowels should NOT be slurred over (as is done with unstressed vowels in English speech).

10 **#1.27:** Sometimes the names of the letters ξ, π, φ, χ and ψ are spelt as ξεῖ, πεῖ, φεῖ, χεῖ, and ψεῖ; sometimes as ξῖ, πῖ, φῖ, χῖ and ψῖ. The latter is the spelling used by Liddell and Scott's Greek-English Lexicon, and is the one recommended.

11 **#1.46:** Allen (pp. 33f.) records that "There is in fact a tradition, preserved in Priscian (*Grammatici Latini*, ii, p.30) as ascribed by Varro to Ion (probably of Chios), that the *ng* sound represented by γ in ἄγκυρα etc. had a special name in Greek, and that this name was ἄγμα." This reference shows that the designation *agma* was not widely attested in Greek, and the term has almost never been adopted by the authors of modern Greek Grammars. Yet nasal γ (*ng*) is a very different phoneme from palatal γ (*g*), with which it has nothing in common beyond the fact that they are both written the same way. Nasal γ is actually not a separate phoneme in Greek. Nasal γ takes the place of ν before palatals (for example: verb μιαινω adds the suffix -κα in the perfect, and its perfect stem μεμιαν- + -κα becomes μεμίαγκα). Moreover, ν and nasal γ occur in different environments — if there is any context where ν and nasal γ can both occur, then the two words are identical and the difference is purely one of spelling (for example: one can find ἐνγράφω and ἐγγράφω as alternative ways of spelling the same word). Thus as ν becomes γ before a palatal and as there are no minimally different pairs in Greek (words which differ only in that one has ν and the other had nasal γ, with a difference in meaning between the two), this indicates that nasal γ is the allophone of ν before palatals. This conclusion shows that nasal γ is totally distinct from palatal γ, and it would frequently be helpful to have a different term to designate γ when it is *ng*. As *agma* has not won favour, I propose for this purpose the term *enga* (ἔγγα) as embodying the phenomenon itself and by its affinity with ἐγγύς, *near*, indicating that *gamma* is only *enga* when next to a palatal.

12 **#1.72:** "Word division was generally not customary in writing in the period of the rise of the N.T. and for a long time thereafter . . . There is no word division in the oldest extant manuscripts; it remains imperfectly developed even in late manuscripts (to fifteenth century A.D.). . . It is certain that the authors of the N.T. could have used punctuation just as other people did at that time, not only in manuscripts, but sometimes also in letters and documents. However, whether the N.T. books were punctuated no one knows, and it is unknown, moreover, where and how they were punctuated, since no authentic traditions have been handed down. Modern editors are compelled to provide their own punctuation and hence often their own interpretation. That latter is very definitely the case, e.g. when a mark of interrogation occurs (found in manuscripts in the ninth century A.D. at the earliest)." (Blass-Debrunner-Funk, pp. 8 and 10.) "Ancient writing knew very little of so obvious a help to reading as punctuation . . . The oldest N.T. uncials have none of these adjuncts . . . obviously no argument towards a right punctuation can be drawn from the barrenness of the earlier or the abundance of the later signs. A fuller system is observed by the later uncials . . . It will be clear that there is little probability that any punctuation worth counting (as) such was present in the N.T. autographs." (Moulton II, pp. 47-48.)

13 **#1.83:** "In morphological analysis . . . one divides or 'cuts' forms of actual utterances into minimal segments, or sequences of phonemes, to which it is possible to assign meanings . . . Such phoneme sequences or form-segments are known in current usage as *morphs.*" (Lounsbury, p. 379.) For a more comprehensive discussion of this and related terms, see #E3.

14 **#1.83:** The *lexal* is the lexical morph of a word in the particular shape (i.e., phonemes and spelling) that it has as it is found in any form of any word; i.e. it is the part of any word which carries the meaning of that word which would be given for that word in a lexicon. For a more comprehensive discussion of this and related terms, see #E3.11 and Footnote 39.

15 **#2.28:** The convenient term *flexion* is taken over from Moulton, *A Grammar of N.T. Greek*, Vol. II, "Accidence and Word Formation", where it is used throughout.

16 **#2.4:** The forms for the cases in a flexion are given by some grammarians in the order used here, and by others in the order: Nominative, Genitive, Dative, Accusative, Vocative. The order given here has been adopted only after the most careful consideration of the two alternative orders, and a discussion of these alternatives will be found in Footnote 36.

17 **#2.72:** *Mood* is the more usual term used for this feature of the verb, but *mode* is the term preferred by a number of scholars, from Robertson in his Grammar (1908) and Davis in his (1923) to Hockett (1958) in his *Course in Modern Linguistics* (p. 237). Both forms of the term derive from the Latin *modus.* In its general usage in English, the word *mood* has the connotation "a frame of mind or a state of feelings" (Oxford English Dictionary), which is inappropriate in relation to this feature of the verb, whereas *mode* conveys the idea of *manner* (cf. "mode of life", "mode of travel", "mode of dress", etc.), which *is* appropriate to the grammatical feature, which is concerned with the *manner of action* of the verb. *Mode* is therefore to be preferred as being the clearer term, and not misleading because of its general implications (as is the word *mood* when used for this feature of grammar).

18 **#3.62:** The terms *punctiliar* and *durative* are those advocated by Moulton in Vol. I of his *Grammar,* p. 109. Sometimes the term *linear* will be found used by some grammarians in lieu of *durative.* The remaining aspect could be termed *perfect* (Moulton's term), or *perfective* (the term, along with punctiliar and durative, used by Blass-Debrunner-Funk in *A Greek Grammar of the N.T.*; vide p. 166). In this present book the latter term, *perfective,* has been preferred in order to avoid the ambiguity of having the same term for the aspect and for one of the three tenses (perfect, pluperfect, future perfect) by which that aspect can be expressed.

19 **#4.32:** McKay, p. 215.

20 **#4.33:** The future tense really stands outside the aspect system — whether it is durative or punctiliar in sense will be derived from its lexical meaning or from its context. (A future perfect tense exists for when the perfective aspect is required, and in practice it is found little used.) Thus Blass-Debrunner-Funk, p. 178: "The future is the only tense which expresses only a level of time and not an *Aktionsart* (aspect), so that completed and durative action are not distinguished."

21 **#4.43:** For a more comprehensive discussion of the concept of a process morph, see #E3.14-E3.18, and Footnote 40.

22 **#9.82:** Robertson, *Short G.*, p. 306.

23 **#9.83:** Robertson, *Short G.*, p. 311.

24 **#9.83:** Robertson, *Short G.*, pp. 162f.; p. 311.

25 **#9.83:** Turner, p. 119, lists the 68 NT usages of the optatives as Luke/Acts 28, Paul 31, I & II Peter 4, Jude 2, Mark 2, Hebrews 1.

26 **#9.86:** Turner, pp. 118f.

27 **#B1.32:** It is standard practice for linguistic science to say (as for example does Nida on p. 1 of *Morphology*), ". . . the written form of the language is entirely secondary (in fact quite irrelevant) as far as the descriptive linguist is concerned"; i.e. the basic form of language is the oral utterance. But this truism must of necessity be modified in dealing with a "dead" language where (by definition) there are no living persons for whom it is a mother tongue, so that we are dealing exclusively with written records from the past and these are the only "utterances" in the language that we have. Moreover, it is the aim of the student of NT Greek to learn this language so as to be able to understand one of these "utterances" in particular, namely, the Greek NT. Therefore a linguistic analysis of NT Greek must of necessity be concerned with the form in which the language is written, not the form in which it was spoken — the more so, as the latter was not uniform, and in any case is only imperfectly known to us.

28 **#B1.4:** Approximately twenty years ago Charles Fries wrote (*Linguistics and Reading*, p.79): "Of course there had been efforts to apply the developing linguistic knowledge even during the first period of Modern Linguistic Science. Whitney, in 1875, speaks of linguistic science as 'bringing about a re-cast of the old methods of teaching even familiar and long-studied languages, like Latin and Greek'." But the recent developments of linguistic science in the techniques of the analysis of a language are not being utilized in the study of NT Greek, even in the more serious and thoughtful books being published. To venture upon a concrete example:

I would consider that on many grounds the most thorough and most valuable textbook on the NT Greek language to be published in the last decade or two would be the two-volume *Handbook of New Testament Greek* by W.S. LaSor. Among the many excellent features of this book are its approach of allowing students to work on the biblical text from the outset (he uses Acts), encouraging students to analyze the forms of words, not just to memorize them, and explaining the basic phonological rules which enable multitudes of so-called irregular words to be seen as completely regular in terms of the functioning of the Greek language. His treatment of morphology and morphemes, in particular (§ 20), is clear, accurate, and helpful, noting for example that "The inflected part is called the ending. More properly, the inflectional elements should be designated as morphemes, since they are not always at the end of a word. A morpheme is a meaningful unit of (a) form" (§ 20.3). But the book's actual analysis of NT Greek does not implement this in practice. Thus in § 24.312 σ, κ, θη, etc. are classified not as morphs or morphemes but as *infixes* (rather than as *suffixes* — an *infix* is something inserted into the stem or root of a word); and it has not been recognized that the aorist indicator is -σα-, not -σ-, and the perfect active indicator is -κα-, not -κ-, whereas morphemic analysis on linguistic lines would identify this at once, and would see the -σ- and -κ- forms as being allomorphs resulting from the elision of the -α- before a following vowel. This type of comment on the book could be multiplied. This is not a criticism of a valuable and scholarly book by a highly competent author; it is a factual statement about the extent of the application in practice of the principles of modern linguistic science to the analysis and teaching of NT Greek — and I am not aware of any other book which begins to do all that Professor LaSor has sought to do.

This gap to which I draw attention is the one which I am seeking to fill with the present volume. To my knowledge, this is the first attempt at the rigorous application to a dead language of the kind of comprehensive analysis, on the basis of the principles of linguistic science, which is being regularly applied in the present-day study of numerous "living" (i.e., spoken) languages. (An excellent and eminently praiseworthy start in this direction has been made in the volume *The Morphology of Koine Greek As Used In the Apocalypse of St. John* by G. Mussies, but, as the title itself indicates, the scope of this quite detailed work of 386 pages has specific limitations.)

Behind the present volume lies a completely fresh analysis of the koine Greek language found in the N.T., an analysis carried out on the basis of the principles of linguistic science. I have sought to make this analysis as thorough as possible, but it would be too much to hope that I have succeeded in making it completely comprehensive or consistent.

Moreover, I want to make it absolutely clear that I am not asserting that the approach followed in this book is necessarily the only way in which Greek could be linguistically analyzed. But I do consider that the analysis which has been made is a valid one, and an acceptable one, and one which is able to account for the observable data of Greek, especially in regard to questions of phonemics and morphology, and I firmly believe that this approach (both at the level of theoretical linguistics and at the level of practical teaching of the language) constitutes a distinct advance upon traditional methods. It is my sincere hope that publication of this present book will be followed by dialogue between those of us who have the privilege of teaching the Greek N.T., dialogue which will lead to an increased efficiency in the way in which we each carry out this work, as measured by the number of students who come to us to be taught how to read the Greek N.T. and who thereafter actually do make regular use of the N.T. in Greek, to the enrichment of their life and ministry.

29 **#B3.06:** The comments in **#A0.15** are very relevant to these factors.

30 **#B4.3:** Refer here to the comments given in Footnote 1.

31 **#C0.33:** Much current linguistic study centres in "grammarians' interest not in the actual texts but in what is linguistically possible. Their interest does not lie, therefore, in the actual utterances of the native speaker of a language, but rather with what he CAN say. This concerns his 'knowledge' of the language, his 'competence', not what he does at any time, the sentences he actually produces, which are a matter only of 'performance'. According to the theory, the native speaker of a language has 'internalized a set of rules' which form the basis of his ability to speak and to understand his language. It is the knowlege of these rules that is the object of the linguist's attention, not the actual sentences he produces." (Palmer, p. 156.) Although Palmer questions the ultimate value of "the distinction between competence and performance", he considers that "methodologically it has much to be said for it." (p. 157.) It is at times highly relevant, therefore, to consider, in seeking to understand κοινή Greek, not merely the word forms which happen to occur in the N.T. but also the forms which could have occurred had the author chosen to use them, and which would have been understood by his hearers if he *had* used them. This is a recognition that the forms an author used were a selection made from a wider range available to him.

32 **#C3.86:** Robertson, *Short G.*, pp. 289f.

33 **#C8.02:** When this book (or any other book that discusses grammar) talks about "rules", these must never be thought of as arbitrary decisions made by some committee of grammarians about how the language is to operate, which all the citizens then carefully learn, and follow. A moment's reflection will show that a "rule" of grammar is empirically derived: that is, it is a statement about a recurring feature of a language which has been noted by observation and analysis of how the language functions. The pattern of language use comes first: later come the "rules" which attempt to explain the nature of that pattern of language use. And, in Greek as in other languages, there will be examples found aplenty where the general rules have been broken by this author or that one.

34 **#C8.05:** "There is no reason but a historical one for any irregularities, and historical reasons are not really any reasons. They are just statements that the irregularity has been in the language for a long time. It does not tell us just how the complexity arose. We do know something about these irregularities, namely, that they occur in all languages, that they are very persistent, especially if they occur in some frequently used form of the language, and that some irregularities are constantly disappearing and others being introduced." (Nida, *Learning*, p. 15.)

35 **#C8.85:** Goodwin, p. 151.

36 **#D0.14:** There are two different patterns of order which are in use for the case forms of the Declensions. These are, respectively: Nominative, (vocative,) accusative, genitive, dative; and, Nominative, genitive, dative, accusative (,vocative). The order of the forms has no function apart from providing the framework for memorization (and later recall) of forms by a student of the language.

I have not found any author who compares the two patterns for case order and gives a reasoned argument in favour of either one in preference to the other. Yet it seems to me that one of these two orders is more logical than the other, accords with the linguistic change which is occurring in the word, and provides a much clearer and more useful memory framework for the student. So let me present the evidence for this for the consideration of teachers.

Many words have a strong linguistic link between their nominative and accusative forms, and between their genitive and dative forms, but show a linguistic change between the first pair of these forms and the second pair. It is therefore a logical arrangement (and a pedagogical advantage) to place together two forms (the nominative and the accusative) that are closely related, the second member of the pair being directly derived from the first in many instances, than to separate them by two other forms (the genitive and the dative) which interrupt the pattern.

Similarly, the vocative is closely related to the nominative, frequently consisting of the word stem which differs in the nominative only in being lengthened or in some other small particular. Where there is a difference of stem between nominative/accusative and genitive/dative, the vocative has the same stem as the former pair. And where no separate vocative is in use, it is the nominative which is used in lieu. This makes quite a strong case for the vocative being placed with the nominative.

One can add that apart from these linguistic considerations there is also the syntactic one that the accusative is "more of a kind" with the nominative (both being directly in relation to a verb) than with the genitive and dative.

The affinities between the nominative, (vocative,) and accusative can be seen in the following flexions, which allow the linguistic logic of this order of arrangement to be recognized:

N	δόξα	ἔργον	πόλις	πατήρ	ἀνήρ	γυνή
V	—		πόλι	πάτερ	ἄνερ	γύναι
A	δόξαν	ἔργον	πόλιν	πατέρα	ἄνδρα	γυναῖκα
G	δόξης	ἔργου	πόλεως	πατρός	ἀνδρός	γυναικός
D	δόξῃ	ἔργῳ	πόλει	πατρί	ἀνδρί	γυναικί

N	σῶμα	πολύς	πολύ	μέγας	μέγα	τίς	τί
V	—	—	—	—	—	—	—
A	σῶμα	πολύν	πολύ	μέγαν	μέγα	τίνα	τί
G	σώματος	πολλοῦ		μεγάλου		τίνος	
D	σώματι	πολλῷ		μεγάλῳ		τίνι	

I have not seen any rationale for the other pattern of case order, and the sole argument that I myself can think of for it is that placing the genitive immediately after the nominative brings together the two declension forms which are used to identify a word and its stem and declension (i.e. the lexicon will give the nominative and genitive singular forms for a word). This is not a compelling (or even relevant) reason for deciding upon a basis for the order of caseforms in a paradigm. In view of the linguistic and pedagogic reasons for the above order of forms, I think it is reasonable to recommend this as the order for adoption in the classroom.

37 **#D0.26:** For a more comprehensive discussion of the zero morph, see #E3.15-E3.19, and Footnote 41.

38 **#D1.63:** The explanation of this apparent irregularity is that this noun originally had a digamma stem.

39 **#E3.11:** The *lexical morph* is the part of any form of any word (and in single-morph words it will be the entire word) which conveys the *lexical meaning* of the word, i.e. the base meaning which is given in a lexicon. For convenience of use, I have coined the word *lexal* for *lexical morph* (and in particular for each allomorph of the lexical morph) as a term of specific reference for this particular morph. The lexical morph of a word may be modified by juxtaposition with other phonemes. Thus in the form θλίβω, the lexical morph appears as θλιβ; but in other forms from this same word it will appear as θλιμ (τέθλιμμαι), θλιπ (τέθλιπται) and θλιφ (τέθλιφθε). Each of these forms of the lexical morph is the *lexal* in that particular word form, and thus all the lexals of the one word are variant forms of the same morph, i.e. *allomorphs* (#E3.2). As all the allomorphs of a given morph constitute together the morpheme for that function (#E3.21), so all the lexals of a given lexical morph constitute together the *lexeme* for that word. *Lexeme* is used in this sense (or approximately this sense) by linguists; e.g. Lyons, p. 197, uses the "term *lexeme* to denote the more 'abstract' units which occur in different inflexional 'forms' according to the syntactic rules involved in the generation of sentences", and on p. 289 in referring specifically to Greek and Latin he says, "it is clear that variation in the forms of a lexeme according to the syntax of the language was regarded as deviation from its normal 'upright' form." The term *lexal* thus fills a descriptive terminological gap. As a *phoneme* is represented by (and made up of) its *allophones*, and a *morpheme* is represented by (and made up of) its *allomorphs*, so a *lexeme* is represented by (and made up of) its "allolexes" or — I suggest, a more euphoneous alternative term — by its *lexals*.

40 **#E3.14:** The term and concept *process morph* is based upon the work of a number of linguists. Thus Zellig Harris wrote in 1944 (p. 199), "The difference between two partially similar forms is frequently described as a process which yields one form out of the other. Thus, when bases or themes have several vocalic forms, the various forms are said to be the result of vowel-change processes operating upon the base or theme." In 1954 Hockett wrote in an article "Two Models of Grammatical Description" (in Joos, pp. 386-399), about the alternative models of the analysis of words as "item and process" and as "item and arrangement", and he himself opted for the former method of analysis as preferable. My own approach accepts some input from both views in identifying word forms as resulting from the adding of affixes to roots and also from the operation of specific processes of change upon them. Thus λύω is augmented (and it is recognized as augmented) by the presence of the affix -ε- in front of the stem (as in the form ἔλυον) while ἀγαπάω is augmented (and is recognized as augmented) by the lengthening of the initial vowel (as in the form ἠγάπησα). Each of these alternatives is morphologically significant and has identical signification: it indicates past time. So each is a morph, and as they both have identical significance they are two allomorphs of the "Greek past time morpheme" (which in fact also has other, less common, allomorphs). But the first augment, the *syllabic augment*, is an *affix*, an *additive morph*, and the second type of augment, the *temporal augment*, is a *process of change* from an initial short vowel (of whatever kind) in the root to its corresponding long vowel. Thus this second kind of morph is a *process morph*.

41 **#E3.15:** Nida (p. 46 of *Morphology*) defines and describes the two types of *zero morphs* which can be found: **(a)** The *allomorphic zero*, where some forms do not show a particular grammatical morph which is found with a specific meaning in some other forms or other words. He illustrates this type of zero morph with the words *sheep, trout, elk, salmon* and *grouse*, which in the plural have zero where other words would have one of the English plural morphs. Thus it can be said that some words add zero in forming their plural, so zero is an allomorph of the English plural morpheme, along with all the other allomorphs for making a word plural. Another example of an English allomorphic zero would be the zero for a past time morph on "let" in the sentence "he let me come", compared with the affix morph which indicates past time in "petted" (from "pet") and the process morph in "got" (from "get"). A Greek example would be the zero augment added to such verbs as εὑρίσκω (aorist, εὗρον).

(b) The *morphemic zero*, where a particular morph is not used in a particular form and by its absence identifies the form. Nida illustrates this with an example of verb pronouns from the Totonac language where the third person singular form is indicated by the *absence* of a pronoun, all the other forms in the flexion having such a pronoun affix. This is exactly parallel with the Greek Third Conjugation aorist active, where the third person singular is similarly indicated by a zero morph (as in e.g. ἔγνω); so also the first person singular in the First Conjugation aorist and perfect active (as in e.g. ἔλυσα, λέλυκα).

42 **#E4.05** Hockett (pp. 290ff.) compares the construction of the various forms of inflected words in a language like Greek to a train picking up trucks in a freightyard. The "locomotive" is the stem (or lexical morph); the "trucks" are the various grammatical morphs, each carrying a particular "load" of meaning. The total meaning "load" conveyed by the entire train (word form) depends upon which individual morphs are picked up. This is a very helpful model which I have made use of elsewhere. Two other models which Hockett gives in this section are: a maze, with several tracks which one can follow, these determining the "meaning areas" one can pass through; and, a rollercoaster, with "meaning" able to follow one of two or three parabolic curves from a particular "point of meaning" to land on another "point of meaning" (one of the alternative options possible), from whence one "bounces" to the next; the total meaning of the word being the sum of all the "points of meaning", i.e., morphs, which one touched. These (and the "switch" description which I have used here) are all models to explain the meaning content of morphs and their arrangement in a word. Each one can make a contribution to understanding morphological function; and other models could also be suggested (e.g., the morphs are like pieces of a jigsaw puzzle, each one contributing a little to your understanding of the whole — when you fit them all together in the correct sequence, it gives you the total meaning of the entire picture). See further, #A3.4, #A6.

43 **#E4.07:** The reduplicating of the initial consonant of a verb root, to denote perfect aspect, goes back to Indo-European, the original ancestor of the Greek language. In that language the augment, -ε-, was originally an independent adverb which came to be more and more restricted in use to the position in front of a finite indicative verb, where it indicated past time, and in the process of time it then came to function as an actual part of the verb form. (Cowgill pp. 135-137; Diamond pp. 131-132.) The use of certain adverbs as prepositions (as separate words) in front of verbs was developing in early Greek, and in Homer (1000 BC) these prepositions are often separated from the following verb (Robertson *Short G.*, p. 248; Cowgill p. 138). By the time of Classical Greek (c. 500 BC) eighteen particular adverbs could be used in the "pre-position" with verbs, i.e. actually attached to a verb as a prefix (and therefore coming in front of the augment, which in turn came in front of reduplication, if two or all three of these occurred together). "The use of prepositions in composition with Greek verbs was slow at first, but became very common in the κοινή." (Robertson, *Short G.*, p. 181; and more fully see *Historical R.*, pp. 553-5.)

44 **#E4.08:** In parsing, one should first identify the form within its immediate number subgroup (i.e., *person* for a verb, *case* for a noun), and then which section of the flexion it comes from (*singular* or *plural*), and then name the flexion itself (*gender* for adjectives, etc.; *tense* for a verb), then, for a verb, the *mode*, and then to which of the macro divisions of the paradigm it belongs: *active, middle* or *passive* voice). When a middle *form* can have either middle *or* passive *meaning*, it should be identified as: middle/passive.

45 **#E4.11:** Though each of the prepositions will sometimes be followed by an augment in a past-tense form of such a verb — see Footnote 47.

46 **#E4.13:** "In the New Testament there occur 320 words that are used here for the first time in Greek literature", but some of these are likely to have been in current spoken use, rather than specifically coined by the biblical author, and "in that case accidentally unmentioned in earlier literature." (Mussies, pp. 113f.)

47 **#E4.27** In addition, verbs which have two prefixed prepositions sometimes take an augment after each. Thus ἀποκαθίστημι regularly takes the double syllabic augment, as in ἀπεκατέστη (Mark 8:25). But other verbs with two prepositions will augment only the verb lexal: διακατελέγχομαι becomes διακατηλέγχετο (Acts 18:28).

APPENDIX G

GREEK VOCABULARY AND INDEX

G1. COMMON NEW TESTAMENT WORDS

G1.1 There are 300 words which occur fifty times or more in the Greek New Testament. These are the "common New Testament words", and all of them are used in the GNT Selections given in the nine Lessons of the Beginner's Course, where they are identified by being marked with an asterisk, *.

G1.2 All these words should be learnt, preferably from the Selections in the Lessons where they occur, i.e. it is preferable to learn them at the point where they are being used. Use this List to assess your progress, by seeing how well you are succeeding in learning them.

G1.3 This Table gives the following information: Word number in the List; Lesson where that word was introduced (L), the Paradigm in Appendix C or D which that word follows or the reference to the Paragraph where that word is mainly discussed (Para); the word; the number of its occurrences in the New Testament; and an English equivalent — different parts of a word's area of meaning may be given, separated by an oblique, /.

G1.4 The "common New Testament words", occurring fifty times or more, are:

NO.	L	PARA	WORD, FREQUENCY, MEANING
1	7	D4.2	ἀγαθός, ή, όν (104) good
2	5	C1.2	ἀγαπάω (141) love
3	9	D1.2	ἀγάπη, ης, ἡ (116) love
4	2	D4.2	ἀγαπητός, ή, όν (61) beloved
5	2	D2.1	ἄγγελος, ου, ὁ (175) angel/ messenger
6	5	D4.1	ἅγιος, α, ον (233) holy/ consecrated/saint
7	3	C2.7	ἄγω (66) lead/bring/go
8	3	D2.1	ἀδελφός, οῦ, ὁ (343) brother/ fellow believer
9	5	D3.9	αἷμα, τος, τό (97) blood
10	6	C1.8	αἴρω (101) take up/lift up/ remove
11	9	C1.3	αἰτέω (70) ask/request/demand
12	1	D3.14	αἰών, ῶνος, ὁ (123) age/world/ eternity
13	5	D4.1	αἰώνιος, ον (70) eternal/ unending
14	4	C1.3	ἀκολουθέω (90) follow
15	2	C8.76	ἀκούω (427) hear/give heed to
16	4	D1.1	ἀλήθεια, ας, ἡ (109) truth/ truthfulness
17	2		ἀλλά (635) but/on the contrary
18	8	D6.9	ἀλλήλους, ων, οις (100) one another
19	5	D6.2	ἄλλος, ης, ο (155) another/other
20	5	D1.1	ἁμαρτία, ας, ἡ (173) sin/ sin offering
21	3		ἀμήν (126) truly/in truth/ indeed/amen
22	4		ἄν (166) -ever (as in "whenever")
23	8	C3.4	ἀναβαίνω (81) ascend/go up
24	5	D3.32	ἀνήρ, ἀνδρός, ὁ (216) husband/ man
25	1	D2.1	ἄνθρωπος, ου, ὁ (548) human being/man
26	9	C3.1a	ἀνίστημι (107) raise/rise/ stand up
27	4	C4.3	ἀνοίγω (78) open

28 4 C2.8   ἀπέρχομαι (116) depart/leave/ come away/go away
29 3 A4.2   ἀπό (645) from
30 8 C2.4   ἀποθνῄσκω (113) die
31 6 C1.9c   ἀποκρίνομαι (231) answer
32 8 C1.89   ἀποκτείνω (74) kill
33 9 C3.2   ἀπόλλυμι (90) destroy/ruin (midd. perish)
34 5 C1.1   ἀπολύω (65) release/send away/ divorce/forgive
35 2 C1.89   ἀποστέλλω (131) send away
36 7 D2.1   ἀπόστολος, ου, ὁ (79) apostle/ messenger
37 2 D2.1   ἄρτος, ου, ὁ (97) bread/a loaf/ food
38 2 D1.2   ἀρχή, ῆς, ἡ (55) beginning/ruler/ authority
39 9 D3.4   ἀρχιερεύς, έως, ὁ (122) high priest
40 9 C1.6   ἄρχω (85) rule (midd. begin)
41 9 C1.7   ἀσπάζομαι (59) greet/welcome
42 1 D6.3   αὐτός, ή, ὁ (5534) he-she-it-they/self/same
43 6 C3.1   ἀφίημι (142) send away/ forgive/leave/allow
44 1 C2.2   βάλλω (122) throw/put/place
45 5 C1.7   βαπτίζω (77) baptize
46 2 D1.1   βασιλεία, ας, ἡ (162) reign/ kingdom
47 2 D3.4   βασιλεύς, έως, ὁ (115) king
48 2 C1.5   βλέπω (132) see/look (at)
49 3 2.95   γάρ (1036) for
50 9 C1.2   γεννάω (97) beget/bear/ give birth to
51 3 D1.2   γῆ, γῆς, ἡ (248) earth/ground/ land
52 7 C2.1   γίνομαι (667) become/happen
53 5 C3.5   γινώσκω (221) know
54 5 D1.3   γλῶσσα ης ἡ (50) tongue/ language
55 4 D3.4   γραμματεύς έως ὁ (62) scribe
56 7 D1.2   γραφή ῆς ἡ (50) scripture
57 1 C1.5   γράφω (190) write
58 5 D3.26   γυνή γυναικός ἡ (209) wife/ woman
59 4 D2.2   δαιμόνιον ου τό (63) demon
60 2 2.95   δέ (2771) and/but
61 9 9.95   δεῖ (102) it is necessary
62 9 D4.1   δεξιός ά όν (54) right (-hand)
63 9 C1.6   δέχομαι (56) receive
64 5 8.62   διά (666) because of/through
65 8 D2.1   διδάσκαλος ου ὁ (59) teacher
66 4 C5.5   διδάσκω (95) teach

67 4 C3.1c   δίδωμι (416) give
68 7 D4.1   δίκαιος α ον (79) righteous/just
69 4 D1.2   δικαιοσύνη ης ἡ (91) righteous-ness
70 9   διό (53) therefore
71 5 C1.3   δοκέω (62) think/presume/seem
72 3 D1.3   δόξα ης ἡ (165) glory
73 8 C1.7   δοξάζω (61) glorify/honour
74 4 D2.1   δοῦλος ου ὁ (124) slave
75 7 C3.3   δύναμαι (209) be able/can/ capable of
76 1 D3.2   δύναμις εως ἡ (118) power/ miracle
77 3 D6.7   δύο (136) two
78 9   δώδεκα (75) twelve
79 4 4.45   ἐάν (343) if (ever)
80 5 D6.8   ἑαυτόν ην ὁ (320) himself/ herself/itself/oneself/-selves
81 6 C1.8a   ἐγείρω (143) raise (up)/rouse
82 2 D6.3   ἐγώ (1713) I/me/my
83 5 D3.5   ἔθνος ους τό (162) nation/ heathen/gentile
84 5 4.45   εἰ (513) if
85 3 C2.8   εἶδον (336) I saw
86 2 C3.3   εἰμί (2450) be/exist
87 3 C2.8   εἶπον (925) I said/spoke/told
88 4 D1.2   εἰρήνη ης ἡ (91) peace
89 3 8.63   εἰς (1753) into/for
90 4 D6.7   εἷς μία ἕν (ἑνός) (337) one
91 4 C2.8   εἰσέρχομαι (192) enter
92 8   εἴτε (65) whether . . . or . . .
93 2 8.64   ἐκ/ἐξ (915) out of
94 8 D4.2   ἕκαστος η ον (81) each/every
95 3 C2.2   ἐκβάλλω (81) throw out/ send away/drive
96 3 9.13   ἐκεῖ (95) there (= in that place)
97 3 D6.2   ἐκεῖνος η ο (243) that (one)/ those
98 9 D1.1   ἐκκλησία ας ἡ (114) church/ assembly
99 5 D3.8   ἐλπίς ίδος ἡ (53) hope
100 2 D4.2   ἐμός ἐμή ἐμόν (76) my
101 2 8.65   ἐν (2713) in/by means of/with
102 4 D1.2   ἐντολή ῆς ἡ (68) commandment
103 8 8.66   ἐνώπιον (93) in front of
104 3 C2.8   ἐξέρχομαι (216) come out/ go out
105 5 D1.1   ἐξουσία ας ἡ (102) authority/ right
106 3 8.66   ἔξω (62) outside
107 9 D1.1   ἐπαγγελία ας ἡ (52) promise
108 8 C1.2   ἐπερωτάω (56) ask (a question)
109 5 8.61   ἐπί (878) on/upon/at/against/ with

110	9		ἑπτά (87) seven
111	1	D2.2	ἔργον ου τό (169) work/deed/ action
112	6	C2.8	ἔρχομαι (631) come/go
113	7	C2.8	[ἔρω] (96) say/speak/tell
114	8	C1.2	ἐρωτάω (62) ask (a question)
115	7	C2.8	ἐσθίω (158) eat/consume
116	8	D4.2	ἔσχατος η ον (52) last
117	9	D4.1	ἕτερος α ον (98) other/different
118	6		ἔτι (92) still/yet/longer
119	6	C1.7	εὐαγγελίζω/-ομαι (54) preach the gospel
120	2	D2.2	εὐαγγέλιον ου τό (76) gospel/ good news
121	3		εὐθύς (54) immediately
122	4	C2.4	εὑρίσκω (176) find
123	2	C2.7	ἔχω (705) have
124	4	8.66	ἕως (145) until
125	7	C8.08	ζάω (140) live/be alive
126	9	C1.3	ζητέω (117) seek
127	1	D1.2	ζωή ῆς ἡ (135) life
128	3		ἤ (342) or/than
129	9		ἤδη (60) already
130	3	D6.3	ἡμεῖς (856) we/us/our
131	1	D1.1	ἡμέρα ας ἡ (388) day
132	3	D1.3	θάλασσα ης ἡ (91) sea
133	6	D2.1	θάνατος ου ὁ (120) death
134	5	D3.9	θέλημα ματος τό (62) will/wish
135	4	C1.8	θέλω (207) wish/want/will
136	1	D2.1	θεός ου ὁ and ἡ (1314) God/ god/goddess
137	8	C1.3	θεωρέω (58) watch/observe
138	6	D2.1	θρόνος ου ὁ (62) throne
139	1	D4.1	ἴδιος α ον (113) one's own
140	2		ἰδού (200) look!/behold!/see!
141	6	D2.2	ἱερόν ου τό (70) temple
142	8	D2.2	ἱμάτιον ου τό (60) garment/ clothing
143	4	4.45	ἵνα (673) in order that/that
144	7	C3.1a	ἵστημι (152) stand
145	5	E2.92	κἀγώ (84) and I/I also
146	7	C3.3	κάθημαι (91) sit (down)
147	3	E2.63	καθώς (178) just as
148	2		καί (8947) and/also/even
149	8	D2.1	καιρός ου ὁ (85) time/occasion/ season
150	9	D4.2	κακός ή όν (50) bad
151	6	C1.48	καλέω (148) call
152	2	D4.2	καλός ή όν (99) good
153	1	D1.1	καρδία ας ἡ (156) heart
154	4	D2.1	καρπός οῦ ὁ (66) fruit
155	8	8.62	κατά (471) according to/against/ down
156	7	C3.4	καταβαίνω (81) go down/ come down
157	9	D1.2	κεφαλή ῆς ἡ (75) head
158	4	C1.6	κηρύσσω (61) preach/proclaim
159	2	D2.1	κόσμος ου ὁ (185) world
160	9	C8.84	κράζω (55) cry out/shout
161	9	C1.9c	κρίνω (114) judge/decide
162	2	D2.1	κύριος ου ὁ (718) lord/sir
163	6	C1.3	λαλέω (298) speak/converse/ chat/chatter
164	6	C2.34	λαμβάνω (258) take/receive
165	1	D2.1	λαός οῦ ὁ (141) a people
166	2	C2.8	λέγω (1318) say/speak/tell
167	5	D2.1	λίθος ου ὁ (58) a stone
168	6	D2.1	λόγος ου ὁ (331) word/saying/ message
169	7	D4.2	λοιπός ή όν (55) remainder/ remaining/rest
170	3	D1.5	μαθητής οῦ ὁ (262) disciple
171	5	D4.1	μακάριος α ον (50) blessed/ fortunate
172	9	9.37	μᾶλλον (80) more/rather
173	7	C1.3	μαρτυρέω (76) testify/bear witness
174	4	D4.43	μέγας μεγάλη μέγα (μεγάλου) (194) great/large
175	5	C1.88	μέλλω (110) intend/ be about to/be impending
176	5		μέν (181) (contrastive) on the one hand
177	7	C1.88	μένω (118) remain
178	3	D4.2	μέσος η ον (56) middle/ (in the) midst
179	3	8.62	μετά (467) after/with
180	4	4.49	μή (1055) not/no
181	9		μηδέ (57) and not/not even/ neither-nor
182	5	D6.7	μηδείς μηδεμία μηδέν (85) no-one/nothing
183	5	D3.32	μήτηρ μητρός ἡ (84) mother
184	8	D4.2	μόνος η ον (66) only/alone
185	2	D4.1	νεκρός ά όν (128) dead/ dead person
186	1	D2.1	νόμος ου ὁ (191) law
187	8		νῦν (148) now
188	3	D3.6	νύξ νυκτός ἡ (61) night
189	2	D6.1	ὁ ἡ τό (19,734) article: the (definiteness)
190	3	D2.4	ὁδός οῦ ἡ (101) way/road
191	7	7.52	οἶδα (321) I know
192	9	D1.1	οἰκία ας ἡ (94) house/household
193	1	D2.1	οἶκος ου ὁ (112) house/ household

194	1	D4.2	ὅλος η ον (108) whole/complete
195	3	D3.9	ὄνομα ματος τό (228) name
196	6	9.13	ὅπου (82) where
197	9	9.13	ὅπως (53) in order that/how
198	7	C2.8	ὁράω (114) see (pass.: appear)
199	4	D3.5	ὄρος ους τό (62) mountain
200	4	D6.2	ὅς ἥ ὅ (1369) who/which/what/that
201	6	7.11	ὅσος η ον (110) as great/much/many as
202	7	7.15	ὅστις ἥτις ὅ τι (154) who(ever)/which(ever)
203	6	4.45	ὅταν (123) whenever
204	4	9.13	ὅτε (102) when/while
205	2		ὅτι (1285) that/because/"
206	2	4.49	οὐ/οὐκ/οὐχ (1619) not/no
207	5		οὐδέ (139) and not/not even/neither-nor
208	5	D6.7	οὐδείς οὐδεμία οὐδέν (226) no-one/nothing
209	2	2.95	οὖν (493) then/therefore
210	1	D2.1	οὐρανός οῦ ὁ (272) heaven
211	6		οὔτε (91) neither/nor
212	2	D6.4	οὗτος αὕτη τοῦτο (1388) this (one)/these
213	4	9.13	οὕτως (208) thus/so
214	2	4.49	οὐχί (53) not/no
215	4	D2.1	ὀφθαλμός οῦ ὁ (100) eye
216	7	D2.1	ὄχλος ου ὁ (174) crowd
217	8	D2.2	παιδίον ου τό (52) child/infant
218	3		πάλιν (139) again
219	3	8.61	παρά (191) beside
220	7	D1.2	παραβολή ῆς ἡ (50) parable
221	8	C3.1c	παραδίδωμι (120) deliver up/hand over/betray/pass on
222	5	C1.48	παρακαλέω (109) encourage/request/exhort/comfort
223	5	D4.6	πᾶς πᾶσα πᾶν (παντός) (1226) all/every/each
224	3	D3.32	πατήρ πατρός ὁ (4:5) father
225	7	C8.63	πείθω (52) persuade/trust in
226	5	C8.63	πέμπω (79) send
227	3	8.62	περί (331) about/around/concerning
228	6	C1.3	περιπατέω (95) walk (around)
229	9	C2.31	πίνω (73) drink
230	8	C2.1	πίπτω (90) fall
231	3	C1.1	πιστεύω (241) believe/trust
232	5	D3.2	πίστις εως ἡ (243) faith/trust
233	4	D4.2	πιστός ή όν (67) believing/faithful/trustworthy
234	4	9.35	πλείων πλεῖον (55) more (than)
235	4	C1.4	πληρόω (86) fulfill/accomplish/fill
236	9	D2.2	πλοῖον ου τό (66) boat
237	3	D3.9	πνεῦμα ματος τό (379) spirit/wind/breath
238	4	C1.3	ποιέω (565) do/carry out/practise/make/produce
239	5	D3.2	πόλις πόλεως ἡ (161) city
240	5	D4.42	πολύς πολλή πολύ (353) much/many
241	2	D4.1	πονηρός ά όν (78) evil/bad/the Evil One
242	6	C1.1	πορεύομαι (150) go/proceed/journey
243	5	D3.8	πούς ποδός ὁ (93) foot
244	8	D4.1	πρεσβύτερος α ον (65) older/elder
245	8	8.61	πρός (696) to/towards/with
246	4	C2.8	προσέρχομαι (87) approach/come to
247	9	C1.6	προσεύχομαι (86) pray
248	8	C1.3	προσκυνέω (59) worship
249	2	D2.2	πρόσωπον ου τό (74) face
250	1	D1.5	προφήτης ου ὁ (144) prophet
251	9	9.23	πρῶτον (60) firstly/first
252	5	D4.2	πρῶτος η ον (92) first
253	5	D3.11	πῦρ πυρός τό (71) fire
254	9	9.13	πῶς (104) how?/in what way?
255	1	D3.9	ῥῆμα ματος τό (68) word/object
256	1	D3.29	σάββατον ου τό (68) sabbath
257	5	D3.6	σάρξ σαρκός ἡ (147) flesh
258	9	D2.2	σημεῖον ου τό (77) sign/miracle
259	5	D1.1	σοφία ας ἡ (51) wisdom
260	4	C1.8b	σπείρω (52) sow
261	9	D3.9	στόμα ματος τό (78) mouth
262	2	D6.3	σύ (1057) you/your (singular)
263	7	8.65	σύν (127) with
264	5	C2.7	συνάγω (59) gather (together)
265	4	D1.2	συναγωγή ῆς ἡ (56) synagogue
266	4	C1.7	σώζω (106) save/rescue/deliver/cure
267	5	D3.9	σῶμα σώματος τό (142) body
268	8	E6.32	τέ (201) and/both/untranslated
269	5	D2.2	τέκνον ου τό (99) child
270	6	C1.3	τηρέω (70) keep/observe/watch
271	9	C3.1b	τίθημι (101) place/put
272	2	D6.5	τίς τί (τίνος) (552) who?/which?/what?/why?
273	4	D6.6	τις τι (τινός) (518) some/any/a certain
274	7	7.13	τοιοῦτος τοιαύτη τοιοῦτον (56) of such a kind
275	1	D2.1	τόπος ου ὁ (95) place
276	4	9.13	τότε (159) then
277	3	D6.7	τρεῖς τρία (τριῶν) (67) three
278	4	D4.2	τυφλός ή όν (50) blind

279 5 D3.13   ὕδωρ ὕδατος τό (76) water
280 1 D2.1   υἱός οὗ ὁ (375) son
281 2 D6.3   ὑμεῖς (1830) you/your (plural)
282 4 C2.7   ὑπάγω (79) go (one's way)/ depart
283 6 C1.6   ὑπάρχω (60) be/exist/be present
284 5 8.62   ὑπέρ (1490 beyond/ for the sake of
285 8 8.62   ὑπό (217) under/by
286 4 C2.8   φέρω (66) carry/bring
287 7 C2.8   φημί (66) say
288 8 C1.3   φοβέομαι (95) fear/be afraid of

289 1 D1.2   φωνή ῆς ἡ (137) voice/sound
290 2 D3.10   φῶς φωτός τό (73) light
291 9 C1.89   χαίρω (74) rejoice
292 9 D1.1   χαρά ᾶς ἡ (59) joy
293 5 D3.28   χάρις χάριτος ἡ (155) grace
294 5 D3.31   χείρ χειρός ἡ (176) hand
295 1 D2.1   χρόνος ου ὁ (54) time
296 1 D1.2   ψυχή ῆς ἡ (101) soul/life
297 4   ὧδε (61) here
298 1 D1.1   ὥρα ας ἡ (106) hour
299 3 9.13   ὡς (505) as/like/how/that
300 5   ὥστε (84) so that/thus

G2.   INDEX TO GREEK NEW TESTAMENT SELECTIONS

G2.1 The Selections given at the end of each Lesson are extracts from the Greek New Testament. At times — especially for the early Lessons — only part of a verse has been used.

G2.2 The Selections are taken from these New Testament passages:

1:24-26	L5/12	11:18	L4/11	23:9	L9/24	**1 TIMOTHY**
1:29	L2/14	11:21-25	L9/21			5:18 · L7/25
1:32-34	L7/16	11:25-27	L4/12	**ROMANS**		
1:34	L2/2	11:55	L4/13	7:12-13	L7/22	**HEBREWS**
2:5	L7/17	12:21	L4/14	13:10	L9/25	1:10 · L2/21
2:13	L4/6	12:34	L3/21			11:38 · L7/26
4:39-45	L7/31	12:41	L3/22	**1 CORINTHIANS**		
4:40	L8/8	12:49-50	L7/21	2:16	L5/16	**JAMES**
5:17-18	L9/17	13:12-14	L8/9	3:17	L7/23	5:7-8 · L5/19
5:43	L7/18	14:1	L3/23			5:16 · L9/29
6:2	L9/18	14:6	L5/14	**EPHESIANS**		
6:3-4	L4/7	14:11	L5/15	2:17	L6/12	**1 JOHN**
6:9	L7/19	14:27	L4/15	4:4-6	L5/17	2:25 · L9/30
6:19-20	L9/19	16:4	L3/24	4:25	L9/26	
6:31	L7/20	16:22	L9/22			**REVELATION**
6:48	L2/7	18:20	L6/10	**PHILIPPIANS**		1:8 · L2/12
6:50	L2/8	18:28	L3/25	1:20-21	L8/11	1:17 · L9/31
7:37	L9/20	18:33, 36	L2/28	2:22-24	L7/24	3:7-8 · L7/27
8:12	L2/9	19:4	L3/26	3:20	L6/13	3:14 · L7/28
8:33	L4/8	19:8-9	L2/10			3:21 · L8/12
8:39	L3/17	19:14	L2/11	**COLOSSIANS**		4:1 · L3/30
8:45-46	L4/9	20:19, 21	L4/16	1:17-18	L9/27	4:11 · L6/14
9:13-14	L4/10	20:28	L3/27			5:9-12 · L5/22
9:28	L3/18	21:8	L3/28; L8/10	**1 THESSALONIANS**		5:14 · L8/13
9:35-36	L6/9			3:2	L5/18	11:12 · L8/14
10:3, 7	L3/19	**ACTS**				15:4 · L8/15
10:26-30	L5/13	5:29	L9/23	**2 THESSALONIANS**		20:5-6 · L7/29
10:36	L3/20	8:21	L3/29	3:3	L4/17	21:2 · L7/30
11:17	L9/21	16:3	L6/11	3:10	L9/28	21:3-5 · L6/15
						22:8-13 · L8/16

G3.   VOCABULARY AND INDEX TO GREEK WORDS

G3.1   This is a combined Vocabulary and Index. All Greek words discussed or used in this book are listed here in alphabetical order, and an English equivalent is given.

G3.2   A hyphen in front of a word indicates that that word does not occur in the New Testament in its simplex form but only in compound forms. A word in square brackets is an obsolete form. The number in brackets after a Greek word is the number of times that that word occurs in the New Testament. This refers only to the word given and does not include its compounds, which may be much more frequent — for example, ἀγγέλλω occurs only once in the N.T. but the total occurrences with all its compounds is 131; στέλλω occurs only twice in the N.T. but the total occurrences with all its compounds is 166. An asterisk, *, indicates a word occurring 50 or more times in the N.T.

G3.3   A summarized English meaning is given next. It must always be borne in mind that the area of meaning of a Greek word is usually much wider than can be conveyed in summarized form by a few English equivalents: this Vocabulary is intended primarily as a memory aid and reference guide, and not as a substitute for your Lexicon, which should also be consulted as required.

G3.4   After the English equivalent(s), the main reference in the book for that word is given. For words with inflection, this will usually be in Appendices C, D, E or F, and this initial reference is then followed in sequence by all the other references in those Appendices. References in the Beginner's Course and Appendix A then follow. The listing of a word in a Vocabulary is shown by V. Thus 7V indicates that the word is given in the Vocabulary (in the Explanatory Notes) of Lesson 7. Some wellknown proper names used in Selections are not listed in the Vocabularies, but they are given in this Index, indicated by S. Thus 2S means that this name is not listed in the Vocabulary for Lesson 2 but is used in one or more of the Sentences.

G3.5   It has been the intention of this book to deal with every word which is "regularly irregular", that is, which consistently used irregular forms. Thus in general all irregular nouns and verbs of the Greek New Testament should be listed here. An exception is proper nouns, which are not treated exhaustively. Words which have some irregular forms in the usage of certain N.T. writers or in particular N.T. manuscripts but are usually regular may be omitted — it is not practical to include all such minor variations.

G3.6   The Greek words used or referred to in this book are:

*ἄλλος η ο (155) other/another D6.2 E3.21 5V
6V 7.11 7V
ἀλοάω (3) thresh 7V
ἀλόη ης ἡ (1) aloes D1.64
ἅλς ἁλός ὁ (1) salt D3.11
ἄλφα (3) alpha 1.27 1.37
ἁμαρτάνω (43) sin C2.33 7.36
*ἁμαρτία ας ἡ (173) sin/a sin/sin offering 6V
ἁμαρτωλός όν (47) sinful/a sinner 7V 9V
ἀμέθυστος ου ἡ (1) amcthyst D2.44
*ἀμήν (126) truly/in truth/indeed/amen 3V 7V
ἀμήτωρ ἀμῆτορ (1) motherless D4.9
ἄμμος ου ἡ (5) sand D2.44
ἀμνός ἀμνοῦ ὁ (4) lamb D3.37 2V
ἄμπελος ου ἡ (9) vine D2.44
ἀμύνομαι (1) come to help C1.89 C7.5
ἀμφί- (-) on both sides 8.64
ἀμφιέννυμι (3) clothe/dress C3.2
*ἄν (166) -ever (indefiniteness) 4.45 E2.27
E2.92 4V 7.15 9V
ἀνά (13) up 8.63 8.69
*ἀναβαίνω (81) come up/go up/ascend 8V 9V
ἀναβλέπω (25) see again/look up 4V
ἀναθάλλω (1) revive C2.2 C1.83 C1.89
ἀνακράζω (5) cry out/shout C2.6 (C8.84 C4.3)
ἀναλίσκω (2) destroy C5.5
ἀναπίπτω (12) recline at table/lean back 8V
ἀνάστασις εως ἡ (42) resurrection 4V 7V 8V 9V
ἀνατέλλω (9) rise C1.8b C1.83 C1.85 C1.89
C8.61 C8.64 9.71
ἀναφέρω (9) lead up/bring up 8V
Ἀνδρέας ου ὁ (13) Andrew 3.17 3V
ἀνέρχομαι (3) come/go up 4.81 4V
ἀνῆλθον (suppletive of ἀνέρχομαι) I came/
went up 4.81 4V
*ἀνήρ ἀνδρός ὁ (216) husband/man D3.32 F36
5.43 5.44 5V 7V
*ἄνθρωπος ου ὁ (548) human being/man 1.27
E6.27 2.29 2.31 8.42
*ἀνίστημι (107) raise/rise/stand up 9V
*ἀνοίγω (78) open C4.3 E4.27 E4.38 4.62 4V
9V
ἀντί (22) instead of 8.64 8.69 9V
ἄξιος α ον (41) worthy of/in keeping with 5V
6V 7V
ἀπαγγέλλω (46) announce/report 6V 7V
ἀπάγω (15) lead away E6.28
ἀπαρνέομαι (11) deny/disown/utterly
renounce 6V
ἅπας ἅπασα ἅπαν ἅπαντος (35) each/every/
all D4.6 D3.20 7.27
ἀπάτωρ ἀπάτορ (1) fatherless D4.9
ἀπεκδέχομαι (8) await expectantly 6V

*ἀπέρχομαι (116) come away/go away/depart/
leave 4V 9V
ἀπέχω (19) receive in full/be distant 3.71 3V 8V
*ἀπῆλθον (suppletive of ἀπέρχομαι) I came/
went away 4V 6V
ἄπιστος ον (23) unbelieving/unfaithful D4.03
ἁπλοῦς ῆ οῦν (2) healthy D4.3
*ἀπό (645) from 8.64 8.69 A4.2 E3.22 3.71 3V
8.44 8.71 8.74
ἀποδίδωμι (47) repay (midd. sell) 6.17 8V
*ἀποθνήσκω (113) die (C2.4 C2.96 C7.6) 6.95
7.36 8V
ἀποκαθίστημι (8) restore F47 9V
*ἀποκρίνομαι (231) answer (C1.9c) C7.5 6.18
6V 7.82 8.45 9V
*ἀποκτείνω (74) kill C1.9b C1.84 C1.85 C1.89
C4.52 C8.61 8V 9.71 9V
*ἀπόλλυμι (90) destroy/ruin (midd. perish) C3.2
C1.88 C4.3 C7.7 9V
Ἀπολλῶς ῶ ὁ (10) Apollos D2.41
ἀπολογέομαι (10) defend oneself C7.5
*ἀπολύω (65) release/send away/divorce/forgive
5V E6.28
ἀπονέμω (1) render/show (respect) C1.89
*ἀποστέλλω (131) send out/away 2V (see
στέλλω)
*ἀπόστολος ου ὁ (79) apostle/messenger 7V
ἀποτίθημι (9) put away/cast off 9V
ἅπτω (39) light (midd. touch) C5.7 C7.5 6.17
6.18 8.44
Ἄραψ Ἄραβος ὁ (1) Arabian D3.7
ἀργυροῦς ᾶ οῦν (3) silvern D4.3
ἀρέσκω (17) please C5.5 E4.43
ἀρήν ἀρνός ὁ (1) lamb D3.37
ἀριθμός οῦ ὁ (18) number 5V
ἀρκέω (8) be sufficient C1.48
ἄρκος ου ὁ and ἡ (1) bear D2.45
ἀρνέομαι (32) deny C7.5 6.18
ἀρνίον ου τό (30) lamb D3.37 5V
ἁρπάζω (14) snatch/take by force C4.4
C4.53 5V
ἄρσην εν (ενος) (9) male 5V
*ἄρτος ου ὁ (97) bread/a loaf/food 2V
*ἀρχή ἀρχῆς ἡ (55) beginning/ruler/authority
2V 7V E3.31
*ἀρχιερεύς έως ὁ (122) high priest 9V
ἄρχομαι begin: middle of ἄρχω
*ἄρχω (85) rule (midd. begin) C1.6 C4.54 C7.5
E2.62 E3.31 6.17 6.18 8.44 9.71 9V
ἄρχων οντος ὁ (37) ruler D3.18 D3.09 E2.36
E2.42 E2.44 E3.31 5.39 5.44 5.65 5V
6.58 7.63
ἀσθενέω (33) be sick/ill/weak 9V

*ἀσπάζομαι (59) greet/welcome C7.5 6.18 9V
ἀστήρ ἀστέρος ὁ (24) star D3.12 D3.09
   D3.32 E2.36 5.31 5.36 5.43 5V
ἀστράπτω (2) flash/dazzle C5.7
ἄστρον ου τό (4) star D3.12
αὐξάνω (23) increase C5.31 E4.36
*αὐτός ή ὁ (5534) he/she/it/they/-self/(the)
   same D6.3 1.33 2.52 3.31 3.32 3.33 6.22
   7V 8V A3.21 A3.24 A3.25
ἀφανίζω (5) ruin/destroy 6V
ἄφεσις εως ἡ (17) forgiveness
*ἀφίημι (142) send away/forgive/leave/allow
   (C3.1 C3.85) D5.32 E2.61 E4.17 6V
   7.48 8V
ἀφικνέομαι (1) reach C2.32 C7.5
ἀφίστημι (14) withdraw/depart E2.23 8.69
ἀφοράω (2) see 7V
ἀφορίζω (10) separate C8.88
ἄφρων ἄφρον (11) foolish D4.8 5.67 9.35
ἄχρι (48) until/as far as 8.66 7V
ἄψινθος ου/ὁ/ἡ (2) wormwood D2.45
βαθύνω (1) go deep C1.89
-βαίνω (-) go C3.4 C3.86 C6.2 C7.6 D5.12
   D5.32 E2.84 E3.34 E4.12 E4.13 7.43
   7.45 9.57 9.59
*βάλλω (122) throw/put/place C2.2 C1.83
   C1.89 C2.96 C6.2 C6.22 E4.13 E4.42
   1.27 3.61 3.63 3.71 3.81 3.93 6.71 6.72
   6.73 7.36 7.41 9.59 A3.31
*βαπτίζω (77) baptize 5V 6V
βάπτισμα ματος τό (20) baptism 3V 5V
βαπτιστής οῦ ὁ (12) baptist 9V
βάπτω (4) dip C5.7
βαρύς βαρεῖα βαρύ (6) heavy/hard D4.4 5.64
   5.65
βάσανος ου ἡ (3) torment D2.44
*βασιλεία ας ἡ (162) kingdom/reign 2V 3.42
*βασιλεύς εως ὁ (115) king D3.4 D0.27 D3.2
   E2.17 2V 5.20 5.24 5.50
βασιλεύω (21) rule/reign 5V
βασίλισσα ης ἡ (4) queen D1.65
βασκαίνω (1) bewitch C1.89 C1.84
βάτος ου ὁ/ἡ (5) thornbush D2.45
βέλτιον (1) very well (9.35) 9.37
Βηθλέεμ (8) Bethlehem 1.35 1.64
βήρυλλος ου ὁ/ἡ (1) beryl D2.45
-βιβάζω (-) cause to go/put E4.12
βιβλίον ου τό (34) book/scroll/statement (of
   divorce) 5V
βίβλος ου ἡ (10) book D2.44
βιβρώσκω (1) consume C5.1 C5.5
βλάπτω (1) harm/injure C5.7
βλαστάνω (4) sprout/produce C5.31 4V
βλαστάω (variant form of βλαστάνω) 4V

*βλέπω (132) see/look (at) C1.5 E2.61 2V 9.71
   A2.47 A2.48
βοή ῆς ἡ (1) shout/cry D1.64
βόσκω (9) feed/tend C5.5
βούλομαι (37) want/wish/be willing C1.88
   C1.89 C7.5 6.18
βοῦς βοός ὁ (8) ox D3.3 D3.4 7V
βραδύνω (2) be delayed/negligent about C1.89
βρῶσις εως ἡ (11) corrosion/rust 6V
βύσσος ου ἡ (1) fine linen D2.44
γάγγραινα ης ἡ (1) gangrene D1.65
γάζα ης ἡ (1) treasury D1.65
γάλα γάλακτος τό (5) milk D3.6
γαμέω (28) marry C8.92
γαμίσκω (1) give in marriage C5.5
*γάρ (1036) for 2.95 E3.11 3V A2.63
γαστήρ γαστρός ἡ (9) womb D3.32
γέεννα ης ἡ (12) gehenna D1.65
γελάω (2) laugh C1.48
γενεά ᾶς ἡ (43) generation/period 9V
γένεσις εως ἡ (5) birth 9V
*γεννάω (97) beget/bear/give birth to 9V
γένος γένους τό (21) race D3.5 D0.27 D4.7
   5.20 5.25 5.26 5.50 5.67 5V
γεύομαι (15) taste C7.5
*γῆ γῆς ἡ (248) earth/ground/land 3V
γῆρας (-) τό (1) old age D3.5
γηράσκω (2) grow old C5.5
*γίνομαι (667) become/happen C2.1 C1.88
   C1.89 C2.97 C4.3 C6.2 C7.5 E2.55 6.18
   7.36 7.51 7V
*γινώσκω (221) know C3.5 C3.86 C6.2 C7.6
   D5.32 E2.16 E2.54 E2.84 E3.19 E3.33
   5V 7.43 7.45 9.57 9.59 9V
*γλῶσσα ης ἡ (50) tongue/language D1.65 5V
γνωρίζω (25) make known C8.89
γόνυ γόνατος τό (12) knee D3.29 5.46
*γραμματεύς εως ὁ (62) scribe 4V
*γραφη ῆς ἡ (50) scripture 7V
*γράφω (190) write C1.5 C4.4 C4.53 C4.54
   1.27 7V 9.71 9.92
*γυνή γυναικός ἡ (209) wife/woman D3.26
   F36 5.43 5.44 5V 8.42
δαιμονίζομαι (13) be demon-possessed C7.5
*δαιμόνιον ου τό (63) demon 4V 9V
δάκρυ δάκρυος τό (10, with δάκρυον) a tear
   D3.1
δάκρυον ου τό (10, with δάκρυ) a tear D3.1 6V
*δέ (2771) and/but 2.95 E2.27 2V 4.93 7.14
   8.83(b) A2.63 A3.64
*δεῖ (102) it is necessary/must 9.95 9V
δείκνυμι (33) show C3.2 C6.1 C6.2 D5.31 7.46
δέκα (25) ten 9V
δένδρον ου τό (25) tree 5V

δεξιός ά όν (54) right (-hand) 9V
δέομαι (22) entreat/beseech C7.5 C8.76
   E2.17 6.18
δέρω (15) thrash/strike/hit C1.89 C1.84 C1.85
   C4.4 C4.53 C8.61 E2.43 4.27
*δέχομαι (56) receive C7.5 6.18 9V
δέω (43) bind/tie C1.48
*διά (666) because of/through 8.62 8.69 5V
   8.71 9V
διὰ τί (26) why? 4V
διακατελέγχομαι (1) refute F47
διακονέω (36) serve/minister E4.18 9V
διάκονος ου ὁ and ἡ (29) servant/deacon
   D2.45 7V 9V
διακόσιοι αι α (8) two hundred 8V
διακρίνω (19) evaluate/discern 9V
διάλεκτος ου ἡ (6) language/dialect D2.44
διαλλάσσω (1) reconcile E2.84
διανέμω (1) spread C1.88 C1.89
*διδάσκαλος ου ὁ (59) teacher 8V
*διδάσκω (95) teach C5.5 4V 6V 7V
διδαχή ῆς ἡ (30) teaching 9V
*δίδωμι (416) give C3.1 C3.1c C3.85 C3.87
   C6.1 C6.2 D5.05 D5.31 D5.32 D5.34
   E2.16 E3.18 E4.39 E4.77 4V 6V 7.46
   9.59 9.89 9V
διέξοδος ου ἡ (1) thoroughfare D2.44
*δίκαιος α ον (79) righteous/just 7V 9.22
*δικαιοσύνη ης ἡ (91) righteousness 4V
δικαίως (5) justly/rightly 9.22
δίκτυον ου τό (12) net 8V
*διό (53) therefore 9V
διορύσσω (4) dig through/break through 6V
διπλοῦς ῆ οῦν (4) double D4.3
διψάω (16) thirst 9V
διώκω (45) persecute/seek after C1.6 9.71
*δοκέω (62) think/presume/seem 5V 9V
δοκιμή ῆς ἡ (7) worth/character 7V
δοκός οῦ ἡ (6) log/beam of wood D2.44
*δόξα ης ἡ (165) glory D1.3 D1.65 D1.66 D4.6
   D5.31 F36 3.11 3.15 3V 5.64 6.58 7.63
   A3.13
*δοξάζω (61) glorify/honour C1.7 E2.64 8V
   9.71
δουλεύω (25) be enslaved/serve 4.82 4V 7V
   8.45
*δοῦλος ου ὁ (124) slave 4V 9V
*δύναμαι (209) be able/can/capable of C3.3
   C6.1 C7.5 E4.27 4.61 6.18 7.46 7.47 7V
   9.89 9V
*δύναμις εως ἡ (118) power/miracle 1.27 2.29
   5V
δυνατός ή όν (32) powerful/the Almighty 7V

δύνω (2) sink/set (of sun) C3.6 C6.2 E2.84
   7.43 7.45 9.57
*δύο (136) two D6.7 E6.17 3V
*δώδεκα (75) twelve 9V
*ἐάν (343) if (ever) 1.37 4.45 4V 7V
*ἐὰν μή (62) except/unless 4V
*ἑαυτόν ἑαυτήν ἑαυτό ἑαυτοῦ (320) him-
   self/herself/itself/oneself/ ourselves/your-
   selves/themselves D6.8 5V 6V 9V
ἐάω (11) allow/leave C1.48 C8.74
ἐγγίζω (42) draw near/approach C8.88 4V 8V
ἐγγράφω (3) write/record E2.06 E2.77 E2.79
ἐγγύς (31) near/close to 4V E2.06 F11 9.37
*ἐγείρω (143) raise (up)/rouse C1.8a C1.84
   C1.85 C1.89 E4.38 6V 8V 9.71
ἐγκαλέω (7) accuse E2.77
ἐγκόπτω (ἐνκόπτω) (5) hinder/prevent E2.79
ἐγχρίω (1) rub on E3.22
*ἐγώ (1713) I/me/my D6.3 E2.92 E6.32 1.37
   2.52 2V 3.33 6.22 A3.21 A3.22
ἐδαφίζω (1) raze totally C8.88
ἐθίζω (1) accustom C8.74
*ἔθνος ους τό (162) nation/heathen/Gentile 5V
   9V
[ἔθω] (4) be accustomed C8.63 C8.74 7.54
*εἰ (513) if 4.45 E6.31 2.86 5V 8V 9V
*εἰ μή (107) except/unless 4V 5V 9V
*εἶδον (336) I saw C2.8 C8.74 D5.04 E2.24
   3.66 3V 7.33 7.35 7.52 A3.31
[εἴκω] (2) be like C8.63
*εἰμί (2450) be/exist C3.3 C6.1 C7.6 D5.05
   E2.46 E3.23 E6.32 1.37 1.65 2.76 2.81
   2.86 2.87 2V 3.81 3.93 6.23 6.41 6.42
   9.91 9.92 9.93 A2.16 A2.17
-εἶμι (-) go/will go C3.3
*εἶπον (925) I said/spoke/told C2.8 3.66 3V
   7.33 7.34 7.35 A3.33
*εἰρήνη ης ἡ (91) peace 1.33 2.29 4V
εἰρηνοποιός οῦ ὁ (1) peacemaker 8V
*εἰς (1753) into/for 8.63 A4.2 E3.11 E6.31 3V
   5.66 5V 7V 8.71 8.74
*εἷς μία ἕν ἑνός (337) one D6.7 D3.09 D3.17
   E2.36 4V 5.66
*εἰσέρχομαι (192) enter 4V 9V
εἰσῆλθον (suppletive of εἰσέρχομαι) I entered
   4V
εἴσοδος ου ἡ (5) entrance D2.44
*εἴτε (65) whether ... or ... /if ... if ... 8V
εἴωθα — see ἔθω 7.54
*ἐκ/ἐξ (915) out of 8.64 8.69 A4.2 E3.21 E6.31
   1.64 1.65 2.65 2V 3.71 8.44 8.71 8.74
   9.23
*ἕκαστος η ον (81) each/every 7.11 8V 9V
*ἐκβάλλω (81) throw out/send away/drive 3.71
   3.72 3.93 3V 4V
*ἐκεῖ (95) there (= in that place) E1.3 E2.92 3V
   9.13 9.23
ἐκεῖθεν (27) thence/from there 9.13

*ἐκεῖνος η ο (243) that (one)/those D6.2 E2.92
  3.36 3V 7.11 7.27 9.23 9V
*ἐκκλησία ας ἡ (114) church/assembly 9V
ἐκλεκτός ή όν (22) elect/chosen 6V
ἐκπετάννυμι (1) hold out C3.2
ἐκπλήσσω (13) amaze/astound/astonish 9V
ἐκχύννω (11) pour out (C5.32 C8.76 C8.77)
  E2.86
ἐκών ἐκοῦσα ἐκόν ἐκοντός (2) willing D4.5
  D3.16 D3.18 5.65 5.67 5V
ἐλαία ας ἡ (15) olive (-tree) 4V
ἐλάσσων or ἐλάττων ον (4) less 9.35
ἐλαύνω (5) drive/row C5.34 E4.38
ἐλάχιστος η ον (14) least 4V 9.35
ἐλεάω/ἐλεέω (32) be merciful 4V 7V
ἐλέγχω (17) convict/correct E4.38
ἑλκόομαι (1) be covered with sores C8.74
ἕλκω (8) drag/pull C8.74
Ἕλλην Ἕλληνος ὁ (26) Greek D3.15 6V
Ἑλληνίς ίδος ἡ (2) Greek woman F3
ἐλπίζω (31) hope/expect C8.88 E4.36 7V
*ἐλπίς ίδος ἡ (53) hope 5V
ἐμαυτόν ἐμαυτήν ἐμαυτό ἐμαυτοῦ (37) myself
  D6.8 5V 6.22 7V
ἐμβαίνω (17) embark/get into E2.77
ἐμβάλλω (1) throw (in) E2.06
ἐμβριμάομαι (5) be moved with anger/deep
  feeling C7.5
ἐμέω (1) vomit out/spit out C1.48
ἐμμένω (4) continue in E2.77
*ἐμός ἐμή ἐμόν (76) my 2.51 2.53 2V 3V 6.22
  7.22
ἔμπροσθεν (48) in front of 8.66 8V
ἐμφανίζω (10) manifest (pass.: appear) 7V
*ἐν (2713) in/by means of/with 8.65 E3.11
  E3.12 E3.22 E6.31 2.65 2.66 2V 3V 4.92
  5.66 8.71 8.74 9V A5.21
ἔναντι (2) before/in the presence of 3V
ἐναντίος α ον (8) opposite E2.92
ἐνδιδύσκω (2) clothe in C5.5
ἐνδύω (28) clothe/put on 6.14
ἔνειμι (1) be inside E3.12
ἐνθάδε (8) hither/to here/here 9.13
ἔνθεν (2) hence/from here 9.13
ἐννεύω (1) enquire by signs E2.77
ἐντέλλομαι (15) command C1.89 C1.83
  C1.85 C7.5 C8.61 C8.64 6V
ἐντεῦθεν (9) hence/from here 9.13
*ἐντολή ῆς ἡ (68) commandment 4V 7V
ἐντός (2) within/inside/among E3.12 3V
ἐντρέπω (9) make ashamed E2.77
*ἐνώπιον (93) in front of 8.66 8V
ἕξ (13) six 8V
ἐξαλείφω (5) wipe away 6V
ἐξανίστημι (3) raise up 8V
ἐξαυτῆς (6) immediately 7V
*ἐξέρχομαι (216) come/go out 3.71 3.94 3V
  (E6.28)
ἔξεστι(ν) (31) it is permitted/lawful 9.95
ἐξήκοντα (9) sixty 8V

*ἐξῆλθον (suppletive of ἐξέρχομαι) I came out
  3.71 3.94 3V E6.28
ἔξοδος ου ἡ (3) departure/Exodus D2.44
ἐξουθενέω (11) despise E4.37
*ἐξουσία ας ἡ (102) authority/right 5V 6V
*ἔξω (62) outside 8.66 3V 9.23
ἔοικα — see εἴκω
ἑορτή ῆς ἡ (25) feast/festival 1.37 4V 9V
*ἐπαγγελία ας ἡ (52) promise 9V
ἐπαγγέλλομαι (15) promise/claim (C1.8a)
  C7.5 9V
ἐπαίρω (19) raise/lift up E6.28
*ἐπερωτάω (56) ask (a question) 8V 9V
*ἐπί (878) on/upon/at/against/with 8.61 8.69
  5V 7V 8.71
ἐπιγινώσκω (44) know/recognize 9V
ἐπιζητέω (13) desire/search for 9V
ἐπιθυμέω (16) desire/long (for) 7V
ἐπικέλλω (1) run aground C1.89 C1.83
ἐπιλύω (2) explain 7V
ἐπιράπτω (1) sew on C5.7
ἐπισκέπτομαι (11) visit/care about C5.7 C7.5
ἐπισπείρω (1) sow over/resow 4V
ἐπίσταμαι (14) understand C3.3 C7.5
ἐπιστρέφω (36) return/turn around 4V
ἐπιτιμάω (29) command/order/rebuke 4V
ἐπιφαύσκω (1) shine upon C5.5
ἐπιφώσκω (2) dawn C5.5
*ἑπτά (87) seven 9V
ἐργάζομαι (41) work/perform C7.5 C8.74
  6.18 9V
ἐργάτης ου ὁ (16) workman 7V
*ἔργον ου τό (169) work/deed action D2.2 F36
  1.27 1.32 1.37 2.29 2.4 7V A2.12 A2.13
  A2.23
ἐρημία ας ἡ (4) deserted place 3V 7V
ἔρημος ου ἡ (34) desert(ed place) D2.44 3V
ἔρις ἔριδος ἡ (9) strife D3.28 5V
ἔριφος ου ὁ and ἡ (2) kid/goat D2.45
*ἔρχομαι (631) come/go C2.8 C7.5 E4.13 3.63
  3.66 6.18 6V 7.33 7V 9V
*[ἔρω] (96) say/speak/tell C2.8 C8.74 7.33
  7.34
*ἐρωτάω (62) ask (a question) 8V
*ἐσθίω (65) eat/consume C2.8 C4.2 C7.6 7.33
  7.51 7V 9V
*ἔσχατος η ον (52) last 8V 9.35 9V
*ἕτερος α ον (98) other/different 7.11 9V
*ἔτι (92) still/yet/longer 6V 9V
ἑτοιμάζω (41) prepare 7V
ἔτος ους τό (49) year 7V
εὖ (5) well E3.11 E4.14 9.37
*εὐαγγελίζω/-ομαι (54) preach the gospel C7.2
  C7.5 E4.14 6.18 6V
*εὐαγγέλιον ου τό (76) gospel/good news 2V
εὐδοκέω (21) be pleased/take delight in 4V
εὐθύνω (2) make straight C1.89
*εὐθύς (54) immediately 3V
*εὑρίσκω (176) find C2.4 E4.37 F41 4V 7.36
  7V 9.59 9V

εὐφραίνω (14) make glad C1.89 C1.84
εὐχαριστέω (38) give thanks 1.33
εὔχομαι (7) pray C7.5 (6.18) 9V
*ἔφαγον/φάγομαι (93) (√ φαγ; suppletive of
    ἐσθίω) I ate/I will eat C2.8 C4.2 C7.6
    7.33 7.51
ἐφάλλομαι (1) jump on C2.2 C1.83 C1.89
    C7.5
ἐχθρός ά όν (32) enemy/hostile 4V 8V
ἔχιδνα ης ἡ (5) snake D1.65
*ἔχω (705) have C2.7 C2.96 C2.97 C8.74 E1.3
    E2.57 E2.85 E4.13 2V 3.71 7.36 A2.49
*ἕως (145) until/as far as 8.66 4V
*ζάω (140) live/be alive C8.07 C8.08 5V 7V
ζέω (2) boil (with zeal) C8.76
*ζητέω (117) seek E4.35 9V
ζιζάνιον ου τό (8) darnel (a weed) 2V
*ζωή ῆς ἡ (135) life D1.64 E4.14 1.27 2.29
ζώννυμι (3) gird/dress C3.2
ζῷον ου τό (23) living creature 5V
ζωοποιέω (11) make alive E4.14
*ἤ (342) or/than 3V 9.38 9V
ἡγεμών όνος ὁ (19) leader D3.16 D3.09 D4.8
    E2.36 E2.44 5.31 5.37 5.67 5.68 5V
ἡγέομαι (28) think/lead C7.5 6.18
ἡδέως ἥδιστα (3,2) gladly, most gladly 9.37
*ἤδη (60) already 9V
ἥκω (26) be present/have come C4.3 8V
*ἦλθον (√ ἐλθ; suppletive of ἔρχομαι) I came
    C2.8 E2.64 E4.38 E6.28 3.61 3.63 3.66
    3.71 3.81 3.82 3.94 3V 7.33 A3.32
Ἡλίας ου ὁ (29) Elijah 3V
ἡλίκος η ον (2) how large/great/small 7.11
ἥλιος ου ὁ (32) the sun 8V
*ἡμεῖς (856) we/us/our D6.3 3.33 A3.21 A3.23
*ἡμέρα ας ἡ (388) day 1.27 1.37 2.29 2.52 3V
ἥμισυς ἡμίσεια ἥμισυ (5) half D4.4
Ἡρῴδης ου ὁ (43) Herod 8S
Ἡσαΐας ου ὁ (22) Isaiah 1.71 3V
ἥσσων ἧσσον (2) worse/less 9.35 9.37
*θάλασσα ης ἡ (91) sea D1.65 3V
*θάνατος ου ὁ (120) death 6V 7V
θάπτω (11) bury C4.4 C5.7
θαυμάζω (42) marvel at 7V
θεάομαι (22) look at/observe C1.48 C7.5 6.18
    7V
*θέλημα ματος τό (62) will/wish 5V 6V
*θέλω (207) wish/want/will C1.88 C1.89 E4.27
    4.58 4.61 4V 6V 7V 9V
*θεός οῦ ὁ and ἡ (1314) God/god/goddess
    D2.45 1.27 1.84 2.29 2.53 3.23 Λ2.43
θεραπεύω (43) heal/cure 4V
θερμαίνω (6) warm C1.89 C1.84
*θεωρέω (58) watch/observe 8V 9V
θῆλυς εια υ (5) female 5V

θησαυρίζω (8) store up/gather 6V
θησαυρός οῦ ὁ (17) treasure/storehouse 6V
θιγγάνω (3) touch C2.34
θλίβω (10) press hard/oppress C1.5 E2.61
    E4.33 F39 9.71
θνήσκω (9) die C2.4 C2.96 C7.6 E4.33 6.95
    7.36
θρίξ τριχός ἡ (15) hair D3.26 E2.85 9V
*θρόνος ου ὁ (62) throne 6V
θυγάτηρ θυγατρός ἡ (28) daughter D3.32
    5.42 5V
θύελλα ης ἡ (1) whirlwind D1.65
θύρα ας ἡ (39) door/gate 3.42 3V
θυρωρός οῦ ὁ and ἡ (4) doorkeeper D2.43
    D2.45
θύω (13) sacrifice/kill E2.83
Θωμᾶς ᾶ ὁ (11) Thomas 3S
ἰάομαι (26) heal/cure/restore C1.48 C7.5
    E4.37 6.18 9V
Ἰακώβ (26) Jacob 2.98
ἴδε (28) look!/behold!/see! 2V
*ἴδιος α ον (113) one's own 1.27 2.51 7V 9V
*ἰδού (200) look!/behold!/see! 2V
*[ἴδω] (336) see C2.8 C8.74 D5.04 E2.24 7.52
ἱερεύς έως ὁ priest 5V
*ἱερόν οῦ τό (70) temple 6V 9V
*Ἱεροσόλυμα ων τά (63) Jerusalem 4V
-ἵημι (-) send C3.1 C3.85 (D5.32) E4.12
    E4.77 7.48
*Ἰησοῦς οῦ ὁ (908) Jesus/Joshua D2.3 1.46
ἱλάσκομαι (2) propitiate C5.5 C7.5
ἱμάς ἱμάντος ὁ (4) strap D3.20
*ἱμάτιον ου τό (60) garment/clothing 8V
*ἵνα (673) in order that/that 4.45 4V
*Ἰουδαῖος α ον (193) a Jew/Jewish 2S
Ἰσαάκ (20) Isaac 2S
ἴσος η ον (8) equal/the same 9V
ἱστάνω (1) stand C9.2
*ἵστημι (152) stand C3.1 C3.1a C3.86 C3.87
    C6.1 C6.2 C8.93 C9.2 D5.12 D5.31
    D5.32 D5.33 D5.37 E2.84 E4.13 E4.39
    7.43 7.45 7.46 7.47 8.69 9V
ἰσχύς ἰσχύος ἡ (10) strength/might 5V
ἰχθύς ἰχθύος ὁ (20) fish D3.1 1.71 5.20 5.23
    5.24 5.50 5V 8V
*Ἰωάννης ου ὁ (135) John 2S
Ἰωνᾶς ᾶ ὁ (9) Jonah 9V
ἰῶτα (1) iota/jot 1.27 1.46 4V
*κἀγώ (84) and I/I also E2.92 5V 7V
καθαίρω (1) clean/prune C1.89 C1.84 E2.43
καθαρίζω (31) make clean C8.88 6V
καθαρός ά όν (26) clean/pure 7V
καθεύδω (22) sleep 4V

*κάθημαι (91) sit down C3.3 C7.5 E4.17 6.18 7.48

καθίζω (45) be seated/sit 8V

*καθώς (178) just as 3V 7V 9V E2.63

*καί (8947) and/also/even 2V 9V E2.92 E3.11 A2.63

Καϊάφας α ὁ (9) Caiaphas 3S

καινός ή όν (42) new 5V 7V

*καιρός οῦ ὁ (85) time/occasion 8V 9V

καίω (12) burn C4.4 C8.75 C8.76

κἀκεῖ (10) and there/there also E2.92

κἀκεῖνος (20) and that one/that one also E2.92

κακολογέω (4) speak evil of E4.14

*κακός ή όν (50) bad E4.14 9.22 9.35 9V

κακῶς (16) badly 9.22 9.37

*καλέω (148) call C1.48 6V 7V 8V

καλλιέλαιος ου ἡ (1) cultivated olive D2.44

*καλός ή όν (99) good D4.2 D4.05 2V 9.22 9.34 9V

καλύπτω (8) cover/hide/conceal C1.5 C5.7 9.71

καλῶς (37) rightly/well 8V 9.22 9.37

κάμηλος ου ὁ and ἡ (6) camel D2.45

κάμινος ου ἡ (4) furnace D2.44

κάμνω (2) be ill C2.31

κάμπτω (4) bend (the knee) C5.7

κἄν (15) and if/even if E2.92

*καρδία ας ἡ (156) heart D1.1 D0.27 D1.61 D1.63 D1.65 D4.4 D5.13 E6.27 1.27 2.29 3.11 3.14 3.17 3V 5.64 A3.12

*καρπός οῦ ὁ (66) fruit 4V

*κατά (471) according to/against/down 8.62 8.69

*καταβαίνω (81) go down/come down 7V

καταβαρύνω (1) weigh down C1.89

κατάγνυμι (4) break C3.2 C4.4

κατακυριεύω (4) lord it over 9V

καταλαμβάνω (15) obtain (midd. realize) 6.17

καταλείπω (23) leave (behind)/forsake 8V 9V

καταλύω (17) do away with/destroy 4V

καταράομαι (5) curse C1.48 C7.5

καταρτίζω (13) mend/make complete C8.89

κατέναντι (9) opposite 4V

κατεξουσιάζω (2) exercise authority over 9V

κατήγωρ ορος ὁ (1) accuser D3.13

κατοικέω (44) settle down/dwell 9V

καυχάομαι (37) boast C7.5 6.18

κεῖμαι (24) lie down C3.3 C7.5 5V 6.18 7.48

κείρω (4) shear C1.89 C1.84 6.14

κεραία ας ἡ (2) stroke of a letter 4V

κεράννυμι (2) mix/pour C3.2

κέρας κέρατος τό (11) horn D3.10

κερδαίνω (17) gain/win C5.33

κέρδος ους τό (3) gain 8V

*κεφαλή ῆς ἡ (75) head 9V

*κηρύσσω (61) preach/proclaim C1.6 E2.62 4V 9.71

κιβωτός οῦ ἡ (6) box/ark D2.44

κίχρημι (1) lend C3.1

κλαίω (38) weep/cry C8.76

κλάω (14) break (bread) C1.48

κλείς κλειδός ἡ (6) key D3.28 5V 7V

κλείω (16) shut/lock C8.91 7V

κλέπτης ου ὁ (16) thief 6V

κλέπτω (13) steal C5.7 6V

κληρονόμος ου ὁ and ἡ (15) heir D2.45

κλῆσις εως ἡ (11) calling 5V

κλίνω (7) incline/lay down/bow down C1.89 C1.86

κοιμάομαι (18) sleep C7.5

κοινός ή όν (14) common/unclean F2 F3 F7 F43

κολλάομαι (12) join/cleave to/unite with C7.5

κομίζω (11) carry/bring/buy C8.85 C8.88

κοπιάω (23) toil/labour/work hard C1.48

κόπτω (8) cut C4.4 C4.54 C5.7

κορέννυμι (2) fill C3.2

κοσμέω (10) decorate/adorn 7V

κοσμοκράτωρ ορος ὁ (1) world ruler D3.13

*κόσμος ου ὁ (185) world 2V 6V 7V

*κράζω (55) cry out/shout C4.3 C8.84 (C2.6) 9V

κρατέω (47) take hold of/seize/arrest 9V

κράτιστος η ον (4) most excellent 9.35

κραυγή ῆς ἡ (6) crying/shouting 6V

κρέας (-) τό (2) meat D3.5

κρείσσων or κρείττων ον (19) better 9.35 9.37

κρεμάννυμι (7) hang C3.2

κρίθινος η ον (2) made of barley 7V

κρίμα ματος τό (27) judgement 5V

*κρίνω (114) judge/decide C1.9c C1.86 C1.89 E2.18 E2.43 E6.26 4.27 9.71 9V

κρούω (9) knock 9V

κρυπτός ή όν (17) secret/hidden 6V

κρύπτω (19) conceal/hide/cover C4.4 C4.54 C5.7

κτήτωρ ορος ὁ (1) possessor D3.13

κτίζω (15) create 6V

κτίσις εως ἡ (19) creation/creature 5V 7V

κύπτω (3) stoop down C5.7

*κύριος ου ὁ (718) lord/sir 2.4 2V D0.27 E3.13 E3.36 1.35 5.20 8.18 8.42 A2.12 A2.13 A2.24 A2.42 A2.43

κύων κυνός ὁ (5) dog D3.35

κώμη ης ἡ (27) village 4V 8V

κώνωψ κώνωπος ὁ (1) gnat/mosquito D3.7

κωφός ή όν (14) deaf/dumb 6V

λαγχάνω (4) obtain (by lot) C2.34

λαῖλαψ απος ἡ (3) storm/squall D3.7

*λαλέω (298) speak/converse/chat/chatter C1.3
  C6.1 E2.18 E2.32 E4.42 E6.26 6.95 6V
  7V 9.71

*λαμβάνω (258) take/receive C2.34 C7.6 E3.33
  E4.13 6V 7.36 7.37 7V 9.59

λάμπω (7) shine C4.52 8V

λανθάνω (6) be hidden/lose sight of C2.34
  E2.64

*λαός οῦ ὁ (141) people 1.27 2.29 6V 9V

*λέγω (1318) say/speak/tell C2.8 C8.64 E3.31
  2V 3.66 7.33 7.34 9V A2.48

λείπω (6) leave/lack C2.5 C4.52 C8.63 7.36

λεπρός οῦ ὁ (9) leper 6V

λευκαίνω (2) whiten C1.89 C1.84

λευκός ή όν (24) white/shining 8V

ληνός οῦ ὁ/ἡ (5) winepress D2.45

λίβανος ου ὁ/ἡ (2) frankincense D2.45

*λίθος ου ὁ (58) stone 5V

λιμός οῦ ὁ/ἡ (12) hunger/famine D2.45

λίψ λιβός ὁ (1) south-west wind/facing s.w.
  D3.7 E2.66 5.34

λογίζομαι (40) account/reckon C7.5 6.18

*λόγος ου ὁ (331) word/saying/message D2.1
  C8.64 D2.43 E3.31 6V

*λοιπός ή όν (55) remainder/remaining/rest 7V

λύκος ου ὁ (6) wolf 3V

λυμαίνομαι (1) harass C1.89 C1.84 C7.5

λύπη ης ἡ (15) grief/sorrow/pain 9V

λύτρον ου τό (2) ransom 9V

λύω (42) loose/release C1.1 C0.2 C0.4 C6.1
  C6.2 D3.09 D4.5 D5.04 D5.1 E2.18
  E2.24 E2.35 E2.42 E2.45 E2.56 E2.84
  E3.12 E3.18 E3.19 E3.32 E3.34 E3.35
  E4.08 E4.09 E4.34 E6.17 E6.28 F40
  F41 2.76 2.78 2.81 2.87 3.51 3.64 3.93
  3.94 4.21 4.35 4.37 4.39 4.76 5.65 6.23
  6.25 6.27 6.28 6.29 6.34 6.41 6.50 6.57
  6.58 6.6 6.71 6.72 6.8 7.41 7.63 7.64
  7.81 9.59 9.65 9.71 9.73 9.89 9.96 9V
  A2.14 A2.15 A2.44 A2.45 A2.46 A2.48
  A2.63 A5.22

μαθητεύω (4) disciplicize/make a disciple 6V

*μαθητής οῦ ὁ (262) disciple D1.5 D1.61
  D1.66 3.11 3.16 3.17 3.18 3V 8.42

μαίνομαι (5) be insane/out of one's mind
  C1.89 C1.84 C7.5

μακαρίζω (2) regard as blessed C8.88

*μακάριος α ον (50) blessed/fortunate 5V 6V

μακράν (10) far/far away 3V

μάλιστα (12) most of all/especially 9.37

*μᾶλλον (80) more/rather 9.37 9V

μανθάνω (25) learn/discover C2.34 E4.43
  7.36

μάννα τό (4) manna 7V

μαραίνω (1) wither away C1.89 C1.84

μάρμαρος ου ὁ/ἡ (1) marble D2.45

*μαρτυρέω (76) testify/bear witness 7V

μαρτύρομαι (5) testify/urge C1.89 C7.5

μάρτυς μάρτυρος ὁ (35) witness D3.31 7V

μάχαιρα ης ἡ (29) sword D1.65 9V

μεγαλύνω (8) magnify/hold in honour/extend
  C1.89 8V

*μέγας μεγάλη μέγα μεγάλου (194) great/large
  D4.43 F36 4V 5.65 7V 9.35 9V

μεγιστάν ᾶνος ὁ (3) person of high status
  D3.15

μέγιστος η ον (1) greatest 9.35

μεθίστημι (5) remove/mislead E2.63

μεθύσκομαι (4) get drunk C5.5 C7.5

μείζων μεῖζον (48) greater 9.35

μέλας μέλαινα μέλαν (6) black D4.6 D4.05

μέλι μέλιτος τό (4) honey D3.8 D3.9

*μέλλω (110) intend/be about to C1.88 C1.89
  4.61 5V 8V 9V

μέλος ους τό (34) limb/part/member 9V

μέλω (10) (impers.) it is of concern C1.88
  C1.89 9.95

μεμβράνα ης ἡ (1) parchment D1.65

*μέν (181) indicates contrast; μὲν ... δέ ... on
  the one hand ... on the other hand ... 5V
  7V 9V

*μένω (118) remain C1.88 C1.89 C1.84 E2.43
  7V 8V 9.59

μέριμνα ης ἡ (6) concern D1.65

μέρος ους τό (42) part 7V

*μέσος η ον (56) middle/(in the) midst 3V
  A3.65

*μετά (467) after/with 8.62 8.69 3V A3.62

μεταμέλομαι (6) regret C1.89 C7.5

μεταμορφόομαι (4) be transformed 8V

μετάνοια ας ἡ (22) repentance 7V

μετοικίζω (2) make to move C8.88

μέχρι (20) until/as far as 8.66

*μή (1055) not/no 4.46 4.49 E3.22 4.83

*μηδέ (57) and not/not even/neither-nor 5.66 9V

*μηδείς μηδεμία μηδέν (85) no-one/nothing
  D6.7 5.66

μηκύνω (1) grow C1.89

μήν μηνός ὁ (18) month D3.15 5.37

μήτε (34) neither/nor 9V

*μήτηρ μητρός ἡ (84) mother D3.32 5.42 5V
  7V

μιαίνω (5) defile/contaminate C1.89 C1.84

μίγνυμι (4) mix C3.2 C4.52

μικρός ά όν (30) little/small 9.35

μιμνήσκω (23) remember C5.1 C5.5 E3.32
  6V

μισθός οῦ ὁ (29) wages/reward 3.42 3V 7V 8V
μνημεῖον ου τό (37) tomb/grave 9V
μοιχαλίς ίδος ἡ (7) adulteress/adulterous 9V
μοιχάομαι (4) commit adultery C7.5
μολύνω (3) defile/contaminate C1.89
*μόνος η ον (66) only/alone 1.27 2.51 8V 9V
μόσχος ου ὁ and ἡ (6) calf/young bull/ox D2.45
μύλος ου ὁ (4) mill 6V
μυριάς άδος ἡ (8) myriad/ten thousand 5V
μώλωψ μώλωπος ὁ (1) wound D3.7
μωραίνω (4) make foolish/tasteless C1.89 C1.84
*Μωϋσῆς έως ὁ (81) Moses 3S
ναί (34) yes/certainly/indeed 4V
ναός οῦ ὁ (45) temple/sactuary 7V
νάρδος ου ἡ (2) oil of nard D2.44
ναῦς (-) ἡ (1) ship D3.3
νεανίας ου ὁ (4) young man D1.4 D1.66 E3.36 3.11 3.17 8.42
*νεκρός ά όν (128) dead/dead person 2V 6V 7V
νέος νέα νέον (23) young/new D4.3 5V
νεφέλη ης ἡ (25) cloud 2V
νεωκόρος ου ὁ and ἡ (1) templekeeper D2.45
νεώτερος α ον (11) younger 5V
νῆσος ου ἡ (9) island D2.44
νικάω (28) conquer/overcome E4.34 8V
νιπτήρ ῆρος ὁ (1) washbasin D3.11
νίπτω (17) wash C5.7 6.14 8V
νομίζω (15) think/suppose/consider 4.83 4V
*νόμος ου ὁ (191) law 1.27 2.29 7V A2.42
νόσος ου ἡ (11) illness D2.44
νοῦς νοός ὁ (24) mind D3.3 5V
νύμφη ης ἡ (8) bride 7V
*νῦν (148) now 8V 9V E3.11
*νύξ νυκτός ἡ (61) night D3.6 3V 5.38 5V 8V
νύσσω (1) prick/pierce/stab C4.4
ξηραίνω (15) dry up/wither C1.9a C1.84 C1.89 9.71
ξύλον ου τό (20) wood/tree/club 1.27 2.29 9V
*ὁ ἡ τό (19,734) the (definiteness) D6.1 E6.31 2.4 4.93 7.11 7.14 8.8 A2.16 A2.17 A2.21 A2.24
ὄγδοος η ον (5) eighth D4.3
ὅδε ἥδε τόδε (10) this 7.11 7.14
*ὁδός οῦ ἡ (101) way/road D2.44 3V
ὁδούς ὁδόντος ὁ (12) tooth D3.19 E2.42
ὅθεν (15) whence/from where/wherefore 9.13
*οἶδα (321) I know 7.52 C4.3 7.54 7V
*οἰκία ας ἡ (94) house/household 9V
οἰκοδεσπότης ου ὁ (12) master 4V
οἰκοδομέω (40) build/build up E4.36 5V
*οἶκος ου ὁ (112) house/household 1.33 2.29

ὀικτίρω (2) have compassion on C1.88 C1.89
οἰνοπότης ου ὁ (2) wine-drinker/drunkard 9V
οἶνος ου ὁ (34) wine 9V
οἶος α ον (14) of what kind/such as 7.11
*ὅλος η ον (108) whole/complete 1.27 1.37 2.51 7.27
ὁμείρομαι (1) yearn for/long for C1.89 C7.5
ὁμιλέω (4) converse/speak with 8V
ὄμνυμι (26) vow/take an oath C3.2
ὅμοιος α ον (45) like/similar 9.22
ὁμοίως (31) similarly/likewise 9.22
ὄναρ (-) τό (6) dream D3.13
ὀνίνημι (1) benefit C3.1 C6.2
*ὄνομα ατος τό (228) name E2.92 3.42 3V 5V
ὄνος ου ὁ and ἡ (6) donkey/ass D2.45
ὀπίσω (35) after/behind 8.66 5V 6V
ὁποῖος α ον (5) of what kind/such as 7.11
*ὅπου (82) where 9.13 6V
*ὅπως (53) in order that 9.13 9V
*ὁράω (114) see (pass. appear) C2.8 C7.6 C8.74 E4.38 3.66 4.61 7.33 7V
ὀργή ῆς ἡ (36) wrath/anger 1.32
*ὄρος ους τό (62) mountain 4V
ὀρύσσω (3) dig E4.38
ὀρχέομαι (4) dance C7.5
*ὅς ἥ ὅ (1369) who/which/what/that (relative) D6.2 4.14 7.11 7.15
ὁσάκις (3) whenever/as often as 9.13
ὅσιος α ον (8) holy 8V
*ὅσος η ον (110) as great/much/many as 7.11 6V 9V
*ὅστις ἥτις ὅ τι (154) who(ever)/which(ever) 7.11 7.15 7V 8V
ὀστοῦν οῦ τό (4) bone D2.41
*ὅταν (123) whenever 6V
*ὅτε (102) when/while 4V 9.13 7V 8V
*ὅτι (1285) that/because/" 1.73 2V 7.15 7V
*οὐ/οὐκ/οὐχ (1619) not/no 1.64 2.96 E3.11 E3.22 E6.31 E6.34 2V 4.49
οὗ (25) where 9.13 3V
οὐαί (45) woe to/alas for 9V
*οὐδέ (139) and not/not even/neither-nor 5V 7V E2.27 5.66
*οὐδείς οὐδεμία οὐδέν (226) no-one/nothing D6.7 5.66 5V 6V 7V
οὐκέτι (48) no longer 5V
*οὖν (493) then/therefore 2.95 2V A2.63
οὐράνιος ον (9) heavenly 3V
*οὐρανός οῦ ὁ (272) heaven 1.33 2.29
οὖς ὠτός τό (36) ear D3.30 5.46 5V
*οὔτε (91) neither/nor 6V
*οὗτος αὕτη τοῦτο (1388) this (one)/these D6.4 1.37 2.53 2V 3.32 3.33 3.35 6.22 7.11 7.13 7.14 7.27 9.23 9V A3.26

*οὕτως (208) thus/so 4V 9.13 9.23
*οὐχί (53) not/no 2V 4V
ὀφείλω (35) owe/ought C1.89 C1.83 8V
*ὀφθαλμός οῦ ὁ (100) eye 4V
ὀχλοποιέω (1) gather a crowd E4.14
*ὄχλος ου ὁ (174) crowd E4.14 7V
ὀψάριον ου τό (5) (small) fish 7V
παιδάριον ου τό (1) a small boy 7V
*παιδίον ου τό (52) child/infant 8V 9V
παίζω (1) dance/play C8.84
παῖς παιδός ὁ and ἡ (24) child/boy/girl/servant
     D3.8 E2.66 4V 5.31 5.32 5.35 5.45 5V
παίω (5) strike/hit C2.99
*πάλιν (139) again 3V E3.11
παντοκράτωρ ορος ὁ (10) the Almighty D3.13
πάντοτε (41) always 6V 8V
*παρά (191) beside 8.61 8.69 3V
*παραβολή ης ἡ (50) parable 7V
παράδεισος ου ὁ (3) paradise 6V
*παραδίδωμι (120) deliver up/hand over/be-
     tray/pass on 8V 9V
*παρακαλέω (109) encourage/request/exhort/
     comfort 5V
παραλαμβάνω (49) take along/take away/take
     with one 6V 8V 9V
παράλιος ου ἡ (1) seacoast D2.44
παρασκευή ῆς ἡ (6) day of preparation D1.64
παρέρχομαι (29) pass away/by 4V
παρῆλθον (suppletive of παρέρχομαι) I passed
     away/by 4V
παρθένος ου ὁ and ἡ (15) virgin D2.45 3.23
πάροδος ου ἡ (1) passage/passing by D2.44
παροξύνω (2) irritate C1.89
παροργίζω (2) make angry/resentful C8.88
παροτρύνω (1) incite C1.89
παρρησία ας ἡ (31) openness (dat.: openly,
     plainly, freely) 6V
*πᾶς πᾶσα πᾶν παντός (1226) each/every/all
     D4.6 D3.20 5.64 5.65 5V 7.27
πάσχα τό (29) Passover 4V
πάσχω (42) suffer C2.4 C2.97 C8.63 E2.64
     7.36 9V
πατάσσω (10) strike/hit C2.99
*πατήρ πατρός ὁ (415) father D3.32 E2.52
     F36 3V 5.42 5.43 5.44 7V 8.42
πειθαρχέω (4) give the obedience due 9V
*πείθω (52) persuade/trust in C8.63 E2.64 6.17
     7V
πεινάω (23) be hungry/hunger C1.48
*πέμπω (79) send C8.63 5V 7V
πένθος ους τό (5) sorrow/sadness/grief/
     mourning 6V
πέντε (38) five 7V
πέραν (23) across/the other side 9.37

πέρας πέρατος τό (4) end D3.10
*περί (331) about 8.62 8.69 E2.22 E2.25 E2.26
     3V
*περιπατέω (95) walk (around) 6V 9V
περισσεύω (39) exceed/overflow 4V
περιστερά ᾶς ἡ (10) dove/pigeon 7V
περιτέμνω (17) circumcise C2.31 (C1.89)
     C2.96
*Πέτρος ου ὁ (154) Peter 2S
πήγνυμι (1) fasten/set up (a tent) C3.2
πηλίκος (2) how large/great? 7.11
πηλός οῦ ὁ (6) clay/mud 4V
πῆχυς πήχεως ὁ (4) a cubit D3.2 D4.4 8V
πικραίνω (4) make bitter C1.89 C1.84
*Πιλᾶτος ου ὁ (55) Pilate 2S
πίμπλημι (24) fill C3.1
πίμπρημι (1) burn/swell up C3.1
*πίνω (73) drink C2.31 C2.97 C4.2 C7.6 C8.63
     7.36 7.51 9V
πιπράσκω (9) sell C5.1 C5.5
*πίπτω (90) fall C2.1 C2.97 C7.6 C8.63 E2.53
     6.95 7.36 8V 9V
*πιστεύω (241) believe/trust 3V 8.45 A3.53
*πίστις εως ἡ (243) faith 5V
*πιστός ή όν (67) believing/faithful/trustworthy
     D4.03 4V 6V 7V
πλανάω (39) lead astray/mislead/deceive 7V
πλατύνω (3) enlarge/open wide C1.89
πλεῖστος η ον (4) most 9.35 9.37
*πλείων πλεῖον (55) more (than) 4V 9.35 9.37
πλέκω (3) weave/plait C4.4 C4.54 C8.63
πλέω (6) sail C8.76
πληθύνω (12) increase/multiply C1.89
πλήμμυρα ης ἡ (1) flood D1.65
*πληρόω (86) fulfil/accomplish/fill C1.4 C6.1
     E2.32 4V 8V 9.71
πλήρωμα ματος τό (17) fulfilling/complete-
     ness 9V
πλησίον (17) near/neighbour 9V
πλήσσω (1) strike/hit C4.4 C2.99 C8.63
πλοιάριον ου τό (6) (small) boat 8V
*πλοῖον ου τό (66) boat 9V
πλοῦς πλοός ὁ (3) voyage D3.3
πλύνω (3) wash C1.89
*πνεῦμα ματος τό (379) spirit/wind/breath 3.42
     3V 5V
πνέω (7) breathe/blow (of wind) C8.76 E4.34
πνίγω (3) choke/drown C4.4
πνοή ῆς ἡ (2) wind/breath D1.64
πόθεν (28) from where?/where? 2V 9.13
*ποιέω (565) do/carry out/practise/make/pro-
     duce 4V 6V 7V
ποιμαίνω (11) shepherd/rule C1.89 C1.84

ποιμήν ένος ὁ (18) shepherd D3.17 D3.09
    E2.44 5.37 5V

ποῖος α ον (32) of what kind? 7.11

*πόλις πόλεως ἡ (161) a city D3.2 D0.27
    D3.13 D3.28 D4.4 E2.17 E6.24 F36
    5.20 5.24 5.65 7V

πολίτευμα ματος τό (1) place of citizenship 6V

πολλάκις (17) often/frequently 9.13

*πολύς πολλή πολύ πολλοῦ (353) much/many
    D4.42 F36 5.65 5V 9.35 9.37

*πονηρός ά όν (78) evil/bad/the Evil One 2V
    9V

πόνος ου ὁ (4) pain/suffering/labour 6V

*πορεύομαι (15) go/proceed/journey C7.5 6.18
    6V 9V

πορφυροῦς ᾶ οῦν (4) purple D4.3

ποσάκις (3) how often? 9.13

πόσος η ον (27) how much/many? 7.11

ποταπός ή όν (6) of what kind? 7.11

πότε (19) when? 9.13

ποτέ (29) once/at some time 9.13 4V

πότερος (1) which of two?/whether 7.11

ποῦ (47) where? 9.13

πού (4) somewhere 9.13

*πούς ποδός ὁ (93) foot D3.8 D3.09 E2.36 5V
    8V

πραιτώριον ου τό (8) residence (of governor,
    etc.) 3V

πράκτωρ ορος ὁ (2) court officer D3.13

*πρεσβύτερος α ον (65) older/elder 8V

πρό (47) before/prior to 8.64 8.69 E2.22
    E2.25 E2.26 E3.11 2.65 2V

πρόβατον ου τό (37) sheep 3.42 3V

*πρός (696) to/towards/with 8.61 A4.2 5V 8.71
    8.74

*προσέρχομαι (87) approach/come to (some-
    one, etc.) 4V

*προσεύχομαι (86) pray (C7.5) 6.18 8.45 9V

*προσῆλθον (suppletive of προσέρχομαι) I
    approached 4V

προσκαλέω (29) call to oneself 9V

*προσκυνέω (59) worship 8V

προστίθημι (18) add (to)/proceed E2.83

*πρόσωπον ου τό (74) face 2V

προϋπάρχω (2) be previously 1.71

*προφήτης ου ὁ (144) prophet 1.27 2.29 3V

προφήτις ιδος ἡ (2) prophetess D3.28

πρύμνα ης ἡ (3) ship's stern D1.65

πρῷρα ης ἡ (2) ship's prow/bow D1.65

*πρῶτον (6) firstly/first 9.23 9V

*πρῶτος η ον (93) first 5V 6V 7V 9.23 9V

πταίω (5) stumble/go wrong E4.35

πτέρνα ης ἡ (1) heel D1.65

πτύρω (1) frighten C1.89

πτωχός ή όν (34) poor D4.05 6V

πυνθάνομαι (11) inquire C2.34 C7.5

*πῦρ πυρός τό (71) fire D3.11 5.46 5V

πῶλος ου ὁ (12) colt/foal 4V

πώποτε (6) at any time 4V

*πῶς (104) how?/in what way? 9.13 9V

Ραββι Ραββουνι (17) Rabbi 4V

ῥάβδος ου ἡ (12) rod/staff D2.44

ῥέω (1) flow C4.4 C8.76

ῥήγνυμι (7) break up/burst C3.2

*ῥῆμα ματος τό (68) word/object 1.27 1.38
    2.29 5V

ῥήτωρ ορος ὁ (1) spokesman D3.13

ῥίζα ης ἡ (16) root D1.65

ῥίπτω (8) cast down C5.7 E4.32

Ῥόδος ου ἡ (1) Rhodes D2.44

ῥύομαι (17) rescue/deliver C7.5

ῥυπαίνομαι (1) be impure C1.89 C1.84 C7.5

ῥώννυμι (1) strengthen C3.2

*σάββατον ου τό (68) sabbath D3.29 1.27 2.29
    2V

σαίνομαι (1) be disturbed C1.89 C1.84 C7.5

σάπφειρος ου ἡ (1) sapphire D2.44

*σάρξ σαρκός ἡ (147) flesh D3.6 E2.66 5.31
    5.34 5.43 5V

σβέννυμι (6) extinguish/quench C3.2

σεαυτόν σεαυτήν σεαυτό σεαυτοῦ (43) your-
    self (sg) D6.8 5V 6.22 6V

σέβομαι (10) worship C7.5

σημαίνω (6) indicate C1.89 C1.84 E2.43
    E3.17 E4.43

*σημεῖον ου τό (77) sign/miracle 9V

σήμερον (41) today/this very day 6V

σήπω (1) decay C4.3

σής σητός ὁ (3) (clothes-)moth 6V

σιδηροῦς ᾶ οῦν (5) iron D4.3

σίναπι σινάπεως τό (5) mustard D3.2

σῖτος ου ὁ (14) wheat 4V

σκανδαλίζω (29) cause to stumble/give offence/
    anger 6V

σκάπτω (3) dig C5.7 E4.35

σκηνή ῆς ἡ (20) dwelling/tabernacle 6V

σκόλοψ οπος ὁ (1) splinter/thorn D3.7

σκηνόω (5) live/dwell 6V

σκληρύνω (6) harden/make stubborn C1.89

σκύλλω (4) trouble/annoy C1.89 C1.83 4.27

σμάραγδος ου ὁ/ἡ (1) emerald D2.45

σμύρνα ης ἡ (2) myrrh D1.65

σορός οῦ ἡ (1) coffin D2.44

σός σή σόν (27) your (singular) 2V 6.22 7.22
    7V

*σοφία ας ἡ (51) wisdom 5V

σοφός ή όν (20) wise 9.33
σπάω (2) draw (one's sword) C1.48
σπεῖρα ης ἡ (7) cohort D1.65
*σπείρω (52) sow C1.89 C1.84 C1.85 C4.4
C8.61 E2.43 4.27 4V
σπεκουλάτωρ ορος ὁ (1) executioner D3.13
σπέρμα ματος τό (44) seed/descendent 2V 8V
σπεύδω (6) hasten/hurry C1.7 E2.64 9.71
σπλαγχνίζομαι (12) have compassion C7.5
σποδός οῦ ἡ (3) ashes D2.44
στάδιον ου τό (7) a stade (about 200 metres)
8V
στάμνος ου ἡ (1) a jar D4.22
στατήρ ηρος ὁ (2) stater (a coin) D3.11
σταυρός οῦ ὁ (27) cross 6V
στέλλω (2) send (midd. avoid) C1.89 C1.83
C1.85 C4.4 C8.61 D5.17 (2V) 4.27
στενάζω (6) groan/sigh/grumble C8.84
στερεός ά όν (4) solid D4.3
στήκω (12) stand/stand firm C8.93
στηρίζω (14) strengthen/fix C8.84 4V
στοά ᾶς ἡ (4) porch/portico 3.14 D1.63 F38
*στόμα ματος τό (78) mouth 9V
στρέφω (22) turn C4.4 C8.63 7V
στρώννυμι (6) spread/furnish C3.2
*σύ (1057) you/your (singular) D6.3 E6.32
2.66 2V 3.33 6.22 A3.21
συγγενής οῦς ὁ (11) kinsman/relative D4.7
συγκληρονόμος ου ὁ and ἡ (4) fellowheir
D2.45
συζεύγνυμι (2) join together C3.2
συζητέω (10) discuss 8V
συζωοποιέω (2) make alive together with
E4.14
συκάμινος ου ἡ (1) mulberry tree D2.44
συλλαλέω (6) talk/converse with 8V
συμβαίνω (8) happen/come about E2.06 8V
συμπορεύομαι (4) walk with/go with 8V
*σύν (127) with 7V 8.65
*συνάγω (59) gather 5V 7V
*συναγωγή ῆς ἡ (56) synagogue 4V 6V
συνανάκειμαι (7) sit at table with (C3.3)
E4.11 7V
συνέρχομαι (30) come together 6V
συνθρύπτω (1) break (one's heart) C5.7
συνίστημι (16) hold together/cohere 9V
συντέλεια ας ἡ (6) completion/end 6V
σύρω (5) drag C1.89 C4.52 E2.43 4.27 8V
9.59
συστρέφω (2) gather around/together 8V
σφάζω (10) slaughter/slay C4.4 C8.84
σφραγίς ῖδος ἡ (16) seal 5V
*σώζω (106) save/rescue/deliver/cure 4V 6V

*σῶμα σώματος τό (142) body D3.9 F36 5.44
5.45 5.50 5V 9V
σωτήρ ηρος ὁ (24) saviour D3.11 5.31 5.32
5.36 5.46 5V 6V
ταπεινόω (14) humble 7V
τάσσω (10) appoint/arrange/order C4.4 C4.53
C4.54
ταχέως (10) soon/swiftly 7V 9.37
ταχύ (18) soon/quickly 8V
*τέ (201) and/both 8V E6.32
-τείνω (-) stretch C1.89 C1.84 E4.12
*τέκνον ου τό (99) child 5V 8V
τέλειος α ον (19) perfect/complete/mature 3V
τελευτή ῆς ἡ (1) end/death 8V
τελέω (28) finish/bring to completion C1.48
7V
τέλος ους τό (41) end 8V
τελώνης ου ὁ (21) tax-collector 9V
-τέμνω (-) cut C1.89 (C2.31) E4.12
τέρας τέρατος τό (16) wonder/marvel D3.10
τέσσαρες τέσσαρα (41) four 9V
τετραπλοῦς ῆ οῦν (1) fourfold D4.3
τηλικοῦτος (4) so large/so great 7.11 7.13
*τηρέω (70) keep/observe/watch 6V
*τίθημι (101) place/put C3.1 C3.1b C3.85
C3.87 C6.1 C6.2 D5.31 D5.32 D5.35
D5.37 E2.44 E2.83 E4.09 E4.13 E4.39
E4.77 7.46 7.48 9.59 9V
τίκτω (81) bear/give birth to C2.1 C2.96 C7.6
C8.63 7.36
τίλλω (3) pluck C1.89 C1.83
τιμάω (21) honour/set a price on C1.2 C6.1
C8.08 E2.18 E2.24 E2.32 9.71
τιμή ῆς ἡ (41) honour/value/respect 5V 6V
τίνω (1) pay/suffer C5.31
*τίς τί τίνος (552) who?/which?/what?/why?
D6.5 E6.25 F36 2V 5.68 7.11
*τις τι τινός (518) some/any/a certain D6.6
E6.32 F36 2.31 4V 5.68 5V 7.11 7.15
8.81
τοιόσδε (1) of such a kind 7.11
*τοιοῦτος (56) of such a kind 7.11 7.13 7V
*τόπος ου ὁ (95) place 1.27 2.29
τοσοῦτος (19) so much/many/great 7.11 7.13
7V
*τότε (159) then 9.13 4V
τοὐναντίον (3) on the contrary E2.92
τοὔνομα (1) the name E2.92
τράπεζα ης ἡ (15) table/bank D1.65
*τρεῖς τρία τριῶν (67) three D6.7 3V
τρέμω (3) tremble C1.89
-τρέπω (-) turn C4.4 C8.63 E4.12
τρέφω (9) nourish/feed C4.4 C8.63 C8.64
E2.85

τρέχω (19) run C2.8 7.33

τρίβος ου ἡ (3) beaten path D2.44

-τρίβω (-) rub C4.4 C4.53 C4.54 E4.12

τρίτος η ον (48) third 8V

τροφός οῦ ἡ (1) nurse D2.44

τυγχάνω (12) happen/obtain C2.34

τύπτω (13) strike/hit C5.7 C2.99

*τυφλός ή όν 950) blind 4V 6V

ὑγιαίνω (12) be healthy/sound C1.89 C1.84

*ὕδωρ ὕδατος τό (76) water D3.13 5.46 5V 7V A5.21

*υἱός οῦ ὁ (375) son 1.33 1.37 1.46 2.29 8.42

*ὑμεῖς (1830) you/your (plural) D6.3 2V 3.33 A3.21 A3.23

*ὑπάγω (79) go (one's way)/depart 4V 7V 9V

*ὑπάρχω (60) be/exist/be present 6V

*ὑπέρ (149) beyond/for the sake of 8.62 5V 9V

ὑπήκοος ον (3) obedient D4.3

*ὑπό (217) under/by 8.62 8.69 8.71

ὑποκριτής οῦ ὁ (17) hypocrite 1.27 2.29

ὕσσωπος (-ον) ου ὁ/ἡ/τό (2) hyssop D2.45

ὑστερέω (16) lack E4.37

ὑψηλός ή όν (11) high/exalted 8V 9.33

ὑψόω (20) exalt 7V

φάγος ου ὁ (2) glutton 9V

φαίνω (30) shine (midd. appear) C1.89 C1.84 C4.4 C7.6 4.27

φανερός ά όν (18) known/open/evident/visible 4V

φάσκω (3) assert C5.5

φείδομαι (10) spare C7.5

*φέρω (66) carry/bring C2.8 C1.84 C1.89 C2.97 C8.63 E4.13 E4.27 E4.38 4V 7.33 7.35

φεύγω (31) flee/escape C2.5 C4.3 C7.6 5V 7.36

*φημί (66) say C2.8 C3.3 2.76 7.33 7.34

φθάνω (7) precede/reach C5.31

φθείρω (8) ruin/corrupt/destroy C1.8b C1.84 C1.85 C1.89 C4.4 C8.61 9.71

φιλέω (25) have deep feeling for/love/kiss C8.85 9V

φίλος ου ὁ (29) friend 8V 9V

φιμόω (7) muzzle/silence 7V

φλόξ φλογός ἡ (7) flame D3.09

*φοβέομαι (95) fear C7.5 6.18 8V 9V

φορέω (6) wear C1.48 E4.33

φράσσω (3) close up/silence C4.4

φρέαρ φρέατος τό (7) well D3.13

φυλάσσω (32) guard/keep 4V 6.14

φυλή ῆς ἡ (31) tribe 5V

φύω (3) grow up/sprout C3.7 C4.4 9.57

φωνέω (42) call 4V

*φωνή ῆς ἡ (137) voice/sound D1.2 D0.27 D1.61 D1.64 1.27 2.29 3.11 3.13 3.16 5.64 A3.11 A3.13 A3.52

*φῶς φωτός τό (73) light D3.10 D5.13 2V 5V

φωστήρ ῆρος ὁ (2) radiance D3.11

φωτίζω (11) give light to C8.89

*χαίρω (74) rejoice C1.89 C1.84 C4.4 C7.6 9V

χάλαζα ης ἡ (4) hail D1.65

χαλάω (7) let down/lower C1.48

χαλκολίβανος (-ον) ου ὁ/ἡ/τό (2) burnished bronze D2.45

χαλκοῦς ῆ οῦν (1) made of copper/brass/ bronze D4.3

*χαρά ᾶς ἡ (59) joy 9V

χαρακτήρ ῆρος ὁ (1) exact likeness D3.11

χαρίζομαι (23) grant/forgive C7.5 6.18

*χάρις χάριτος ἡ (155) grace D3.28 5V

*χείρ χειρός η (176) hand D3.31 D3.11 5.36 5V

*χείρων ον (11) worse 9.35 9V

-χέω (-) pour C8.76 C8.77 C8.87 C8.88 C9.2 E2.17 E4.12

χιλιάς άδος ἡ (23) thousand 5V 7V

χορτάζω (15) feed/satisfy with food 7V

χόρτος ου ὁ (15) grass 4V

χοῦς χοός ὁ (2) dust D3.3

χράομαι (11) use C7.5

χρεία ας ἡ (49) need 4V

*Χριστός οῦ ὁ (536) Christ/Messiah/ anointed 2V

χρίω (5) anoint E4.33

χρονίζω (5) take a long time C8.89

*χρόνος ου ὁ (54) time 1.27 2.29

χρυσοῦς σῆ σοῦν (18) golden D4.3

-χύννω (-) pour C5.32 C8.76 C8.77 C9.2 E4.12

χωλός ή όν (14) lame/crippled 6V

χωρίς (41) without/apart from 8.66 7V

ψάλλω (5) sing C1.89 C1.83

ψεύδομαι (12) deceive/lie C7.5

ψεῦδος ους τό (10) falsehood/lying/lie 9V

ψηφίζω (2) figure out E4.35

ψῆφος ου ἡ (3) pebble/vote D2.44

*ψυχή ῆς ἡ (101) soul/life 1.27 2.29

ψύχω (1) cool down C4.4

ὦ (17) O! 8.42

*ὧδε (61) here 4V 7V E6.17 9V

ὠδίν ὠδῖνος ἡ (4) birth-pains D3.15

ὠδίνω (3) be in pain (in labour) C1.89 C1.86

-ωθέω (-) thrust C5.4

*ὥρα ας ἡ (106) hour E6.17 1.27 2.29

*ὡς (505) as/like/how/that 3V 9.13 E6.31

*ὥστε (84) so that/thus 5V 7V

APPENDIX I

INDEX TO TOPICS

References are to Paragraphs: a reference beginning with a *number* refers to the Lesson with that number in the nine Lessons of the Beginner's Course; a reference beginning with a *letter* refers to the Appendix with that letter.